Janie's journal

Volume 6

2010-2015

Also by Janie Tippett

Four Lines a Day

Janie's Journal
Vol 1: 1984-1987
Vol 2: 1988-1991
Vol 3: 1992-1996
Vol 4: 1997-2004
Vol 5: 2005-2009
Vol 6: 2010-2015

Janie's work appears in
the following anthologies:

Talking On Paper: An Anthology
of Oregon Letters and Diaries

Crazy Woman Creek:
Women Rewrite the American West

Janie's Journal

Volume 6

2010-2015

Janie Tippett

Lucky Marmot Press

www.luckymarmotpress.com

Wallowa, Oregon

JANIE'S JOURNAL, VOLUME SIX: 2010-2015
was originally published in the weekly Agri-Times NW.
These columns are collected here with permission of the publisher.

All photos were taken by Janie Tippett as part of her photojournalism
for Agri-Times NW, except where noted in the captions.
All photos are used with permission.

The cover photo shows Janie's faithful border collie, Daisy, on the home
ranch on Tenderfoot Valley Road outside Joseph, Oregon. Chief Joseph
Mountain dominates the background.

ISBN 978-1-7334833-1-5 (paperback)
ISBN 978-1-9565300-0-1 (ebook)

This volume was collected, digitized, edited, and published by
Lucky Marmot Press in Wallowa, Oregon.
https://www.luckymarmotpress.com

Historic Eggleson barn off Highway 82 between Enterprise and Joseph.

2010

January 4—Well, the holidays are over and we're beginning a new year. I feel overwhelmed with gratitude as I gaze out my window on this foggy, cold morning. I am grateful for the safety of my family, who braved winter roads and airplane flights to reach their various destinations.

The last to leave was granddaughter Mona Lee, who drove off yesterday to spend time with her cousin in La Grande before returning to Challis, Idaho. I miss having her along on my daily walks with Halley, sipping tea at the kitchen table, her morning hugs, her jolly spirit, and generous heart.

It has been an emotional time. Our thoughts don't stray far from baby Jacob, who, along with his parents and brother and sister, was flown from Okinawa to Honolulu, Hawaii for intensive medical care. Daughter Ramona's flight was rerouted so she could be with her family. Our little boy is still hanging in there, his mom, Maria, is much improved, and his sister and brother have started school in Hawaii. One day at a time.

Frasch's cows are cleaning up the oat and barley stubble on Doug's old ranch, the throaty croak of ravens shatters the foggy silence, occasional V's of geese or ducks light in the grain fields to feed, and flocks of starlings whirl over Prairie Creek. I cut open one of those huge baking squashes whose vines strangled our garden last summer, and as I write, half is baking in the oven for pies, and the remainder will accompany pork chops for supper.

We have invited son-in-law Charley to join us, as Ramona won't be back until the 15th.

Approaching the chicken house yesterday morning, I heard what sort'a sounded like a crow. Definitely not Piglet's, my rooster, but similar. Closer inspection of my flock revealed one pullet with spurs. Whoops! Dang it! That pullet will never lay eggs.

Doug and I were alone on New Year's Eve. Well, not really, we had the Blue Moon, the second of two moons in December, to brighten Prairie Creek. I made my own crust and baked a pizza, and we spent a quiet evening at home bringing in 2010.

The next morning, New Year's Day, Doug treated Mona and I to breakfast at the Mountainaire Cafe in Joseph. The town looked cold and deserted, but there was a crowd in the popular eatery, still gay with Christmas decorations and music. That week was spent treating various members of our family to lunch, which was fun for Mona as she doesn't get to see them often.

One noon we were joined by Myrna and Jenny Moore, who drove up from Bear Gulch. Redeeming my 4-H Radio Auction certificate, we gathered at Calderas for black bean soup and artisan bread. We ate upstairs in the balcony, which was a dining experience, from your table, you can look out over the town of Joseph.

Before Adele flew back to Texas, we met at El Bajio in Enterprise for excellent Mexican food. It was a welcome break for this cook. And now everyone is off leading their own lives, and the holidays are only memories kept alive by the telling of stories.

January 5—A freezing rain left a glaze of ice on everything, so bad Phyllis Webb and Christine Anderson were "iced in" and couldn't attend our weekly writer's group. We are in the midst of this year's Big Read, and the county is reading *To Kill a Mockingbird* by Harper Lee. We were thrilled to have Charles Shields speak at our big Kickoff event. Charles, a Harper Lee scholar, wrote Lee's biography, entitled *Mockingbird*, a great book that gives a fascinating insight into an author's life.

January 6—This morning, following a light snowfall, Phyllis and I walked around Joseph and ended up at Mutiny, a new brew pub that featured rockfish fajitas for lunch. Yum.

My sister Kathryn sent another box of tangerines and grapefruit from her backyard trees. How sweet is that? My Aracuna pullets began laying their first blue eggs today as well.

We lost another old time cattleman this month. Native Reid Johnson, of Wallowa, was widely-known, not only as a cattleman, but as a productive member of our community as well. Although he lived a long, full life, Reid will be missed.

January 10—I drove to Alder Slope with a kettle of homemade chicken noodle soup for grandson James, who was battling another sore throat. Happy to report that the soup did the trick; he improved dramatically.

Later that afternoon, Doug and I drove to Imnaha to escape the icy cold, and to treat ourselves to those famous chicken strips and fries, served up by the new managers at the old Imnaha Store and Tavern.

Carol Pepsick, of Estacada, shown here with one of her lead dogs, came in 6th in the 100-mile Eagle Cap Extreme sled dog race—her first distance race.

January 11—A Chinook wind whispered down Prairie Creek this morning, following a persimmon-colored sunrise that melted over Locke's hill. A warm wind out of the south, with gusts up to 35 mph. The hollow roar of which was all-consuming, icy fields melting under its breath.

January 12—A thick fog blanketed Joseph when I was there on Main Street to help with the Eagle Cap Extreme Sled Dog Race vet checks.

Later, at another vet check in Enterprise, I ran into Agri-Times NW columnist John Groupe, who seized an opportunity to join the Ollokot volunteer team, as they were short a veterinarian.

While handing out drop bags to the mushers, I was visited by grandson James, who had sought me out to say goodbye before flying off to the east coast to be a Marine. We won't hear from him again until he completes basic training. These grandchildren are hard on grandma's heart strings.

Tonight I drove to Joseph High School and purchased two "drive-by beef tri-tip dinners," prepared by Randy Garnett for their FFA chapter's money-raising event. You could smell that beef barbecuing all over Joseph. Judging by the lineup of cars, Wallowa Countians are still eating beef.

January 17—The sled dogs left Ferguson Ridge around 1:30 p.m. on the 13th, and we members of the Salt Creek Summit checkpoint crew were there when they came through. What a treat to watch those "still fresh" dogs swish on past. It was one of those bluebird days above the fog, and such a welcome contrast to the valley, which was melting and free of snow. At that higher elevation there was a good base of new snow, crisp air, cobalt skies and bright sunshine.

Once again, Billy Snodgrass of Dubois, Wyoming, won the 200-mile race with his team of 12 dogs in 35 hours and 3 minutes. Those teams that made the trip to Halfway and back experienced high winds that, at times, completely obliterated the trail. Although I didn't work at Ollokot this year, granddaughter Becky did, and reported everything went well. Much warmer this year, so much so that some brave team members, Becky included, jumped into the frigid waters of the upper Imnaha! Tough gal, that Becky.

Without much sleep, she was there with us on Saturday as we helped her dad, son Todd, move 320 head of his Marr Flat cows from Big Sheep to Hayden, where the herd spent the night. Halley, who dubs this The Event of the Year, walked and trotted with me behind those cows for 9 miles. Fun for both of us, as we wound our way up the Imnaha Highway along Little Sheep Creek.

Daughter-in-law Angie, her daughter Becky, Grandson Buck's wife Chelsea and her mother Carol and father Mark DeJong, who drove over from McCall, Idaho, all rode horseback. Son Todd took the lead in his pickup, and grandson Buck alternated riding and driving a pickup with the stock trailer. At one point little great-granddaughter Lucy rode with her grandpa. The weather was great for trailing cattle, cool and sunny.

The next afternoon, around 2:00 o'clock, we looked out the living room window to see the herd trailing down Echo Canyon. By the time the last cow filed into the holding pasture and the horses were unsaddled and loaded in the trailer, this grandma had two casseroles of tamale pie, a tossed salad, and sourdough biscuits on the table. After being in the saddle on a cold January day, you can imagine those appetites.

For dessert I'd spent the morning building a fresh lemon pie, heaped with golden meringue. There were nine of us, including little cowgirls Lucy and her baby sister Katelyn. Early the next morning Todd and Buck were there to open the gate, and trail the cows to the old Snyder Place, where they'll be fed hay, and calve out until spring, when grass returns to the canyons.

January 20—This morning found Phyllis and I hiking a trail that winds up Devil's Gulch. A very interesting ramble in January, when the weather is snowy and cold "on top."

The trail begins on the south side of Little Sheep Creek, and slowly gains elevation between outcroppings of the colorful rock formations typical of the Imnaha canyon country. Thickets of aspen and tall cottonwoods grow in the gulch, along with alder, sarvisberry, elderberry, snowberry, wild rose bramble, clematis, and the occasional poison oak. A small creek appears, and disappears, and the trail crosses it in several places.

We climbed higher, skirting great open bunch grass slopes, and side canyons beckoning beyond. The trail, littered with last fall's rotting leaves, smelled of wild things: old bear scat, fresh coyote and coon, and we saw scrapings on tree trunks from deer and elk antlers. At last we rounded a bend, and there stood the rustic one-room cabin we'd been searching for. Weathered in lovely shades of rich browns, it hunched in a clearing above the live creek.

Here we sat on stumps and ate our lunches while the warm canyon sunlight poured down. Tender green watercress flourished in a spring that fed the creek, and we stared up toward Clear Lake Ridge, which was wearing a spattering of snow.

By the time we started back down the trail, the sun had slipped beyond the Western rims, and the brief canyon daylight was fast disappearing. A bitter chill settled in as we hastened back to the car. Devil's Gulch is owned by The Nature Conservancy and is open to the public. There are no dogs or overnight camping allowed, and you pack out what you pack in, to help maintain the beauty of the place by respecting its wildness.

January 21—Doug and I drove into Enterprise to watch the Wallowa/Union County Wrestling tournament. Wrestling is a wonderful sport for growing boys, and there was plenty of action. A proud great-grandma was I, when great-grandson Ronan and granddaughter Ashlyn belted out the Star Spangled Banner. Ronan's dad, our grandson Chad, is the Enterprise wrestling coach.

January 22—Phyllis and I hiked the newly-opened trail near the Old Chief Joseph Monument at the foot of the lake. The trail was very icy in places, and we had to watch our step, but were rewarded as we walked beneath a pair of bald eagles perched on a cottonwood limb above the trail. Later, we warmed up with soup and shrimp tacos at "Mutiny" in Joseph.

After spending days creating a new sourdough bread recipe, our daughter Lori and husband Larry arrived just as the finished product, baked in the dutch oven, was ready to sample. Oven fried chicken, and tossed salad went well with the bread, which was eagerly devoured. The couple spent the night, and the next morning Doug treated us to breakfast at the Mountainaire Cafe in Joseph before they departed.

Yet one more old-timer has left us. Ken Kooch, whose son Reid and wife Linda continue to operate the same "Century Farm" that former generations of Kooches have capably managed in the past. Ken and wife Rowena were my neighbors, long ago, when I lived on Alder Slope. Ken, a very upbeat person, always had a smile for everyone.

January 25—Banana cake in the oven, Doug playing cribbage with "the boys," Halley waiting for a walk, and the chickens fed. Prairie Creek is shrouded in fog this late January morning. Frosty "whiskers" grow on the apple tree limbs and chicken wire fence, Hough's cows appear ghost-like across the road, slicking up their ration of hay scattered across the snowy field. My world appears shrunken and muted. Save for the ticking of the clock, there is no other sound.

It's been a busy January however, and to update everyone, baby Jacob is gaining weight. He now weighs over three pounds. I took venison pasta soup to Ramona, who returned from Honolulu on the 19th with a nasty cold, just in time for her ewes to begin lambing. At last count there were ten.

We had a short visit from Lyman and Wilma, who drove up from the canyons to escape a bout of cabin fever. We understand Lyman has been "twittered." I'll leave it at that. While Ramona was gone, we had Charley over for supper one night for pork chops and baked squash.

January 26—I spotted two foxes on Prairie Creek on my way to our weekly Writer's Group.

January 29—Daughter-in-law Angie helped me serve at our Community Dining Center in Enterprise. We represented the CowBelles, who are becoming an endangered species. Since every table was filled, Angie and I were kept very busy waiting on everyone.

More bald eagles along Prairie Creek, waiting to snatch up every placenta. The birds look forward to these "afterbirth treats" all year. I noticed the Marr Flat cows are beginning to calve.

Granddaughter Chelsie and her mom Annie hosted a baby shower for Maria and baby Jacob on a recent Saturday. Great granddaughters Riley Ann, Ashlyn, and Jada met us at the door with flowers for our hair. The long dining room table was decorated with fruit to resemble a Hawaiian theme—pineapples, grapes, and kiwis.

Annie prepared a delicious ham garnished with a pineapple-orange glaze, and served with steamed fruited rice. Chelsie baked cup cakes, decorated with palm trees, and we had us a feast. Granddaughter Carrie dialed Maria in Honolulu and we all talked to her. It was like she was there with us, as Carrie had sent the photos she took with her phone across the oceans to Maria. Go figure!

Anyway, we are happy to know baby Jacob continues to gain and grow strong on his mother's milk. Then we all participated in a hula-hoop contest, which wasn't a pretty sight for us oldsters, but our youngsters performed like we USED to.

January 31—Doug and I attended the annual Wallowa County Chamber of Commerce Annual Citizen's Award Banquet, held in Cloverleaf Hall. After a scrumptious prime rib dinner, we were filled with pride when son Todd and wife Angie received the Entrepreneur award. They were chosen for their beef promotion efforts to market their Marr Flat Cattle Company beef. Some of their natural beef has traveled as far away as New York. Todd, humbled, gave credit to his nephew Buck Matthews and wife Chelsea, as well as secretary Susan Hobbs.

We were pleasantly surprised, as well, when our neighbors Tom and Donna Butterfield were awarded the Agriculture Award. Couldn't have gone to a more deserving family.

February 1—Early this morning, the January Moon (the Wolf Moon) hovered over Ruby Peak in a pink blush of sky that reflected upon the snowy ridges of Chief Joseph Mountain. We enjoyed the sight, before the fog moved in.

February 8—The sun is shining! After days of foggy, frozen cold and limited visibility, we can now enjoy those glorious mountains again. We missed them. The last day of January left us with six inches of new snow, hard, crusty and glittering under the bright sun. It has taken me over a week to stomp a trail around the old ranch. Each day I return less tired, as my pathway is flattened.

Halley's ever-sensitive nose sniffs out mouse tunnels, and when a warm rodent scent sends her digging, she often comes up with a furry little field mouse. After flipping the poor thing in the air, my sadistic Halley watches, fascinated, as the mouse regains its feet and stands on its quivering hind legs, boxing with its tiny paws in a futile attempt to fend off my fearless dog.

The Tippett Ranch on Prairie Creek on a "blue bird" morning. Bunk house on right, chicken house in far left.

When mamma kitty follows us, I send Halley off on a wild deer chase, thus allowing a very willing kitty to end the mouse's suffering. Two crunchy gulps, end of tail, tale.

Later, down along the creek, I pause to watch a great blue heron fish in a bit of open water. Suddenly aware of me, the large bird utters a throaty croak and lifts off. At that moment a V of geese flies over, several ravens tease Halley, and from the top of Locke's hill a pack of coyotes, young and old mingled together, begin to talk. The sun is out, the snow sparkles, the frost-encrusted willow limbs drop their load onto thin ice, and, for that one perfect moment, the world is at peace.

One of my fans, Bob Lundy, who farms in Madras, sent me (via a friend) a bag of garlic. Thanks to Bob, the chili I cooked up for yesterday's Super Bowl Sunday was mighty tasty.

February 10—It's the 10th already and the sun is still out, however a chill wind is kicking up. Phyllis is home from Hawaii, and we'll most likely go for a snowshoe hike this afternoon.

February 14—Great-granddaughter Brenna appeared at our door bearing two huge heart-shaped cookies, all frosted pink, which she'd baked with her grandma Ramona. Brenna, who lives in La Grande, spends a great deal of time on her grandma and poppa Charley's ranch. This

Halley, Janie's border collie, loves the snow.

little miss is starting a sheep project, and enjoys feeding the bummer lambs.

February 16—I hosted our writing group. After our morning class I ladled up steaming bowls of Italian soup, which we slurped down with chunks of fresh french bread supplied by Phyllis. While the gals played Scrabble on the kitchen table, I got out the rolling pin and baked a squash pie to go with the huckleberry cream pie I'd made earlier that morning.

Both pies were auctioned off this evening at the Wallowa County Stockgrowers "Dollars for Scholars" dinner. People sitting at various tables pooled their money and purchased the pies for dessert. Naturally, son Todd and grandson Buck bid up my pies, and therefore gained the winning bids. Eileen Williams, our Extension agent's wife, had donated two lemon pies that fetched well over $100 each. Proceeds go to college scholarships for our local young people.

Randy Garnett and his Apple Flat Catering crew had cooked up a scrumptious prime rib dinner.

February 17—Anne Werner and I hiked the steep East Moraine of Wallowa Lake. A sunny morning deteriorated into a cold cloudy afternoon, but no matter, we enjoyed the views from on top, and our lunches, which were eaten while perched on huge glacial boulders.

Doug drove out to the hills to have a look-see after our long winter, and reported plenty of elk.

The sun reappeared in late afternoon, so Halley and I took off across Hough's pastures, crossed three irrigation ditches, and climbed the hill to look for buttercups. Due to the mildness of our winter, I suspected there might be some yellow drops near some warm rocks. However, my searching revealed only the shiny green leaves of buttercup plants.

February 22—Winter Fishtrap, held at the historic Wallowa Lake Lodge, was very stimulating in the sunny weather. The theme was "What We Learn From Women," and our three presenters—Molly Gloss, Ursula Le Guin, and Tony Vogt—were terrific. The food was excellent, and I was thrilled to be with two of my "Syringa Sisters", Barb and Mary, who shared a room at the old Lodge.

Open mic is one of the richest segments of the program, and this year, due to the theme, attendees from all over the West presented some outstanding essays and poems. I'll always remember Ray Bilderback's essay about the influence exerted by his aunt, who lived on a farm in the Placer County foothills near where I grew up. This theme reaffirmed the importance of women's roles in our lives.

I returned to the ranch just in time Sunday for Halley and I to jump in the pickup with Doug and go fishing on Imnaha. No fish, but we soaked up plenty of sunshine and, later, devoured piping hot chicken strips and french fries at the old Tav on Main Street (the only street) Imnaha.

Driving home we noticed a brand new crop of calves being born along Sheep Creek. And now the snow has turned to rain, at least here on Prairie Creek, and it's lunch time.

February 24—Rare spurts of sunlight stream in the kitchen window as I write. At least five red wing blackbirds are at the feeder this morning. All males, whom, I'm told, return early to select their nest sites before the arrival of their dull-colored mates. These shiny black birds with their feathered red wings flash cheerfully in the sunlight.

Mt. Howard is adrift in snow clouds, and it appears to be snowing out north as well. Earlier, snow sputtered from the skies, while Halley and I took our walk around the old ranch. Startled by a flock of wild honkers in the oat stubble, Halley nearly took flight herself in an effort to catch one. Honking their alarm, the heavy birds simply circled, then landed a short distance away, where they continued feeding. Apparently they thought Halley wasn't much of a threat.

The lovely song of a single meadowlark drifted from the leafless willows by the creek. Another sign of an early spring was the arrival of robins in Enterprise yesterday.

The Moore boys just chugged past in their two old trucks, hauling hay for their cattle down Bear Gulch. Nice folks.

Last evening Doug and I drove into Enterprise to attend the grade school talent show, a money-raiser for the 6th grade field trip. For their act, great-granddaughters Riley Ann, Ashlyn, and Jada sang a quirky little song, and I was reminded of myself, so long ago, in grade-school, giggling and singing at the same time. The place was packed, as the local populace always turns out when their children perform.

We left during intermission and drove up the road to Joseph in time to view some rare old footage, transferred to DVDs, of Red's Horse Ranch in its heyday. There was Red Higgins himself, red bearded, smoking his pipe, treating the movie star's children to a wilderness ranch experience.

There were scenes of hay being cut on the landing strip meadow using an old horse-drawn mower, raked with a buck rake, and stacked and forklifted up to the hay mow of the same barn that still stands there today. There were Red's private quarters, where Doug and I spent our honeymoon in 1978, and the old swimming hole I swam in just this past summer.

Our Wallowa County Museum organized this showing, which also featured an early film, shot by Jerry Gildermeister, of raising the water level of Minam Lake for irrigation purposes. Teams of draft horses were used, as this was and still is a wilderness area.

My father would have loved viewing this film, which showed those powerful horses pulling Fresno scrapers to build an earthen dam at one end of the lake. Those same horses hauled in huge culverts, mounted on sleds, up those six rugged miles from Two Pan Trailhead.

Phyllis and I did get away to cross-country ski up Ferguson Ridge on a sunny afternoon when the snow was in perfect condition. Taking advantage of another nice day, we skied around the head of the lake before the ice began to melt. Then we celebrated the opening of The Glacier Grill, which has been closed all winter, by chowing down on Italian sausage dogs with "the works."

February 25—I climbed the hill to search for the first buttercup again…and found one! Beneath the same warm rock as last year.

This evening we met Lyman and Wilma at the Imnaha Store and Tavern for the weekly community dinner. The pool table, covered with a cloth, held both smoked and roasted turkey, plus all the dishes that go with. Hungry folks from up and downriver, and "on top," stomped through the door, grabbed a plate, and chowed down. We sat in a booth with Lyman and Wilma and helped them celebrate their wedding anniversary and Wilma's birthday. We won't tell her age, 'cause since she married Lyman she still looks like a bride.

Another old-timer passed away. This time a woman, Carol Coppin, who lived for years with her husband Cleve at what was once an old fort, built early-on for protection from the Indians, who proved not to be a threat. Carol gave of herself to the community for years, from the Museum Board to the Library and many other volunteer jobs. Her work continues at the old bank building that now serves as our Wallowa County Museum. Hopefully, her dream of a research and archival storage room will soon become a reality.

February 27—Several of us participated in a training meeting for volunteers to man the new Alvin and Betty Josephy Library, which is now up and running. The Josephys, who made their summer home here at the north end of the moraine for years, left a legacy to be treasured, and the library, housed in the Coffin House, which is home to Fishtrap, contains invaluable research material for anyone interested in writing about the West. Alvin, a world-famous writer, produced a body of work that staggers the imagination. It is hoped that historians and writers will take advantage of this Western goldmine.

February 28—It was 40 degrees and balmy when folks from all over the county converged on the Hurricane Creek Grange Hall to celebrate the grand finale of the Big Read. Those Grange ladies baked their famous pies, a volunteer group bar-b-cued Southern spare ribs, and the community arrived bearing Southern side dishes, grits, cornbread, Mardi Gras salad, pickled okra, chicken and noodles, buttermilk biscuits, baked beans, and more food than the crowd could eat.

Since this year's book was *To Kill a Mockingbird,* Hurricane Creek Grange Hall's kitchen smelled of Southern cook'in. Mark Mathabane, author of *Kaffir Boy,* was our speaker, and the silence was so thick you could hear the creek outside as Mark spoke softly about his growing up under Apartheid in South Africa. He told us that, without the love and inspiration of his mother and grandmother, he would not be here today. They both stressed the importance of education, and saw to it that he got one.

Driving home under the full "Snow" Moon, I pondered Mark's words. Perhaps it takes extreme hardship to become human, but Mark stressed the importance of being kind, giving love, and caring for others more than yourself.

Happy to report baby Jacob is on the gain again, after a brief setback. Grandson Shawn will be deployed to Camp Pendleton in California, where his family will join him.

March 2—Phyllis and I decided to drive up to Salt Creek Summit, not knowing what we'd find in the way of skiing conditions. No snow whatsoever here on the valley floor, so we were pleasantly surprised to find perfect snow for cross-country when we arrived. After donning our skis we slid and glided over clean, fresh snow, following the Sled Dog Race route through sunlight and cloud shadows, fresh air, the odor of pine and fir, and a cool breeze which kept the snow from melting.

At noon we skied back to the parking lot, ate our lunches, then skied (without jackets) to the log cabin and around the frozen pond. Now, with this fresh snow, we can't wait to return.

March 4—Got a call from granddaughter Mona Lee. "Hi Grandma, I'm over at Buck and Chelsea's, leaving tomorrow. Wondered if we could do lunch."

"Sure," I replied, and so there we were at noon, seated at the big table in the back room at Cloud Nine Bakery. At the last minute son Todd, wife Angie, grandson Buck, and wife Chelsea and two girls Lucy and Katelyn joined us. Mona Lee will work on the fire suppression crew for the Challis National Forest again this year. It was good to see her.

March 5—On this gorgeous morning, Doug and I were winding our way down Buford to cross the Grande Ronde, then up Rattlesnake. Destination: Clarkston, Washington to attend the Lee Earl Memorial Scholarship Cowboy Poetry Gathering. Bob Fauste (aka Smoke Wade), Doug's nephew, had kept us informed on the event, and another nephew Wayne Tippett and wife Diane invited us to come stay with them.

Pulling into Clarkston was like entering another time zone. Of course Doug always has to tip his hat as we drive past his old high school, but the first trees were abloom, as was the brilliant forsythia. Daffodils and crocuses dazzled us in sunlight. It must have been 70 degrees.

We met up with Wayne at the Elks Club, a sprawling building that perches on a rim above the Snake River. Myriad windows look down upon the river and Clarkston. Smoke Wade greeted us and showed us the many venues, where performers from five states and B.C. were either singing, strumming a guitar, playing the fiddle, or reciting cowboy poetry. It was impossible to take it all in.

Wayne joined us for lunch there in the dining room, where we were entertained by more talented performers.

Afternoon found us wandering around, visiting old friends, like Helen Beard, who lives up Asotin Creek, and some of Doug's old classmates. Doug and I found a comfortable seat near the fire pit and spent a couple of hours enjoying the music, especially what's known as "The Train Wreck." I'll always remember the faces of those oldsters (and youngsters) standing around the fireplace, others wandering in, placing the fiddle under their chins, strapping on their guitars, bringing the harmonica to their lips and making music.

"Key of G," they'd say, and off they'd go, feeding off each other. It was a train wreck, a good one, and we could have spent all day there.

This evening we were joined by Doug's brother Jack, and his lovely wife Blanche, who, along with son Wayne and wife Diane, sponsored two of the tables. During, and after, a bite-size steak dinner, we were entertained until nearly 9:00 by more performers.

Smoke Wade, who was chairman of organizing the event, recited a poem about his two uncles, Biden and Doug, who operated the last two deeded cattle ranches on the Snake River. Later, while a group named Lonesome Dove played danceable music, Doug asked me to dance. Young Joshua Crosby brought down the house with his John Denver-like voice and guitar pick'in. Joshua hails from Kooskia, Idaho.

After, we followed Wayne and Diane to their lovely home on a hill above Clarkston, where we spent a restful night.

The next morning Diane treated us to the best breakfast in town. I'd given her a dozen fresh pullet eggs, which she scrambled and served with bacon, muffins, fruit, yogurt and hash brown potatoes. Diane knows how to cook a cow camp breakfast. Jack and Blanche drove over to join us, and I wish I'd had a tape recorder when it came time to for those two to tell stories about growing up on Joseph Creek.

"I remember," said Doug, "the time I picked up a cat by the tail and threw it onto the back of the milk cow when Ben was milking her. Sure was fun to see that bucket go sailing and Ben end in up in the gutter."

Then Jack. "Once the team ran away with me while I was pulling a slip. They headed to the house and mom thought I'd been run over. Dead. But there I was, clinging to the collars in the middle of the team."

On the way home, Doug and I pulled into Boggan's where you cross the Grande Ronde, and split one of their world-famous milkshakes.

Halley was glad to see us when we returned to the ranch. After chores and a walk in the sunshine, we made it to the Blue Mountain Old Time Fiddlers show at Cloverleaf Hall. The Wallowa County Fair Board, under Randy Garnett's able culinary guidance, served a bar-b-cued pork dinner before the fiddle playing commenced.

The hall was filled with folks who love toe-tappin' music, and it was fun to visit with our neighbors like Ardis and Harold Klages. A year older now, young Bailey Vernam played her little fiddle again, as did our favorite Prairie Creek Girls: Ryya, Lexi, Hannah and Landra. M.C. Denny Langford kept the crowd busy eating cucumber canapés and listening to the same jokes, year after year…and just being Denny.

Larry Schnetzky, our very talented local musician who performed at the Lee Earl do'ins, made it across the canyons to play the fiddle, sing, play the piano, and accompany on the guitar. After all that, he still had enough energy to dance a jig with his daughter. We noticed several old folks couples out on the dance floor kick'in up their heels or slowly dancing the waltz, as well as small fry whizzing around like they have for years in all the old halls scattered throughout Wallowa County.

We regulars couldn't help remembering those who have passed on: Charley Trump, Len Samples and Spencer Bacon come to mind.

Still snowing at noon. Time to braise ribs for supper.

March 8—Never fails. Just when you think spring has sprung, and everyone worries about fruit trees blooming too early, it happens—March, that is. This one in particular came in like a soft warm lamb but has morphed into a snowy-maned lion.

We did have several days of unseasonably sunny mild weather, which allowed the buttercups to bloom on Hough's hill, calves to bask in warmth, and me to prune the forsythia, pull the old hollyhock stalks, clean and line the chicken nests with straw, spread manure on the rhubarb, and walk with Halley in shirt sleeves. That was yesterday. This morning we slogged through three inches of fresh snow.

No complaint here, however, as this snow is soft, and full of moisture, and that's good.

Son Ken, who has been grading and graveling our lane, and installing a new culvert, will have to wait for things to dry out to finish his job.

March 26—The day after our return from California, I joined three other gals down at the Writer's Retreat on the Upper Imnaha, to clean the log lodge after the long winter. We had quite a time. The pump needed priming and the wood furnace fan motor wouldn't kick on, so I called Ken Stein, the mayor of Imnaha, who drove upriver with wife Pat and solved myriad problems for us. For his most appreciated efforts, I promised Ken a coconut cream pie.

*Young Bailey Vernam, Enterprise, entertains at the Blue Mountain Old Time
Fiddler Show in Cloverleaf Hall.*

March 27—Dawned sunny and breezy, so, for the first time all winter, I hung my laundry on the line.

This afternoon Karl Patton, our neighbor who lives up Echo Canyon just east of us, came down to look at some machinery he's buying from Doug.

"Last night was pretty wild," he said. "Had a visit from the wolf pack." And Karl proceeded to fill Doug in on the details. That explained why Halley had set up such a terrible ruckus in the early hours of the morning. Apparently the wolves were eyeing his calving cows.

Now we hear an airplane flying low, hazing the wolves away from the ranches. What next? The wolf pack is supposed to stay on the Divide, but they don't know that. Besides, the easy hunting is here on Prairie Creek. Until they're gone, I guess Halley and I won't venture over the eastern hills, as I hear wolves consider cow dogs a threat to their territory.

I've noticed the white-tails are taking refuge in the willows down along the irrigation ditch lately. Can imagine those wolves are making them nervous too.

March 31—Phyllis and I headed down into the canyons to hike the Devil's Gulch trail again. And so, for those of you who would like to go along on the hike with us, here we go.

The morning was cloudy and mild, but coolish enough for a jacket. Just right for hiking. We parked our car, crossed the narrow wooden bridge that spans Little Sheep Creek, and made our way through the hiker's small gate. It was quiet and only a faint breeze stirred the frosted winter grasses.

We were the only ones on the trail. Birds were vocal, and fluttered and fed about us: Rufus-sided towhees, black-cap chickadees, grouse, quail, robins, woodpeckers, jays, and sparrows; above, hawks sailed the thermals. The trail told its own story of coyotes, deer, coon, elk and skunk. The bushes were still dormant, just budding, and the only greening was the wild gooseberry.

The small creek sang its springtime song, running happily full of melting snows coming from Clear Lake Ridge. There were patches of snow in the shaded bottoms, under the wild rose bramble and poison oak. We climbed steadily out of the rocky creek, crossing it several times, and hiked a high trail that flanked the steep canyon sides. Above, billowy clouds, white as alabaster, accumulated in a brilliant blue sky. The cusp of spring mingled with the smells of lingering winter.

The trail borders a huge cut bank of Mt. Mazama ash, where little canyon rodents have dug tunnels deep inside. Large Ponderosas appear, and they, and Douglas firs, make a green statement in an otherwise colorless landscape. Cottonwoods, Syringa, Sarvis, Alder and willow, all leafless, follow the creek.

It is nearly 12:30 when hunger drives us to some flat rocks under a fragrant Pine to break open our lunches of tuna salad sandwiches on whole wheat bread, with plenty of lettuce. From the rocky rims above drifts the haunting, descending call of a canyon wren. While thus engaged, a dreamlike phenomenon sweeps down the canyon…it begins to snow, feathery flakes floating through shafts of sunlight. The clouds close their ranks and the wind rises, but we want to hike the final mile to the cabin.

So, onward and upward we trudge. Suddenly—there it is, in a clearing, just like the last time we visited this place. It has stopped snowing, so I snap some photos of the rich weathered wooden cabin. I wonder about the stories this small one-room shack could tell, with its bunk bed, crude table, and shelves. Suddenly the clouds turned black, and the wind had a bite, so we hurried back to our car, arriving in half the time it took to climb the trail.

Later, after a hot soak in the tub and fixing supper, I am at the OK Theatre joining a standing-room-only crowd to take in the Soroptimist Idol show. The Soroptimist is our local thrift shop. If laughter is good for your health, then we all received a good dose of medicine that night. Our local folks really know how to put on a show and raise money for college scholarships at the same time.

Wallowa County might not have a Saks Fifth Ave clothing store, but you should've seen what those folks found at the thrift shop!

April 1—We awoke to over three inches of snow, and more to come. No April Fool's either. Must do something with the leftover ham for supper. See you next time.

April 6—Yesterday morning at this time, the snow was falling straight down relentlessly, blanketing Prairie Creek with a coverlet of fat wet flakes. Now, at noon, the morning icicles have melted, and snow from the roof is dripping onto the budding daffodils that have appeared alongside the house. Sunlight streams through the large picture window, opening the red osier dogwood blooms, clustered in my Ted Juve pottery vase. Two newborn kittens curl around each other in the sunshine out in the woodshed, and waxy golden buttercups drink the snowmelt on Hough's hill.

Easter Sunday sunrise was short-lived, obliterated by dark clouds pushed by gusty winds. Upper Prairie Creek was a whiteout. Daughter

Phyllis Webb inspects an old cabin up Devil's Gulch near Imnaha.

Ramona and hubby Charley spent the day bringing in chilled newborn calves. Unable to attend our Easter dinner, the couple, as well as other ranchers around the valley, have had very little sleep. Spring is put on hold. However, each time the snow melts, the grass appears taller and greener.

We'd invited Lyman and Wilma to join our family for Easter dinner. Looking out the window was quite a contrast to leafing through my album to show off my Placer County, California, photos in full spring dress.

I'd spent Saturday baking a coconut custard pie topped with toasted coconut meringue, an Easter sweet roll braid with orange frosting, carameled yams, and refrigerator cloverleaf rolls.

Sunday morning after chores, the ham, purchased at the F.F.A. fat stock auction at the County Fair, baked slowly at low heat while I prepared a salad, baked the rolls, cooked frozen corn from our garden, and mashed potatoes. Yum! It was a pleasant afternoon—inside, that is.

Later, son Todd and wife Angie joined us for pie. All this moisture is Lyman's, and especially Wilma's, fault. You see, she went to our local thrift shop and bought me a teeny weeny polka-dot bikini to wear whenever I do the rain dance. Well, let me tell you, once that thing is on, it's pretty confining,and when you're dancing and rain turns to hail, well…it's just not pretty.

Yesterday I got a call from Barb Warnock, a neighbor of Lyman and Wilma's on the upper Imnaha.

"Janie, you can stop that dancin' now, we got enough rain." Knowing Barb, she's wantin' to get out in her garden. Seems I wasn't helping the situation at all.

Got a surprise call from grandson James, who's graduated from Marine officer's training school in Quantico, Virginia.

"I made it grandma." He said he was the only young man in his platoon raised in the country, and attributes that to his making it through a difficult training period.

Another Marine grandson, Shawn, has been deployed to Camp Pendleton, and was just recently reunited with wife Maria, son Jack, daughter Savannah Rose, and baby Jacob, who now weighs 5 lbs and remains hospitalized.

Our Navy grandson Josh is back in Southern California, having returned from Afghanistan on a tour of duty. Wife Desiree and children Wyatt and Ryder haven't seen him for nine long months.

Granddaughter Adele has graduated with an associate degree in Culinary Arts and is back in Wallowa County. We had lunch at the Outlaw Restaurant in Joseph the other day, and this pretty blond Miss tells me she's working on the ranch, riding colts and feeding cattle.

"Missed the ranch work," she says. Hopefully she will be able to continue her studies at Eastern Oregon University in La Grande, where she has set her sights on a degree in Nutrition.

April 19—Experiencing spring along the upper Imnaha has become a necessary part of my life. I need that yearly fix.

Having arrived here yesterday morning, I've just returned from a walk up Indian Creek, eaten breakfast, and seated myself at my desk, which affords a view of where I just hiked. Everything about this place is inspiring. The greening canyons, frothy blooms on cherry and plum, fragrant violets sprinkled on the lawn, daffodils nourished from the flotsam of former floods, and the songs of the kingfisher, dipper, and canyon wren. The air itself, filtered by last night's star-cooled sky and warmed now by the morning sun, which makes its way down the western canyon.

I am the "den mom" for this week's shift of four writers, Richelle Graves, Melissa Riordan, Pat Cason and Julianna Waters, who've traveled long distances to retreat and write. Being a local, and thus the first to arrive, I received a frantic phone call from Pat, who had driven from Hood River.

"Janie, is there supposed to be snow on the road?"

"No," I answered. "You must've taken the wrong road, better turn around. I suspect you're headed for Hat Point."

"I can't turn around here, and there's this sheer drop-off, thousands of feet down, and rocks and snow in the road, but I'll try." Pat had left her car and walked out to where she could receive cell phone service, which is, otherwise, nonexistent here in the canyons.

"You'll be fine," I said. "Just be sure and take the road that turns upriver at the store. See you soon."

Pat did make it, having triumphed over her fear.

Melissa and Richelle arrived just as I was serving up supper, and Julianna is due tomorrow. So far we've been blessed with blue skies and plenty of sunshine. It's been a busy week.

On Wednesday Halley and I joined son Todd and his crew of cowboys and cowgirls down past Peekaboo, where over 400 head of cows and calves had spent the night after being trailed from Enterprise to OK Gulch, and thence, the next day, down South Lightning to Peekaboo, across the road from Little Sheep Creek. It was fun moseying along behind the cattle. Of course, this is the highlight of Halley's year. My young border collie joined seven other happy cow dogs.

Later in the morning, here came great-granddaughters: one-year-old Katelyn, pushed in a stroller by mom Chelsea, and her three-year-old sister Lucy riding "Rose," led by Lucy's daddy Buck. I wish all children could experience what those lucky little girls did that day. The weather smiled on us, and only we who endure long winters can really appreciate what spring offers along Wallowa County's back roads.

We munched our lunches as we hiked behind, allowing cows and calves to take their time, grazing as they ambled along. It was nearing two o'clock when the lead turned off the highway and headed up the narrow, rocky road that follows Big Sheep Creek. A few miles up the canyon, the cattle were left to scatter for the night.

Then, on Saturday, cowboys and cowgirls, children and cow dogs converged from miles around for the annual branding. Another beautiful day, and a long day, wherein the crew never took a break until the last calf was branded and reunited with its mom.

The scene was a photographer's dream, full of action, setting, color, and a chance to capture a way of life that might be fading in other parts of the West, but appears alive and well in Wallowa County. Yep, as I looked around at that herd of youngsters wearing old hats and boots, twirling ropes, and mimicking their dads and moms, it was obvious there'd be plenty of future cowboys and cowgirls.

Blooming sarvisberry dotted the hillsides, willows were leafing out, the meadow was green, and Big Sheep, rushing full of meltwater, was draining the snows from the high plateau country known as Marr Flat. The trees were filled with nesting crows, hawks and magpies, and the air was filled with the sound of bawling cows and calves. Huge thunderheads, heavy with dark bellies, formed over the rims, and Oregon grape splashed yellow among the rock outcroppings.

It was late afternoon when daughter-in-law Angie, who was part of the ground crew, fired up the bar-b-cue, and grilled patties of juicy Marr Flat natural beef burgers. I'd contributed a huge potato salad and a large pan of huckleberry-raspberry-strawberry cobbler. The sun had already slipped over the Western rim by the time the tired but happy crew loaded their horses, dogs and kids, and rattled down the rocky road to home.

Nearly every weekend will find this crew at a branding. Their only pay is the camaraderie of being with their own kind, and the satisfaction of a job well done, all the while honing their skills. Of course the food is always a draw, and for their children the experience is priceless.

Must admit I was a bit beat myself upon returning to Prairie Creek. Just watching all that action made me tired. To bed early, as I headed back into the canyons the next morning.

April 20—Imnaha Writer's Retreat—Our weather is changing now, at noon. Before the clouds appeared I arose early and hiked downriver to have oatmeal and canned pears with Lyman and Wilma, which tasted mighty good after that long walk. Leaving Lyman spading and raking his garden spot, and Wilma chasing birds away so they wouldn't fly over the garden, I retraced my steps back to the cabin where I spied a small flock of wild turkeys across the river, and two Mule tail does picking their way across the steep hillside.

Lyman's daughter Vicky Marks, who drives the Imnaha school bus, stopped to say hello. I tripped back across the retreat bridge before ten o'clock, and, after a good soak in the tub, returned to this column.

April 21—Last evening, while seated around the fireplace and staring into the comforting flames, thunder echoed off the rims and sudden flashes of lightning lit up the canyon walls. The fireworks, short-lived, rumbled off down the Imnaha. In the middle of the night I woke to the steady patter of rain on the tin roof, and water dripping off the eaves. My window was open and the air felt tropical.

When the phone rang this morning, I knew it would be Lyman.

"Hey, your rain dance worked. Thanks," he said, "Just got my wheat in the ground."

"No problem," I replied. "Any time."

On my walk upriver this morning I spotted a lone cow elk grazing a high green bench. Above her, foggy pockets of mists curled around the rims, tugging at the Ponderosas marching up the steep draws. A lovely sight. The river was high and frothy with malt-colored snowmelt, swollen with water from many musical creeks dashing down the grassy draws. Narrow waterfalls trickled down rocky gorges and the greening canyon responded positively to the warm rains. Since we've been here, the cherry blossoms have exploded and the bees are already at work.

April 25—It was a productive week. The rain ceased and the landscape was warmed with bright sunlight on Friday morning, so we decided to hike the Saddle Creek trail, a 2500 ft. elevation gain to the Rim Trail that looks down on Hells canyon.

That story will have to wait for next time, however. Back to Prairie Creek.

Doug and I spent the day working in the yard. While he pruned raspberries, I cleaned out flower beds and raked the lawn. That hike up Freezeout really got me in shape.

A hawk is making a stick nest in one of the willows out front, Melvilles no-till-drilled the fields, and Halley is very happy to see me. Feeling blessed, as this will be the third spring I've witnessed this year. The first was in California in March, then Imnaha in April, and now Prairie Creek in May.

May 10—A weak sun sifts through a cloudy haze this morning, and rain is expected by afternoon—at least, that's what the weather man on our local radio predicted.

Yesterday was pretty near perfect for Mother's Day, weatherwise and otherwise. After two long walks with Halley over the springtime hills, son Todd and daughter Ramona (and spouses) treated us to dinner at Vali's near Wallowa Lake. Can still taste that fried chicken. Young Mike Vali and wife, Dione, have taken over the chefs duties from Mike Sr., and dear Maggie, who has the stamina of a horse, serves up the delicious food along with her jovial manner and hugs for all.

Our children checked in to wish me a Happy Day, and daughter Jackie mentioned there would be a hanging basket of flowers with my name on it at the Alder Slope Nursery. Although she didn't arrive on Mother's Day, my most exciting gift was an 8-month-old Jersey heifer. I named her Fawn. Grandson Buck and wife Chelsea, along with daughters

Phil Ketscher, on horse, helps at the Marr Flat Cattle Company's branding on Big Sheep Creek.

Lucy and Katelyn, delivered her. She is absolutely beautiful! And, after a few days of intense work on my part, at the end of a rope halter, she is now broke to lead. More on Fawn in my next column.

Last week you needed to possess a lot of faith to know it was spring around here. We had six inches of snow! On the positive side, after that spring snow melted into the ground, the grass was as high as Halley's eye. Good thing, 'cause son Ken and Grandson Rowdy turned some of their heifers, cows and calves into our pastures.

A week ago Saturday, Ken, Rowdy, his brother Chad, and sister Chelsie, and their spouses and children, all showed up to work the heifers. It was cold that morning, with a freezing wind blowing down the Prairie, as the entire family pitched in to help at the chutes. All of Ken's grandchildren clipped eartags in their own heifer's ears. In addition to a number, every tag was marked with that child's name. Of course, after the heifers were turned out, this great-grandma had to photograph her herd of kids perched on the fence.

Luckily, I had a large kettle of soup simmering on the stove, to warm up those big and little tummies when they trooped into the kitchen. Let me tell you, it takes a heap of soup to feed 20 hungry cowboys and cowgirls. It was fun seeing Rowdy and Kasey, who had driven up from Mt. Vernon with their cows and calves, although we missed seeing

Cade Cunningham, left, and Katie Hoffman, both of Enterprise, on the fence at the Marr Flat Cattle Company branding on Big Sheep Creek.

great-grandchildren Cutter and Nevada, who opted to stay with grandma Annie to explore her loft full of goodies.

On Saturday Doug and I drove to the Tri-Cities to help daughter Lori celebrate her 50th birthday. Lori's hubby Larry tended to the cooking, which included a bit of help from a local barbecue catering service. Finger-lickin' ribs, chicken and coleslaw tasted twice as good eaten out on the sunny deck—that is, until a thunderstorm swept over Richland.

Another big event was meeting six-month old great-granddaughter Seely Jo, who provided the entertainment.

May 12—Since I promised to finish telling about our hike up Freeze-out while at the Writer's retreat on the Upper Imnaha, here goes.

The trail was muddy at the bottom after those warm rains, but dried up quickly as it does in the canyons. Yellow Fawn Lilies nodded their heads near cool, seepy springs, and, as we zigzagged our way upward, our eyes feasted on the gifts of the rain: Mountain Blue-bells, Yellow Bells, the first Indian Paint Brush, and acres of yellow Cous, the Biscuit Root. Since it was a new experience for Pat and Julianna, they thanked me profusely during the entire trek.

Each switchback brought into view a new wonder. Since it was clear and sunny, we were able to gaze westward to the snowy Wallowas, which had appeared suddenly when we were halfway up. Higher and higher we climbed, through lush bunch grass, past bees working on blooming gooseberry bushes, past gorgeous rock formations and tiered rims ending in sky.

At noon we sank down on a grassy promontory, sprinkled with wild Shooting Stars and Pussy Toes, then broke out peanut butter and apricot jam spread on sourdough bread I'd baked the day before.

Several chukars called on the opposite hillside, and a wee chipmunk twittered on a rock, begging for crumbs. As we climbed, there came the usual question…"How much farther?" which I refused to answer, until we were only steps away from the top of the Saddle. Then: we were there!

The air was thin and an icy breeze refreshed our lungs. To the east yawned the breaks of the Snake River canyon. We were straddling the Imnaha and the Snake.

Snow covered the old Freezeout burn, and a few brave wildflowers clung to the loose scree. We took photos of ourselves by the Rim Trail sign, and stared down at the Saddle Creek Trail, nine miles to Snake River. My day pack yielded an aged chocolate bar, and we celebrated.

To escape the wind, which was now chilling, we opted to start down. It was much calmer going back, but hard on the knees. Julianna, who suffers from a bad back, bravely stuck it out, and we made it to the trailhead safely. Always another triumph for me to hike that trail. My two companions were 20 years my junior, so it felt good keeping up with them.

The memory I'll always cherish from that hike will be the sight of Julianna, an accomplished musician and song writer, stumbling up that steep trail, pen in one hand and note-book in the other, composing a song, humming the melody as she hiked.

That night, in front of the fireplace, we listened to that song, which came straight from the heart, her lyrics capturing the essence of that wild canyon landscape on a perfect day in May.

Our Writers Group meets at Christine's cabin on the west side of Wallowa Lake now. Very pleasant, looking out to the East Moraine and watching the wavelets below.

Rancher neighbor Lois Hough helped me serve for CowBelles at the Community Dining Center this time. Fun to visit Lois, who lives just down the road from us. Of course we had to discuss the wolf issue, which is a very real concern for all the livestock people hereabouts, especially since there has been the first confirmed calf killed by a wolf last week.

At the annual Wallowa County Grain Growers dinner meeting, I sat next to my old friend Ruth Baremore, who has a twinkle in her eye and enjoys a good joke. Ruth is still Wallowa County's number one cowgirl.

Lots going on this time of year. A couple weeks ago, Halley, our Calico cat and I hoofed it over the hill to the Liberty Grange Hall. We were almost there when I caught a whiff of sourdough hotcakes. Leaving my companions waiting outside, I joined Doug for a great breakfast served up to the teamsters, who drive the draft animals which pull the plows and dies for the annual Lee Scott Memorial Plowing Bee held at the Larry and Juanita Waters' ranch.

Back home, I tended to chores before Halley and I wandered up the road to take in the Plowing Bee. My border collie and I accepted a free ride in a buck-board, pulled by a powerful team of blond-maned Belgians named "Gus" and "Call," owned by Bill Myers of Hermiston. Larry drove his team of mules, "Sis" and "Ernie," and Julie Kooch, a local mule skinner, plowed with her team of Belgian cross mules "Mattie" and "Lucy." Brian Cook from Irrigon, was there with his team of dark mules.

As they plowed, the sun streamed down occasionally between dark clouds that blotted out the blue Prairie skies.

The Liberty Grange members grilled hamburgers and of course I wolfed one down before hiking back home.

One dark and stormy night found me in the midst of a squawking clutter of chickens roosting in my chicken house, clipping wings on my new pullets. Yuk! Doug was complaining 'cause they fly out and scratch in his raspberry patch.

Doug and I, being past grand marshals of Hells Canyon Mule Days, were invited to the annual dinner held at the Outlaw Restaurant in Joseph. Honored this year is Doug's brother Biden and wife Betty, who used to ranch down on Jim Creek near the Snake River. The family continues to ranch on the Zumwalt and near Enterprise.

The Honorary Grand Marshal was our own hired man for so many years, Doug's cousin Ben Tippett. In fact, it came close to being a Tippett reunion that evening as cousin Wayne Tippett and his wife Diane drove Doug's brother Jack and wife Blanche over from Clarkston for the big event. There were other family members there, too, and whopper stories were told. Just ask Biden's sister Barbara sometime about how she "branded" her brother—*Ouch!*—with a red hot poker yet.

The big news, however, was that Ben went off and got married...yep, to a pretty gal named Sandy. And now, like the weather man promised, and much to Lyman Goucher's delight, it's raining. Lyman called us to say he'd just hand-seeded three acres of alfalfa and he'd appreciate a little rain. No, I didn't put on that itsy, bitsy teeny weeny bikini to do the rain dance!

May 15—After spending the morning building a coconut cream pie, Doug and I headed for Imnaha to attend the long-awaited BIG BASH at the old Store and Tavern. Remember all those dollar bills tacked to the ceiling? Well they aren't there anymore, at least the old dusty ones aren't. For years those bills were saved for a BIG PARTY for when Dave and Sally sold the place. Well, the sale went through, and the new owners are doing a great job, so the Tanzeys threw a whing ding.

It was a beautiful day. Sunshine, 70 degrees, scent of locust tree blossoms in the air, fragrant lilacs hanging from an old lilac "tree" in the beer garden where we downed a hot dog and sipped a local IPA brew. There were a lot of young folks there we hadn't seen before, but then we took inventory and realized many of the old-timers have left us.

And the coconut cream pie? Well, you remember that was payment to Ken Stein for performing repairs at the Writer's Retreat upriver. Ken enjoyed showing off his $100 pie.

The grain and Canola fields that were "no-till-drilled" earlier are all

Brian Cook, of Irrigon, discing with his team of mules at the annual Lee Scott Memorial Plowing Bee held at the Waters' ranch in Joseph.

A few of Janie Tippett's great-grandkids at the Tippett ranch, working grandpa Ken's cattle on a cold, windy day. L-R: Ashlyn Gray, Riley Ann Gray, Gwenllian Nash, Jada Gray, Gavin Nash, Kennon Nash, Ronan Nash and Gideon Gray.

sprouting. The cherry and plum trees planted in the chicken pen are beginning to bloom. And every morning, while digging worms in that rich soil where I've thrown out kitchen scraps for years, my eager hens perch on the shovel, anticipating a wiggly breakfast. Yum!

Last week I attended the Enterprise Grade School music program. Great-grandson Gideon had called. "Better come hear us grandma," he said. So, I attended, along with half the community who were in various ways related to the grade schoolers. Wallowa County is proud of its new crop of youngsters, and this grandma was especially thrilled with Gideon, his twin Jada, his sisters Ashlyn and Riley Ann, who all performed well. And, when Riley Ann sang "One Tin Soldier" a capella, tears welled up in my eyes. It so reminded me of my father, who used to sing to his milk cows in the dairy barn when I was Riley's age.

More bad wolf news! Son Todd lost a calf near Big Sheep Creek. A confirmed wolf kill. Now Oregon is faced with the same problems most of the Western states have been battling for ten years. Doug attended a wolf meeting in La Grande on Saturday and reported it was very productive. As a result, five ranchers have been granted permits to shoot a wolf when they see one killing their livestock.

Then, a couple of nights ago, my friend Phyllis lost her little donkey to a wild animal attack. Phyllis and her husband Fred suspected a cougar, bear, or wolf. The donkey was kept right next to the house. Later it was determined a a black bear had killed the little pack animal. The bear returned the following night, tore down all of Phyllis' hummingbird feeders, left its huge paw prints on her kitchen windows, then ambled back to the slain donkey to feed…but Mr. Bear had a surprise. He was captured in a snare and subsequently shot.

Last I heard his hide was being saved. Phyllis said it was a very large black bear, which is sort of unusual, as most of the bears they've seen up there are brown or cinnamon-colored. Phyllis says she guesses you have to expect things like that when you live on the edge of the wilderness.

Last Saturday Kathy and I drove over to the Opera House in Elgin and took in the play "Joseph and the Amazing Technicolor Dreamcoat," which was a smashing success. Well presented, with a large, local, talented cast and showy costumes, great lighting and props. We sat front row balcony, which afforded a splendid view. The singing was superb, and, although I'll probably never attend a New York play, this, in my opinion, would rival it.

The sun is out, which is nice, 'cause this morning I planted three different kinds of lettuce and set out more flowers.

During all that rain and snow last week, Lyman and Wilma called.

"Better go hide yourself in the closet, we have snow down on the upper Imnaha." Sometimes you just can't please these folks.

"It's all your fault," I piped back. "You're irrigatin' too soon."

May 24—Oh, it feels good to be out planting the garden! Here, in Wallowa County, where winters are long, and spring is an extension of winter, it's especially gratifying to dig in warm, friable soil again. Yesterday I planted the Yukon Gold and Red potatoes, transplanted more strawberries, and set out the remainder of my herbs in pots.

Last week I transplanted the Walla Walla Sweet onions I'd "heeled in" earlier, as well as a row of cabbage plants I purchased at our Alder Slope Nursery. Actually, I visited this lovely place to check out the hanging basket of flowers my daughter Jackie gave me for Mother's Day. I left carting armloads of starts. I couldn't resist. Pam and Randy Slinker do a fantastic job of tempting us. Their greenhouses are bursting with vigorously growing and colorful plants. The sun actually came out that day, so those of us in that delightful setting responded like the plants, blossoming as well as we wandered among that jungle of geraniums, petunias and tomato plants.

Then whoops, two days later the temperatures zipped down to 28. My garden fairy said to bring my plants inside, and I obeyed. Last week we had at least five inches of snow here on Prairie Creek. No matter, it melted before nightfall, and all this moisture is making for a gloriously green May. Wildflowers are rampant and blooming more profusely than they have for years.

It has been a good morning. Our old Calico mamma kitty's surviving kitten, a colorful Calico, has been romping around the woodshed. Down in the cow pasture, one of Ken and Rowdy's late calvers has birthed her baby during the night. The new calf is up and nursing and, like the kitten, kicking up its heels.

On our walk this morning Halley and I spotted two wild mallard nests, and noticed a Red tail hawk setting on its eggs, high in one of the old Cottonwoods along the creek. And best of all, grandson James called from Quantico, Virginia were he is now a lieutenant in the U.S. Marines. So good to hear his voice, although he's a very homesick young man and missing Wallowa County. I didn't have the heart to tell James I baked the first rhubarb pie yesterday…his favorite. He tells me he won't be home until November.

Before our walk this morning, and after the chickens were fed, Halley and I hoofed it down to the calving shed and tended to Fawn, my eight-month-old Jersey heifer. I still can't believe my good fortune at acquiring

Fawn, Janie's Jersey heifer, slips out of her halter.

this young future milk cow. Joe Platz, who lives in Union, was visiting with grandson Buck one day, and mentioned he had this heifer he would be willing to give away, if he could have the first calf, to raise for locker beef. "My grandma probably would," said Buck, and that's all it took.

Fawn was a bit feisty after Buck and Chelsea dropped her off, not yet used to her new home. It took about a week of working with her, slipping a rope halter over her head and letting her drag it around, tying her up each morning while Halley and I walked, and brushing and petting her.

It all paid off, except she learned how to slip out of that rope halter—a very clever little bovine. Now, however, she has tamed down and comes running when she sees me, anticipating her cup of grain and a brushing. She was pretty lonesome until Ken and Rowdy's cattle arrived. I won't breed her until she's grown out, so therefore she can't be pastured with the other cattle. That young Angus bull would surely fall in love with my young Jerz.

A pair of Swainson's hawks has been building a nest out of limbs they've tweaked from the ancient willow in the front pasture by our house. The nest was nearly complete when a wild windstorm blew it away. Undaunted, the pair rebuilt, and now it appears the female is setting.

May 26—Phyllis and I wandered around in the woods at the base of the East Moraine hunting morels. Although it was an invigorating hike, it wasn't warm enough for mushrooms yet, so we treated ourselves to lunch at the Glacier Grill, situated across from the Wallowa Lake Lodge. Their cook creates a mean Reuben sandwich.

Fishermen were out on the lake in spite of sprinkling rain showers, hauling in more record Kokanee, the landlocked Sockeye Salmon that appear to be very prolific this spring.

May 27—This morning I put together an elk steak and noodle recipe to simmer all day in the crockpot, and this evening I drove the 30 miles to attend the Imnaha end-of-school program. School marm Shari Warnock is down to six students this year.

After adding my crockpot dish to one of Imnaha's famous potlucks, I visited with Lyman and Wilma, who had driven downriver for the event. The river was running high and fragrant roses bloomed alongside the church. After stuffing ourselves with potluck, we took a seat in the church pews and watched the students perform their rendition of "Snow White and the Three Dwarfs," as well as various recitations and musical selections.

The show brought back memories of when my grandchildren Buck and Mona Lee, now grown, performed on that same stage. Outside, the sun burst forth after the rain, and the canyon was bathed in that startling evening light which illuminated every blade of grass, every cottonwood leaf, and every fragrant lilac bloom.

May 29—Son Todd drove Doug out to the Divide to show him where his cows were grazing out on Three Buck. Early the next morning Doug headed out there with the four-wheeler loaded on his pickup to perform "wolf patrol." About all one can do is report a kill, as the chances of being there DURING a kill is very rare, as these wily predators strike at night. There have been several more kills this past week. Very worrisome for local ranchers, nice folks who don't deserve to be in this unfair situation, which is not of their making.

I attended the first Farmer's Market of the season in Joseph that morning. What a festive place! The sun shone on the many vendors' booths, including tables of early spring greens, cooking demos, and a petting zoo with a calf, goat and sheep; The Prairie Creek Girls fiddled and Arrowhead Ranch sold their produce and homemade chocolates. Anne and Jim Shelly, who live up Hurricane Creek, offered their FireWorks pottery, and Wendy McCullough her goat milk soaps.

The air was filled with the aroma of grilling grass-fed beef, served with grilled bok choy and asparagus, crunchy fresh radishes, and new green onions, not to mention Joseph's Wildflower Bakery cookies and cinnamon rolls. Joanie Fluitt took orders for their Prairie Creek Grass-Fed beef. It was a real open-air market. I purchased an armload of greens, and a cherry tomato plant for my garden. Rising above all the festivities were our brilliant white Wallowas.

Doug and I spent Memorial Day weekend at home, except to attend the branding at Triple Creek Ranches on upper Prairie Creek. Luckily, the rain held off until the last calf was worked and the last bite of their famous picnic was eaten. The cowboys and cowgirls who help with this branding look forward all year to that meal, served up by the McKinley family and neighbors who treat us to the best food in the West.

The McKinleys, very generous with their hospitality, serve us King Crab legs simmered in garlic butter, thick steaks grilled outside on an open fire, dutch oven peach and berry cobblers, and fresh fruit salads. Neighbors add scalloped potatoes, beans, and breads, oh my! All eaten outdoors in that magnificent setting. It just don't get any better than this.

Had a nice visit over the phone with neighboring rancher Lois Hough, who just lost a calf to a wolf kill. "Up near Pine Tree Gulch," she said. Everyone wonders where the wolves will strike next. I took a walk up on the hills with Halley that afternoon, to check out a place where I'd spotted a coyote that morning. I'd been planting my garden when I heard it, yipping and carrying on for a half hour or more. I found its tracks near a large badger hole, saw where it had stood on its haunches howling.

Later, returning across the fields, Halley and I came face to face with a badger, who hissed at us as we slowly backed away. About then I looked up to see seven nervous white-tails pause briefly on the skyline, before dashing away over the hill. It rained again on June first, when our Writer's Group met at Christine's cabin on the West side of the lake. After our writing session, to celebrate Sharon Sherlock's birthday, we all drove to the East side of the lake to the Glacier Grill where we all enjoyed a delicious meal.

Last Saturday, after volunteering 'til 1:00 at the Alvin Josephy Library, located in Fishtrap House, I hunted mushrooms in the woods near the ski run road, and came home with enough fresh morels to saute in butter for supper. Yum!

The next evening Doug and I joined daughter Ramona, husband Charley, and friends and family for a potluck on Upper Prairie Creek. The occasion, organized that very morning, was in honor of visiting rancher friends from Red Bluff, California. I added my potato salad to a potluck which included Myrna Moore's homemade bread, Ramona's bar-b-cued pork ribs and beans, and strawberry-rhubarb sauce over ice cream. Good thing I spend a good deal of time hiking and working in the garden, or all these potlucks would do me in.

"Wolf talk" dominated the conversations that evening.

June 7—"June is bustin' out all over," that is, whenever it stops raining long enough to notice. Nevertheless, It IS pretty spectacular here in Wallowa County right now, and the displays of GREEN rival Ireland's. When the sun does peek out, this landscape of mountain, prairie, and canyon is bathed in spring light.

The rains have been soft and warm as of late, and therefore melting the high mountain snows. Reports of rivers overflowing, docks on Snake River being washed away, and mud slides on our Wallowa Mountain Loop Road are just a few of the problems caused by too much rain. All in all, the rain has blessed the country. The grass in the hills and canyons is stirrup high, our strawberry plants are blooming, as are their wild cousins in the woods, mushroom hunting hasn't been this good in years, and my sprouting garden is thriving and growing.

Fifty-seven years ago today, my second child, a son named Kenneth, was born in Highland Hospital in Auburn, California. This afternoon a bunch of heifers, six pairs and one bull, belonging to Ken and his sons, graze our lush pastures. Two more late calves were born last week. The sun is out at the moment, and those babies are stretched out soaking it up.

Down in the barn lot my Jersey heifer Fawn is keeping the grass grazed down in the corrals. Regardless of the weather, Halley and I make our daily rounds of the old ranch, noticing hawk nests, baby killdeer, wild mallards, muskrats, and Great Blue Herons along the irrigation ditch that is now running bank to bank. I fill my senses with shiny new leaves on the cottonwoods, rain-washed skies, and glimpses of blinding snowfields that are rapidly diminishing.

June 8—Sunny and warm all day. At our Writer's Group this morning we sat out on Christine's deck and watched the fishermen float past while we read our pieces and wrote.

Now it's afternoon. Doug is mowing the lawn and I must put a period to this column.

June 11—I spent most of the day in the kitchen baking pies—Shaker Lemon, raspberry/blackberry, and sour cream raisin—for the annual

Erica Reininger sells her organic produce at the Farmer's Market in Joseph every Saturday.

Lynne Sampson Curry, a professional chef, demonstrates how to cook grass-fed beef. Lynne also uses local produce to serve with the beef.

Beth Gibans has many talents—she's a chef who runs a catering service and operates Backyards Gardens in Joseph. Her produce is always sought after at the Wallowa County Farmer's Markets.

Wallowa Mountain Cruise, when the vintage cars chug into town. We members of our Museum Board sold pies right there on Main Street in front of the Museum until the last slice was gone. Huckleberry pie slices sold for $5 while the others went for $3. Several whole pies sold for $20. Money collected was added to the building fund for the remodel of the old firehall, to provide needed space to the Museum.

That evening found Doug and me chowing down on Sammy Garnett's bar-b-cued tri-tip sandwiches before taking in the Blue Mountain Old Time Fiddlers Show, held this time in the Enterprise high school multipurpose room.

Denny Langford, emcee for the show, kept things lively as he introduced the players, who included Little Bailey Vernam with her fiddle tunes, The Prairie Creek Girls, Sam Schaafsma, Maggie Collins and her dad Tim, and many others who drove from miles around to create this great event of toe-tapping merriment. Oldsters, their bones creaking, rose up from their seats to waltz around the room, stepping a bit more livelier as they remembered when they were young.

June 13—Phyllis and I drove out the Zumwalt Road to see the wildflowers, which are pretty spectacular this year.

June 14—The sun warmed a 70 degree day, and on my walk I discovered a white-tail fawn hidden in the tall grasses on the rocky hill above our house.

June 15—Ice on the windshield this morning. Frost nipped the tomatoes and pepper plants. Picked our succulent rhubarb and baked a juicy pie, then called son Todd, who, along with Kevin and grandson Buck, arrived before the pie cooled. Since they'd been doctoring a heifer and the weather was cold and stormy, Todd built a fire in the wood cookstove to dry off.

I couldn't help but think of grandson James, stationed in faraway Virginia, a lieutenant now in the Marines. How he loves rhubarb pie. Wish he'd been there.

This afternoon, son Todd brought me another calf, as company for Fawn, who has been very lonely. Seems this little heifer's mamma wouldn't claim her and she'd been fending for herself. I named her Rhubarb! A pie for a calf. Not bad.

June 19—My friend Pat Cason and I drove the 37 miles out to Wallowa County's North End to attend the annual Flora School Days. It was a lovely day, with enormous cottony clouds floating through a rain-washed sky, and golden Mule Ears, Lupine, Indian Paint brush, pink phlox, camas, and wild geranium carpeting the rolling green hills. Flora, though dubbed a ghost town, is still inhabited by a few souls who live by today's standards while enjoying peace and quiet as well as wildlife.

After parking in a wildflower-strewn field, we ambled over to where numerous early-day skills were being reenacted. We watched soap making, candle making, horse shoeing, silver smithing, plowing with a rusted single-share plow, quilting, sewing on treadle sewing machines, rug making, butter churning, grinding whole grains, dutch oven cooking, charcoal making, and many more homesteader survival skills.

Artist Gene Hayes was there, selling his lovely watercolors that depict local scenes. The North End Grange women displayed and sold their famous pies, a long wooden table laden with them. You purchased tickets for the meal, which included a slice of pie.

Although thunderheads rumbled in the distance, the June sun was warm as we joined a long line of folks waiting to be served grilled chicken, a heaping ladle full of beans from a simmering copper kettle slung over a low fire, coleslaw tossed with dressing made of homemade apple cider vinegar from the "apple squeezin" party held up at Chuck and Kris Fraser's ranch last fall, corn muffins baked in a wood cookstove, and freshly-churned butter. Once served, we sat down to oil cloth-covered tables to chow down and visit our neighbors. Talk centered on the challenges we're all dealing with in our gardens this year.

Vanessa Thompson stirs tallow to which she will add lye to make soap at the recent "Flora Days" held in Wallowa County's North End.

June 22—How green is my valley? Well, let me tell you, it's REALLY green, brilliant green, in every hue imaginable, due to nearly 3 inches of rain that soaked our pastures, fields, and hills. Our nights are now mild and our days sunny. Prairie Creek appears almost tropical.

The Summer Solstice has come and gone, and last evening Halley and I walked until dark to savor the year's longest day. A pair of Barn owls flew from the machine shed to begin their nightly hunt, and the pair of hawks, tending their babies in the ancient willow, were pretty nervous as one of the owls swooped down to snatch one of their offspring. The parent hawks flew into such a rage, they were able to discourage the owl from gulping down its anticipated meal.

After several torrential down pours, my garden picked itself up and, as of today, continues to survive this erratic weather. Potatoes, lettuce, radishes, beets, onions, shallots, corn, beans, squash and carrots are thriving; however, the pepper, cucumber and tomato plants look a bit bedraggled.

Yesterday morning our book group met at Phyllis' pretty place perched on the side of a mountain above Hurricane Creek. Her irises were in full bloom, and the views of Sacajawea out the living room window and the Seven Devils out the kitchen window, were pretty fabulous.

Sunday evening found Doug and me at Vali's Delicatessen at Wallowa Lake, celebrating our 32nd Wedding anniversary. Son Todd and wife Angie had received money from an anonymous source to treat us to dinner for the occasion. After we were seated, they told us the meal was compliments of our Auburn, California, friends, Fred and Sandra Hubbard. What a generous and delicious surprise! We'd just talked to them on the phone, mentioning that we'd have to hang up so as not to be late to Vali's!

Ever-cheerful Maggie served us, and her son Mike Jr. and wife Dione outdid themselves on the Schnitzel, Au Gratin potatoes, Sweet sour beets, and homemade rolls. Desert was apple strudel and tiny cream puffs filled with coffee ice cream. Yum.

All the while, rain-soaked clouds emptied themselves as the waters of Wallowa Lake lapped at the picnic area. 'Tis the season of violent thunderstorms and rainbows.

Last Sunday afternoon, during another "frog-strangler" downpour, some of us music-lovers attended a piano recital staged in the old Dobbin House, not too far from where we live. This charming older home, which features locally-quarried Bowlby Stone, was built by early-day cattle and sheep baron Jay Dobbin. Although it suffered a fire in its upper story, the house is still in great condition, thanks to the folks who own it. A large solid home, built with beautiful wood planed at local mills.

Wallowa County's number one angel, Gail Swart, enthralled us as her nimble fingers flew over the keys, sending waterfalls of beautiful music to pour forth into the spacious rooms of that grand old house. Gail's gratitude for life and her love of humanity flows from her heart to her music, another of her treasured gifts to our community.

Peter Donovan, a gifted pianist, performed duets with Gail, as well as treated us to solo pieces that appeared to be very difficult. We hardly noticed the rain sluicing down outside the many windows. The affair benefited both Fishtrap and The Wallowa Valley Music Alliance. A wonderful way to spend a rainy Sunday.

Contented cattle graze the lush spring pastures on the Mt. Joseph ranch, south of the town of Joseph, Oregon.

The season of myriad activities has begun, and all too soon our brief, beautiful summer will have ended. Ken's and Rowdy's cows, calves, heifers and Angus bull are sleek and shiny, up to their flanks in grass. My hens are laying ten eggs per day, and in a few days those first tender radishes will be ready to pull.

I regret to report another wolf kill last night. On upper Prairie Creek, this time. My heart goes out to the rancher, who has lost yet another calf. Hopefully, something will be done, and soon.

Time to start supper and pull the clothes off the line. It didn't rain all day—yeah!

June 23—Grandson James turned 24 today.

This evening there was a persimmon-colored sunset, one of many we've enjoyed lately on Prairie Creek. Stormed all day.

June 24—Rain-cleansed skies greeted Halley and me as we hiked the East Moraine this morning. After that first vigorous uphill pull, we ambled along the five-mile-long ridge with nary a care. While Halley investigated with her nose, I paused often to photograph the display of wildflowers: golden Mule Ears, brilliant Indian Paint Brush, Lupine and Clarkia against the stunning back drop of snow-splotched Chief Joseph Mountain. All the while, we walked in view of Wallowa Lake below.

Aside from a den of foxes, a multitude of meadowlarks, a mule deer doe and twin fawns, plus a young buck in the velvet, we were the only ones up there. Enormous glacial boulders graced our route, and one generous rock contained a deep hole full of rain water that literally saved Halley's life. The top of the Moraine is a waterless place. I was having to ration my own water, after deciding to hike the entire length, which meant wiggling my aging body beneath the seven-foot high elk fence.

The afternoon heated up and thunderheads accumulated overhead while I perched on a rock overlooking the lake to eat my sandwich. Halley, her tongue lolling to the side, flopped down in the shade of the boulder. I'd made a plan and hoped for the best. After walking down an old wagon road that wound into thick timber, I struck off toward a remembered creek, crossed the water, and continued downward until I arrived smack dab in Jean Wiggins' back yard.

Luckily Jean was home, and delivered Halley and me back to where we'd parked our pickup at the foot of the lake. Just as we arrived, a thunderstorm exploded over the Wallowas and rain pelted our windshield all the way home.

Doug, just home from the hills, reported seeing hundreds of elk.

June 25—I called the Gouchers on Imnaha and learned that Lyman was haying his first cutting. He said son Craig was helping.

That night our resident barn owls flew against the full "Wild Rose" June moon.

June 26—Today was the Amy Hafer Memorial Run/walk, which began at our new hospital. Nearly 250 participants turned out in a gorgeous morning to run/walk the scenic course that climbs uphill toward Ant Flat. All along the route bloomed the wild blue flax, and our return route blessed us with a cool, refreshing breeze. I completed the 5K in less than an hour. Didn't receive a ribbon, as I was competing with 60-year-olds.

That afternoon Doug and I attended the annual Joseph Ranch Rodeo, held in the Harley Tucker Memorial arena. Although the Marr Flat team didn't win this year, they did "rock" in the team branding. 2010 top honors went to the Baremore Ranch team. Ruth Baremore's tough grandsons really showed their stuff.

Great-granddaughter Lucy ran in the stick horse race, held for the little tots.

June 27—I was invited out to Lost Prairie for lunch with friends Al and Nellie Habegger. Words fail when it comes to describing their place, which includes a log home they built themselves, Nellie's garden, their view of Lost Prairie on the breaks of the Grande Ronde, and the lovely countryside and forests that comprise their property. Both true stewards of the land, this couple can be commended for their efforts.

Al showed me his successful grafting of apple tree limbs and his propagating of native bunch grasses. Nellie served a delicious meal, cooked earlier on her Monarch wood range. Since they have no electricity, save for a generator and solar panels, she does her cooking while the fire is burning in the morning. It was a memorable visit.

On the way out I was thrilled to see a mother grouse and her little brood, who appeared suddenly alongside the road.

June 28—Up at 4:30 a.m., reuniting one of grandson Rowdy's calves with its mother, both of whom had been bawling all night. My reward was viewing the waning full moon hanging over the Wallowas, bathed in the blush of predawn light.

June 29—I hoed my garden with renewed vigor, hoping for no more natural disasters. So far, so good. We're enjoying fresh lettuce, spinach, radishes, onions, and strawberries. The Canola field, planted in one of our former hayfields, is in full mustard-colored bloom.

I photographed it this morning.

July 2—Doug took great-grandsons Clayton and Cole fishing early on the lake. Although Grandpa Charley caught the biggest Kokanee, the boys caught their share. Later in the morning, I treated us all to breakfast at the Cheyenne Cafe in Joseph.

July 3—I joined other 5K runners and walkers up the South Fork of the Lostine River for the annual 4th of July event. It was a lovely cool morning in sunlight and shadow. Fueled by wild rose-scented air, and the sounds and sights of the Lostine River flashing past, I bested my previous time. And, since the Rotary Club offers a 70+ age class, I won—no competition again—and received a bright blue ribbon to hang on my wall.

I had enough energy left to wander along Main Street and enjoy Lostine's Giant Flea Market. Ran into Doug at the Lions Club booth and gobbled down a hamburger smothered in fried Walla Walla Sweet onions. Wandering back to my car, I purchased some lavender soap, a bouquet of fresh lavender and a potted plant from Lavenders R Us.

On the way home I left the lavender bouquet off with Chelsea and Buck, who were celebrating their sixth wedding anniversary that day. I have a busy week ahead, cooking for the Outpost Writer's workshop way out at Billy Meadows.

July 5—Safe in their airy nest, perched high in our ancient willow, the baby hawks wobble their fuzzy heads in anticipation of their next meal. I love watching the parent red-tails take turns bringing them tidbits of ground squirrels and other rodents. Because the nest is visible from our living room window, I'm able to observe their antics through my binoculars.

The 4th of July ended with a final thunderous boom, followed by the bursting of myriad fiery sparks, co-mingling into a grand finale of fireworks that sizzled down upon the dark waters of Wallowa Lake. Members of our family, plus friends, parked midway on the East moraine, compliments of a friend, to view the 45-minute annual display. Far below, the lake glittered with tiny green lights shining from a flotilla of small boats, all grouped at the north end of the lake.

Way high up on the southern ridge of Chief Joseph Mountain, we spied more pinpricks of lights. Were these energetic hikers? Hundreds of cars lined the lake shore, stretching nearly to Joseph. When the show ended, earlier clouds had dissipated and, led by Venus, the natural display of stars took the stage, their silent beauty in contrast to man's noisy display.

Earlier, family and friends had gathered at Kate and Heimo Ladinig's rustic new home on Upper Prairie Creek under the East Moraine, to visit and chow down on Heimo's grilled tri-tip, salmon and vegetables. The rest of us filled in with salads and desserts. I contributed some of Myrna Moore's peaches I'd frozen last summer, baked under a cobbler crust.

We ate on the patio with that awesome view spread before us: the sweep of Wallowas, acres of lush hay fields, and dark thunderheads that threatened but didn't wet us. A brisk wind died down before sunset, and that familiar low, golden light treated us to another special Prairie Creek evening.

One of my banty hens hatched out a lone chick, which seems to be thriving.

Three of the California great-grandkids are here visiting their grand-parents, Charley and Ramona, so it's been fun seeing them. Clayton and Cole are through showing and selling their 4-H steers, and Halley sold her market goat, so they were free to visit Camp Run-a-Muck, which I understand has been renamed Camp-Earn-a-Muck. In other words, the kids are being put to work on the ranch.

My garden picked itself up again, after being hammered with mothball-size hailstones last week.

And the big news—My book, published by Pika Press, is on sale now at the Bookloft in Enterprise. The title is *Four Lines a Day*, the true story

Halley enjoys the view from the east moraine of Wallowa Lake during a recent hike.

of ranch woman Mary Marks, who loaned me the diaries she faithfully kept all those years she lived on Imnaha. Sadly, Mary passed away just before her 90th birthday.

July 10—Stanlynn showed up to load my dutch ovens, pots, pans and assorted cooking utensils that we would need to feed 16 people from Sunday 'til Thursday at Billy Meadows.

Later in the morning, grocery lists in hand, we shopped for foodstuffs at the Dollar Stretcher and Safeway. A big job.

July 20—After feeding and watering my chickens, I was traipsing down the path to the house when I noticed a pickup slow down in the road. Curious, I looked out front to see a herd of cows, calves, and one bull! They looked familiar...could it be? It was. Son Ken's cattle had apparently just escaped from their pasture.

I jumped in the car and drove to get ahead of them, and close a gate that opened into a lush field of oats. They then turned tail and headed up the road toward another open gate that led to a wheat field. While maneuvering my car to head off the frisky bull, I noticed someone had unlatched the gate to their pasture.

Of course, this always happens when I'm alone. And although Halley is a cow dog at heart, her role is more that of companion, since we

Members of the 2010 Chief Joseph Days Court participated in the Joseph Ranch Rodeo. Queen Alex McCadden (holding Cody Cunningham), Emily Howerton, and Jesse Kohlhepp.

Smiling for the camera in the Baremore Ranch Team that won top honors at the recent Joseph Ranch Rodeo, held at the Harley Tucker arena. From left: Travis Bales, Randy Baremore (holding spurs he won for top hand), Brandon Burgess, and Cody Baremore.

don't run cattle anymore. So, she obediently stayed in the yard whilst her mistress turned the herd toward the open gate. Thankfully, the errant cattle filed into their pasture and, after securing the gate, I further fortified the latch with baling twine.

This set the tone for the morning, and I won't bore you with all the sordid details, but it is now 3:30 and I'm just now sitting down to begin this column. Summertime in Wallowa County is here.

On Sunday morning, the 11th, I awoke at dawn and, after chores and a final weeding of my garden, headed to Stanlynn's. We spent a good deal of time loading and packing coolers full of perishables, our sleeping bags, a portable barbecue, and other items into her pickup.

Stanlynn Daugherty, who for years ran a llama packing service up Hurricane Creek, is a pro when it comes to packing, plus she is considerably younger than me. Those days when I helped pack mules and ride into wilderness camps to cook for deluxe elk and deer hunts are over. Therefore, I helped carry stuff to the pickup but left packing to the PRO. Nice. I would need to conserve my energy for other activities such as dutch oven cooking in a fire pit.

At last, we were off to some of Wallowa County's little-visited outback. Loaded for bear, we headed out the North Highway, turned east onto the Charolais Road, thence along Elk creek to Crow Creek, crossing Chesnimnus Creek where that creek joins Crow Creek and becomes Joseph Creek, before we headed up Red Hill. After a brief stop at the Red Hill fire lookout to gaze down upon the awesome view of the "Chesnim," the faraway Findley Buttes and the distant Wallowas, we proceeded past Coyote and thence to Billy Meadows.

As we drove into the Forest Service Guard Station where I cooked last year, we noticed considerable activity. Previously we'd been informed that a roofing crew would be installing a new shake roof on the historic CCC cabin, which is where the Fishtrap "Outposters" would be participating in their writing workshop.

A large truck cab attached to a trailer was parked in front of a modern "Module" that would serve as our kitchen. Luckily, there was still room to back the pickup against the steps so we could unload our stuff. The peace of the meadow was shattered by the roar of a generator. The Outposters would be arriving around 6:00 p.m., and we were assured the crew would leave by that time.

We began the monumental task of unloading, sorting and putting away foodstuffs in the module kitchen, situated up hill from the historic cabin. By 6:00 we had the first meal under control, and could see the roofing crew outside eating their evening meal. The generator roared on. No sign of our Outposters.

6:30 came and went—and suddenly the generator was turned off, the roofers packed up and left, and the diesel truck roared and rumbled up the road. Silence! The meadow returned to its lovely peaceful self, and shortly thereafter, here came the van driven by Jon Rombach, who would serve as camp manager, full of writers along with instructors Charles Goodrich and Robert Michael Pyle.

We'd made a potato salad, laid out fixings for some of those bar-b-cued Marr Flat Natural Beef burgers, cooked corn on the cob, and sliced watermelon. After the participants were settled in, their tents pitched among forest and meadow, they trooped in to eat. It was such a lovely, warm evening, we enjoyed our meal around the campfire pit.

Thus began the second year of the Fishtrap Outpost Writing project and Werner Residency at Billy Meadows. Needless to say, Stanlynn and I fell into our beds that night: real beds with mattresses to throw our sleeping bags on, while the writers, and Jon, a wild river guide and humor columnists for our local paper, chose to "rough it in the Outback."

Billy Meadows is a lovely spot, and all manner of wildflowers bloomed profusely. False Hellebore spiked tall in the lush grassy meadows and lined a tiny stream. The meadows were fringed by Aspen thickets and thick conifer forests. There was no traffic on the spur road, and since we didn't use electricity, there was no hum of appliances, no phones ringing, no e-mail, no television; just the natural sounds of birds and breezes singing in the pines.

Everything was lush and green due to our late wet spring. And, juxtaposed to last year, we had no violent thunderstorms, hail, rain nor cold. One sunny day followed another, and with the exception of one morning, when the meadow sparkled with frost, the weather smiled on us.

Monday morning we arose early to begin breakfast. I prepared cowboy coffee by bringing my large granite-ware pot to the boil, then dropping one of Doug's socks (clean, of course) filled with fresh ground coffee into the pot. Coffee was ready every morning by 7:00. Then I fried bacon, and kept it warm in the dutch oven while I cooked a griddle full of fresh eggs. We served country food at every meal.

After breakfast we laid out lunch fixings and everyone "brown-bagged" it before attending their writing workshop held inside the old CCC cabin. That evening we served two large lasagnas Stanlynn and I had previously prepared at home and frozen. It was a fabulous five days, full of work as well as fun.

Tuesday morning, virtually everyone, including Jon Rombach, who drove the van, and Stanlynn, who drove Bob Pyle, left to spend the day at Buckhorn Lookout. Naturalist Jan Hohmann arrived to lead a nature hike. I had Billy Meadows all to myself!

I began by baking sourdough bread in the gas oven that is situated in the CCC Cabin. By noon I had traipsed back and forth from that oven to the module many times, toting peach cobblers and fragrant bread. Then I lit a fire in the firepit and let it burn down before I placed my heavy dutch ovens full of pot roast, shallots, carrots and garlic among the hot coals.

By the time everyone returned I had the potatoes peeled and, while they cooked, Stanlynn put together a salad. After Jon mashed the spuds, we feasted. The dutch oven meal was done to perfection, and served from the kettles nestled in the campfire coals.

Later, we fed the fire and, while Jon and Stanlynn did the dishes, I retreated to the campfire to join a sing-along, accompanied by Donald Witten strumming his guitar. Soon, two more of our group appeared with harmonica and fiddle. Sparks drifted skyward to join a star-filled night. Gas lights glowed from the windows, and wild things watched from the forests.

The next day I took time to photograph and write in my journal. Stanlynn prepared a delicious meal of grilled chicken kabobs that night.

One morning I treated them to sourdough pancakes hot off the griddle, and after everyone ate their fill, there were several left. Stanlynn suggested we dry them in the sun. That evening, to relieve the tensions of writing, we all engaged in a wild game of pancake frisbee. What a joy cooking for this congenial group of writers who hailed from all over the country.

On Thursday morning, after everyone was fed and lunches made, Jon helped Stanlynn and me load our gear. By some miracle we were all able to arrive at the Fishtrap Gathering at Wallowa Lake by 3:30 that afternoon to participate in the Outposters presentation of which all of us were a part, even the cooks and camp manager.

A program posted at the door revealed that I was scheduled to read from my new book at 5:00 p.m. That happened, and I was honored and moved to tears by the appearance of my daughter Jackie, visiting from Challis, Idaho, along with her son Buck, his wife Chelsea, and two of my great-granddaughters, Lucy and Katelyn, who had come to hear Grandma Janie read from *Four Lines a Day*. My family presented me with a lovely bouquet of flowers, and then I was seated at a table set up outside on the lawn to sign books. It was, perhaps, one of my proudest moments.

Summer Fishtrap was very stimulating and many old friends showed up to honor me. For starters were Eric Ottem, Steve Reed, and Tom Hampson, who attended the first Writer's Retreat on Imnaha, many years ago. And, Bobbie Ulrich, one of our Syringa Sisters, was there and working on her new book, due out in November.

The conference ended Sunday morning, followed by a gathering of Fishtrap attendees at Alvin Josephy's writing studio situated at the base of the East Moraine. We all felt Alvin's presence there, as well as his wife Betty's. Hard to believe they are no longer with us. Alvin's son Al, and his wife Melissa, were gracious enough to continue the tradition in this lovely place.

I returned that afternoon to Prairie Creek to find Doug had done a commendable job of watering my gardens and tending my chickens and Halley. Daughter Jackie and childhood chum spent three nights here.

On Monday morning I hosted our monthly book group on the lawn, and served the traditional strawberry shortcake by 9:00.

The next day I finally found time to sort through and put away the Billy Meadows stuff. And now it is Chief Joseph Days, with company coming and the first rodeo tonight. Like I say, summers here are crazy, everyone is frantically busy. Must get ready for the rodeo. Joseph is full of tourists and hype for the big weekend. See you next time. Take time to enjoy the summer.

July 30—Neighbor Lois Hough and I served for CowBelles at the senior meal site.

August 1—Grandson James called from Virginia, where he is stationed in the Marines. He misses Wallowa County.

August 3—Melvin and Mary Lou Brink hosted us old employees of the Wallowa Memorial Hospital at her lovely home in rural Enterprise.

August 4—Granddaughter Adele showed up at my door clutching a handful of Indian Paint Brush. She'd backpacked up McCully creek to have some alone time. Proud of her! Spent the night up in McCully basin with her dog. That's my girl.

Old-timer 100 year-old Kate Wilde went to join "her Will." She was buried in the Prairie Creek cemetery at the same time a professional film crew was shooting a documentary on the Jidge Tippett family here on the old ranch.

Doug Tippett smiles as he proudly shows off the Chinook Salmon he caught recently in the Imnaha River.

Abundant irrigation water from melting snow in the Wallowa Valley. Farmer Doug Tippett ranch, now owned by Richard and March Frasch.

It was also county fair time, and I had entered veggies and photos again. Great-grandson Gideon won second place in the watermelon seed spitting contest, I purchased great-granddaughter Riley Ann's 4-H market lamb, and Doug bid on and "turned" Rebecca Cummins' market steer. The photo shoot was quite an experience and I'd spent a good deal of time watering lawns and tending flowers so our yard would be presentable for the occasion.

Doug's 91-year-old brother Jack drove from Clarkston, Washington, with wife Blanche, as well as his brother Biden and wife Betty, and his sister Barbara Fredrick, all of whom live in Enterprise. Horses were provided by son Todd for the four siblings to mount up for the photographer. Lunch was catered by Doug's niece Patsy Tippett from Portland, whose son from New York, Dylan Coulter, was the photographer.

The next day the film crew and the Tippetts traveled out to Buckhorn Lookout, and I stayed to do the fair. Lyman and Wilma came up from the canyons and joined us for the F.F.A. barbecue held before the auction.

What a summer, and only a portion of it recorded in my daily journal. My life is busy beyond busy, as Doug's niece Patsy described it. But the last few nights I have stepped outside to gaze up at the clear night sky and witness the falling stars, the annual Perseids meteor shower. We, who choose to live here, should accept this life as the greatest gift of all, and be forever grateful.

August 15—It's Sunday morning and, for the first time in weeks, I've stolen a bit of precious time to pause in the midst of a life that seems not mine anymore. Perhaps it's just August in Wallowa County, but it finally FEELS like summer so everyone squeezes everything into this brief period before fall. It's been a very odd year, weather-wise...and otherwise. A writer friend mentioned recently that after you have a book published, your life is forever changed. And since my book is now out there, this seems to be my fate.

Yesterday it was HOT! And out at Maxville, the historic logging community that lies north of Wallowa Town, things came to life again during Maxville Days! Gwen Trice, daughter of Lucky Trice, who logged the woods near Maxville during those early years, is responsible for this annual picnic that celebrates her heritage.

Our home town of Joseph hosted the popular annual Bronze, Brews and Blues Festival yesterday, too. I didn't go to town, but can imagine the place was full of blues lovers, swilling local brews and ogling the bronzes that punctuate Main Street. Yesterday's events also included class and family reunions, a youth horse clinic, a large wedding, and a birthday party down on Little Sheep Creek.

I opted to attend the party, which honored my friend Ruth on her 80th birthday. Phyllis came over and we drove down together. What a beautiful setting for a party. A new house, built next to a historic barn and designed like the barn, afforded views of the creek splashing its way down through a meadow fringed by forest, and beyond, the Wallowas. From the sleeping loft, the windows look out on the breaks of the canyon country. This unique country home serves as an example of what can be achieved when a retired couple works together to live their dream. Truly, a labor of love.

Back home for a short breather, before driving to the Enterprise Community Church to attend the wedding of Sterling Shetler and Alyse Fisher, granddaughter of well-known local ranchers Mack and Marian Birkmaier. Since Sterling has been employed by our son-in-law Charley Phillips, who manages the Cross Sabres ranch on Tucker Down Road, our family has witnessed the blossoming of Sterling and Alyse's romance. Therefore, these two delightful young people have been included in our family gatherings for quite some time.

The old church was filled to overflowing, a testament to Sterling and Alyses' popularity. Those of us who witnessed this marriage will never forget it. Pastor Gerald Raedeke performed the simple ceremony, a ceremony that truly touched our hearts, because true love and commitment is so rare in today's troubled world. There they were, Alyse, a beautiful bride, inside and out, and her handsome cowboy, whom Pastor Raedeke described as a young man who "worked for a living."

The reception was held at "The Blue Barn," up Tenderfoot Valley Road a quarter mile from our place. Don Harker and Nancy Knoble, who purchased "the old Hockett place," have done a commendable job of restoring the old barn. with a new paint job and a cleaning and polishing of the old hay mow, to the extent that this landmark barn is now in demand for weddings and receptions.

Just two weeks ago I attended the wedding of Clayton Lowe and Casey Montgomery there, the ceremony performed in the horse arena whilst goats nibbled the cloth on the guestbook table, chickens and one turkey clucked, scratched and crowed, and neighboring rancher Robert Butterfield swathed hay during the couple's wedding vows.

Another hot afternoon when great thunderheads rolled across Prairie Creek and busted loose with rain and hail, though by some miracle the weather held off until the bride and groom were pronounced man and wife. Earlier, neighbor Larry Waters had delivered the bride, clad in her long white gown, in his mule-drawn buggy. When everyone climbed

Ashley Exon, of Enterprise, smiles as she shows off her Reserve Champion 4-H Market Steer at the Wallowa County Fair.

B.J. Warnock, FFA member from Imnaha, who belongs to the Joseph High School Chapter, with his Champion Market Steer at the Wallowa County Fair.

Tres hermanos caballero

From left: Jack Tippett, 91, of Clarkston, Washington; Biden Tippett, 84, of Enterprise; and Doug Tippett, 79, of Joseph, pose for a photo shoot held recently at the Tippett Ranch on Prairie Creek.

Phyllis Webb pauses along the trail up Hurricane Creek during a recent hike. Sacajawea Peak is in the distance.

the wooden stairs to the hay mow, the rain turned to hail and, while the bride and groom danced, the Imnaha band was drowned out by the steady drumming of hail on the tin roof. It was a wonderful wedding.

And that scene was repeated again yesterday, with food served near the old horse stalls and carried up to the hay loft for music, dancing, and folks visiting. Down below lay those chickens, goats and the pastoral scene of Prairie Creek, with its tidy farms and ranches, and always there, our Wallowas, bare-boned, awaiting the first early snows of autumn.

Warm yesterday in the mow, but also so much merriment and visiting that no one cared. The bride was lovely and loving, and the groom smitten with his "gem." I sat on a bale of straw and visited my neighbor Lois Hough, who, with her husband Don, own the ranch across the road from us.

While observing everyone enjoying themselves and visiting, it struck me that what Don and Nancy are doing here, opening their barn for these young people and their families and friends, is also sustaining a sense of rural community and lifestyle that hearkens back to the early days before television, computers and automobiles—back to a time when neighbors and friends gathered to celebrate the joining of two lives.

Given the opportunity, folks love to get together, especially busy ranchers and farmers who never take time to visit like they did in the "old days," when everyone brought food and danced and remembered their own weddings. This is a place for children to race around and dance, too, and grandmas and great-grandmas, like me, to dance with a son-in-law and a great-granddaughter.

With all good intentions I began this column several times, only to be thwarted by my complicated life. Help! Yesterday was also my youngest son Todd's birthday. I remembered the day he was born, in Sacramento, California. It was HOT that day too, but I had other things on my mind. It was air-conditioned in the Sutter Memorial Hospital, so I didn't notice the heat; I was overjoyed with a brand new son.

Today, Todd and his wife Angie have two sons and two daughters, and the eldest of those two sons, Josh and his lovely wife Desiree, have two sons of their own, Wyatt Richard and Ryder Todd. Josh is in the Navy, stationed in San Diego. The young family was here visiting recently.

Todd's other son, James, is stationed in Virginia and a lieutenant in the U.S. Marines. Daughter Adele, recently graduated from Culinary school in Austin, Texas, and is presently training colts on the home ranch while cooking at Terminal Gravity, a local brew pub in Enterprise. Daughter Becky recently opened a coffee shop in La Grande. The years roll on.

Daughter Jackie and husband Bill traveled from Challis, Idaho, to Union, where they spent their time keeping track of Grandson Buck and wife Chelsea's little girls, Lucy and Katelyn—no small job!—whilst mom and dad conducted a Rodeo Bible Camp. Busy time for that family. They were in the midst of moving to their modest little house and down-sizing.

Because our family LOVES to get together, I planned a picnic here last Thursday evening. Our family is HUGE. They all came, with the exception of granddaughter Adele, who had to work; son Ken, who was working on a contract job in Dayton, Washington; and granddaughters Becky and Carrie. That meant there were 30 of us.

Every day last week it rained, thundered, and was generally unsettled, but on that Thursday the weather was perfect. The cars rolled in, children spilled out. Homemade ice cream was cranked and the children gravitated to the raspberry patch, holding kittens and picking berries. Fifteen great-grandchildren, ages 10 and under. Parents took a head count as they disappeared in the garden. Justin grilled hamburgers, the ham I'd had in the oven all afternoon was carved, the family brought more food, including Chelsie, who baked chocolate sheet cakes to celebrate three birthdays and one anniversary. Uncles organized foot races for the kids, and we all cheered them on.

As the sun slipped behind the Wallowas it was chilly enough to break out the jackets. Everyone left just before dark, and a great silence fell over Prairie Creek. The kittens came out of hiding, Halley missed the children, Doug crept off to bed, and I stayed up just long enough to put things away.

My last thoughts as I drifted off to sleep had to do with how blessed we are with this large, wonderful family. I have made pesto from my garden basil, put up the first batch of raspberry freezer jam, and we are eating Walla Walla sweet onions, potatoes, and strawberries.

August 30—"My life is a poem I might have writ, if I had the time to live and utter it." This is a quote from Thoreau I memorized as a young girl. Henry David seems to have hit the nail on the head when it comes to describing my life. Lately, I've been so busy living my life, I scarcely have time to write about it. It is four o'clock in the morning, and this column was due on Friday.

On Friday I was lying in the warm sand, on a sunny beach in Neskowin, Oregon. Next to me, reclining in a beach chair, was my dear friend and writer, Bobbie Ulrich.

On the other side of Bobbie sat Barb, reading my book, *Four Lines a Day*, while above us, seated amongst the tall beach grasses and boulders, rested Mary and Jessica. You got it! We "Syringa Sisters" were meeting for our 14th year, to recharge our batteries, write, hike, laugh, eat, cry, and grow another year older.

I can feel it now: the soft golden sand, the gentle sunlight. I can smell the salt air and watch the incoming tide, as it washes around Proposal Rock, near where Slab Creek empties into the Pacific. I hear again the cry of gulls as they wade the foamy swells to snatch the first bits of meat in a broken crab leg or clam shell. I hear the cawing of ravens and my mind's eye sees the wild geese wheeling over the turquoise waves, fluorescent in the morning light.

I can smell the sea weed and kelp, some attached to mussel shells, and remember the young mother who appeared up the beach, with her mother and father, to set up a tiny tent into which she plopped her baby while she allowed her two toddlers to play in the sand with their toys. Only they didn't play with the toys—they played with the sand, sifting it between their fingers, marveling, like me, at the wonder of it all.

It had been 32 years since I'd been to the ocean. My mother loved the sea. My sisters love it, and go there whenever they get the chance. But I am a mountain girl, I thought. Always will be. Only, now I understand why mamma loved it so. I was wearing her pink jacket embroidered with wildflowers that Friday morning, to ward off the fresh sea breeze. In essence, I took a part of my mother to Neskowin. I could feel her presence in the warm pockets of salt air, in the cry of the gulls, and I imagined her footprints in the sand. Oh my, one writes strange things before daylight.

"Piglet," my rooster, just crowed, and over Hough's hill the wailing of coyotes breaks the silence of Prairie Creek. I open the living room door, which faces east. At five o'clock the sky is brightening. What woke me early was Doug arising to check the temperature, which was under forty. Since he has been caretaking my garden during my week's absence, he was afraid it would freeze—and it came close while I was gone.

We awoke yesterday morning to see the first snow blanketing the Wallowas, and the clouds have cleared, and you know what that can mean here on Prairie Creek…goodbye, garden, even when it's at its most beautiful; corn ripening, beans ready to pick and can, sauerkraut to make, pickles to can, and goodness! What of the zucchini and my prolific baking squash? Speaking of which—my squash is climbing the apple tree again, and trailing along the garden fence, its tendrils heading toward the rows of corn and having babies along the way. Only the babies aren't anywhere near mature. What they need are warm nights and hot days. But this seems like fall. Is fall. School starts today. Where did summer go? Was I not watching?

5:30 a.m. Just stepped out on the carport to check the temp. 45 and falling. Doug set the sprinklers going on the garden, which will keep it from freezing, even though everything will be sheathed in ice.

We used to get our first freeze the morning after Labor Day.

While outside I gazed toward the west to see Venus the morning star, glittering in the cold dawn sky above snow-spattered Chief Joseph Mountain. The sight brings to mind the fate of "Morning Star," my Arab mare that had to be put down several months ago because she couldn't make it through another winter. The damage to her joints, due to a second bout of founder, was just too severe. I am just now able to write about it.

My yearling Jersey heifer Fawn, and her mate, the black heifer son Todd gave me, are living the good life. They have shade, running water, green grass, and a cup of grain every morning, plus plenty of TLC.

Halley sticks to me like a tick ever since my week-long absence. It's good to be home. August on the calendar was so full, and marked up with so many dates, I will be glad to flip the page to September, where Doug and I will grow another year older one day apart. It's just a blur.

We attended the Stockgrowers Ranch Rodeo, with its World Champion Rock jack building contest and dinner-dance that night. I got the winning bid on Pat Daugherty's first place rock jack, the proceeds of which, along with other donations, will be given to the Moores to offset medical expenses due to cancer in the family. Good things happen here in our valley.

Then there was the dinner here for our old gang on a perfect summer evening. Doug grilled that huge salmon he caught in the Imnaha and Jeannie Wiggins added more, and our friends brought food, and Bob Hall and I cranked out a freezer of ice cream for over an hour before we found out the dasher wasn't engaged, but we fixed it and the ice cream was the best ever. We sprinkled huckleberries over the top and sat on the lawn and visited until the sun sank behind the Wallowas.

I had planned to have a book signing during the rodeo the next morning, but my friend Phyllis sold my books 'cause I wanted to watch grandson Rowdy in the horse race, and sons Ken and Todd contest in the rodeo, and great-grandson Cutter Chief and great-granddaughter Lucy in the stick horse race, and grandson Buck and his wife compete in various events.

Well, that next morning, Sunday, I drove to La Grande, left my car with granddaughter Carrie, and met up with Syringa Sisters Jessica and Mary. Then I sat in the back seat for 10 hours until we arrived in Neskowin, on the Oregon Coast.

Neskowin. I'd been dreaming of that trip for months.

And now the birds are awakening and joining Piglet here on Prairie Creek, and I'm tired and will e-mail this column. I'm not even going to edit it, just send it on. Good luck, Sterling

P.S. It is 32 degrees on the carport, and falling... at 6:15 am.

September 13—It is 2:25 a.m, and here is me, sitting in my bathrobe at my kitchen table, surrounded by reminders of this past week: myriad birthday cards for Doug and me, who turned 79 and 77 on the 8th and 9th, respectively; the official program for the 30th annual Hells Canyon Mule Days; stacks of correspondence that remains to be answered; my daily journal, in whose pages I haven't had time to record my life for days; a packet of photos of my incredible camping trip to Cayuse Flat; a bouquet of flowers from my dear friend Richelle, who operates Central Copy in Enterprise and taught me how to print out my own digital photos; a button for Hells Canyon Mule Days; and the program for the Max Walker Memorial cowboy gathering held every year as part of Mule Days.

All of these moments represent what has transpired in a mere heart-beat of my life. It is typical of all of us who live here in this beautiful place. We must squeeze these events in before winter, in this brief beautiful time before the snows come, before the nine months arrive when we can't do outside things like Mule Days, camping, or Cycle Oregon.

And God truly smiled on us these past few days, 'cause after no summer at all—or so it seemed—there suddenly appeared Indian Summer with its lovely, warm, almost-hot afternoons, star-filled nights, and crisp sunny mornings. No wind, just gentle breezes, and our beloved Wallowas standing bare and purple-hued, stark against the bluest of skies.

The early snows of last week, that dusted Sacajawea and Aneroid Mountain, melted and vanished under a September sun that seemed to radiate more warmth than it did in August. A gift, 'cause Mule Days broke records in attendance, as did Cycle Oregon.

The 2,200 riders came together in a living, breathing, teeming tent city of humanity which included myriad local volunteers; its wheeled community of semi trucks full of showers, food services, and bicycle repair shops; tents full of massage parlors serving smoothies, chai tea, beer, wine, and ice cream.

The folks, young and old, riding bikes or strolling around our local golf course, crossing Trout Creek to walk to dinner under an enormous tent near where a stage was erected and our local talent, like Brady

Goss, Janis Carper and the Alibis, performed to an audience of thousands who stood in awe of Ruby Peak rising to the west and the new moon suspended above, the evening star Venus appearing in a salmon-colored sky, with an American Flag spotlighted, waving in a mere breath of air against those darkening Wallowas.

All around them, beauty and quiet and unpolluted skies, and a white-tail doe, up from the creek to the dry hill, startled to see a stage where loud music played, and so many lights, and so many humans, all sprawled out where the previous night there had only been the dry grass and a rusted manure spreader.

I returned from that sprawling Cycle Oregon encampment just a few hours ago. It was around 8:30 p.m. when I drove back to the quiet world of Prairie Creek, where Halley eagerly greeted me. After answering phone messages and eating a bite of supper, I tumbled into bed beside my sleeping husband.

At 2:00 a.m. I awoke and lay there awake, with words wanting to get out of my head. Giving up on further sleep, I succumbed to the call of my laptop, so this is what you get for a column that was due on Friday. Sorry, Sterling, for once again pushing my deadline to its final hour.

I spent all weekend at Mule Days, which began last Friday and included the Max Walker Memorial Cowboy Gathering. This event broke records for attendance due to the efforts of Sondra Lozier and family, plus hundreds of local volunteers. A big draw was the appearance of Doug's nephew, Smoke Wade, who M.C.'d this annual event to honor the early Snake River cattlemen, including Doug, his brother Biden and wife Betty (the 2010 grand marshals) and Ben Tippett, Doug's cousin, who was honorary grand marshal.

It was a proud moment for the Tippetts and all the other early day cattleman. Smoke, a Tippett himself, honored his family and an era that has slipped away. There are no more family-owned ranches now along that section of the Snake.

That evening celebrated our early ranching culture, as well as the original inhabitants of this beautiful valley, Chief Joseph and his Wallowa Band of Nez Perce. Lest we forget, they were here first and, now, like the Nez Perce, the culture of our early ranching families along the Snake has all but disappeared. However, the West has always been in flux, always changing and good things are happening, but more on that later.

Saturday morning found Doug and me waiting for the mule-drawn covered wagon driven by Julie Kooch to arrive across from Les Schwab, where the annual Mule Days non-motorized parade was forming. Only thing was...no Julie.

Labor Day campout. L-R James Royes (3), Lucy Matthews (3), Addie Royes (7) and Lilly Royes (5) with Halley, Janie Tippett's border collie are camping on Cayuse Flat in Wallowa County.

Larry Waters drives a team of mules, pulling grand marshals Biden and Betty Tippett. L-R Juana Malaxa, Doug Tippett, Marge Onaindia. All past grand marshals of the Hells Canyon Mule Days.

Young Sam Schaafsma, Upper Prairie Creek, plays the fiddle at a Blue Mountain Old Time Fiddler show in Enterprise. Landra Skovlin at right.

Doug and I found Marge and Juana, other past grand marshals, and soon there appeared 84-year-old Fred Talbott, mounted on a more controllable mule than last year, and 82-year-old Dick Hammond leading a riderless horse, wearing past Grand Marshal Gene Marr's boots and hat on its saddle. Oldster Arnold Shaffer rode his horse, and Carmen Kohlhepp was seen on the street, but wasn't with us. So there we were, waiting for Julie, when Sondra comes by with the news.

"Julie was driving her team to town when a wheel fell off her wagon."

The parade was supposed to start in 15 minutes, but it didn't, and pretty soon, here comes Julie, her big draft mules clattering down the street toward us. We all climbed aboard and off we went. Not on schedule, but then, these things happened along the Oregon Trail and folks just dealt with them, and the crowds of folks who came to see the parade just had to wait for a wheel on a covered wagon to be repaired. No big deal. The parade was worth the wait.

Doug and I ate a lot of those Marr Flat Natural Beef burgers, and took in many events. I recited son Todd's tear-jerking poem in the beef show barn during the Cowboy Poetry jam that afternoon. We also took in the Jim Probert pork bar-b-cue Saturday night.

Yesterday I attended the fabulous quilt show and, finally, after the wild-wooly-dusty team branding event, I headed down Medical Drive, past our new hospital, to Cycle Oregon. Oh my! Was told by those in charge that I could not enter the area, would have to park somewhere and walk to the encampment. However, they let me drive into a field to take a photo if I wouldn't get out of my car...then get the heck back out!

Suddenly realizing I was in rancher Wayne Lathrop's driveway, I drove to his house, parked, and asked Wayne's permission to leave my car there, as it was just across the fence from Cycle Oregon. Such a different culture, so juxtaposed to our ranching culture.

I inquired as to Wayne's wife's condition. Not good. My dear friend JoAnn had suffered yet another stroke, was in the hospital in La Grande. JoAnn, one of the best of our old-time Cowbelles. We continue to pray for you and Wayne.

It was a lovely evening as I strolled into the midst of Cycle Oregon, snapping photos of a tent city that sprang up along Trout Creek and covered our lovely golf course, with its view of Ruby Peak. The air was soft and warm with the late summer sun sinking behind the Wallowas.

For all of its humanity, there was a relaxed feeling in the air. Folks appeared from showers and stood in lines to eat, everyone in awe of this beautiful place. It was as if everyone felt hushed and reverent, stunned by the beauty of it all. I purchased a glass of iced tea and found a chair in front of the outdoor stage.

Immediately I spotted Janis Carper, one of our Fishtrap staff, who designed and printed the cover for my book. Janis was in charge of the music. Then, who should appear but my neighbor Lois Hough, a rancher who lives down the road, to sit beside me. Lois had arrived early to volunteer serving last night's dinner.

I'd seen other locals: Jane Wiggins, Rosie Reynolds, Cheryl Kooch, and many more; familiar faces in a sea of folks from all over the world. We were the lucky ones. We get to live here! We were surrounded by folks who envied us, as fascinated with our lifestyles as we were of theirs.

The first man I sat by said he was from John Day. Did he know Kasey Nash, married to grandson Rowdy, the veterinarian in John Day? Why, of course. Kasey had just treated his horse before he left for Cycle Oregon. Small world.

The second fellow and his wife were from Corvallis, a friendly retired couple living in a 104-year-old house, downsizing, living simply, riding bikes. They were in their seventies with bodies like forty-year-olds. I met a woman from Michigan and another from Wyoming, both wonderful folks, like you and me.

Then, after Brady's piano playing, there appeared on stage Jonathan Nicholas, the person who thought up Cycle Oregon. He stood up there and told about the early history of the Wallowa Valley, and how we ranchers were being bought out and how things are changing. Nils Christofferson, head of Wallowa Resources, explained how they were helping sustain the young ranchers so they would stay on the land and have jobs, so they could live here in this place.

I sensed the audience really listening to him, feeling this shared dream from the west side of our state. At least with those there last night with Cycle Oregon, I sensed a barrier breaking. We all want the same things. I sensed a shift in understanding of us and them, there under that star-studded sky, of city and country, and I felt HOPE for the future of Wallowa County, which cannot rely only on tourism, but must rely also on a natural resource-based economy.

Nils stood there before us and said he'd just ridden down the trail from the high lakes in this beautiful day, where his family and friends had celebrated his father's birthday in the midst of the Eagle Cap Wilderness. Nils didn't mention it, but I knew granddaughter Adele had been the wilderness cook for that celebration.

Later, when Jonathan left the stage, I made my way through the crowd and gave him a hug. You see Jonathan is a member of our Fishtrap

Advisory board, and our literary organization has relied on his advice over the years. A long time ago I took a journalism workshop under Jonathan at Summer Fishtrap.

Looking out over that sea of faces, that living, breathing community of thousands, I asked Jonathan what he thought of his dream child, which was Cycle Oregon. His eyes said it all. Cycle Oregon will not only leave money behind for our county, but those 2,200 bikers will peddle down Buford and up Rattlesnake this morning with a greater understanding of our culture, thanks to Jonathan, Nils, Janis Carper, her local musicians, and all those local volunteers who mingled and truly got to know these folks…who were, like us, just folks.

I made my way back in the dark to a gate along a dusty road to my car, and thought about Wayne and his beloved JoAnn as I drove back out to Prairie Creek. All was asleep under a starry sky.

Now, it's nearly six o'clock on Monday morning, As daylight seeps in to steal the night away, another perfect day begins. I hear my banty rooster Piglet's first "cock-a-doodle do." I must get some sleep.

September 27—3:00 a.m. In spite of good intentions, here I am again, seated at my kitchen table, talking to my laptop with my fingers, hoping a column will appear on the screen in front of me.

It occurs to me that I've written this column for over 26 years, and a lot of what happened during those 26 years is recorded therein. And, if I choose to drag out one of those first columns, I'll recognize the voice of a much younger woman…a 51-year-old woman, five years into her second marriage, who, in addition to her own four children, took on her husband's three.

That woman rode horseback beside her cowboy in the hills. She rode with top hands Ben Tippett and Mike McFetridge every summer and fall, trailing cattle from summer range into the valley; then, after the long cold winters, trailing the cattle from the home place here on Prairie Creek and turning those cattle to grass on what newcomers refer to as the Zumwalt Prairie, which to us are "the hills" of Wet Salmon Creek, the Johnson pasture, the Red Barn pasture (the barn torn down now) and, my favorite, Butte Creek west of Greenwood Butte.

I can just now report that Doug sold those properties a few years back. Quite frequently, Doug returns to the hills, but my trips back to that beloved prairie are few. The memories are too fresh.

It's hard when you love that wild beautiful prairie, knowing where the hawks will build their nests, where the coyotes will den, where the sticky geraniums will bloom, where, in spring, the hills will be splashed with balsamroot, phlox and yellow bells, the native grasses having been grazed over a hundred years, first by the Nez Perce ponies and cattle, then by the first cattlemen, whose descendants kept it in the family and loved the land.

Some families have hung on, and I applaud them. I have faith in our present generation. They are the hope of our future. And here in Wallowa County, we have some of the best cowboys, cattlemen, cattlewomen, and stewards of the land found anywhere in the West.

Oh my, the things one thinks about in those dark hours before dawn, when Prairie Creek is all moon-washed under the waning September moon. When I stepped outside about an hour ago, Halley greeted me by yawning and stretching, wondering if we were going to walk, or what?

It's now 50 degrees on the carport, and last evening was so mild, Halley and I DID walk around the old ranch, taking our time. After a long day of being around people, I needed time to process everything, to listen to the land, hear the water song of the creek, savor the golden air, stare upward into the yellowing cottonwoods, watch the white-tails leap away through the oat field, and, from the top of the hill, look down to see Tom Butterfield harvesting his grain. What a sight, there in that Indian Summer evening, to watch the dusty chaff boil up as the old harvester made its way up and down those golden rows of wheat.

Looking all around, I saw clouds of dust hovering over other fields as farmers worked late to get the harvested grain in, lest it rain or the air dampen. Some of those farmers worked way into the night. These are good farmers, quietly going about their business, maintaining old equipment and keeping those generational ranches going during these hard times. Their sons and daughters have what it takes. I'm betting on them.

Yesterday, the Joseph United Methodist Church celebrated its 100th anniversary. It was quite a day. Members of that church donated many hours to making their celebration memorable, and I wouldn't have missed a minute of it.

The church service began at 10:30, shortly after I arrived to sit with an overflowing crowd. The morning sun streamed through the six original stained glass windows in the sanctuary, which have just recently been cleaned with the old leading replaced with a stronger alloy. Former local Prairie Creek farmer Malcolm Dawson's father, George Dawson, and uncle, Harry Dawson, donated lumber for the church's frame 100 years ago. Most of the stone used in the building was quarried from Guy Gorsline's land, which lies east of Joseph on the road to Kinney Lake. Lots of volunteer labor went into the building of the church that proudly stands today.

The stories that were told yesterday were amazing, and demonstrate over the years the love and desire each generation shares to keep the church alive. And alive it is, in an era where many rural places of worship are drying up, closing their doors due to hard economic times. Not so our church. During a tour we were shown the bell tower, where I was tempted to pull the rope and ring the bell. We were led downward into dank earth, where the foundation was laid and where one could smell the glacial drift and observe the geology of the nearby moraine in layers, like it was for eons.

After the service we all drove to the United Methodist Camp for potluck and more stories, also of the history of the camp itself, which is home to Summer Fishtrap Writer's conference. I sat beside Ray Cook of Mill Valley, California, who traveled up for the occasion, bringing an old Cook family Bible dated from 1886. His grandfather, Rev. Luther A. Cook was a pastor at the Methodist churches in Wallowa, then Joseph, from 1914-1916, and his great-grandmother Elizabeth A. Cook is buried in Wallowa. I had recognized Ray from attending last summer's Fishtrap in that very lodge.

My friends "Skye in the Road" sang and played gospel music, as did husband and wife Mike Hale and Sara Miller, neighbors who live on the Dawson farm west of us on Prairie Creek. Native Wallowa Countian Ben Boswell was M.C., and his Ben-isms made us laugh. Malcolm Dawson's mother, Minnie, sang in the choir, and Malcolm's wife, Jean, and daughter Lisa continue to sing every Sunday.

This old church is here to stay, and our community will see to it that it does. That's how we do things here in Wallowa County. I'm betting the church, with its rich history, will be going strong for the next 100 years. And, who knows, perhaps one day I will sing in the choir. They told me yesterday all it took was "to show up."

It's now five thirty and the moon has aligned with the morning star, which is about to disappear behind Ruby Peak. The temperature has dropped to 45 and Halley is asleep in her dog house. Soon a new day will begin, another perfect Indian Summer Day, and I have not reported on the past weeks as my calendar has been too full. I promised to tell about our Labor Day camping trip to Cayuse Flat, but that can't happen, as I must get some rest. My kitchen table is covered with canned pickled beets, sauerkraut, pears, blackberry jelly and seven-day sweet pickles. I must carry them to the cellar.

Last week friends Sheryle, Sara, Barbara and Pat, along with others, helped me dig potatoes and store them in the cellar, harvest corn, and pick up windfall apples. Sara and her helper gleaned my garden and that produce was donated to the Slow Food project and given away to needy families. That's how we take care of our own here. My friends are all preserving and putting food by for winter.

On the 20th, our mountains wore a fresh sifting of snow and we had a couple of frosty mornings. Our garden was saved by the sprinkler system, when Doug and I arose in the early hours to turn the water on. I have frozen corn, pear sauce, strawberry jam, dried keeping onions, garlic and shallots—this is all work, but not really. My garden is my solace, my respite from the rigors of life.

Pat Cason and I drove to the Elgin Opera House and took in a performance of "Seven Brides For Seven Brothers." Wonderful! We then traveled to Imnaha and set rat traps for the pack rats that have invaded the Writer's Retreat. It is a pack rat year, as reports come in from cow camps and cabins up and down the river.

There was a dance in the Blue Barn down the road. I square danced with great-granddaughter Gwenllian, and her neighbors when we changed partners in old-time dancing. It was so much fun.

The night of the Autumn Equinox I visited briefly with my dear friend Tom Hampson, who traveled with his wife, Woesha, from Portland, to speak at a Fishtrap-sponsored program on Oregon Indians. I also spoke recently to two book groups about my book, which they chose to read for this month's read. Funny, but I haven't had time to read my own book from beginning to end myself. Just too busy.

The book, by the way, seems to be selling well, and hopefully sometime soon we will have a local book-signing at the Bookloft in Enterprise.

Pam, Barbara and I returned to the retreat on the upper Imnaha to clean and check traps. No, we didn't catch one...a good thing. Maybe they left.

We readied the cabin for Fishtrap's October Writer's Retreat, which is nearly upon us. It was a very long, hard work day, but beautiful on Imnaha, where the apples are falling, the air is golden, the river song present, and we dined on the sunny deck. I will return with my five writers during the third week of October. Can't wait.

Had a nice visit with Lyman and Wilma when Pat and I went down to pick blackberries and Lyman fixed us fresh tomato soup.

A few days later, Doug and I drove down to pick pears and blackberries, and we ate lunch there: fresh corn on the cob, Imnaha tomatoes, and grilled sandwiches. Lyman and Wilma are doing fine. Lyman finished putting up his hay and continues, at age 82, to change his own hand irrigation lines. His fields are green and the elk come to graze his high green benches.

The seasons roll and we all roll with them. Must put a period to this column and get some rest. Let me tell you, it hasn't been easy. No one's life is. Life is hard. Instead of portraying the hardness, I chose to write about the good times, lived in one of the most beautiful places on earth. I continue to write with overflowing gratitude about this place, its seasons, and the wonderful people who choose to live here.

October 9—Indian Summer! My favorite time of year. Having survived the first killing frosts, my garden is so happy! Sunflowers with their happy faces, blue bachelor buttons, calendulas and marigolds, bright as coins, and you should see the Icelandic poppies! More brilliant and numerous now than in summer. We are still feasting on corn, cabbage, Swiss chard, and eggplant, and my tomatoes continue to ripen.

On Prairie Creek yet! One of my favorite meals begins by traipsing into my wonderful garden and filling my pail with tiny yellow crookneck and zucchini squash, egg plant, onions, shallots, garlic, peppers, carrots, corn, tomatoes, Swiss chard and anything else I can glean from these end-of-garden veggies.

After slicing, I stir-fry them in olive oil, and serve with a liberal amount of fresh goat cheese crumpled on top. My neighbor, Nancy Knoble, milks her goats and makes delicious, nutritious cheeses to sell in the Sheep Shed, a shop on Joseph's Main Street that she operates with another friend, Sally, who markets her hand-dyed yarns there as well. The Sheep Shed also sells my book, as well as artwork created by Wallowa County artists.

I promised to tell about our trip to Cayuse Flat, so here goes.

Grandson Buck and wife Chelsea invited me to a campout on Cayuse Flat over the Labor Day weekend. I was thrilled to be revisiting this special place, as hadn't been there in many years. In fact, the last time I was there was when daughter Jackie, husband Bill and their two small children worked for Imnaha rancher Wilson Wilde, and the young family used to spend their summers up there at Cayuse Cow camp, riding herd on the cattle. Oftentimes Doug and I would join a family outing there in the summer.

So, I squeezed into their pickup, previously loaded with frypans, garden veggies, tents, sleeping bags, a cot for me, bar-b-cue grill, two happy campers (great-granddaughters Lucy and Katelyn) and three equally happy border collies, including Halley.

Off we rattled down Sheep Creek, to Imnaha, then passed the store and headed up the narrow dirt road that leads to Hat Point. This road is not for the timid. Nor is it for anyone who is afraid of sheer drop offs without the aid of guard rails. I love it! As you climb higher and higher, and look down upon the Imnaha River canyon, the views are outrageous. Up there several miles, we turned off onto a narrow rutty dirt road to drive through a patch of timber and *voila*, there it was. Cayuse Flat. The dear familiar cow camp that was home for Buck and his sister Mona for all those summers.

Beyond the small cluster of buildings stretched the wide, grassy flat, perched there between the breaks of the Imnaha canyons and the head waters of Horse Creek. Upward, to the southeast, lay the fire tower at Hat Point, which affords a breathtaking view of Hells Canyon and the Snake River. Sprinkled with the season's fading wildflowers, the mature ungrazed bunch grasses grew rank and tall. It appeared no one had occupied the cabin since Bill and Jackie lived there, at least not during the entire summer, like they used to do. The little cabin looked lonely there against that wild high prairie.

Buck, like me, was excited to be there, excited about bringing his wife and two little girls back to visit, to let them experience the freedom of growing up in such a place. In a grove of corrals and loading chute, we met up with Buck and Chelsea's friends, Luke and Callie Royes, and their three children, Addie, Lilly and James, who are growing up with my great-granddaughters, Lucy and Katelyn, just like Luke and Buck grew up friends in the canyons together.

A wind was blowing across the flat and the two young mothers weren't too sure about this camping adventure, but I was thrilled to be there, and acted as cheerleader. The children loved it, as all children do. Of course Buck and Luke couldn't wait to check out the elk hunting, 'cause they had tags for bow season. So, in spite of the cold, and absence of the "boys" this grandma forged ahead with enthusiasm. After all, we were camping in one of the most beautiful places in the county, and who cared about a little wind and cold?

Tents were pitched, a fire was built, my cot was assembled, foam pad, two sleeping bags, and since I didn't bring a tent, I set up camp in the small horse barn nearby. Upon entering the barn, I noticed this adorable little wood rat scampering around the rafters. I called the children to come see. Halley, meanwhile, was whining and running back and forth in a futile effort to catch the small rodent with the beady little eyes and perky ears. The children named the rat "Tom." Such glee as the children laughingly called out "run, Tom, run." The sound of genuine childish laughter made my day. Even baby Kate giggled.

On the other hand, the two young mothers were horrified, and never did set foot in my bedroom/barn. My faithful Halley kept "Tom" from chewing on my pony tail and sleeping bag during the nights, so I slept well. Good dog.

The following two days whizzed by. Memories were made, witnessing sunsets that flamed and died beyond the Zumwalt Prairie, sitting around the campfire singing with the children, being served Callie and Chelsea's cooking, which included sourdough pancakes with strawberry jam, sausage, grilled pork loin, homemade veggie/pork soup simmered in the granite-ware coffee pot, sourdough biscuits baked in two fry pans on top of the camp stove, with Luke's fried potatoes and eggs. That first night we slicked up the apple pie I'd baked at home that morning, using some of our windfall apples. Such fun.

Obviously, in addition to being the cheerleader, my happy role was to entertain the children, and thanks to "Tom" the pack rat, that job was a cinch. He became a real pet. The children and I also took walks in the woods, where we discovered several hunting camps. We stumbled onto an old outhouse, and were hugely amused to find a pack rat nest of gigantic proportions built over the "hole." So, you see, my job was the BEST. No camp chores, just hiking around with these youngsters.

On Monday we broke camp, loaded our gear, kids, and dogs, and took off, saying a last goodbye to Cayuse Flat. Buck, raised in the canyons, drove us safely down the steep winding road to Imnaha, where we stopped at the store for fruit juice before heading up Sheep Creek and "on top." Memories are kept alive by the photos we took.

Life for me here on Prairie Creek has been so cram full of living I've scarcely had time to think. The book continues to sell well, but comes with more speaking engagements.

More food "put by" for winter. Doug located some peaches for me, as well as Lyman and Wilma. They are canned and frozen for cobblers. I put up more strawberry freezer jam, and, yesterday, after I dug the horse radish roots, Doug peeled them and I ground them with vinegar—outside, so I wouldn't cry.

A week ago last Saturday, Richelle Chitwood, Pat Cason and I met at 6:00 a.m. at the Hurricane Creek trailhead, and by dawn's early light we headed up the trail to LeGore Mine. Those of you who have hiked this trail know how steep it is. The elevation gain is amazing.

It was a warm Indian Summer day, and the aspen and choke cherry leaves were just beginning to color. Falls Creek splashed down the rocky face and then faded into the distance as we climbed higher. Pat and Richelle, being much younger, were very kind to me...they packed my

Janie Tippett on Hurricane Divide looking down to Le Gore Lake, (Oregon's highest lake), October 1, 1993—when she was 60 years old. Photo by Linda Grevin.

water and hiked slowly. At one point Pat decided to forge ahead, but Richelle stayed with me.

Upward we trudged, sometimes on hands and knees, where the trail was so steep and filled with sliding rocks that skirted narrow ledges hanging precariously above the yawning Falls Creek gorge. We hiked through the familiar Mountain Mahogany thicket, and soon arrived at the first creek. I was thrilled, as hadn't trekked this trail since 1993, 17 years ago, when I was 60 years old. It was such perfect weather.

Richelle and I shouted for joy as we looked down upon a hanging meadow, to see the creek, originating from LeGore Lake, splashing its way through the grass on its way to the falls far below. We watched the sun break clean over Chief Joseph Mountain, and marveled at Sacajawea Peak, the final snow fields melting and gleaming in the morning sun. At this point we could stare upward towards Twin Peaks, knowing LeGore Lake was nearby. Such a sight.

It was 1:30 in the afternoon when we reached the second creek—dry now in autumn—and scrambled up to the LeGore mine entrance. After writing in the journal that is stored in an old ammunition can, we photographed and marveled at the view of Twin Peaks above. We'd made it! The feeling of elation I felt can't be put into words.

Janie at the entrance to Le Gore mine and lake, October 2, 2010 at age 77. Photo by Richelle Chitwood.

After scrambling down the rocky creek bed to the trail, we continued on up toward the crumbling LeGore log cabin. Earlier, we paused briefly alongside the trail to eat lunch with Pat, whom we'd caught up with. At that point Pat decided to start back.

It was 4:30 when Richelle and I turned around and headed down the trail. Long story short...it got dark on us! Really dark, and we were far from the trailhead and our cars. I discovered a small flashlight in my pack, which Richelle tied to the rear of her pack. I followed that swinging light, which reminded me of a light bobbing back and forth on a horse's tail.

Finally, we could hear the water flowing over Falls Creek. Nearly there, but each step was made difficult by rocks. I didn't want to fall, and didn't, but it was nearly 9:00 p.m. when we stumbled out in to the parking lot. We'd been in motion for 15 hours.

I felt great, the stars were brilliant, and the night so mild you could have camped out without a blanket. And, there was Richelle's husband and friends driving up for a search and rescue. Let me tell you, they were very relieved to see us. And guess what? The battery in my tiny flashlight chose that moment to die. There is a God.

So much more to report, but I've been up since 4:30 and must get this column e-mailed.

Yesterday found me singing in the choir at the Joseph United Methodist Church, with some of the most wonderful folks to be found anywhere. And guess what? They let me ring the bell, 25 times. It seems, lately, I've been crossing things off my "Bucket List."

Life is good. Must get to making mincemeat. Simmered the neck of the buck son Todd bagged opening morning, and have it already ground and waiting in the fridge.

Next time I'll write about my oldest great-grandson Clayton's visit, as well as a Halloween harvest party on Alder Slope with family. Enjoy the fall.

October 20—Here is me again, along the old Imnaha at the Fishtrap Writer's Retreat. This time I chose the "tree house," which isn't really a tree house, but rather a small one-room log cabin constructed above a lower story cellar-type room, which is built into the side of a hill. Thus the upper story juts out over the lawn, and the front door opens onto a small deck that appears to be perched in the midst of a very old apple tree.

A goodly portion of my book was written in this cozy cabin. Whereas in April my view is of apple blossoms, October brings the fruit to fruition in such abundance. Heirloom apples—possibly planted by Auntie Louise Marks; anyway, I like to think so—tempt me to pluck those apples, tote them across the way to the spacious lodge kitchen, and peel them for a pie whilst gazing from the kitchen sink to watch the falling leaves drift upon the sun-struck surface of the river.

Tomorrow, I say to myself. Tomorrow we are inviting Lyman and Wilma up for supper. This morning, you MUST write.

Indian Summer continues in a year that is very different than usual, and somehow feels a month behind. No golden leaves here. They are as green as spring, and the lawn, groomed by Dr. Driver, appears Irish green. The canyon grasses sport new growth since the last rains amid unseasonably warm days and nights. These last precious days that dwindle down, like the song, seem strange here as compared to other Octobers.

Only the light itself is golden, and falls slanting, soft and warm, to melt the recent frosted bottoms. The sun takes its time, advancing slowly down the western canyon wall to bathe my cabin in autumn light. It takes its time breaking clean over the eastern rims. It's already 10:00 o'clock before its sudden light spills onto my deck. And since we four—Mary Lou, Helen, Margie and I—arrived last Sunday, the days have been remarkable in their brilliance and beauty. Writing can be extremely difficult when Indian summer beckons and "calls each vagabond by name."

Yesterday morning, awaking before dawn, I kindled a fire in my tiny stove, did a bit of journaling, and then hiked downriver to Lyman and Wilma's for breakfast, which has become a sort of tradition. It was a long, cold walk, as the sun hadn't worked its way down to the road yet, which made Lyman's floured elk steaks and Wilma's quiche taste marvelous. Especially welcome was the coffee perked on a wood stove, laced with sugar and carnation milk from a can, not to mention the conversation among old friends.

Lyman was anxious to get back on the tractor, working up a piece of ground in preparation for seeding a small crop of wheat. So he drove me back to the retreat, where I continued to work on this column. I am alone in my little cabin during the day, but at night there is a visitor, a silently-padding black bear who quietly slips down Indian Creek to gorge itself before winter—*crunch, crunch, slurp, slurp*—on the apples that litter the ground beneath my deck. Her (Mary Lou says she's a girl) great piles of undigested apples make traipsing uphill to my "lovely" outhouse a challenge. Especially at night, when I am not so much concerned with the peaceful bear, but her droppings...which are rather amazing, both in size and number.

Janie's new book:

Order your autographed copy today!

Fill out the form below and mail a check to:

Pika Press
PO Box 38
Enterprise, OR 97828

Four Lines A Day
$15 plus $3 shipping per order

Name:

Address:

City/State: _____ Zip: ____

Agritimes NW

Advertisement in Agri-Times for Janie's new book, Four Lines a Day.

Cider pressing at the Joseph Farmer's Market. This booth offered free cider and ginger cookies.

Mt. Joseph as seen from Ben Tippett's ranch on Prairie Creek.

Melville Ranches harvesting wheat on the former Doug Tippett Cattle Ranch, located Prairie Creek.

Haven't seen any wild turkeys this fall. Is it the bear? A cougar? Wolves? Who knows. There also seems to be an absence of deer, whose tawny shapes used to appear at dusk to nibble the numerous windfalls. I have glimpsed quail or Hungarian Partridge skittering off into wild rose bramble, and the usual kingfisher flying above the river, but the bear, or bears (we've seen smaller paw prints in the mud) seem to have marked their territory, due, I suspect, to the abundance of apples.

It's been a bit disconcerting to the other three gals who are staying in the lodge, to know there are bears about their abode. Especially so, in light of the huge paw and nose prints left the other night on the sliding glass door that opens into the living room. Perhaps the bear is literary and yearns to join our story-telling, when we group around the fireplace in the evening.

Needless to say the gals have been locking doors at night, as have I, which seems rather futile. In the event the bears run out of apples or yearn to taste our food, the bear, or bears, will simply rip off a door and break in. Not a comforting thought, but one my husband threw out there. Thanks, Doug.

October 29—The days have passed, and since this is the month with five Fridays I realized my deadline was a week off. And, since those perfect Indian Summer days just kept on and on, I procrastinated in finishing this column.

As planned, we did invite Lyman and Wilma up for supper. We all pitched in and prepared roast pork, mashed potatoes, gravy, freshly stewed applesauce, sourdough biscuits, pickled beets, coleslaw, and dessert...dutch apple pie. We feasted on hearty fall fare, as the nights were cold and appetites were keen.

We were honored also to have Fishtrap's interim Executive Director drive down and join us as well. Barbara Dills was delighted to meet Lyman and his Wilma, and a merry time was had by all.

On Friday we decided to hike up Freezeout Creek. Knowing the road was washed out, and wanting to see just where, we all piled into the car and headed up the narrow dirt road until we came to the washout, which was rather impressive. A water spout apparently did a real number up there, and this will not be an easy fix. So, armed with day packs and lunches, we struck out up the road to the trailhead.

Noon came and went and we were hungry, so selected some rocks to sit upon and enjoyed our food before finishing our hike to the trailhead. Mary Lou and Margie opted not to climb the trail, so Helen and I took off through the Ponderosa pines and quickly came to the long switchbacks that climbed ever higher, affording a spectacular view of the canyons.

Late afternoon shadows began darkening the draws, and we were only halfway to the saddle, so after much photographing and savoring that last perfect day, we slowly made our way down to the trailhead. Mary Lou and Margie had already headed back to the car, as a bitter chill settled into Freezeout canyon. To the west, we could see a cold front moving in, which would, indeed, signal an end to those perfect warm evening.

Home to our lodge to make a pot of soup.

The next day we cleaned the lodge and my cabin, packed up, and said goodbye to this special place.

On top I was plunged into my life, which hasn't slowed since and given no sign it will. Doug informed me that Halley came in heat, and broke the news that the daddy-to-be might be one of neighboring rancher Dwayne Voss's hounds. I must say she has good taste, as they are handsome dogs. Halley was very happy to see me, but continued her nocturnal visits for a couple of nights before she decided the romance was over and stayed home. Now there is snow on the Wallowas, and the slopes are golden-tinged with tamarack groves that contrast brightly with the evergreens. A lovely time, even though it is suddenly very COLD.

So much more to report, but tonight is a book signing at the Bookloft for me, and today was a doozy. It was CowBelles turn to serve at the senior center, and neighbor Lois Hough and I had great help from my granddaughter-in-law Chelsea, who is organizing another CowBelle organization soon among her rancher gal friends. Lois and I are looking forward to attending, to be served by this very capable younger generation. Long live the CowBelles. Old-timer Mary Lou Brink is offering her home for the first organizational meeting.

Halloween is Sunday. Must make caramel apples for our little trick or treaters. I see Doug has his stash of candied corn ready for the spooky night.

Have been visiting our friend Arnie in the hospital, as his wife Barbara is not doing so well. Our prayers are with you both. I took Barbara some asters growing alongside the house, and Arnie said they grew those flowers where he lived in Switzerland. Arnie is also reading my book as he sits by his beloved wife's bedside.

After I cover the carrots and parsnips with straw and dirt, the garden will be put to sleep. It's hard to believe it's almost November. Must poke a period to this column and get supper before the book signing. See you next time.

November 11—On this Veterans Day I was dusting my book shelves and came across a small faded green book, put together by Cecilia Cooper and published in 1924, that I suspect might have been required reading for one of my mother's English classes. Mamma's name, Blanche Wilson, is written on the first page. Obviously, this book has been used and abused. Perhaps small hands once occupied themselves by cutting several pages with a scissors—possibly my younger sisters or brother, or me? We'll never know.

The pages are filled with poems, written by favorite authors of the time. When I opened the worn little book my eyes fell on the famous poem entitled "In Flanders Fields," written by John McCrae.

In Flanders fields the poppies blow
Between the crosses, row on row,
That mark our place; and in the sky
The larks, still bravely singing, fly
Scarce heard amid the guns below.

We are the Dead. Short days ago
We lived, felt dawn, saw sunset glow,
Loved and were loved, and now we lie,
In Flanders fields.

Take up our quarrel with the foe:
To you from failing hands we throw
The torch; be yours to hold it high.
If ye break faith with us who die
We shall not sleep, though poppies grow
In Flanders fields.

Late on Tuesday evening came a knock on our door, and who should be filling the doorway? Grandson James. Lt. James Nash, as a matter of fact. It seems everyone had conspired to keep this a secret from Grandma. I knew son Todd had flown back to Virginia for James' Marine Officer's graduation, and supposed Todd was back, but what no one told me was that James flew back with him! Not only did he fly back, he'd just filled his bull elk tag!

Since I hadn't laid eyes on this grandson since January, you can imagine my surprise, seeing this muscular lad standing there grinning and covered with blood. Next to him was his dad, also grinning. After the two of them disappeared into that bitterly cold night to unload James' elk in Doug's shop, I bundled up and followed suit.

Later, after taking photos, I retreated to the house to fix father and son something to eat. It was such a happy surprise, and now I must spoil my Marine grandson with some home cookin'. I understand James' sister Adele, who recently returned from Italy, was as surprised as I.

Tuesday was a very emotional day for me, as that morning I had driven to the Lostine Presbyterian Church to attend my friend Barbara Uppiano's very moving memorial service conducted by Kathy Johnson.

Upon returning to Enterprise, I drove to the hospital to look in on Christine, one of our Tuesday Writer's Group friends, who has been recovering from a recent fall. Upon entering her room I found Christine's daughter Kris in the process of moving her mom to Alpine House Assisted Living in Joseph. Naturally, I helped with the transition. So, by the time grandson James appeared that evening, I'd run the gamut from sorrow to sheer joy!

November is here, with its shorter days, frosty mornings, and occasional snow showers. Son Todd stopped by on his way home from Big Sheep to check his cows, and reports the feed is the best he's seen in years. The cattle ranchers hereabouts are all happy about their fat calves, which they attribute to the abundance and quality of this exceptional fall feed.

Grandson Rowdy has hauled his heifers, which spent spring, summer and fall grazing our pastures, down to the home ranch in Mt. Vernon near John Day. Son Ken weaned his calves and hauled the mamma cows away yesterday. My Jersey heifer, Fawn, and her companion, Rhubarb, are thriving, and wearing their winter coats. I have been feeding them hay and grain for several weeks now.

My hens are molting, which means their egg production took a dive. All the fields have been harvested, and my garden has been laid to rest. And, I guess, time will tell if my Halley is bred to Voss's hound. In the meantime my border collie runs like a deer, after the deer, so they won't jump the garden fence and nibble on the fruit trees.

My book continues to sell well, and folks seem to enjoy it, which makes me feel good, 'cause it was a labor of love, both for Mary Marks and for that special place in the heart we know as Imnaha.

We lost another old-timer, Russell Dotson, last week. I traveled to Imnaha to attend his celebration of life, which was held in the church near the bridge and conducted by his son, Pastor Dan Dotson. Numerous entertaining stories were told by the old-timers, and the canyons never looked lovelier on that November day.

Rays of sunlight sliced through the clouds, illuminating the golden cottonwoods that line Sheep Creek, as well as the lingering patches of Sumac that flamed under those high tiered rims. Of course, due to recent warm rains followed by bright sunny days, the canyons appeared green as spring. While partaking of an ample potluck served up by members of the church, I enjoyed visiting old and new friends.

Being a writer means my house ALWAYS needs cleaning, and after such a busy summer and fall, the dust was accumulating daily.

Luckily, I found a super hard-working gal by the name of Andi Mitchell, who just whips in with her brooms, mops and rags and makes that dust fly. So, for the time-being, our mud-room and back porch are clean, and now Andi is tackling the rest of the house, room by room. It is my hope that some day I will actually have an office. In the meantime, I'll just write here at the same kitchen table I've used for over 26 years.

One evening last week, we invited our rancher/farmer neighbors Tom and Donna Butterfield over for dinner. Since Tom gave me permission to scoop up several pails of spilled wheat around their storage bins after harvest, I promised him a meal. You see, I was most grateful for this wheat to feed my chickens, so I found another pork roast in the freezer and came up with enough small apples to make a pie.

It was a fun supper, as Tom and Donna and Doug and I go back a long way, to when both of our operations included the raising of seed potatoes.

Next we'll invite Arnie over for supper. He must be missing his wife Barbara very much.

Halley and I have resumed our morning walks, regardless of weather. Our route is always the same: around Doug's old ranch, which now consists of stubblefields of wheat, oats and canola, following the irrigation ditch, where ducks, pheasants, and white-tail deer abound. Ice rims the waterways now, on these bright golden mornings, when we feel the icy breath of those glorious snowfields.

Thankful for our full canning cupboard and the Marr Flat Natural Beef in the freezer, and James promises he'll share some of his elk steaks.

November 12—The center of my joy are my grandchildren and great-grandchildren. This morning I received a phone call from great-granddaughter Riley Ann. "Hi Grandma, want to hear me play my fiddle?"

"Sure," I answered.

"I'm going to play Boiling Down The Cabbage," stated sweet little Riley, and I could picture her there, on the other end of the phone in her home in Enterprise, placing the fiddle under her chin and drawing back the bow. Those happy little notes reflected her love of music, which made me feel mighty proud,

Then her sister Ashlyn played a piece on the piano, which brought tears to my eyes. Ashlyn's teacher is Wallowa County's beloved music teacher Gail Swart. Rebecca Lenahan, Riley's teacher, is equally gifted when it comes to working with young people We had an extended Halloween Trick or Treat here on Prairie Creek, Friday evening granddaughter Chelsie and hubby Justin, and their four ghosts and goblins spooked us with their costumes.

November 13—Granddaughter Adele was here for lunch today. I spent the morning making slow food for her: homemade chicken noodle soup, sourdough bread, and rhubarb pie, using frozen rhubarb. Adele, just back from attending the Slow Food Conference, called "Terra Madre" in Torino, Italy, treated us to a slide show of her experiences. Such as the olive harvest in Tuscany, the conference, the outdoor markets, and oh my, the rustic Italian and other ethnic foods from all over the world. Adele transported us to Italy via her beautiful expressive photos.

This granddaughter, who recently graduated from the Cordon Bleu Cooking School in Austin, Texas, has a dream of one day becoming a restaurant owner and chef. Our young cowgirl, who trains horses and cooks in a local eatery, is very well qualified for the job, as she is a member of a generational family who were among the first white settlers in the Wallowa Valley. Born here, Adele has experienced both the raising and the preparing of natural beef. Terra Madre honors small producers and helps them succeed, and my wish is that Adele's dream can, in time, become reality.

November 14—Had choir practice this morning at 9:00, followed by Sunday School, followed by the church service, followed by a delicious brunch, then home to work on this column before leaving at 3:30 to pick up great-granddaughters Riley Ann and Ashlyn to accompany me to the Inland Northwest Musicians concert held at the Enterprise High School gym.

What a wonderful performance—and a surprise to see Kaye Garver, pastor of our church, playing the french horn, as well as other familiar faces. Music for the soul.

On Thursday James flies back to Quantico, Virginia. We have two other grandsons serving our country. Shawn in the Marines and Josh in the Navy. We all pray for peace and an end to this terrible war, so our boys can stay home and be with their families, and continue their careers. This is our prayer for Thanksgiving.

November 16—We invited Lyman and Wilma to lunch here at our place. It was fun visiting with them. I'd spent the morning cooking spaghetti and baking a blueberry pie.

November 18—Doug and I invited our friend Arnie over for supper this evening. Our friend is missing his Barbara very much. Arnie stayed and watched the "Wolf" documentary on OPB with us before returning home to Enterprise.

Received another gift, a box of lovingly-packed persimmons and mandarin oranges from our friend Fred, who lives in Auburn, California. What a treat to have our mail lady deliver freshly-picked fruit on a snowy afternoon. Thanks again, Fred!

November 19—Lyman called. "Need some help down here, my son Craig just sent fresh crab, could you come down and help us eat it?"

"No problem," I replied. "We'll be there."

So, after I fixed a macaroni salad, we headed up Sheep Creek Hill and drove down into the canyons. The November moon, only days away from being full, glowed brightly above those dark rims. A lovely night to travel. Warm, welcoming lights greeted us at Lyman and Wilma's log home.

Then, from several miles upriver, other neighbors began to arrive. Newspapers were spread on the table, then here came Lyman toting a huge panful of fresh crab. We were just sitting down to crack crab when, who should walk in with his son Dave, but 93-year-old "Doc" Morgan, who made his way to the table, sat himself down, and went to eating. As in years past, Doc, our favorite retired veterinarian, won the contest by eating the most crab.

We certainly thank Craig, a crab fisherman who lives in McKinleyville, California, for this generous treat that has become a tradition over the years, and on the upper Imnaha, yet. So far from the ocean. A jolly time was had by all, and the 70 mile-round-trip was certainly worthwhile.

Back to Prairie Creek on that cold November night, drenched in moonlight.

November 21—Last week I suggested Doug redeem the gift certificate for the Cheyenne Cafe's "chicken fried steak breakfast for two" he'd purchased at the recent 4-H radio auction. So, on this Sunday morning, we met there at the "local's table" where I was the only female.

My goodness! Did those boys lay it on—the most amazing bits of misinformation and kidding I'd heard in years. The chicken fried steak was tops. Naturally, there was more food than I could manage, so an old Alder Slope friend came to my rescue. Al Slinker savored every bite.

Thus fortified, I arrived at the Methodist church in time for Choir practice; outside brutally cold, inside warm and cozy with friends.

November 24—It's the day before Thanksgiving and all through our house waft the smells of tomorrow's feast: squash and mincemeat pies, bubbling cranberry sauce, and yams, drenched in brown sugar and butter. Even the colorful maple leaves, collected earlier to decorate the table, give off an earthy harvest smell. Good thing I preserved these seasonal offerings, 'cause this morning we have snow on the ground and the temperature is poised around zero. Factor in the wind chill and, well, you get the picture. It's cold!

Jake Moore, who is staying at daughter Ramona and husband's Charley's ranch while they're in California, told me it got down to 19 below there on Upper Prairie Creek.

Tomorrow twenty members of our family will gather here to partake of the traditional turkey dinner and all the trimmings. The remainder of our extended family has been traveling miles over winter roads, and this mom/grandma/great-grandma is extremely thankful that they all arrived at their various destinations safely—though all with stories that range from driving through a whiteout snow storm at the Diamond Lake cutoff, to pulling a stock trailer, loaded with 4-H steers, over the snowy Sierras to Lodi, California.

It's been a few years since we've experienced an Arctic blast as cold as this before Thanksgiving. Long john weather. I was so bundled up this morning, forking hay to my heifers and tending my chickens, I could scarcely move. Ten below is going to take some adjustment.

In yesterday's mail came a generous gift from George Hixon of Pendleton, a longtime fan of this column, who called a few days ago to ask if we would like a copy of his book, *Tales of a Mule Twister,* plus an enlarged photograph of George and Bill Schaan perched on the seat of a long wooden wagon, with a banner that reads, "Baker Livestock Auction Inc."

Reins in hand, these two old-timers posed on the Hayes Ranch off Hurricane Creek Rd, with a 20 mule team hitch. 20 mules! All as white as the snowy Wallowa peaks that rear behind them. 87-year-old George writes that he broke and drove this team for 13 years.

He also says folks have been after him for 20 years to write a book,

Krebs' sheep graze the fall grasses along the north highway between Enterprise and Snow Hollow Hill.

and it finally got done. Bill says most of the people involved with the mules are gone now. His book can be purchased at Betty's Books in Baker City, or online. Doug and I have really enjoyed reading Bill's account, which is illustrated with wonderful old photographs.

After several trips to the hills, Doug has yet to fill his Zumwalt cow elk tag. I tagged along last weekend to photograph and lend a hand lest he shoot one. Like I say, it's hard to return to Wet Salmon Creek and that high rolling prairie that holds so many memories, knowing Doug doesn't own land there anymore.

There is a story around every bend in the road, like the little stand of Ponderosa pines our family planted over 30 years ago above the creek on a sloping north-facing hillside…in the rain, on Mother's Day. The kids protested, but gamely slipped in the greasy mud as they dug holes to plant those tiny seedlings. The pines that survived porcupines, drought, deer, elk and cattle seem to be making it in that mostly treeless land.

We did see elk. Hundreds of them, though from a distance and on posted land. No hunting allowed. Gone are the days when old-time landowners allowed hunting by permission. Doug's brother Biden and son Casey still own Tippett land out on Pine Creek, and we stopped to visit with nephew Casey, who was out checking cattle, hunters, and fences.

While jouncing down rocky Dorrance Grade in Doug's old pickup, the dark shape I spotted standing in a shady draw turned out to be a wolf. After staring at us for a matter of seconds, the animal fled uphill and disappeared over the ridge.

Back home to Prairie Creek in time for me to put together a dish for the potluck at the Anne and Jim Shelly's FireWorks Pottery and Arrowhead Ranch Chocolates party and sale held at Shelly's studio up Hurricane Creek, a benefit for Fishtrap.

Historic landmark Dorrance "pink" barn, along Crow Creek. This ranch was where Tom and Bill Dorrance were raised.

Then I drove down the hill to the Hurricane Creek Grange, where another one of those wonderful old-timey dances was already in progress. Folks laughed, danced to fiddle music, and had a great time. I danced with young Jake Moore, and oftentimes we gals danced with gals. I suspect I might have been the oldest gal on the dance floor. Not to worry if you're young at heart.

That evening brought back memories of growing up in the foothills of the Sierras, and dancing the Virginia Reel in old Mt. Pleasant Hall. Long ago, when we hillbilly kids were in 4-H, back in the 40s and 50s.

Good to see the Prairie Creek Girls there: Lexi and Ryya Fluitt, Hannah Schaafsma, and Landra Skovlin. Punch and cookies in the kitchen for refreshment. I love old Grange Halls. Lately, here in our county, there seems to be a resurgence of good old-fashioned fun. Hats off to the organizers, like Laura Skovlin, who calls the dances, and our local musicians who come out of the woods to provide the fiddlin', pickin', and flutin'.

November 26—Now 'tis the day after Thanksgiving and the house is silent, and yesterday's aromas of turkey, dressing, gravy, mashed potatoes, and sounds of laughter, and visiting, and children singing is in memory land.

How I loved having family around, hugging, loving, eating, laughing, and giving thanks for being together. We are all so grateful for living here in this beautiful place. Because I had two turkeys to roast, I fired up the old Monarch wood stove and baked the second bird in that oven.

This weekend kicks off the annual Joseph Community Christmas bazaars, and I'll be baking a lemon pie, as our church is serving lunch.

Rock jack built by the Moore boys near Dry Salmon Creek.

Old Midway Stage stop along Zumwalt Road, northeast of Enterprise.

Birkmaier Ranch cattle graze fall bunch grass near the head of Butte Creek in the hills north of Enterprise.

Road to Zumwalt Prairie—old homestead shack on the right.

November 26, continued…—Doug is off to the hills again in hopes of spotting an elk close enough to shoot. As November wanes, the temps have warmed a bit. Ten above this morning. Halley and I have resumed our winter walks around the old ranch. This morning hundreds of wild mallards landed in the stubblefields to feed on spilled grain.

December 1—Foggy, with frozen whiskers of hoarfrost decorating every willow limb, rail fence, and weed. After chores and my early morning walk, I baked a batch of persimmon cookies while Andi cleaned the front room.

December 2—A Blue Bird Day, bright sunlight spilling over pristine snow; I kept my camera in hand during our morning walk. Shuffling through deep, powdery snow was tiring, but also gratifying, as Prairie Creek appeared silent and lovely under a bluebird sky.

Back in my kitchen I baked a pear pie and set a cast-iron skillet full of sourdough biscuits to rise. One of those Marr Flat Natural Beef roasts baked slowly in the wood cook stove oven, and by five o'clock that evening Grandson Buck, wife Chelsea, and their two little girls, Lucy and baby Kate, arrived. Potatoes were mashed, gravy made, and we sat down to enjoy a special meal, my way of saying thank you to Buck for locating and hauling my hay.

In the middle of the night I awakened to stare out our bedroom window, as shifting curtains of pale, green light wavered on the horizon…Northern lights.

December 4—Temperatures moderated. Snow turned to slush and mud. After chores I got busy in my kitchen, baking two loaves of sourdough bread and a blackberry pie before noon. Doug settled in to watch football on TV while I drove into Enterprise for a book signing of local authors at the Bookloft, which was followed by the annual Winterfest parade down Main Street, with its lighted tractors and Santa Claus.

December 5—The day broke clear, sunny and 12 above zero. After doing chores and leaving a hearty soup simmering in the crockpot, I made it to choir practice by 9 o'clock. After church I hurried home to set the table for company. We were expecting granddaughter Adele and her friend Rawleigh for lunch.

Around 1:30 the couple drove in, bearing our perfect Christmas tree. It's always refreshing to be around young people, and we all enjoyed soup and sourdough bread, topped off with blackberry pie. I'll cook a meal anytime for a tree delivered and set up in our living room.

By five o'clock friend Phyllis and I were singing Christmas carols in the Great Room at the historic Wallowa Lake Lodge, where we joined friends and neighbors for another one of Gail Swart's special Christmas presents to our Community. After a stuffed Cornish game hen dinner, served in the old Lodge's rustic dining room, we munched Gail's Christmas cookies while being entertained by a variety of local talent.

Gail played the piano next to a large decorated tree, while several of her students sang or played instruments, a testimony to this beloved teacher and friend who has touched so many lives here in Wallowa County.

Returning to Prairie Creek, we found our lane full of glittering ice crystals, and I was filled with Christmas spirit.

December 6—Spent the day decorating our tree and stringing lights along the rail fence in the yard. Snow fell steadily and softly over the landscape.

December 7—A cold fog crept down Hough's meadow and our world ceased to exist beyond the yard fence. Hoarfrost coated everything again and the temperature turned bitterly cold. Then, in the night, the warm breath of a Chinook wind came out of the south and melted the snow, leaving slushy water pooling everywhere...that is, with the exception of our driveway, which had formed a solid sheet of ice. Forty degrees seemed positively balmy as I skated my way to the barn.

Venison stew in the dutch oven, Andi here to clean my bookshelves, and the wind rising. Christmas cards in the mail box, and thoughts of family from afar.

December 9—Melting snow drips off our roof, and the frozen fields Halley and I wandered over this morning are turning slushy. They weren't that way earlier, when each step sounded a cold *crunch, crunch.* I wonder if the hundreds of Canadian Honkers that filled our Prairie Creek skies with "goose music" are still feeding on the neighbor's grain fields?

How I look forward to our morning walks, no two alike.

After carrying water to my chickens, feeding them their wheat, dumping out the kitchen "chicken bucket," and checking their supply of oyster shell, Halley and I head for the old barn, where I fork hay to my two heifers. This is high quality alfalfa hay, put up in 100 lb. bales by Upper Prairie Creek rancher Mike Coppin. Three tons were delivered by grandson Buck.

Then we walk to the calving shed where I pour two coffee cans full of grain in wooden boxes for the heifers. After forking manure into the manure spreader, Halley forges ahead in anticipation, down the road to a metal gate that opens into our old calving pasture, where we ramble over a familiar route that circles the old ranch. I take note that the irrigation ditch is still frozen over. Between blue breaks of open water, coon prints and deer tracks crisscross the snow-encrusted ice.

Frasch's Angus heifers are still cleaning up the oat and wheat stubble, as well as rank grasses that line the ditch banks. Always curious, the heifers stand and stare at our passing. Halley, by the way, isn't as fleet afoot as she's been in the past. Methinks—no, me knows—she is heavy with child... 'er, puppies.

From across the frozen fields we listen to the mournful howls of Voss's hound dogs. Will her puppies be half hound? Or border collie? Or both? Halley's due date is Christmas. Anyone need a puppy?

From the top of the hill I look down to see Hough's hired man pushing flakes of hay off a flatbed truck as it slowly lurches its way over frozen cowpies. Munching hay as they go, a long line of black cattle trail behind. This scene is repeated all over the valley this time of year. A passing Raven croaks, a Bald Eagle perches on a center pivot while its mate swoops down to snatch a duck in the midst of a band of feeding mallards, and two hawks surf the windy thermals over Prairie skies.

Inside our cozy home, a fir tree is decorated, stockings hang from the fireplace mantel, and two nativity scenes define the Yule season. All over Wallowa County it's beginning to look a lot like Christmas, which is only days away. Doug is playing cribbage down at ye old Range Rider again, with "the boys."

Christmas cards wait to be addressed and mailed, and sweet breads must be baked. But mostly, Christmas is enjoyed, more so, since realizing I can no longer purchase gifts for everyone. Our family is just too large... this means no shopping. Amazing, how freeing that is. Yet I still am allowed the joy of giving, in the form of dinners for family and friends, letting them know I love them through my cooking.

Our writing group is meeting again at Ruth Wineteer's place on the hill above Enterprise, where we spend the morning reading and writing. Oftentimes, after eating our lunches, we gather around Ruth's table for an afternoon of Scrabble. Missing Christine, when we used to meet at her cabin on the lake. Ruth and I did visit our 87-year-old friend recently, who seems very content in her cozy room at Alpine House Assisted Living in Joseph.

December 11—As I finish up this column, I reflect on last night's traditional Cioppino party here at our house. What fun. I spent the morning baking sourdough bread and simmering the soup base for this special seafood supper. Toward evening, friends appeared bearing scallops, shrimp and white fish to toss into the pot simmering away on the old Monarch. After desserts provided by our guests, we retired to the living room to read cowboy poetry and share tall tales. That's the good thing about winter here, when we take time to gather and visit with friends and neighbors, and wonder why we don't do it more often.

Discovered a surprise on the back porch: a box of apples and a bottle of wine from our friend and fan of this column, Frank Millar, who used to live here and says he misses Wallowa County. He left a note, saying he'd been fishing and stopped in on his way home. Thanks, Frank.

December 26—As scattered blizzards swirl around the house and Prairie Creek is cloaked in early darkness, I reflect on those eventful days leading up to Christmas, as well as to Christmas itself. Just Doug and I here this evening, our tree cheerily lit, and a bright patchwork tablecloth we used for yesterday's dinner still graces the table where I write.

All is quiet, save for the occasional contented grunting sounds coming from the back porch. Yep! Halley had her puppies. All black and white border collies. Seven of 'em, and not a runt in the litter. All roly-poly healthy puppies. Born on the late afternoon of the Winter Solstice, following the Eclipse of the full December moon the night before. These are very special puppies. Four girls and three boys.

I'd driven home from Enterprise and noticed Halley wasn't there to greet me, so I searched the woodshed and other places I'd noticed her digging. Darkness descended and it was well below freezing by the time I made my way to the hay barn. A wee cry of distress led me to an opening between two bales of hay, where lay a newly-born puppy, protesting the cold world into which it had been dropped. A few feet away, in a hole dug in some loose hay, reposed Halley with four more puppies. I hurried to the house for a cardboard box in which to transport the mass of squirming puppies to the back porch.

After spreading down a layer of old sheets and a discarded pair of overalls, I placed the puppies carefully on their bed. Halley appeared quite contented. Everyone who comes through the back door has to hold a puppy and wish they could take one home. Who can resist? They all resemble Halley, who obviously chose neighboring rancher Dwayne Voss's border collie, rather than his hound as Doug led me to believe.

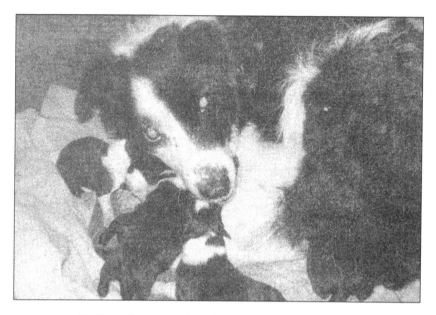

Halley's "winter solstice" puppies—three days old.

Janie's two heifers enjoy their alfalfa hay on a cold winter morning.

January 5—On New Year's Day, daughter Linda and son Jordan, who live in Salem, arrived late in the afternoon. Linda called that morning to say they were coming, so I put a ham in the oven and baked scalloped potatoes for supper. We had a nice visit, even though it was below zero much of the time they were here.

Just hours after they left, son Steve flew in from Alabama, and the next day daughter Lori drove over from the Tri-Cities. I was busy in the kitchen cooking, worrying about my heifer, and juggling the Sled Dog Races that were scheduled to begin on Thursday. It was good to see our grown children, who live out of the county. I mixed up the sourdough jug, made waffles for breakfast, and simmered leftover ham in a kettle with beans. Since granddaughter Mona Lee was still visiting, we had several get-togethers with family before she traveled on.

The night before Steve and Lori left, we all met at Terminal Gravity, a popular brew pub and eatery in Enterprise that, in addition to quality locally-brewed beer, serves up fine food. Of course we are bragging, 'cause our young chef, granddaughter Adele, runs the kitchen there. The place was packed, and we sat around a large table upstairs to enjoy Adele's cooking, which was pretty impressive.

Although I didn't participate in the Eagle Cap Extreme Sled Dog Races as much as in previous years, I did enjoy the show. The day before the race I helped hand out bags to the mushers during vet check on Main Street Joseph.

It was foggy cold that morning, and several of us fled to the newly-opened Arrowhead Chocolate Shop to thaw out. Located in the old Chief Joseph Hotel, this local hangout has been very well-received by our community. I ordered a foamy mug of mocha, topped with whipped cream and drizzled with chocolate. The chocolate is made right there while you watch. Displays of mouth-watering fresh chocolates, in every form, tempt one to purchase treats for gifts, or to enjoy later. The Reiningers live on Alder Slope, and we applaud this new family-owned business in Wallowa County.

A 12-dog team of sled dogs crosses Salt Creek Summit on the first lap of the Eagle Cap Extreme Sled Dog races, held recently in Wallowa Co. Photo by Mona Matthews.

January 6—Mona Lee and I drove to Salt Creek Summit to photograph the sled dogs as they passed the checkpoint. As planned, we arrived an hour before the first teams were expected, in hopes of snowshoeing in the nearby woods. It was sunny there at that elevation, and much warmer than in the fog-shrouded valley below. Large frost crystals, in rainbow colors, glittered from the clean surface of deep snow as we made our way through the woods. We passed one other couple cross-country skiing, and stopped to visit. Other than that, we had that white wilderness to ourselves.

Emerging from the trees, we heard barking. The first team was fast approaching. It was exciting to be there to watch those athletic dogs, their tongues hanging out, panting with the effort it took to pull a sled uphill in that sudden warmth. Sled dogs and mushers both prefer cold conditions.

Mona Lee, who positioned herself alongside the trail, captured some great images as team after team passed us. After the last musher waved goodbye and disappeared around the bend, we snowshoed up the trail to the Salt Creek checkpoint tents and visited the crew. This is the crew I would've been part of, had I not opted to stay home with our visiting family.

Janie Tippett at Salt Creek Summit, snow shoeing with her granddaughter and watching sled dogs. Photo by Mona Matthews.

January 8—After cooking up a big kettle of vegetable/beef soup, Mona and I drove down Sheep Creek to Bear Gulch, where we visited the Moore family: Larry, Myrna, Jake and Jenny. It was fun being in their modest little house, supping soup and visiting our long-time friends. After munching Myrna's bear claw pastries, Mona presented an interesting slide show of her recent trip to the Philippines.

The Moores are in the cattle business, and the brothers operate a small saw mill in the canyons. Myrna runs the library in Imnaha, which is set up in the school at the Bridge. I remarked how pleasant it was there, with the winter sun spilling down upon the Moore house near the creek…and then, suddenly, the sun disappeared.

"Goes behind that high rim," said Larry, "We'll get one more shot of it before long." And, sure enough, the sun reappeared just as we were getting ready to leave. There are places in the canyons where, in winter, the sun never shines. Walled in on both sides, waiting for the days to lengthen.

Now our county is in the midst of The Big Read, and this year's selection is Mark Twain's *Tom Sawyer*. This annual event fills the darkest, coldest days of winter with many stimulating programs that relate to the book and author. Our kickoff was held last Sunday evening at the Odd Fellows Hall in Enterprise, where a packed audience listened to Dr. Cindy Lovell, who is the executive director of the Mark Twain Boyhood Home and Museum in Hannibal, Missouri.

January 10—Attended the viewing of "Mark Twain Tonight," the 1999 film featuring Hal Holbrook. There, on a clear cold night, in the Mutiny eatery in Joseph, we were transported back to more than a century of old humor, as real as if it were performed by Twain himself.

January 11—Mona leaves tomorrow, so I roasted a "drunk" chicken, cooked in a pottery bowl that contained a hollow filled with beer, along with various root vegetables roasted in garlic and olive oil. Since Mona's birthday is January 27th, and she'll be in Seattle then, I baked her a sourdough chocolate cake with raspberry/strawberry filling, served with whipped cream. Great-granddaughter Lucy stuck candles in the cake. A good time was had by all, except for Mona's brother Buck, who had been gathering cattle up Big Sheep canyon all day and was too late for the party.

January 12—The latest Arctic blast has loosened its hold. As opposed to yesterday's zero degree reading, our thermometer registered a balmy 25 when I went out to chore this morning. Due to several inches of recent snow, Prairie Creek seems muffled in white stillness, which means shuffling through soft snow to the barn.

I'm greeted by Halley, who spends most of her time there now, rather than the back porch. Her brood of seven puppies quickly outgrew their quarters, plus it was beginning to smell like a kennel out there. After constructing a barricade of bales and creating a cozy nest in loose hay, I transported the seven roly-poly babies to the barn. When they aren't snoozing in a black and white heap, they tumble about, bark, growl and play, like puppies do. Nothing cheers my winter-weary soul like watching Halley's border collie puppies.

Every morning my two heifers wade through the snow to the feeder, where they munch their alfalfa hay. My naughty Jersey is allowed to eat a small portion of grain again. You see, last week she pushed the gate latch open in the barn, and pretty much demolished a sack of oats, cob and molasses...not good. Not good at all.

In fact, if I hadn't called the Red Barn Veterinary Clinic to administer all sorts of oily concoctions and other remedies, she wouldn't have survived her major tummy ache. Obviously, my other heifer, Rhubarb, didn't share in the feast. You should have seen my Jerz. It wasn't pretty. Every morning for several days I expected to find her dead.

Thanks to Dr. Karl Zwanzinger, an experienced large animal vet, Fawn lives.

January 14—Tomorrow morning I'll be down at Big Sheep Creek, walking behind son Todd's Marr Flat cattle, beginning their three-day drive to the valley. Other cowgirls and cowboys will be a horseback. This time Halley will have to stay home. I won't tell her.

January 29—Doug and I drove to the newly reopened Imnaha Store and Tavern to meet Lyman and Wilma for lunch. Nice to see a good crowd socializing and munching Sally's famous chicken gizzards, hamburgers, or shrimp 'n chips. Much warmer in the canyons, plus a complete absence of snow, and Lyman remarked, "Sure could use some moisture, things are pretty dry."

"Same on top," we told him.

February 7—This morning would have been nice if it weren't for the wind. Undeterred in my determination to make good my commitment to walk every morning, Halley and I struck out along our familiar route. Bundled up in outer and inner wear, I stayed warm, and actually found the wind invigorating. The periodic splashes of sunshine, streaming from the open prairie's wind-cleansed skies, lifted my spirits. Clouds, pushed

Lynne Sampson Curry and her two little girls, Molly and Cecil, ride behind 350 Marr Flat cows while they are being trailed from Big Sheep Creek to the valley where they will soon calve.

by the wind, skittered overhead with dizzying speed. And dark boiling masses of them sped toward us before emptying sleet that stung my cheeks. Rather than dreading and simply enduring the wind, I embraced it, became its friend.

Opting not to slide under the solar-powered electric fence, I chose to walk alongside the irrigation ditch toward the county road, and thus added more mileage to my usual route. Two Bald eagles, perched in a leafless cottonwood, their feathers flailing in the wind, stared down at me. A pair of Red tail hawks glided aloft, just for fun. Hough's black cows and calves munched their hay, ravens croaked, and Halley, tail-wagging, dug furiously at the entrance to a field mouse's tunnel.

Ice groaned and crackled in the large ditch and, as we neared home, there were Halley's remaining puppies, playing next to the barn. Between bites of alfalfa hay, my two heifers watched the puppies. The chores were done, my walk was over, and I felt energized enough to tackle housework...ugh!

This evening found me joining other friends at Mutiny, a local eatery in Joseph, viewing our Fishtrap-sponsored "The Adventures of Huckleberry Finn," a 1960 film that celebrates our Big Read selection, Mark Twain's *Tom Sawyer.* Our Big Read helps fill the void created in midwinter here in Wallowa County. Local participation grows each year, and it's very rewarding to see folks actually reading rather than sitting in front of some electronic device. Curling up with a book, is much more personal.

February 9—The Amaryllis bulb I've been watching grow on my kitchen counter has suddenly burst into bloom. Six brilliant blooms, the color of a blossoming Trumpet vine, somewhere between red and orange. There are two tall stalks, and each one sports four blooms. I've moved the plant to the kitchen table where I can enjoy it while I write, in hopes it will inspire me to wax cheerful in an otherwise dull morning.

Another bone-chilling morning in a succession of them. However, today there is an absence of wind.

February 10—This evening I rode out with Steve and Angie Rubin to La Grande, where we took in the production of "Flashback to the 60s." This rollicking, fun-filled, toe-tapping, singing and dancing evening was staged by the Eastern Oregon University's Chamber Choir and Music Department. Remember all those great songs? "Leaving on a Jet Plane," "The Sound of Silence," "Itsy Bitsy, Teenie Weenie, Yellow Polka Dot Bikini," "Hit the Road, Jack," and "My Girl?" Well, those young people, backed up (and later joined) by the music faculty, were fabulous! Such energy.

A large part of our populace showed up on a cold night to fill the Enterprise OK Theatre to view a fully-restored 1938 original version of "The Adventures of Tom Sawyer," starring Tommy Kelly, and Wallowa County's own Walter Brennan. However, there we all were, waiting for Becky and Tom to be rescued from the cave, when the film stopped...so Doug and I opted to leave. We knew Mark Twain wouldn't leave them there. We'd read the book.

Halley's puppies are gone, save two. Jan Botham will be by soon to take one to her grandchildren, who are, at the present time, in Bend. Our prayers are with little Remi, Jan's granddaughter, who has undergone another surgery.

A letter, dated January 18th and mailed to Pika Press, has just reached me. It was written by Lois Lehman of Rice, Washington, who says she just finished reading my book, *Four Lines a Day*, which brought back memories of her own childhood. Lois was born in 1922 in Davenport, Washington, and says her father's parents had the first dairy in Davenport, and her mom's parents homesteaded what was known as the Half Way House, which was at the De Tillian Bridge on the county line between Lincoln County and Stevens County.

She writes, *I spent a lot of time throwing rocks in the river while playing with my brothers there under the bridge. The backwater of the Columbia River has the site all covered up. The fall of 1924 was a crop failure and my folks were ready to find a new home. I had three older brothers which helped to make the move easier. Dad loaded all he could make stay on a 4-wheeled wagon, which was mostly small tools and our household goods. The back seat of the Model T was filled with bedding, clothes, and special possessions. It was a very long day getting to our destination, which was a small town in Stevens County called Chewelah, where the grass was greener.*

Lois recalls the local dances. *Many nights I would lay on the bench alongside of an old pot bellied stove and sleep, after I got tired of dancing with all the neighbor kids. I loved to dance and later on my husband and I danced until they closed down the halls and the Granges consolidated.*

Lois also writes, *If there was time left over from taking care of us children, my mother pitched the loose hay and helped build the stacks. I had the pleasure of driving the horse that pulled the hay up with a derrick to get it into the barn. Our family grew grain crops, and hay, and had beef cattle and dairy cows, and pigs and chickens. I rode the saddle horse herding the cows and taking the cows to their pastures for the day.* Thanks, Lois. I really loved hearing from you, and I'm glad you enjoyed my book.

Now, the sun is shining. Must get outside and go for another walk with Halley.

February 12—While Halley and I were walking up Tenderfoot Valley Road, my gaze wandered upward to our Wallowa's highest peaks to discover "snow smoke," a phenomenon created as fresh snows are whipped aloft by fierce winds. To entertain warmer thoughts, I remembered sitting in the Christian church yesterday evening, listening to Matt Cooper on piano and Lisa Robertson on violin, performing in concert. Both Matt and Lisa are Eastern Oregon University Music Professors and their passion for playing their instruments is something rare to behold. We are so fortunate to have the Wallowa Valley Music Alliance bring programs of this caliber to our isolated area.

After chores and a walk, I made it to choir practice at our church. On Sundays I'm happy to report the bell ringing task seems to have fallen on yours truly. I love it!

This afternoon Doug and I drove down to Imnaha again, and ordered up some of Sally's crisp chicken while warming ourselves by the barrel stove in the old store and tavern.

We returned to Prairie Creek just in time to meet Jan Botham and her twin grandsons, who were here to pick up their puppy. Of course

The "Farmer's Ditch," frozen over in winter, provides stock water for cattle and horses. Water runs under the ice. The photo was taken on Janie Tippett's morning walk.

The old "Wade" place on Alder Slope, near Enterprise, is now known as The Red Barn Veterinary Clinic." The photo was taken during a February snow storm.

we couldn't leave one puppy here all by itself, so grandma Jan said each boy should have one. One little fellow, clutching the second puppy to him, said, "This will be the best dog I'll ever have." Which kinda made me tear up.

As a follow up to this story, a letter arrived in our mailbox today from Jan, who reports the boys "Have been taking their puppies on sleds, down a slide, and mostly racing with them on foot." Can't you just see those two little boys with Halley's puppies? Jan says their little sister Remi is home now, and they're hoping for some follow-up care at Stanford University.

February 13—Doug joined nephew Casey, brother Biden and wife Betty, in attending his sister-in-law Blanche Tippett's 90th birthday in Clarkston, Washington. Since I had previously purchased a ticket to our Big Read Grand Finale, I opted to stay home. It was truly "An Evening with Mark Twain," portrayed by Kurt Sutton, who was full of Twain's "hilarious witticism, wisdom, and humor." At the end of his program we were all singing along with Kurt/Mark while he played old songs like "Red River Valley" on his banjo.

Around 5 o'clock the old Hurricane Creek Grange Hall had filled up with folks bearing fragrant dishes of black-eyed peas, hush puppies, beans, and salads, to accompany roaster pans heaped with oven-fried catfish, served up by members of Fishtrap, which sponsored the event. Once again those Grange ladies baked their famous homemade pies, lemon, custard, berry, pumpkin, apple, and chocolate. So many choices.

On the program I noticed a quote from Mark Twain: *All of us contain Music and Truth, but most of us can't get it out.*

February 14—On Valentine's Day I treated myself to one of Arrowhead Chocolate's yummy mochas. After Erica mixes the foamy hot drink, she lets you lick the chocolate from the spoon…chocolate which is created there as you watch. This unique chocolate shop is located in the old red brick Chief Joseph Hotel on Main Street.

I joined Ryya and Lexi, our Prairie Creek girls, and their dad, plus other friends, at a sunny table with a view of snowy Chief Joseph Mountain.

February 15—Our "Write People" met at Ruth Wineteer's place, high on the hill above Enterprise, where you look out on the scenic winterscape of Alder Slope. After our writing session, we ate our lunches before launching into a challenging game of Scrabble.

Last week I carried one of those big squashes, raised in my garden, up from the basement and baked it slowly with brown sugar and butter. Yum! A few days later I mashed the leftover squash and turned it into a tasty pie. My canning cupboard is emptying its shelves of peaches, pears, tomatoes, cherries, pickles and preserves. Nothing tastes as good in winter as these fruits of summer.

Great-granddaughter Riley Ann played her fiddle over the phone for me last week. An old familiar hoe-down tune. Thanks Riley, I'm very proud of your progress and can't wait to hear you someday at the Old Time Fiddlers Show.

More of our old-timers have left us. JoAnn Lathrop, who was in Cow-Belles with me, passed away last week, as did Ted Juve's mom, Dorothy, a longtime neighbor on Alder Slope. And we lost Jim Birkmaier, whom Doug and I share fond memories of hunting elk out on the Zumwalt Prairie. There we'd be…way out there in those windswept hills, hands freezing, shooting our cow elk, then helping gut and load those huge animals into the truck. Patti (Jim's wife) and I were often the only women for miles around.

February 22—Our weather has changed considerably since my last column. What was that I said about no snow or moisture? About it being dry both in the canyons and here "on top"? Not now. For starters, we received a foot of snow, and before that soft wet layer could settle, we got dumped on again. Snow over my boot tops when I break trail to the chicken pen or slog for the barn. My mother's heart goes out to those baby calves born during this bitter cold spell. Not only do we have snow, but frequent freezing winds that plummet temperatures into the teens. Sympathy, too, for the calving crews, who stumble out of bed—if they're lucky enough to get in one—to rescue newborns before they freeze down.

Lyman reports they have the same amount of snow on the Upper Imnaha as we do here on Prairie Creek, which he claims is highly unusual for late February. He says he's helping Dan Warnock load hay, and misses the cow/calf business. Of course he was mostly through calving by this time.

Well, the wolves have made a kill. Guess they've been living on elk and deer up 'til now. Karl Patton's herd again, in the hills due east of our place. This time the pack brought down two pregnant cows and devoured the calves in their bellies. One cow had twins.

Our neighbor Lois Hough called one evening to warn me about my two heifers.

"Did you hear the wolves howl?" she asked me. I had, I replied, for two mornings in a row, just before the attack on Karl's cows. So, here we go again, dealing with a problem that remains unsolved. Ranchers continuing to cooperate with Agency people in hopes some solution can be reached. Hopefully a common sense approach will allow ranchers to protect their animals from these carnivores. For it is a given, these wolves will continue to feast on domestic livestock as well as elk and deer.

February 23—Long, tapering icicles hang from the eaves of our house, barn, bunkhouse and shop. A frigid wind is blowing loose snow into high drifts, as Alaskan air brings zero temps to our valley. And, it's great-granddaughter Kate's second birthday. Happy Birthday, baby Kate!

February 24—An impressive amount of snow fell, adding another layer to our white world. Robin Martin, who lives beneath Sheep Creek Hill, hosted a luncheon for some of us church ladies that day. The Martins' home is situated at the end of a long lane, and Robin's husband David had done an admirable job of plowing the road so we women could drive in. The rustic house, with its large windows and high ceiling, affords sweeping views southwestward, to the wintry Wallowas, and northeastward, to the breaks of the Imnaha Canyon.

After heaping fresh greens onto our plates and adding a variety of colorful veggies, shrimp and hard boiled eggs to create our own salads, we gathered around a large wooden dining table. It was a most welcome winter interlude, seated there with the sun streaming through those windows, while outside the brilliance of snow cloaked the evergreens. And, of course, we could see Little Sheep Creek, meandering through a winter-white meadow. This beauty is why we live here in all seasons...

February 25—Our temperature registered zero degrees this morning. A real challenge to do my chores while protecting my skin from the brutal cold.

Later this morning, I drove into our local hospital to visit my old friend and hiking buddy, Scotty, who recently suffered a serious fall. Scotty, born in Scotland, is one tough gal. I'm betting she'll be up and around again before long. Although Scotty has a few years on me, it always took a lot of effort to keep up with her as we trod those many trails together.

This evening Winter Fishtrap began at Wallowa Lake Lodge. Another challenge, keeping that old lodge warm. However, the friendly atmosphere and stimulating conversations helped.

February 26—This morning it was 11 below zero as I bundled up early to chore, and to be ready when Andi Mitchell picked me up in her four-wheel-drive to return to Winter Fishtrap. Driving alongside the lake we noticed a thin skin of ice that hadn't been there before.

The day whizzed by as we delved into the theme—"Getting Small"— and explored many new ideas about living simply, eating Slow Food, building smaller houses, and reducing debt loads by ridding ourselves of "stuff." Which all sounded wonderful, until we realized the "doing" takes a great deal of courage and commitment.

In keeping with Slow Food, our Saturday night dinner, prepared in the lodge kitchen, was an adventure in eating locally. Cooked by chef Lynne Sampson Curry, who was aided by our own granddaughter Adele, the food was truly tasty. 75 folks at a sit-down dinner. The meal featured Grass-Fed Strip Loin Stuffed With Wild Rice, Wheat Berries and Mushrooms in a Balsamic-Red Wine Sauce. Carman Ranch in Wallowa supplied the beef. The wild rice was the only item on the menu that wasn't grown locally. It had been ordered from Minnesota, the home of Winona LaDuke, who was our keynote speaker.

It was good to see old friends Charles Goodrich and Amy Minato again. Kate Power and Steve Einhorn, now settling into their slower, simpler life in Olympia, offered ukulele lessons to us. A large crowd of us trooped down to the basement where Steve and Kate brought forth 30 ukes for us to practice on. A merry old time was had by all, and we emerged playing several simple tunes.

February 27—10 degrees felt positively warm. Except, during the night, furious winds had created high drifts and my car got mired down in our lane. So, I was late to the final session of Winter Fishtrap. After Doug returned from the Cheyenne Cafe, I took the four-wheel drive pickup. Those wild winds continued without letup, and the drifts grew higher and higher as loose snow from the prairie formed long ridges over our raspberry patch, garden, chicken pen and barnyard...and, mostly, our lane.

Grandson James, a Marine, stationed at Fort Knox, Kentucky, called this afternoon. It was so good to hear his voice.

March 5—As a result of those continuing storms, I was snowed in from Monday 'til Thursday. It was kinda nice. Talk about living simply. I just concentrated on feeding my animals and keeping warm. The drifts were so high I used a ski pole to climb them. Keeping us fed was no problem, as I've been doing Slow Food since before it was given a name, cooking with what's on hand—and around here there's always plenty.

On the last day of February three-foot drifts buried our yard fence, and I had to dig out the gate to the chicken pen. I got in a lot of reading.

Reread Isabella Bird's *A Lady's Life in the Rocky Mountains,* as well as several other books I'd dreamed about all summer.

Admirers of this column continue to spoil me. Thanks to Bob Lundy of Madras, for the garlic and potatoes raised in his garden. And, just yesterday, granddaughter Adele delivered a gallon of Organic milk from Allen Voortman who, along with his wife Cheryl, operate the Pride and Joy Dairy in Granger, Washington. This gallon of fresh milk had that old-fashioned cream rising to the top and I couldn't wait to drink a tall, cold glass with my lunch yesterday. Reminds me of the milk we drank as kids, growing up with our family dairy on Oakcrest Ranch in Northern California. Thanks again, Allen. Hopefully, my Jersey will freshen next March.

Such a joy seeing Joe with his eager little puppy, Luna, walking the streets of Enterprise. She reminds me so much of her mother Halley at that age.

March 6—All day March mini-blizzards have erupted over Prairie Creek, snow like goose down fluttering from the skies. Now, at three o'clock, a Chinook wind shreds those dark snow clouds to reveal openings of clean blue; this warming trend will, hopefully, aid in the rapid shrinking of hardened drifts that have held our house hostage and buried our picnic table and yard fence.

My Jersey heifer and her pal are relaxed in the sun next to the calving shed, chewing their cuds; the Aracuna pullets are laying extra large blue eggs; carrots and parsnips grow sweet beneath sloping banks of drifted snow; the first robins and red-winged blackbirds have returned; and Halley is happy because we've resumed our long rambles around the old ranch.

Last week I treated granddaughter Adele to lunch at El Bajio in Enterprise, the occasion being a belated birthday gift. Her dad, son Todd, joined us to say hello before returning to the calving cows. A busy season for ranchers now.

March blew in with another blizzard and we're still locked in a winter world, with snow piled around the house, lining the lane, and smothering our garden. Wind gusts up to 43 miles an hour tore half the roof off Triple Creek Ranch's hay shed on Liberty Road. I guess winter isn't through with us yet.

Saw three coyotes hunting mice under the snow the other morning in Hough's field. No more wolf kills that we know of, here locally, anyway.

Buttercup report: Ken Hunt, who lives on Big Sheep Creek, says they're blooming on an open canyon side near the mouth of Big Sheep.

The first calves are arriving in Wallowa County. Shown here are the Marr Flatt Cows and calves who are wintering southeast of Enterprise. Some of these calves were born when the temperatures dropped below zero.

Thanks, Ken. You made my day!

March 17—For St. Patrick's Day I spent the day preparing the traditional corned beef 'n cabbage, 'n carrots 'n potatoes meal and invited guests over. This is a meal I love cooking and sharing.

March 23—Halley and I have just returned from our morning jaunt, a familiar route that winds through fields and pastures on the old ranch. I'm guessing the same pair of Red Tails that reared their young in a high stick nest perched in an old cottonwood last year, are preparing for this spring's brood. Two weeks ago I observed them mating, and every morning they greet us with their warning cries.

While walking the high Western banks that border the Farmer's ditch, I was reminded of Alaska! The scene was positively glacial. Deep irregular cracks lined hardened drifts that clung to the eastern banks, and chunks of snow and ice were sliding into the water like calving glaciers.

Yesterday's new snow had melted, and this morning's 20 degree temps frosted Prairie Creek. The earlier sunshine, which allowed me to hang sheets on the line, has fled. And now those ominous clouds, plus a rising wind, promise more rain and snow. Our calendar informs us that we are three days into spring... Wallowa County spring!

Doug bet me a dollar I couldn't find buttercups on Hough's hill, so naturally, I had to prove him wrong, and did, after enduring a long blizzardy hike. There they were, blooming between snow banks in a sheltered draw. The first purple crocuses are opening their buds alongside the house this morning, and last Sunday, while on a trip to Imnaha, I savored the scent of blooming violets. Flocks of robins search the fields for leftover grains and dream of feasting on our summer raspberries.

Wild geese honk their way across the skies, still feeding on the stubblefields and making their rounds of the many ponds, creeks, and Wallowa Lake. Often, I hear them during a snow squall, winging their way to and fro. Many honkers are beginning to "pair up," ready to start nesting.

Yesterday, after meeting with our weekly writing group, I dropped in to visit one of our members, Christine Anderson, who now resides in the Wallowa Valley Care Center. While chatting with Christine, a local band, who call themselves "The Last Stand," appeared to entertain the residents. I was kindly invited to stay, and was glad I did. Three guys—one playing an electric steel guitar, the other two singing, while strumming their guitars—and one gal, who sang, took us back in time as we listened to those Western tunes we grew up with. Because the words were still imprinted on my memory, I couldn't help singing along.

Speaking of great country music, Doug and I attended the Blue Mountain Old Time Fiddlers Show in Cloverleaf Hall on March 5th. We arrived early enough to chow down on another one of Apple Flat Catering's roast pork dinners before the show began. We were surprised to see old-time rancher and fiddler Lester Kiesecker, and his wife Clarice, who used to live in Troy. In fact there were several generations of Kieseckers performing that evening.

Talented little Bailey Vernam, another year older and more accomplished, also played her tunes, as did the Prairie Creek girls Ryya, Lexi and Landra, whom we've watched grow up. Len Samples would have been proud of his two sons, Caleb and Tyson. Fiddlers, piano players, and singers, from Palmer Junction to No Name City, took turns on stage while we all clapped to toe-tapping tunes.

Returning to our cars in the parking lot, all of us had to wait for ice on the windshield to melt before driving home. The next morning I joined Doug for breakfast at the Cheyenne Cafe in Joseph before church. As usual we sat at the "locals" table, where the familiar chatter and banter accompanies each bite of ham and eggs. Those old-timers never tire of ribbing each other unmercifully.

Three days in a row I baked a pie. The first, a raspberry pie, was baked as a going-away present for granddaughter Adele, who is moving to Portland to pursue her culinary career. Then, the next day, my friend and fellow writer Idella Allen, who'd just returned from Arizona with fresh lemons, gave us some. So, of course I baked a lemon pie, using 8 of my fresh eggs and one of those huge Arizona lemons. Then granddaughter Chelsie's hubby, Justin, called and wondered if I would bake a berry pie for Chelsie's birthday.

"Sure," I said, and thawed out a package of Imnaha blackberries. Noth'ins as lov'in as pie from Grandma Janie's oven.

March 24—After feeding my heifers this morning, I took Halley to the Red Barn Veterinary Clinic on Alder Slope, as she had an appointment to be spayed. Leaving my sad-eyed dog there, I returned to the ranch to feed my chickens and take a walk...without Halley!

Reminds me of the phone call I received this week, from a rancher who lives due east of us, across the Snake River in Idaho. He said he runs 1400 head of cows and needed more dogs, since three of his dogs had been killed by wolves! He'd seen the ad in Agri-Times about Halley's puppies and wondered if there were any left. I told him the last two left nearly a month ago. I did give him my son Todd's number, however, as he and wife Angie have some really well-bred border collie pups right now.

Yesterday afternoon Doug appeared at the kitchen door, beaming and bearing a large, bright steelhead.

"Been fish'in," he said. I knew the fishing had been good on Imnaha, but didn't know he'd gone. Then, with a fishy grin, he explained that the Fish and Wildlife Department had been giving fresh steelhead away at the Community Dining Center that day, and he'd eaten there with the "Old Folks!" He also hinted that I might clean it, so I did. After freezing half, I slid the other half in the oven. Yum!

March 25—Now it's Friday, and Halley is home, not chasing sparrows, or cats, or racing around the chicken pen, but soaking up sunshine—yes, the sun is shining—on a dry patch of lawn.

I see a small section of my row of parsnips is exposed. Well, the straw and dirt I heaped on them last fall, anyway. At last that huge snowbank is shrinking, meadowlarks are singing, and my pullets are flying over the chicken fence. Limbs litter the lawn between snow drifts, and the manure in the barn, where my heifers find refuge during snow squalls, needs to be spread on the fields.

An apple pie bakes in the oven, and Doug is home after breakfast with "the boys" in town. Time to e-mail this column.

This sign, located on highway 84 in Island City, near La Grande, Oregon, was sponsored by the Education Committee of the Wallowa Co. Stockgrowers. Photo by Doug Tippett.

March 26—Doug and I drove to Enterprise to pick up Doug's brother Biden and wife Betty, then headed out north, down Buford and up Rattlesnake to Clarkston, Washington, to attend Doug's brother Jack and wife Blanche's 70th wedding anniversary. Yep, 70th! 92-year-old Jack and his 90-year-old bride looked radiant. A large crowd of family and friends gathered in the elegant Sternwheeler Room, which afforded a view of the Snake River and surrounding hills.

On the way home we pulled into Boggan's Oasis on the Grande Ronde River for one of those famous milk shakes. Turns out they were in the midst of a dinner for the fishermen who were receiving prizes for catching the largest steelhead.

Judging by all the photos displayed, they all looked like winners.

March 27—Jackie and I drove to Lostine to attend the Miracle Worker, a play staged by the Mid-Valley Theatre Company. This production about the life of Helen Keller was professionally done under the direction Wallowa County's own Kate Loftus. Amazing acting. That last performance was so packed, more chairs had to be set up in the old gym at the Providence Academy.

April 1—No April Fool, the first day of April was truly amazing! Warm and balmy, nearly 60 degrees. Daughter Jackie, from Challis, Idaho, who has been in the county visiting her two granddaughters Lucy and Katelyn all week, left this morning. We'd had such a good time while she was here, driving to Imnaha with the two little girls to visit the school where her daughter Mona Lee was the last student to receive a certificate from 8th grade. Today there are only three pupils, one of whom, a kindergartner, is seldom present, as that student lives miles away on a narrow, winding dirt road that leads to Dug Bar. School Marm Claudia Boswell, and husband Ben, who live in Lostine, stay in a trailer parked near the school.

While there we paid a visit to the Imnaha Library, also housed in the two-room school. We were greeted by Librarian Myrna Moore, who invited Lucy and Katelyn to choose toys from the Children's Treasure Chest. Since it was lunch time, we trooped into the Imnaha Store and Tavern and seated ourselves in one of those old wooden booths. While Sally was cooking up our chicken strips, Lucy commented on the many dollar bills tacked to the ceiling. After being closed for a few months, it's great to have this popular gathering place open again.

Jackie took her granddaughters across the street—Imnaha's only street—into the tiny post office, one of the oldest in the state, in continuous operation well over 100 years, to say hello to postmistress Bonnie Marks. Apricot trees, Forsythia, and bulbs were beginning to bloom at that lower elevation, and several steelhead fishermen were plying the waters under the bridge. Up near Camp Creek we stopped to watch a colorful Turkey Gobbler strut his stuff for his harem.

We were saddened to learn of the death of 93-year-old "Doc" Morgan, a longtime friend who lived in a tidy little house just above the river near the bridge. We'll always remember this kind gentleman, a veterinarian, who retired to Imnaha to raise roses and go fishing. "Doc" and his wife Betty raised 10 children. We treasure memories of those crab feeds at Lyman's when our friend "Doc" would always win the prize for eating the most crab. Goodbye, old buddy.

Like I said, the day was so mild and sunny that I struck off across Hough's fields to celebrate the day. Halley ranged ahead to terrorize ground squirrels, and soon we were wandering the "wolf hills," hoping, of course, we wouldn't encounter any. Half way up a steep draw, I rested on a flat rock, soaking up the sun, while surrounded by an explosion of buttercups. Just the merest breeze and the bluest of skies, the earth awakening from its long winter sleep.

I took it all in. The blinding Wallowa snow fields, fertile Prairie Creek spread out below, the smell of pungent sage amid the melting snowbanks, and red-tails hunting squeaky squirrels. After reaching the ridge top,

Snow melting on East Moraine of Wallowa Lake, while Bonneville Mountain displays the winter snow pack. The Alford Ranch is in the foreground.

Halley and I followed a cow path that led to another pasture, where we startled several wild mallards swimming in the irrigation ditch. While sauntering down Echo Canyon, I noticed our neighbor Lois in her yard and waved a greeting.

Also today, Doug hooked the tractor up to his 70 year-old John Deere manure spreader, which I'd spent the winter forking manure from my two heifers into. The old spreader had been parked in the barn where the cattle spent their winter nights. I watched him *put-put*-ing out to the pasture.

Doug says that same manure spreader used to belong to Harley Tucker, whom he supposed used it to haul manure accumulated from his famous Bucking Bulls. I loved watching how the old spreader still worked, how it spun the chunks of manure out the back, sending it flying over the fields. And the sight brought back memories of my own childhood, when my father operated one just like it. It's kind'a rare these days to see the old manure spreaders still being used. Chemical fertilizers, broadcast from elaborate machines, have replaced them.

April 2—I drove to Wallowa Town to attend a concert performed by the Wallowa County Orchestra and Chorale, held in the High School gymnasium. Delighted to see granddaughter-in-law Amy playing in the violin section. It was a wonderful evening of music and our county is very proud of these musicians, who mastered some very difficult selections.

Like I said, that huge snow bank slowly dissipated over the parsnips and carrots, so I hunted up a digging fork, removed the straw, and dug a pailful. Honest to Pete, there's nothing so sweet as wintered-over parsnips. Couldn't wait to simmer those fresh root veggies alongside a pot roast in my dutch oven.

April 4—A small vase of Forsythia sprigs brightens the kitchen table where I write. Their golden presence provides proof that, down near the mouth of Big Sheep Creek, it is, indeed, spring. It would be here, too, "on top" if it weren't for the pin pricks of sleet pinging against the windows, or the bone-chilling wind and leaden skies. If it were warm and sunny, perhaps I'd notice the row of garlic sprouting in the garden, the first red burls of rhubarb pushing through the ground, the robins and blackbirds seeking nest material, and the absence of the snowbank covering the parsnips. But for now, I am content, after doing my morning chores, to stay inside where it's warm.

My peacefulness is shattered, however, by the frantic scratching of a bird who has unwisely chosen the stove pipe, which is connected to our wood cook stove, to build a nest. I say unwisely, because it is now trapped in the pipe. So, I must DEAL with it.

After several futile attempts to coax the bird into the firebox, I gave up for the night. I did manage to open the draft enough to glimpse a very black bird, made even blacker by the insides of the stovepipe. As the bird eyed me through the sooty dust, Doug, who ISN'T fond of Starlings, suggested I simply let it die there and scoop it out later. However, visions of that trapped bird stayed with me all night, and by morning I had a plan.

Luckily, the bird had fallen into the fire box, and luckier still, there was no fire. So, I opened the little door under the lid and attached a plastic bag, then took the poker and poked the bird into the bag. It worked!

Outside, I let the bird free, and away it flew.

April 6—A blizzard rages outside this afternoon Snow flakes swirl around the house and stick to everything. Our world is white again. Wilma calls from Imnaha and says it's a blizzard down there too, says a coon ate all but three of their hens; they set a live trap and caught their cat first, but caught the coon the second night.

Speaking of cats, as I write, our mamma calico kitty is somewhere birthing a batch of kittens. My Jersey heifer is in heat. I'll breed her next month to calve in March.

Scene of the annual Marr Flat Cattle Company branding at the Big Sheep Creek corrals on Blue Meadow.

April 7—The ground was white this morning. It was under 30 degrees when I went out to chore and take Halley for her walk.

Last night I attended the annual Soroptimist of Wallowa County annual Fashion Show. This year they staged a "Musical." I'm telling you, our Ok Theatre was filled to overflowing! Let our residents put on a benefit with local folks acting, singing and dancing and people come out of the woods, prairies, canyons and hills in droves. It was hilarious, a spoof about a Wallowa County couple visiting New York and trying to decide which musical to attend.

Right there on the stage of our OK Theatre appeared Julie Andrews from the "Sound of Music," complete with the Von Trapp children singing Doe a Deer; Dorothy from the "Wizard of Oz" and "Toto;" Mary Poppins, and lots of CATS. Our local talent brought the house down. And most of their costumes were provided by the Soroptimist Thrift Shop!

And now, it is hailing.

Our prayers are with grandson Shawn, who has been deployed to Afghanistan again, and our thoughts with wife Maria and children Jackson, Savannah Rose, and little Jacob.

April 16—Drove down to Big Sheep canyon to attend the annual Marr Flat Cattle Co. branding. Since the sun was actually shining, for the first time in days, there was an impressive turnout of cowboys, cow-

Wallowa County Sheriff Fred Steen hones his cowboy skills, along with other locals at the Marr Flat Cattle Company branding.

girls, cowdogs and cow kids. Recent rains, plus the impact of numerous pickups and horse trailers that preceded me, made the road pretty greasy, but Doug's four-wheel drive pickup made it just fine.

When I pulled into Blue Meadow, son Todd and his able crew were already working the cows. The calves, separated from their mammas, milled about the corral. What a setting for a branding. The long green meadow, the weathered wooden corrals, the towering rim rock ridges rising east and west, Big Sheep Creek flowing under the bridge, the greening canyons under a blue sky scattered with April clouds, and that balmy canyon air.

After such a long winter everyone yearned to be outside, doing spring things, and branding is what our ranching families most look forward to. This is a chance to combine work and play. Zane and Jesse Anderson were there with their portable bar-b-cue, and the meaty aroma of roasting beef wafted in the breeze. While the crew worked the cows, Halley and I took a hike up the meadow and across the bridge.

When we returned the cowboys were heading and heeling calves, quite often five at a time, became there was a large ground crew ready to brand and vaccinate. Such activity! Young and old, girls and boys. A new crop of youngsters, another year older, straddled the fence. A real photo op, what with all the western trappings: chaps, spurs, ketch ropes and a variety of hats and boots. Cow dogs barked, cows bawled, and the air was filled with the smell of scorched hair and smoke.

Grandson Buck's wife Chelsea arrived with yeast donuts, freshly-made in her kitchen. Todd's wife Angie pulled in with more food, and I added my potato salad to the tailgate picnic. Around 1:30 the crew broke for lunch. That's when the first drops of rain splattered down. Just after those juicy roasts were sliced and plates heaped with beans, bread and salads, those clouds broke loose. I mean, it flat-out poured. Cowboys, with water dripping off their hats, didn't let that bother them. They filled their plates and fled to horse trailers and pickups to gobble down their meal.

Then, as quickly as it appeared, the storm moved on up the canyon. The cowboys shook off the rain and returned to the corrals to finish branding the tail end of over 300 calves. According to old-timers, Blue Meadow has seen a lot of brandings over the years, and this wasn't the first time it rained, nor will it be the last.

April 18—Unlike Aprils past here at the Writer's Retreat on Upper Imnaha, when cherry trees were bursting with bloom, the lawn was dotted with tulips and daffodils, and apple trees were an explosion of pink, nothing is blooming. Save for the startling yellow forsythia bush near the river, the upper Imnaha seems nearly a month behind with spring. However, on my way in yesterday morning, I noticed an abundance of wild plums and Sarvis in full bloom a couple of miles down the road toward Lyman's place.

Since we were here last October, there appears to have been a visitor—a beaver, who, before moving on, proceeded to gnaw its way through several fruit trees. These once prolific pear and plum trees have been reduced to a pile of wood chips that surround a pointy stump.

So here I am again, not in the "tree house" cabin this time, but in my familiar room upstairs in the log lodge, seated at a writing table in front of a sliding glass door that opens onto a deck with a view up Indian Creek. As I write, several pairs of cows and calves are grazing their way along the steep bunch grass slopes. Rising above, the high tiered rims capture the sun's first rays to announce a day that, for the moment, appears free of clouds. However, a heavy frost dulls the lawn, which means I'll need to go downstairs and fire up the wood furnace.

This week we are five: Katey Schultz, our Fishtrap Writer in Residence, who's been here for two weeks; Molly Gloss (well-known author of *The Jump-Off Creek* and *Hearts of Horses*; Bette Husted, who wrote *Above the Clearwater*; and Mary Emerick, who is working on a memoir, and yours truly.

We settled in yesterday. I was the first to arrive, and by the time I pushed two cart loads of gear and groceries across the bridge, and lugged my "stuff" upstairs, I was ready for a break. So, after fixing myself something to eat I indulged in a nap. The days leading up to my being here were pretty hectic.

This morning I took a long walk up-county, and even though frost lay thick on the river bottoms, the sun shown intermittently. Most every draw boasted a waterfall sifting down over blackened basalt, creating its own music. Crows swooped above, cawing loudly, and several wild turkeys fed in a high green field. Gary Marks' cows nibbled hay from long wooden feeders while their calves slipped through the fence to sun themselves alongside the road.

Good to be back in cow country.

April 19—Arising early on this clear frosty morning, I started a fire in the wood furnace before bundling up to hike downriver to visit Lyman and Wilma, which has become a sort of tradition. While hiking along I gazed across the river to see numerous deer, plus a small herd of elk, grazing the high benches. I stopped to visit Cynthia Warnock, who was on her way to Enterprise, and it was 8:00 when I hiked up Lyman's driveway.

Since the sun had just cleared the snowy eastern ridge, I plopped down in a porch swing to soak up the warmth and the view. Turning my head at the sound of a tractor motor, I spied Lyman feeding cattle up the road. After surprising Wilma, who was dusting the fireplace, I was invited into their cozy log home. While visiting and sipping coffee laced with sugar and plenty of canned cow, in walked Lyman.

Later a knock on the door produced neighbor Barbara Warnock, who is recovering nicely from hip surgery. Meanwhile, outside, a single cloud on the horizon had multiplied and a north wind was rising, so I left to "hoof it" upriver. By afternoon it was sleeting and snowing.

I called Doug last night to see how he was managing without me, and he was just taking a batch of sourdough biscuits out of the oven to go with the beans I'd cooked for him.

April 21—We awoke to rain drumming on the tin roof. Daylight revealed more snow on the high rims and ridges. Good weather for writing. Busy carrying wood from the wood shed and keeping the furnace going. Snowed again that evening as we gathered around the fireplace to read our writings to each other.

On Friday I drove out "on top" to attend grandson Buck and wife Chelsea's branding. A cold wind blew there near Eggleson Corner, but with the help of many friends the work was accomplished. This spring continues to be an ongoing challenge for ranchers, who must work their cattle before turnout time, not to mention farmers trying to work their fields and seed their crops. The "windows" of opportunity are few.

Meanwhile, back at the retreat I'd baked a loaf of sourdough bread before heading out, and this evening I slid a casserole of lasagna in the oven. We'd invited Lyman and Wilma for supper. A good time was had by all, and Wilma made it across the swinging bridge, even though Lyman shook it.

April 24—Returned to Prairie Creek yesterday, Saturday, and actually made it to the Easter Sunday sunrise service by 8:00 this morning. Almost forgot to ring the bell, but the congregation waited patiently while this old lady climbed the stairs to the bell tower.

In my absence our 24th great-grandchild, Callen James, was born to Colin and Lacey Hemphill.

April 28—Doug and I attended the annual dinner/meeting of the Wallowa County Grain Growers where, after a delicious roast beef dinner prepared by members of the Hurricane Creek Grange, I won a $200 gift certificate door prize.

April 29—Three of us former CowBelles donated our services at the Enterprise Community Dining Center. Neighbors Lois Hough and Mary Lou Brink and I were kept busy serving a large crowd of seniors a chicken fried steak dinner, prepared by the staff at Community Connection.

That evening, and far into the night, I could hear Melvilles no-till-drilling their grain crop over the hill. Other neighboring farmers have their crops in as well. A faint green mist of leaves brightens the ancient willows that line the Farmers Ditch, and yesterday the dandelions appeared.

April 30—I left in a snow storm to drive down into the canyons to the confluence of Big Sheep Creek and Little Sheep Creek. At Lightning Creek the sun burst forth, blue sky appeared between cottony clouds, and the air was balmy.

Last January I'd purchased a small acreage with a crude cabin there at the confluence. Across the creek from my cabin lies a long meadow in full sun, and I offered it to members of our church to use for a community garden. On this bright Saturday they staged a work day to construct a high deer fence, and over twelve folks turned out to help. While volunteers dug post holes and strung fence, I attended to various chores around the house and yard, which included burning limbs and doing some cleaning inside the old house.

At noon, I set up a lawn chair in the yard, where I rested and munched my sandwich while I gazed around at that perfect spring day; three cherry trees in full bloom, pink flowering quince, the apple trees in bloom, the rushing sound of the creek, a ruby red hummingbird seeking nectar in the quince, and those canyon rims rising all around. It was one of those rare moments in time I shall always remember. Work in the cabin could wait.

By late afternoon, when the sun was about to dip over a rim, the crew finished the deer fence! More about this garden project later.

The Imnaha pack of wolves has killed again, twice, taking one of son Todd's calves on the Divide, and another one of Karl Patton's across the way from our place on Prairie Creek. Fortunately, positive legislation is in the works. Many local ranchers have been working hard to effect this change.

May 3—Our writer's group met up Hurricane Creek at Phyllis' house on the mountain. The view from her living room is dominated by Sacajawea Peak, which we glimpsed periodically through sleet shot with sunlight.

May 4—Doug and I joined numerous other past grand marshals at the Outlaw Restaurant in Joseph to announce the 2011 Hells Canyon Mule Days Grand Marshals.

Tip Proctor of Enterprise was chosen, while George Hixon of Pendleton will serve as Honorary Grand Marshal of the 31st Annual event, to be held September 9-11 in Enterprise. Both are very deserving of the honor. Tip and wife Ruth of 62 years, have worked on ranches all their lives, including locally for the McClarans. Tip operated his own team when he was only 12 years old.

George has authored a book entitled *Tales of a Mule Twister* that chronicles his experiences during the training and showing of a 20 mule team. George traveled all over the West with that matched white team during the 70s and 80s.

May 9—Lyman and Wilma stopped by for lunch on their way to town. It was good to see them.

May 10—Our Writer's Group had a difficult time concentrating on writing when we met at Idella Allen's lovely home on Barton Heights above Joseph. We were granted another one of those rare spring mornings. Over the years Idella and husband Herb have planted hundreds of daffodils in their spacious yard, and they were all in full bloom, as were other perennials. Their lovingly-restored older home commands a stunning view of the Wallowas, which were brilliant with fresh snow. Idella served us homemade clam chowder for lunch and it just don't get any better than that.

May 12—If I'd been writing this column yesterday, you'd be reading about how sunny and warm it was, how the sky was the color of a robin's egg, how our brilliant snowy Wallowas contrasted with green pastures, and how I hung the laundry on the line for the first time in months. But today seems as if yesterday never existed. Today there is no blue sky, and those glorious mountains are shrouded in wet clouds. A fine sprinkling of rain soaks into the fields and another layer of snow falls at the higher elevations. Not that this moisture isn't what the germinating crops and grass needs, it's just that we haven't seen much sun lately.

Yesterday Doug and I talked about roto-tilling the garden and mowing the lawn, but today we've retreated to the house where it's warm.

Despite the weather, last weekend was typically busy.

Saturday, the 7th, Larry and Juanita Waters hosted the 13th Annual Lee Scott Memorial Plowing Bee at their ranch here on Tenderfoot Valley Road. Luckily the rain held off until several teams of horses and mules were harnessed and hooked up to various vintage plows and discs, to till one of Larry's fields. Folks traveled from afar, hauling their draft animals over the mountains to camp on the Waters Ranch.

Saturday evening they enjoyed a potluck at the Liberty Grange Hall, which included fiddle music as well as food. These families who farm with horses and mules included Julie Kooch, Vicki Leonard, and Larry Waters, from Wallowa County; Marvin Brisk, from Halfway; Laura Bruland, from Haines; Brian Cook, from Irrigon; and Bill Myers, from Hermiston. Some of the restored horse-drawn farm equipment dated back to the 1850s.

I hiked out into the field and photographed the teams. Those I talked to commented on how the soil was just perfect for plowing, not too dry nor muddy. Smelling that freshly-turned earth and listening to the quiet, broken only by the jangle of harness as the faithful draft animals plodded up and down the furrows, proved very pleasurable. As opposed to a noisy tractor, one could still enjoy the song of a Prairie Creek meadowlark.

That afternoon Doug and I joined a crowd of folks who gathered in the Enterprise Community Church to celebrate the life of our beloved friend "Doc" Doug Morgan, who passed away recently at the age of 93. The surviving nine of Doug and wife Betty's 10 children were in attendance. Many tributes and stories were shared about "Doc" who, at one time, was the only veterinarian in Wallowa County.

Rancher Melvin Brink, who raised his family way out on the Zumwalt, told how he came to town to get Doc to pull a calf. Doc insisted they eat first, and invited Melvin to join his family for supper before heading out the long road to Melvin's ranch. After an extremely difficult delivery, Doc drove all the way back to town and only charged $20 for the call.

We'll always remember Doc living out his later years in his beloved home on Imnaha, and how he enjoyed those crab feeds up at Lyman's place.

On Sunday, Mother's Day, the Plowing Bee was canceled due to foul weather. That is, the plowing was but the traditional Teamsters Breakfast, prepared in the Liberty Grange Hall, was served as planned. In years past I've always hiked over the hill and met Doug there for breakfast. So as not to disappoint Halley, who was anticipating her morning walk, I decided to go for it. Bundling up against the cold and wearing my chore boots, I struck off in freezing rain that turned to wet snow before I reached the old hall.

Directly across the county road from the Grange Hall, I came to one of those wire gates. Let's just say I had a confrontation with that contraption and the gate won. Like most women, I just left the thing lying on the ground. Doug would deal with it later. Since it was on his old ranch, he'd probably constructed it.

Leaving Halley outside, I entered the warm cozy kitchen and joined Doug for a cup of coffee before lining up to fill our plates with "hot off the griddle" pancakes, sausage and eggs. After listening to many tales of long (and not so long) ago, I headed back over the fields and up the hill to feed my chickens.

Shortly after 11:00 I was climbing the stairs to ring the church bell. We had a wonderful Mother's Day Service.

Later that day our children honored me in a variety of loving ways. Yesterday I dug the last of the parsnips and carrots in the garden, and last week I pruned the raspberries.

May 14—Doug and I attended a graduation party for Ryya and Lexi Fluitt. Not your ordinary High School graduation, as these two lovely sisters have been homeschooled. We, along with their many friends, have watched these two Prairie Creek girls grow up and admired their many skills, which include being top ranch hands, cowgirls, fiddle players, and just plain wholesome country girls.

The event was held at the Liberty Grange Hall, just across the road

Lori Meyers, shown here with Gus and Cal, who have been harnessed to participate in the annual Lee Scott Memorial Plowing Bee, held recently at the Waters' Ranch near Joseph. Lori and her husband Bill live in Hermiston.

Laura Bruland from Haines breaks ground with a two bottom plow pulled by a six-horse-and-mule hitch. Laura is one of several teamsters who participated in the event.

Marvin Brisk hauled his team from Halfway to take part in the 13th annual plowing bee.

from our place. Folks came from the canyons, hills and valleys bearing potluck dishes, and the family provided their own Fluitt Farm Natural Beef burgers. Afterwards the Skyline Band gathered on the old stage upstairs and provided some "foot-stompin" music for dancing. We enjoyed watching the younger (and not so young) generations expend all that energy.

Lyman and Wilma, who'd come up for the party, spent the night at our house as they are headed to Boise early the next morning.

May 16—After a day of sunshine, it rained, and this morning the snowline was at Ferguson Ridge again. Tucker's Mare, the snow shape of a horse, just isn't happening yet. The melting mare is covered yet again with another layer of snow.

Once again we met at Idella Allen's lovely home on Barton Heights, this time to discuss our monthly book club's selection. While it rained and sleeted on her colorful daffodils, we gals indulged ourselves in Idella's warm-from-the-oven rhubarb custard pie, which put us in a great mood to talk about the book.

We learned that about 18 inches of spring snow fell out north. After dark, the nearly-full May moon sailed in and out of wet clouds.

May 18—This evening son Todd delivered a young Angus bull to breed my two heifers, who, for months, as they're come in heat, have gazed longingly across the road at Hough's bulls.

Since my Jersey was just coming in heat, she was very aggressive, so much so the visiting bull acted pretty intimidated. Worried that he wouldn't get the job done, I voiced my concern to Doug, who said, "Don't worry, he'll figure it out." Which, of course, he did. The young bull not only bred the Jerz, he tended to the black heifer the next day. Hopefully, come next March, I'll be milking a cow again.

May 20—We were treated to a bright, sunny day, and Robin showed up to roto-till our garden. The willows that line the Farmer's ditch are leafing out, and the pair of hawks have hatched their babies in the old cottonwood. This afternoon I cut the first tender asparagus and we ate the last of the stored baking squash.

May 21—We joined a throng of Erma Tippett's friends and family, who gathered from far and near at the Enterprise Elks Lodge to celebrate the life of a grand lady. Born in Enterprise in 1914, Erma was best remembered for when she ran the Cowboy Bar Tavern, the Gold Room Restaurant, and the Chief Joseph Apartments in Joseph for 29 years, along with her husband Ben Tippett, and continued after his death in 1968.

The affair was a potluck, and a long table groaned with food. I'd contributed a platter of deviled eggs. It was fun visiting other Tippetts, like Bob, Merilee, and Patsy, who traveled from out of the county. Erma grew up in the Imnaha area, and her mother Josie Hays, who was a Zumwalt, lived to be nearly 102. Josie told me once, at age 100, that the Zumwalt area was named after her.

Erma worked at the Imnaha store when she was nine years old. She and Ben bought the Cowboy Bar in 1951, when it had a reputation for being a wild place. One of her customers was movie actor Walter Brennan, who owned a ranch in the Imnaha area. Walter nicknamed Erma "Miss Kitty." Erma might have seemed tough on the outside, but she befriended and helped many people who were in need.

May 25—My childhood chum Sandra, and her daughter Pam, left early this morning. It was a short visit. Having left Auburn, California, on Friday, and spent the weekend with relatives in Portland, they arrived here late Monday afternoon. I'd gone out near the bunkhouse to pick the first succulent stalks of rhubarb and bake a pie, and later roasted a plump chicken and peeled the last of our stored potatoes from the garden to cook garlic mashed potatoes.

Since it'd been raining most of their trip, Sandra and Pam were eager to enter a warm kitchen and inhale the homey smells of supper cooking. Due to health problems, Sandra's hubby Fred was not able to travel to this altitude, and therefore we missed his presence. With only one day to enjoy our visitors, we crammed in many memory-making experiences.

Tuesday morning we headed down into the canyons to show them my newly-purchased property on Big Sheep Creek, and of course it was raining, but our dampened spirits lifted when we spied the blooming wild sarvisberry bushes and those golden clumps of arrowleaf balsamroot appearing on the steep hill sides. Little Sheep Creek was running bank to bank with snowmelt and rain run-off.

Down at the confluence of Big Sheep Creek the swollen waters raced swiftly toward the Imnaha, less than three miles downstream. And, in my yard, verdant spring gone amuck; a tangled growth of yellow roses cascading over a sagging fence, bushes of white and lavender lilacs, clumps of iris, tiny green cherries dangling from the limbs of three older trees, blooming apple, pear, apricot and plum trees—hopefully forming fruit—and a knee-high lawn.

Standing there in the misty warm rain, you could feel the lush growth, breathe in the scent of fragrant new cottonwood and alder leaves, hear the frothy water tumbling past, and gaze across the creek to the newly-fenced and roto-tilled garden. Hidden among the limbs of locust trees, myriad birds sang in the rain. Scattered on the rocky hillsides we spied patches of pink phlox and more balsamroot. And those immense tiered rims towered above all, their slopes wearing a carpet of soft green grass.

From the car I unloaded a potted Syringa bush, a gift from my Syringa Sisters, to plant later. Since we had a lunch date in Joseph, we hurried on down to Imnaha "town," which consists of a post office, store and tavern, for a brief stop to show Pam the Wooden Indian-fronted Tav, with its dollar bills tacked on the ceiling, before we headed up "On Top." The Imnaha River, the color of malted milk, rolled high and wild under the bridge, rushing toward its confluence with the Snake.

Naturally, due to those persistent rain clouds cloaking our Wallowas, there WERE no mountains! Since this was a first-time visit for Pam, all she had was our word that they existed.

We did meet up with Doug and Ramona at the Outlaw Restaurant, where we enjoyed a most delicious meal. Ramona and Pam, who were children together when we lived near Auburn, California, hadn't seen each other since the 1950s. After Doug left us girls to "do" the shops, we walked up the street to Arrowhead Chocolates—a must if you're in

"Farmers Ditch" running high. Wallowa Lake is very full and water is being released due to heavy rains and melting snows.

Joseph—before wandering in and out of places like Lamb Trading, The Sheep Shed, and Simply Sandy's.

Back at the ranch, while taking a walk along Tenderfoot Valley Road, we were startled by the sudden appearance of Ruby Peak rising out of the rainy mists, followed by Chief Joseph Mountain emerging in all its snowy glory.

Doug treated us again that evening, when we feasted at the Embers Brew Haus in Joseph, and savored some of our local Terminal Gravity beer. Then it was home to resume the traditional cribbage tournament.

Now, as I write, we miss our friends.

May 27—One of my former 4-H Sourdough Shutterbug members, Tony Yost, stopped by to pick up some sourdough starter. We had a nice visit. Tony, his wife and two girls live in Baker City.

May 28—Made a brief visit to this season's first Farmer's Market in Joseph. The rain held off for awhile, and as usual, the event was very well-planned, with fresh produce offered by Back Yard Gardens, the educational Magic Garden Booth, Fluitt's natural beef, Wendy's goat milk soap, FireWorks Pottery, salad demos by Lynne Sampson Curry, and a talented guy and gal strumming dulcimer and guitar.

Meanwhile, the aroma of bar-b-cued beef hoagie sandwiches drew folks to Randy Garnett's Apple Flat Catering wagon. Alder Slope Nursery was offering planting demos, and tourists as well as locals were taking advantage of the brief sunshine to stroll around the market. There was even a petting zoo for children, consisting of goats and sheep.

May 29—Grandson Buck and wife Chelsea invited us over for bar-b-cued hamburgers and rhubarb/strawberry pie. Great-granddaughter Lucy ran out to greet us. "They're here!" she hollered to sister Kate. Of course it rained, but we were snug in their cozy little home.

May 30—It also rained on Memorial Day, which didn't discourage the first hummingbirds sipping at our feeder.

June 1—June swirled in cloudy and warm, and Phyllis and I traipsed up and down the forested slopes of the East Moraine in search of mushrooms. Just cool enough for hiking, we happened upon small patches of morels in the most unexpected places. Also we spied the emerging pink Calypso Orchids, and of course the open sunny slopes of the East moraine are smothered in clumps of golden balsamroot.

Noon found us over a mountain mile from our car and our lunches. So, we hoofed it in haste, following a game trail back, and shut the car doors before the rain hit. We each had a bag full, and that evening my tasty morels were browned in garlic butter and served with sirloin steaks. Yum!

Grandson Rowdy, wife Kasey, and their two children Cutter and Nevada, hauled up several pairs and some yearlings from the ranch in Mt. Vernon to help graze down our lush pastures.

June 3—Saturday dawned clear, sunny and WARM, which was a blessing because that was the day many of us who live here on Prairie Creek look forward to all year—the Triple Creek Branding! Held at the scenic ranch headquarters on Tucker Down Road, southeast of our place. Several members of our family was there helping, along with other neighbors, who hauled their saddle horses to rope around 75 calves. It was very entertaining for those of us who lined the corral fence, soaking up that welcome sun, visiting friends, and photographing. Our snowy Wallowas were drop-dead gorgeous against those brilliant green fields.

The cowboys and cowgirls worked together in a beautifully orchestrated way to head, heel, and stretch out husky calves for the ground crew to work them. It was art in action. Skills learned over a long period of time were put to good use. Son Todd was roping with a 60 ft. braided rawhide riata, which had been a gift.

When the last calf was branded, the cows and calves were driven down the road to a new pasture and the crew, plus us onlookers, ambled across to the ranch house lawn.

On the way over I grabbed the platter of deviled eggs I'd had on ice for the potluck table. And what a table it was! Pans of King Crab legs simmered in butter next to platters of thick juicy steaks, grilled to perfection, and casseroles of beans, scalloped potatoes, bowls of salads, strawberries, melons, and pineapple.

Brent McKinley and wife Connie, along with several of their nine children, are always so generous, and truly enjoy having neighbors over. Connie graciously thanked everyone for helping and saw to it everyone had more than enough to eat. We had to pinch ourselves to see if all of this was indeed, real.

I mean, that warm sunshine, those enormous crab legs, a babbling brook splashing down beside the lawn, those stunning mountains, and our cowboys and cowgirls chowing down. Pretty soon, here came one of the boys carrying two huge cast-iron dutch ovens, and plopped them down on the grass. The lids were lifted to expose cobblers, steaming in thick berry and peach juices. Of course we had to sample some for dessert.

After visiting several of our great-grandchildren, grandchildren, and children, we headed down the road to home. Full as ticks and drowsy from the warmth of rare sunshine, we felt truly blessed.

June 8—Occasional spurts of sunlight punctuate an otherwise gray, soggy morning. And when the sun does shine, the green lushness is so brilliant it takes your breath away. The snowy mountains play peek-a-boo with purple rain clouds.

Dandelion fluff drifts over the prairie, apple blossoms, that have waited so long to open, are profuse on the gnarled heirloom tree, my Aracuna hens announce they are laying large blue eggs, Halley is napping after our morning walk along the Farmer's ditch, and a rhubarb pie is bubbling over in the oven.

Doug is in Salem, attending grandson Brady's high school graduation, and I'm riding herd on what's left of our ranch.

June 11—Yesterday I baked raspberry and Dutch apple pies for the Wallowa Mountain Cruise antique car show today, along with other members of the Museum Board. The pies were sold for our annual money-raising project. Sales were brisk and, lucky for us, the rain held off until the last slice of pie was sold.

The snowy Wallowas provide a showy backdrop for their branding scene held in Triple Creek Ranch between rain showers.

This evening I drove into Cloverleaf Hall to partake of Apple Flat Catering's bar-b-cued beef dinner, followed by the Blue Mountain Old Time Fiddlers June show. Doug, who prefers not to sit that long, decided to stay home this time.

As usual, I delighted in the variety of old-time music and fiddle playing. Be-whiskered oldsters, young'uns like Bailey Vernam, and teens like our Prairie Creek Girls, kept our toes tapping. A newly-formed local group, who call them themselves Homemade Jam, really made a hit with the audience, as they played instruments that ranged from auto harp to fiddle with vocals thrown in. Not only did they play well, they were having fun.

June 12—Over a hundred of us gathered at the Wallowa Lake Methodist Camp to honor two couples who have, over the years, given of their time, energy and money to help create our unique community. Don and Rosemary Green, and Malcolm and Jean Dawson were roasted, toasted, and congratulated. The affair was preceded by another one of Wallowa County's famous potlucks, of which there have recently been many. Folks seem to outdo themselves with the delectable dishes they prepare.

Neighbor and fellow former CowBelle Mary Lou Brink commented that it's a shame we don't do this for all deserving folks before they die.

"It's so good to have these celebrations of life where people can attend their own parties," she said.

June 13—Drove to Imnaha to transplant my Syringa bush, as it was a cool, drippy day. The snowballs were in bloom, and a covey of quail came trooping out from under the blackberry bushes to welcome me.

June 14—Our Writer's Group drove out to Flora, thence to Courtney Butte to poet Cathy Putnam's old farm house. The drive out was gorgeous, and we stopped to photograph the Krebs' flocks of sheep grazing the long, green meadows near the North Highway. Miles of Mule Ears, lupine and pink Phlox dotted the hills and lined roadways. Farm fields in Flora, under snow for so long, remained waterlogged. Many grain fields were not yet planted, and we understand some won't be.

Large bushes of blooming lilacs greeted us at Cathy's rustic garden gate, and the smell of baking biscuits mingled with the scent of lilacs as we made our way slowly through her yard. It was a brilliant sunshiny day. Cathy's hubby Dan baked the biscuits, as she has recently undergone shoulder surgery which limits her activity. Upon entering the old farm house kitchen we, of course, had to sample a hot-from-the-oven biscuit, slathered in butter and marmalade, with a cup of tea, before we read our writings.

At noon we spread a tablecloth on the picnic table under the trees and ate the lunches we'd brought. A fitting way to celebrate the Summer Solstice.

Later, at home, Doug returned from fishing the Snake River where he caught a nice bass which he filleted for supper. He reported traveling the Loop road which is now open after a very long winter.

June 17—Doug and I celebrated our 33rd Wedding Anniversary by joining the "old folks" at the Family Dining Center in Enterprise. The pot roast was delicious.

This evening I gathered with the Juve family and friends at another Potluck, this one at the Joseph Community Center, to honor their mother, grandmother and friend, Dorothy Juve, who passed away early in the spring. It was good to see Dorothy's family, as they were my neighbors when I lived on Alder Slope. Dorothy and her husband Arnold were some of the kindest folks I'd ever met, and it appeared others thought so too, judging from the many treasured stories that were shared.

Their son Ted has been an especially good friend all through the years. He goes by the name Olaf and is a potter of great fame. His pottery graces many a home far and near, and is in great demand. He is now making pots from local clay.

Krebs' sheep graze the green meadows off the north highway to Lewiston.

Springtime near the confluence of Big Sheep Creek near Imnaha.

Blue Mountain Old Time Fiddlers performing at Cloverleaf Hall.

June 19—For Father's Day I treated Doug to dinner at the Glacier Grill at Wallowa Lake. Doug ordered Fish and Chips, and I had the beer-battered Halibut, which was yummy. Tourists have invaded our Lake now, but that is good. It was amusing to watch them, especially the young families with children. I always love to watch youngsters being with their parents as a family. We also marveled at the array and variety of dogs that vacation with their owners.

Both Doug and I were saddened to learn of the passing of Roger Pond. So many folks will miss his sense of humor laced with common sense. We just know, Roger, that you are somewhere in "The Back Forty," resting from your labors here on earth.

June 23—Today is grandson James' birthday. He called me the other day from North Carolina, where he is stationed while serving in the U.S. Marines. It was so good to hear his voice. And another Marine grandson, Shawn, who is serving in Afghanistan, is always in our prayers. Shawn's parents, Charley and Ramona are just recently returned from California, where they traveled to watch their grandchildren, Clayton, Cole and Halley, show their 4-H and F.F.A. project animals at the local County Fair.

Charley and Ramona brought back with them son Shawn and wife Maria's two children, Jackson and Savannah Rose, who will spend a month on grandpa and grandma's ranch. My great-grandchildren tell me their little brother Jacob, who had such a hard time of it after he was born, is doing just fine. Jacob was our miracle baby, born on Okinawa when Shawn was stationed there with his family.

This morning dawned cloudy and cool, unlike yesterday, when temperatures shot up over 70! Last evening's thunder-showers didn't amount to much, and I never thought it would happen, but I was actually glad to have it cool down. We just aren't used to such a drastic change in the weather.

Doug and I arose early yesterday morning, while it was still cool, to drive to my place on Sheep Creek, to deal with the waist-high lawn. However, we were defeated by the newfangled grass eater Doug had recently purchased. It wouldn't start!

So, after I transplanted a red climbing rose by the back porch, and watered the recently-planted Syringa bush and the Rainier Cherry tree son Todd planted for Mother's Day, we headed back up the canyon to Prairie Creek.

Before we left, we did drive across the bridge to visit the "Magic Garden" and drop off some pipe fittings for their irrigation setup. Steve and Angie Rubin were working in the garden, and those 100 growing tomato plants made me hunger for warm off-the-vine tomatoes with thick slices of bacon in a sandwich later this summer. The canyons are still green, and now the sweet scent of Syringa floats in the warm air. All manner of wildflowers bloom up and down the draws and sunny slopes. Tiny pears, apples and cherries peek through thick foliage in my orchard.

Ken and Rowdy's cattle haven't begun to catch up with the lush feed growing in our pastures. My garden is flourishing due to recent rains, followed by warm days and mild nights. Cabbages, potatoes, onions and lettuces are especially happy. I love being out in my garden weeding, especially when I lean on the hoe to rest, look up at the nearby snowy Wallowas, and feel the warmth of sunshine here on Prairie Creek.

A few of the ranchers are beginning to irrigate, and Lyman called yesterday from the Upper Imnaha, informing me I was NOT to let it rain today. He has hay down.

It's been a very busy month thus far.

June 24—Doug and I arose early to beat the heat and headed down to my Sheep Creek property. Wearing snake boots, and armed with a weed eater that WORKED, we attacked weeds and waist-high lawn, then raked and stacked our hay.

June 25—I entered the annual Amy Hafer Memorial Run/Walk again. It was a lovely morning, and I joined others in the 5K Women-Over-60 Walk category. The course was mostly uphill toward Ant Flat, where wild honeysuckle, Lupine and Flax lined the route. I finished the three-miles in an hour, not rushing, just sauntering along without pausing to rest.

June 26—Made it to church on time, to ring the bell.

This evening son Todd arrived to pick up his bull, assuming my Jerz and Rhubarb, the black heifer, are now bred. The bull obviously didn't want to go home. He jumped over a barrier near the trailer and we had to run him into the corral again.

June 28—Doug and I returned to Sheep Creek to move an old refrigerator I'd purchased into the cabin. Since we couldn't locate our dolly, we borrowed one from Dave and Sally down at the Imnaha Store. While there, Sally fixed us sandwiches and treated us to warm Long Johns she'd made that morning, baked in honor of her dad, Ken Stein, who celebrated his 80th birthday that day. Sally told us a large turnout of locals had gathered at the old wooden table that morning to enjoy those Long Johns, which resemble maple bars, with their coffee.

"An old Imnaha recipe," said Sally. "I only bake 'em for dad's birthday."

Growing in a rocky pasture on my property are numerous Syringa bushes, and the sweet scent of Mock Orange, released by the summer heat, was very pleasant. Cherries are ripening on the old trees, and the soft green slopes beneath the high tiered rims are carpeted with delicate pink phlox. Due to all those late spring rains, the canyons are still green.

June 29—My 25th great-grandchild was born, a girl, Arianwyn Nash, who joins four brothers and a very happy sister. Welcome to our family, Arianwyn.

This morning Lyman, his son Craig, and wife Wilma invited Doug and me to join them for breakfast at Friends Cafe in Enterprise. A real treat for me. Craig, the crab fisherman from Eureka, California, was on his way home after helping his dad put up the first cutting of hay. The hay was baled without rain damage, thanks to me, the weather girl.

June 30—I spent the day hauling furniture, dishes and plunder to the cabin on Sheep Creek. Also scrubbing kitchen cupboards, sweeping floors, and cleaning the old fridge. In the afternoon I heard the familiar *swish-swish* sound of sprinklers and looked across the creek to see the crew from our church had gotten the timed irrigation going in their Magic Garden. Yeah!

Soon the electrician drove in to start mine. Resting from my labors, I plunked down in a lawn chair on the deck under the shady grape arbor and relaxed. Myriad swallow tail butterflies floated in the summer air, birds of every description burst into song, hawks glided above the rim rocks, Sheep Creek splashed past, and a soft breeze cooled my sweaty body. Another defining moment.

In the past I've been filled with doubts about purchasing this property, but not so this day. All was falling into place. I sat there until the sun slipped behind a rim and a delicious coolness wafted from the creek.

Driving home, saffron clouds clustered in the narrow canyon sky, and the evening sunset over Prairie Creek plunked a period to a perfect day.

July 1—Several weeks ago, daughter Ramona called to say I should mark July 1st on my calendar. Doug and I were to be at Wallowa Lake Lodge at 6:30. She said nothing else. A mystery. So, there we were, at the appointed date and time, to join son Ken and wife Annie, and daughter Ramona and hubby Charley. For what?

Well, turns out 50 years ago I'd "put on" a wedding for my sister-in-law Janice Ingle, and this July 1st would have been Janice and husband Warren's 50th wedding anniversary. Warren, however, passed away after they'd been married 47 years.

Janice got to thinking about it, and wanted to let me know just how much she appreciated all I'd done to make their day special. So she was treating me and my family to this surprise dinner. Janice had enlarged a photo of that long-ago happy occasion and, standing next to the newlyweds, were son Ken and daughter Ramona as young children. Members of the wedding party. 50 years ago!

Janice, even though not present, was there in spirit, as was Warren. We all laughed as we recalled that hot day in Davis, California, when the candles, placed near the flowery altar, bent over in the heat. Our meals were delicious, and son Ken, who had been working on a rigorous job out of the county and hadn't taken time to eat much, really chowed down. It was rather amazing.

The historic old lodge is a great get-a-way, and Gail Swart's piano playing added to the ambiance.

July 2—There I was again, another year older, boarding the bus that took us runners and walkers up the Lostine River to drop us off for the start of another race. However, the word RACE is not in my vocabulary, as I near 78 years. Consequently, when everyone took off, yours truly "ambled" the three miles downriver to the small town of Lostine. Always a beautiful course, and over 100 participants showed up this year. For once I did have walkers behind me, and managed to win the second place medal for Women 70 and Over.

Doug met me at the finish line and, since he wasn't hungry and I was, I left him to nap in the pickup while I strolled up the street to the annual Lostine Flea Market to find myself a hamburger.

Later I returned to purchase a beef steak heirloom tomato plant for the Imnaha garden, and a birdhouse mounted on an old shovel.

July 3—Friend Pat Cason and I drove down to the cabin, where I planted the tomato, finished cleaning, hung pictures on the walls, and irrigated the lawns, Syringa, rose bush and new cherry tree. Resting from our labors under the grape arbor, we were entertained by a frisky little cottontail that appeared to live there with a doe and new fawn.

Now, back at home this afternoon, a corner of my front room is piled with dutch ovens, cooking kettles, sleeping bag and other gear, waiting to be transported to Billy Meadows later this week. On Friday, neighbor Nancy Knoble and I will shop for groceries to prepare fifteen meals for when she helps me cook for the Fishtrap Outpost Writers workshop out at the Billy Meadows Guard Station.

This will be my third year of taking on this task. We leave Saturday and prepare the first meal that evening, ending with lunch on the following Thursday. Then it's back to Fishtrap summer conference to give a presentation. The next day, Friday, four "Syringa Sisters," who will have spent the week at Billy Meadows Workshop, will travel to Sheep Creek, where we'll all spend the night. So that's the reason I've been rushing to get the cabin ready. Our time there will suffice as our annual get-together, our 15th.

After, I will return to Prairie Creek just in time to welcome son Steve's family, who are flying in from Alabama to spend a week with us. It's a typical Wallowa County summer.

Hope all you in Agri-Times Land are having a good one.

July 5—The 4th of July is history. It was different this year, at least for us. Our families have grown so, and lately tend to branch off and do their own thing instead of gathering for large get-togethers. Since we are still growing, logistics are exhausting. Instead, yesterday was spent in total relaxation, which was nice. After tending to our own yard, irrigating the lawns and vegetable garden, we just enjoyed being here, not having to go anywhere, cook anything, or worry about entertaining anyone. Because we live on Prairie Creek amid peace and quiet, surrounded by ranches and farms where present activities are limited to irrigating and haying, and the views in all directions are stupendous…why leave?

The old-fashioned yellow rose that grows so profusely alongside our bunkhouse is in full flower, nearly a month late. The vegetable garden is

Mountain snows water upper Prairie Creek Ranch and farmland. Stored in Wallowa Lake and flowing our over the valley in irrigation ditches, the melted snows are seen here in myriad sprinklers.

flourishing in the summer heat which begats mild nights. The pastures are up to the cows' eyes, and they are glossy and fat.

For several days in a row, there have been Robin's egg blue skies, and now the ancient willows are pregnant with cotton fluff which floats in the air.

Last evening, after Doug went to bed, I curled up in a chair and lost myself in a good book. Around 10:00 o'clock I realized the annual fireworks display at Wallowa Lake was about to begin. So, with Halley at my heels, I waded through chin-high meadow grass up the hill to watch the show.

A new moon sliced into Sheep Ridge, and several pairs of eyes glowed in the grasses. At first I thought they were white-tail deer, but then realized those curious cows were following us. So, there we were, bovine, canine, and human, standing under the stars watching an explosions of sparks bloom above the East Moraine of Wallowa Lake. It was one of those defining moments in life. I don't know what thrilled me the most, the moon and brilliance of stars or the man-made short-lived sparkles. Mother Nature's was free and Man's was not.

Summer continues to roll on with its myriad activities.

July 25—Weather-wise, summer has made itself known. Yesterday our thermometer shot up to 90 on the carport! Today is pleasantly cooler. My laying hens have finally calmed down after our company left. Son Steve, wife Jennifer, and their children, Bailey and Stetson, aka "The Alabama Tornadoes", have departed after a week's visit.

During their stay my chickens were "fed," checked, chased, and treated to kitchen scraps every hour on the hour. The children camped at the nests waiting for an egg to be laid, then, while still warm-in-hand, fetched the eggs to the house.

Our neighbors the Houghs are haying, long furrows of fragrant meadow hay quivering and falling to the swather. It's a beautiful time in our valley. My garden is producing. We savored beets with tops, swiss chard, Walla Walla onions, radishes, new potatoes in cream sauced with bacon, and lettuces for last night's supper.

Ben and his grandson have been irrigating our pastures with the hand lines, and all over Prairie Creek the second cuttings are growing furiously. Hay stacks are multiplying, and folks drive by with pickups and trailers stacked with winter wood.

On July 9th, neighbor Nancy Knoble drove her truck down and we proceeded to load it with supplies and food to feed twenty people for six days. We left, me driving her Subaru, and she her truck. 30 miles later, we pulled into Billy Meadows Guard Station on a lovely clear morning.

Before heading out north, we made a brief stop in Enterprise as "The Bowlby Bash" was in progress, and it would be my only chance to see grandson Chad and son Ronan's entry in the Soap Box Derby—a creative backhoe, featuring a garden shovel brake!

After settling in to Billy Meadows, we began shucking corn for the first meal, preparing a fresh garden salad with marinated shrimp, and cutting Wild Flour Bakery bread.

The van load of writers appeared on schedule and I was thrilled to see my "Syringa Sisters," who elected to take Dr. Robert Pyle's workshop, known as the Outpost Workshop, at Billy Meadows. This would suffice as our annual outing, a tradition that has endured for fifteen years, since we met in Pyle's class as part of Summer Fishtrap Conference at Wallowa Lake, and wrote about Syringa! And now, the eldest of us is 83, and we continue to meet every summer.

I had an exceptional crew this year. In addition to Nancy, Nick Lunde was hired as camp director. He lit propane pilot lights and tended the coals for my dutch oven cooking, lifted heavy pots and kettles, did dishes, and even proved his talent for cooking, which included baking sourdough pancakes after I mixed the batter.

Nancy, a great cook herself, in addition to cookie baking, prepared a chicken shish kabob dinner one evening that was a hit. Nancy also treated everyone to goat milk cheese, which she makes using milk from her own goats. You can buy this cheese at her shop, "The Sheep Shed," in Joseph. It's both delicious and nutritious.

Each morning I was up at dawn, filling my huge granite-ware pot with cold Billy Meadows water and bringing it to the boil before adding a (clean) sock full of coffee. Cowboy coffee proved very popular with this crowd. The Marr Flat Hamburgers, grilled outside, as well as the pot roast cooked in the dutch oven in the coals were consumed with relish. That mountain air, and the fact that the writers all slept out in tents made for healthy appetites. Nancy disappeared down to the CCC cabin to bake a batch of fresh cookies, which she did every day.

This rustic cabin, along with the environment adjacent to Billy Meadows, provided an inspiring outdoor classroom. Even though there was a generator, we didn't use it, so no electricity, no phone, no cell phone service, no computer—we were "off the grid," and it was Heaven.

The cooking stove top in the module where I cooked was propane, as were the refrigerator and freezers. Three long tables, set end to end, seated everyone at once in the living room. The first night's meal, and others, were eaten outside around the campfire pit.

Every evening we gathered at the fire to read our writings, sing, and visit. One night we roasted marshmallows and made s'mores, and oftentimes the waxing July Moon rose through the Ponderosas. Once a bull elk bugled from afar, and the coyotes yipped and yammered. Myriad birds warbled, twittered and flitted about, and the False Hellebore in the meadow bloomed creamy white.

My friend Ellie Waterston acted as intern instructor, as she is in training for next summer. Ellie gave me the idea for the title of my book, *Four Lines a Day*, which, by the way, is in its second printing. Ellie, a former rancher, hails from Bend and is the founder of "The Nature of Words" writing center there. She has authored several books. I'm reading *Where the Crooked River Rises*, and find it most interesting. Lots of Eastern Oregon history therein.

Nancy and I were invited to join the writing classes, which we did when time allowed, so I was able to begin another project. One day, naturalist Jan Hohmann joined us, and the next morning, after making lunches, the entire class took off to spend a day at Buckhorn Lookout. All returned with enough fodder to write about for days. Just walking to the clothesline to hang out dish towels and my coffee sock, I sidestepped Penstemon and Prairie smoke. The wildflowers were gorgeous. Mosquitoes were not so welcome, but inspired writers, who could be seen perched on stumps and sprawled under trees, scribbling pen to paper, to accomplish a great deal of swatting.

One day, to escape my kitchen duties, I strode out to hike along McCarty Rd. Lovely clouds floated overhead and a breeze blew the mosquitoes away. Succumbing to a faint trail that led to a more defined road, grown over with grass and lined with wild roses, I veered off back in the direction of Billy Meadows. Adventure!

I knew a ridge separated me from the meadows, so I continued on in the hopes the trail/road would lead me back. An hour later, knowing I'd gone too far, I jumped a large white-tail buck, then came to a stock pond. Below the pond I came to a crossroad. A sign read *Road 0202*, which meant nothing.

Long story short, I came out on the main road not far from Coyote campground! Which meant I had to hoof it back a few miles to Billy Meadows. A shower and a cup of tea revived me enough to make it through supper. Being the cook and a local, I found myself playing the role of wildflower identifier, history buff, confidant, mother, and cheerleader. Normal for me.

On Thursday morning we packed up—no small feat—and posed for a group photo on the steps of the CCC Cabin before we headed down McCarty Road to Chesnimnus Creek, thence past Birkmaier's ranch on Crow Creek to Elk Creek and out the North Highway to home. Nancy and I managed to make it to Wallowa Lake Camp in time to hear the Outpost presenters, who looked well fed. Robert Michael Pyle was proud of their writings.

I spent that night at home, while the gals stayed at the lake.

The next afternoon, we headed down to my Sheep Creek cabin. That evening we grilled Imnaha-caught salmon, tossed salad greens from my garden, sliced sourdough bread I'd baked previously and frozen, and sat out by the creek to savor the canyon views. After supper we hiked across the bridge to visit the "Magic Garden," which is thriving, and visited neighbor Ken Hunt.

Returning to the cabin we sat at creekside and watched the full July moon glow, then free itself from the eastern Rim. I mean, it don't get any better than that!

Later, the gals laid their sleeping bags out next to the creek, while I chose a cot in the screened-in sleeping porch. My view was of those tiered steep rims and the moon-washed canyon. The creek lulled us to sleep.

Wallowa County Cowbelle Reunion at Mary Lou Brink's home in rural Enterprise. BACK ROW. L-R Shirley Parker, Janie Tippett, Jean Cook, Paula Boston, Ardis Klages, Barbara Warnock, [unknown], Ann Hays, Lois Hough, Davise McFetridge, Bonnie Marks, Marla McFetridge, Judy Stilson. FRONT ROW: L-R Helen Jones, Mary Hays, Zua Birkmaier, Marilyn Johnson, Mary Lou Brink, Marian Birkmaier, Elaine Morse, Pat Murrill and Wilma Goucher. Photo by Melvin Brink.

Next morning we made sourdough toast smeared with cherry preserves I'd made the week before from the cherry trees out front. The resident doe and twin fawns, plus a cottontail, and covey of quail kept us entertained. Reluctantly, we left, and met again at Arrowhead Chocolates in Joseph for a mocha topped with whipped cream, a fitting farewell for Barb and Bobbie, heading for Portland, and Jessica and Mary to Boise. Until next year!

Monday found me at our monthly book group, then serving a dinner outside on our picnic table that evening, for grandson Shawn's wife Maria and her family, which included great-grandchildren Savannah Rose, Jackson, and baby Jacob, our miracle baby, who was born on Okinawa, flown to Hawaii, and finally to the States, all the while in intensive care. Weighing a mere few pounds, Jacob's story has proven there's power in prayer. Today he is a normal, happy 18-month old.

Our prayers remain with Shawn, our Marine, serving his third hitch in Afghanistan.

The next morning I hosted our weekly writer's group to a salad luncheon after we read and wrote. Just before the gals arrived, in drove son Steve and his family. More cooking for me, which is what I love.

On the last night, Doug treated us all to a dinner at Vali's at Wallowa Lake. Shish Kabob night! And I got another reprieve when we all met at the Cheyenne Cafe for breakfast the next morning before they took off. Grandkids Bailey and Stetson were crying crocodile tears. They had spent the night before with Uncle Charley and Aunt Ramona at Camp Runamuck Ranch, and although there was cow manure dried on their jeans and s'more marshmallow in their hair, they didn't want to leave.

There's nothing like good old summertime, and now this is Chief Joseph Days week. This past Saturday evening I attended the Tamkaliks celebration in Wallowa, but we'll save that story for next time.

August 3—I perused the second edition of my book, which is just out, complete with a map this time. Folks wanted to know where all those cow camps were located, and where was this Imnaha anyhow? The Bookloft in Enterprise is selling them, as well as other stores around Wallowa County. The title is *Four Lines a Day*.

August 6—I baked popovers for great-grandchildren Lucy and Katelyn, and then we visited the Saturday Farmer's Market in Joseph.

Jackie took home some of Sally B Farms' goat milk soap, and I purchased two bottles of local fruit wine made by Scott Lathrop, who is starting a local wine business here.

Later, Jackie left with her family to drive to Union for a week of Rodeo Bible Camp, where she will tend to her grandchildren Lucy and Katelyn, and be joined by hubby Bill from Challis, Idaho, while her son Buck and wife Chelsea conduct the camp. Busy summer for these young folks, who manage to weave parenting, haying, moving cattle, weed spraying, and Chelsea's RN duties at our local hospital, into their busy lives.

In the afternoon, I attended a bar-b-cue and concert hosted by Alvin Josephy Jr. and his wife, Melissa, who live in Seattle but are vacationing at their summer home situated on the north end of the east moraine of Wallowa Lake. There, pond-side, we savored salmon grilled by Joe McCormack while seated around the campfire pit listening to well-known folk singer Hank Cramer.

It was a wonderful warm evening and the lapping of the water, the fluttering of the cottonwoods, and the birdsong that accompanied our meal and songs was very relaxing.

August 10—Once more my kitchen table/office reflects the season. Jars of canned Bing cherries, pickled beets, raspberry freezer jam, and six pints of pie cherries I managed to cheat the Robins out of.

On my left, the Wallowa County Fair Premium book informs me that Cloverleaf Hall is open to the public today. Yesterday it was only open to exhibitors, like me, entering their perishables.

Monday morning found me there, armed with my Photography Division entries. Yesterday morning it was up at dawn, pulling beets, digging potatoes, cutting squash, lettuce and chard, arranging an herb basket, and plucking a large blue delphinium. Fairitis...there's no cure. It's in the blood since youth, so may as well stay involved.

It's a beautiful morning. A little on the coolish side, and our garden is flourishing, as are our bodies as we digest those nutritious vegetables growing there. Oftentimes, if I'm hungry, I graze up and down the rows: a leaf of chard, a sun-ripened strawberry, a taste of basil, a bite of Walla Walla Sweet onion, a pinch of dill, or a sniff of calendula or bachelor button which add color to my garden.

Rowdy and Ken's cattle have yet to catch up to the grasses that sway above their backs. My hens are laying nine eggs per day. The Houghs have stacked their first cutting of meadow hay, our resident wild honkers are flying from field to field again, as their goslings are now teenagers; swallows and blackbirds flock together, coyotes wail plaintively at dawn, and Halley answers with her long drawn-out howl.

I promised to write about the recent Tamkaliks Celebration held in Wallowa. Again it was a very moving experience for me, as well as the others who attended that Saturday evening's events. Arriving in late afternoon, I wandered around the many booths, admired the Indian beadwork, and purchased a rug for my Sheep Creek cabin. After setting up my chair on the perimeter of the dance pavilion, I plopped down to soak up the atmosphere.

The Grand Entry was very colorful and emotional, as these proud people danced sedately to the beat of the drum as they circled the dancing area. A prayer was recited about how all men were created equal, how we should all respect one another and acknowledge a power higher than us, a creator. They wore feathers and bells and elk teeth and beads, all backlit by the fiery sun sinking slowly in the west.

Cottonwood drift floated in the air like summer snow, all intermingled with smells of sage, frybread, and a cool dampness seeping from the nearby river, where tepees caught the golden light of a summer evening.

August 16—We had a surprise visit from Chuck and Dinah Hemphill, who ranch in Pilot Rock. Granddaughter Lacey, married to their son Colin, lives on the ranch with our two great-grandkids, Seely and Callen.

I invited Chuck and Dinah for supper, which always begins with a trip to the garden. After digging potatoes, picking chard, lettuce and broccoli, Dinah and I retreated to the kitchen to prepare creamed new potatoes with parsley, fried elk steak, salad, and veggies, topped off with slices of double chocolate zucchini cake with cream cheese frosting.

August 17—In the evening, Diane and Chuck, who had been staying in their motor home at the Lake, walked up to the Wallowa Lake State Park amphitheater to listen to me read from my book for a Fishtrap Literary event. Good thing, or we wouldn't have had an audience, save for the participants. Seems there was a mix-up in advertising the event.

Son Ken and his family completed another setting of hand irrigation lines over our pasture, and all through the fair and the Stockgrowers doings, we picked raspberries and made jam or froze them. Also busy in the garden, freezing broccoli and making dill pickles.

Last Thursday our Writer's Group traveled out north to the RimRock Inn for lunch and celebrated two birthdays. What a treat, sitting out on the sunny deck, in a soft summer breeze to savor delicious sandwiches, as well as the awesome view of Joseph Creek Canyon.

Later that week our group drove to my Sheep Creek place to pick blackberries and eat lunch under the grape arbor. After a tour of the "Magic Garden," which is truly magic, we picked buckets of berries and transparent apples from my orchard. This morning I made a huge pie using those apples.

Summer is waning, our brief beautiful summer. Better make the most of it. Grandson Ethan is coming for supper and the mountains are calling.

August 23—A canner full of peaches, three pints of apple butter, and a humongus apple pie remind me of what I've been up to lately on this lazy, warm, summer afternoon here on Prairie Creek. The garden languishes in its fullness, freshly watered and ripening in the tropical heat. Corn, squashes, green beans, potatoes, cabbages, broccoli, strawberries and raspberries are reaching peak flavor. The southwestern baking squash is climbing the apple tree in the garden, and threatening to do battle with the zucchini and rows of cabbage.

We wish this could go on forever, but alas, the days are shortening and the nights are noticeably cooler. Afternoon breezes dry out the hills east of us and irrigation is constant. Second cuttings are going up without rain-damage. The threat of fires is always present.

Received word last evening of our friend Dave Moore's passing. Known hereabouts as the "Moore Boys," Dave and his brothers are respected for their excellent fence building. The brothers also run cattle, and operate a small sawmill down along Sheep Creek. Lately, due to Dave's lingering illness, the mill has been silent.

Our heart goes out to the family down there in Bear Gulch. All those miles of wandering fences, fortified with Rock Jacks, that knit together our hills, valleys, and canyons, will remain a monument to the Moore Boys' fine work. Adios, old friend. How fitting that the winning Rock Jack, built by Tom Birkmaier of Crow Creek, at the recent World Champion Rock Jack Building Contest, was once again auctioned off with the money donated to the Moores. Dave died less than two days later.

This last Saturday was one of those marathon days. It all began with the annual Stockgrowers breakfast meeting chaired by son Todd, Wallowa County Stockgrowers president. Although it was a short meeting, it covered a lot of territory. We heard a wolf update by Rod Childers, a California report by Bill Hoyt and Kay Teisl, an introduction to Angie Dietrich's Wolf Book, and a Wallowa County Stockgrowers Education Committee update by local ranchers Ramona Phillips, Lori Schaafsma, Terry Tienhaara, and Lori Butterfield.

The escalating problem of wolves, brought about due to the introduction of Canadian Gray Wolves to our area, dominated the meeting. To date there are ten wolves in the Imnaha pack, six in the Wenaha, seven in Umatilla, one in Fossil, and tracks found near Ladd Canyon. The costs to ranchers, both in terms of money and their ability to cope with these predators, is unreal. Keeping their cool has been, to put it mildly, almost beyond belief.

Latest hit is upper Prairie Creek rancher Denny Johnson, who has lost several head that were NOT confirmed as wolf kills when all evidence pointed to their being otherwise. These are good people, hardworking tax payers who contribute to the community on every level. Denny runs cattle on the Divide, as does son Todd and others.

Our sincere hope is that the video being made by the Wallowa County Stock Growers Education Committee will enlighten the voting public on the truth. A film clip was shown at the dinner that night in Cloverleaf Hall. Filmed by Mark Bales, a native Wallowa Countian, this documentary is professionally done.

At noon the annual Ranch Rodeo began with the Rock Jack Building Championship. Inside of an hour those contestants split tamarack logs and assembled them into the traditional Rock Jack, complete with rocks to anchor them. They were works of art! And the sweat rolled down the backs of those muscular men as they toiled under the August sun. Tom Birkmaier, who ranches on Crow Creek and who has been the subject of a great deal of kidding, won! Perhaps it was the birth of his first son that sparked his energy, but he did it. Way to go, Tom.

Grandson Buck was in charge of the stick horse race for the youngsters, who had to ride their steeds to a tethered goat, grab the ribbon from the goat's tail, then ride back to the finish line. I was a proud great-grandma watching Cutter and his sister Nevada focus on winning. They'd traveled with parents Rowdy and Kasey all the way from Mt Vernon to compete. Also competing were Buck's children, Lucy and Katelyn, who were joined by a "herd" of future cowboys and cowgirls all growing up together here. It was an exciting, fast-paced rodeo, and the proceeds all go towards college scholarships for Ag students in Wallowa County.

Watching sons Todd and Ken, along with grandsons Rowdy and Buck, compete, was fun for Doug and me. Lots of dust flew during the horse races, cow penning, team brandings, and cow dog competitions. A large crowd showed up, which was amazing. As per usual, Wallowa County had a calendar full of events competing that weekend.

"I won $185.00 in the Calcutta," exclaimed Carol Wallace, who, along with hubby Ed, had traveled from Clarkston, Washington, to attend. Half of that money from those winnings went to the F.F.A. program. Then it was home to put together a garden salad, and return to Cloverleaf Hall to join Doug at the annual Stockgrowers dinner/dance.

Randy Garnett and his Apple Flat Catering did a bang up job of grilling those tri-tips, served up with beans, baked potatoes and Cattlewomen's salads. A record crowd gathered from near and far, taking time from haying, checking cattle, and irrigating, to socialize. The Cattleman of the Year was awarded to Perry Johnson of Wallowa, whose wife, Donna, was ill, and not able to attend.

I had the honor of awarding the Honorary Cattleman plaque to none other than Lyman Goucher. Lyman, however was absent. He'd gone home during the rodeo, as wife Wilma said he was tired, and he got away before we could stop him. Because this was a surprise, we couldn't tell him. Daughter Vicki Marks, of Imnaha, accepted the award on his behalf.

Doug and I were too tired to stay for the dance. It had been a long day. Music floated outside as we left, a band named "Last Call" fiddling away into the night. I bet Mack and Marian Birkmaier were out there on the dance floor. I'd heard Marian say, "Mack and I went and took a nap, now we're ready to party." Good for you two.

Last Sunday I made it to a naming ceremony for baby Arianwyn at their family's church, then made it to my church in time to ring the

Dylan Denton (left) meets Doug Tippett, who, along with wife Janie, sponsor the coveted Jidge Tippett award, given annually to the best beef project at the Wallowa County fair. A belt buckle has been awarded.

bell. At our church, it's wise to lock your car, else you'll find zucchini on the seats. Lately there is zucchini in the pews as well. It seems the Imnaha Magic Garden is doing well, and I can attest to that! The potluck after church at Wallowa Lake State Park leaned heavily toward zucchini casseroles and desserts.

The Wallowa County Fair was another success story, with a mind-boggling amount of volunteerism keeping everything turning like a well-oiled wagon wheel. Great-granddaughter Riley Ann made us proud showing her 4-H lamb, and my photography garnered ribbons, as did my veggies. Couldn't beat Imnaha gardener Barb Warnock in potatoes and squash, though. She's a pro.

That was a busy week. On Grange Day we indulged in marionberry pie and ice cream, eaten in the shade on a picnic table while visiting neighboring ranchers Ardis and Harold Klages. And, of course, one has to sample those "fair burgers," grilled at the food booth.

On Saturday we attended the awards, followed by the Joseph F.F.A. bar-b-cue. Charley Warnock sure knows how to grill tri-tip Beef over fruit wood coals. Yum. The fat stock auction that evening set records for the number of animals and the money they fetched. I purchased a hog for our freezer and Doug "turned" a steer. Riley Ann cried crocodile tears over her lamb.

Short on funds, our fair was long on volunteers, and so it goes in Wallowa County. We aren't going to let our fair die. All deserved blue ribbons. And if you looked around you would have seen several generations of 4-H'ers and F.F.A. members running the show. As it should be. That's what builds and maintains community. Our local resources should be sustained and the most important of all are our citizens.

I thought about that on the way home late that night, and just as I drove down our lane, a falling star on the southern horizon added an exclamation point to the thought.

August 24—We had a Museum Board meeting at the Wallowa County Museum to discuss plans for an Open House to show off our newly-remodeled firehouse addition, which includes an office with an archival storage room and new display area for larger items. This project has been a long time in the completion and we are most grateful to those who contributed both money and time to make this happen.

August 26—I arose early and whipped up a fry pan full of German apple pancake, which I served hot-out-of-the-oven, along with fresh strawberries, to Doug's nieces, Jenni Tippett and Pat Tippett, visiting from California and Portland. For a brief time these sisters lived with their parents down the road at what is now the Hough Ranch.

By 6:30 we were headed down to my Sheep Creek cabin and property. While the sisters picked wild blackberries, I puttered around cleaning the cabin. They loved it down there and were astounded by the "Magic Garden," which has taken off in this heat. Surrounded by the dry canyons and towering rim rocks, this oasis is green and flourishing under its timed irrigation, loaded now with such an abundance of produce and tended by dedicated gardeners who donate produce to the school lunch program in Joseph, as well as other worthy programs in the county.

A big harvest party is scheduled in the future.

August 27—I got in and canned pickled beets so I could attend the popular Irving Berlin Musical "Annie Get Your Gun" at the Elgin Opera House this afternoon. It was wonderful! Full of energy, laughter, and lively music. Perfectly cast, and a great joy to both observers and performers.

I made it back in time to attend a special dinner prepared by Jenni and Pat at their cousin's cabin at the lake. The meal featured produce out of both of their aunt's gardens, and for dessert, we savored a blackberry cobbler from those Sheep Creek berries.

August 28—Doug crept to the chicken pen with his trusty gun and shot the spotted skunk who'd been sucking eggs!

Made it to church in time to ring the bell, while Doug headed to Imnaha to deliver a bed frame he'd purchased for the cabin at a yard sale.

August 29—Last night, sheet lightning played on the horizons east and north. We feared for fires. This morning, we learned one had been ignited near McGraw.

I've been hitting the yard sales locally, and hit it lucky. Nearly furnished my cabin. Small desk, rocking chair, more beds, and odds and ends needed in the kitchen. It's been fun!

One evening Doug and I headed down so I could do some cleaning, then drove the couple more miles to the Imnaha Store and Tav for fish and chips for me, chicken gizzards for Doug. We added our names to the rattlesnake count written on the freezer. Doug is ahead of me, as he killed two on the highway that day.

September 4—Frost rimmed my garden this morning, and ice glazed the corn stalks where the sprinklers ran all night. Luckily, those sprinklers saved the veggies and it didn't take long for the September sun to warm up Prairie Creek.

Halley and I just returned from a long walk up the hill, following a track flanked by golden wheat, the trail dusty with white-tail prints. We flushed a covey of Hungarian Partridge and a cock pheasant.

September brings cobalt skies cleansed by crisp mornings, while our afternoons and evenings glow with the gentle sun's slanting rays of early autumn. Still canning pickles, and the kitchen is filled with the salty odor of sauerkraut fermenting in my large crock. A few days ago I cut five enormous heads of cabbages fresh from the garden and wheelbarrowed them to Doug, who was waiting at the picnic table with his antique kraut cutter to wash, trim, cut, core, and begin shredding the crisp cabbage into large bowls, which I then layered with pickling salt and pounded with a wooden mallet to get the juices flowing. I can taste those Reuben sandwiches this winter, not to mention German sausages on a bun smothered in kraut.

The two rows of ever-bearing strawberries decided to come on, so in addition to freezing some, I cooked up a batch of strawberry/blueberry jam. Thankfully the raspberries are spent. So am I. Our family gleaned enough for their winter larders, as did friends.

From left: Wallowa County Stockgrowers Secretary Cynthia Warnock and Ranch Rodeo chairman Scott Shear present the rock jack trophy to Tom Birkmaier of Crow Creek.

Over a hundred folks came from near and far to attend the annual apple squeez'in held at Chuck and Kris Fraser's ranch on Upper Prairie Creek.

John Groupe and the Mounted Pendleton Roundup Band play a tune at the Cowboy Breakfast at the recent Chief Joseph Days.

Prairie Creek rancher Lois Hough drives the tractor under her sun shade.

Chad Nash solves the problem of living in the "frost zone." He designed and built his own irrigation and raises food for his family.

Sara Miller of "Bunchgrass Beef" ready to do a demo at the Joseph Farmer's Market.

Robin Martin showed up at my kitchen door the other morning with a bucket full of wax beans she'd picked from our garden down on Sheep Creek, so I carried the pressure cooker up from the basement and canned them. Thank you Robin!

Strands of wild geese waver overhead during the mornings and evenings, and crickets play their tiny violins in concert among the fall grasses. Taking advantage of these warm days I washed blankets and sheets, then hung the bedding on the clothesline to dry. Also called grandson James, a Marine stationed at Camp Lejeune in North Carolina, living off base on Emerald Isle, to see if he escaped Hurricane Irene. He assured me he was fine, and had moved inland to a friend's place.

September 7—Just took a canner full of sauerkraut out to cool on the kitchen table.

It was quite the Labor Day weekend. Doug and I left late Sunday afternoon in our camper and drove to Ollokot Campground on the Upper Imnaha, where we set up lawn chairs above the river and read and unwound.

Early next morning we headed through the mountains and down North Pine Creek, to Pine Valley and Halfway, to attend the 90th annual Baker County Fair. As usual we drove straight to the Lions Club Cowboy breakfast to chow down on huckleberry pancakes, ham, eggs, hashbrowns, coffee, orange juice and that melon bar with its juicy, sweet slices of local cantaloupe and watermelons. Let me tell you, we were pretty hungry by that time, and that breakfast lasted well into the afternoon.

Doug visited his friend Bill Shields, who demonstrated his copper washing machine and wringer, said he was washing his underwear, and there it was, *plop, plosh*-ing around in sudsy water. He even wrung it out for us.

Sipping fresh lemonade, we wandered around the exhibits and I did some photographing. At 1:00 we were seated in the old grandstand, taking in the rodeo, which featured mule races, mule chariot cow roping, steer and bull riding, ranch horse bucking contests, cowhide races, and wild cow milking. The gray mule I picked won its race, but Doug won the other two.

September 8—Well, we pulled it off. The SURPRISE birthday party for Doug. Thanks to our visitor Mike Wright, a shirttail relative of Doug's, who had flown in from Missouri for a visit.

I asked Doug if he would like to take Mike to Imnaha, to show him the country and end up at the Tavern for dinner to celebrate his 80th birthday. He agreed, thinking this would be low key. Meanwhile, I scurried around and loaded the car with the necessary items and food for the surprise at my cabin on Sheep Creek. Mike kept Doug occupied and he didn't suspect a thing.

I proposed to drive down this morning to do some work on the place, and Mike and Doug could drive down later to pick me up. All agreed. I spent the day setting up tables, chairs, frying chicken, preparing mak'ins for homemade ice cream, and thawing Imnaha river salmon for grilling outside.

It was a lovely evening, and at 5:00 o'clock, here came the invited guests...and precisely at 5:30, Mike drove in with Doug, who thought they were just going to stop and look at the cabin and property. Boy, was he surprised! Our friends contributed salads, potatoes, rolls and a birthday cake. Dirk Wiggins cranked the ice cream and we dined beside the cool creek, where we breathed in the blackberry-scented air.

Later we conducted a tour of the Magic Garden on the other side of the creek. All in all, a wonderful evening with our gang, all of whom are now over 80 save for yours truly. I needed those lesser years after cleaning up and tumbling into bed 25 miles away on Prairie Creek.

September 9—Today was MY 78th birthday, which we celebrated that evening with a shish kabob dinner at Vali's Alpine Delicatessen. Waiting for our reserved table, we drove to the bridge and gazed down at the spawning kokanee, turned bright orange now, as they filled the West Fork of the Wallowa River.

Our kitchen table spilled over with cards and birthday gifts from our extended family.

The valley was filled with a smoky haze, as the Cactus Mountain fire burned out of control in the Snake River Canyon. Luckily, the buildings at Dug Bar were saved.

September 11—Yesterday I canned mixed pickles before joining Doug and other past grand marshals of Hells Canyon Mule Days, to climb into Julie Kooch's mule-drawn wagon and ride in the parade. We were a bit crowded this year, so I sat on Doug's lap!

A horse with an empty saddle was led in the parade. Bob Casey was one of the founders of Mule Days. His enthusiasm never wavered for many worthwhile community dreams.

While waiting for the Grand Entry, we ordered some of those juicy Marr Flat hamburgers, prepared by daughter-in-law Angie and grand-daughter Becky.

Julie Kooch, Enterprise, drives her mule drawn wagon load of Hells Canyon Mule Days past grand marshals. Honorary 2011 Grand Marshal George Hixon, standing. Inside wagon L-R: Juana Malaxa, Marge Onaindia, Fred Talbott, Betty Tippett, Janie Tippett, Doug Tippett, Mike Brennan, Biden Tippett, Dick Hammond.

The weather was perfect this weekend and while listening to open mic cowboy poetry in the outdoor show ring, mules brayed their own brand of poetry. Our guest Mike borrowed a guitar and sang a song he'd dedicated to me and his wife, Kathy.

That evening we joined a LONG line of folks waiting to chow down on the traditional Jim Probert bar-b-cue pork dinner. Jim, however wasn't there. Jim is gone now, and so it was appropriate that his family carry on the tradition. They did Jim proud. The meal was delicious, and a record-breaking crowd was fed. Music by "Soul Renovation" mingled with the braying of mules as we waited and visited friends.

This morning found me joining two other food judges to determine winners of the annual Dutch Oven Cooking Contest. Not an easy job, as every dish was yummy.

Across the fence from those steaming kettles, Bull Whack'in Cass's 1,333 lb. Brown Swiss Ox chewed his cud. Between bites of each dish prepared, we cleansed our mouths by eating grapes and sipping water.

September 12—Doug and Mike took me to breakfast at the Cheyenne Cafe before we three headed out the Zumwalt Road, ending up at Buckhorn Lookout. As the sun rose over the Seven Devils in Idaho, we spied a herd of Mule deer bucks grazing the dry hills. The view of the Imnaha River Canyon, as well as the breaks of the Snake River, was awesome, and we could see the smoke sleeping between the canyons near Cactus Mountain. We were the only ones there, and the silence was palpable.

A circuitous route landed us at the Imnaha Store and Tavern for lunch. Sally makes a mean Reuben sandwich, which Doug and I split. After a stop at my orchard to pick pears, we headed up on top.

This evening we dined outside, enjoying the first corn-on-the-cob from my Prairie Creek garden. Later, we watched the full September "fire" moon, glowing hugely, rise over Hough's hill.

September 13—Mike left today, and I spent that week canning pears, digging horse radish roots and grinding horseradish, freezing corn, putting up more pickles, digging garlic, simmering pear/apple butter in the crockpot, and putting up blackberry jelly from a flat of blackberries Doug picked at the Sheep Creek place. Even started a bottle of blackberry wine.

September 17—Attended a dance at neighbor Nancy Knoble's Blue Barn. The wooden floor of that old hay mow was trembling with stomping feet doing the "do-si-do, ala-mand left, swing your pardner," as young and old responded to the caller's terms. I danced the first dance with 3rd grader great-grandson Ronan, who never missed a beat. He and sister Gwenllian, and brother Kennon attend these dances regularly, and are pretty darn good.

Mamma Amy plays a mean fiddle and daddy Chad was in charge of baby Arianwyn, so I offered to hold my great-granddaughter whilst her parents danced. As I held this baby girl in my arms, her wide eyes watched the dancers and bored into the scene before her. As we swayed to the beat of the fiddling, Arianwyn felt the rhythm and remembered music way back in her ancestry until, at last, she fell asleep and I laid her in her carrier on a bale of straw.

Dancers, in need of refreshment, gulped down apple cider, and cookies. Thanks, Nancy, for offering your wonderfully restored historic barn to our community.

September 18—Our church enjoyed a potluck down at my Sheep Creek property after services.

September 19—Canned apple sauce from the windfalls picked under our heirloom apple tree.

September 20—I hosted our WRITE Group here. We met outside on the lawn, and all brought food for lunch. I treated everyone to a cream pie, piled high with strawberries just picked that morning.

September 22—Doug and I drove to Sheep Ridge, high under Ruby Peak, to see the TV towers and gaze at the valley below. It was a warm, hazy morning, and far below we could see Enterprise and Lostine. We also saw the pens where the Big Horn Sheep are trapped.

September 24—I attended the Healthy Futures dinner and auction at Cloverleaf Hall, which was transformed into a swanky eatery. A meal of prime rib and salmon was served by the Enterprise Future Business Leaders of America members. As usual, Apple Flat Catering did a bang up job with the meal, and thousands of dollars were raised to purchase new equipment for our local hospital.

I had donated a basket of sourdough bread, apple butter, cherry jelly and a signed copy of the second edition of book for the silent auction.

September 25—It clouded up today, looked like rain, and Lyman and Wilma called to ask me to do the rain dance. All I got for my efforts were a few sprinkles. Sorry, guys.

And tonight is the long-awaited Harvest celebration dinner for the Magic Garden, a free dinner prepared by members of our church for the community.

Yesterday I helped churn butter and donated eggs for the zucchini cakes. More about that later. Enjoy this lovely fall weather.

September 28—Halley and I have just returned from our morning walk on this coolish morning. The garden has escaped two frosts, and the strawberries are still bearing, as is the last of the corn and zucchini. The potatoes await their digging, and the sunflowers and cosmos are radiant during these endless warm days. Actually our weather, for weeks now, has more resembled August than September. No appreciable rain. Good news for those putting up late cuttings of hay and harvesting grain, but bad news for the natural feed in the hills, canyons and divides where many cattle still graze.

The Imnaha pack of wolves has struck again, this time killing one of son Todd's calves on private property up near the Divide. Todd and wife Angie were in San Diego at the time, visiting their new granddaughter, born to their son Josh and wife Desiree, stationed there in the Navy. The new little Miss is named after her two grandmothers: Vivian Angela. Wee Vivian is our 26th great-granddaughter.

Neighbor Scott Shear rode out to discover this latest kill. Fortunately for Todd, the authorities deemed it a confirmed wolf kill, which means two more wolves from the Imnaha pack will have to be euthanized. Progress, albeit slow, is happening, due to the Wallowa County Stockgrowers and a group of women ranchers who have formed an education committee.

Doug and I attended a showing of a professional video put together and funded by local people on wolf depredation in Wallowa County. This is a very effective tool in defending the ranchers' story.

Melvilles have begun harvesting the fields of mature wheat growing on Doug's old ranch. Every morning Halley and I make our way on paths that wind through this golden harvest. Often times we flush pheasant, Huns, and white-tails.

September 30—A busy day. Lois Hough, Judy Stilson and I served for CowBelles at the Community meal site. Doug called us the "Prairie Creek Girls," as we ranch wives all live on adjoining ranches. At the conclusion of the meal, here came daughter Jackie, who had driven in from Challis, Idaho, to help me with daughter Ramona's 60th birthday party. We just go from one party to another!

The remainder of the day was spent purchasing items for the party and picking up the gigantic cake I'd ordered at Cloud 9 Bakery. Then we transported everything up to the Mt. Joseph Ranch, where the party was scheduled for tomorrow evening. Originally we had planned this to be a surprise, but word leaked out as time went along and Ramona was inviting her friends. Therefore, we had no idea how many to plan for.

October 1—It was a perfectly beautiful evening, so warm that most folks stayed outside.

This morning Jackie and I decorated tables with autumn leaves, small candles, and photos of Ramona's family. I carted my huge pots of blooming geraniums and a blue enamelware coffee pot full of cosmos and sunflowers to decorate the dinning room. I also brought along family photo albums. It was a lot of fun. Son Todd took charge of the meat, and grilled hamburgers.

This evening a caravan of cars drove up the long lane to the rustic log lodge and parked beneath the tall Ponderosas. The view of the valley below, and the fact that this place is situated on the slopes of Chief Joseph Mountain, made for a very scenic setting. Friends and family carried in salads and hot dishes, which were added to the feast. Jackie sauteed ten Walla Walla Sweet onions to go on those burgers.

My younger daughter insisted we light 60 candles on her sister's cake, so we did. And, while Myrna Moore held a piece of cardboard to shield the blaze from the breeze, we sang Happy Birthday. A great time was had by all, and five of our seven children were able to attend, as well as several relatives who traveled from afar.

The highlight of the party was our traditional family storytelling time. Of course, Jackie had to tell the story about the time Ramona coaxed brother Ken into the rabbit hutch when he was about two years old, and left him there with alfalfa hay and water. Ken elaborated on the story, and remarked that, by the time his mother discovered him, he was pretty sad, plus it was summertime, and Ken recalls he was potty-trained shortly after that.

We hope this party convinces Ramona that turning 60 isn't all that bad. And as a mother, I felt blessed seeing my children enjoying being together.

October 2—Bade goodbye to daughter Jackie and attended church, then came home and canned tomato juice.

October 3—Took my former sister-in-law Nancy Tanner to Sheep Creek, where we found Beth Gibans, David Martin and Ken Hunt cleaning the irrigation ditch above the Magic Garden. After picking tomatoes and peppers, we returned to Prairie Creek.

October 4—Awoke to the season's first snow blanketing the Wallowas. This is the first day we turned heat on in the house.

October 6—Awoke to find an inch of snow here on Prairie Creek! The maple tree, its leaves burdened with snow, drooped, as did the fir tree in the front yard.

October 7—Returned to my Sheep Creek cabin to plant daffodils and transplant a honeysuckle vine. Beautiful, rain-washed morning. Enjoyed my lunch sitting out under the grape arbor, which is full of dangling Concord grapes.

October 8—Attended friend Ruth Wineteer's yard sale and came away with two end tables for my cabin.

October 11—Headed down to Sheep Creek again to deliver my tables and pick those grapes to make jelly.

Melvilles have baled straw and are now adding more line to their center Pivot irrigation system. It's a crisp, clear fall day, and next Sunday

I leave for the upper Imnaha and the Fishtrap Writer's Retreat for a week. See ya later.

October 13—I arose early to put up six pints of Concord grape jelly from those grapes I gathered before the BULL. Then Doug hooked up our long stock trailer, and we took off for the Divide to help son Todd haul his calves to the valley. The Kiser place, as it's known, is a lovely spot, situated on a high, wide, grassy plateau, with distant views of the Wallowas. Well-maintained wooden corrals held bawling calves that had been separated from their mammas.

After Doug backed up to the loading chute for our load, other stock trucks and trailers arrived. Todd pointed off over a hill to where his most recent wolf kill had been discovered, and told us a mile further on was the site of yet another kill. Again, it saddens me, as a mother, to know my son is suffering mental anguish over this ongoing wolf problem. Those opposed to any sort of lethal removal of these carnivores should spend just one day with a rancher. If the tables were turned, and a pack of snarling wolves were set free in their daily lives, perhaps they would understand.

The latest kill breaks my heart. A cow, partially eaten in her extremities and still alive when found, showed signs of great struggle and had to be shot. This is not a pretty picture, and some uninformed folks are participating in "wolf howls." This is actually happening now in our County. It keeps me awake at night wondering what sort of person could participate in these eco-tourism activities, knowing, if they do, who is paying this terrible price for their entertainment.

October 14—We awoke to a drippy warm rain. The Northwood Maple was ablaze with color. Canned the seven-day sweet pickles, then drove down to my Sheep Creek place to pick apples for the the annual Apple Squeeze'in tomorrow. Also harvested the last of the corn, tomatoes and pears.

October 15—Our first killing frost this morning. 28 degrees on the clothesline post. Prairie Creek sparkles now at 8:00 am. as the sun spills over the frosty meadows. Before sunup I watched last night's full moon sink beyond Sheep Ridge. Goodbye petunias, cosmos and garden. I must cut the large baking squash, including those suspended from apple tree limbs in one corner of my garden. Those runaway squash vines climbed the tree and birthed babies.

I've had plenty of help harvesting windfalls under the ancient apple tree that grows between the chicken pen and house. For the past two mornings, a coyote has come sneaking in to grasp an apple in its teeth before slyly retreating behind the raspberry canes to chew its tasty morsel. After nervously devouring around ten juicy apples, it trots off over the hill. Halley seems fascinated with this apple-eating carnivore, and even more amazing are the two hens that often fly over the chicken pen, pecking apples right alongside Mr. Coyote! Something's wrong with this picture.

Then there's son Ken's calves that squirm under the electric fence to gobble down more apples. Luckily, there are plenty to go around. I've canned and frozen apple slices for winter pies, made apple butter, apple sauce, apple cakes, and apple pies. And those pears trees in my Sheep Creek orchard just won't quit, either. In addition to canning them, I've preserved 9 pints of pear butter to sell at our upcoming church bazaar.

Talked to Lyman on the phone the other evening and asked if he and Wilma were still canning pears.

"There's still pears, but we quit," he said. Earlier he'd mentioned that they get up of a morning and do a canner a day.

We've had a couple of refreshing rains to calm the dust and green the grasses. I've been stowing away garden tools and sprinklers, while Doug has carried the hoses to the pump house.

Last week Doug and I got in and dug the spuds. What a job! We now have eight sacks of beautiful potatoes stored in our cellar. Took most of the afternoon, as these two senior citizens bent to their task. I picked the largest green tomatoes, which are now ripening in the house.

Opening morning of buck deer season resounded with shots over the hill, and fewer bucks seen the next day. Doug says his days of deer hunting are over.

"The fun stops after you pull the trigger and have to deal with gutting and skinning the deer," he says. Guess we'll have to rely on our grown sons and grandsons to provide us with venison.

The community Harvest Party was a resounding success! Approximately 300 people gathered in the Joseph High School Cafeteria to enjoy the vegetables and fruits of our labors. Such a colorful and nutritious array of food, including an enormous salad bar featuring tomatoes, peppers, cucumbers, onions and lettuce, all grown either in our Magic Garden or locally.

A delicious spaghetti sauce, made with those Sheep Creek tomatoes and herbs, was served over penne pasta along with locally baked sourdough bread, chocolate zucchini brownies topped with frozen local raspberries, and hand-cranked ice cream. The butter I'd churned the day before was served with the bread. Children were allowed to crank ice cream, churn butter, press apples for cider, and make carrot juice after the meal. An award was given to the child who raised the largest cabbage.

Angie Rubin and I were honored with silver angel wing necklaces for our contribution to the project. Kudos to all those hardworking church folks who brought this dream to fruition, and mostly to Robin Martin, who dreamed the dream.

October 16—Low-lying wet clouds obscured our mountains as I opened a jar of mincemeat, added sliced pears, and baked a large pie for the apple crushing party. While baking the pie, I listened to the 4-H Radio Auction on our local KWVR radio station.

Later I arrived, bearing the warm pie, which was placed on a long table set up in the shop that held other mouth-watering potluck. I was just in time to slurp down two raw oysters; then Doug and his friend Bill arrived, and we three went to work. Dumping the apples Bill brought from Idaho in the bin, turning the crank to chop them, after which the chopped apples were caught below in round, slatted wooden tubs. When these tubs were full, we cranked down hard on the press until all that golden juice flowed into a bucket. Many varieties of apples were used, which produced a delectable drink.

The foggy day didn't deter the crowd that converged on Chuck and Kris Fraser's ranch. An entire field was filled with rigs. And the food! Oh my! A whole hog, tended all night by Chuck, sizzled in a homemade bar-b-cue on wheels that sported a smoke stack. Lyle Witherite was there, fryer chicken halves broasting away. There was a tub of freshly-caught crab, and then, of course, the long procession of folks carrying in salads, beans, potatoes and platters of sliced tomatoes and pickles.

Children climbed the pulp pile and chased each other over bales of straw. Chris' laying hens cackled, McCully Creek splashed past Chuck's new honey-extracting shed, and two groups of local musicians played fiddles, accordion, auto harp, and guitars, whilst singing old-timey folk songs. A few brave souls peeled horse radish roots and ground them into sauce, and everyone kept busy working and visiting. A grand time had by all.

Late that afternoon the clouds lifted to reveal our snowy Wallowas and, full as a tick, I drove home. Up late that night canning apple juice, and packing to leave for the Writer's Retreat on the Upper Imnaha.

October 23—The morning after the apple squeezing party, I headed down into the canyons and turned upriver. It was raining when I stopped at Lyman and Wilma's to drop off newspapers for fire starter. Lucky for me the rain ceased before I pushed three cart loads of food and other belongings across the swinging bridge that spans the Imnaha River.

After settling into the Tree House log cabin, I brewed myself a cup of tea. Thus refreshed, I baked a pear pie, cooked up a pot of potato-vegetable-bacon soup, and baked a pan of cornbread for the other three writers, who arrived that evening from out of the county.

It was a most productive week, filled with writing, cooking, eating, hiking, reading and resting. I got five chapters done on my novel.

On Thursday evening we invited Lyman and Wilma for supper. Wilma managed to hang onto the bridge railings so she wouldn't be upset by Lyman shaking the bridge. Those kids! I served them Marr Flat Beef pot roast, mashed potatoes, gravy, carrots and sourdough bread.

We made a fire in the fireplace every evening, while reading what we'd written during the day. Every evening Becky Hyde and I were treated to the lovely voices of Julianna Waters and Richelle Graves, two talented songwriters. No bears bothered us this year, only the elusive beaver that is now gnawing down two more trees. The snap, crackle, pop of my little wood stove in the cabin took the chill off enough to allow for a comfortable writing studio. Really felt the absence of apples this year, as well as color. All the leaves were still green!

Called Doug every evening, and found he'd driven one day clear to Dug Bar, his old ranch.

Yesterday, Saturday, we cleaned house, pushed our carts across the river, and said goodbye.

Back at home on Prairie Creek in the afternoon, I took the already-fried donuts out of the freezer to thaw, grabbed a basket of pressed fall leaves, and headed for Joseph to our Museum Open House. Pretty tired, so didn't stay long, but a large crowd attended to view the new addition of an office and display room…and to consume those donuts and cider.

After church this morning, Halley and I hiked up Hurricane Creek, making it nearly to Slick Rock before turning back. The fall colors had peaked that crisp, clear, fall day, and Sacagawea never looked lovelier, her lower green slopes accentuated with golden tamarack trees. Glittering Aspen thickets and yellowing cottonwoods lined the creek that tumbled down from the high country, and of course that fresh snow contrasted with all that autumn color. It was a fitting farewell to the season.

October 26—Andi Mitchell and I drove down to my Sheep Creek cabin this morning, to clean a storage area situated off the kitchen, a large walk-in room lined with shelves and insulated with sawdust between the walls. Built in the 1940s, this room will serve as future storage for canned goods and root vegetables. We also coiled up all the irrigating hoses on the lawn, and stored them in the pump house.

A couple of weeks ago those two infamous bulls, who roam, free-ranging, through the small settlement of Imnaha and on up the creek, visited my place. Even though the gate was closed, they must have entered by the creek side. While Andi tackled the canning room, I shoveled great piles of bull S., scattered around the house, and used it to fertilize the cherry trees. The bulls also did a number on the grapes hanging from the arbor, and nibbled my newly-tram-planted honeysuckle vine. I was not happy, but neither are my neighbors, who have, and still are, experiencing similar destruction.

However, nothing could spoil such a lovely fall day on Sheep Creek. The cabin's tin roof was littered with golden leaves that continued to fall on us as we sat in lawn chairs alongside the creek. It was magical there, staring up toward Middlepoint as a kingfisher skimmed over the water. We'd paused at noon to make sandwiches from slices of crisp bacon and the tomatoes I'd picked a week ago in the garden.

Then, sipping tea with thick wedges of applesauce gingerbread, while soaking up the autumn sunlight, I told Andi about coming home from the Writer's Retreat last Saturday, when I stopped to show my friends this place, and how we were entertained by a family of otters! Squeaking at us, laughing almost, they caught bright trout, carried them to a large rock, and devoured them.

We took a walk across the bridge, up past the gar-den, which is all put to sleep for winter, and opened a gate that put us on a deer trail to an old orchard. Here we picked apples, walnuts, and more green pears. Every time I visit my place I discover more fruit trees. Hopefully I'll soon have a wood cook stove in the kitchen, and start up the electric heat so we can spend some time there during the winter months.

It's been in the 20s these past mornings here "on top" with heavy frosts and keen clear days. The willows are yellowing, and my garden is through bearing, save for Swiss chard and carrots. After digging a good supply of carrots, I covered the rest with straw and dirt.

Ben was here while I was on the upper Imnaha, cleaning out the chicken house, and shaking straw on the floors. He dumped the rich chicken manure on my garden. The baking squash has been harvested, and I picked most of the bright, red eating apples off the dwarf tree.

Our Writer's Group met here yesterday. After reading our pieces, we supped Idella's turkey noodle soup and savored warm applesauce gingerbread. I also served cider, simmered with apple slices.

October 27—Now it is nearly noon on the 27th, and my kitchen is filled with the aroma of sourdough bread. Two loaves baked for Connie Dunham, who captured the winning bid for my two loaves at the 4-H Radio Auction.

We invited Ben for supper as a thank you for cleaning out my chicken house. We had a nice visit over sourdough biscuits, potatoes 'n gravy and roasted Cornish Game hens.

Must get this column e-mailed.

October 28—Took the eight pints of pear butter I'd canned to our church's annual bazaar. The church was crammed with gift baskets, caramel corn, fudge, and home-made aprons. The aroma of coffee, fresh cinnamon rolls, and chicken soup floated up from the kitchen.

October 29—After church, Doug and I drove to Imnaha for lunch before stopping at my Sheep Creek place to harvest more of the walnuts and delicious apples that grow beyond the Magic Garden. We noted the garden had been cleared of old vines and tilled, after the last acorn squash was picked.

Then it was home where I got in and baked an apple pie for the Halloween party at Buhler's Mt. Joseph Ranch this evening. Susan and her crew did a bang-up job of decorating the old log building with colorful leaves, cornstalks, pumpkins and bales of straw, and there was a cheerful fire in the wood stove. We sat at long tables chowing down on delectable potluck and visiting friends.

October 30—We were visited by trick or treaters, great-granddaughters Lucy and Katelyn. Pappa Doug made sure their bags were full before they left. One of our Marine grandsons, James, called to say hello, and told us he would be visited soon by cousin Mona Lee, who had flown back East to visit friends. James said he'd talked Mona into extending her stay so he could take her to the Officer's Ball.

Our hearts were relieved and gladdened when our other Marine grandson Shawn made it safely home from Afghanistan to be with his wife Maria and their three children. The latest exciting news is that they will be here for Thanksgiving!

October 31—I baked two loaves of ground flax seed bread, and later this evening we were visited by more great-grandchildren—Riley Ann, Ashlyn, Gideon and Jada—all outfitted in elaborate costumes. Gideon, a mummy, was thirsty, and since his mouth was taped shut, grandma had to give him a straw to drink with.

November 1—I baked a tomato pie using those ripening tomatoes I gleaned before the frost. Our writer's group met here this morning, so at noon we sampled the pie, which contained corn, cheese and onions baked in a cheesy crust. Very yummy.

Two of our members have fled south for the winter, Maxine Stone to Mexico, and Ruth Wineteer, who, at 82, put her house up for sale, sold all her belongings, moved into a small used motor home, and hit the road. She says she'll write a column called "Ruth on the Road."

Last we heard, they were doing just fine. "They" meaning Ruth and "Cody," her large black lab, who rides shotgun in the passenger seat!

November 4—It snowed three inches and Doug invited me to meet him at the Range Rider in Enterprise for lunch. Otherwise known as the local watering Hole, this eatery and bar is decorated with all sorts of western memorabilia, the owners are most hospitable, and the food is excellent. We heard Taco Nights are standing room only.

After leaving Doug, I stopped in to visit Christine, one of our writer's group members, who now resides in our local Nursing Home. We ended up playing a long game of Scrabble. Chris, nearly 90, whooped me! Said she learned to play Scrabble when she was teaching Eskimo children in Alaska.

November 7—Snow crunched under our tires as Doug and I headed out to the hills this morning to help grandson Buck and wife Chelsea haul in their weaned calves. We, along with three other folks, driving pickups and pulling long stock trailers, met out along Crow Creek around 9:00. The cows were in one large corral and their calves in another, the one closest to the loading chute.

The clear, crisp 15 degree-morning had begun to warm up by the time we arrived at the "Pink Barn." Granddaughter-in-law Chelsea, with great-granddaughters Lucy and Katelyn in tow, drove one of the rigs, and Buck and Colin pulled the other two trailers. The old Dorrance place lies about 17 miles north of our ranch. A familiar landmark over the years, when Doug and I trailed X Quarter Circle cattle to and from the valley. Now, all these years later, we would be hauling in Lazy J calves wearing my old brand, which has been transferred to Buck and Chelsea.

Four-year-old Lucy was right in the thick of it, helping her mom push calves into the holding pen. Baby Kate opted to stay in the warm pickup cab.

Last week Buck and Chelsea joined other ranchers to gather cattle that run on a huge chunk of canyon land which comprises the Swamp Creek Grazing Allotment.

Four-year-old Lucy Matthews helps parents Buck and Chelsea load weaned calves to ship.

This scarecrow sitting along the Imnaha Highway hopes to thumb a ride to Dug Bar. Middlepoint & Big Sheep Canyon in back ground.

Buck and Chelsea's Lazy J pairs, along with those other brands, were sorted on a high ridge before being trailed down to the Dorrance corrals, a feat that required long cold hours in the saddle, not to mention back-riding for missing cattle.

Before we took off with our second load of calves, Buck said, "I think you have a flat tire on your pickup," which we did. Ah, youth! Buck had that tire changed in minutes.

Soon we were off, driving the long gravel road back to Enterprise, where longtime cattle-buyer Wayne Cook, and his rancher helper Rod Childers, were there to receive the calves.

Our warm Indian Summer-like weather ended abruptly with several 16 degree mornings and three inches of snow that lingers yet. More snow in the forecast. Shocked by the cold, the willow leaves turned brown before being whisked away by 50-mile-per-hour winds that left us without power one evening. No problem—we simply crawled into bed early between flannel sheets.

I've begun feeding my two heifers hay again, as well as two bulls son Todd is pasturing here. Grandson Rowdy, wife Kasey, and children Cutter and Nevada were here a week or so ago to haul their critters back to Mt. Vernon.

November 8—I've just returned from a long walk with Halley, and the short winter days are upon us. At 4:30 the sun has already disappeared over Chief Joseph Mountain. The hoard of starlings that have been feeding on the frozen windfall apples have gone to bed, and a bitter chill has settled over Prairie Creek. Think I'll cook up a kettle of clam chowder for supper.

November 11—Doug and I drove to Sheep Creek to do some winterizing before crossing the bridge to harvest more English walnuts. Just before we crossed the bridge, a flock of wild turkeys scurried to creekside, then flew to a nearby cottonwood.

The afternoon was golden and warm, the air mild, and we spent a pleasurable hour hunting for walnuts under a litter of leaves. At home we set the walnuts to dry under the wood stove.

November 13—We were up early yesterday to pull the gooseneck trailer to the old Dorrance Place on Crow Creek again. This time we hauled Buck's cows. Nearly there, we ran into Yost cattle being trailed to upper Prairie Creek. James told us some of Buck's cows had broken through the fence and joined them. We made two trips to the Cummings place, which Buck has rented to winter his cattle, and the cows were turned out on a dry hill covered with plenty of fall feed.

After the second load, we trooped into the Range Rider for lunch. There we found James Yost. "My 'mule' had a flat tire," he said. "Left the cowgirls with the herd."

While I attended church this morning, Doug helped Buck haul the cows that had been sorted out of the Yost cattle.

November 14—Played Scrabble with my friend Christine who resides in the Nursing Home. Yep! She beat me again.

November 15—Four coyotes appeared in front of Halley and I on one of our walks around the old ranch. Playfully, they coaxed Halley away, then back she'd race, one coyote chasing her—then off again with my border collie as the aggressor. Fearful they were trying to lure her away and attack, I called her off. They seemed quite fearless.

Our weekly Write Group meets every Tuesday morning at Cloud 9 Bakery in Enterprise now. No more homemade lunches in our homes; we simply order soup and sandwiches there. This is a more central place for us to meet in winter.

Our Ruth has made it as far as Shady Cove, Oregon, where she is waiting for the snows to slack off in the Siskyous before she heads south.

Doug plays an occasional game with "the boys" at the Range Rider, when they're open. Thanksgiving looms. For the first time in years, our large extended family will not gather here at the ranch, but at oldest son Ken's place on Alder Slope. Last I heard there will be close to 40 of us.

One of our Marine grandsons, Shawn, and his family will be driving up from San Diego, as well as oldest granddaughter Tammy and her family from Lodi, California. However, this grandma will be cooking one of the turkeys, as well as preparing dressing, mashed potatoes and gravy. I expect there will be a mincemeat pie as well.

Hope everyone in Agri-Times land has a great Thanksgiving.

November 21—I was nearly swept off my feet by gusty winds while carrying a flake of hay up the hill to my chickens. Flying snow stung my face as I fought to push the gate open into the pen. The old chicken house rattled and shook, and my hens and two roosters opted to stay in the roost. One by one they appeared, when I tossed them the flake of leafy alfalfa, and began pecking at the fragrant leaves.

With three inches of snow on the ground and small drifts forming, I imagined they were ready for a taste of summer. My hens are on strike since the bitter cold weather set in, but thanks to wheat gleaned from our neighbor's fields during harvest, they are eating well. As a thank you for the generosity of those farm families, I baked two dutch apple pies and delivered them warm to their kitchens. What a surprise to receive my pie plates returned full! A chocolate pie with real whipped cream from Anna Butterfield, and cinnamon rolls from Karen Patton.

This windy morning a contrast to yesterday's foggy one, when Halley and my heifers grew hoarfrost whiskers. But then, later in the morning, the fog burned off, exposing a polished blue sky and brilliant snowfields.

Sun streamed through the stained glass windows of our old stone church, and I was happy to find the rope—which I'd broken a couple weeks before—had been replaced with a new one. I remembered pulling down with all my might on the knotted rope to ring the church bell, only to have it drop, frayed, in my hands! After only one ding dong... silence. Embarrassing. Nothing to do but race downstairs, rope in hand, to explain what had happened.

Returning to the ranch after church yesterday, I headed down into the canyons to my Sheep Creek cabin to check on things. A different world down there. Nearly 60 degrees, no snow, and a smattering of golden leaves clinging to the old cottonwoods along the creek. I spent a contented two hours sweeping leaves off the porch, putting lawn chairs under cover, cleaning floors inside the cabin, and simply resting in that peaceful setting.

A covey of quail chittered from the blackberry thickets, and a kingfisher flew up the creek. Middlepoint beckoned, and I vowed one day to climb its terraced sides to explore a high meadow that peeks out under the highest rim.

On the way home last evening I stopped in to share a cup of tea with friends Myrna, Larry and Jenny Moore, who live up Bear Gulch. It's always so homey there in their modest little house.

The sun had slipped over the canyon rims, and a fall chill was in the air. Warmth from their wood stove, not to mention delicious aromas coming from the oven, tended to distill my thoughts to the basics of life. Out along the creek Myrna's hens were scratching in the garden, and a new puppy dragged dog blankets around the yard.

November 25—It snowed and blowed all night. Have been haying my two heifers and Todd's two bulls again, as the dry feed lacks nutrition this time of year.

Though Thanksgiving is now history, fond memories linger. Not only were we blessed with a large, loving family, but sunshine as well. While eldest son Ken carved the ham, grandson Buck sliced a turkey.

Annie's kitchen buzzed with talk whilst granddaughters-in-laws helped with meal preparations.

Tables were set up in three rooms, decorated with fall leaves, pilgrims and pumpkins. Myriad great-grandchildren (all cousins) playing in an upstairs loft playroom. Baby Arianwyn passed around from lap to lap. Eldest daughter Ramona and I both contributed stuffed turkeys, gravy, and desserts, while other family members brought more pies, vegetables, salads and appetizers. Annie's counters groaned with food.

Overflowing into the dinning room, 33 of us formed a wavering circle, and held hands while grandson Chad said the blessing. Sun streamed through the windows into Ken and Annie's festively decorated home while we gorged ourselves on the traditional Thanksgiving feast. Snow-clad Ruby Peak, brilliant in sunlight, was visible out the windows.

As in past family gatherings the children entertained us. Lochlan and Gavin were at our table, as well as baby Jacob, our miracle baby, nearly two now. Jacob finally wound down and fell asleep eating mashed potatoes! Although I missed having Thanksgiving at our house, I must admit I enjoyed not having all that work.

November 26—That monotonous wind laid down, which made 30 degrees seem warm. I spent the afternoon roasting the last of my garden tomatoes to make a delicious pasta sauce to store in the freezer.

This evening I joined Agri-Times columnists John and Mrs. Groupe at Lear's in Enterprise to take in a musical benefit for our local museum. After partaking of a yummy pasta dinner cooked by Steve Lear, we were entertained by a local musical group, "Homemade Jam," followed by the "Ruby Gap Mules."

Robin Fairchild, who grew up on Alder Slope, brought her musicians to Wallowa County to "give something back to the community." Robin is an extremely talented fiddle player and possesses a clear sweet singing voice as well. The "Ruby Gap Mules" collection of old folk tunes was very well received by a large turnout of folks.

November 28—I loaded up Halley and drove down to Sheep Creek. Since it was such a lovely warm afternoon, nearly 60 degrees down there, we did some exploring across the creek. Because the rattlesnakes are denned up for the winter, it felt safe wandering to the far corners of the property, where I discovered an old weathered sheep shed, a small loading chute, and fallen-down corrals, hidden away beyond tall weeds and grasses. It was fun tromping around, and we happened upon the last sweet apples clinging to the trees in the old orchard. Using a long stick I knocked enough off the limbs to fill my jacket pockets.

Returning to the cabin we surprised our resident cottontail, which scurried out from under the porch. The brief winter sun was just slipping behind the canyon rims as we headed back up the road.

Back home in my Prairie Creek kitchen, I cooked up a kettle of turkey noodle soup.

November 29—Granddaughter Mona Lee, who has been visiting her brother Buck and wife Chelsea, and nieces Lucy and Katelyn, moved in with us for a few days. I fixed a roast pork dinner that night in her honor. Mona brought up photos on her computer, taken during her recent visit with Marine grandson James, who is stationed in North Carolina. My favorite photo was of the two of them, all dressed up, attending the Traditional Marine Ball. Cousin Mona had been James' date.

Continued sad news for local ranchers. Two more wolf kills, this time in the Zumwalt hills. The Ketscher's cow was found Thanksgiving morning with her unborn calf eaten out of her womb and left there to die. This brings the total depredation number to four cows, just since the no-kill order was stopped. The order ceased due to opposition from organizations and individuals who see the wolves as a good thing.

We have a tough battle ahead, dealing with a large segment of our population not educated in the ways of animal agriculture, and more alarming yet, who don't seem to care. Unfortunately, there's much more at stake here. This is taking its toll on our local culture and heritage, the very same attributes that continue to draw folks to our area in the first place.

On a happier note a box of persimmons, mandarin oranges, and pomegranates was plucked from our mail box last week. A generous gift from our Auburn, California friends Fred and Sandra.

November 30—Lyman called from Imnaha. "Hey, we need help down here, just got a shipment of crab." Doug and I, along with other friends, were more than willing to help Lyman out. I put together a macaroni salad and grabbed some leftover cake from the freezer, and we headed down to Imnaha, then turned upriver to Lyman and Wilma's cozy log home.

After newspapers were spread out on the kitchen table, Lyman carried out two enormous roaster pans full of fresh crab. The room got pretty quiet as we ate our fill, save for the sounds of cracking crab. Many thanks to Lyman's son Craig, the fisherman who sent us this treat that has, over the years, become a tradition. Several of us old-timers fondly recalled our old friend Doc Morgan, who always won the contest for eating the most crab.

Although it was spitting snow "on top" the long drive was worth it.

December 1—The day dawned clear and sunny. This evening grand-daughter Mona and I attended the annual LDS Christmas Musical program, which is open to the community. We were awed by the live Nativity Scene, the fragrant fresh-cut Christmas trees, and over 100 miniature Nativity Scenes displayed around the room.

Naturally, this grandma was very proud of our Little Drummer Boy, great-grandson Ronan, who never missed a beat. Ronan's mom, Amy, her fingers strumming a harp, sang a Christmas carol in her clear young voice, which pleased everyone. Then there was that bevy of great-grandchildren, joining other youngsters in singing joyously under granddaughter Chelsie's directing.

December 2—Mona and I did the holiday bazaars in Joseph and Enterprise before treating ourselves to lunch at Mutiny on Main Street Joseph. Yum! Good food.

December 3—We awoke to a salmon-colored sunrise, although it was bitterly cold, with a faint breeze blowing. Despite the cold, Mona and I opted to hike the Iwetemlaykin trail. This 62-acre site is located above the Old Chief Joseph Monument, near the foot of Wallowa Lake. Iwetemlaykin, which means "at the edge of the lake," in Nez Perce, is a lovely area, and as you top the first rise you sense the closeness of snowy Chief Joseph Mountain.

Mona, who runs marathons, ran ahead while I ambled along in the rear. As I walked along the edge of the frozen Knight's Pond, Mona was already running back down the trail.

After lunch I drove to the Methodist church to begin our holiday choir practice, then headed home to get dressed for Gail Swart and Wallowa Lake Lodge's annual Christmas Caroling Party. I had purchased a ticket for Mona Lee as well. Although there was a lack of snow, the lights in the old Lodge beckoned in the darkness.

Once inside, we relaxed in the Great Room, with its cozy fire, friendly folks, and a mounted moose head wearing a stocking cap. Sipping hot spiced cider, we visited with friends before joining everyone in singing Christmas carols. Our local Bell Choir performed, following our Christmas Caroling. It was magical to be seated there in the old lodge, listening to those bells we associate with Christmas.

Mona and I were pretty hungry by the time we ambled into the dining room to sit at long tables with neighbors and friends, and partake of Mediterranean stuffed chicken breasts, wild rice pilaf, green beans, salad, and hot-from-the-oven rolls. While numerous platters of Gail's homemade Christmas cookies were passed around, we were entertained by local talent. Gail herself, of course, the star, treated us to her own musical Christmas card which filled the room with LOVE.

December 7—We live in a land of contrasts. Whereas my last column conjured up images of yours truly struggling against a blizzard to open the gate to her chicken pen, this one finds Halley and me just returning from a sunny jaunt around the old ranch, and a complete absence of snow and wind, the former having been blown away by the latter, a south wind that evaporated every vestige of white stuff save for a few hardened drifts left in the barrow pits.

Frasch's black cattle have been turned into the stubble field, and the Farmer's Ditch is nearly frozen over. Several white-tail deer bound off the hill and cross the road to Locke's field at daylight every morning, and our resident honkers congregate in neighboring fields to feed on spilled grain.

December 10—It was 10 degrees today when Son Ken and wife Annie helped me haul a sofa and recliner—a gift from the Martins, who live along Little Sheep Creek—down to the cabin. After Ken did some chores for me, I treated us to lunch at the Imnaha Store and Tavern. Sally and Dave had the old barrel stove fired up, and we enjoyed visiting friends who came through the door.

Doug came down with a cold about that time, and naturally, I caught the bug a few days later, which turned out fine, 'cause I nursed him back to health so he could help me. In spite of feeling miserable, I was able to read six books!

In our mail box appeared sister Kathy's annual gift to us. A box of tangerines, picked from her tree in Roseville, California. Am sure all that vitamin C helped chase away our colds.

December 13—A foggy 17 degrees, with hoarfrost coating every tree limb, fence post and blade of grass.

This afternoon Buck hauled 15 bales of alfalfa hay from Mike Coppin's ranch, which was nice of him. My held-over stack was shrinking. Wolves killed another heifer up Grouse Creek on the Upper Imnaha; came right into where the cattle had been corralled next to the house.

Later, another heifer was found in the same area. Much in the news lately about a wolf called OR-7, who has become an international hero, having traveled many miles away from its Imnaha pack. Oregon Wild is conducting a contest for children to give OR-7 a name.

This wolf isn't a hero in my eyes. He's the wolf that attacked and viciously killed two of son Todd's calves. Others in this pack have run cows so hard they bleed from their noses, and two fine young bred heifers had their calves ripped out of them while they were still alive. One heifer, her calf literally pulled out of her womb, staggered in shock to the main herd, where she was discovered by her owner and had to be shot.

The wolves in these cases didn't eat the cow, just the tender unborn calf, which is like candy to them. Just as there is black and white, there is right and wrong. And this senseless killing, and blaming of honest hard-working ranchers for being anti-wolf, is WRONG. Terribly wrong. It's unfair to create a hero for children at the expense of the ranching community when ranchers aren't allowed to protect their private property, much less receive a fair compensation.

It's a good thing to love wild animals. We, who live close to the land, enjoy our wildlife, and we do not hate wolves. However, special interest groups who would like to see cattle ranching on public lands come to an end are putting pressure on those agencies that manage wolves to let these dangerous predators multiply and go on killing with no empathy whatsoever for the rancher or his livestock.

The general public needs to know the truth about the introduction of the Canadian Grey wolf, a species that was NEVER indigenous to Wallowa County. OR-7 is being romanticized, his every move tracked by his radio collar, and the news media often portray OR-7 as an animal actor, a true version of the Walt Disney film, likened to "The Incredible Journey."

Just today I understand he has crossed over into California. Northern California ranchers best be prepared to suffer as our ranchers have, because the way things are going in Oregon, the wolf is here to stay. Hopefully, through education, the wolf can be sensibly managed.

Wallowa County is cattle country, and historically, that industry contributes mightily to the area's economy, not to mention its culture. Can you imagine driving into the Wallowa Valley and not seeing ranches? Ranches are our open space, and ranchers are the best stewards of the land. People in opposition need to visit them and see for themselves. Ranchers are not the bad guys. They are the glue that holds our communities together.

OK, off my soapbox.

Let's all hope the year 2012 brings an element of common sense to this very important issue...an issue that could greatly affect Wallowa County's quality of life.

December 29—A warm sun streams through our living room windows to expose numerous dust bunnies residing under the living room sofa. This is the dust of Christmas. Add four little great-grandchildren, running to and fro, trailing cracker crumbs, and, well...you get the picture. I should be cleaning house, but I can't bear to take down the tree just yet, so I procrastinate.

This morning I bask in happy memories of being together with loved ones. Our Christmas was full of youthful exuberance. Having uncles, aunties, moms, dads, grand-, and great-grandparents all in one room makes children happy, and in our family children command the center of attention.

Amid Prairie Creek's snowless landscape the temperature was nearly 40 degrees when I ventured out to chore this morning. The mild air was filled with the sounds of quacking and honking of ducks and geese as numerous waterfowl waver and wheel downward to land in the stubblefields. Son Todd came for his bulls this week, so I'm back to feeding my two heifers.

We awoke early this morning to find granddaughter Mona Lee packing up to leave us. Mona, who has been dividing her time between brother Buck, wife Chelsea, and her two nieces Lucy and Katelyn, has been such a help, and we'll miss her joyful presence. Mona's massage therapy school begins next week in Portland.

Yesterday morning daughter Jackie, hubby Bill, Buck (their son) and wife Chelsea, and the little girls, plus Mona and I, caravaned into the Imnaha country to visit my place along Sheep Creek. Doug opted to spend the day playing cards with his cronies at the Range Rider.

A warm rain splattered my windshield as we descended into the canyons, making it seem more like March than the end of December. After all the hubbub of Christmas it was a pleasant change to sink into a comfortable chair and stare out at the dry canyon sides drinking in that welcome warm rain...and to be far removed from TVs, cell phones, and other so-called modern conveniences. While the children explored the cabin, we adults simply rested.

On the way home, Bill, Jackie, Mona and I pulled into Bear Gulch to visit Larry, Myrna and Jenny Moore. Since Bill and Jackie raised their family in the Imnaha canyons, it was fun to reconnect with old friends. Buck, Chelsea and the little girls went on ahead, and by the time we arrived back at the ranch, Chelsea was heating leftover prime rib and making sandwiches.

Later, son Todd, who was on his way home after checking his cattle up Big Sheep Creek, stopped in and polished off the remainder of that roast. The guys had their eyes on the mincemeat pie, and soon, that too was reduced significantly. When Doug returned that evening with a fresh loaf of Italian bread, we sat down to French dip soup made with the last of the broth and rib meat. Our 20 pound Christmas dinner prime rib provided eight meals!

The Christmas Eve Candlelight service at the Joseph Methodist church was well attended by our community, and proved to be a special night for me, because one entire pew was filled with family. Katelyn and Lucy waved to their great-grandma, seated in the choir loft, and familiar faces lit by candlelight were wreathed in smiles. The stained glass windows, the warm colors of the wood work, and a beautifully decorated Christmas tree (that nearly touched the ceiling) provided a perfect setting for our version of "Silent Night, Holy Night" in Joseph, Oregon.

Daughter Ramona and husband Charley arrived safely in California to deliver their precious cargo of F.F.A. and 4-H steers, and granddaughter Halley's horse. After spending Christmas with their family in Lodi, they are now on their way home.

Doug and I had 15 here for Christmas dinner, which, in addition to the prime rib, included mashed potatoes, rich beef gravy, salad, and a loaf of Chelsea's dutch oven bread. I'd baked huckleberry cream and mincemeat pies the day before. Daughter Jackie and husband Bill arrived late Christmas evening, after everyone had left, having driven straight through from Challis, Idaho, leaving after their Sunday morning church service.

I heated up their prime rib dinner, and after they'd eaten, the couple nearly fell asleep at the kitchen table.

Granddaughter Lacey, husband Colin, and their children Seely and Callen, drove over from Pilot Rock to be with us for Christmas dinner. And we were pleased to have the DeJongs from McCall, Idaho, join us this year. Mark and Carol are Chelsea's parents.

Our Mona, who had requested the huckleberry cream pie, sent a photo of her holding that delectable dessert to her cousin James. Of course she couldn't wait to gloat over James' favorite pie. Mona received an almost instant reply. Imagine, an image making its way to Mississippi, where James was spending Christmas with friends!

December 30—Three of us former CowBelles, Lois Hough, Mary Lou Brink and yours truly, volunteered to serve the Friday meal at our local community dining center in Enterprise. We women always enjoy a chance to visit about old times.

Happy New Year to all of out in Agri-Times land, and hang in there ranchers, we love you!

December 31—Snug in our cozy home on Prairie Creek, Doug and I celebrated New Year's Eve alone. I'd made a kettle of oyster stew for supper, and after a bit of reading, we were fast asleep when 2012 arrived.

I recall younger days, when we would attend the big New Years Eve Dance at our local Elks Club, and dance, well beyond midnight, then join friends at the old Circle T Cafe in Enterprise for a whopping big breakfast. Those days are gone now, as are many of our old-time friends.

In Charlie Russell's era, this is how they dealt with wolves. Photograph of an oil print by the artist Charlie Russell, dated 1902.

2012

January 1—The New Year's Day sky was bluebird blue. Halley joined me on my round of chores, tending the chickens and throwing flakes of hay to my two heifers. Then I drove to Joseph and joined Doug for breakfast at the Cheyenne Cafe. The locals were in their usual state of joviality, ribbing each other and telling "betcha can't top this" stories.

Full of ham and eggs, I drove up the road just in time to see over 30 brave—or crazy—folks of all ages dive into the frigid waters of Wallowa Lake. Each year this Polar Bear Plunge seems to grow in popularity. Although they didn't stay in long, everyone seemed to be having a good time. What a way to begin a new year! I was glad to enter the warmth of our church and join our choir.

This afternoon I roasted two Cornish game hens and made a macaroni salad for our New Year's dinner, after which I hung up my new 2012 Wallowa County Calendar and made a few resolutions. Mostly I was grateful and thankful for the safe return of family members who traveled long distances over the holidays.

January 3—39, sunny and warm. January in Wallowa County? Two coyotes appeared this morning, sniffed around, then sat on their haunches to stare through the chicken wire fence at my poultry. Thankfully, Halley began to bark, which sent the pair trotting off over the hill. Halley and I have been running into these two lately on our morning jaunts around the old ranch. Once she took off after one, but the other coyote took off after my border collie and I decided to keep Halley close after that episode.

January, thus far, has been unseasonably mild...so mild several of our "snow bird" friends have opted to remain here in Wallowa County, rather than travel south for the winter. We do need moisture, whatever form it takes. Lyman Goucher, who ranches on the Upper Imnaha, reports two creeks on his place, that normally flow all winter, are now completely dry.

This past Sunday afternoon Doug and I attended the 50th wedding anniversary celebration for Dave and Darlene Turner, who live southwest of us here on Prairie Creek. Dave and Darlene's roots are deeply entwined in Wallowa County's history. The couple have raised three daughters, who have followed in their mother's footsteps by becoming members of the Chief Joseph Days Court. Over the years Dave and Darlene have given generously of their time for the annual Chief Joseph Days celebration.

Our County mourns the death of Mike Vali, who along with his wife, Maggie, operated the popular Wallowa Lake Alpine Delicatessen for over 30 years. Mike, who has been in failing heath for some time, passed away in Portland. Hopefully, during the summer season, Maggie, along with the couple's son, Mike and wife Dione, will continue offering the same famous menu they have in the past.

Granddaughter Adele called the other day from Austin, Texas, where she is working and spending the winter. She says on her days off she volunteers teaching horsemanship as therapy for young people. Our young miss will be returning to Wallowa County in June.

Her brother, grandson James, called from North Carolina, where he is stationed with the Marines. He's pretty homesick for Wallowa County and was eager to hear about family.

January 6—I finally dismantled Christmas, dragging the small tree to the chicken pen to join those of Christmases past. Down our road I spotted a pair of bald eagles, waiting for those first placentas.

January 9—At dawn this morning I peered out the bedroom window to see the nearly full January moon, the "Wolf Moon," hovering over Sheep Ridge. A rag of purple cloud draped eerily around its midsection.

My border collie Halley didn't get much sleep last night. Coyotes, or perhaps wolves, kept her barking well into the night. The infamous Imnaha wolf pack is coming in close again. A couple of mornings ago, during the dark predawn hours, they killed a young replacement heifer on Triple Creek Ranch. These cattle are managed by Scott and Kelly Shear. Triple Creek Ranch lies just southeast of us, up Tucker Down Road.

Numerous sightings have been reported lately, as well as the odd wolf-killed deer carcass. This heifer most probably died of a heart attack, as a result of severe trauma experienced while those wolves tore out chunks of her hindquarters while she was still alive. The photos of that unfortunate heifer, documented on a cell phone camera, were not pretty.

These are not wolves killing in the wilderness, or Forest Service grazing lands. These wolves are coming in and around our homes on private property. Until certain environmental groups lift the stay imposed on the legal disposing of problem wolves, this senseless killing will continue.

A night range rider has been hired to scare these predators away from where the cattle are wintering, but wolves cannot be seen in the dark and these wolves attack under cover of darkness. Electrified fencing and other scare tactics have proven useless in the past, yet more money is being spent to continue this worthless effort. Last year a wolf was spotted INSIDE the fencing.

At this date there is no compensation for those who lose livestock due to wolves. How could you compensate for a young replacement heifer worth $1500? You couldn't. Because, had she been allowed to live, she had the potential to produce ten calves. Do the math. It's a very frustrating time for our local ranchers. They need all the support they can get.

Thankfully, our local rancher gals who comprise the Canadian Grey Wolf Education Committee are doing a fine job for the Stockgrowers, and it is up to us to spread their message, sharing "the rest of the story" to our misinformed public.

January 12—The past two mornings have been clear, cold and 10 degrees. The skiff of snow we had last Tuesday is still on the ground. Time for long johns and flannel sheets.

January 18—Son Todd and his crew of cowboys and one cowgirl (wife Angie) started his herd of cows trailing from Big Sheep canyon to the Snyder place east of Enterprise. A three-day drive. These cows have grazed on natural bunch grass as they ranged over thousands of acres that include Marr Flat, the Divide, and all that steep canyon country in between. They've been moved around on that range since last April, having been trailed to the canyons after their calves were born. The cows were in great shape, considering they haven't had a bite of hay since that time.

I decided not to walk in back of Todd's cows this year, and missed it very much. However, that morning on Prairie Creek, the snow was blowing so hard I couldn't see our mountains, it was 16 degrees, and I knew the road up Sheep Creek hill would be icy. In other words, it was COLD! All day I thought about son Ken, who'd saddled his horse here at dawn, and Todd's hired man, Pat Dougherty, and Todd's wife Angie, and knew how tough they'd have to be. I'd been there myself over the years.

After the weather warmed somewhat, I decided to drive down and see how far they'd gotten, and there was Ken down at the barn, unsaddling his horse. They'd made it to the pasture at Hayden by 1:00 o'clock, a record.

Early next morning, when the riders started the cows up Hayden canyon, a warm Chinook blew out of the south. All the snow melted and wet clouds swept over the hills, spilling a fine spring-like rain over the hardened patches of ice. I'd started a fire in the wood cook stove and the house was so warm I opened the kitchen window. All morning I cooked two casseroles of tamale pie, a fry pan of sourdough biscuits, a tossed salad, and a large blackberry cobbler.

Todd, who'd been spreading flakes of hay in Stilson's pasture where the cows would overnight, stopped in to say the herd should be arriving around 2:00. Then he left to drive up Echo Canyon to see if he could spot them. Angie had called earlier, saying they were "on top."

It began to rain, but there was a complete absence of wind, which was a blessing. I kept looking for the lead cows to come into sight around a bend of the road that leads to our neighbors, the Pattons. And, pretty soon, here they came, plodding along, nearly 400 head scattered out like ants crawling downhill.

Finally there they were, the wet and weary cowboys and cowgirl, bringing up the rear. Grandson Buck, who'd spent the morning hauling me another load of alfalfa hay from Mike Coppin's barn, came into the kitchen and smelled those sourdough biscuits, so of course I invited him to stay for dinner.

Doug returned from the Range Rider and asked Buck to help him put chains on his tractor while we waited for the crew to tend to their horses. Pretty soon they all trooped in, washed up and wasted no time seating themselves around the kitchen table. I had steaming cups of hot chocolate and coffee for them, and then brought out the food. One of the joys of life is feeding hungry folks good food.

Buck, who had been hoisting 110 lb. bales, was just as hungry as the bedraggled cowhands. Between the warmth of the stove and the food, everyone relaxed a bit before returning to Hayden to drive back the pickup and stock trailer. I did the dishes and, with little time to spare, loaded the four dozen cookies I'd baked the day before, and made it to the Methodist Church by 5:30.

Idella and I were in charge of refreshments for the Big Read Lecture, presented by BeeBee Tan Beck, who talked about Chinese customs and cooking. Am afraid I was too weary to absorb any tips on Chinese cuisine, especially after preparing stick-to-the-ribs cowboy cooking.

One tough cowgirl. Angie Nash, nearing the end of a 2-day, 25-mile cattle drive on a cold January day. Cattle were driven from Big Sheep Creek to Prairie Creek.

January 19—At daylight Pat showed up to turn the herd out onto the gravel county road, and before noon the cows reached the end of their long trek. Here they'll be fed hay daily, and begin to calve in late February and on into March.

January 26—Wallowa County's Eagle Cap Extreme Sled Dog races will begin at one o'clock this afternoon at our local "Fergi" ski area on Ferguson Ridge, which lies south of Tucker Down Road. The snowy ski runs are visible from my kitchen window. I sure hope it's snowing up there, and not raining, like it is here. At this lower elevation, there IS no snow.

While tending my chores this morning it was a balmy 37 degrees. However, living here on Prairie Creek for 34 winters has taught me that our weather can change in mere minutes.

Just last week, on the 21st to be exact, the temperature dropped 10 degrees in 10 minutes. I'd gone out to throw hay to my heifers in the midst of a morning so mild, the sparrows were singing. However, "Out North" an unusually dark cloud appeared to be moving our way, and by the time I emerged from the chicken house, Prairie Creek was enveloped in a swirling blizzard. With chattering teeth and a snow-plastered face, I fled to the warmth of my kitchen to watch, again, the rapid transformation of dull colorless prairie to winter white.

I understand a record six 12-dog teams are registered for the annual Sled Dog event, with a total of seventeen mushers entered in the various races. For the first time in three years I did not volunteer to help. Perhaps if I were younger, but for now I'll cherish those memories of being a member of the '09 Ollokot team. Naturally, I'll be thinking of those adventurous mushers and their courageous dogs as they leave the starting line an hour from now.

Our ever-changing weather continues to be an adventure in itself. As predicted, strong winds out of the west have risen, and high on Mt. Howard and East Peak snow "banners" unfurl into a cold blue sky. Can imagine that blowing snow along those lonely backcountry trails. A real challenge for this year's entrants, not to mention snow showers in tonight's forecast.

Tuesday morning I met with our Write Group at Cloud 9 Bakery in Enterprise for our weekly session. Then it was back to my kitchen to bake desserts for the annual Stockgrowers "Dollars for Scholars" dinner and auction at Cloverleaf Hall.

That evening Doug and I joined a record crowd of predominately young ranchers and their families to enjoy another one of Randy Garnett's famous prime rib dinners. Which was followed by the anticipated Dessert Auction. Craig Nichols, offering his auctioneering skills, livened up the action. After a spirited bidding war over my raspberry cobbler, the table next to us won. The final bid: $260.

As a matter of fact, all the other scrumptious pies, cakes, cheesecakes and cobblers, created by our county's generous cooks, fetched outrageous prices. Doug purchased a cake, then offered it for resale. Great-granddaughter Lucy had her eye on a glossy three-tiered cherry chocolate cake, baked by Marjorie Hudson. So, Jeff Dawson, who was sitting at our table, offered the final bid. Thanks Jeff. Buck, Lucy's daddy, cut the cake, and we savored every forkful.

Proceeds from silent and live auction donations, plus desserts, amounted to $5,800 toward college scholarships for our local youth enrolled in ag-related fields. The Stockgrowers also awarded money to deserving F.F.A. members to purchase heifers for their projects, and the Wallowa County Hay Growers donated hay to feed those heifers. Anna Rinehart, and

Joseph and Wyatt Smith, all of Imnaha, were awarded checks to purchase heifers. Every effort to encourage the continuation of the livestock industry and agriculture in Wallowa County is to be applauded.

There were several old-timers sprinkled among the newer generation of ranchers, among them Marilyn Johnson of Wallowa, who, along with her late husband Reid, contributed so much to the cattle industry, including their daughter Sara Lynn, who organized the very successful event. Cynthia Warnock, an upper Imnaha rancher, contributes as well to all Stockgrower projects.

It was good to see Dave and Shirley Parker of Highview Ranch there, as well as a table full of lower valley ranchers. Thanks for buying my chocolate pie! Other Ag-related scholarships offered included the Jim Probert/Helen Boucher Memorial scholarships, as well as a scholarship in memory of Doris Goucher.

After Sara Lynn welcomed the large turnout, she suggested we shouldn't talk about wolves—rather, we were encouraged to take a break, visit with our neighbors, and have a good time. Judging from the number of youngsters running around Cloverleaf Hall, there appears to be no shortage of future generation ranchers.

January 27—During the night those threatening snow clouds evaporated, and the stars and a crescent moon shone in a storm-polished sky. Can imagine the mushers riding those snowy wilderness trails were awed by the mountain night, with its brilliance of cold stars.

They say sled dogs perform better when the temperatures are 10 below or 10 above.

A friend to many, Vaden Flock, of Snake River Road, Asotin, Washington, passed away last week. We'll miss seeing him at the annual Ploughing Bee held at our neighbor's ranch every spring. I can still hear the bells Vaden attached to the harnesses worn by his beautiful team of mules.

Must get this column e-mailed. Am running late. Before the sun sinks over the mountain, Halley and I need a walk.

January 29—Doug treated me to breakfast at the Cheyenne Cafe before I attended church. Our Magic Garden committee is busy with plans for a bigger and better garden on my Sheep Creek property come spring. More volunteers from the community are needed, and welcome.

I'm still the official bell ringer, a job I love. There's something nostalgic about a small sleepy town on Sunday morning. I like to imagine folks listening for the pealing of the bell while gazing with gratitude at our snowy Wallowas.

January 30—Son Ken stopped by to check on his horses and visit. We polished off the last of the clam chowder I'd made for our Write Group earlier in the week.

January 31—Ken and son-in-law Charley hauled some poles Doug had stored in Ben's barn on the other side of the ranch. I'd found a frozen apple pie in the freezer and thawed it out for the "boys." It was 36 degrees this morning!

February 1—30 degrees.

February 3—After grandson Buck and his two little girls, Lucy and Katelyn, fed their cows, they picked me up and we drove down to my Sheep Creek place. It was so sunny and mild, we ate our picnic lunch beside the creek. Buck's wife Chelsea was working at the hospital that day, so daddy had the girls. Buck, using his chain saw, cut down broken limbs on the old apple and cherry trees, while the girls and I drug the smaller limbs to the fire. Buck cut some of the larger fruit wood into stove-length pieces, which were added to the wood pile.

We spent most of the day there, and were pleasantly surprised to discover the angle of the winter sun, on its journey Westward, continued to spread its warmth well into the late afternoon. Due to the canyon's numerous high rims, the sun is mostly blocked this time of year, which means many other locations receive little or no winter sun.

At day's end I treated Buck and his little helpers to chicken gizzards and fries at the Imnaha Store and Tavern.

"Gizzards, that's what you order when you come here," said Buck, who grew up along the Imnaha.

Later, eating ice cream bars, we all piled back in the pickup. Leaving Imnaha we spotted a flock of wild turkeys feeding in a pasture near the old Duckett place. The waxing February moon sailed high above Middlepoint as we made our way back to the valley.

February 7—I met with our Write Group at Cloud 9 Bakery, a weekly session we all look forward to.

Yesterday I attended our monthly Museum Board meeting at the county Extension Office. We are planning the Grand Opening of our newly-remodeled Firehall addition to the Museum in June.

February 8—Sometime in the night the full February moon was smothered in clouds. What a sight it was at twilight, rising over Hough's hill. Huge and bright against a sky still blushing with sunset colors.

Observing full moons from our living room window, for nearly 33 years now, never ceases to evoke a sense of wonder.

This morning's gray cloud cover presents a drastic change to what we've become accustomed to, which have been crisp, cold, clear days void of any threat of snow or rain. Morning temps stuck around 17 degrees meant continued ice in the irrigation ditches, and Wallowa Lake was completely frozen over. However, down in the canyons, there are signs of spring. My daffodils peek through a layer of dead leaves, the willows bordering the creek are budding, and the grass is greening. And it's 20 degrees warmer!

By midday here "on top," however, the sun manages to convey a bit of winter warmth and there are hints of seasonal change. My hens have decided to lay again, big blue Aracuna eggs; my Jersey heifer is making up a nice little udder, and son Todd's Marr Flat cows are beginning to calve, which means bald eagles have taken up residence in the tall cottonwoods growing along Prairie Creek, and hundred of ducks and geese are feeding alongside the cattle. Ravens join the eagles in cleaning up those placenta potlucks.

According to one of the locals, steelhead fishing on the Imnaha river is very slow, the water too low. Now, as I write, the sun is bursting through defined white clouds and blue sky appears to dominate. Although we do need moisture in some form, preferably snow to hide all the ugly junk strewn around the ranch, it's lovely to be out and about with Halley.

Winter seems to bring on sickness, especially to those who must work outside, like our cowboys, exposed to all types of weather. Both sons Ken and Todd have suffered pneumonia or lung-related problems, aggravated by chores that must be done regardless, even if they're suffering a cold. Cattle must be fed every day.

Our prayers are with Crow Creek rancher Tom Birkmaier, whose truck ran over him while he was feeding cattle. I understand Tom, using a crutch, is back to ranch work again. Luckily the injuries weren't as bad as they could've been.

Older cowboys suffer too, Doug came down with a doozy of a cold this past weekend, and refused to see the Doc. Just the week before, I'd hauled him into our local medical clinic to have an ugly head wound stapled together. Wearing cowboy boots, he'd slipped on our icy driveway, feet flying out from under him—*wham*—to land on the back of his head. Not a pretty sight! Happy to report the staples have been removed, leaving a dim scar and a new respect for hidden ice.

His cold is under control, and yesterday he was back playing cards with "the boys" at Ye Olde Range Rider.

No reported wolf kills by the "Imnaha Pack" since the most recent, "Annie," the saddle mule owned by Shawn and Shelly Steen, local outfitters who manage the Minam Lodge. Annie was found eaten on private property on the Divide, and deemed a "probable wolf kill."

Will Voss has been hired as Range Rider to discourage wolves from coming in and around livestock, which helps, as calving season is here. However, ranches are so far-flung in our county, Will can't be everywhere at once. To make matters worse, the pack alpha male's radio collar has ceased to transmit a signal. Not good.

Our county continues to mourn the frequent loss of its old-timers. Former owner of the Courthouse Ranch up Big Sheep Creek, Howard Borgerding (just shy of his 90th birthday) passed on recently. Howard's wife Carol and I were in CowBelles together. Carol passed away some time ago.

Tex Miller and Don Martin, two of Doug's card-playing buddies, left us recently as well.

The white-tail deer we used to see here early of a morning and late in the evening have disappeared. As have the coyotes. Wolves have been spotted nearby, and neighbor Lois Hough and I hear them at night, as does Halley, who howls as mournfully when they do. We don't know if their presence has anything to do with the disappearance of the deer or coyotes.

February 9—Would you believe it's raining and 33 degrees! The cold drizzle began last night. No doubt we'll have snow soon. After all, it IS calving season.

February 12—It was misty, rainy, and 33 degrees, a recipe for fog.

Yesterday evening, daughter Ramona and husband Charley joined us in attending a Lincoln Day Dinner at the VFW Hall in Enterprise. It was fun visiting old rancher friends Mack and Marian Birkmaier, before sit'in down to a thick juicy steak dinner with our neighbors.

The evening proved to be another one of those famous dessert auctions to raise money. Ramona's raspberry cobbler sold for $100, even though she'd left it home. No problem—I would deliver it to Carolyn in church the next morning. Then I got carried away and purchased a peanut butter pie, baked by Judy Wortman, for $100. Judy's luscious pie would travel to church also, and those Methodists ate every crumb.

Before church on Sunday, Doug treated me to breakfast at the Cheyenne Cafe. Fresh snow had fallen in the backcountry and the place was packed with snowmobilers who had driven their machines from Halfway to Joseph. Most were married couples and all were in a merry mood and hungry, chowing down on heaping platters of Cheyenne's Cafe's famous Country breakfasts.

February 13—The weather was so mild and breezy I hung my washing on the line to dry. This afternoon Doug and I drove out to the hills, where we spotted 30 head of elk bunched together on a hill off North Pine Rd. Although the roads were pretty greasy, they were free of snow drifts. Not many winters can you drive out there in February!

It was nearly dark when we returned to the ranch in a snow squall.

February 14—As Valentine's Day dawned, a pink Alpine glow appeared briefly on our snowy mountain tops.

Spent the morning preparing a special salad for a church luncheon hosted by Kathy and Bob Reitman, who live in Enterprise. This couple's charming Victorian home, built in 1910, has been lovingly restored. Sunshine flooded through the dining room window as we enjoyed our delicious meal. And what'a you know, across the street, on the elementary school playground, I spied several of my great-grandchildren romping around during recess.

Kathy and Bob also have a dog named Halley—short for Hallelujah!

Two great-granddaughters, Lucy and Katelyn appeared at our door with their Valentine, a plate full of brownies and a card with their photo on it. Since it was lunch time I offered the little family a fridge-full of leftovers. Our younger generation invigorates. Love 'em.

I baked a cobbler using those canned Sheep Creek cherries for Doug's Valentine, and he surprised me with a small heart-shaped box of chocolates.

February 15—Called granddaughter Adele today, and sang her Happy Birthday. Hard to believe our young Miss is 24! Adele is in San Antonio, Texas, celebrating her big day with two girlfriends. I told her about the time I'd flown to San Antonio for a "Women Writing the West" conference, many years ago, and how I enjoyed the River Walk and visiting the Alamo.

"We can look right down on the River Walk from our motel," she said. "And we're planning on doing that very thing today."

Baked an acorn squash, raised in our garden down on Sheep Creek, for supper. Also pork chops from Raymond Seal's 4-H hog, along with wax beans canned last fall. Opened a jar of pickled beets too. Slow Food!

February 16—A pot of beans and ham hocks simmered on the stove all day, and this evening I attended a program sponsored by Fishtrap and Wallowa Resources entitled "Wallowa County in Transition: New Stories from the Old West."

The event, held in the Hurricane Creek Grange Hall, drew a good crowd. The panel discussion, moderated by Liza Jane Nichols, explored the subject of Creative Markets for Traditional Products. Panelists were Jill McClaran of the McClaran Ranch, Jim Zacharias of JayZee Lumber, and Larry Davis and Nicole Bellows of Northwest Goat Grazers and Happy Chick Farms.

This down-to-earth discussion enlightened the audience on how generational and newcomers to Wallowa County are adapting to change. All agreed they want to live here in this beautiful place, but it's tough to make a living. Listening to this younger generation, who are coming up with creative ways to survive, like taking risks and working hard at their dreams, gives us hope for the future, which can be a pretty scary place.

The next program in this series, entitled "Keeping Traditions Alive: The Next Generation on our Working Lands," is scheduled for March 14th. Same time, same place. Son Todd will moderate this panel, which will explore the future of our working lands, asking how the children of present day ranchers, farmers, and foresters can own land and make a living.

February 17—Son Ken and his grandsons Ronan, Kennon, and Gideon stopped by to feed their horses. They were on their way to work on Upper Prairie Creek. Grandma just happened to have cookies for them.

Later, grandson Buck arrived, along with daughters Katelyn and Lucy. Chelsea, their mom, having worked at the hospital all night, was sleeping. So, while Buck welded his trailer, I entertained the little girls, which included letting them chase my chickens, an activity popular years ago with all my grandchildren. With the same look of glee, Lucy (with daddy's help) actually caught one. It was all very exciting and fun, and three days later the hens began laying again!

February 18—Marine grandson James called from North Carolina. Over the miles, he described the country and how warm it was there, to his grandma, who has never been any farther east than Woonsocket South Dakota in 1951.

This evening I drove to Enterprise and climbed the old stairs to the Odd Fellows Hall, where an old time square dance was in progress. Granddaughter-in-law Amy played the fiddle, and other musicians, which included a hammered dulcimer, made great country music.

Out on the dance floor, swinging each other around, were great-grandchildren Gwenllian and Ronan. Lined up on the benches were

Kennon, Gavin and Lochlan.

"Where's baby Arianwyn?" I asked the little boys.

"Oh, she's asleep over there."

I added my apple snacks to a long table of food, then joined my kiddies. They told me their daddy was attending a meeting in Montana, which meant Amy had managed to get her six children there by herself.

Other large families were there too, like the Pat Matthews family. It was like stepping back into the pages of Mary Marks' diaries, reading how Kid would do the calling and Mary would join the square dancers so long ago, in the old Grange Hall on the upper Imnaha.

February 22—On this Washington's Birthday and Ash Wednesday, the day after Fat Tuesday, a west wind is gusting over 40 miles an hour, flailing tree limbs and lifting Halley's dog house off the carport. The warm wind rose in the night and evaporated every trace of snow here on middle and lower Prairie Creek. The snowline has only retreated to timberline on Upper Prairie Creek, however, and it appears to be snowing on East Peak and Mt. Howard, while Chief Joseph Mountain and Ruby Peak remain invisible due to swirling storms.

Our outside thermometer registered 44 degrees when I went out to throw hay to my heifers this morning. After feeding and watering my chickens, Halley and I walked.down to the cellar to replenish my potato supply here at the house. Each week I gave potatoes to our grandchildren's families. They have a lot of mouths to feed.

Which brings to mind my friend Mary Marks, who used to say when planting potatoes in her garden, "I always plant a few extra spuds, somebody might need a potato." A typical remark from Mary, who never forgot about growing up during hard times.

The Amaryllis bulb on my kitchen table has burst into bloom. Its variegated red, trumpet-like flowers cheer my winter-worn spirit.

One red-winged blackbird and one robin have taken up residence in our yard. At the feeder I've spotted red polls and various species of sparrows. A large barred owl can be heard calling in the evenings, and a pair of Red Tail hawks are mating near the stick nest in the old cottonwood growing along the Farmer's ditch.

Wild geese and ducks calf be seen feeding in the fields and ditches, but nary a white-tail or coyote. Halley still barks at night, but stays close to the porch. Neighbor Darla Klages hears the wolves too, but I'm happy to report there have been no KNOWN kills lately. Our Range Rider must be doing his job, as calving season is well under way.

Received a phone call yesterday from Allen Voortman, who owns the Pride and Joy Dairy in Granger, Washington. We talked a long time. He speaks my language. We both share a passion for milk cows, chickens, lambs, beef, home grown veggies, and Slow Food. We understand the benefits of wholesome homegrown food and what it can do for one's health, energy and ability to think clearly. Allen is living proof of the advantages of eating natural foods, which we both agree promotes overall mental health and prevents, and cures, many modern maladies.

Allen's enthusiasm and his zest for living is contagious. This man is living his dream. Articles have been written about his honor system Farm Stand where he sells whole milk, eggs, grass-fed beef, and other farm-grown products directly to his happy customers. Allen's operation is diversified, and he believes strongly in raising wholesome foods to feed local folks. Agri-Times has featured articles on his unique farm in the past. He's quite a guy. Can't wait to meet him, as he reminds me so much of my father.

Allen asked about my Jersey, and as a loyal fan of this column he says he's anticipating my first-calf heifer's freshening as much as our family is. Can't wait for that nutritious whole milk and cream. Doug and I, plus our children, were raised on it.

Another fan, Nancy Doherty, who lives in Milton-Freewater, sent me a Valentine card with a note telling me that a photo of her two grandsons, Nicky and Macey, showing lambs in pee wee showmanship, was published under my column several weeks ago. Thanks for the card, Nancy.

February 23—All that mud is frozen again. The skiff of snow that fell in the night is gone, the sun is bursting through snow clouds, and the sky is a cold blue. Snowing in the mountains, and daughter Jackie just called from Boise, on her way from Challis to see her granddaughters.

Our Baby Kate is three years old today.

February 24—I forked the straw covering off my row of carrots in the garden, and dug a bucket full of the sweetest carrots you ever tasted. I also received a fan letter from Gloria Mensah of Bethesda, Maryland, who worked at Wallowa Lake Lodge with Irene Wiggins from 1955 to 1957. Gloria has many fond memories of Wallowa County, and tells me reading this column makes her wish she was here.

February 27—10 degrees here on Prairie Creek, unofficially the coldest spot in Oregon.

This evening Doug and I drove down into the canyons, stopping

*Built in 1906, this rare octagonal barn near Joseph has had many owners.
It is presently owned by Triple Creek Ranch.*

Curious horses pose atop the far north end of the Wallowa Lake east moraine.

at Bear Gulch to visit Larry Moore, before proceeding to the Imnaha Church, where we chowed down at a benefit Taco Feed. We visited Lyman and Wilma, as well as other old friends like Pat and Ken Stein, Barbara Warnock, and Myrna Moore, who was helping with the tacos.

After eating, we all joined into a game of Bingo. Doug and I hadn't played for years! It was fun. Commissioner Susan Roberts was there, as well as several others from "on top."

February 28—This morning I received a phone call from my sister Kathy in California, informing me that our cousin Marsha Wilson had been involved in a serious car wreck. She was in an ICU neuro trauma center. Prayers for Marsha.

Then, just as I walked into the house, returning from my weekly Writer's Group, Doug was on the phone with daughter Ramona, who'd called to say John Rysdam had been killed. He was working with the county road crew north of Elgin at the time of the accident. He was our granddaughter-in-law Kasey's daddy, father-in-law to our grandson Rowdy, and Poppa to our great-grandchildren Cutter and Nevada, who live in Mt Vernon, Oregon. John was only 60 years old. More prayers.

However...Fawn calved tonight, a Jersey/Angus bull calf, during one of the worst blizzards we've had all winter. Following the events of the day, you can understand why Fawn's calving ended the day on a happier note.

Like I already mentioned, it was a wild night. The wind was howling, the tin on the roof was rattling, and snow sifted through the cracks of the old barn when my Jersey first-calf heifer went into labor. Fawn was quite the drama queen.

All through my childhood, growing up on a dairy, I'd witnessed many animal births, but never have I heard such bawling and carrying on as exhibited by this little gal. She'd paw the ground, bawl, lay down, get up, and begin all over again. Two front feet appeared, then nothing. I went to the house to fix supper, and later, bundled up against the storm, returned. No progress! Fawn was bawling so loud, you could hear her for miles.

Alarmed, I called son Todd. His wife Angie answered, saying he'd just gotten out of the shower, and would call me back. He'd not had any sleep the night before. Todd and his helper Pat are calving out over 400 head of cows.

"I was just wondering what veterinarian you would recommend?" I asked my son.

"You don't need to do that, mom. I'll be right over. And he hung up.

Fawn, Janie's jersey, with her newborn bull calf. Born February 28 during a Prairie Creek blizzard. The calf was named 'Leap' for leap year. Note the snow that blew through the cracks in the old barn.

I felt bad calling for help. All this reinforced my respect for all our local cattle ranchers who were outside on such a night. My heifer was out of the wind and snow, laboring in a sheltered barn. So I waited, there in the old barn, in the midst of that freezing night, peering down the road for Todd's headlights.

Just before he and granddaughter Becky pulled up in the pickup, my Jerz bawled loud enough to wake the dead, and out slid a slimy calf. I quickly removed the sack from its nose and mucous from its mouth, whereupon the little cinnamon-colored bull took a big gulp of air and bawled.

Fawn, a good mamma, was up in a flash, licking and cleaning her little guy, when Todd and Becky burst through the door carrying the calf puller. I could see the look of relief in Todd's eyes. Obviously, all was well. The pair turned and disappeared back into the blizzard, leaving me to see to my little herd.

It was midnight before I crawled into bed beside my sleeping husband, who tells me HIS days of calving are over, and he doesn't miss it a bit! I felt like I'd been on an emotional roller coaster all day. I named the little bull Leap, 'cause of Leap Year.

February 29—This morning I was up before dawn, milking out colostrum to freeze for grandson Buck, who's also in the midst of calving. Doug thinks I'm nuts, but I just love being out in the cow barn again. However, when I walked back to the house this morning carrying my plastic container of colostrum, Doug, just back from the Grain Growers, presented me with a shiny new milk pail, the only one he could find in the county. He'd tied a red ribbon to the handle!

March 1—March came in like both a lamb and a lion. Calm in the morning, yet 20 degrees cold, with a typical mixed bag of alternating sun and snow showers.

March 2—We had a new snowfall, 20 degrees. Good news! Cousin Marsha was taken off the ventilator and continues to improve daily. Doug accompanied daughter Ramona and husband Charley to Summerville for John Rysdam's funeral. My prayers went to the Rysdam family.

Meanwhile, I attended the World Day of Prayer, held at our Methodist Church in Joseph, and my hands were full of milk cow chores.

March 3—It was melting and drippy and MUDDY. I cooked a big pot of chicken soup for grandson Buck, who'd been hit with a nasty stomach flu bug. Buck's wife Chelsea works shifts at the local hospital, and Buck was calving, feeding and taking care of his little girls. Like so many young ranch families all over Eastern Oregon, this couple juggles many roles to realize their dreams while earning a living in the country they love.

This evening Doug and I picked up great grandkids Riley Ann, Ashlyn, and twins Jada and Gideon, and attended the Blue Mountain Old Time Fiddlers show at Cloverleaf Hall. Poppa Doug treated us all to one of Randy Garnett's famous pork dinners before the show began. Four generations of our family were in attendance to cheer for our Riley Ann, who played three fiddle tunes.

Denny Langford bestowed the honor of Sheriff on son Ken, and Gideon asked his great grandma to dance. It made my day. The "Prairie Creek Girls" and our local group "Homemade Jam," as well as other locals made this show special. A large turnout of toe-tapping, clapping folks enjoyed the fun-filled evening.

The Imnaha wolf pack has struck again. Our neighbor, Dave Talbott, who ranches just over the hill, had to have a two-year-old cow put down as a result of injuries sustained by wolves. The cow's unborn calf was dead due to the attack, and the cow was running a high temperature. Two more cows had confirmed injuries, and Dave is missing one of

11 year old Riley Ann Gray plays her fiddle tunes at the recent Blue Mt Old Time Fiddler Show, held at Cloverleaf Hall in Enterprise. Riley is the daughter of Justin and Chelsie Gray, granddaughter of Ken and Annie Nash all of Enterprise. Great granddaughter of Doug and Janie Tippett.

his newborn calves. Sadly, a bill that would allow a kill order on these chronic livestock predators failed to pass in Salem recently.

This month marks the 28th year I have been writing Janie's Journal for Agri-Times. I remember, because that was the year Virgil Rupp started up this little paper, which is still going strong thanks to Sterling Allen and his able staff. I will always remember the date, as March 1984 was the year my dairyman father, Matthew James Bachman, died.

March 8—Normally, I'd be seated at my kitchen table writing this column. Like I was doing yesterday morning, when I actually began to write. And when, before the sun's warmth burst over Hough's hill, it was 10 degrees! When Prairie Creek lay stunned by cold, under sunny skies that dazzled our mountain snowfields.

But right this moment, this afternoon, I'm down here on Sheep Creek with my laptop set up on my screened-in porch. The thermometer here registers 65 degrees. Soothed by creeksong, gladdened by birdsong, warmed by sunshine, and awed by the awakening of canyon springtime, I find the quiet I seek. I'm "off the grid"—except for this laptop.

Several robins, taking advantage of Halley sleeping at my feet, hop about the greening lawn. Quail call from the blackberry bramble, March sunlight saturates the bunch grass-covered canyon sides, and the tiered rims of Middlepoint tower above. A mild breeze rattles the tall dead grasses alongside the creek, and the lawn is littered with black walnuts.

My daffodils are budding, as are the flowering quince and forsythia bushes, all of which are a few warm days from bursting into bloom. Buds on the old apricot and cherry trees are swelling, and we pray it doesn't freeze before the fruit sets. Steelhead swim silently upstream to spawn—that is, unless the fish are diverted into the nearby holding pond managed by Fish and Wildlife. Across the creek our Magic Garden awaits the tiller to till in the green manure crop.

Earlier, Halley and I took a jaunt up the road to see what we could see, and just beyond the garden, there they were: clumps of golden waxy buttercups!

When we first arrived I drug a lawn chair out beside the creek and ate my chicken sandwich. Then, naturally, it was time for a nap, so am only just now beginning to write. But it's hard to stay focused. My eyes keep straying to the creek.

My mind, which won't settle down, wanders to our family Easter Sunday picnic, my Syringa Sisters annual week together in June, my California sisters visiting in July, and my spring writers group retreat, all coming up soon, all happening down here. My mind also dwells on

Celebrating her third birthday on the "Fergi" ski slopes with her grandma Carol and grandpa Mark DeJong, Katelyn Matthews rides in her "pack pack." Shown on right is Kate's other grandma, Jackie Matthews. Katelyn is the daughter of Buck and Chelsea Matthews, ranchers in Wallowa County.

the garden across the creek, and on my desire for a swinging bridge, and my mouth hungers when I look forward to those first ripe tomatoes.

Doug has driven out to La Grande to attend the Livestock auction. The day is mine. Lots of water has run under the bridge this past week. Lets see if I can recall it.

Allen Voortman sent a gallon of his "Pride and Joy Dairy" whole milk to me, via a neighbor. Thanks, Allen. I want you to know it was the nourishment provided by your milk that enabled me to survive this past week. Now, thanks to Fawn, we GOT MILK!

Leap will be two weeks old come Tuesday, and let me tell you, I'm in shape again. Between forking manure, carrying buckets of water, feeding hay, halter-breaking Leap, and milking a cow again, I should be. I love it! Once a dairymaid, always a dairymaid. I really missed my milk cows.

Daughter Jackie arrived safely. We had such a good visit. Took a four-generation walk with Buck's family and went skiing at Fergie. Five-year-old Lucy is a real pro, and three-year-old sister Katelyn made two runs from the top of the T-Bar, riding in her backpack, strapped to Poppa Mark's back. It was a beautiful day on the slopes and the snow was excellent.

This evening my friend Pat Cason treated me to the "Opera To Go" at the Elgin Opera House. A wonderful musical performance of professional singers from the Portland Opera.

March 14—Doug and I attended the second lecture series sponsored by Fishtrap and Wallowa Resources, held at the Hurricane Creek Grange Hall. The event was well attended. Son Todd led the discussion, and grandson Buck was one of the panelists. Listening to these younger generation loggers, farmers and ranchers tell their stories was riveting.

Living here in our beautiful valley has never been easy, but these young people, who are taking enormous risks to follow their dreams and who aren't afraid to work, are making a living. They all credited our sense of community, which is alive and well in Wallowa County. There's something to be said for making a living doing what you love. 'Tis the way it should be.

March 17—We had friends over for our traditional St. Patrick's Day corned beef 'n cabbage, along with spuds and carrots from the garden. Since Jean Falbo doesn't bake pies, and hubby Clem loves lemon, I whipped up one of my famous Farm Journal Cookbook's four-star lemon pies. Yum! Of course, those fresh eggs are a must.

After Clem, Jean and Pat Cason left, Jeff Dawson stayed to visit Doug while I joined the three of them at the Liberty Grange Hall, where an old time country dance was in progress, just west of us on Liberty Road, across the road from our old ranch. The hall was full of stomping young people, old folks, and babes in arms. Someone called out square dances, and dancers were somewhat tangled up, but eventually catching on. Everyone was laughing and having a good time.

Granddaughter-in-law Amy was playing the fiddle, and great-grandson Ronan was playing his own little guitar. Other musicians, including my friend Pat, playing her flute, were making good music, and the floor jumped with activity. I visited with two more of my great grandchildren: Gwenllian and Kennon.

When I returned home, Jeff and Doug were still visiting! I washed dishes and crashed.

March 19—Our book group discussed our March read, *Crows in the Autumn Sky* by Ted Sabine, who was there! What a treat to meet this astonishing author. I highly recommend this book to just about everyone. You can order copies from the Bookloft in Enterprise.

Since our family raised two pet crows years ago, I purchased books for my children. Doug read the book and so did Lyman, and they couldn't put it down. Now Mike Fluitt and Chuck Fraser have my copy.

March 20—Ted Sabine, along with his interesting wife Maggie and their friend Linda, visited us the next day. I took them on a trip to the barn to see Fawn and Leap. For almost a month now, I've been milking my little Jersey morning and night, and our families have been guzzling her nutritious milk. However, breaking a first calf heifer to milk wasn't as easy as it used to be. Like I mentioned earlier, I don't have quite the stamina I did at, say, 60!

First off, my Jerz decided she didn't like the stanchion, so we did everything HER way. Suits me fine, as she stands quietly anywhere and allows me to milk, just as long as her wooden box of rolled barley is placed in front of her. This being my first experience with Jerseys, Fawn is teaching me.

Beginning when I was five years old, when my daddy taught me to milk, I always milked Guernseys, and later, after being married at age 17, I milked most all dairy breeds: Brown Swiss, Holsteins, Simmental crosses…but no Jerseys. So this feisty little beast has tested me to the limit.

However, we've come to a complete understanding, and I'm in Heaven. It isn't work when you are doing something you love, and so I spend far too much time in the barn, playing with Leap, while Halley amuses herself attempting to reach the skunks and coons who inhabit the dark recesses under the old barn's rock foundation.

March 21—The Vernal Equinox marches off the March calendar. Today was a typical Wallowa County first day of spring—It snowed three inches. Our Writer's Group met around our usual table in the back room of Cloud Nine Bakery. We normally eat lunch there, but that day, on a whim, we decided to try out Ye Olde Range Rider.

As we gals burst through the door, there they were, Doug and his cronies, engaged in an intense game of pinochle. And since my hubby appeared to be "in the chips," I anticipated his treating me to lunch. Then who should walk in but Lyman and Wilma? So Doug joined us, and we had ourselves a party. Let me tell you, Jan and Mark Baughn know how to make you feel welcome, and their food is tops!

March 22—Our grandson James, a Lieutenant in the Marines, surprised us with a visit, and brought along his Danielle for us to meet.

"Could you teach Danielle to make a pie, grandma?" asked my grownup grandson.

"Sure," says I. "Come early Monday before supper and we'll have a go at it."

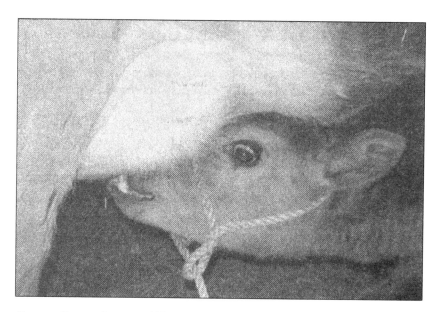

Leap, a Jersey Angus calf born February 27th, enjoys his mommy's milk.

Old cronies playing pinochle at the "Range Rider" in Enterprise. L-R around the table: Dick Hammond, Chris Hansen, Harold Lay, Jerry Winegar, Doug Tippett, Charley Johnson, Dick Lathrop, and Jack Poulson.

Whew! That was a busy day. Baked sourdough bread that morning, went to the canning cupboard for applesauce and pickled dilled green beans, slid a pork roast into the oven along with a casserole of yams, thawed out a package of Sheep Creek blackberries, milked the cow, and tended to other chores.

Danielle passed Pie Baking 101 with straight As, and I tucked away the memories made that evening for safe keeping in my heart. Our prayers are with James, who will know early this summer if he will be deployed to Afghanistan or not. James, at the end of his Marine commitment, plans to attend the University of Idaho, where he will be going for his MFA in Literature and Creative Writing.

Grandson Shawn, a career Marine, is now in North Carolina for training, and grandson Josh is still stationed in the Navy in San Diego. Prayers for all young people serving our country.

March 23—Harold Klages, our 86-year-old neighboring rancher, passed away recently, and his funeral was held today in the Grace Lutheran Church in Enterprise. Harold died peacefully in his home on the ranch that he, along with his beloved wife Ardis and son Alan, have been operating for many years, the same ranch Harold's dad Henry established.

The simple service was a happy occasion, as Harold would have wished. The place was packed. It was an honor to know Harold. He and Ardis have been my hero and heroine for the 34 years I've lived on Prairie Creek.

March 31—Just flipped my calendar to April, couldn't bear to look at March another day. Of course, growing older might have something to do with this breathless feeling of always being behind. You should see my March calendar—unbelievable! Every single day was full to the brim with this business of LIVING! And now it's nearly 9:00 p.m. and I'm just now sitting down to my kitchen table to miss another deadline.

I had all good intentions, but family comes first and, like most writers, I'm really good at finding excuses to avoid writing. So, when grandson Buck and his two helpers, Lucy and Katelyn, appeared at my door this morning, I quite happily turned off my computer.

Buck was here to haul a few bales of hay from the ham closer to the feeder, so it would be handier for Doug to feed my heifers this next week, as I'll be attending the annual Fishtrap Writer's Retreat on the Upper Imnaha. I leave in the morning and I'm not even packed!

When Buck and the girls arrived, the Prairie Creek wind was whipping my clothes on the line, banging the chicken pen gate, rattling the tin roof on the cow barn, and blowing us sideways as we made our way to the hay barn.

Earlier this 50 degree morning, it had been raining, which meant high up on the mountain slopes, our deep snow pack would be melting. I called Lyman and Wilma.

"River's pretty high," they said, and reported a warm wind blowing down the canyon. Lyman had been planting radishes in his garden.

After our hay-hauling chore was completed, the girls and I leaned into the wind and fought our way to the chicken house to gather eggs, then retreated to the kitchen for glasses of cold Jersey milk mixed with ovaltine. Since mom Chelsea was working at the hospital, Buck and his two little girls had hayed their cows at the Cummings place, and seen to their new calves. Now they had time to kill before joining mom at the hospital for lunch.

We had a nice visit, which included a slide show of grandma's photos. Lucy and Katelyn were very amused to see themselves participating in many events I'd caught on camera this past year.

Then I got busy packing for Imnaha, doing chores, folding clothes, cooking liver and onions for supper, watching Laurence Welk on TV, phoning our friends Sandra and Fred in Auburn, California, and well, you see how it is. That fierce wind laid down, it began to rain, then snow, then rain, and methinks by morning all will be white for April Fools Day.

So you see, this is pretty typical of what happened all month. Every Sunday I attended our church and rang the bell. And, whenever the sun came out, I headed to my Sheep Creek place to escape winter and enjoy spring, which is already happening in the canyons—apricot trees in bloom, daffodils nodding their golden heads, violets running rampant over my lawn, pink flowering quince budding, bright yellow sprays of Forsythia, greening grass, the creek running full of snowmelt, and wild turkey gobblers fanning their tails, strutting to and fro to impress their harem of hens.

It's always hard to leave, to drive back "on top" to our snowy world.

April 1—After Harold Klages' service last week, I ran into young Sam Morgan, son of our old friend Doc Morgan. Sam is a veterinarian like his dad, who left us a year or so ago. Sam mentioned he had a bummer lamb, and would I like it?

"Sure" said I, without hesitation.

But that's another story for another time, as time is running out and it's Sunday morning and there is a blizzard happening outside...and that's no April Fools!

I went to bed at 10:00 last night and got up at 4:30 this a.m. to work on this column. Doug got up and did my dishes and fed my heifers. The calf is turned out with the cow, and the lamb was given to my great-grandkids.

Now I must pack for the retreat, drive to Joseph, ring the bell at church, head down into the canyons to Imnaha, then turn upriver to the Writer's Retreat. I'll be off the grid for a week. Adios. See ya next time!

April 12—3:30 a.m. Wishing to write by moonlight, rather than electric light, I resign myself to sitting here at my kitchen table, while outside glows the April moon—half a moon, sailing through islands of luminous clouds in a sky pierced by the brightest stars in the universe.

I imagine this moon tinged with pink, as April is the month of the "pink moon," so named for the bright pink phlox now beginning to bloom between the rocks in our canyon's wild places…and not so wild places, like our Alder Slope Nursery, where, attracted to their color, I purchased several plants. Later, perhaps this afternoon, I'll fill my planter down at my Sheep Creek place with these pretties, to celebrate the "pink" moon.

Here on Prairie Creek, the "boys" who have been chomping the bit, waiting for just the right time to "farm," are hard at it. Up our road I spied Jake Moore rolling Butterfield's leased hayfield, and across the way, there was Greg Brink, plowing up a storm, literally, as the calm morning morphed into a windy, rainy afternoon. Not enough rain to deter Greg, who was moving right along.

Driving to town the other day I waved to Anna Butterfield on the tractor, roll'in, roll'in, roll'in their hay fields. Other rancher/farmers are burn'in, burn'in, burn'in, including my hubby. Another spring ritual. Prairie Creek is beginning to green. With every snowfall the grass grows another inch. As in past Aprils, I recall old-timer Mike McFetridge's words, "Snow don't lay long on green grass."

My Jersey milk cow Fawn, and her sidekick, Rhubarb, are actually grazing. Not to say they aren't still running to their feeder for alfalfa hay, but soon my chores will lessen. A pair of honkers are considering nesting in the cow pasture, and in my chicken house, "Henny Penny" is setting on three eggs. Our Calico mamma kitty birthed her spring litter of kittens in an old rusty barrel, and yellow and lavender crocuses are blooming alongside the house.

All over the valley I hear the sound of bawling cows and calves being trailed to their summer ranges. "Turn out time" has arrived, which means brandings, an event all ranch families look forward to. The back of winter is broken!

I promised to finish the "lamb" story, so here goes. The day after Harold Klages' funeral, I drove to Sam Morgan's veterinary clinic to pick up my bummer. I'd been thinking of a name, perhaps Sam, for obvious reasons, but Sam became Samantha, for obvious reasons. Samantha, a wee black ewe lamb, greeted me from the depths of a cardboard box as she was loaded into my car, along with a sack of milk replacer and a plastic pop bottle with a nipple attached.

After thanking Sam, who seemed relieved to find someone who would take her, I sped back to the ranch. Since it was nearing feeding time, I mixed up a bottle and, leaving Samantha in her box in the car, changed clothes to meet my friend Phyllis at Mutiny in Joseph. Like Roger Pond used to say, it's hard to look cool when there's a sheep in the back of your car...but I did, and met my old friend as planned. We had a great visit over a delicious lunch, and then I let Phyllis feed the lamb.

Back home I pondered how best to break the news to Doug. Since I was milking Fawn twice a day, and tending other myriad chores, I just knew he would think me totally wacky. So I let it go for a day or two. Then, while talking with my childhood chum Sandra over the phone, I blurted out an aside: "I have a bummer lamb," and Doug simply rolled his eyes in resignation. It was a done deal—my deal, not his.

I'd made a snuggly little nest with hay bales for Samantha, and she thrived. Children came to see her. She was an Easter lamb. She followed me everywhere—to milk the Jersey, to feed the chickens, and to run alongside Halley and the cats. But I was leaving for the April Fishtrap Writer's Retreat, so what to do? I'd hire a lamb sitter...my great-grandkids!

Long story short, Samantha is now a 4-H project for Ashlyn, and she'll make a fine breeding ewe. I must call Sam, as in Morgan, and ask if Samantha's mother is still alive. The old ewe looked pretty tough after the birth of twins, one of whom died. Little Samantha has a loving home and, although I miss her tagging after me, it WAS a chore to mix her bottle, what with all my other chores!

I did e-mail my column that Sunday morning before loading my car to drive to Joseph, where I shopped for groceries and ran into our church just in time to ring the bell, then headed down into the canyons. It was raining when I pulled up to the Imnaha Store and Tav to order a "hamburger to go." I was starved, but had no time to eat. I drove upriver, parked at my friend Pam's place, gobbled down my lunch, and caught a few *zzzz*'s.

Feeling enormously restored, I continued on upriver. It was still raining when I stopped at Lyman and Wilma's to give them some Jersey cream. Luckily, the rain ceased as I pushed three cart-loads of groceries and all my "stuff" across that swinging bridge, the Imnaha, full of chocolate-colored snowmelt, roaring its way downriver beneath me.

Feeling weary after putting groceries away and lugging stuff upstairs, I put the kettle on for tea. Then, across the bridge, appeared Cathy Love, who had driven all the way from Sacramento, California. What a delight to meet this gal, who was cheerful, 45 years old, a school teacher, loved to kayak, a great poet, strong and smart. Cathy pitched in to help from the moment she arrived. She carted all the wood from across the river, then split and stacked it on the porch. It turns out Cathy was awarded one of our Write People's Sally Bowerman scholarships for Summer Fishtrap last year. She says she was most grateful to be chosen as one of the recipients.

Shortly thereafter appeared Robin and Steven from Portland, youngsters really, the ages of my older grandchildren. Both poets. Finally, Jim arrived, lugging his musical instruments and recording equipment across the bridge. Jim had driven cross-country from Arlington, Virginia. Another poet, plus songwriter, photographer, and podcaster.

All week I was inspired by poets. Jim taught me how to write haikus and I was hooked. To relax before working on my novel, I wrote numerous poems.

That evening I cooked up a kettle of potato soup and we all settled in. Steven chose the tree house this time, so I wrote in my old room upstairs that commanded a view up Indian Creek. It was a most productive, creative week.

On Thursday we all pitched in to stage the Imnaha Retreat's social event of the year. Cathy made name cards for each place setting while I prepared the meal, which featured Marr Flat Natural Beef roast, mashed potatoes, rich beef gravy, sourdough bread, salad, carrots simmered in beef broth, pickled beets, and Imnaha apricot cobbler, with ice cream provided by Ben. Since all the writers, save for Cathy, were vegetarians, I was craving red meat.

We had invited Ben from our Fishtrap staff, along with Cameron Scott, Fishtrap's writer-in-residence, Wilma and Lyman from downriver, and our Imnaha poet Robin Townsend, who lives near the Bridge. It was a wonderful evening! An eclectic mix of folks, celebrating the arrival of spring. We gathered in Indian Creek Lodge to feast on Slow Food, Slam poetry, heartfelt haikus, soulful sonnets, and homemade music by Jim and Ben. As in years past, Lyman shook the bridge when Wilma walked across. And, as usual, she got back at her hubby by swinging the swaying bridge when it was his turn. Those kids!

One morning we awoke to see it snowing, lightly, magically, into the river, and onto the daffodils, the violets, the forsythia and the budding fruit trees, a mystical moment before it began to stick. Over four inches later, it ceased, and spring was put on hold.

A murder of crows cawed in protest, and the pair of wild honkers who'd adopted us hunkered down alongside the rushing, hissing river. Our two Portlanders snapped many photos. It was pristinely lovely and conducive to writing. We stoked up the wood furnace and built a fire in the fireplace, and we five had a most productive day.

The next morning Steven spotted our beaver in the river. So far he, or she, has chewed down two pear trees and three apple trees. We can't believe this eager beaver is planning on damming the Imnaha!

I took numerous hikes up Indian Creek, and along the old wagon road. On a rare sunny afternoon, I took Steven and Cathy up the Freezeout road to the Saddle Creek trailhead. A real challenge, as the road was filled with snow. We hiked far enough up the snowy switchback trail to enjoy great canyon views. Our experiences included observing great billowing clouds form in the purest of blue skies, feeling warm sunshine on our faces, slipping and sliding up the snowy/muddy trail, smelling the fragrant Ponderosas, and listening to birdsong, interspersed with deep silence. All quite magical to city folk.

On a ridge far above us, Steven spotted a lone wolf, while on the trail we stepped in numerous elk and deer prints.

Saturday morning everyone pitched in and cleaned the lodge for the next shift, then Cathy set her camera on auto for a group photo. Hugs and goodbyes. Wonderful new friends, will I ever see you again? Cathy followed me down the gravel river road and we stopped for yummy shrimp baskets at the Tav. Yes, they serve really good shrimp!

Then we stopped at my Sheep Crik place. Those daffodils I planted last fall are all blooming.

Later, back home on Prairie Creek, I signed a copy of my book for Cathy, and she met Doug with a hug. Of course my border collie Halley was ecstatic to see me!

After unpacking, I thawed out two of those 4-H hogs' hams, which I stuck in the oven around 4:00 a.m. Easter Sunday morning. Then, by the Grace of God, I made it to church before the 8:00 o'clock Sunrise Service, early enough to help Ben Boswell with the "Special Effects," which involved lighting candles.

All went well, 'cept the thing to light the candles went out, and, well, someone came to the rescue, and the candles eventually got lit. First I broke the rope that rings the bell, and now this!

Three-day cattle drive. Angie Nash and Duane Van Leuven bring up the rear of the herd of Marr Flat cattle being trailed from Enterprise to Big Sheep Creek near Imnaha.

Sunlight streamed through the stained glass windows, and the service turned out to be most memorable. Thanks, Ben.

Then it was home to load those steaming hams and other picnic stuff into the car, and head to my Sheep Creek place, where Doug appeared later, bearing chairs and the horseshoe pitching set. Around 2:30 nearly 30 members of our family, plus friends, gathered for an Easter potluck.

April 16—I drove down along Sheep Creek, parked my car at Jenny Moore's place, and caught up to son Todd's annual spring trailing of his cows and calves to Big Sheep Canyon. It was a beautiful morning. Halley joined the other cow dogs and enjoyed working with them. Wild Sarvis and arrowleaf balsamroot bloomed on the canyon sides, and Sheep Creek splashed happily alongside the road.

I did some photographing and, when the cattle single-filed across the bridge that spans the creek just below the confluence, Halley and I veered off to my place. A fine warm rain began to fall just as the last of 320 head trailed out of sight, the end of a three-day drive that began at the old Snyder ranch near Enterprise.

Earlier I had visited briefly with Jenny's mom, Myrna, who'd been feeding their cattle near Bear Gulch. Also waved to Maya Lowe driving the Imnaha school bus. At my place the cherry trees were in full bloom, as well as the flowering quince. Leafing out willows and cottonwoods were a welcome sight.

After spending several hours working around the place, I hitched a ride with Myrna Moore back to my car.

April 17—Attended grandson Buck's branding at Stangel's buffalo corrals off the North Highway.

April 18—Doug and I arrived at those same Stangel's corrals again this morning, to help Buck haul his calves to Swamp Creek. Large cattle trucks, one owned my Danny Baremore of Wallowa, transported the cows. I visited briefly with Danny, inquiring about his mom, Ruth, Wallowa County's number one cowgirl, an amazing woman. I must visit my old friend soon. Hi there, Ruth!

Rain threatened as the cows and calves "mothered up." Buck's dad, Bill, who'd driven over from Challis, Idaho, to help with the branding and turning out, was enjoying being with his son in this beautiful meadow, watching the cows graze the holding pasture there on Swamp Creek. Buttercups dotted the meadow and Elk Mountain dominated the background.

Doug treated everyone to freshly-baked apple fritters he'd purchased earlier at our local Cloud Nine Bakery. Buck and Bill would spend the next three days trailing the pairs to Buck's Swamp Creek Allotment, which runs into Joseph Creek, in steep canyon country, big country, where they will spend the summer.

As we left it began to rain. Good for the grass.

April 20—I spent the morning building a huge potato salad for son Todd's branding the next day up Big Sheep. That evening my friend Pat and I spent the night at my cabin, and the next morning we hiked up the road to Blue Meadow. The morning was hot and we were glad when Doug, who'd picked up my potato salad and Pat's pie, stopped to give us a ride.

As usual, cowboys and their families converged from miles around, and the crew was just finishing working the cows. The aroma of roasting beef permeated the air, as the local portable bar-b-cue wagon was parked in the meadow. Lots of photographers lined the fences, and this grandma was happy as many other family were in attendance. Great-grandchildren ran around, greatly entertained by frogs in the water trough, or riding their pony. Daughter-in-law Angie and her crew served up the salads and provided buns to build beef sandwiches to the hungry crew.

Pat and I left with Doug early in the afternoon, as Pat was scheduled to play her flute at the old time country dance that evening. I lingered at the cabin, resting and relaxing. It was after six when the last cowboy's trailer rumbled across the bridge, a long day for the cowboys and cowgirls.

April 21—After church this morning, I joined cowgirls Ryya and Lexie in Mad Mary's, then rode to Lostine with Jane Wiggins, Maggie Vali, and Jo Bollman to attend the Mid-Valley Theatre Company's performance of "The Music Man."

Let me tell you, we are so lucky to have Kate Loftus living here. She and her helpers staged one of the most ambitious plays ever, and it was a smash. Standing room only. Held in the old Lostine school gym, this production was their 24th, and more than 31,000 volunteer hours have been recorded since they began in 1995—5,000 hours on this show alone. I've been humming "76 Trombones" ever since.

We lost another old-timer last week. 95-year-old Marvin Dawson, better known at "Mutt." A fine old cowboy. A real cowboy. He lived a good life.

April 25—Can this be April? It's over 70 degrees this afternoon, and earlier in the week temperatures soared into the 80s. What gives? A warm wind blows across Prairie Creek this afternoon, drying out all those fields our neighbors seeded late into the night, to beat those predicted rains. Rains that never came, in spite of dramatic thunder heads and flashes of heat lightning over Hells Canyon. We remember last spring when everything was rain, rain, rain. We wait and wonder...what next?

A pair of red tail hawks is building a nest in one of the ancient willows growing alongside the irrigation ditch in our old horse pasture. My Jerz and Rhubarb are grazing the succulent new grasses in the cow pasture, while Leap, now a steer, soaks up the sun in his own enclosure.

Every morning and evening I attempt to lure my Jerz into the milking parlour with grain. I say attempt, as most times—with a great deal of patience—I am successful. Then there are other times, when I simply run out of time, and then my independent little heifer wins. The stanchion is the problem. She doesn't like it! The only way she'll put her head in that wooden contraption is for me to lead her in. Naturally, when my wily little cow sees me coming at her with a halter, she takes off for the West 20.

It's especially frustrating on Tuesday mornings, when I'm scheduled to be in Enterprise for our writer's group. She senses my urgency, and I resent having to hurry through my chores. Being in the cow barn provides much-needed solace, an escape from my busy life. It's a link to my childhood. Quite simply, I love my cows.

I envy my bovine friends. They live on "cow time", which is to say they have no sense of time. They aren't always rushing hither and thither. Their needs are simple, and provided by man...or, in this case, woman. I'm beginning to think my Jerz is smarter than me. Perhaps she's trying to tell me something. Like, stop to smell the cow barn, or something like that. So my first calf heifer and I blunder along. If I'm relaxed, Fawn trots right in. If I'm hurried, she stands at the open door, chewing her cud!

Meanwhile Leap, penned behind us, drools in anticipation of his breakfast. In due time mamma warily wanders inside, whereupon I come out of hiding and shut the door. Long story short, I emerge carrying a bucket of rich Jersey milk. Milking three times a week usually supplies our needs, unless I plan on making ice cream, cheese or butter. Since I don't milk all four quarters, Leap finishes up my job.

However, just when we are establishing a routine, my Jerz comes up with another trick. I'm not tied to night and morning milkings...Leap takes care of that! And if I must be gone, he's happily turned out to pasture with mom. Meanwhile, Rhubarb, the black heifer calf son Todd gave me, now weighs around 1200 lbs and appears to be pregnant, and making up an udder.

Well, wouldn't ya know, my good-natured Gelbvieh comes lumbering into the barn without so much as a hidey-ho, just pokes her head in the stanchion and slurps Fawn's expensive molasses-flavored grain in two swipes of her enormous black tongue. Rhubarb isn't a milk cow—she's a beef cow. So now I must separate these two "buds" before milking time. Like I say, cows have always been part of my life. They provides entertainment, exercise, and nutritious milk.

Discovered a second family of kittens in the flower bed. Halley is shedding, and another hen is setting. Cousin Grady Bronson, who works at the local feed store, says baby chicks are coming soon.

We've been enjoying asparagus from the garden. Also an abundance of fresh eggs. There are a few potatoes left in the cellar, and I dug the last of the carrots before Tina roto-tilled the garden this week. A large area out front has been seeded to wildflowers, and Doug mowed the lawn yesterday. Spring has sprung!

April 26—4:45 p.m. Well, here I am, down at my cabin writing studio on Sheep Creek. However, I am just now beginning to write. You see, Doug and I have invited family and friends to a get-together on Saturday, and today is Thursday. And, well, the place needed tidying up.

I didn't leave Prairie Creek until noon. First I ran errands in Joseph, then, being starved, stopped at the Cheyenne Cafe for some nourishment. Finally on my way, I drove in a soft April rain, followed by a downpour, to Sheep Creek.

Along the way I noticed how Sheep Creek was rising, and by the time I got here the waters had been swollen by the confluences of Devils

Gulch, Bear Gulch, and, of course, Big Sheep, which is just up the creek from here. As I write, the chocolate-colored snowmelt swirls past, only a few yards away and visible through my screen porch. The waters are bank-to-bank and rising.

The thirsty canyons are drinking up the moisture, my lilacs are blooming, and spent cherry blossoms litter the lawn. I can see cows grazing the green canyon sides across the road. Halley, curled up on the porch, watches me write. The only sounds come from the rushing water and the popping and snapping of my wood cookstove. It's cozy and warm here, far away from the madding crowd. Through a curtain of rain I glimpse the Magic Garden's green manure crop of vetch and rye, and anticipate next month's planting day.

I've been invited to the Writer's Retreat on the Upper Imnaha for supper. Must get ready to leave. Ought to be exciting seeing the Imnaha at flood stage, and walking across that swinging bridge to visit old friends. However that will be a story for another time.

April 28—As planned, our old gang converged down here at Sheep Creek for one of our annual get-togethers. It turned out well, albeit a bit too chilly to eat outside. Daughter Lori and hubby Larry drove over from Richland, Washington, to join us. Larry cranked the ice cream freezer, and that batch was especially yummy, 'cause earlier I'd cooked a custard using Jersey cream and six of my fresh eggs.

I seared two Marr Flat Natural Beef roasts with onions, garlic and carrots in my dutch oven, then fired up my wood cook stove and cooked them in the oven on low heat for several hours. Our guests supplied salads and rolls, and I boiled up a pot of cowboy coffee to go with the ice cream. A jolly time was had by all.

The afternoon warmed enough for a walk up Big Sheep to visit neighbors. Arrowleaf balsamroot, pink phlox, yellow bells and sarvis bloomed among the bunch grasses. We stopped along the way to smell the lilacs, savoring the full flush of canyon spring time.

Last week Doug and I hauled three trailer loads of cows and calves to the Kiser Corrals on the Divide for son Todd. Todd and his cowboy Pat also hauled several loads. It was a cold windy morning out on that high grassy plateau, but the views of the distant Wallowas, and old homesteads were wonderful. Todd told us how those first tender grasses were being grazed by over 1000 head of elk. He tells us the elk move up the ridge as the snow melts.

On the last load Todd had stopped in Joseph to pick up an order of hamburgers at the R&R. So there we were sitting in our warm pickup

Tip Proctor, of Enterprise, drives a team of mules owned by his son Rondo Proctor of Lakeview, Oregon, at the recent plowing bee. The mules' names are Puss and Kate.

chowing down, when Todd's cell phone rang: "Hi, this is James." Our Marine grandson, calling from Twenty Nine Palms, California. This was surreal. I mean, here we were: James' dad, and his grandma and granddad eating hamburgers in a pickup parked way out on the Divide. We learned that James will be deployed to Afghanistan in July. Before he leaves he will be coming home. I'll bake his favorite pie.

The other day I visited James' sister Adele. She's home for the summer now, having spent the winter in Austin, Texas. She was training a colt, and came racing across the green pasture to meet me. Says she's been helping her folks with ranch work. She introduced me to an orphan calf she was bottle feeding.

April 30—1:00 a.m. Here is me, back at my kitchen table on Prairie Creek while the world sleeps and leaves me alone, typing the final draft of this column. After going to bed at 6:30 p.m. last evening, I arose at 10:00 p.m. and hopefully now I'm ready to put a period to this scribbling.

Those chicks came in at the local co-op. Six Barred Rock pullets are thriving in my chicken house, three each snuggled under Henny Penny and my other broody hen, keeping warm during these 30 degree mornings. Yep—frost again!

10:00 p.m. My calendar is so marked up with events I can't read

Julie Kooch, Enterprise, drives her team of mules to plow a furrow at the 14th Annual Lee Scott Memorial Plowing Bee.

it anymore. All winter we wait for spring, and suddenly we're there, caught up in a wave of seasonal change that demands attention, the days so full of living we fall into bed at night.

The weeks fly by and now it's nearly May. Samantha is growing, and being loved and well-cared-for by four of my great grandchildren. In talking with Sam the vet, I learn that Samantha's mother did die, after a valiant fight.

May 2—Doug and I attended the Hells Canyon Mule Days 2012 Grand Marshal dinner at the Outlaw restaurant in Joseph. A very deserving couple, Grant and Barbara Warnock of Imnaha, were chosen grand marshals this year. Duke and Rhea Lathrop of Lostine are the Honorary Grand Marshals. A large crowd, which included many past grand marshals, was in attendance.

Sondra Lozier and her committee are doing a great job as usual. The 32nd annual Hells Canyon Mule Days will be held on the 7th-9th of September at the Wallowa County Fairgrounds. It was fun visiting with Juana and Marge, past grand marshals, as well as Mike Brennan, who is now 90 years old.

This past weekend was the Annual Lee Scott Memorial Ploughing Bee held up the road at Larry and Juanita Waters' Ranch. Doug and I took in the Potluck Saturday night at the nearby Liberty Grange. Afterwards we enjoyed listening to the music of "Homemade Jam" while a passel of children raced around the old dance floor and several couples danced.

I arose at dawn the next morning. Milked my cow and did chores, then Halley and I hoofed it over the hill to the old grange hall, where we met Doug, who'd driven over. After a hearty breakfast of sourdough pancakes, sausage and eggs, Halley and I hiked back to the ranch. The morning was chilly, but the afternoon was lovely.

After church I stopped by again to photograph, visit friends, and eat lunch in the field. What a treat to watch powerful teams of horses and mules pull the old plows and discs. And now I must drive back up on top to Prairie Creek.

Later, as I was driving down Sheep Creek hill I met daughter Ramona and hubby Charley moving cows and calves to their grass ranch. And further down the hill I waved to son Ken, driving a grader, smoothing out the ground for a new fence, being built by Triple Creek Ranch, which used to be the old Cross Sabres Ranch. Times, they are a-changing.

May 9—Well, here is me again, down at my Sheep Creek cabin. I'm drawn to this place because it provides a quiet haven for my cherished writing time. All windows are open to spring. Borne on a clean breeze, the scent of newly-mown hay wafts through my screened porch. Not really hay, rather, vetch and rye, being pulverized by the mower. The Magic Garden's green manure crop.

From across the creek, above its joyful splashings, I listen to the thrumming of David's new tractor, and the whirring of its mower attachment. I watch lithe Lynn bend down to break dry mullen stalks, and sticker teasels. This willowy woman gardener has volunteered to help clean up and fence my former pasture, where young apricot, apple and quince trees are being transplanted. This fertile section of my property, relatively free of rocks, provides an ideal location for our garden: full sun, with ground that lies below my irrigation ditch.

What has been dubbed "The Magic Garden" is being expanded this year to include a large corn patch. We're going to plant Golden Jubilee, just like Bud Harshfield (now deceased) used to do in the 60s and 70s on his ranch, which lies just up the creek from here. We older folks remember how sweet that corn tasted...and waited, in anticipation, for midsummer, when Bud would drive his old pickup up the winding canyon road to Joseph, loaded with freshly-picked ears of corn.

Swollen with meltwater, Sheep Creek swirls past, on its way to empty into the Imnaha a mere three miles from here. The high country, that Big Sheep drains, is melting into summer. Tiny green fruit dangles from the cherry tree's limbs and I was surprised to spy a few apricots. We haven't had much of a harvest in recent years, but there appears to be a fine crop of pears, and several varieties of apples are in their later stages of bloom.

The Roopers have mown my lawn twice. Ross and Linda's motor home is parked in a grove of Locust trees west of the cabin. Like last year, the couple plans to come and go on weekends, to work in the Magic Garden, and irrigate and mow my lawn. They love it here, and, in fact, used to rent this house, so they are familiar with the irrigation setup, plus they provide much-needed help when it comes to troubleshooting water pumps and plumbing.

The air is filled with birdsong. Quail call from the blackberry thickets, noisy chukars scurry into rocky clefts in the canyon sides, chickadees flit about in the leafy grape arbor and feed on box elder bugs, mergansers fly low over the creek, and a lone crow hops about the lawn, gargling in crow language. Haven't spotted a rattlesnake yet; in fact I've only seen one on the property since I've owned it.

The air is saturated with the fragrance of lilacs, and a lovely lemon-colored rose crawls along the weathered fence that encloses my orchard. Am pleased to see cherries on the semi-dwarf Rainier son Todd gave me for Mother's Day last May.

Next to my famous "Rock Jack," snowballs have burst into bloom. This Rock Jack, built by son Todd's cowboy Pat Dougherty, was the winner of the annual World Champion Rock Jack Building Contest, held at the Stockgrowers Ranch Rodeo two years ago. It serves as a memorial for Dave Moore, one of the well-known Moore Boys, of fence-building fame, who lost his battle with cancer last year. The Moores are fine folks and live a few miles up the creek at Bear Gulch.

Wild blackberries are beginning to bloom, and the arrowleaf balsam-root is wilting in this unseasonable heat. We pray for rain. Native bunch grasses are maturing, the wild fiddleneck blooms orange alongside the roads, and Thornbrush shows off its brilliant white blossoms. The pungent leaf-scent of cottonwood, willow and red osier dogwood mingles with creek water smell.

Taking a break from writing, I wander outside along the creek. And, today, for some unexplained reason, I am remembering editor emeritus Virgil Rupp, who used to tell me to slow down and enjoy life.

"That's what it's all about," he'd say. Well, Virgil, here I am. Wish you were here to share.

Virgil, who left us years ago, loved to wander alone in the high desert country, just poking around, looking for rocks and enjoying the natural world.

I crept out of bed at 4:30 this morning on Prairie Creek to milk my Jersey before tending to other chores. My two hens agreed to share the job of mothering. Those six chicks have it made with two moms. I spend far too much time out in the chicken pen, digging worms and being entertained as the chicks play tug-of-war with those wiggly morsels of protein.

Yesterday son Ken hauled his backhoe over so he and Doug could build a new panel fence to replace the rotting wooden one. Which is really nice, 'cause now I can separate Leap from mom when I need house milk.

On Tuesday our Writer's Group met at Idella Allen's lovely home on Barton Heights. Where, in addition to reading our writing, we feasted our eyes on hundreds of blooming daffodils as we helped ourselves to cool salads and Idella's traditional warm-from-the-oven Rhubarb crisp. It was a lovely sunny morning, with Chief Joseph Mountain still clad in brilliant snow, luring us outside to eat at the picnic table.

I promised to continue the story of my trip upriver to the Fishtrap Writer's Retreat that rainy evening when the Imnaha was at flood stage. Well, let me tell you, it was something to see, what with logs and other flotsam bouncing above those high muddy waves. In several places upriver, water spilled over the banks and flooded low-lying meadows. The Imnaha was on a rampage.

The warm rain continued as I made my way over the swinging bridge at the Driver place. The island between Driver's log lodge and Mary Mark's old house was completely covered with water. Fishtrap's new Executive Director, Ann Powers, had prepared a hearty crockpot full of grass-fed beef stew, and I so enjoyed seeing old friends Tom and Woesha Hampson again. Anxious to be back down the road on such a night, I bid goodbye to my friends and tripped back over the bridge to my car—and it was still raining!

Back at the cabin, I could hear the roar of the water as it rose ever higher. Before I headed home I aimed my flashlight over the creek. So far so good. Both the river and the creek crested that night, but no damage done.

These past two weeks have been so full of living, there was simply no time left for me to write in my journal, so am relying on my calendar to recall just what transpired. The Jerz and I did eventually come to a compromise, and she now trots willingly into the milking parlour and stands with her head in the stanchion, if I don't close it. Works for me, and she never moves or offers to kick.

Allen Voortman and I have long discussions about dairy cows over the phone. Allen is coming for a visit soon, and I must bake him a rhubarb pie. Can't wait to meet this guy. We think alike when it comes to raising our own food.

May 15—Our "Write People" gathered around a picnic table at the Enterprise City Park. It was a lovely warm morning and we were seated next to the river. The accommodating owners of the Range Rider had reserved a table for our lunch, which was delicious.

This evening I attended the 82nd Annual Enterprise F.F.A. Spring Banquet. Sons Ken and Todd, plus daughter Jackie, were all members of this oldest F.F.A. chapter in Oregon. The meal, catered by Enterprise Mayor Steve Lear and served up by the Enterprise High School Future Business Leaders of America Chapter, was super.

The awards won by the Enterprise F.F.A. chapter were very impressive, as was the caliber of these Future Farmers, whose motto says it all: *Learning to Do. Doing to Learn. Earning to Live. Living to Serve.* I deem these young people to be Wallowa County's most valuable resource. Yours truly was especially proud when son Todd was chosen one of the distinguished service award recipients. Unfortunately, Todd was too busy tending his cattle operation to attend.

May 17—I was a guest of the United Methodist Church Women's annual salad luncheon, held in the lovely Wallowa Lake home of Janie Wiggins. After feasting on fabulous salads and enjoying views of the West Fork of the Wallowa River, as seen from Janie's large picture window, we were treated to a program by Fishtrap's Story Teller Kathy Hunter, who recently attended a storytelling conference in China.

May 18—I hosted our weekly writers group down at my Sheep Creek place. What fun we had! Perfect weather and time to write, stare up at the canyons, listen to the burbling creek, smell the clean air, and feast on potluck picnic. Upon arriving we were greeted by a resident rattlesnake, who slithered away from us as fast as it could. Evidently not a literary snake! We never saw another one again. The place was ours.

A tiny chickadee, totally oblivious to us, carried on with its nest building in the birdhouse, which was situated in the midst of our meeting. Quoting Emily Dickinson, *Happiness is a little thing with feathers that sings in our hearts,* or something like that. My covey of Quail announced their presence, and the resident crow hopped about nearby.

The weather was "purely perfect" and hasn't been that good since. We ate, read to ourselves, wrote, and read our work to each other, all outside next to the creek. We were seven gals and by late afternoon all had to leave, save Amy Roseberry, Leita Barlow and I. We three spent the night in my cabin. A long walk in the canyon twilight, a gourmet dinner, a bit of poetry, and a good night's sleep refreshed us all.

May 19—Out of bed at first light, I peered through the screen porch up Big Sheep Canyon to see a lone bull elk grazing his way around a steep, grassy hillside…followed by a Mule doe, obviously heavy with fawn. While making coffee, I glanced out my kitchen window just as the elk and doe disappeared into a steep draw.

A kingfisher, flying up the creek, broke the morning silence, and soon Leita and Amy were awake. Amy cooked breakfast by being creative with my fresh eggs, and soon we were packing up to leave. A busy day ahead for the three of us.

By 1:00 o'clock I was busy in the kitchen at the Joseph Civic Center, making lemonade and helping Janie Wiggins, who was organizing the salads we had asked folks to bring. The occasion? A long-in-the-planning Memorial celebration for Mike Vali, who passed away last year. Mike's wife Maggie, as well as their son Mike and daughter Monica, had planned this event so Mike's many friends could attend.

There were nearly 300 folks there, and a group of volunteers kept the food coming. Randy Garnett and his family catered the bar-b-cued pork, roasted chickens, beans and grilled fresh asparagus. Mike Jr. baked the rolls, and wife Dione created her special pastries. It was a huge success, and Maggie was touched by this outpouring of love for her extraordinary man.

For over 30 years the couple operated Vali's Delicatessen at Wallowa Lake, which is just now open for the season. Mike Jr. and wife Dione tend to the cooking, and Maggie, well, she's still the hostess/waitress with the mostess.

It was good to visit old friends Pat and Linde Irwin, who drove all the way from Friday Harbor to attend.

May 20—After church this morning, Doug and I drove to Imnaha to attend Wayne Marks' 94th birthday celebration at the Imnaha Church. Good to visit friends, including Lyman and Wilma. It was a gorgeous afternoon.

Wayne, a cousin of Kid Marks, looks great. Guess living on Imnaha all his life agrees with him. Wayne still lives in the same house he and Gladys lived in all those years. Gladys has been gone a long time now, but I fondly remember her as one of our Imnaha CowBelles.

May 22—Allen Voortman arrived with a milk cow and three calves for son Ken's family. Allen, who has been a fan of this column for a long time, phoned that he was on his way. This happy man owns the "Pride and Joy Dairy" in Granger, Washington. As promised, I'd spent the morning cleaning house and baking him a rhubarb pie.

This evening I prepared a roast pork dinner, complete with the last of our garden potatoes and gravy. Seven o'clock came and went…no Allen. Son Ken and wife Annie had come for supper as well, so as to be here to help with the cow and calves.

We were just finishing eating when Allen pulled in with his stock trailer, and two border collies riding on the bed of his pickup. Turns out he'd taken a wrong turn and ended up at Wallowa Lake. Since this was his first visit to Wallowa County, Allen had spent a good deal of time gawking at the scenery.

After eating supper, Doug went to bed and Ken, Annie, Allen and I went out to the calving shed to unload the cow and calf. It began to rain, and the rain on the tin roof was deafening. Ken and Allen were soaked through by the time the cow and those three calves were under cover. I mean, it poured down in bucket-fulls. After the cow was milked and the calves were nursed, Ken and Annie left, and Allen and I headed for the house.

May 23—Allen was up by daylight, seated in a chair in the living room, reading my book, *Four Lines a Day.* While we were eating breakfast, Ken appeared at the kitchen door. He had saved some milk for my chickens, after letting the calves nurse. He was on his way to work.

Later I acted as tour guide and drove Allen around the county, ending up at the Imnaha Store and Tav. Allen bought me a hamburger, and lobbed a dollar bill on a thumb tack that stuck to the ceiling on his first try! Of course we talked the entire time about COWS! And, since Allen had business with Mike Fluitt up Tucker Down Road, he had to leave.

"I'll be back," he promised. And off he went. This generous man is to be appreciated for helping my son find a milk cow, He and Annie have ten milk-drinking grandkids. Before Allen left, the rain clouds lifted long enough to expose those glorious snow-covered mountains. Allen's zest for life and love of cows reminds me so much of my dad, it was like I'd always known him. Our family really enjoyed meeting him.

May 26—Earlier this week—can't remember when, too busy—I began this column. Unfortunately, my earlier efforts have vanished. Apparently not saved by this "expletives deleted" laptop, that prefers to eat my writing. So, being as I can't bring them back to life, my words are locked up in this electronic device that is supposed to SAVE TIME. When, in actuality, I find myself spending far too much of my valuable time deleting e-mails, answering e-mails, or simply dealing with its whims.

Take yesterday, for instance, when I loaded my computer in the car and drove down to Sheep Crik to help plant the Magic Garden. Planting potatoes and squash was pure joy—the camaraderie of fellow volunteers digging in that rich soil, taking time to enjoy the beauty of the canyons, listening to the singing birds, the creek song, and smelling the sweet-scented locust tree's blooms. It was, indeed, magic.

Alas, after everyone left, it was time to resume my column, and the magic disappeared. Nothing to do but start over. But the sun was out, and a lawn chair beckoned. So, bird book in hand, I identified a pair of Western Tanagers, observed the comings and goings of a little chickadee building a nest in my bird house (built on a shovel), and simply relaxed... even took a nap.

Before I knew it: time to head home, supper to fix, Jersey in heat, Dave Parker due at 6:00 o'clock to artificially inseminate my little milk cow. It all got done and I fell into bed. So here is me, seated at the kitchen table, beginning all over again.

We are experiencing a typical May—rain, frost, sleet, hail, clouds, mists, cold, and snow at timberline. After all it IS Memorial Day Weekend. So what's new? We desperately needed the moisture, but not the cold.

The "boys," including son Ken, who has started up our handline sprinklers, are irrigating. Many of our Prairie Creek neighbors have installed center pivots, which move like giant erector-set monsters over Prairie Creek's fertile fields. Gone are most of the handlines that provided jobs for our children and developed character, as well as a work ethic.

My Jersey, having been artificially inseminated last evening, is taking it easy this morning. Lying down chewing her cud, as opposed to yesterday, when she was driving poor Rhubarb nuts. At the moment Leap wants to play with his mamma but she's not interested.

Yesterday was typical of the entire week: up at 5:00 a.m. to chore, pack a lunch, and head to the canyons for a day of gardening and writing. Home by 5:00 o'clock to make supper, and, aided by son Ken, persuade my Jerz to put her head in the chute gate, in the calving shed, so Dave could A.I. her. No way, Jose! Anything resembling a stanchion won't do. So I traipsed through the pasture to the milking parlor to fetch a rope halter. After tying her securely, the deed was accomplished with a minimum of trauma to my drama queen.

We, Dave Parker and I, are keeping our toes crossed in hopes that, in due time, Fawn produces a fine Guernsey/Jersey HEIFER calf. Dave, along with wife Shirley and son Jeff, operate the Highview Ranch on Alder Slope, where they've raised purebred Limousine cattle for years.

Their children grew up with my children, and Dave has been the official ABS (American Breeders Service) representative here in Wallowa County for 45 years. Amazing, isn't it? Wife Shirley just came up with that info yesterday, and Dave was dumbfounded. At an age when most men are retired, he still has the touch, and, in fact, had just artificially inseminated several head of Gelbvieh heifers for son Todd. Dave commented that he even took time for a hamburger in Joseph between jobs.

The Parker's daughter Carol, following in her father's footsteps, practiced some artificial insemination in Minnesota. According to Shirley, nearly all of those old Minnesota dairy farmers and their little dairies are a thing of the past.

After Dave left, Ken drove his newly-purchased milk cow, Clover, in to milk, before allowing three calves to nurse. More about this later.

Luckily, I got my garden here on Prairie Creek planted before the rains. Radishes, lettuce, spinach and onions are happy, as are the transplanted strawberries.

Yesterday several of us volunteered to plant potatoes, squash, and other veggies in the Magic Garden on Big Sheep. Later, the corn, melons, and over 200 Beef Steak tomato plants will go in. Students at the Joseph School started the plants in their greenhouse. They've had fun with this project, which was inspired by the Joseph United Methodist Church under the able leadership of project manager Robin Martin.

Come harvest time, the students will be eating healthful "slow food" in their school. As a reward for working in the garden, all community volunteers will be allowed to harvest vegetables for their families.

May 27—Now, it's Memorial Day. I arose at five to complete this column, but guess what? Yep—a gate was left open, and my Jerz and Rhubarb were mixed in with Ken's four yearlings. Leap was bawling in another pasture, and, well, an hour later, after tromping through knee-high wet grass, I finally got everyone sorted out.

They say exercise is good for the brain—therefore, this gal's brain is telling her to quit this writing and eat breakfast. Ken just showed up to milk his "humble cow, Clover."

Later this morning I picked a bouquet of phlox and tulips to place on grandson Bart's grave for Memorial Day. It was a lovely morning up there, in the midst of the Prairie Creek Cemetery, on a hill that commands a view of farm and ranch lands, and the east moraine of Wallowa Lake.

Doug and I were invited to dinner at Brian and Pat Adelhardt's lovely Wallowa Lake cabin, which provided a pleasant break in my busy life. Pat is a good cook and her meal featured prime rib and fresh asparagus. The weather was warm enough to sit on their patio before dinner. Pat is a member of our Writers Group.

May 29—Our Write People group carpooled at Safeway and drove out the north highway to Flora and beyond, to meet with our poet friend Cathy.

As in years past, we enjoyed the drive. We passed Stangel's buffalo cows and new calves, and Krebs' sheep turned out to graze their long green meadows; the herders and their dogs and wagons, the full stock ponds, the newly leafed-out aspen thickets, our snowy mountains rising in the distance; pink phlox, cous and larkspur blooming in the forests; and the not-so-ghost-town of Flora, not to mention the food, fun and camaraderie awaiting us at Cathy's old farm house.

There were eight of us, who read our writing to each other and tucked yet another precious memory away.

May 31—I attended, along with a throng of others, the book signing of my friend Lynne Curry, whose recently published cook book *Pure Beef* was sold out that night at the Bookloft. After the signing we convened at Gypsy Java for a feast featuring local grass-fed beef. Yum.

Enjoyed visiting with Lynne's hubby Ben, who was born and raised out Flora way, as well as granddaughter Adele, who helped in Lynne's kitchen, taste-testing each recipe included in the book. Lynne has done an excellent job of telling the rancher's story, as well as researching beef from birth to butchering. It's a beautiful book.

That evening, our young chef, granddaughter Adele, served tongue tacos she'd prepared herself. Delicious!

Earlier that day I'd visited the Joseph School's Magic Garden. David Martin was in the greenhouse helping students with re-potting tomato plants started earlier this spring. In the Magic garden plot, north of the high school, wife Robin was supervising the planting of their school garden. You never saw such energy, and those kids were obviously having fun.

Robin and David, members of the Joseph United Methodist Church, aided by other community volunteers, are taking risks to change the world, one person at a time. Their Magic Garden project, which includes other locations including my property on Sheep Creek, is really taking off.

Community gardens are sprouting up all over our valley, growing local food for local people. We have good soil here, and our folks are volunteering to make sure people are eating healthy homegrown food. The Joseph schools will be using these vegetables in their lunch program when classes resume this fall.

I spend every spare moment down at my place on the creek, to work outside and complete projects inside. Doesn't feel like work, really, being there "far from the madding crowd."

June 2—Our Writers group carpooled again, and headed out north to the RimRock Inn, where manager and cook Melanie prepared a six-course meal for us. The occasion was the book-signing for our Cathy, whose chapbook of poetry, *Always*, published by Finishing Line Press, has recently been released.

One of our senior members, Christine Anderson, who resides in the nursing home in Enterprise, was driven out by her daughter Kris and son John—a nice surprise for Cathy. The meal, served in that lovely setting, was truly a gourmet treat. Near the Flora junction, the RimRock Inn perches above scenic Joseph Creek Canyon.

Cathy Putnam's chapbook, as well as Lynne Curry's cookbook, is available at the Bookloft in Enterprise. Talked to Darlene Turner the other day, and she mentioned that the Count-Down to Chief Joseph Days Ranch Rodeo is fast approaching, June 29th and 30th. The trail ride on the east moraine of Wallowa Lake will take place on the 29th, with the rodeo on the 30th.

This year there is a $1200 added purse. Presently there are 8 teams entered, and they would like to have 12. The rodeo is a fundraiser for the popular Chief Joseph Days rodeo, and fun for both participants as well as spectators. Ranches from Eastern Oregon form teams, who then compete in various events. Team points are tallied at the end of the rodeo.

June 3—Nephew Bob Tippett, wife Merilee, of Pasco, and their Aunt Lorna Waltz, of Pendleton, appeared, as expected, at our church. Bob told me when he was a boy, their family lived across the street from the Joseph United Methodist Church, and he remembered when Rev. White let him climb the stairs to ring the bell. Well, everyone knows that's my job now. They say I'm the head ding-a-ling.

However, that morning I let Bob ring the bell, which was a nostalgia trip for him. The three of them stayed for church, and afterwards we all drove to upper Prairie Creek, where the Triple Creek Ranch branding was already in progress.

The rains slackened long enough for a beautiful sunny interlude. Our newly white washed Wallowas put on a show, as did the local cowboys and cowgirls. Doug, not feeling up to par, joined us for a while and then drove home.

Son Todd and daughter Adele were in the thick of it, as were other friends and neighbors. Grandson Buck, awaiting the birth of his son, was not in the corral roping this year. Son Ken showed up after church with his extended family, which meant 10 of my great-grandchildren were running around, which pleased this grandma no end. Daughter Ramona and hubby Charley were also in attendance.

Triple Creek ranch owners, Brent and Connie McKinley, aided by their family and neighbors, host a feed that is looked forward to every spring with wild anticipation. Namely, King Crab legs, thick and juicy grilled beef steaks, and dutch oven cobblers. The sun blessed us with its presence and the creek splashed happily past as folks visited and partook of this rare gourmet fare.

Earlier I'd baked a rhubarb crisp, which was added to the groaning desert table. There were side dishes too, scalloped potatoes, baked beans, a variety of salads and bowls of blueberries, raspberries and strawberries. A colorful feast, arrayed on long tablecloth-covered tables. Our mountains gleamed white above the green prairie. We who live here are so blessed.

June 4—Whitman College's "Semester in the West" class, accompanied by Phil Brick, Ellen Morris Bishop, and Holly Akenson arrived at our ranch. I have spoken to this group in the past; they are a joy! A great group of students, who hail from all over the U.S.

The class had just come off the Divide, where son Todd had given them permission to camp. You could tell they were pretty happy about being here in Wallowa County. While they were grouped around me on the lawn, in drove Bob, Merilee, Lorna and Doug.

After the Whitman students left, Doug and I climbed in with our guests, and we headed to the hills for another adventure. Our destination: the Zumwalt Prairie and beyond, a nostalgic trip for nephew Bob, whose father's family, who is Doug's family, settled much of that country in the late 1800s. Lorna, bird and wildflower books in hand, began identifying flora and fauna—of which there were many.

Storm clouds building over the Prairie provided spectacular viewing. There was an absence of traffic that day, and we had the Prairie to ourselves, save an occasional rancher in his pickup, border collies riding in back. Views of the distant Seven Devils mountains that separate

Idaho and Oregon, as well as the awesome breaks of the Imnaha, were breathtaking—due in part to dramatic cloud shadows racing across acres of grassy green Prairie.

We hiked the Horned Lark Trail and spied a herd of elk grazing the opposite hillside. Views of the Wallowas, and the sweeping grass lands provided endless photo opts. In Bob's new rig, we continued out past Zumwalt to the Steen Ranch and Thomason Meadows, places ripe with Tippett history. We were in "Tippett Country."

We picnicked in the meadow and listened to Doug's stories about his family's heritage in the "Chesnim" as Chesnimnus Creek gurgled past, just as it did long ago when Doug fished it as a boy. Then, on to Buckhorn Lookout, where the scene below was, well indescribable. You just have to see it for yourself.

The Indian paint brush and arrowleaf balsamroot resembled a garden there on the breaks of the Imnaha, and the views of canyon after canyon, clear to the Bitterroots, was amazing. Far below, gleaming in sunlight, snaked the Imnaha River.

However, having nearly worn our cameras out, we returned to Bob and Merilee's rig, to find it LOCKED. With the keys inside. After several unsuccessful tries to break the window with a rock, Bob picked up a boulder and got the job done. Not pretty, but we were able to return to the valley, where it was pouring down rain and continued to do so as we drove to dinner at the Glacier Grill at Wallowa Lake. I mean, it poured. A real frog-strangler.

June 5—Doug said his goodbyes to our guests the next morning at the Cheyenne Cafe, while I stayed home to milk my cow.

Our 28th great-grandchild arrived on this Tuesday. He's finally here! Cooper William, born to Buck and Chelsea Matthews, who live in Enterprise. He's a big one—9 lbs, 8 oz—and about as handsome as they come. Welcome to our family, baby Cooper.

Sisters Lucy and Katelyn are pretty excited, as well as Grandma Jackie and Grandpa Bill, who live in Challis, Idaho. In fact, grandma Jackie's on her way to Wallowa County right pronto. Grandpa Mark and Grandma Carol, of McCall, Idaho, were here for the big event.

Last evening, while cuddling this newest babe in my arms, I felt truly blessed.

Prayers for Lyman Goucher, who suffered heart problems this past week, and will be traveling to Spokane Monday for continued treatment.

It's been pretty wild around here. So what's new? I've done some culling in the chicken pen. My handsome rooster, son of Piglet, has a new home. And his OWN harem. He even has a name, which, at the moment, escapes me. I sent along three older hens as well, and well, they are laying eggs, which surprises me. I mean, these old gals had some age on them!

Did some downsizing in the kitten department too. Desperate, I called the Humane Society, who suggested sending a photo I'd taken of our five "darling" kittens out into cyberspace. Lo and hold on, a woman in Joseph responded and immediately took two, and then all I had to do was walk into Arrowhead Chocolates and another friend took the remaining three, as I just happened to have them in Halley's dog carrier in the trunk of my car. Whew!

June 6—Stanlynn and I drove down to my Sheep Creek place to ready the cabin for the Syringa Sisters, who will be here Sunday through Saturday. Busy week ahead—our annual get-together. Can't wait.

The wild Syringa in the canyons is in full bloom and the sweet-scented air will welcome them. We will be six this year, with the addition of Thea Pyle, Bob Pyle's wife. We all met in a workshop conducted by Bob Pyle sixteen years ago. Thea had gathered a cluster of syringa for our class, and Bob gave us an assignment to write about it, and we did...and we're still writing about it all these years later.

June 7—Son Ken's 59th birthday.

My garden was nipped by frost. An incredibly busy summer ahead. Grandson James flying in soon. A bridal shower for granddaughter Carrie on Saturday, the day I come out of the canyons. A party for James the next day, before he is deployed to Afghanistan. Same day as Father's Day, which is also Doug and I's 34th wedding anniversary. So, if I may survive all this...see you next time.

June 8—Those "June rains," so critical to the health of our grasslands, are happening. The Wallowas, shrouded in mists, peek out just long enough to expose their brilliant new coverlet of snow. Yep, like the old-timers say, "Gotta have those June rains."

Our hills, canyons, high plateaus, and valleys are a kaleidoscope of greens. The irrigated crops are lush: alfalfa, grains, peas, pasture lands and grain hay. Not so lush is my vegetable garden, nipped by frost two nights ago. Although it'll survive, as it always does, the potatoes and squash look pretty sad.

Not so on Imnaha, where gardens below the frost line are flourishing. My Jerz and her calf Leap, as well as Rhubarb, my pregnant Gelbvieh heifer, shed out and shiny, are grazing knee-deep grass, drinking clean running water, breathing clear mountain air, and shading up under the ancient willows when the sun DOES shine.

Son Ken's Holstein/Jersey milk cow, Clover, is producing three gallons per milking and raising three calves to boot under those same conditions. Ken stops by on his way to and from work every morning and night to milk his cow and let the calves nurse. Consequently, six of he and wife Annie's grandchildren—Ronan, Gwenllian, Kennon, Gavin, Lochlan, and baby Arianwyn—are thriving, with roses in their cheeks due to Clover's nutritious milk.

In his spare time, Ken is building facilities at home so he can haul Clover and her calves to Alder Slope.

Thanks again to Allen Voortman, whose generosity knows no bounds.

June 9—After packing up for our week's stay here, I ran into the Farmer's Market in Joseph to purchase fresh salad greens and asparagus. The streets of Joseph were lined with vintage cars, as the Wallowa Mountain Cruise was in progress, which meant The Friends of the Museum were selling pies. It was the first time in years I hadn't been involved with that project, but I was just too busy. However, I did purchase Diane Turner's two pecan pies—one to take to the creek and one for Doug, who would be without his cook all week.

Then I flew home, unloaded my produce, and took off in the pickup to climb Elk Mountain with Ken's family. No time to record this trek, but it was quite the experience, and since I'd always wanted to see the view from the mountain I wasn't disappointed. In spite of sleet and freezing wind on top I managed to take some great photos.

Home just in time to attend the Old Time Fiddlers contest in Cloverleaf Hall with Doug. I was able to make it through the night thanks to Randy Garnett, whose family cooked up a tasty meal, which centered around his famous bar-b-cued beef.

That day set the pace for all the days to come.

June 10—I drove into Joseph to ring the church bell and attend the service, then head down to the cabin to greet my Syringa sisters. Bobbie, Barbara and Thea, driving from Portland, arrived first, followed by Jessica and Mary, who hadn't left Boise until noon. There we were, another year older, meeting like we have for sixteen years, since first we met at Thea's husband Bob's workshop at Summer Fishtrap.

We were thrilled to have Thea join us for the first time this year. We call her our original Syringa Sister, as Thea gathered the bouquet of Syringa so long ago for us to write about in Bob's class.

The Syringa Sisters on the Divide. Wallowa is in the background. Photo by 6th Syringa Sister, Janie Tippett. L-R: Mary Smith, Teah Pyle, Barbara Fankhouser, Bobbie Ulrich, and Jessica White.

"Homemade Jam" a Wallowa Co. musical group perform during the Blue Mountain Old-Time Fiddler Show, held recently in Cloverleaf Hall.

Thea, who has been battling cancer for years, made our week special. She, like her famous husband, knew so much about butterflies, birds and other flora and fauna we were constantly amazed. Not only was the Syringa blooming, but every variety of wildflower appeared for Thea, as did every species of bird, every butterfly, and every insect that inhabits the canyon.

We ate gourmet meals, took long early morning and late evening walks, soaked up the sunshine near the creek, read our writing around a campfire at night, looked at photo albums of years past, and spent Monday night on The Divide, thanks to son Todd, who let us camp near the Kiser Corrals.

I'll never forget that night full of stars, coyote cries, and elk squealing in the nearby draw. Of course, Todd's cows came around curious and bulls bellowed, which made for a fun time with my city friends. The views of the distant Wallowas and the Seven Devils against that high grassy plateau were awesome. The quiet was so restoring.

We read from the book, *Around the Cat's Back,* as we were camping in the area where the book was written. We took a drive that evening to the Cat's Back and gazed down upon the breaks of Big Sheep. So much country, the gals were awed.

We made a hasty exit that next morning and broke camp early, as it had begun to rain. Not a cold rain, however, and I'd gotten up early to stir up our campfire so we could have coffee. Since we were so close to our Prairie Creek ranch, we all descended on Doug and took showers, then headed into the Old Town Cafe for a tasty breakfast.

Then back to our cabin on the creek for a wonderful week, which included helping plant the Magic Garden. I volunteered my sisters to help that day, when nearly 20 people converged to transplant more tomatoes, set out pepper plants, and plant melons and numerous other seeds. It was fun! And Bobbie even wrote about it, as she hadn't had her hands in the soil planting since she was a little girl. Bobbie's career as a U.P.I. reporter, and later as a writer for the Oregonian, took her on a very different path.

One morning I took them upriver to visit Barbara Warnock, who was out in her beautiful garden. Barb graciously invited us in to see her family photos, and she generously shared some of her first strawberries. Then we drove up to visit Lyman and Wilma. Well, we visited Wilma, but Lyman, he was busy swathing hay. 84 years old and still going strong.

On Saturday we packed up early and left the cabin clean so Sterling Allen and his wife could use it for a couple of days, then met for goodbyes at Arrowhead Chocolates in Joseph. Then back to our separate lives until next time.

Meanwhile, back at the ranch on Prairie Creek, things were happening! A bridal shower brunch, staged by my granddaughter Tamara, up from Lodi, California, for the occasion. In fact, her whole family, which consisted of hubby Matt and my great-grandchildren, Clayton nearly 17, Cole not far behind, and Halley Jane. Fun times. They put on the brunch and carried in delicious food prepared by Tamara for this shower for her sister, granddaughter Carrie, held on our front lawn.

Our Carrie is getting married to her Joel Bushman out on the Phillips grass ranch on July 14th, and things will be exciting, as if they aren't already. But it's all good, and we enjoyed seeing our California family, who stayed for a longer visit.

June 17—Doug and I celebrated our 34th anniversary, on Father's Day, at granddaughter Adele's home, where she staged a going-away party for her brother James, home on leave before being deployed to Afghanistan. It was an emotional time for all of us, and our prayers are with grandson James.

June 21—The Summer Solstice. James and his girlfriend Danielle stopped in. James wanted his grandma to teach Danielle how to make a rhubarb pie, so I did. Danielle was a quick learner and she made two, and then Danielle and I got to cooking and whomped up a meal, which consisted of grilled ribs, steaks and pork chops, oven roasted potatoes, a big salad and garlic bread.

By 5:00 James had done the grilling outside, and Danielle and I had the other food ready. Grandson Buck stopped by on his way back from the Divide and Buck's sister Mona was here visiting as well. It was one of those treasured moments with family.

June 23—Today is James' 26th birthday and also the Amy Hafer Memorial run/walk, where I completed the three-mile 5K walk again, before meeting daughter Ramona, Mona, James and Danielle at Mutiny for lunch. Then the final goodbye to James. Another emotional day for me. Hard to focus on a column.

Summer marches on, without slackening. The wedding looms; son Steve and his family are en route from Alabama to Washington where Steve is being transferred to another job. They will be here on the 5th.

My garden is flourishing, as is the one on Big Sheep. Fawn's AI took, she is bred, Leap is huge, Rhubarb will calve soon. Cooper is growing and attended his first rodeo on Saturday, the Ranch Rodeo in Joseph.

Things are hopping here in Wallowa County. See you next time, gotta get this e-mailed.

June 25—Well, I survived the past two weeks…barely. At the moment my life is peaceful beyond belief. Peaceful and quiet, save for the creek's song and the squawking of a juvenile crow. The sound of flowing water soothes the soul, washes away all those frenzied hours spent participating in my extremely full life, leaving nothing behind but memories. Cherished memories, captured in photos, filling yet another album.

You guessed it, I'm seated at my little desk down here on Big Sheep Creek. Through the window, ripening cherries glisten red on leafy limbs. The fruit tastes of summer. Earlier, bucket in hand, I walked across the bridge to the Magic Garden, where I was greeted by Sugar, an 18-year-old Appaloosa mare belonging to my neighbors Nathan and Joanna. Sugar grazes the high grasses growing outside the garden fence.

After pausing to admire the hills of squash, rows of potato plants, and those beautiful Beefsteak tomatoes, I made my way past our new corn and pumpkin patch to an old orchard. Carrying buckets of water, dipped from the irrigation ditch above, I carefully watered the newly-planted quince, apricot, peach and English walnut trees. Ever aware of rattlesnakes, I created a great deal of commotion to warn them of my presence.

Beyond lies the old orchard with its heirloom apple trees. Pear, cherry, plum and apricot trees are also growing fruit. However the apricots are rather scarce again this year.

The Magic Garden is responding to this sunny dry heat, so characteristic of Imnaha's lower elevation. While driving down Sheep Creek this morning I opened my windows to savor the prolific Syringa, whose blossoms saturate our June canyons with it's sweet "mock orange" scent.

Returning to my cabin, I ran into my neighbor Ken Hunt, who, along with wife Maggie, live up the road a piece. While we visited, here came son Todd rumbling across the bridge in his pickup, pulling a stock trailer, border collies and saddle horse in tow. Todd was headed up Big Sheep to check his cattle that are grazing their way up toward Marr Flat.

Hard to believe just last week we six Syringa Sisters spent seven days here.

June 29—While I was seated on a bench in front of Arrowhead Chocolates, sipping an Italian soda, waiting for the ranch teams entered in the Ranch Rodeo to ride down Main Street, three of those Whitman college students, who have remained in Wallowa County as interns for various organizations this summer, stopped to visit. Together we

Adele Nash, Enterprise, was a member of the Marr Flat Cattle Company team that competed at the recent Ranch Rodeo held at the Harley Tucker Memorial Arena in Joseph. Adele is Janie Tippett's granddaughter.

watched the "parade," the first ever for this Count Down to Chief Joseph Days Rodeo.

After waiting for a long time, we finally heard the clopping of shod hoofs approaching, and suddenly—they were there, before clattering on down Main Street. We cheered son Todd, grandson Buck, and granddaughter Adele, the Marr Flat Cattle Company team, who were all grins. And, since my young friends from widely scattered places had never seen a rodeo, I invited them to join me.

What fun to be with these young people, and what fun for this grandma to watch her family perform together as a team. Buck's little family appeared—wife Chelsea, girls Lucy and Katelyn, and month-old baby Cooper taking in his first rodeo. The Yost ranch teams took top honors, but all our local cowboys and cowgirls had gangs of fun competing, performing in timed events the things they do out on their ranches on a regular basis. My young friends were all eyes and ears.

Teams competing this year were Barremore Ranch, Circle P Ranch, Marr Flat Cattle Company, Quail Run Ranch, Bar K Y Ranch, Triple Creek Cattle Company, Skid Row Cattle Company, Yost Quarter Horses, and Yost Ranches. I thought my student friends would faint dead away when George Kohlhepp rode his saddle bronc and got bucked off, and ended up draped over the arena fence like a wet noodle! However, George, raised on Snake River, is one tough hombre. He threw his hat in the air, climbed down off the fence, and stalked off toward the chutes.

Last Friday morning son Steve and his family from Alabama arrived to hook our fifth wheel travel trailer to Doug's diesel pickup and leave for Union Gap, Washington, where Steve is beginning a new job. Grandson Stetson had come down with a nasty virus, and the trip had not been fun for any of them.

Last we heard, they were living in a trailer park until they could find a house to rent or purchase. They report it's very hot in Union Gap, too. Doug and I had spent a good deal of time cleaning out the trailer, as well as his camper, which is being borrowed for the wedding party.

July 2—I'm seated at my kitchen table and trying to finish this column. The pace hasn't slowed. I fully intended to have this completed yesterday, but as I was returning from church, Doug flagged me down on the highway as he was headed into town.

"Steve and Leslie Dorrance are here in Joseph," he said. "They want us to meet them at the Cheyenne Cafe for lunch." It'd been over 25 years since we'd seen this couple. Of course we'd visited Tom and Bill Dorrance many years ago at their ranch on Toro Mt, when Doug and I used to spend a few weeks each winter visiting my California relatives. Of course, Tom and brother Bill have long since passed on, and the years have disappeared with alarming speed.

So, there on the street in front of the Cheyenne Cafe, we met up with Steve and Leslie, whom we hadn't seen in years.

Since the cafe was full to the brim with tourists, we opted to drive to Imnaha for lunch. There, Steve and Leslie remembered seeing Steve's uncle Jim, as had we, seated at the Riverside Cafe, then owned by his daughter, Phyllis White. Of course, because that is closed now, and since renamed the Hells Canyon Road House, we seated ourselves at the Imnaha Store and Tav. We had a great lunch served up by Dave and Sally Tanzey's daughter, Heather, and Doug and Steve talked about the old "Dorrance and Tippett" times on Snake River, Imnaha, Joseph, and Crow Creek.

On our way home, we stopped at my place on Big Sheep. Steve commented that it would be pretty easy to just stay there. While Doug picked a pail of cherries, we walked across the bridge to see the gardens, then down to visit saddlemaker Ken Hunt. Steve and Leslie enjoyed talking to Ken about rawhide and saddle making.

We drove back up on top where Leslie and I raided my garden and put together a huge salad for a light supper. Son Todd, just off the Divide, joined us. We talked late into the night, and, of course, this column was put on hold. Todd had to arise early too, as he was having to swim his cows and calves across the creek to a new section of his Forest Service permit land. A big job, with an early start to beat the heat of day.

We said goodbye, as Steve and Leslie would spend the night at a motel in Enterprise and then head out to Crow Creek where they plan to visit the old "Pink Barn" and house site of Church and Minnie Dorrance, the place where Steve's father Bill and uncles Jim and Tom grew up.

July 3—Our Write People carpooled to Cricket Flat, where we were hosted by one of our members, Annette Byrd, at her and hubby Kimber's cattle ranch. The road in was a bit of a challenge, and I opted to walk. A lovely walk, and the final hill helped get me in shape for the Lostine River walk. As usual we all brought gourmet food, feasted, read, and had a Hatty birthday party for Annette.

On the way in we had stopped to photograph the sagging Mt. Pleasant church/school, which has an interesting history.

July 4—We were invited to our upper Prairie Creek neighbor's lovely home for a potluck. Kate and Heimo Ladinig's place is situated at the base of the East Moraine.

It was a beautiful evening, with the low golden light flooding the grasses, and ranch lands below, that comprise Upper Prairie Creek. We sat out on the patio with the mountains exhaling the last of their snowy cool breath upon us. I had baked a cherry pie that morning and hand-cranked a big freezer of ice cream, using some of Clover's rich milk, that son Ken had given me.

As of late I've turned Leap in with his mom. No time to milk. Thank goodness for that big steer calf, who gladly takes all Fawn's milk. When things calm down this fall, I'll go back to milking.

July 5—I enjoyed a great visit with old friend Barbara Dills who was interim director of Fishtrap last year. Barb, who now lives in Colorado is here to attend Summer Fishtrap.

Later this evening, I drove to Big Sheep Creek to take a load of supplies down in readiness for my sister's visit. Steve Dorrance and wife Leslie ended up spending two more days here in the county, after hooking up with son Todd, who persuaded them to take part in the "Pink Barn" proceedings on Crow Creek.

I talked to Leslie the morning they were pulling out to return to their ranch near Salinas, California, on Toro Mt, and she said, "We're getting outta town before we buy a place here."

July 11—Yesterday was my mother's birthday. Had she lived past her 95th year, mamma would be well over the century mark now. I think about her today, as I often do when I'm swamped with demands on my time from family, husband, chores and community. She'll always be my role model when it comes to coping with events that, at the time, appear a bit overwhelming.

I'll always remember how my mother, as calmly as she could under varied circumstances, handled with grace every emergency, every disrupting turn-of-events, as well as the numerous outcomes wrought by family dynamics, all of which demanded a lot of her precious time, time she didn't have an abundance of. She always referred to "time as the enemy."

Mamma was a dairyman's wife and mother of five. She canned fruit, led a 4-H group, and sewed costumes for musical plays that she wrote the script for and directed as well. These plays were performed for our small rural community at Mt. Pleasant Hall way back in the '40s. She kept the dairy records, paid the bills, tended the baby calves, and washed all the dairy work. Twice a day, for days. Then she returned to the house to wash diapers with a wringer washer, hang them on the line, nurse her babies, and cook a nourishing meal for her family.

Being the oldest child, and intensely interested in our Guernsey cows, the job of washing and scrubbing the dairy parlor was often my responsibility, therefore I was old enough to remember how hard my mother worked. Mamma could be relied on, it was as simple as that. I can't say I remain as calm as mamma in like situations, but I try. Because of her. Today, when the weather is HOT and there seems never enough time to meet the ever-increasing challenges of heading up a very large family, I yearn for her wisdom. Oh well, life is good.

The countdown to the BIG WEDDING has begun. It all happens Saturday. Which means every bed in our house will be occupied by out-of-town family members, which translates into yours truly washing sheets, making beds, and preparing for my two California sisters, Caroline and Kathy, plus Caroline's hubby Duane, to stay at my place on Big Sheep Creek. There's no room at the Inn here on Prairie Creek.

Thanks to my new friend Jacquie, who pitched in to disturb long-sleeping dust bunnies, who have resided under beds and in corners of our living room for longer than I care to admit. We are ready. Well, as ready as one can be, at a time when everything else is happening here in Wallowa County.

Naturally, July is the hottest time of year, as well as the busiest. The heat brings on the garden, which is bolting, in summer's tropical fashion. This means we are weeding, watering, and harvesting the first greens: spinach, lettuces, chard, radishes, beets and onions. How good they taste, and make us feel.

All over the valley farmers and ranchers are frantically swathing, raking, baling and stacking a bumper crop of hay. My friend and neighbor Lois Hough is making rounds with the hay rake as I write. Every afternoon thunder clouds swarm in, billowing up over the Wallowas, creating celestial palaces of alabaster, brilliant in their whiteness against the clean blue skies.

Monday night's heat lightning out North and over Hells Canyon created a light show that rivaled our 4th of July fireworks at the lake. We worry about fires. This morning a Forest Service helicopter flew over Prairie Creek.

Yesterday, when I was picking apricots on the lower Imnaha with my friend Eric, a Whitman college student who is spending the summer in Wallowa County as an intern for the Maxville Heritage Project) the temperature hovered around 100 degrees. The sun-ripened fruit tasted sweet and hot, like savoring stewed apricots. Earlier that morning, while I readied the cabin for company, Eric picked the last of my cherries. After returning to Prairie Creek with our fruit, Eric, who had asked if he could help me can fruit this summer, left, too hot to can.

Later, refreshed by a short nap, I got busy and canned a batch of apricot jam, then froze the cherries and remaining apricots. Finished up before preparing beef tacos for supper. Son Ken, here to change pipes and tend his cow, joined us later at the picnic table. Luckily, here on Prairie Creek, evenings cool down and relaxing on our lawn is a very pleasant way to unwind after a sweltering day of labor.

While we were at Big Sheep Creek we checked on The Magic Garden, which is thriving. You should see those tomato plants! Can't wait. Yum!

Every Thursday morning Robin Martin and hubby David drive down for the BIG WEED. This generous family who lives up the creek at the old Harshfield place have been such a help. In return for their labors, these children and their folks will receive a share in our garden's bounty.

Sugar, the little Appaloosa mare, has responded to grazing the high grasses growing around the garden, and appears to be content.

The annual Summer Fishtrap Writer's Conference is in progress all this week at the United Methodist Camp at Wallowa Lake. It's the first one I've missed in our literary organization's 25-year history.

Fishtrap's Outpost Workshop, the one I've cooked for the past three years, isn't being held at Billy Meadows this year. The week-long workshop is being conducted by Ellie Waterston on the Zumwalt Prairie Preserve at the Summer House, now owned by Nature Conservancy. Taking my place this year is my neighbor Nancy Knoble, who was being aided by Nick Lunde until he was called out to fight fire.

Tomorrow evening I will drive out the Zumwalt Road and partake of Nancy's dutch oven cooking in MY dutch ovens that she borrowed, and give a short talk around the campfire. Am looking forward to this experience. I was imagining how it must have been Monday night, out there on that big lonesome prairie with its wide open skies, witnessing that awesome display of lightning. Lots of fodder for writing.

I've been driving to the Wallowa Camp at the Lake each evening to listen to this Summer's Fishtrap presenters. Meeting longtime writer friends Teresa Jordan and Hal Cannon, Tom and Woesha Hampson, Kim and Perrin Stafford, and Mike Andrews, to name a few—all friends I've made through my affiliation with Fishtrap over the years.

Kathy Murphy, from Sacramento, California, called when she hit town, and we met at "Friends" restaurant in Enterprise for breakfast. I hadn't seen her since last April's Writer's Retreat on Imnaha.

I've opened the front door to a late afternoon breeze, which wafts the scent of newly-mown hay into our living room. Hough's meadow hay is curing, and soon they will be out with their loader stackers that spit out "bread loaf" hay stacks. It's a lovely time of year, and a bumper crop of hay, some dampened by passing thunder showers, but mostly going up nicely. Our neighbors are all so busy!

Center pivot lines spew out jets of water, as do wheel lines. Son Ken, in addition to milking his cow, "Clover" and letting the calves nurse, is changing hand lines here on our place. This, after putting in a full day working on upper Prairie Creek. Son Todd and grandson Buck, and son-in-law Charley, all in the cattle business, are equally as busy.

Last Saturday was the annual Lostine River walk/run. In the 70+ category I placed first with a time of 1:02:42—not bad for a 78-year-old. The walk was enjoyable, even though it was hot in the sun. Both the 10K and 5K course follows the rushing clear waters of the Lostine river into town, and my 5K (three miles) went fast. Cattle and horses grazing along the way in green pastures, birds singing, and wild daisies and lupine blooming alongside the road kept me entertained. After crossing the finish line I joined Maureen Krebs and Pat Cason to stroll through Lostine's annual Flea Market.

On the way home I pulled in to visit my granddaughter Adele Nash at the Six Ranch, and gifted her the medal grandma had won. Prayers for her brother James, now in Afghanistan.

After a refreshing shower, and fixing supper for Doug, I took myself out to the RimRock Inn, where I savored a delicious meal while looking out over the Joseph Creek Canyon. Once there, I joined friends Larry and Donna Bacon from Lost Prairie, Harvey and Ginger Gilworth, who ranch on Grouse Flats, and Cowboy poet Ken Overcast, who'd traveled with his wife and granddaughters from his ranch in Montana to perform that evening.

We listened to wonderful fiddle-playing by their lovely granddaughter, who, accompanied by her grandpa on the guitar, made her fiddle sing—not to mention, entertaining cowboy poetry and stories by Ken.

A sudden thunderstorm erupted and a warm rain fell, so Ken and his granddaughter couldn't perform on the outdoor stage. No matter. The evening fed my soul. On the long drive home, windows rolled down, I savored the warm summer smell of wet sage wafting up from Joseph Creek Canyon.

July 12—I must wind up this column, and get ready to drive out to Zumwalt and join the Outposters. My sisters will be here in the morning. The Big Wedding is nearly here! A very large family reunion in the making.

July 20—I volunteered to help Beulah Wynans in the raffle ticket booth at the 22nd Tamkaliks Celebration held at the Pow Wow grounds in Wallowa. It was a windy evening, which created a few problems when it came to anchoring things down, but I enjoyed watching the colorful participants perform their traditional dances and music, and celebrate their culture. This annual event is held in recognition of the Nez Perce presence in Wallowa County, the former Homeland of Chief Joseph and his Wallowa Band of Nez Perce.

Marine grandson Shawn, wife Maria, and children Jackson, Savannah Rose and Jacob remained after the wedding for an extended visit—an excuse for a family get-together. Son Todd and wife Angie hosted the picnic at their place on Alder Slope. Todd grilled sirloin and the rest of the family contributed salads and other potluck dishes. With help from younger members of our family, I churned a freezer of homemade ice cream. It was very pleasant there in the yard, and a good time was had by all. Baby Cooper was passed around from cousin to auntie and back to mom again.

Chief Joseph Days weather conditions couldn't have been more perfect. The action-packed week flew by. Great-grandchildren Lucy and Katelyn joined their young friends walking in the Jr. Parade Friday morning, and a good crowd turned out. I'd met other members of our family to attend the Wednesday Family Night performance of the Rodeo. Daughter Lori and husband Larry spent the weekend with us.

Our Methodist Church entered a float in the parade, and yours truly volunteered to ride on it. Wearing old-timey clothing and hats we sat on church pews and sang from our hymnals, while Claudia Boswell accompanied us on an ancient organ. Great-granddaughters Lucy and Katelyn sat beside me which proved to be gangs of fun for all of us. Throngs of people lined Joseph's Main Street.

On Saturday evening I was in the stands to cheer on Son Todd, along with grandsons Buck and Chad who all took part in the wild cow milking event. All I can say is it was WILD, and the cow Chad mugged must have been dry. Can't say those Corriente types resembled any milk cow I've ever milked.

On Sunday I joined Doug and other Tippetts at the Cowboy Breakfast, and chowed down on a grilled steak, which gave me the energy to walk from the Methodist Church, where I then parked my car, to the rodeo arena to attend Cowboy Church. Walking back in the late morning heat proved a bit to much, however, so I hitched a ride with neighbor Juanita Waters, who delivered me to the Methodist Church in time to ring the bell.

Must admit it's a relief to us locals when Monday rolls around and we have our town back to ourselves, well almost, as it IS tourist season. However, tourist don't often stray far from Joseph and Wallowa Lake. And, out here in the countryside, haying and irrigating quietly continues on our beautiful ranches.

We guess there's no finer place to live than here on Prairie Creek, where, during the cool of evening, we can watch the juvenile hawks fly into the ancient willows and feel the coolness of the irrigated fields and dry hills. Where we can savor the quiet and eat a meal outside, picked from the garden. Our many drop-in summer visitors constantly make us aware of our good fortune, lest we take it for granted.

We lost another old-timer. George Justice passed away on July 23rd. He was born December 4, 1917, which means he's seen a lot of changes. George was one of the kindest persons one could know, and he always had a smile for everyone. He will be missed by many.

The summer marches on, the days are shortening; so much to do, not enough time. Must harvest the broccoli and freeze it, and then there's those ripening strawberries, and peas to shell. And the watering.

Doug's nephew Mike, here visiting at the lake, was our guest one evening, the occasion being his 56th birthday. I cooked up a pot of spaghetti and served a large garden salad, which we ate outside on the picnic table. Candles adorned a blackberry cobbler which served as a birthday cake.

This year we only had one great-grandchild showing in 4-H. First-year Ashlyn made us proud when she won a blue/choice on her lamb, and then reserve Champion Jr. Sheep Showman. A few years back, or so it seems, son Ken showed his steers in 4-H and F.F.A., followed by his daughter Chelsie showing her animals, and now Chelsie's daughter is keeping the tradition alive.

There were many generational families participating in the fair this year. In fact, in most cases, the fair superintendents were former 4-H and F.F.A. members. Our County Fair is pretty precious, and the outpouring of volunteerism is awesome. It's all about helping each other and having a good time doing it.

Last evening Doug and I attended the awards program, followed by the annual F.F.A. bar-b-cue, followed by the Fat Stock auction. Local support was tremendous, and those youngsters have a head start on their college funds. I had the winning bid on Ashlyn's lamb, pretty expensive meat. $5.50/lb. Oh well, should be yummy. Ashlyn presented me with a loaf of homemade bread as a thank you.

July 23—Although not as cool as Prairie Creek was early this morning, this afternoon on Big Sheep Creek is quite pleasant. What a relief! We Wallowa Countians aren't used to such heat. Yep, I'm down here to write my column.

This place provides the seclusion I seek, a place where the world leaves me alone. And, after the proceeding days, I need to be alone! To collect my thoughts and spend quiet time contemplating the butterflies and ripening blackberries, listening to the creek, feeling the soft breezes that rustle the cottonwood leaves, and glimpsing the tiny brood of quail, hatched just weeks ago.

The Magic Garden is thriving. I picked a few zucchinis to take home. Mine "on top," are just now beginning to bloom. My garden on Prairie Creek is a wild runaway jungle of flowers and vegetables. Just inside the gate you are startled by a patch of blue bachelor buttons, while others are scattered among the potatoes. Bright golden marigolds mark the long rows of carrots, beets and corn. Cosmos and carrots share common ground, and several colorful varieties of sunflowers turn their pretty heads to catch the sun. All prolific volunteers from gardens past.

Volunteers, including children, weed the "magic garden" on Big Sheep Creek

Last week I dug the first Yukon gold potatoes, and we are enjoying chard, lettuces and broccoli. And, wonder of wonders: three ripe tomatoes, grown in a tub, placed in the garden's full sun.

As I was leaving the ranch to drive to the Magic Garden's "Big Weed" last Thursday morning, I checked my large Gelbvieh heifer, Rhubarb, as she was "making up" pretty good, and lo and behold, there was a little black calf standing next to her. Somewhat bewildered by such a SMALL calf, born of my very LARGE heifer, I parked the car in the middle of our lane, bailed out, and ran for the pasture. And what to my wondering eyes should appear, but a considerably larger calf. Yep…twins, both heifers.

In the half hour since I'd last checked my first-calf heifer, she'd not only birthed two healthy calves but expelled her placenta as well. When I arrived on the scene, Rhubarb was splashing her way across a wide, deep and rushing irrigation ditch. In an attempt to follow mamma, the smaller of the two was tottering on the brink. Nearby, staring at me with expressive brown eyes, the larger twin lay curled in a nest of high grass.

Scooping the smaller one up in my arms, I plunged into the water just in time to hand my precious bundle to son Ken, who, lucky for me, had arrived to milk his cow. After gently placing the calf next to mom, he sloshed across to fetch the other twin. Whew! Saved. That full head of water might have spelled disaster for my newborns. Not until both little heifers found a teat and went to nursing did I relax.

After a complete change of clothes I continued on my way. Just up the road on Doug's old ranch, I spied a white-tail doe standing in a grain field, tiny spotted fawns flanking her sides. 'Twas a morning for twins.

I left you last time just before driving out the Zumwalt road to the Nature Conservancy, which proved to be another "adventure." You see, the gate to the Summer Place was locked with a combination lock. And there I was on a hot evening, hungry and tired after a day of labor, and not looking forward to a mile and a half hike to earn my supper. But that's what happened.

Fortunately, a blissful breeze sprang up and the walk proved both pleasant and interesting. I enjoyed the quiet, savored the warm summer scents of waning wildflowers, and startled several Mule does grazing the green draws. Curious cattle, allowed to graze Conservancy bunch grass range, stared at me as I wended my way through the hills. Finally, I crested the last hill and looked down on the Summer Place, a scatter of old ranch buildings that lay at the head of Camp Creek.

The treeless prairie provided no shade. Further down the creek, to the north, a large barn squatted at the base of a hill. It was hot and the workshop participants were also seeking shelter from the sun. Nancy felt badly about the gate being locked, but had her hands full with cooking duties. Nick Lunde had been called out on a fire, and she was short-handed. There was no campfire due to dry conditions, so my audience sat around the picnic table. The dutch oven beef pot roast had been cooked on a gas stove in the kitchen.

I enjoyed visiting the workshop instructor, my old friend Ellie Waterston, and meeting her class of participants. Any earlier discomfort was more than made up for by being driven back to the gate by a descendant of the Findleys, an early Wallowa County pioneer family, who had signed up for the Outpost workshop.

The next day my sisters Caroline and Kathy, plus Caroline's hubby Duane, pulled in from California. We relaxed after a late lunch until more out-of-town family began to arrive. Niece Debbie Kollenberg drove in, and since all beds were taken, the five of us headed for Big Sheep Creek. We settled in and, because it was the first time my relatives had seen my place, they spent the afternoon exploring. Such precious memories were made.

We had shrimp salad for supper, featuring fresh garden greens, and garlic bread. We ate all of our meals outside, next to the creek. My sisters and I slept on cots, set up inside the screened porch, which reminded us of our girlhood summers so long ago, growing up on Oakcrest Ranch in the Placer County foothills.

Toward the early hours of the morning the intense heat broke, and for the duration of our stay the days were quite pleasant. At dawn we were serenaded by a family of coyote puppies, whose den is located under the tiered rims that rise above the Magic Garden.

Myriad birds sang the mornings awake. And, since my younger sisters are serious "birders," the two could be seen peering through binoculars or prowling under the trees, identification book in hand, identifying some rare bird. Our resident quail, western tanagers, and wood peewees, plus the dippers and Great Blue Herons that frequent the creek, kept them busy. Other fauna included a couple of rattlesnakes, one a mere baby.

Then it was Saturday morning, the BIG WEDDING day. I got busy in the kitchen and whipped up a hearty breakfast of ham, scrambled eggs, sauteed veggies, toast and apricot jam. We lingered over coffee, savoring the quiet, and relaxed. While gazing up toward Middlepoint, we witnessed the rising sun that sent brilliant shafts of light down upon the Magic Garden. A new day beginning, and us there to see it happen.

Early afternoon found us dressing for the wedding, then heading up "on top" to Sheep Creek hill, where we turned north onto daughter Ramona and hubby Charley's grass ranch. Following a long line of vehicles chugging their slow way along a rutted, grassy road filled with cow pies and rocks, we finally wound slowly up a hill and parked. Great-grandsons Clayton and Cole manned the gates to keep the Phillips cattle in.

We joined a throng of people, all walking towards the lip of Imnaha Canyon country. A July thunder storm was brewing, swirling mists partially hid the Wallowas, and the smell of rain was in the air. The surrounding view was stunning. Northward, blue distances revealed the soft outlines of The Buttes, landmarks to the rolling Zumwalt Prairie. To the southeast rose the jagged crest of the Seven Devils in Idaho, and a slow turn to the right brought into view the Divide, Ferguson Ridge, East Peak and the entire Wallowa Chain.

The views were awesome, but even more awesome were those enormous black clouds racing our way, their bellies full of rain.

The appointed hour came and went—no sign of the bridal party. Cars were still wending their way through the pasture. Everyone sensed the impending storm. For me, the matriarch, it felt surreal to see such a gathering, nearly 300 guests seated in chairs on the brink of the canyons with a storm approaching. Relatives from several states, all gathered at this place, waited.

And then, Marine grandson Shawn was escorting me down the

bumpy aisle to a seat in the front row, where I was soon joined by daughter Ramona, the mother of the bride. To our left stood great-granddaughters Halley Jane and Riley Ann next to daughter-in-law Amy, playing their fiddles. Riley Ann's sister Ashlyn held their music, which fluttered as a cool wind began to rise.

The ominous bank of clouds moved closer. Strains of Edelweiss, my father's favorite tune, floated in the summer air. Then, here came the bridesmaids, attired in blue, followed by great-granddaughters Lucy and Katelyn, clad in frothy white dresses, tripping down the aisle, sprinkling daisy petals. And then, during the lull before the storm, our lovely Carrie, curly tendrils of brown hair caught in the breeze, truly a vision in white as she clutched her father's arm, escorted to the simple altar where stood son Todd, who performed the brief ceremony.

Good thing it was brief. That cloud meant business. Because no flowers could rival the views, vases of wild daisies adorned either side of the altar. Then it was over. Joel kissed his bride, and Mr. and Mrs. Bushman walked toward the Wallowas. Granddaughter Lacey, official photographer, recorded the scene and took professional photos.

The crowd dispersed rapidly after the first drops began to fall. The wind rose, and the last folks carrying chairs to a stock trailer got pretty soaked. Great peals of thunder echoed over the high plateau, and lightning ripped blue-black clouds to shreds. It poured buckets. The road was a creek. Windshield wipers couldn't handle the deluge. Driving down Sheep Creek Hill, the procession of cars moved at a snail's pace. It poured all the way to the reception.

A feast, prepared by Randy Garnett and his Apple Flat Catering, awaited us at the Liberty Grange Hall. Bar-b-cued beef and all the trimmings. The old Grange hall bulged with family and friends, fiddles played, and young and old danced into the night. The wedding cake was cut.

The skies cleared and a golden evening light flooded Prairie Creek, providing the perfect lighting for photos. Children fell asleep, including baby Cooper. Our niece Debbie, who'd driven alone from California, left earlier to drive as far as Baker City. It was late when the four of us returned to Big Sheep.

The next day we hiked, relaxed, and played Scrabble. The rain caused the canyon primroses to bloom. Caroline picked up some windfall transparent apples in my orchard, so I baked a cobbler.

We invited cousin Janet and my daughter Jackie down for dinner that Sunday. I grilled the steelhead a friend had caught in the creek out

2012 Chief Joseph Days court: queen Kylie Willis and princess Emily Ketscher chowing down at the cowboy breakfast.

front earlier this spring, and we roasted corn on the cob. Duane set up my hammock, and we all took turns trying it out.

Every morning, at first light, we'd hear these strange sounds, which proved to be four baby Screech owls fledging on the lawn.

Time passed, and before we knew it, it was Monday, and I got a call from Doug "there's a bunch of women here, they say it's Book Group and you were supposed to make strawberry shortcake." Oh my! I was away from my calendar and totally forgot. Oh well—a rain check.

On Tuesday we cleaned the cabin and drove out to the ranch. That night Doug joined us for dinner at the Glacier Grill at Wallowa Lake. My sisters and Duane left next morning. I still miss them.

July 30—Chief Joseph Days is history, and that's why I'm late with this column. I was able to maintain my energy thanks to Allen Voortman's "Pride and Joy Dairy." Allen brought me a couple jugs of his delicious "salad bar milk". Thanks, Allen.

August 7—A cool breeze sweeps away the heat of day this evening. During the hottest part of the afternoon our outside thermometer registered 96 degrees. Too hot to accomplish much of anything, so after supper, which we eat outside, I relaxed until it cooled off enough to pick raspberries...again. This is the fourth picking. My freezer is filling with jam, along with frozen berries for winter pies and cobblers.

Between Doug and I, our blackberry supply is being replenished as well. Sheep Creek blackberries will continue to ripen for some time. We understand there's a good huckleberry crop this year, but haven't found time to pick. All in all, a "berry" good year.

This afternoon Doug returned from Big Sheep with two flats of black berries, and reports it was 102 outside while eating lunch at the Imnaha Store and Tav. I talked to Lyman and Wilma this afternoon, and they said it was 104 upriver.

Arose at dawn this morning to gather my veggies, herbs and flowers to enter in the fair. Yep, it's County Fair Time. Yesterday I entered my photography. We who love our fair should make an effort to help fill the classes. It seemed to me Cloverleaf Hall could have used more entries in the Land Products and Baked Goods Divisions this year. The joy of entering is simply participating in the competition, and it doesn't matter if you win or loose.

This unique small-town experience provides an opportunity to show-case one's garden, hobbies, or homemaking skills. My garden here is riotous with growth, bearing much more than we can use, therefore much is given away to our large family and friends.

The other evening I drove down to Big Sheep to pick enough black-berries for two pies, which I baked early next morning for our Museum Benefit Pie Sale/Contest held at the Farmer's Market in Joseph.

The Magic Garden is producing as well, under the able care of vol-unteers, who, like me, enjoy just being there. What a special place. I especially love picking blackberries in the morning cool as the sun breaks over Middlepoint, spilling light over the rows of corn, squash, melons, tomatoes, potatoes, pumpkins, cucumbers and myriad other vegetables, all thriving in this summer heat.

As I was weeding the potatoes, the timed sprinkler irrigation came on. Nothing like a shower on a hot morning to cool you off.

Rhubarb's twin heifer calves are a constant joy! I love watching them run around the pasture in the cool of evening. I've named them "Caroline" and "Kathy" after my two younger sisters.

August 10—I hosted our local book group today…and actually re-membered the gals were scheduled to meet here this time! Arising early, I'd baked shortcakes, which were heaped with freshly-picked strawber-ries and real whipped cream. This homegrown treat has become an annual summer tradition.

It was a lovely morning on Prairie Creek, so we gathered around the picnic table on the lawn to discuss our August read.

August 12—I've just returned from church, where David Martin announced that there was plenty of free zucchini for the taking, and if you didn't take some, better make sure your car was locked!

August 25—On the golden summer evening, a large crowd of folks gathered at neighbor Nancy Knoble's ranch just up the road, for the annual Wallowa Resources dinner and fundraiser auctions. Randy Garnett, of Apple Flat Catering, served up his juicy grilled local beef, and Beth Gibans, of Backyard Gardens, used fresh produce to create yummy dishes to compliment McClaran Ranch beef. Guests were seated at long tables in Nancy's large arena, in the midst of Prairie Creek's fertile farmlands with a view of our Wallowas.

Since I needed some shut-eye before our aforementioned backpack adventure, I opted out of the barn dance that followed in the loft of Nancy's Blue Barn. I understand it was a real hoe down, and the music was great.

After church the next morning, I returned to Prairie Creek to pack my car with food and gear for our stay at Sheep Creek, and thence into the wilderness.

Months in the planning, this adventure couldn't have gone more smoothly. Bobbie Ulrich, one of our Syringa Sisters, has always pleaded with the remaining four of us to include at least one overnight backpacking trip in conjunction with our annual summer get-togethers. However, for the past five years, various circumstances beyond our control have prevented us from striking off into the wilderness.

So, I suggested Bobbie meet me at my cabin on Sheep Creek in late August. We'd backpack into the Blue Hole, hiking the reasonably level trail that follows the Upper Imnaha River into the Eagle Cap Wilderness.

The weeks prior have been hectic for both of us. Bobbie was busy entertaining relatives at her cabin on Priest Lake, while I was in the midst of preserving summer's bounty from the gardens, making sauerkraut, canning pickles, picking raspberries, strawberries and blackberries to jam and freeze, as well as attending myriad chores associated with the garden on Sheep Creek, in addition to my own here on Prairie Creek.

On that Monday, however, Bobbie drove in around 4:30, and, after unloading her gear, we relaxed and later walked over to the Magic Garden and "picked and dug" our supper. I'd thawed out a package of great-granddaughter Ashlyn's 4-H lamb chops, and invited my neighbors Ken and Maggie Hunt.

Standing there, in the midst of the garden, Bobbie was thrilled to see the row of healthy cantaloupe plants she and the Syringa Sisters helped plant in June. Scattered among the sprawling vines we spied several green cantaloupes. After digging Yukon gold spuds, gathering a few tomatoes, cucumbers, eggplant and peppers, we traipsed across the bridge to my cabin. Bobbie relaxed while I cooked. She'd had a long drive.

Despite the smoke, which cast a surreal glow over the canyons, the evening was lovely. I grilled the lamb chops with roasted garlic, and baked the potatoes, peppers and eggplant. Earlier I'd grated coleslaw from one of my cabbages, and soaked cukes and onions in vinegar. I'd also baked a blackberry pie using those abundant berries growing everywhere.

Ken and Maggie walked down the road and joined us. Crickets sang their little songs, and the smoke cleared somewhat. We ate outside, next to the creek. The lamb was mild and tender. The veggies were a gift from the canyons. It was a special meal, and later we witnessed the nearly full August moon push its way up just south of Middlepoint.

After Maggie and Ken left, Bobbie and I did the dishes and hit the hay. A long day loomed on the morrow.

Amazingly, by next morning the smoke had cleared somewhat, but later reappeared when a hot wind began to blow. We took our time packing our backpacks, and just before 4:00 o'clock we headed to the Imnaha Store, where Bobbie was able to secure a small can of gas for her tiny camping stove.

The settlement of Imnaha was buzzing with firefighting hotshot crews, who had traveled from afar, as well as firefighting equipment. A large poster proclaimed the latest fire statistics.

Area: 68,569 Acres
Cause: Lightning
Percent contained: 40%
Total personnel: 810
Date started: 8/20/12

On the way upriver we stopped briefly to visit Lyman and Wilma, who were resting up after freezing corn picked that morning from their garden. It was still very hot, and the smoke lingered.

However, the skies cleared as we drove the long, dusty gravel road that winds along the Imnaha river, through beautiful ranch country where hay was being baled. Apparently the wind had shifted. The skies were a fallish hue of blue. We rumbled onto the pavement at the mouth of Gumboot and drove to Indian Crossing, our jump-off place!

It was shortly after six when we shouldered our packs and took off up the trail. Evening descended on the high country, cool and delicious. We savored the sight of Ponderosa Pines that grew thickly near the trailhead. To our left ambled the lovely wild river. We had the trail to ourselves.

At first there were the usual misgivings. Could we do this? Could we reach the Blue Hole before dark? Would we run into a bear? The sign at the trailhead warned of an unlikely encounter with wolves, and offered detailed instructions on how to protect ourselves. The measures were so humorous I almost wished we would see one, so I could throw Bobbie's camp stove at it.

Being familiar with the country, I remained confident but sensed Bobbie was a bit fearful of what lay ahead. I totally understood. My extraordinary friend was five years my senior. Not until we were on the way out the next day did Bobbie confess she'd had reservations about fulfilling her wish.

I set a sedate pace. Slowly, as we plodded along, using our walking sticks, I imagined the picture we made: two aging white-haired ladies, packs on their backs, attentive to rocks in the trail lest they stumble, stopping often to gaze at the river, the last of the Indian Paint Brush, and the purple asters that brushed against their pant legs... the anticipation of adventure written on their weathered faces, mixed with amazement at how good it felt.

Thus, when three fishermen returning down the trail stopped to chat, I understood their startled expressions and read their minds. We were not your usual sight at the end of the day.

"Better get on up the trail," they said, "Be dark soon. Nice to meet ya, good luck."

Our packs rode well, as we'd selected a minimum of gear. We passed the old pack station where, so many years ago, our crew had outfitted themselves before starting up the trail to the "Forks" of the Imnaha, when I'd cooked for Manford Isley's deluxe deer camps. In my mind's eye I recalled the sight of those large pack strings of horses and mules *clip-clop*-ing up that lovely trail amidst the glorious October colors of cottonwood and tamarack.

A slight rise in the trail brought us to a spring-fed creek, which we navigated by crossing a large flattened log. Earlier we'd entered the old burn, with its stark blackened trees surrounded by thick new growth. Often, in the quickening twilight, we'd catch breathtaking glimpses of the clear, cold river, flanked by gravel bars, which I likened to scenes in Alaska.

It was quiet, save for occasional rapids in the river. A sharp barking noise, which I guessed was a fox, followed us for a quarter mile, then ceased. We flushed two Blue Grouse and I wished for my shotgun. Fried grouse for breakfast would have been nice.

The sun sank, the cool of evening descended, the crickets sang, and finally, after two miles, a sign read, *Blue Hole.* We'd made it. High fives! Thrilled with this accomplishment, we slid out of those wearisome packs, made our simple camp, and walked to the river, where we heard a great splashing. Migrating salmon were spawning!

Before total darkness descended, we scrambled up on the rocks to gaze down upon the awesome gorge that forms the Blue Hole. It is here the salmon are trapped by a sheer rock face, thus blocking their migration further up the Imnaha. Far below we glimpsed their fins swirling in the last light of day.

A half hour later the nearly full moon slid over the low eastern ridge. Far in the distance, down in the hot canyons, we saw a fiery glow—the lower Imnaha fires were still burning.

The night was incredibly mild. We were all alone, had the place to ourselves. We savored the quiet, the river, the Ponderosas, the damp smell of ferns and mixed conifer forest. We sat on a log and ate our simple supper of sandwiches, earlier prepared, then crawled into our sleeping bags with only thin pads to protect us from the hard ground. The moon washed our faces.

The night was long. We imagined bears smelling what we'd eaten for supper. Eventually, the moon also went to bed, leaving the stars numerous and brilliant as the hours passed. Finally, light seeped in and we must have slept some. Bobbie said she heard me snoring SOFTLY.

Mercifully, dawn arrived. An alpine squirrel chirped, and I was up!

Leaving Bobbie sleeping, I scrambled back up those high rocks to photograph the gorge at sun-up. Back in camp I found Bobbie struggling with her little butane stove to heat water for coffee. Finally, after a few choice words—success! Bobbie has to have her coffee.

It was so nice being there, enjoying the wildness and the quiet, watching the salmon floundering around the Blue Hole. A golden mantled squirrel and an enormous hawk-like bird entertained us while we ate breakfast and stuffed our scattered gear into our packs.

It was after ten when we left our campsite and started down the trail. To our amazement we weren't even stiff! Stopping often to photograph and document our trip, we stomped the dust off our shoes at the trailhead before noon. We'd done it!

We stopped at the Store and Tav to report in to Sally and order a hamburger, which tasted mighty good. The settlement of Imnaha was still full of fire fighters, and the road from Fence Creek to Dug Bar was still closed.

August 31—After a busy morning of chores, which included making a batch of strawberry freezer jam, baking a blackberry cobbler, tending my chickens, preparing dried garlic for storage, salting my cattle, irrigating the garden, lawn and flowers, and taking Halley for a long walk, I'm finally sitting myself down to write a column.

It's not easy, cause there's a hint of Indian Summer in the air, and I find myself drawn outside. Fortunately, the prevailing winds are currently blowing smoke from our huge Cache Creek fire away from our valley this afternoon. Other times we've not been so lucky.

In addition to Bobbie and I's backpack to Blue Hole, which couldn't have gone more smoothly, a heap o' living has transpired these past three weeks.

As usual, summer accelerated. There was the surprise birthday party for son Todd's 50th, held at Buhler's Mt. Joseph Ranch, not to mention our weekly Write People's gatherings, to read and dine on gourmet lunches at Pat Adelhart's Wallowa Lake cabin and Maxine's cute little house in Enterprise. There was the CowBelle reunion at Mary Lou Brink's lovely ranch home, plus those drop-in summer visitors.

Doug and I attended the annual Stockgrowers marathon weekend, where we somehow survived the breakfast meeting, the Ranch Rodeo and World Championship Rock Jack Building Contest, and the awards/dinner that night at Cloverleaf Hall. Whew! That was a fun day, albeit hot and exhausting for us oldies.

The Rock Jack Building event was, as usual, a big draw. This year teams of two competed for the prize. Son Todd and B.J. Warnock built their rock jack in the fastest time, 6 minutes and 54 seconds; however, quality counted as well as speed. When the final judging was completed by veteran rock jack builders Tom Butterfield, Doug Tippett, and Dave Parker, the team of Doug Peterson and Matt Profit placed first, with Todd and B.J. coming in second.

Cynthia Warnock, B.J.'s mother, the first woman to ever compete in this event, teamed up with another son, Tyrel, and built a rock jack in 8 minutes and 50 seconds. Pretty impressive for this Upper Imnaha gal, who also serves as the Stockgrowers Secretary.

Cynthia Warnock, Imnaha, is the first woman to enter the rock jack building contest. She teamed up with her son Tyrel.

Ranch rodeo contestants included many of our great-grandchildren, children and grandchildren. New this year was the wild sheep milking contest. Great-grandson Cutter, who traveled all the way from John Day with his dad Rowdy to compete, had a great time. Cutter's mom Kasey, a veterinarian, had to work that day, so she and little sister Nevada couldn't make it. Once again we applaud the hours of volunteer labor that goes into making this all happen.

After the rodeo, I drove home, tossed a salad from lettuce I'd picked in the garden that morning, and returned to join Doug at the annual dinner at Cloverleaf Hall. The Warnock boys bar-b-cued tasty tri-tip beef, and salads were donated by us old-timey CowBelles. The hall was packed with young families with children as well as us old-timers.

During the awards, we were very proud and pleased when Doug's cousin Ben won the distinguished Cattleman Of the Year plaque. Dennis Sheehy of Wallowa was the recipient of the Grassman of the Year award. Proceeds from auctioning off the winning rock jack were donated to the Oregon Cattlemen's Fund to help those ranchers who lost stock, fences and grass during those devastating range fires.

This mom was especially gratified when son Todd received a standing ovation as outgoing president of the Wallowa County Stockgrowers. Our new president is Triple Creek cattle foreman and cattleman Scott Shear.

September 13—The air is fragrant with the flavors of fall. Crickets chirp all through the days now, and a soft breeze rustles the cottonwood leaves clinging to the tall trees that grow alongside the creek. I am quite alone, except for the family of quail scratching around under the blackberry bramble.

Last week, while I was down here on Sheep Creek, sitting in a rocking chair on the deck beneath the grape arbor, half drowsy with sleep, something caught my eye. No less than 26 wild turkeys paraded past me. There appeared to be several families. The half-grown turkeys reminded me of a group of gangly teenagers, while their parents were ever on the alert, hunting grasshoppers, eyeing the ripening grapes, and nudging their boisterous broods out of harm's way.

On my way down into the canyons this morning I passed son Todd's cowboy, Pat Dougherty, who'd just come off the Divide. I guessed he'd been up there since early morning, checking on the cattle.

Two nights ago Todd lost a calf on private land, an obvious wolf kill deemed so by our local Government trapper…and pronounced UN-CONFIRMED by ODFW. Ironically, and sadly, the calf had a name. Had, in fact, been named this spring, by a visiting student from a Portland Environmental School. The calf's name was Emily.

For several years now a group of Portland area students are hosted by ranch families, who include them in their daily labors. This student, who couldn't own her own calf, was allowed to name one of Todd's calves. It was a generous effort to bridge the urban/rural gap, and an attempt to educate folks from different lifestyles on where their food comes from. To better acquaint them with our rural culture here in Eastern Oregon.

"Emily" is now the latest victim of an increasing number of wolf kills. There are far more wolves roaming our canyons, valleys, prairies and high divides than have previously been reported. Wolves were known to have been in the area during this latest kill; another Divide area rancher, Denny Johnson, lost a calf a few days ago, and a Baker County rancher lost a cow.

Local ranchers have shown remarkable patience when it comes to dealing with laws crafted by folks who appear to have no conscience. Every time an animal is killed—or worse yet, maimed, to suffer a lingering death—there goes the rancher's profit margin.

More important is the stress created, knowing livestock you've protected and cared for in a husbandly manner might be sacrificed for the sake of bringing back wolves who never lived here. Something is wrong here. Canadian Gray Wolves are not indigenous to Wallowa County, These predators are strangling our culture like an invasive weed.

This past June, while us "Syringa Sisters" were camped at the Kiser Corrals on the Divide, Todd's cows and calves peered at us over the fence. My "city sisters," were enthralled by their curiosity, and the fact that these cattle grazed such as vast country, a country that is ridden by cowboys who spend hours in the saddle, checking their herds through summer, fall and early winter, constantly moving the cattle, to avoid overgrazing. It is a chilling thought that this calf was savagely attacked not far from where we gals spent the night last June.

Thank you, Bob and Helen Lundy, who live in Madras, for having your friend deliver that welcome bag of garlic. I cook a lot with garlic, and my crop was rather sparse this year. Bob and Helen are faithful readers of Agri-Times.

Another long-time fan of this column, Ruth Baremore, whom us locals refer to as "Wallowa County's Number One Cowgirl," still lives in her own home in Wallowa. I think of you often, Ruth, and hope to visit one of these days.

Another old-timer, Jean Butler, who was raised on the Divide, passed away on August 29th. Doug and I joined a large crowd at the Prairie Creek Cemetery to wish him farewell. Among other community services, Jean served for many years on our Museum Board, and will be missed.

Doug and I will also attend services at the Prairie Creek Cemetery on Saturday for our old friend Bob Wiggins, who passed away August 18th. I'll always remember Bob as "Clem Stretchett," a pen name he used, while writing letters-to-the-editor of our local newspaper, The Wallowa County Chieftain.

Bob's recounting about the "Side Hill Gouger," that elusive creature who inhabits our canyon country, is legend. If you've ever wondered about those terraced trails that wind around those steep sidehills, you'll find your answer in Bob's story.

Mule Days is history, and speaking of old-timers, we PAST Grand Marshals somehow managed to hoist ourselves up into Julie Kooch's mule-drawn wagon for another Grand Parade. It was old home week. Here came Fred Talbott, Merle Hawkins, Marge Onaindia and Juana Malaxa, Biden and Betty Tippett, Dick Hammond, and Doug and I. Arnold Schaeffer, still spry enough to climb in the saddle, rode his mule.

Julie's handsome team pulled us down Main Street, and delivered us back to the fairgrounds, where we later joined the Grand Entry. 2012

Grant and Barbara Warnock of Imnaha are the 2012 grand marshals of Hells Canyon Mule Days, September 7-9 at the Wallowa County Fairgrounds.

Former Hells Canyon Mule Day Grand Marshals in parade. Left to right: Doug Tippett, Dick Hammond, Merle Hawkins, Fred Talbott, Janie Tippett, Marge Onaindia, Betty Tippett, in back of Betty is Juana Malaxa, Julie Kooch in driver's seat, and Biden Tippett. Photo by Cynthia Warnock.

Grand Marshals Grant and Barbara Warnock, from Imnaha, rode in the wagon ahead of us.

Honorary Grand Marshal, Duke Lathrop, of Lostine, was unable to join the parade this year. Duke, battling cancer, was missed. However, wife Rhea rode in a horse-drawn buggy. Prayers for Duke.

As in years past, the Marr Flat hamburger stand was pretty popular. Doug and I ate our share. Daughter-in-law Angie, granddaughter Becky, and Marr Flat Cattle Co. secretary, Susan Hobbs, grilled over 500 of those thick, juicy burgers.

On Friday evening I attended the Max Walker Memorial Cowboy Gathering. The indoor arena of our County Fairgrounds was packed, and the event was a great coming-together of Cowboy poetry and music.

On Saturday another large crowd stood in line for the yummy Jim Probert Memorial pork barbecue, followed by the mule and horse auction. It was perfect weather for all those mule lovers, who traveled into our County.

On Sunday two other gals and I spent the greater part of the day volunteering as official judges for the Dutch Oven Cookoff, where we willingly tasted, then rated, the mouth-watering recipes prepared in those briquette-fired iron kettles.

This year Doug Martin and Matt Pelton, who competed as a team in this year's International Dutch Oven Society World Champion Cook-Off, and now hold the world title, were at Mule Days. They had a separate booth, where they demonstrated their art of Dutch Oven Cooking. What fun visiting them. I learned several new tips. Winners of this year's cookoff were the Henry Fork Hashers, who took first place, and the Shorts Family, who came in a close second.

"Bull Whackin' Kass" was at Mule Days again this year with her Old World Oxen Living History. Her 18-year-old 3,400 lb ox, "Ezra," was showing his age, placidly chewing his cud in a pen constructed inside the grounds. "Kass" and her oxen are popular with the youngsters, who are allowed to prepare food outside a chuck wagon as they learn more about life on the Oregon Trail.

After returning from my backpack to the Blue Hole, granddaughter Mona Lee called from Portland to say she and two friends would be up to spend a few days while attending a friend's wedding. What fun we had! What delightful young people.

I got in and cooked up a home-grown meal for them that first evening, which was warm enough to eat outside. Grass-fed beef, mashed Yukon gold potatoes, corn on the cob, coleslaw, pickled beets, and blackberry cobbler for dessert. A typical "I love you" grandma meal. Such a joy to watch grateful young people enjoy their food.

Before leaving, they spent one night down on Sheep Creek. Mona, born and raised here, enjoyed showing the canyons to her friends.

In today's mailbox I found a gift from Mona's friends—a box of Trader Joe's goodies with a heart felt note thanking us for our country hospitality.

September 14—This morning is the first time in four days we haven't had a heavy frost. My garden has lost its luster. Dead are the brilliant cosmos, zinnias, marigolds, squash, cucumbers, and tomatoes. Anticipating the freeze, I resembled a frenzied squirrel storing food for winter, picking buckets of tomatoes, squash, and herbs. Frost doesn't harm the corn, just dulls the stalks, so I froze enough to last all winter.

One afternoon I dug horseradish roots and ground them with vinegar to store in the fridge, lugged green tomatoes to the basement, dug and dried onions. Those pears I'd brought up from the creek began ripening, so canned a canner full of them, then made a batch of blackberry freezer jam.

The garden on Sheep Creek is thriving; no frost damage there. Robin and her crew harvest buckets of produce and deliver them weekly to the Joseph School, as well as to Community Connection and our local Food Bank. Those big juicy tomatoes we've anticipated are ripening now. Bacon and 'mater sandwiches make great meals.

'Tis Zucchini season. I've been using it in breads, meat loaf, spaghetti sauce and stir-frying it with eggs for breakfast. Picked up windfalls from our old tree and baked a dutch oven apple pie.

Doug and I are a year older, although we'd just as soon cancel birthdays from now on. As usual, our birthdays (one day apart) fell during Mule Days. All seven of our children wished us Happy Birthday, which is amazing, as their lives are so incredibly busy.

Our writer's group met at Cloud Nine Bakery in Enterprise, then treated me to lunch at the Range Rider. Good food, good times. Thanks gals!

On some days our valleys and canyons are cloaked in a smoky haze, as the big Cache Creek fire continues to burn. Containment isn't expected until it rains or snows. Mother Nature started it, and she'll put it out.

Short ribs in the dutch oven, smothered in garden veggies—smells like Fall cooking. Gotta quit writing, bring the clothes in off the line, 'n gather the eggs. Life is good!

Janie Tippett enjoys a quiet moment at the "Blue Hole" located in the upper Imnaha river. Photo by Bobbie Ulrich.

September 16—Doug and I invited daughter Ramona and hubby Charley to join us for dinner at Vali's Alpine Delicatessen at Wallowa Lake. The menu was Schnitzel, cooked by Michael Jr. and served by sweet, feisty Maggie, who has brightened so many lives over the years.

The occasion, to celebrate three birthdays for Charley, Doug and Yours Truly. In true traditional form, Charley "yodeled" for his dessert, baked to perfection by Dione.

September 17—Doug took off for parts unknown today. "Going North" was all he'd say. Alone in his camper. Said he wanted to have an adventurous road trip, which he did. After he left, I spread a map of the Pacific Northwest out on the kitchen table and attempted to track him. That is…whenever he'd answer his cell phone.

Nearly a week elapsed, and my man did indeed make his way north, albeit by a circuitous route. He called from St. Regis, Montana.

"Heading to Missoula," he said. "After I get the starter fixed."

On Friday, he rolled in safe and sound, with many tales to tell.

September 18—I was a dinner guest of Bernice and Frank Bernatot, who live on upper prairie Creek. Driving up to their place, I noticed a large plume of smoke billowing up behind Ruby Peak, which turned out to be a lightning-caused fire on Bald Mountain, only seven miles as the crow flies from Red's Horse Ranch.

Last I heard, that fire had grown to 1200 acres. The setting sun bled red into a smoky haze as we dined on sauerkraut, mashed potatoes and pork roast cooked to perfection in Bernice's German tradition. Frank's contribution was a warm plum kuchen, served with real whipped cream. Trips to my Sheep Creek property to harvest veggies, and water the lawn were frequent and relaxing, in spite of smoky conditions caused by those Idaho fires.

September 21—I cooked a dinner for our Navy grandson Josh and his family before they returned to San Diego. Roasted a beer brisket, found in the freezer, long slow cooking on a bed of caramelized onions and garlic in my dutch oven, along with mashed potatoes, pickled beets, and corn on the cob. Using the last of our windfall apples, I baked a dutch apple pie for dessert. Josh has been stationed near Fallon, NV for several weeks, while his wife Desiree, children, Richard, Ryder and Vivian have been staying with grandma Angie and grandpa Todd on Alder Slope.

September 22—The Autumnal Equinox. Doug and I drove down to visit Wilma. Barbara Warnock and her crew were still cleaning house and helping Wilma, along with Lyman's daughter Vicky Marks, whose husband Gary and son Michael had gotten the sprinklers going and were moving some hay.

On the way home we stopped at the Imnaha Store and Tav for supper. Saturday night on Imnaha was pretty lively. Since the fires were still going, the canyons and valley remained hazy with smoke. Still, we spotted the canyon's first signs of fall: numerous patches of Sumac blazing red against the hillsides.

September 23—I drove to Wallowa this evening, then out Whiskey Creek Road to Troy Road, thence along that gravel road to the "Pignick." I'd been invited as a guest to this money-raising event, sponsored by Slow Food, which benefits the Magic Garden. It was quite the affair, and nearly 95 folks drove those long miles out to Ferre's ranch to enjoy roasted pork-a-la-Steve Arment, and deliciously prepared "locally grown" side dishes.

Beth Gibans, of Outdoor Gardens, and Lynne Sampson Curry, author of *Pure Beef,* held sway in the kitchen. Sara Miller cranked-out homemade ice cream and folks contributed 15 homemade pies. There was live music, and apple pressing, and visiting whilst gazing out upon those rolling dry hills interspersed with Ponderosa Pines...well, you get the picture.

Long tables, decorated with zinnias and other fresh flowers from the Magic Garden, were set up on a rocked patio. The evening was warm, the sky cloudy and still, before a small breeze scudded across those dry hills, bearing the scent of rain. Could it be? It could—and did—rain. No one seemed to mind, however. The moisture was as welcome as the food. A few guests fled indoors, but most rejoiced and continued feasting.

There was no dust on that long drive back to Wallowa.

September 24—It's raining! The first appreciable moisture since July 14th. Our long drought is broken. The neighboring grain fields have been harvested, song birds have headed south, with only an occasional sonnet sung by a migrating meadowlark. The Owls remain as vocal as the coyotes on Hough's hill. As I pick the last ears of corn, the stalks rattle noisily, their brittle, bleached husks no longer green.

Bernice and Frank Bernatot showed up one morning to help dig and sack three varieties of potatoes, which we stored in the cellar.

Cattle plod past on our road, as many ranchers are out of feed. Some folks have been hauling water to their livestock. More wolf kills have been reported.

A melancholy morning here on Prairie Creek. All is silent as the parched hills taste this welcome bit of moisture. I wonder if it's raining in the canyons upriver, where Lyman and Wilma live...only Lyman isn't there anymore. He passed away Tuesday, September 18, there on his ranch. Lyman, such a presence on Imnaha all these years, is gone, leaving a sudden silent void hard to express in words. I suppose, when someone dies, that's always the way.

Those canyon grasses and parched rims seemed drier last week, as I drove the long dusty miles to comfort Wilma. Before turning up hill to the sturdy log home, I glanced at those two familiar pear trees, golden fruit still clinging to their limbs, and saw the ladder.

When you figure Lyman, like most ranchers, lived "on the edge" most of his life, it shouldn't surprise us, when, at age 83, he ultimately met his death by falling off a ladder. Never one to waste anything, Lyman was doing what he'd done every fall, picking pears to can for winter—not just for the two of them, but to produce many jars to be generously given to family and friends.

"As they ripened, we did a canner full each morning," Wilma told me over the phone.

On Imnaha, neighbors and family take care of their own. Barbara Warnock was at the house, hanging clothes on the line and sweeping floors. She'd brought a crockpot of stew the night before, and a peach pie.

Barbara's grandson, Clancy, was splitting kindling and filling the wood box. Donna came down from "on top" to help, bearing roast chicken for lunch. Other neighbors dropped in, left food, and hugged Wilma. Several boxes of pears Lyman had picked that fateful Tuesday sat on the freezer. We sorted them and stored the greener ones in the cooler for Lyman's daughter Vicky to take home. The riper ones were loaded in my pickup.

"I'll make pear butter," I said. Handling and smelling those pears brought back many memories of all those autumns spent helping Lyman and Mary can pears, peeling, coring, making a sticky mess on the kitchen floor as we stuffed jars with sweet white fruit and timed the canner, counting the pings as the lids sealed, our assembly line joking and laughing as we labored.

All gone now, along with those impromptu suppers when Lyman's son, Craig, would UPS fresh crab from the California coast all the way to the Upper Imnaha. And all those years when Doc Morgan came up from the Bridge to "seriously" eat crab.

Memories of earlier times came flooding back. I recalled hunting stories, told while cutting up elk and venison, and freezing the winter supply of meat, the work lightened by the presence of friends. All those fall cow camps, too, "cooking for the boys" and shipping calves. I recall my walks down to Wilma and Lyman's for breakfast during Fishtrap's Writer's Retreats, and inviting the couple up for dinner every October and April.

Am sure many of Lyman's friends feel this same sense of loss, missing as well the way of life he took with him. For me it means no more phone calls to joke about the weather, and that bikini Wilma found at Second Best for me to wear while I did the rain dance.

My mind's eye still sees Lyman every spring out there in his small garden plot, hand spading the earth with a shovel. Over the years he'd built up the soil with mulch and manure, and raised more than enough food for the two of them. I can see him in winter down in the calving shed, visible from the kitchen window, helping a newborn calf stand and nurse. Lyman was a good rancher.

Like Barbara Warnock said, "There's a time to be born and a time to die."

The family asked me to write Lyman's obituary, which I just finished. It was difficult describing his particular life. I detest cold statistics. Those who truly knew Lyman will understand. He was a man small of stature but large in heart. On the Imnaha there are many "Lyman stories," and on Saturday, September 29th, folks will have a chance to share some of those stories, because Lyman's family is inviting friends and neighbors to his ranch for a final feast and farewell.

September 28—I was invited, along with friends, to travel out of our valley to the Historic Elgin Opera House, where we attended a performance of the popular musical, "Fiddler on the Roof." Highly entertaining! Such talent we have in Eastern Oregon.

September 29—Doug and I joined a caravan of cars making their way over the dusty miles to Lyman's ranch on the Upper Imnaha today. Lyman's Memorial was well-attended, and his green irrigated field used for a parking area. Bar-b-cued beef was provided by Apple Flat Catering, care of Randy Garnett and his family. The Garnetts used to live at the mouth of Freezeout.

Friends arrived bearing a parade of side dishes that defies description. Tables set up inside the log home groaned with mouth-watering salads, beans, scalloped potatoes, rolls, pies and cakes. I contributed my apple pie. Oldie Western tunes, played and sung by two members of "Last Call" drifted from the porch.

Folks visited, quietly commenting on how many old-timer funerals and memorials we'd been attending lately.

Wilma, surrounded by family and friends, smiled at me, and carried on. Lyman's son Craig, daughter Vicky, and their families were busy making everyone feel welcome. After a brief blessing spoken by Wilma's brother, pastor of an Idaho church, everyone lined up to fill their plates. Folks ate outside, seated at long tables, or clustered on the deck.

The canyon gifted us with a gorgeous evening as stories gushed forth from friends and neighbors who'd made their way up onto the porch. However, many of us, who had been closest to Lyman, couldn't quite make ourselves walk up there.

Suddenly, all eyes focused on the appearance of a young gal from up Grouse Creek Ranch. Trotting her horse into the field below, she led another horse wearing an empty saddle. All was hushed as she rode down around the pear trees where Lyman met his death. Kicking her horse into a lope, she circled once more, then clattered out onto the county road.

As we were leaving, I glanced up at the eastern ridgeline just as the setting sun's last rays bathed the rimrocks in burnished copper. A fitting tribute to Lyman, who must've witnessed that sight many times there along the Imnaha.

September 30—Every Sunday morning I climb the stairs to ring the bell in the old church tower that graces our Joseph United Methodist Church. I like to think folks who don't attend church enjoy hearing the sound of that bell, ringing out over our beautiful town.

October 4—Early this morning, Wilma's son Craig, and his wife, Pon, drove Wilma to our place here on Prairie Creek. It was still dark. Hurriedly I tended my chickens, and then Wilma and I met Doug, Craig and Pon at the Cheyenne Cafe.

Later, fortified by a hearty breakfast, we went our separate ways, Craig and Pon to California, Wilma and I to Idaho, and Doug back to the ranch. I had offered to drive Wilma over to Grangeville to meet with her daughter, who was trying to locate a house for her mother to move into. Wilma didn't plan to spend the winter alone on Imnaha, and she was anxious to make plans before the first snows came.

It was cold this morning—21 degrees when I'd done my chores. The day warmed as we sped out the North Highway, however, and soon we approached the RimRock Inn, the solitary restaurant perched on the edge of Joseph Creek Canyon. This was an establishment Wilma, along with her first husband, Loren, once ran, and Wilma recalled many stories of those bygone days as we began our winding descent of Buford Grade to the Grande Ronde River. Many of us remember how folks would drive all those miles for a slice of Wilma's mud pie.

Then we were climbing, up and up Rattlesnake, over to Asotin, Washington, thence to Clarkston and Lewiston, following the Clearwater River onto 95 through Lapwai, up Winchester Grade. The miles disappeared into a smoky haze. We exited into the small town of Cottonwood, where we called Wilma's daughter Deb, who would meet us in Grangeville.

After looking at several places to rent, we ate lunch at an old restaurant called Oscar's and secured a motel for the night. We got the last room! The motel was booked full due to fire fighters and road construction crews. The town was filled with a smoky haze.

October 5—The morning dawned frosty cold as we drove out of Grangeville into the foothills, to say goodbye to Wilma's daughter before heading home.

October 10—Another clear Indian Summer day. No frost this morning, no ice-laced grasses under the irrigation lines, no frozen chicken waterer, and no frosty fingers while doing chores. A great stillness prevails. Save for the occasional bawling of my Jerz, who is enduring the emotional loss of her calf, it's pretty quiet here on Prairie Creek.

Activity in my kitchen is even slowing down. Tomatoes are canned, grape jelly made, and more pear butter lines my cellar shelves. As much as I enjoy putting food by for winter, it's a relief to be done. I detest waste, however, and budgeting time to preserve this bounty can be overwhelming.

Yesterday I dug a goodly supply of carrots, and today, I will cover the remainder of the row with grass clippings and dirt. Come spring we will dig sweet carrots that have wintered-over, protected from the hard freeze.

The Magic Garden on my Sheep Creek property got zapped by our sudden cold spell. The beginning of last week, our garden overflowed with orange pumpkins, ripening tomatoes, and maturing squash. Then, overnight, all that lush growth turned to a tangle of slimy vines. Anticipating that fierce freeze, Robin and David Martin and their crew, plus Beth Gibans and hers, harvested all the veggies the day before the dreaded frost. I was down there too, lugging my large baking squash to the cabin, gleaning the last ripened pears and plucking the fragrant Concord grapes dangling from the arbor over my deck. I'd seen those wild turkeys eyeing them.

The Magic Garden was a huge success this year, with over 100 cantaloupe harvested, along with buckets of tomatoes, cucumbers, green peppers, and zucchini, not to mention those pumpkins! A new plot of corn and pumpkins was added this year, and alas, there wasn't a deer fence around the area, therefore a small portion of that bounty fattened the resident wildlife. The Golden Jubilee corn that did survive was sweet and wonderful, however!

The leaves on my brilliant-colored Northwood Maple have succumbed to frost, waiting for a breeze to whisk them off the branches. Prairie Creek appears dulled by the prolonged drought, now followed by frost. Feeling a mother's sympathy for Fawn, my Jersey milk cow, I forked her and Rhubarb a few flakes of hay this morning.

You see, last Sunday afternoon, Joe Platz arrived to pick up Leap. Yep, Fawn's baby went down the road. Her sturdy Angus/cross steer calf lived up to his name when he tried to leap out of the trailer.

I'd planned to continue milking my Jerz, but changed my mind when I found she was nearly dried up. This will give my little cow a good rest before she freshens in the spring.

Doug has been diligently cracking walnuts to store in the freezer for my winter baking, as we'll soon be harvesting a new crop. He also mowed the lawn for the last time.

This "famous" octagonal barn built in 1906 is being restored by its present owners, Brent and Connie McKinley, who also own the Triple Creek Ranch in Joseph.

Yesterday I drained the garden hoses and stored the stakes that mark my garden rows in the pump house. Smoke from those lingering fires has retreated to the northern horizon, and we pray for rain. Stock ponds are drying up and the prolonged dry spell has taken its toll on the weaning weights of calves.

October 13—It rained lightly in the night!

Today is the annual "Apple Squeezin'" party up at Chuck and Kris Fraser's ranch on Upper Prairie Creek. The rain has cleansed the air and brought a crisp clarity to the bare-boned mountains. High on the slopes, still devoid of the first snows, the Tamarack are turning golden.

Allen Voortman and wife Cheryl are on their way over from Granger, Washington, bringing apples and some of their "Pride and Joy Dairy" cream for me to make a freezer full of ice cream.

Yesterday I baked a raspberry pie, and this morning I'll bake a mincemeat pie for the do'ins. Nothing like hand-cranked ice cream to go with those pies. More on the apple squeezing next time.

October 18—After a summer break, our local Book Group resumed meeting today at Fishtrap House, where we selected the book *Meadowlark* by Dawn Wink, a novel based on a true story taken from an early homesteader woman's diaries. The story is set in the Dakotas.

Yesterday I invited son Todd and his son, my grandson Josh, who was home on leave from the Navy, along with Josh's mom, Angie, and granddad, who recently moved here from Colorado, to supper. Todd had taken Josh cow elk hunting on the Divide. After their long, cold, successful hunt, they dove into my meal of roast pork, mashed potatoes, and sauerkraut simmered with apples, bacon and onion.

We finished with slices of the $275 Black Forest cake, featuring brandy-soaked cherries, baked by Carolyn Lochert's daughter and purchased by me at Zeb Ramsden's benefit.

Zeb is the little boy who nearly lost his life after suffering a severe reaction to antibiotics recently. The benefit, organized by locals, filled the Wallowa High school gym to overflowing and raised enough money to help this ranching family with medical expenses. Zeb, who sat in front of son Todd and me, grinned the entire time.

This week I also attended Heidi Muller and Bob Webb's latest CD release of "Dulcimer Moon," which was held at Lear's in Enterprise. It was a magic evening of music, and I recalled the night those two came to Sheep Creek, where we gazed at the full Hunter's moon rise over Middlepoint. Wonderful memories, wonderful friends, soothing music, and a great meal served there at Lear's Main Street Grill.

October 30—Our Write Group met at Cloud Nine Bakery in Enterprise before trooping over to "Bee Charmed" for soup and sandwiches. I returned to Prairie Creek to make caramel apples for our trick or treaters.

October 31—I baked a batch of persimmon cookies from fruit frozen in the freezer.

As tonight is Halloween night, Doug and I opened the door and were pleasantly spooked by a ghostly family consisting of granddaughter Chelsie, hubby Justin and their children, Riley Ann, Ashlyn and the twins, Jada and Gideon. Doug, as usual, was well-prepared with candy, so there were ample treats for all.

November 1—The first of November dawned frost-free and 40 degrees. This afternoon Steve Jones, of A&M Supply in Hermiston, stopped by with two boxes of potatoes, a bag of onions, and a bucket of freshly-dug carrots as big as my arm. He and his hunting companion were on their way to a much-anticipated elk hunting venture.

Steve, whom Doug used to purchase potato chain from over 20 years ago, says he's a big fan of *Janie's Journal.* We really appreciated his

The first snow to cover the Wallowa Mountains occurred during late October.
Shown here is Chief Joseph Mountain as seen from Prairie Creek

generosity, and I spent the remainder of the day dividing produce to give away to our large family. Thanks again, Steve.

The french fries and carrot salad I made to go with fried chicken for supper that night were yummy.

November 2—Frosty and clear when I stepped out to chore.

Late morning found me headed for Sheep Creek to complete some jobs in the cabin. Fall colors were at their peak, and the canyons resembled a watercolor painting. While sauntering across the pasture to check on my English walnut trees, 25 wild turkeys barely acknowledged me, apparently so focused on scratching and pecking bugs and worms in the freshly-tilled Magic Garden that they paid me no heed.

The sun was beginning to disappear behind the rims when I drove down to the bridge and parked at Doc Morgan's old place. I wanted to check on Doc's quince tree in his little orchard perched above the Imnaha River. It's a long story, though one I fondly recall, that began at one of Lyman's famous crab feeds.

You see, as the evening wore on, Doc and I commenced reciting poetry, our favorite being that ancient poem, "The Owl And The Pussy Cat." You know how it goes: *The owl and the pussy cat went to sea, in a beautiful pea green boat.* The poem rambles on, and then, *They dined on mince, and slices of quince, which they ate with a runcible spoon.*

Somehow we got to discussing quinces and runcible spoons, and that spring Doc planted a quince tree. After the next crab feed he went to the library and looked up runcible spoon...which, in the old English tradition, means a spoon with holes in it, or some such thing.

As the years passed, the tree grew and our beloved Doc passed away. Every time Doug and I drove past the little orchard, I glanced at the quince tree. This fall I glimpsed golden fruit hanging from the trees limbs! Hank, one of Doc's sons, who lives there now, had given me permission to pick.

So I thought of you, Doc, as I plucked those lemon-colored, apple-like quinces from your tree. Now all I need is a runcible spoon to eat them. Most folks hereabouts have never heard of quince, but my grandma, Myrtle Wilson, who lived in California, used to make wonderful jelly from this fruit.

On the way home I captured some great photos. Luminous cotton-wood leaves reflected on the waters of Sheep Creek, and castles of clouds built up in a cold blue sky. Our days dwindle down, like the leaves floating in the eddies of the creek, and we savor one last glorious spell before winter sets in.

November 3—This morning it was 37 degrees and cloudy with a wan sun. After a busy day Doug and I drove into Joseph and ordered pizza at Embers Brew Haus for supper.

November 4—We remembered to set our clocks back. I baked a mincemeat pie for Doug and son Todd.

Made it to church to ring the bell, and it was so mild I didn't need a coat. I returned to Prairie Creek to find Doug gone. He returned later that afternoon with walnuts he'd picked under the trees at Sheep Creek. The nuts are now drying under the wood stove.

Good to hear from grandson James in Afghanistan. Our prayers are constantly with him and his comrades.

November 7—A sprinkling of cold rain fell as I walked down to feed my heifers this morning. The twins, wearing their winter coats, came bumbling across the pasture to nibble sweet clover hay. It's probably snowing near timberline, at the base of our cloud-shrouded mountains.

Yesterday's wild winds stripped more leaves from our willow trees. My Barred Rock pullets delight in scratching and pecking among the rotting leaves. You might call them "free ranging"—in other words, they're happy chickens, and I'm happy 'cuz they've begun to lay lovely brown eggs with yolks as yellow as dandelion blossoms.

This past week, having been unseasonably mild and sunny, Halley and I resumed our regular rambles along the irrigation ditches. Flocks of wild mallards, water glittering in their wake, took flight, circled overhead, then, with a great quacking ruckus, landed behind us.

Oftentimes we come upon a Great Blue Heron, who croaks in surprise, flaps its gangly wings, and flies low up the creek. The rank golden grasses, bordering the water, harbor numerous white-tail does and fawns. Halley keeps her nose to the ground, quivering with wild scents.

Son Todd has come for the five-point bull elk hanging in our shop. Can't wait to taste some of that wild meat. Wallowa County is still invaded by elk hunters, typical for the season.

November 8—We woke up this morning to find Prairie Creek fast-forwarded to winter. Wet snow continued to fall while I fed my heifers and tended the chickens. Halley loved it; she's a snow dog. Returning to our warm kitchen, I mixed up a batch of pancakes for breakfast before Doug and I bundled up to climb into the pickup Pulling the stock trailer, we headed out the long gravel Crow Creek road.

Just before we arrived at the "Pink barn," the old Dorrance place, here came granddaughter-in-law Chelsea and her kids in their pickup, towing the first load of calves. We waited in line for grandson Buck to load our trailer, then headed back to Prairie Creek.

It was snowing heavily, and the temperature was dropping by the time the calves were unloaded at Boyd's scales. Other pickups towing trailers pulled in behind us.

The day began early for Buck and his family, Buck told me later. When they were sorting calves from cows, one calf got away and ran down the road. While Buck, along with his little girls, went to retrieve the calf, Chelsea, wearing baby Cooper in a front pack, had the calves nearly all sorted. That's teamwork.

November 9—Still snowing this morning, with an accumulation of around three inches. Our world is white.

Before I put a period to this column, I would like to pay tribute to one of Wallowa County's longtime cattle ranchers, 83-year-old Duke

Lathrop, who passed away on November 2nd. Duke will be sorely missed around the card table at Ye Olde Range Rider.

Tonight I attended the annual Healthy Futures dinner and money raiser to benefit our local Health Care Foundation. Cloverleaf Hall was decked out in uptown finery. Beth Gibans and Lynne Curry did a great job on the meal, which featured locally-grown McClaran Ranch Prime rib.

M.C. Matt Kurtz kept up a lively banter as the evening progressed. Matt was one of my 4-H Sourdough Shutterbugs, as was Eric Johnson, now Joseph High School FFA instructor, who, along with his wife, sat next to me. I am so proud of all of them.

I understand another member, Kurt Ehrler, is now the father of twins, a girl and a boy. Congratulations, Kurt! Kurt's mom Rita called recently to talk about old times, like the time we all hiked into Red's Horse Ranch and slept in the old barn, long before the historic Dude Ranch sold out to the U.S. Forest Service.

Hooked up with a longtime Agri-Times fan while chowing down on one of Heavenly's Marr Flat grass-fed hamburgers last week. He says he worked for Red Higgins, of Red's Horse Ranch, and he told the story of flying chickens into the ranch. Casey, here in the county cow elk hunting with his longtime friend, Darrell Witty, remembered seeing yours truly cooking at Red's a long, long time ago.

I was just walking down the path from my chicken pen one morning last week, when my old buddy Allen Voortman, eyes a-twinkle and bearing jugs of his nutritious Pride and Joy Dairy milk, appeared in our driveway. Allen, who reads "Janie's Journal," knows my Jerz is dry.

Doug and I invited him into the house and fed him some of my aged, homemade cheddar cheese, made using the Jerz's milk. After chewing the fat and telling monstrous tales for a couple of hours, Allen left, but not before this man of many talents let his four border collies out of the trailer to work my cow herd. It was amazing watching these dogs. Responding to Allen's soft whistle, they performed quietly, gently gathering my cows and calves into a curious bunch.

November 10—This morning Doug and I arose early, gulped down our oatmeal, jumped in the pickup, and once more headed out the long Crow Creek road, this time to help Buck and Chelsea haul their cows to the valley. It had snowed during the night and the white stuff continued to fall as we drove out to the hills.

When we pulled up to the "Pink Barn" corrals, daughter-in-law Chelsea, wearing baby Cooper in his front pack, was helping load cows, and Lucy and Katelyn were on the fence waving excitedly. The little girls quickly joined us in the truck to keep warm. Sara Miller and Mike Hale had just finished loading their trailer. Then it was our turn; the cows clattered in, the gate was slammed shut, and Doug pulled off to the side to wait for Buck and Mike Williams.

Chelsea, Sara, and the children, pulling their load of cows, were already headed to the valley. About that time a large stock truck pulled in to be loaded. Then we heard Buck yell, "Poppa Doug, you have a flat tire on your trailer." Deja Vu of last year! Aided by Mike, grandson Buck changed the tire in jig time, and we were on our way.

It had stopped snowing by the time we reached highway 82 at Eggleson corner. Then, as we drove down a slight incline toward Moffit's gravel pit, Doug glanced in his rear view mirror and announced we had two more flat tires on the trailer. We pulled over into the nearest wide spot and stopped. There we sat—what to do? Fortunately, Doug had his cell phone, so called Les Schwab, who said it would be awhile before they could send someone out.

Cars and elk hunters sped past. Those who knew us waved, but no one stopped. The loaded stock truck zoomed past, followed by Buck and Mike, who slowed to a halt, and were mighty relieved when I walked up to tell them Les Schwab was on the way. After what seemed like hours, here came our rescue man, armed with fantastic tools that made short work of our problem.

Meanwhile, the cows, having accepted their fate, had settled down to wait.

Later, after Buck and Mike unloaded our cows at the Cummings place, in drove Chelsea, Sara and the kids, They'd driven clear back out to the corrals and brought in another load. By this time it was well past noon, and my oatmeal had worn off. I was hungry. Doug, who'd chowed down on Chelsea's freshly-baked brownies, wasn't. So, after dropping me off in Enterprise, where I ordered a "Heavenly Hamburger," Doug proceeded to Les Schwab's.

Later, when he picked me up, I asked Doug if he wanted a hamburger, whereupon he grinned and said, "Nope. Had two bags of popcorn."

November 11—The temperature dropped to 14 degrees here on Prairie Creek, with reports of six degrees on Swamp Creek. A bitter wind didn't help.

Later, while climbing the steps to our church, Jean Dawson remarked, "My father used to say, you had to be tough to be old." And I agreed. How I admire Jean and her husband Malcolm, who used to ranch on Prairie

Creek. They ARE tough, taking the cold in stride, making their way to church every Sunday regardless of the weather.

Tonight I baked buttermilk biscuits and stirred up a fry pan of sausage gravy for supper. Also baked one of those Sheep Creek squashes for Thanksgiving pies.

November 13—Our high was a foggy 32 degrees. Doug joined a marathon card game at the Range Rider, which was a good way to spend a cold day. I rang up Wilma in Grangeville, and she was glad to hear from me. Said she was missing her Wallowa County friends, and still settling into her little apartment. Which must seem a far cry from Imnaha.

November 16—Our Sheep Creek writers met at my cabin. I'd picked up two pans of Kelly Shear's famous beef enchiladas that morning before heading into the canyons, as I'd gotten the winning bid at the 4-H radio auction. The others brought potluck. Good food, good times, great writing.

November 17—Duke Lathrop's memorial was held today at the Elk's Lodge in Enterprise. The place was packed. It was pretty obvious Duke had been a "presence" in many folks' lives.

Among other things, Duke was known for his bad jokes. Several of his favorites were recited for the benefit of those who hadn't heard them...like the one Mack Birkmaier told about the old cowboy, who said, "One way to find out who loves you the most, your wife or your dog, is to put your wife and dog in the trunk of the car and leave 'em there for a couple hours. When you open the door, you'll know."

Duke would have loved his memorial. It was upbeat, and left folks with warm feelings. The ninth of 13 children, Duke was raised in the Leap Area north of Lostine. He married Rhea Caudle in 1950, and together they raised dozens of foster children in addition to their two adopted children.

Duke would have enjoyed the food too, tables laden with Wallowa County potluck. I'd spent the morning building a lemon pie.

November 19—Winds gusted to over 55 miles an hour here on Prairie Creek. The old apple tree shuddered, but remained upright; tin was ripped off the machinery shed, however, and a flock of wild white swans, flying overhead, struggled to buck the swift wind currents. Fluttering in vain, they made little progress before landing in a stubblefield to feed.

November 22—The aroma of Thanksgiving dinner lingers in my kitchen as the turkey carcass simmers for tonight's soup—soup as warm and comforting as our family, seated around the table feasting on traditional fare of potatoes, whipped to a high fluffiness by son Todd, giblet gravy, homemade bread stuffing seasoned with sage, tart cranberry sauce, Annie's light rolls, brown sugary baked yams, and, heaped high on the platter, moist slices of dark and white turkey, carved by Doug.

Ashlyn and Riley Ann took charge of the punch, and yours truly contributed her squash and mincemeat pies. There was plenty of whipped cream. We celebrated Thanksgiving and the birthday of daughter-in-law Angie by poking candles in the mincemeat pie.

Although other members of our extended family traveled out-of-county to join relatives, fifteen of us gathered here. We had much to be thankful for. The weather was a mixed bag of sunny, cloudy, mild, and cold. Of course, prayers were offered for those not able to join us, like grandson James in far-off Afghanistan, and Shawn and Josh and their families, who are stationed in the U.S.

Yesterday I ventured down to Sheep Creek to check on my cabin and found everything in order, save for a few fallen limbs, which I dragged to a burning pile. Deer droppings and turkey feathers provided obvious evidence of visitors. My honeysuckle vine and roses bushes were pretty well pruned. The lawn and deck were littered with colorful cottonwood leaves, and the creek, running a bit higher now, splashed happily past.

Here on Prairie Creek, my Barred Rock pullets are laying lovely brown eggs on a regular basis, while my older hens are just coming out of their ugly molt.

One of my pullets thinks she's a border collie. I have to laugh when she joins Halley, running laps around the chicken pen.

Every morning my little bovine family shows up at the hay feeder. They're such an odd little herd—one ponderous Gelbvieh/Angus cow, her furry black twin heifer calves, and the dainty yet feisty Jerz.

November 23—At last, all is quiet. It's nearly 8:00 p.m. and I'm finally sitting down with my "new" (to me) laptop. Everything is foreign and strange. After years of writing on the same "out of date" computer, I'm finding this transition to be extremely difficult. Change does not come easy for an old mare. She's used to routine, and anything that deviates from that is stressful.

In fact, MAJOR STRESS is what she's feeling now. You see, my writers group has been after me for years to update my technology.

"Get rid of dial-up," they'd say. "Too slow." Then, last week, Pat

Adelhart gave me her hubby's outdated computer. He'd apparently purchased a newer one. Another member, Leita, is helping me with this transition. However, after staying up late into the night and transferring years of accumulated data from my old computer to the new one, we were both very weary of the entire process.

Leita, a guru when it comes to modem technology, finally got everything set up so's all I had to do was type, and that's what I'm doing now. Turns out, the only thing I really understand is writing.

Leita left the next morning to travel to her home in Richland, leaving me with this THING. That was last Wednesday. Now on my own, my only link to my friend is via cell phone. Hopefully, she can walk me through it, and perhaps, by some miracle, this column will be sent over the miles to Sterling Allen, my patient editor.

I called Sterling this morning and unloaded my sad story. Being as I'm way past deadline, I thought it best to explain why. Anyhoo, you out there in Agri-Times land may, or may not, read these scribblings. It all depends on if my friend, Richelle, at Central Copy, can successfully retrieve and send it. Leita assures me my words are being recorded on a flash drive inserted to the right of my computer.

Right now I wish for my old Smith Corona typewriter here on the kitchen table. No cords, no blinking lights, no outdated software, hardware, spellcheck, font size, or files. Simply type and correct mistakes with white-out. Then, like in days long past, I would walk out our lane to the mailbox and put the flag up.

Ken has hauled his critters, along with Rhubarb's twin heifers, to a pasture on Alder Slope. He says Ebony's bull calf will be shipped to Vale this week. That leaves Fawn, and her Guernsey heifer calf, Buttercup, plus Rhubarb and her spring calf June Bug, under my care. Since temperatures have been in the single digits as of late—it was down to 8 several mornings in a row—I've been haying my milk cow and her weaned heifer. There's still plenty of feed to sustain the others, who are going into the winter fat and sassy.

Last week Doug hauled 10 bales of alfalfa hay from Mike Coppin's barn on upper Prairie Creek, and let me tell you, my Jerz and Buttercup love it. Plus, I love going out to feed. It sure beats sitting here in front of this computer. Although I enjoy writing, sitting is not my thing!

Last Saturday we discovered a box of freshly-picked tangerines in our mailbox. Thanks to my sister Kathy, who lives in Roseville, California.

Halley, my border collie, snuggles in her new state-of-the-art dog house, which features a woolly pad and flexible plastic door to ward off our recent bitter cold weather. Several of my older hens are showing their age, and molting, which means they aren't laying eggs.

Remember the chicks I slid under that setting hen last spring? Well, I chopped the head off one rooster fryer and we ate him, which left two. These two, a pullet and another rooster, resemble Herefords. At least, that's how my cuz, Stanlynn, describes them. She's right. These red and white birds trundle along like obese cows. What's really scary is that they haven't reached their full growth yet. It's frightening how much they eat.

I was going to butcher the rooster, but now he thinks he's a border collie, which is enormously entertaining. I named him "Allen" after Allen Voortman, so how can we eat him?

The pullet strains to lay an egg, and I wonder if it is stuck. I've observed her for three days and nothing happens. The fellow I purchased the chicks from told me this breed of chicken lays triple-yolk eggs. I'll keep you posted—that is, if anything comes out!

November 26—When I walked out the lane to open our mailbox, I was surprised to see a large package crammed in with our other mail. After carrying the box to the house, I couldn't wait to open it. Out spilled persimmons, mandarin oranges and pomegranates, a gift from our friends, Fred and Sandra Hubbard, who live in Auburn, California.

Doug and I dove right into those oranges, which tasted as sweet as the sunny Sierra foothills.

November 28—I treated granddaughter Adele to lunch at Mutiny in Joseph. Lots to catch up on with this busy little Miss, who tells me she and her other grandma are leaving next week to fly to Australia.

Another granddaughter, Becky, is currently living on a farm in Ireland. This younger generation really gets around.

November 29—The wind, blowing out of the south, creates a steady roar. The predicted rain is yet to arrive. A kettle of beans simmers on the stove.

The Thanksgiving leftovers are gone, and Christmas looms ahead.

December 2—Folks from near and far gathered at the Historic Wallowa Lake Lodge to attend Gail Swart's annual Christmas Caroling Party. To me, this is the event of the Holidays. It just wouldn't be Christmas without it. Gail's warm hospitality was felt in the Great Room as we all joined in singing traditional carols. The old lodge was filled with song as Duff Pace led us, and Gail accompanied on the piano. It was all there, old-fashioned Christmas Spirit, a cheery fire, decorated tree, and smiling faces lifted in song.

Later, after a thrilling performance staged by our local Bell Chorus, we all filed into the dining room to be seated at long festively-decorated tables set with real silver and cloth napkins. While we dined on such fare as herb cream chicken breasts, pork roulade, rice pilaf and green beans, we made new friends or reconnected with old ones.

After trays of homemade Christmas cookies made their way up and down the tables, we were entertained by local talent, not the least of whom included Gail herself, who dedicated a lovely song "Still, Still," to Jane Williams, who now resides in the Nursing Home.

This was followed by a sampling of Wallowa County's incredible talent: Pat Cason playing the flute, Janis Carper on guitar, Heidi Muller on the dulcimer with Bob Webb, blues singer Carolyn Lochert, a reading by Rich Wandschneider of "Stubby Pringle's Christmas," the Hobbs family, Randy Morgan, Duff Pace singing "In This Very Room," Rod Ambroson and wife Mary, and others.

Everyone joined in the singing of "Silent Night" and "White Christmas" before we stepped out into the mountain night. Driving along the lakeshore provided another treat. The waning moon, lighting the face of Chief Joseph Mountain, was reflected in the calm waters of the lake.

Back on Prairie Creek, great velvet clouds, tinged with gold, sped across the night sky as the moon disappeared behind them.

Ken hauled two huge bales of hay he raised on Alder Slope, and stacked them near the feeder, making it handy to feed my little herd.

December 3—Windy weather returned overnight. Prairie Creek felt like an ocean in motion as Halley and I, propelled by the wind, were blown down the hill and swept along the irrigation ditch.

When I returned to the house, I received a call from friend Phyllis, who, along with hubby Fred, moved some time ago to Bend. I miss having Phyllis around to hike the moraine, sip tea in her mountain home, play Scrabble, and cross country ski.

December 4—After our Write Group met in the back room of Cloud 9 Bakery, Pat showed a video, filmed last April, of son Todd's branding up Big Sheep Creek at Blue Meadow. Suddenly we were transported back to those greening canyons, where the bawling of cattle, smoke from the branding fire, cow kids, cow dogs, cowboys, cowgirls, cow ponies and the aroma of roasting beef mingled together.

Thank you Pat and Leita. A job well done.

December 6—Using that California fruit, I baked my mother's recipe for persimmon bars, drizzled with lemon glaze. Earlier this morning, Ken borrowed our pickup and trailer to haul the Moore Boys' calves to the valley.

Another surprise in our mailbox. A box of tangerines from sister Kathryn, who lives in Roseville, California. Since our mandarins were long gone, this sweet, freshly-picked box of citrus was most welcome. Thanks, sis!

On these long winter evenings, my head is usually buried in a book. At the moment I'm reading some collected stories by one of my favorite authors, Wallace Stegner.

December 7—Myrna Moore invited Doug and I down to their place on Bear Gulch for lunch. Sadly, most folks don't take time to visit like they used to. Therefore, we found it very refreshing to visit over Myrna's Taco soup, corn muffins, raspberry cream cheese salad and Christmas cookies. She and husband Larry's modest little home is always full of warmth and friendship. Their daughter Jenny and son Jake joined us as well. Myrna also baked Doug's favorite chocolate cake to send home with us as a thank you for helping with the shipping of their calves.

After I washed the dishes and Myrna dried them—no dishwasher there either—we continued to visit in the living room. We talked about the bobcat that got into Myrna's chickens, and then reminisced about those long-ago K-8 Imnaha school Christmas programs, when our grand-children Mona and Buck, as well as Myrna's Jenny and Jake, attended the little school at the bridge.

December 8—A blizzard blew up out of the north. Blowing snow swirled around the house and I felt sorry for my little herd, but they found shelter near the barn.

December 9—Salmon-colored clouds scudded across the sky before the sun burst bright over Locke's hill. It was 20 degrees. My barred rock pullets are staying in the hen house these days, where it's warmer. I'd pushed a wheelbarrow full of straw from the calving shed to scatter under the roosts and line the nests. Once a week I treat them to a flake of leafy alfalfa.

December 10—Last night's snow is melting, dripping off the eaves and slowly forming icicles. Taking advantage of this brief interlude of warmth, Halley and I took a leisurely saunter around the old ranch. Since the myriad flocks of ducks have moved on, the open waters in the ice-skimmed irrigation ditches were quiet this morning. The skies above

Former Wallowa County CowBelles Judy Stilson, left, and Mary Lou Brink help serve dinner at the dining center in Enterprise.

Prairie Creek weren't, however. They were full of honkers winging their way to another grain field.

At first light I heard a dull thud, followed by another thump. The sound came from the front room window. I peered out to see a Hungarian Partridge floundering in the snow. Halley saw it too, and began pawing around until I called her off. Thankfully, the stunned bird came to its senses long enough to fly off toward the cow pasture. Soon my attention was drawn to a lone coyote hunting across the road. I watched, as, nose down, it followed a snowy mouse tunnel—then suddenly pounced! I hoped the dazed "Hun" was not on Mr. Coyote's breakfast menu as well.

While this drama unfolded, several white-tail does and fawns tippy-toed across the stubble, leaped the fence, and melted into the snowy, sage-dotted hills. So, you see, while Doug is seated at the "Locals" table at the Cheyenne Cafe, jawing with "the boys," I, too, am entertained.

A small canyon fir tree, adorned with ornaments from Christmases past and twinkling with tiny lights, adds warmth and cheer to our short December days. Hanging from our Angel's arm, as she tops the tree, is a small hardened gingerbread man with a string through its head. Written below, in a child's scrawl, reads *James*. The boy is a man now, fighting for freedoms we often take for granted. I pray for an angel to watch over

James and his comrades on that faraway foreign battlefield.

It was a balmy 40 degrees when Judy Stilson, Mary Lou Brink, and I served a tasty roast pork dinner to the "old folks" at the Dining Center in Enterprise. It's always fun visiting with old-timers like Mike Brennan, Shandon Towers, and Wayne Lathrop, to name a few. "Old Timer" Doug Tippett, who apparently hit a winning streak in a card game at the Range Rider, missed out on his dinner.

The so-named "Pineapple Express," with its warm 45-degree-rain, ushered in the month of December.

I called Scotty early on the morning of her birthday, to sing my version of "Happy Birthday" and catch up with my 90+ year-old hiking buddy, who traveled many miles through the Wallowas and canyons with me, and worked on our potato digger all those years. Scotty tells me she's still walking a mile most every day.

From 11:00 'til 2:00 o'clock I helped serve soup and grilled cheese sandwiches from the kitchen at the Joseph Community Center for our Methodist Church—all part of the annual Christmas Bazaar, where other members of our church sold an amazing array of Christmas cookies.

December 14—I drove up on the hill above Enterprise to attend the Night of the Nativity sponsored by the LDS church. More local talent midst a warm Christmas setting that included over 100 nativity scenes displayed along the walls. Of course, this grandma was especially proud when granddaughter-in-law Amy, her sweet voice floating out over the audience, sang an old English folk song while playing her harp, and again when several of our great grandchildren sang in the choir. Gail Swart was there, faithful as always, joining several other locals.

After visiting and munching beautifully decorated cookies, I stepped out into the cold icy night with renewed warm feelings for the season.

December 16—Wallowa County loves Christmas, and a multitude filed into the new Josephy Center for the Arts and Culture this evening, where we enjoyed the annual Community Christmas concert.

This event, sponsored by the Wallowa Valley Music Alliance, was a smash. The acoustics were excellent, the audience was thrilled, and the local talent begs description. The Brann family stole everyone's hearts when they sang their songs. Children are so much a part of what makes Christmas special, and those little ones brought smiles to everyone.

December 17—The wind began a ceaseless roar, and great gusts shook the house, rattled tin sheds, and the limbs on the ancient willows flailed about like great grasping arms. It was dreadful, but luckily we never lost power.

Soft snow fell, drifts piling high in the barrow pits and creating ridges on Tenderfoot Valley road. The temps plummeted. Mercifully the wind laid down, only to rise again later.

December 18—The wind-scoured skies shone with a polished robin's egg blue. The Wallowas wore a sheen of pristine white, and the sun shone coldly on a silent landscape. Prairie Creek was wrapped in breath-taking loveliness. Just when we think we can't take another winter, along comes such a day!

As luck would have it, today is a Tuesday, and our Writer's Group met on Upper Prairie Creek at the home of Pam Royes for our annual noon Christmas potluck. After reading our work, we supped Pam's hot soup, adding our contributions to the meal, all the while gazing out the windows toward Chief Joseph Mountain, a living Christmas card.

Santa, in the form of dairyman Allen Voortman, left three bottles of his Pride and Joy milk in our refrigerator while we were gone. Thanks, Allen. What a treat.

I delivered a fresh-from-the oven cinnamon loaf to our neighbors, the Butterfields, as a belated thank you for allowing me to scoop up spilled wheat for my chickens. What with the price of wheat these days, that really helped.

December 21—Attended the Methodist Ladies' salad luncheon at our church. The wind returned today with renewed vigor.

Delivered another cinnamon loaf to our friend Scotty, who gave me a recipe for chicken rice casserole and a cookie capful of shortbread. Since I had chicken thawing, I made the casserole for supper, which was delicious.

December 22—Ramona and Charley left for Lodi today, hauling a 4-H project steer for their grandson Cole. They reportedly ran into blizzard conditions over Donner Pass and it took them 11 hours to get from Winnemucca to Lodi. They are spending the week there with their family.

The best Christmas gift of all was a phone call on Christmas Eve from grandson James, who is serving with the Marines in Afghanistan. It was so good to hear his voice.

December 24—I busied myself baking wild blackberry pies and cooking up a big kettle of clam chowder. Son Steve and wife Jennifer drove in with their little hats, Bailey and Stetson, just as I was leaving for our Methodist church's Christmas Eve Candlelight Service. Stetson wanted to go with grandma, so we left Steve's family supping soup with Doug and drove over snowy roads to Joseph.

Jennifer's parents, who had flown from Alabama, were also here. All beds were taken. At the church we were delighted to meet up with Buck, Chelsea, and Chelsea's parents, the DeJongs from McCall, Idaho, plus Mona Lee and the newest members of the Matthews family. Lucy, Katelyn and baby Cooper. We took up an entire pew.

It was a lovely service as always, my favorite part being there with family while we lit our candles and sang "Silent Night."

On the way in, I'd taken Stetson on a short detour to see Joseph's decorated homes.

December 25—On the first day of Christmas, my true love gave to me, one shiny milk pail decorated with a red ribbon. And a pair of bog boots.

December 27—The house is quiet for the first time in a LONG while, since the day before Christmas, even, when this place was jumping with nativity activity. It was all good—however, I was wondering how I'd find time to begin this column when things suddenly calmed down. In fact, I'm more relaxed than I've been in months. You see, granddaughter Mona Lee is here, staying on after Christmas.

She just recently completed Massage Therapy school in Portland, and so, this morning, she gave me a massage, the second one I've ever had. Must say I highly recommend this professional little miss who will be starting up her own business in Portland soon. Raised on Imnaha here in Wallowa County, she's got strong hands with a gentle touch. At least, she did for her grandma.

The sun peeked out this morning so Mona is taking a run over the hill and around the country block as I write. Mona's parents, daughter Jackie and hubby Bill, having driven straight through from Challis, Idaho, arrived just in time for Christmas dinner. 21 of us overflowed three rooms to feast on traditional Prime Rib, mashed potatoes, gravy, salad, Chelsea's bread, and grandma's blackberry pies.

After feeding cattle, son-in-law Bill and his son Buck headed out to the Divide this morning, where Buck hopes to fill his cow elk tag.

December 28—And now it's the afternoon of the 28th and a kettle of roast beef ribs and vegetables are simmering on the stove for tonight's soup. I promised a raspberry cobbler, so better put a period to this column. Happy New Year to everyone in Agri-Times Land.

December 29—Our world is composed of hoarfrost, that freezing fog that lasts for days and changes our landscape dramatically. Feathery flakes of frost transformed every frond of grass, every fence line, and ugly piece of junk into a thing of beauty. Fir trees, flocked in white; cow's muzzles, cat whiskers, chicken wire fences, and even Halley sported white feathers. The slightest breeze sent crystals sifting into piles, soft as ashes.

Son-in-law Bill, and wife, Jackie, stayed on after Christmas to enjoy their grandchildren. After breakfast each morning, Bill would drive over to help his son, Buck, hay his cattle at the Cummings place. After feeding one morning, the family headed up Tucker Down Road and enjoyed some skiing at "Fergie," our nickname for Ferguson Ridge, our local ski area. This year, little Miss Kate learned to ski. They reported being out of the fog at that elevation.

December 31—The day dawned zero degrees and hoarfrost continued in our arctic world. I fixed lasagna for supper, and Doug and I were tucked between flannel sheets, sawing logs when 2013 slipped in.

Jackie's family joined son Todd's for New Years Eve.

Over 300 Marr Flat cows being trailed from Big Sheep Creek to the ranch just southeast of Enterprise through Hayden Canyon.

When they topped out it was ten degrees with a north wind blowing.

2013

January 1—On New Year's morning, I whipped up sourdough waffles, pancakes, blackberry jam, bacon 'n eggs, and cowboy coffee—a stick-to-the-ribs breakfast for those of us feeding cattle in bitter cold conditions.

The day warmed to 10 degrees. It seemed surreal watching the Rose Bowl Parade coming from sunny Pasadena, California.

January 2—Jackie and Bill departed to Challis, Idaho, and Mona to Portland. It was 9 degrees this morning, with bare pavement, so, thankfully, they made it home safely.

This afternoon I took a long walk with Halley, who, having been neglected over the holidays, was very eager.

Son Ken hauled more hay for my cow herd, and stacked it for easy feeding. Peering out across Prairie Creek later tonight, across a frozen landscape made visible by muted moonglow, I experienced total silence—broken suddenly by the wailing of coyotes on Hough's hill. Their message conveyed mournfulness and hunger.

January 3—5 degrees. I have the house to myself, Doug having gone to the Cheyenne Cafe to breakfast with "the boys." Again, I went out to chore in the beautiful, brutal cold. My body was warm, but my fingers turned numb while forking hay to my cows and heifers, plus packing water to my chickens.

By ten o'clock the temperature had risen to 10, so I curled up in my overstuffed chair in the living room, spread a blanket over my legs, and lost myself in Norman Maclean's *A River Runs Through It*, which is our County-wide Big Read selection this year.

When I gathered the eggs this afternoon, they were already frozen.

January 4—The dawn sky was stained the color of wild roses when a sudden breeze sent the fog scurrying away, and a sunny day ensued. After chores I fled to the canyons to check on my Sheep Creek property. All appeared fine, but alas, as I was ambling along the creek, I noticed a tall, handsome cottonwood, half eaten near the base. The tree leaned pre-

Beaver working on a cottonwood along Big Sheep Creek

cariously toward the creek and wood chips littered the ground. Beavers! Further inspection down the creek proved just as discouraging. Two more cottonwoods, chewed through, half submerged in the water.

Several mule deer does watched me survey the damage, a Raven croaked overhead, a covey of quail twittered and flew into the blackberry bramble, all as if to say, something should be done. But what? Certainly these beavers don't think they can dam up Sheep Creek...or do they?

I love wildlife but I also love trees, especially these lovely cottonwoods, which only a few months ago shed their golden leaves in great yellow drifts on the lawn.

January 5—A half moon greeted me through the kitchen window before dawn. It was 5 degrees. Busy today, cooking and putting clean sheets on the guest bed, as daughter Lori and hubby Larry will be spending the night. We also invited daughter Ramona and husband Charley for supper, as neither couple were here for Christmas.

The menu was "drunk chicken," achieved by arranging the cavity of a plump chicken over a ceramic bowl filled with beer and garlic, and roasting the bird for several hours until it was crisp on the outside and moist inside. Served with mashed potatoes, Sheep Creek squash, and salad. Ramona contributed peach/blueberry cobbler and whipped cream.

Afterward we watched a video of old movie footage filmed by Doug's mom, Jesse, on Joseph Creek, where the family ranched during the 1940s. We were transported back to a time when Jidge Tippett and his family stacked hay with a swing pole derrick, and all farming was done with a team of mules. A time when Hereford cattle, hundreds of them, grazed the canyons, and steers were driven to the railroad to market, and there were no fences along the way.

January 6—We met Doug's brother, Biden, and wife, Betty, for breakfast at the Cheyenne Cafe in Joseph. After which Lori and Larry left.

This afternoon I took down Christmas. The living room always seems a bit cheerless for a few days afterward. The Christmas cards are still displayed.

January 7—I peered out the window at dawn to see the little fir tree lying on its side, the wind blowing its needles, and remembered the warmth it had brought to our home. Chicken soup simmered on the stove.

January 8—Our Write group met for the first time at our permanent place from now on—the new Josephy Center for Arts and Culture. A very cheerful room, with natural lighting, and warm log walls. We are most appreciative.

After reading our work, we met at Old Town Cafe for a tasty hot breakfast. Tomorrow Todd starts his cows from Big Sheep Creek to Hayden, on the first day of a three-day drive to the valley. I will join them walking behind the herd, and on Friday, I will cook the traditional meal for the cowboys and cowgirls, after the herd trails down Echo Canyon, just east of our ranch.

January 9—A warm wind, rising in the night, has swept the hills of snow. With the exception of odd drifts scattered over the prairie, or filling the barrow pits, that mark the county roads, there appears to be a relaxing from the bitter cold we experienced the end of December and the first of January.

January 12—Doug and I awoke before dawn to the realization that our electricity was off! After lighting candles, firing up the old Monarch, sipping tea and coffee, reporting the outage, and drawing water to drink, we waited. It was well below zero. What was that I wrote in the opening paragraph? About a relaxing of winter's cold? I should know better.

The stars were pricking the sky with icy points of light before daylight filtered in. Just at sunup, I looked out the bedroom window to see the Marr Flat cows trailing through the open wire gate at Stilson's pasture, onto Klages Road, walking stiffly toward their destination at the old Snyder Ranch.

I didn't walk behind the cows as they made their way to Hayden that first day. A blizzard was blowing up here, the snow falling thickly, and somehow it didn't seem like that much fun. Yesterday I concentrated on cooking a hot meal for the riders.

Son Todd had given me several packages of Marr Flat sirloin steaks, with which to build my meal around, and I spent the morning baking a round loaf of sourdough bread in my dutch oven, along with a blackberry cobbler. I tossed a salad, baked potatoes, and set the table. I had the frypans warming on the wood cook stove.

Using my binoculars I kept watching the road that curves down from Echo Canyon. Around 11:30, here they came, the lead of over 300 cows, making their slow way down the narrow snow-filled road. I judged, and rightly so, it would be another hour before the stragglers trailed into Stilsons about a half mile from here. I wasn't going to flop those steaks into my hot cast-iron skillets before I saw the whites of their eyes.

Soon, here they came—first, the one and only cowgirl, daughter-in-law Angie, face red with cold, stiff from being in the saddle, and hungry. Now this is one tough cowgirl. Next was Ken Hunt, equally hungry, one of my neighbors on Big Sheep Creek who had ridden his mustang and was great help, as he knew the terrain. Next came Pat and Todd, who'd had the job of ferrying rigs, dumping out hay for the cows, and feeding the other valley cattle.

Angie said when they "topped out" it felt like it was around 10 degrees with a wind blowing. Everything was a whiteout, hard to tell which direction they were going. There was a great removing of outerwear and washing up in the porch sink, and everyone took a place at our kitchen table with a scraping of chairs.

The old Monarch was fired up, and the steaks were sizzling. I've fed a lot of hungry folks in my lifetime, but these guys and gal were impressive. They wiped out a huge bowl of baked potatoes, a salad, most of that loaf of bread, and enormous amounts of beef steak—all washed down with old fashioned perked coffee made on the range top. And they still had room for blackberry cobbler with whipped cream.

All the while we were eating, stories swirled around the table of other drives, of this drive, and for some reason, all the stories ended up being about rattlesnakes. Kind of a "can you top this" competition. Pat, who is a bit squeamish about snakes, was so visibly shaken, we changed the subject.

Doug returned from his card game at Ye Olde Range Rider after everyone left, and we threw another stick of wood on the fire and read the mail. Now that the electricity has been restored, I must e-mail this column.

January 13—I drove over crunchy, snowy roads to attend our church and ring the bell. The old bell tower was cold, another zero morning, but the exertion of tugging on that rope warmed me. For supper that night I baked cornbread to go with a jar of home-canned Chili, given to us by my friend Idella Allen.

January 14—It seemed even colder, due to a breeze.

January 15—I gave Doug a haircut before he left to join the gang at Cheyenne Cafe in Joseph. After feeding my critters, I drove to the Josephy Center, and joined our Write Group. A good session of reading our writing, then, using the small kitchen facilities, we enjoyed a crockpot of Idella's homemade tomato soup and sourdough bread.

January 16—As frosty crystals sifted past the kitchen window, I set a batch of sweet dough to rise and later baked a pan of cinnamon rolls. In addition to cooking, other wintertime projects take up much of my time, aside from writing... such as labeling photos, placing them in albums, cleaning drawers or cracking walnuts.

Daughter-in-law Angie called one night saying granddaughter Chelsie had called, was worried about the elk hunters. They weren't home yet. It seems Chelsie's daughter, 12-year-old Riley Ann, along with her cousin, Buck, and Uncle Todd, were out hunting and it was dark and very cold. Were they perchance at our place?

"No," I said, then became alarmed myself. Not to worry. I soon raised Todd on his cell phone. He'd been out of range in the canyons. Everything was fine—more than fine, even. Buck had bagged his cow elk, and so had Riley Ann!

Grandson James, Riley's cousin, will be especially pleased, as he took the time to teach Riley how to use her rifle. Lots of nutritious winter meat in those cow elk.

January 17—I stood on the hill and watched rigs pull into the old Liberty Grange Hall for the annual Meeting of the Associated Ditch Company, Doug among them. Another zero degree morning.

This evening I drove to the Hurricane Creek Grange Hall to attend the kickoff for the Wallowa County Reads program. Dr. Jim Hepworth, literature professor at Lewis/Clark college in Lewiston, was the featured speaker. Jim knew Norman Maclean personally, and happened to read the manuscript of *A River Runs Through It* before it was published. Actually, the manuscript was rejected by Eastern publishers and only later published by the University of Chicago Press.

It was all very interesting, and the place was packed in spite of the bitter cold. Grange ladies supplied the pies. My name was among 30 others drawn to attend John Maclean's limited-seating presentation next month, as was granddaughter Adele's.

Ross and Linda Rooper volunteered to wrap my cottonwood trees growing along Sheep Creek with chicken wire. Now we'll see if those beavers can chew through that! For some reason two barred owls have been *hoo-hoo*-ing a lot this past week, just before dawn. Does this mean more snow in the forecast?

January 19—It was 5 degrees as I stared out the living room window. Nothing moved. A lone hawk perched, silent, in the leafless willow, and small bunches of Hough's cows stood hunched like dark sculptures, nary a coyote or a bird; the only moving thing, the sun, exploding over Locke's hill. As if on signal, a raven croaked it's way across the Prairie, and "Piglet," my banty rooster, began crowing the morning awake.

Later that afternoon, as I stood next to her nest one of my Barred Rock pullets plopped an egg into my hand. At least that one didn't freeze. I enjoyed visiting on the phone with Kay Braseth of La Grande, who called to say how much she's enjoyed my column all these years, and how she ran across my book, *Four Lines a Day,* and loved that as well. Kay identifies with the book, as she remembers growing up with similar experiences.

January 21—Matching the date, our temperature rose from zero to 21 degrees by the time Halley and I struck out on our daily walk over the hill. Since I use this same route each time, steps are carved in the hardened snow, which makes walking much easier than breaking new trail.

The temps haven't varied in days. Thankfully, no wind stirs over the prairie during these frigid times. Fog creeps in at night, leaving its frozen crystals behind. Weeds fairly glitter when sunlight floods the hill. It's like walking through a frozen fairyland, until I tromp through snow-crusted stubble down the other side. Ice-flooded irrigation ditches resemble shattered milk glass, and prints of coon, fox, coyote and border collie clutter the snowy surfaces.

Today I saw two golden eagles, a magpie and a flicker. Nothing else was afoot or awing in that wide white expanse of prairie. Beyond, on Bicentennial lane, scattered bunches of white-tail deer foraged on frozen alfalfa poking through the snow. It's been hard on wildlife lately, watercourses frozen, no browse, and frigid temperatures.

Each night the "Wolf" moon grows, sending pangs of hunger gurgling in the stomachs of all the little wild things. My Jerz, heavy with calf, plus Rhubarb and her twins, consume quantities of hay and are fortunate to drink from a heated water trough.

This morning our book group met and discussed Norman Maclean's *A River Runs Through It*, which is also our County Reads selection. Although attendance was short, discussions were long.

Doug is presently reading Norman's son John's book, *Fire on the Mountain*, a page-turning story of the South Canyon fire on Colorado's Storm King Mountain. John writes a detailed account of smoke jumpers finding themselves in harm's way. Fourteen young men and women died fighting that fire.

January 24—What a difference 24 hours makes. It's 35 degrees!

The temps began to moderate yesterday, and it began to rain when Doug and I drove into Cloverleaf Hall to attend the annual Stockgrowers "Dollars for Scholars" dinner. A warm Chinook wind blew its breath across the prairie, and the melting began. When we drove in the yard around 9:00 p.m. it was 40 degrees.

The event, staged by the Wallowa County Stockgrower's committee under the capable hands of Sara Lynn Johnson, should be commended. The total tally of funds derived from the sale of those desserts and silent auction items broke previous records.

Local F.F.A. students interested in starting a beef breeding program are offered a chance for a heifer scholarship. This project, sprouted by son Todd, is in its third year, and this year the scholarships have been expanded to award two additional yearling heifers. Funds were also raised at the Stockgrower's Ranch Rodeo, held in August. This year's winners were Bryce Melville of Wallowa, Justin Exon of Enterprise, and Whitney Evans of Joseph. Income from the project is to be saved for college or post-high school educational expenses.

After chowing down on a hearty prime rib dinner provided by Buzz's Homestyle BBQ, Joseph F.F.A. Instructor Dave Yost donned his auction-eer's hat and kept hands fluttering in the air until the last mouth-watering pie, mile-high chocolate cake, warm apple strudel, and juicy cobbler was sold.

Each table bid on a different item, which was then eaten for dessert. Son Todd won the bid at our table, to the tune of $200—a cost shared by others—and my blackberry cream pie was divided into seven slices and

Cattle share their breakfast with a flock of wild mallards on this frosty, 10-degree morning south of Enterprise.

licked up to the last crumb. My apricot cobbler made its way to grandson Buck's table to the tune of $100. We were eating mighty expensive desserts.

I looked around at the neighboring tables and watched folks cut into Eileen Williams' lemon pies, Angie Dietrich's apple strudel, Margie Hudson's chocolate cherry cake, Darla Klages' tender-crusted pies, and Ramona Phillips' decadent Hershey chocolate pie. And that was just a sample.

Silent auction items included Alan Klages' horseshoe coat rack, antique framed prints, and Karen Patton's sourdough orange rolls. Live auction items, like braided reins and spur straps, fetched even more money for the scholarships.

Highlight of the evening for me was receiving hugs from my great-grandchildren, Lucy, Katelyn and baby Cooper.

January 25—I heard on KWVR that our friend Christine was having a birthday today, so, after purchasing a bouquet of daffodils and a card, I walked into the Nursing Home just as the staff was about to throw her a party. Talk about timing. I found Christine, turning 90, perky and cheerful. Christine is a member of our writing group. Hopefully, her memoirs will be published soon.

Good news! Marine Grandson James, on his way home from Afghanistan, connected with his stepsister Becky in Ireland. Unreal! James will be flying into Portland soon, and then making his way back to Wallowa County. We are all very excited about seeing him.

January 26—It snowed about five inches, and after chores I baked a high apple pie, placed a pork roast in the oven, and invited Doug's cousin, Ben Tippett and our neighbors, Don and Lois Hough for supper. A wonderful way to spend a winter evening.

Later, our guests stepped outside onto our snowy Prairie, hushed in muted moonglow.

January 27—I watched two coyotes hunting mice in Hough's field, just at daylight. Warmed by hot tea, with Halley at my heels, I completed my round of chores, then,

Later, drove to church. At 2:00 o'clock, several of us "Stitch and Bitchers" met at the Sheep Shed to celebrate Lynne Price's birthday. While the others stitched, I perused the hand-knitted caps and then purchased a warm wool one, made by Linda Hilderman. After tea, and slices of decadent chocolate cake, baked by Leslie Moholt, we stepped out into the falling snow.

I returned to Prairie Creek to find one of my Barred Rock pullets taking over Halley's dog house. After a chase with my long wire chicken catcher, I captured my border collie hen and proceeded to clip her wings.

January 28—21 degrees. After chores, I cooked up a kettle of bean soup with hamhocks, carrots, celery, and later added kale. Granddaughter Adele was here for supper after which the two of us drove into the Josephy Center to view "The Ranger, The Cook, and The Hole in the Sky," a film adapted from the story written by Norman Maclean. Beautifully filmed and highly entertaining.

Learned there has been a recent wolf kill, just up the hill east of us, on Karl Patton's ranch. The Imnaha pack killed a cow and ate her unborn calf.

January 31—The temperature soared to 40 degrees yesterday! And today was the same, so while Doug drove to the Livestock Auction in La Grande, I headed for the canyons. At my place on the crick, I was pleased to see that the beavers had moved on, or at least ceased chewing on my cottonwood trees.

I was greeted at the gate by a cock pheasant and his hen, and there was an absence of snow. All the ice had melted alongside the creek. To take the chill off the cabin I built fires in both the wood stove and the cook stove.

A cup of tea, a good book, and it just don't get any better than this. I split kindling for the stoves and filled the wood boxes, then took a long walk down Sheep Creek, accompanied by the music of myriad unseen birds. The canyons were greening and great cloud shadows raced across the rims. A short vacation from winter.

I returned home with a handful of red osier dogwood, which is now budding-out in my Olaf pottery vase. The warm weather continued on into February, and daughter Jackie called from Challis, Idaho, to say it was moderating there as well.

February 2—Dawned clear and sunny all day, although a bit cooler. Our Write group met here at our ranch for a wine-tasting. Since one of our members has been a wine server in posh restaurants all over the U.S., Tatiana led us through this delectable experience. We poured, sloshed, sniffed, rolled the wine around on our tongues, and finally swallowed. For four hours we did this, whilst snacking from trays of mangoes, raspberries, apples, pears, dried apricots, aged cheeses, crackers, and a loaf of sourdough garlic bread, hot from the oven.

By the fourth bottle in the fourth hour, we were nibbling chocolate truffles with a huckleberry wine when Doug returned from Imnaha. He joined in the fun, too, and by the time everyone left, our noses were red and we had laughed a lot. Vowing to do this again soon, we returned to our daily lives.

Most of the wines we tasted were imported, but being as our granddaughter, Tamara Lauchland, and hubby, Matt, raise wine grapes in Lodi, California, I can't say they were superior. We should also support our local winemakers, like Wallowa County's Lathrop County Wines.

February 5—Halley and I just returned from our daily two-mile round-trip hike to Klages' corner. The sun was out when we left, melting the snowy pastures, warming the pavement, and loosening clogged ice in the irrigation ditches, enough to hear running water again. Now a cold breeze blows, and clouds, with snow in their bellies, have replaced the sun.

This morning our Writer's Group met in a many-windowed sunny room upstairs in the large log building in Joseph, which houses the Center for the Arts. After reading and critiquing our work, we wandered up the street to Red Horse Coffee House, sat ourselves down in a sunny corner, and supped potato soup and gourmet sandwiches.

My Jerz grows big in the tummy, Rhubarb's twins are weaned, Doug and Ken fixed a panel so the pair of them can eat hay without competition from the cows, the back of winter appears to be broken, and life is good.

For the first time in years, I didn't take in the Sled Dog Races. Due to unseasonably warm conditions and rain, the 200-mile race was shortened to 150 miles. I did miss seeing the mushers and their brave dogs…however, I didn't relish being stuck in slush at Fergie, where the races began and ended.

February 6—And now it's the sixth, the sun is out, and although the Wallowas are curtained behind snow showers, the temps are rising toward 40 degrees.

When I returned from our Writer's Group yesterday, Doug said I'd missed a visit with our friend, Allen Voortman, who'd stopped by in my absence. Seems he and his border collies have been traveling the stock dog trial circuit, having just returned from Red Bluff, California.

For supper last night I gulped down a fresh, cold glass of Pride and Joy Dairy whole milk with my steak sandwich. And this morning my grape nuts and banana breakfast was made all the more nutritious and delicious by that same milk. Thanks, Allen!

Last evening I drove into Fishtrap House to attend, along with a select group, a presentation by John Maclean, son of famous Norman Maclean, the author of *A River Runs Through It*. What a delightful and educational two hours that was!

John, an author in his own right, sat on a stool, as informal as if he were in the family cabin on Seeley Lake in Montana, and literally took us into the lives of the Macleans, transporting us via words and slides to his father's beloved rivers, giving us an insight into the mind of a man who grew up with these famous first lines from his book:

In our family, there was no clear line between religion and fly fishing. We lived at the junction of great trout rivers in western Montana, and our father was a Presbyterian minister and a fly fisherman who tied his own flies and taught others. He told us about Christ's disciples being fishermen, and we were left to assume, as my brother and I did, that all first-class fishermen on the Sea of Galilee were fly fishermen, and that John, the favorite, was a dry-fly fisherman.

At the end of his talk, I approached John to ask if he would autograph my books, one being *Fire on the Mountain,* his own book, and the other *A River Runs Through It.*

When he smiled and handed me the signed books, I mentioned that my grandson, James, had attended University of Montana Western in

Dillon, and did he remember him? John smiled again and said he sure did, and was much impressed with both his literary and fly-fishing skills.

Of course, I drove home floating on a cloud of pride.

February 7—It snowed five inches. Ken hauled more hay for my cows, and I amused myself in the kitchen by baking a pear-ginger cheese-cake.

This evening I drove through a curtain of softly-falling snow to view "A River Runs Through It." It was magical watching this movie, which was filmed in British Columbia during the summer months. Quite the contrast with the feathery flakes swirling past the massive windows outside the Art Center.

A large crowd was transported to the banks of trout streams, where the drama of this adaptation of the book unfolds in Montana.

February 8—There was an accumulated six inches, and it continued to snow.

On the way to Enterprise I noticed the first baby calf born to son Todd's Marr Flat cows. I dumped several food items in the box at Les Schwab's, where the local F.F.A. Chapters are conducting a food drive for the needy.

February 9—I thawed out sirloin steaks and baked a loaf of sour-dough bread in the dutch oven, as we'd invited our old friend Pat Irwin for supper. Pat and wife, Linde, used to live here in the county, and Linde was one of my faithful hiking buddies. The couple now resides in the San Juan Islands. Pat was here to do some mechanic work on Mike Coppin's tractors. We had a nice visit.

Since Doug and I are both early risers, we awoke Sunday morning to discover our electricity was out again. While Doug started the fire in the wood cook stove, I lit candles and set a kettle of water to heat. Only twenty customers were affected this time, but the outage lasted over two hours. Icicles hung like glass daggers from the eaves when I left for church to ring the bell.

This evening I joined granddaughter Adele in the Multipurpose Room at the Enterprise High School, to participate in the battle of the Book— The Book being *A River Runs Through It.* We, along with Liz Hopkins, formed a team dubbed "The Bunyon Bugs" to compete with other teams in answering questions relating to Norman Maclean's novella.

Thanks to Adele, who not only read the book but retained the minute details needed to answer the trick questions, we made the championship round, but were beat out by "Team Suckerfish."

Preceding the battle, we enjoyed a tasty potluck dinner featuring rainbow trout, grilled to perfection by Joe McCormack of our local Nez Perce tribe. I'd baked a lemon pudding cake for the occasion.

February 11—It was 19 degrees and the sky was the color of a Mountain Blue Bird. Accompanied by Halley, I walked six miles. Spent most of the day outside, as it soared well over 40 degrees.

February 12—Six of our Write Group met this morning at the Josephy Center, after which I left to join granddaughter Adele and her father Todd at El Bajio in Enterprise for lunch, and to celebrate Miss Adele's birthday. A museum board meeting on the 13th at the Extension Office, then home to bake cherry turnovers for Valentine's Day tomorrow.

February 14—The sun streamed over Locke's hill by 7:15 and I spent Valentine's Day down on "the crik," cleaning the cabin, to accommodate our Write Group's potluck on Saturday.

It was over 50 degrees. After much dusting and sweeping I struck off along an old wagon road, and sauntered down Sheep Creek for several miles. At one point I reinforced a rock jack and propped up my line fence on a steep canyon side, before snapping a photo of the cabin far below. My adventurous spirit was itching to climb Middlepoint, but time was of the essence.

It's very pleasant and safe tromping around in February, knowing the rattlesnakes are still in their dens. At that lower elevation there was an absence of snow, and I expect we'll soon be discovering buttercups.

Upon leaving, I noticed the flowering quince was beginning to bud.

February 16—Late last tonight, daughter Linda and her friend Dennis Huber called from the Indian Lodge Motel in Joseph. They'd made it safely here from Salem to spend the long weekend. I mixed the sourdough and invited them for breakfast. By 8:00 a.m. coffee was perking, and sourdough waffles and ham 'n eggs were hot off the griddle when they arrived with an appetite. We were very happy to see them, and had a nice visit whilst the breakfast disappeared in record time.

I dashed out and fed my critters, then loaded the car and took off by 10:00 for the "crik," which allowed me time to start fires in the two stoves and take the chill off the cabin before the gals arrived. Suddenly it was noon, and everyone drove in bearing food and wine.

We were nine in total. Such jabbering and giggling as fruit was sliced, cheeses placed on platters with crackers, bread and other dishes warmed in the oven, and salads plunked on the long trestle table. Then we toasted the beautiful handmade wooden table and benches, crafted by our local wood artist, Steve Arment. We also toasted ourselves and the art of WRITING. We feasted slowly all afternoon, and the day was glorious outside, so we took breaks to wander along the creek.

Since my water pump hadn't been primed yet, the gals were real troopers when it came to dipping buckets of water from the creek to flush the toilet. I'd brought water for drinking and washing. Between the wood cook stove and the primitive water situation, we felt far-removed from civilization, and of course we had no TV, internet, or cell phone service.

At five o'clock most had headed home, and those of us left spent the night. Water was heated on the stove to wash dishes, the floor was swept, and total peace settled on that cabin along Sheep Creek as we wrote and read.

February 17—The earlier sunshine was replaced by thick wet clouds, and it rained all night. We knew "on top," it would be snowing.

I arose early to start the coffee perking on the wood stove, and sneaked in a bit of writing before frying bacon 'n eggs and heating up some leftover sourdough waffles. After a quick clean-up of the cabin, we locked up and reluctantly left.

Meanwhile, back at the ranch, I fed my animals and fixed lunch for daughter Linda, her friend Dennis Huber, Doug and I, before Linda and Dennis took off for the hills. A few minutes later, a swoosh of cold air entered the kitchen and the front door opened to admit James, followed by his pal Kyle. Big hugs for both of them.

I handed James the cabin key and some fresh eggs, and they were off for Sheep Creek. James said he dreamed of staying there the whole time he was in Afghanistan.

I went for a walk to sort everything out, and Halley was glad of that.

This evening I prepared a supper for Linda and Dennis, and we all hit the hay early.

February 18—Whipped up french toast and sausage to fortify our family for their trip back to Salem.

James and Kyle returned later this afternoon having caught fish, practiced setting up James' new wall tent and stove, and generally had a grand time. We are eternally grateful for James' safe return. He looks terrific, and tells us he doesn't have to return to Afghanistan.

February 19—While tossing hay to the cows this morning, my eyes were drawn to a violent kicking motion in Fawn's tight belly. My Jersey's baby must have been anticipating her mother's breakfast as much as she was! There's an extra mouth to feed now. Not Fawn's baby, but Clover's, Ken's nine-year-old milk cow, who joined my herd last week.

This "humble cow" needs a little TLC, having wintered a bit poorly. Not that she didn't receive all she could eat, but methinks Wallowa County's winters are more severe than Granger, Washington's. Since she was, earlier, bonded to Fawn and Rhubarb, Clover is much more content here.

Perhaps because this grand old cow raised three calves and supplied milk for three families last year, she didn't stick to being artificially inseminated. Anyhoo, for whatever reason, she came in heat yesterday. Ken says he'll wait awhile and let the cow regain some flesh, then breed her to calve next February. That way, he can haul her up on Alder Slope to his new milking parlor, and during that normally slow job month, he'll have time to milk her.

Winter is in slow retreat. Snow from the latest storm lingers here on Prairie Creek. It's been an active week.

It was 24 degrees and snowing when our Write People met at the Josephy Art Center. At noon, we walked up the street to the Red Horse Coffee House and ordered steaming bowls of leek and potato soup.

Yesterday, our Book group met at Fishtrap House, and chose *The Snow Child* by Eowyn Ivey, for our March read. An excellent novel, by the way.

Male Redwing blackbirds have invaded the bird feeder, and several returning robins are hopping about the raspberry patch, chirping loudly. This morning, on my way into Joseph, I spotted a small red fox hunting mice in Waters' field. Our two Great Horned owls *hoot-hoo* at dawn from their perch in the hay shed, and a pair of Red tail hawks are eyeing last year's stick nest high in the ancient willows.

February 20—Green leaves appeared on my osier dogwood branches, growing roots in my Olaf pottery vase. A lovely day to be out and about; walked six miles, accompanied by a happy border collie.

February 22—Today, the phone rang.

"Hi grandma, I proposed to Danielle."

Thinking James was going to finish his sentence, I waited. And then it hit me. He PROPOSED to Danielle.

"Congratulations!" I said. "This calls for a celebration. Can you come to dinner tomorrow night?"

"Of course!" he replied. So, I spent that next day cooking James' favorite foods: huckleberry and blackberry cream pie, sourdough bread,

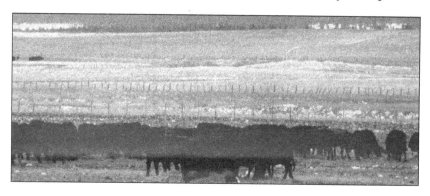

The little black Baldy calf lying in the hay is one of the first babies born in the Wallowa Valley this year. By mid-week it was joined by many more.

and green salad. James' dad, Todd, would furnish and cook the beef. The meal he'd dreamed about in Afghanistan was becoming a reality.

The evening arrived, and the couple showed up just as the sourdough bread was dumped out of the dutch oven. Naturally, slices of bread slathered in butter were consumed, to the point I thought there would be no room for the main meal.

Wrong again. Todd and wife, Angie, entered the kitchen bearing Marr Flat beef tenderloin, plus two rib steaks. While I tended the potatoes, Todd seared the tenderloin, then stuck it in a hot oven. When all was ready, he pan-broiled one of those thick rib steaks and plopped it on James' plate. In wonderment, I watched our Marine not only consume that steak, but slices of tenderloin as well. The meat was cooked to perfection, medium rare, juicy and tender.

Such laughter, gaiety, and love around our table. After two slices of pie, James leaned back and smiled. I wondered what Danielle thought? Would she be expected to cook like this after they were married? She needn't have worried. James' gal can hold her own when it comes to cooking.

February 23—The wind-sculpted snow resembled ocean waves in the barrow pits, and the fields rippled like white desert sand. Snow flakes plastered against our windows created frozen lacey patterns.

Doug and I paid a visit to the Hurricane Creek Grange Flea Market today, and I purchased videos of two classic movies, "Greystoke: The Life of Tarzan," and Rogers and Hammerstein's "Oklahoma," which were in excellent condition and provided us with hours of entertainment.

February 24—I rang the bell in church and offered prayers of gratitude for James' safe return.

February 25—After chores, I joined other women in our church to cut out squares for quilts to be sold at our fall market. Boiled up a beef tongue with herbs and garlic, then, after cooling this delicacy, fried fritters for supper. We sliced the remainder on sourdough bread and spooned on the horseradish. Yum! There is an excellent recipe for tongue fritters in Lynne Curry's "Pure Beef' Cookbook.

John Maclean e-mailed me to say I'd spelled their family name wrong in my column. So take note: Maclean. Sorry, John.

February 26—It was 19 degrees in the morning, so I shut Fawn in the barn that night, lest she calve. At dusk, a full moon rose over Prairie Creek, and my Jersey appeared agitated.

February 28—Granddaughter Carrie was helicoptered to St. Luke's Hospital in Boise, where she was placed in the neonatal unit. Carrie and Joel's baby, not due to be born until the end of June, had other plans. Just before midnight tonight, perfect, precious, and tiny Brylynne was born. She weighed a mere one pound, 10 ounces.

Constant prayers winged their way to Carrie and Brylynne from that moment on.

March 1—It was 32 degrees and the melting began as the day warmed. Mud appeared!

Jeff and Carolyn Dawson invited Doug and I to supper this evening. I baked a loaf of sourdough bread to go with Carolyn's lasagna. A good visit was had by all; however, Carrie and baby Brylynne were constantly on our minds.

Earlier that day, I'd popped in to congratulate Mary Swanson on owning the Bookloft, our local independent book store, for 25 years. What would we do without Mary's little place?

Later that night, I tried, unsuccessfully, to shut Fawn in the calving shed, but she refused to come in. And when my Jersey doesn't want to do something, I may as well forget it. She was swishing her tail and generally throwing a fit, so I knew she was ready to calve.

March 2—The day dawned foggy, damp and cold. Still wearing PJs stuffed into my bogs, a ragged jacket, and cap on my head, I traipsed down to the corral and here came Fawn to meet me…all skinny in the belly, mooing frantically.

I looked for a baby. No baby. Then I heard Clover bawling and found her standing over a shivering calf. Clover had stolen Fawn's calf. For eight years in a row, this "humble" cow had given birth to a calf of her own, and this year she wasn't even pregnant.

My morning's work was cut out for me. Not so gently, I lifted the slimy calf up in my arms and carried it to the gate, then pushed and shoved baby out onto the road and, after a few yards of this, heaved it through the door of the calving shed. All the while, mamma and Clover were tearing alongside in the adjacent corral. I shook out straw, steered baby toward it, and we both fell down and rested.

Regaining my wind, I grunted and pushed open the heavy sliding door to the shed. Whereupon both cows shot in at once. By some miracle, I persuaded Clover to exit, and slammed the door shut. Then I walked over to examine the baby. What luck—a heifer! Marked like her sire, a purebred Guernsey, with white markings on a golden Guernsey hide. She was perfect.

I congratulated Fawn on a job well done and returned to the house to fetch a 7-up bottle and a lamb nipple. After milking some colostrum, I gave the baby a taste. Immediately she went to nursing. I tossed Fawn a flake of alfalfa and headed to the house.

My grimy PJs went into the washer, and I put on clean clothes and finished my chores. I called Dave Parker, who ordered the semen and inseminated my Jerz, to tell him the news. Dave had said he couldn't guarantee a heifer. When I returned later, to check on the calf, she was still shivering, so I covered her with Ken's horse blanket and she drifted off to sleep.

This evening Doug and I attended the Blue Mountain Fiddlers show at Cloverleaf Hall, one of the best we'd ever attended. We arrived early enough to partake of Randy Garnett's Apple Flat roast beef dinner. It was good to visit old friends like Carmen Kohlhepp, our neighbors Juanita and Larry Waters, and Brent and Connie McKinley.

It was impossible to keep from stomp'in your feet and clap'in your hands to those familiar songs. Denny Langford kept everyone entertained with his jokes, and he and his helpers gave away lots of "stuff". The amount of talent displayed that evening would fill two pages, but let's just say we drove home filled with fiddle tunes.

We also checked in on Carrie and Brylynne, who are both hanging in there.

March 3—We received the early morning phone call—our little Angel passed from this earth to Heaven. Our hearts were broken. Brylynne is

Faun's heifer calf, Buttercup—3 days old.

our 28th great-grandchild. I say IS, because she will forever live in our hearts.

Prayers continue for granddaughter Carrie, who was recently placed in the Grand Ronde Hospital in La Grande, where she's bravely fighting complications related to Brylynne's premature birth.

As it's Sunday, I rang the bell at church for Brylynne.

March 4—I spent the day on Sheep Creek, cleaning the cabin and finding the first buttercup. 'Tis the season. My little heifer's name is, of course, "Buttercup."

I made excuses to go outside to enjoy the violets blooming on the lawn, the daffodils and forsythia ready to flower, and walk up the road.

This evening, baked a round loaf of sourdough bread that had risen all day, and delivered it, hot-from-the-oven, to son-in-law Charley. His cook has been helping care for Carrie in La Grande.

March 6—Over the refrigerator hum, I hear the soft hoarse whistling of the Red Wing blackbirds, perched in the apple tree, beyond my kitchen window. One minute the sun is out, the next, rain spits from clouds, swept in by a south wind. At the moment, a snow squall has erupted on upper Prairie Creek, which means our Wallowas are shrouded in white.

This March weather is as unsettled as my mind. It's been an emotional week for our family.

March 9—It was warm and breezy, so I hung my wash on the line.

Later, Halley and I walked around the country block. To Klages' corner, turned south, past Liberty Grange, East, toward Hank Bird's and Waters', then north past the old Hockett place, and Locke's, thence on home. A rather long trek. Baked a pan of brown rice/raisin/pudding, using my fresh Jersey milk and pullet eggs.

March 10—I attended church, rang the bell, then drove to Lostine to attend the afternoon matinee performance of the Mid-Valley Theatre Company production of "The Egg and I." This hilarious comedy, adapted from the book by Betty MacDonald, was well-received, and our local actors did a great job. It was fun seeing our old copper bathtub and my battered milk pail, borrowed for props, used in the play.

March 11—I invited son-in-law Charley, and Doug's cousin, Ben Tippett, who used to work for us, to supper. Pork roast, mashed potatoes with rutabagas, sauerkraut, gravy, pickled beets, applesauce. Fun to cook for appreciative men.

March 12—Allen Voortman blew in, bearing hugs and jugs of his "Pride and Joy Dairy" milk. I told him my Jersey calved and was milking again, but accepted the milk with gratitude, as the great-grandchildren would savor it. Allen had spent the day previous touring Imnaha. The Fluitt girls, who live on Upper Prairie Creek, were his guides.

Our Write Group met at the Josephy Center for the Arts, and after reading and writing, we celebrated two birthdays. I'd spent the earlier part of the morning cooking up a kettle of wild rice chicken soup, and Pat Adelhart brought birthday cake. It was 60 degrees today.

March 13—Our Museum board met at the county Extension Office and we continued with plans to reproduce the long-out-of-print Wallowa County History Book. Son Ken was here with his track hoe, cleaning up some old junk, and the temperature rose to nearly 70.

I ordered supplies to make cheese with my excess milk.

March 15—Our Write Group met at Sheep Creek for a potluck. It was a lovely mild evening and the windows and doors were opened to the fresh, spring-like air. Seated around my new table, we devoured Shrimp Pasta Primavera, salads, sourdough bread and apple dumplings fresh-from-the-oven. After our readings, the group pitched in and helped with the dishes.

When I stepped out of the cabin to drive home, a waxing moon hung over the rim rocks, and diamond bright stars pricked the clear night sky.

It had been a hectic morning. Son Ken, along with his son, Chad, and their family of six children, were here to brand their calves. After loading my car with supplies, I walked down to the corrals to record the big event on my camera. Such entertainment, little ropes swinging toward not-so-little calves, daddy and grandpa helping, branding, ear tagging—all still in progress when I left.

Grandma Annie had dropped off six pizzas, so I drove past to tell granddaughter-in-law Amy that my oven was pre-heating, and to make themselves at home. Then I fled to the canyons.

When I returned just before 10:00 that night, all was in order: dishes done and floor swept.

March 16—Doug and I drove over to La Grande to attend the sad little burial service for our baby Brylynne Saige. I'd purchased some primroses earlier, so placed a potted bright pink one next to the tiny casket. A cold breeze blew there on the hill top at the cemetery, a lovely peaceful place, with lots of trees and great views of the Wallowas to the East.

Only immediate family was in attendance, which included granddaughter Tamara (Carrie's sister) and her daughter Halley Jane, who had just driven in from Lodi, California.

March 17—After church on this Sunday, St. Patrick's Day, I cooked up a corned beef and cabbage dinner for Doug and I. It was good to stay inside and enjoy a hot meal, as it snowed all day.

March 18—Still snowing when our book group met the next morning at Fishtrap House to discuss our latest read, *The Snow Child*, a great book.

March 19—After milking Fawn, throwing hay to my cows and calves, and tending the chickens and various other critters that live here, I managed to get myself to our Writing group at the Art Center by ten o'clock. I'd gotten up early enough to bake a lemon pudding cake using my fresh eggs, milk and the juicy lemons Idella brought back from Arizona. Pat Adelhart contributed a salad, and after our session, we hungry writers feasted on fresh fare.

The Vernal Equinox, a.k.a. the first day of spring, was typical Wallowa County, as blizzards erupted all day and it was freezing cold.

This evening a sizeable segment of our Ag-related community gathered in Cloverleaf Hall for the annual Wallowa County Grain Growers dinner meeting. The Pomona Grange did a first class job of preparing a tri-tip beef dinner with all the trimmings, including pies. It was fun to visit with other ranchers who are in the midst of calving.

March 20—Doug and I hosted friends Jeff and Carolyn, and Steve and Angie, for dinner. We joked and laughed and told tall tales whilst feasting on great-granddaughter Ashlyn's 4-H lamb—half a leg of lamb, roasted to perfection, smothered in garlic, rosemary, thyme and parsley; served with mashed potatoes, gravy, creamed cauliflower and carrots, pickled beets, salad, and another one of those lemon cake puddings.

Winter appetites are sharp, and I LOVE TO COOK.

March 23—I attended a piano and violin recital at the Enterprise Christian Church, and listened with a great deal of pride as great-granddaughter Riley Ann played Beethoven's Minuet in G on her violin. The performing musicians were students of Rebecca Lenahan, and the quality of the performers was a tribute to her talents as a teacher.

Lots of water has raced under the bridge at Sheep Creek since my last column, and I've only touched on the highlights.

On this bright warm morning, I'm happy to report success! In that I managed to lead Fawn to the stanchion in the milking parlour, close it, and milk her. There are advantages to breaking calves to lead. Previously, I've had to let her stand in the calving shed, which means moving around, which means my bucket and I must follow while holding on to a teat. Most aggravating.

Little Miss Buttercup is locked away this morning in a sunny pen where she can see her mommy. Tonight I will milk first, then let baby in to finish the job. When I have to be gone, *voila!* I'll turn Buttercup in with her dam.

Must get down to the crik and prepare for Easter Sunday, as our large extended family will be descending on the violet-strewn lawn to feast and hunt colored eggs, plus eat those chocolate bunnies the Easter Rabbit (Poppa Doug) always contributes.

My wish is that everyone in Agri-Times Land, by the time you read this, will have enjoyed a Happy Easter.

March 25—The morning is cloudy, but mild compared to last week, when mini-blizzards swept over Prairie Creek with great regularity. Spring seems to leap forward before March sends it whirling back to winter.

On the positive side, granddaughter Carrie is recovering slowly, my Jerz is producing milk for our family, Buttercup is balkingly enduring her first lessons in halter breaking, the red wing blackbirds are dominating the feeder, my hens are laying 10 eggs per day, and a batch of squash cupcakes are cooling on the kitchen table where I write.

Chad Nash, Enterprise, teaching his sons Ronan (left) and Kennon how to rope calves.

April 2—When our Write group met at the Josephy Art Center, it was still beautiful weather. As we walked up the street to lunch at the Red Horse Coffee House, we noticed a tour bus parked nearby. You should've seen those cameras clicking, trying to capture our glorious mountains, gleaming white snowfields, nearly blinding in spring sunlight.

As we walked among the tourists, we, too, were struck at the beauty in our back yards. Always a sort of magic here in Wallowa County after such a long winter.

Back on Prairie Creek, son Ken was harrowing the pastures until late that evening, so I invited him to share Easter Sunday leftovers.

April 3—Pink-tinged clouds scudded across the dawn sky, and it would rise to 60 degrees again. Ken finished harrowing. I got bit by the housecleaning bug and plowed into winter's accumulated dust and cobwebs. Also broke down the hollyhock stalks, and burned them, while Doug did other burning of dry grasses around the place.

April 4—I served from noon to four o'clock as a volunteer docent at the Josephy Art Center, which was interesting, as the varied, colorful, and creatively-displayed "Collections" exhibit was still in place.

April 8—I attended, along with a large group of church members, the first meeting of the Magic Garden, at which time we planned our third year of planting. We are expanding this year, and adding more fencing to the garden. Volunteers are planning on digging post holes this Thursday. Many thanks to Robin Martin and her husband, David, who head this very successful mission that has provided tons of fresh vegetables to schools, food banks and the needy.

A very busy week ahead, and I will be leaving Sunday for a week as "Den Mom" at the Fishtrap Writers' Retreat on the Upper Imnaha. Since I don't have a column due that week, for a change, I'll be able to work on my novel.

Buttercup will be happy. She will be spending all that time with mamma.

Doug says, "No way I'm gonna milk your cow."

April 9—Spring snow flurries come and go all afternoon as I sit at my kitchen table, writing on my laptop. Occasionally, I peer outside through the soft wet flakes, to see if my little Buttercup has enough sense to go in the barn, where it's dry, as opposed to hovering out in the wet and cold. The answer is…both. Since she's better able to see mamma outside, she prefers her spacious pen to the warmth of straw bedding. Oh well, she seems to be thriving.

Just minutes ago, as thick flakes danced in the air, I noticed she was inside, and now the sun is out and the snow, which melts on contact with the greening grasses, has evaporated. A low mist curls down the meadow as warmth meets cold. Somewhere a rainbow bursts into bloom.

Using my surplus milk to make cheese has been a new experience for me. After my culture and supplies arrived in the mail, I immediately went to work. Ignoring the booklet's advice to start out making cottage cheese or other soft cheeses, I launched into a recipe for cheddar. Perusing the recipe, I suspected an entire day would have to be devoted to the project…and I was right.

Using 2 gallons of refrigerated whole Jersey milk, I began early in the morning and finished at ten that night. All day I was intimately linked to either the thermometer or the timer. I heated milk, cut curds, stirred curds, salted curds, and pressed them in a makeshift press, using creative objects for weights.

For 12 hours the round of cheese must be pressed at 50 pounds pressure. You should have seen what I used! After weighing each utensil of cast-iron skilletry, sadiron or what-have-you, I added it to the pile, which looked ridiculous but served the purpose. My first attempt has now been air-dried and waxed. Don't know if I'll be able to wait four months to taste it, but I might.

The second cheese I made was Jack cheese, which is now air-drying. If anything, Fawn's production has increased with the arrival of green grass. Even by drinking three glasses of milk per day, cooking custards, milk gravy and other gastronomical dairy delights, I still have excess milk, so my hens are laying 10 eggs per day and the barn cats are fat and/or pregnant.

I was giving the whey, left from cheese-making, to the chickens, when a friend suggested I use it to make bread. Let me tell you, the loaf of round bread I made with that Jack cheese whey was the tastiest ever. Sourdough and whey pair with a passion.

The Walla Walla onion plants Doug brought home from the local co-op are heeled in the garden, the garlic planted last fall is up, the emerging red rhubarb curls have been spread with manure, the seed potatoes are stored in the pump house, and I dug the remainder of the sweet carrots that have been covered all winter with lawn clippings. Some are now simmering, along with parsnips and short ribs, in the dutch oven.

Easter Sunday was hectic but very rewarding. After milking the cow and finishing chores, I drove into Joseph early to attend our Methodist Church's Sunrise Service. It was a glorious morning and the sun streamed through those stained glass windows to illuminate our cross made of willow sticks.

As the congregation decorated the cross with fresh flowers, I climbed the stairs to ring the bell, which pealed out over the little hamlet of Joseph, bearing the joyful news.

Home again to Prairie Creek, to begin oven-frying three pans of chicken, load the car with food prepared yesterday—potato salad, deviled eggs, pickled beets, dill pickles, and the makings for homemade ice cream, not to mention more of that Jersey milk. I left soon thereafter for "the crik," leaving Doug to follow later, as I would be staying on to clean up afterwards.

Sheep Creek was lovely and 70 degrees! My forsythia was in full bloom, as were the daffodils and flowering quince. The recently set out primroses were colorful and happy, and the large apricot tree in the orchard was snowy with blossoms.

After placing the pans of chicken in the oven to finish crisping, I lugged a rocking chair out beside the creek, leaned back, and inhaled the violet-scented air, listened to the rising creek, and closed my eyes. Heaven!

By the time our large, extended family began to arrive, bearing everything from baked ham to Easter cupcakes, it was 2:00 o'clock and everything was ready. Husky sons helped move tables onto the lawn, chairs were set up and table cloths applied, while a bevy of children, dressed in Easter finery, flitted around like butterflies.

We were joined by Big Sheep Creek neighbors, Ken and Maggie Hunt. Son Ken led the blessing, and we fell to what this family does best: EAT.

Later, I produced the ice cream bucket and layered the ice and salt As each great-grandchild, grown grandchild, and son lent an arm, the crank became increasingly harder to turn. The result was rich, creamy and delicious vanilla ice cream. Of course, the last child to turn the crank was rewarded by licking the dasher after it was removed from the can.

Next on the agenda was the infamous chocolate bunny hunt. "Easter Bunny" (Poppa Doug) had been busy. The grown cousins delighted in hiding the bunnies. Naturally, one was appointed to keep the children on the opposite side of the house. No peeking!

Later, when all the bunnies had been discovered, Uncle Todd loaded the herd of big and little kids into his pickup, and they rumbled up Big Sheep Canyon to seek out a rattlesnake den. Granddaughter-in-law Chelsea, baby Cooper, and I, refrained. By the time the noisy gang returned, wide-eyed, proclaiming they'd seen two sleepy little snakes, Chelsea and I had picked up most of the strewn-around-the-lawn picnic.

The sun was beginning to sink over the canyon rim when they all left, including Doug. Since it was so mild, I sank into the rocking chair again and savored the golden-glow-lit saddle south of Middlepoint. When the cabin was in order, I headed home around 7:30, thankful I'd turned Buttercup in with Fawn.

April 10—I milked my cow and finished up chores before baking cream puffs and filling them with a rich custard sauce. By afternoon, yours truly, gussied up in floppy white bonnet (daughter Jackie's wedding hat), frilly blouse and long sheer skirt, packing cream puffs, was off to an afternoon tea held at the new Arts Center in Joseph.

Once in a great while, this gal, after smelling of cow, and wearing jeans, enjoys dressing up like a lady. I'd picked a large bouquet of flowering quince from my Sheep Creek place for decoration.

At the Center I met up with other members of our Writer's Group, who were serving the tea and goodies. What fun we had! I even crooked my little finger and drank from an old tea cup given to me by my Grandma Wilson.

April 11—Our Magic Garden volunteers met at Big Sheep Creek to dig post holes. Ben Boswell bragged that he'd even dug one. A tailgate picnic was prepared and served by Robin Martin, and by noon the posts were all in! Now the fence raising is scheduled for this Thursday.

It was a beautiful spring day and things were a'bloomin down there: cherries, apples, pears and plums. Wild Serviceberry and Oregon Grape decorated the canyons in white and yellow. I took Halley along and she loved it.

April 12—Heavy frost, but that didn't deter the Melvilles, who are busy no-till-drilling our former hay fields.

This evening I attended the Enterprise Education Foundation dinner at Cloverleaf Hall. This annual money-raising event funds the Art and Music program at the school. I came away with the winning bid on a gift certificate to Vali's Alpine Delicatessen at Wallowa Lake for two, an excuse to visit our good friends Maggie and family.

April 13—Buck and Chelsea scheduled their branding for today, and it was a freezing, windy, spitting snow kinda day. However, the branding was accomplished and the younger generation of cow kids made a slide on the hay stack, picnicked, and generally had a great time. I was there long enough to snap a few photos before retreating to the warmth of our house.

This evening I filled the crock pot with beans and hamhocks, and baked sourdough biscuits to leave for Doug, as I would be gone for a week.

April 22—A heavy frost this morning. 22 degrees, and clear. A lot has happened since last I wrote.

The morning of the 14th, after turning Buttercup in with Fawn, I loaded the car, headed to church, rang the bell, and then drove to the Writer's Retreat on Upper Imnaha to spend a glorious week acting as "Den Mom" for five talented friends.

Tom Hampson and wife, Woesha, driving from Portland, had promised a wild salmon filet for supper this evening. So, after carting my belongings across the swinging bridge and settling in an upstairs bedroom, I tended to the sourdough bread that had been rising in my car all morning.

Later, as the loaf emerged, fragrant and crunchy from the dutch oven, the crew arrived. Let me tell you, that bread was nearly eaten before dinner! I tossed a salad, baked potatoes, and made a lemon pudding cake. Gareth, followed by another songwriter, Julianna, appeared, and Carolyn was already there, as she had signed up for two weeks.

Since it was already six o'clock, Tom went into action in the kitchen, marinating one salmon filet in ginger, garlic and olive oil, and before it was shoved into the oven he sprinkled frozen huckleberries over all. Oh my! Meanwhile, Gareth grilled the other filet on the bar-b-cue out on the deck. We feasted.

Since it was cold and raining, and snowing on the rims, we built a fire in the fireplace in addition to the wood furnace. We were all to bed early that first night. Being with three songwriters, a memoirist, and a novelist for a week was pretty inspiring stuff. The first three days were very cold, and we burned stacks of wood, but accomplished a lot of writing.

Each of us took turns preparing supper. Since I love to cook, it provides diversion from serious writing time. I puttered in the kitchen baking such savory delights as gingerbread, apricot upside-down cake, and another loaf of sourdough bread. Gareth intimated he didn't want to go home.

Despite the daily rain and nightly snow showers, we took walks up the game trail that follows Indian Creek, and along the old wagon road that leads to Benjamin and Elizabeth's graves. We shared in dishwashing and housework, and in readings and homemade songs at night around the fireplace. My room afforded a view up Indian creek. Gareth had spoken for the tree house so he could practice singing and playing his guitar.

On Thursday Tom, Woesha, Gareth and I hiked the steep trail to Freezeout Saddle, a greasy, muddy trail, slip-sliding most of the way, but the views were awesome as we zig-zagged up those steep canyon miles. Halfway up, Tom halted, and motioned to me below, where 16 head of elk trailed single file, plodding along the rim trail.

By this time we were encountering patches of melting snow seeping into the trail. Looking back, we began to see the snowy Wallowas stretching toward Cornucopia. A few wildflowers began to appear on the bunch grass covered hill sides: yellow bells, cous, kitten tails, and at the trailhead we'd waded through patches of blooming dog tooth violets.

A frigid breeze assailed us as we reached the final switchback and clumped our way to the saddle. The weathered wooden sign had fallen during the winter, so Tom and Gareth righted it in its rock jack. We took photos, gazed down into the depths of Saddle Creek, and were drawn to continue the nine miles down into Hells Canyon. The high ridges and rim trail were still snow-covered.

Despite the cold, we were elated, especially me, at age 79, to have gained the saddle. We sat on flat rocks to eat our lunches, and marveled

Janie Tippett, elated at hiking to the top of Freezeout Saddle, Hells Canyon below. Photo by Tom Hampson.

at the beauty around us. When our earlier exertion's warmth wore off, we descended, down and around, to where the wind lost its bite.

Nearly at the bottom, the sun streamed down upon a grassy bench and we all staggered toward the spot and flopped down to rest. That moment in time, there in silence so absolute you could hear the drone of a bee, we slept. Breathing the purified air while filmy white clouds formed and dissipated, amidst a rain-washed sky as blue as a bluebird's wing, smelling the awakening earth and warmed by the sun, we felt truly blessed.

Later, after hot showers all around, Tom and Woesha creatively disguised our leftovers, and we fell to eating their delicious concoctions with ravenous appetites.

On Friday we all drove to my Sheep Creek cabin to be joined by my Imnaha writer's group. Thirteen of us gathered around that new table. It was a lovely warm evening. Sunshine after rain. The canyons glistened.

While I prepared a large steelhead, caught earlier by my poet friend Robin, a jam session happened in the living room—Tom on the fiddle, Gareth on guitar, and Julianna on her uke, her lovely voice raised in song. More homemade music filled the little cabin on Sheep Creek as our guests arrived.

The potluck was a success. Steelhead baked slowly in the oven with lemon slices and olive oil, Keith's salad, Pam's brussel sprouts, Ken's sourdough bread, and chili beef. I added pickled beets and, for dessert, a large bowl of custard I'd cooked earlier, served with canned cherries picked from the trees outside.

We toasted creativity and feasted on creative fare...then left the dishes in the sink to retire to my cozy little living room for more music and written words. Poems, essays, memoirs, novels, and fantasy stories, interspersed with songs written by our songwriters. It just don't get any better than this.

The stars were out when we gals rode together back to our log lodge on the upper Imnaha, and the guys followed. It was midnight when we crawled into our beds.

The next morning was hectic. I'd promised a sourdough hot cake breakfast, which I gladly accomplished while everyone pitched in to clean the place for the next shift, as well as pack and haul our belongings across the bridge. We said our sad goodbyes as we prepared to leave and return to our lives OUTSIDE.

Around 11:00 I arrived at my cabin on Sheep Creek, placed the large potato salad I'd made the day before in the fridge, and tackled those dishes left in the sink. Lucky for me, Linda Rooper appeared to help, and we had them done, while visiting, in no time. Her husband, Ross, was mowing my lawn and setting up the irrigation for summer. Soon my friend Pat Adelhart arrived, as did Doug.

Taking my potato salad, and Pat her cookies, we piled in the back of Doug's pickup, plopped ourselves in lawn chairs, and enjoyed the ride up Big Sheep Creek to Blue Meadow, where son Todd's crew of cowboys and cowgirls were already heading and heeling calves, and branding. We placed our food on a long table and joined a throng of onlookers at the corral fence.

Suddenly, I was surrounded by family: three sons, their wives, grandsons, granddaughters, and a swarm of great-grandchildren riding horses or helping with the branding. My niece, Jennifer, along with her friend Billy, had driven up from Roseville, California, for the annual Marr Flat Cattle Co. branding. Rain threatened but didn't spill. Perfect weather. I managed to take my share of photos.

By one o'clock, half the calves were worked so Todd called a lunch break. Sisters Catering grilled pans of juicy Marr Flat burgers served up with all the trimmings, including sauteed onions.

By 2:30 I was bone weary, so Doug and I headed out—me to straighten up the cabin and take a long nap before heading home, while Doug drove

Stetson Tippett, of Selah, Washington, helps break Buttercup, his grandma's Guernsey heifer calf, to lead.

directly back to Prairie Creek. Son Steve, wife Jennifer (Tippett) and their little hats, Bailey and Stetson, who had driven over from Selah, Washington for the branding, came in much later. Grandson Stetson was bruised and banged up from being kicked and then bucked off the calves he tried to ride. Showers for all, and a nice warm bed.

The family left the next morning after a scrambled egg, bacon and hot biscuit breakfast I'd gotten up early to prepare. Church at 11:00, then home for a nap before cooking supper for Jennifer and Billy, who had been staying at a Wallowa Lake cabin.

April 23—Doug and I have just returned from helping grandson Buck haul his cows and calves to Swamp Creek. Yep! It's turnout time—perhaps a little early for most, but the hay piles around the valley are shrinking. However, the grass out there is surprisingly good, much better than last year at this time.

We hauled a load of bawling calves while Buck's dad, Bill Matthews, who drove over from Challis, Idaho, hauled a load, and Buck pulled half a load of calves in addition to two saddle horses. Two of Dan and Sue Baremore's large cattle trucks hauled out the cows. After the cows and calves paired up, Bill and Buck left them to graze awhile before driving them the three miles planned for today.

Buck thinks they'll reach Joseph Creek by Friday, a fine horseback ride for father and son, as the weather promises to be clear and sunny. Buck's three border collies eagerly awaited the journey as well. His wife Chelsea, along with children: Lucy, Katelyn and baby Cooper, brought food out for her menfolk.

It's a busy time for Wallowa County cowboys and cowgirls, with brandings every weekend, plus trailing cows and calves to grass, which seems to keep us busy too.

May 1—Doug and I, along with many other past Hells Canyon Mule Days Grand Marshals, were invited to the annual dinner to honor the 2013 Grand Marshals Larry and Juanita Waters, our neighbors, who, this past weekend, hosted the annual Lee Scott Memorial Ploughing Bee. For a change it was beautiful weather.

Daughter Lori and hubby Larry drove over Saturday, and that evening we celebrated Lori's birthday at Vali's at the lake. Although Maggie wasn't there, we enjoyed Michael and wife Dione, who served a mighty tasty steak dinner. We invited daughter Ramona and husband Charley to join us.

The next morning Halley and I walked over the hill to the Liberty Grange Hall, where we met Doug, Lori, and Larry, and breakfasted on sourdough hot cakes, sausage, and eggs. I could smell those hotcakes coming down the hill.

I managed to get in some photographing of the teams of mules and horses, attend church, and stop again to get shots of a six-mule hitch plowing the field there on the Waters' ranch. It was a perfect morning, with clouds dappling a blue sky.

May 7—The following words are probably the hardest ones I'll ever write.

Our precious grandson, Rowdy, father of Cutter and Nevada Dawn, husband of Kasey, son of my son Ken and wife Annie, is no longer with us. He died suddenly last Sunday. At this writing the cause is unknown and doesn't really matter. Rowdy is dead. There will be a big void in all our lives, especially in his children's lives.

Brian Cook, of Hermiston, rests his draft team while driving during the plowing bee on the Waters' ranch on Prairie Creek.

David Cook drives in posts as Mike Hale waits his turn while building fence at the "Magic Garden" on Sheep Creek.

As I write, our large supportive family is rallying around, converging from miles around to console, plan Rowdy's funeral, and go on with what has to be done during these unfortunate times. Daughter Jackie drove straight through from Challis, Idaho, yesterday. We spent the morning going through my myriad albums, selecting photos to be made into a video to be shown at his service.

Each beloved photo of Rowdy and his family brought on a fresh torrent of tears or laughter at the remembering. Rowdy, standing between his brother Chad and cousin Shawn atop Ruby Peak, Chad holding a stick with a white handkerchief flying in the breeze so relatives far below could look up with binoculars and see us.

Rowdy, who forgot his jacket, was wearing big brother Chad's coat and my old floppy hat. I still have that hat, which used to be red checked and is now faded pink. Rowdy's mom, Annie had admonished Chad before we began the long trek up the peak.

"Take care of your brother now," she told her eldest son. Chad had, and as he shivered in the wind himself, without his jacket, I can imagine he was a bit miffed but he never let on.

The image that breaks my heart now, over the years, is towheaded Rowdy sitting in the midst of a batch of baby chicks I was raising in the barn. I had taken him down there to see them. Doug and I hadn't been married long, so he was just a little tyke. I snapped a photo of him, that, to this day, endures.

For me, that will always be the essence of Rowdy. He was holding a fluffy yellow chick in his cupped hands, talking softly to it, totally absorbed in the magic of those little creatures. Rowdy loved all animals, and had a special way with dogs and horses. He was a superior father as well. His children adored him.

The last time I saw Rowdy was at Buck's branding, a freezing cold day in April. He noticed me sitting in the car and came over to hug me.

"I love you, Grandma," he said, words I will always cherish.

Earlier, braving the wind and cold, I'd snapped what turned out to be the last photos ever taken of my grandson: Rowdy, astride his horse, building a loop to rope a calf, doing what he loved best.

"Never too cold for a branding," he'd said, grinning that little boy Rowdy grin.

After Jackie arrived last evening, she watched granddaughter Lucy play T-ball, then drove up to her brother Ken's place, and later more family got together to talk about Rowdy. Rowdy's uncle Todd is a great storyteller, and Jackie tells me the Rowdy stories tumbled out.

Stories are what we have left. They are the glue that holds us as a family together. Each of us lives his or her own story every day. It is important for the younger generation to hear these stories, because, in the end, these tales of their relatives will define who they are.

Goodbye, my grandson, we'll keep your stories alive by the telling until we meet again in the great beyond.

We've been experiencing warm, verging on hot, days, clear and sunny until great thunder clouds form and disappear every evening. No rain, however, and we desperately need rain. If Lyman were still alive, he would have me doing the rain dance.

Speaking of Lyman, Wilma was in the county recently, staying with Barbara and Grant Warnock on Imnaha. We all had lunch together, and learned that Wilma plans on moving back to Wallowa County. Yeah!

This afternoon, a hot wind blows, so I have the drip hose running on the row of raspberries. My cows and calves are finally off hay and grazing the pasture, and I've begun to weed the strawberries.

Last week Ken hauled a load of his heifers and one steer over to turn out to graze our pastures for the summer. If it doesn't rain soon, Ken will be setting out the hand lines. Time to irrigate.

I picked the first asparagus yesterday, and after our Writer's Group met today, we were invited up to Idella's place for rhubarb crisp. My rhubarb isn't ready to cut yet, so it was a real treat.

My refrigerator was so full of milk, I turned Buttercup out with her mom. I miss milking, but even the chickens couldn't drink it all. My jack cheese is delicious; haven't cut the cheddar yet. Also made a batch of feta cheese using neighbor Nancy Knoble's goat milk. Delicious with fruit, or sprinkled on salads.

The fence-raising, rock-picking day on Sheep Creek went well. 15 volunteers showed up eager to work amidst a glorious canyon morning. Robin provided another yummy lunch, which was eaten in the shade of a newly leafed-out Box Elder tree. Soon the men will till the green manure crop under and ready the garden for planting.

Other volunteers showed up at the Joseph School to transfer vegetable seedlings into pots that will be transplanted to the Sheep Creek garden. I added to a little herb garden plot next to the cabin, and set out more raspberries and rhubarb. The lawn was mowed, the transplanted pansies are thriving, and the irrigation going. The canyons, like the hills, need water. The normally bright pink phlox is faded from the heat.

Doug climbed astride his riding mower and mowed the lawn for the first time. Soon the garden will be tilled here at the Prairie Creek place, and I will be busy planting here "on top", as well as on the crik.

Jackie and I will drive down to Sheep Creek in the morning to pick lilacs with Myrna Moore for the funeral, a peaceful place to mend our broken hearts and melt away a bit of sorrow.

May 12—Mother's Day dawned cloudy and cool, a relief from the hot weather we'd been experiencing. Granddaughter Mona Lee, who stayed on a few days after Rowdy's memorials, attended church with me that morning.

All of our children checked in to make my day special—Ramona with a Desert Rose vase filled with plum blossoms, Todd with the promise of another fruit tree he'll plant on my Sheep Creek place, Jackie having gifted me a hanging plant from Alder Slope Nursery, and Ken with a phone call, "I love you mom," plus cards in the mail.

May 13—Mona and I packed a lunch and headed to Sheep Creek. So wonderful spending time with this granddaughter. We picnicked on tuna salad sandwiches alongside the creek, stared up at Middlepoint, breathed the fresh scent of cottonwood leaves, and listened to the snowmelt waters swirl past. Scattered drops of rain splattered the windshield as we topped out on Sheep Creek hill.

May 14—Our Write Group met at the Josephy Center. Idella brought a crockpot of delicious chicken soup loaded with homemade noodles.

Tina Borgerding showed up that afternoon to till my garden. We found out a calf was attacked by wolves near Three Buck, left alive with festering wounds in its rump. This week a cow belonging to Dwayne Voss was found just east of us near Hayden Creek.

All that was left, after the wolves finished eating, was her head—ear tag still attached.

May 15—35 degrees, which was a relief after that unseasonable heat. Halley and I took a long walk around Doug's old ranch before supper, and I transplanted two rows of Walla Walla Sweet onions in my newly-tilled garden, plus a row of shallots and a package of radish seeds. I also baked a rhubarb pie and crisp with the red fruit given to me by my friend Idella.

May 16—It rained today! Just enough to soften the ground. I planted four rows of seed potatoes: Yukon Gold, Red, Russet, and a new purple variety.

Our United Methodist Women's luncheon at Janie Wiggins' lovely home at Wallowa Lake proved a wonderful break for all of us. We savored a variety of salads, prepared by the gals, whilst feasting our eyes through Janie's floor-to-ceiling windows that commanded a view of the West

Fork of the Wallowa River and the snowy Wallowas. My rhubarb crisp joined the dessert table.

On the way to and fro, I noticed the East Moraine of Wallowa Lake is now blanketed with the golden arrowleaf balsamroot. Those warm days and nights caused them to bloom earlier than usual.

Agri-Times columnist John Groupe stopped by with a lovely potted plant, plus a sympathy card. John understood how we felt. His son, who died at the age of 16, would have been Rowdy's age now. John told us he had just completed a longtime dream of riding horse back from Saddle Creek, following the Snake River trail, and out by way of Cow Creek.

That evening I attended the annual F.F.A. Awards Banquet in Enterprise. I was not familiar with most of the young people because, until our great-grandchildren reach High School, we won't have any in the program. This is a wonderful chapter that our children and grandchildren have belonged to over the years, and son Todd received his second award for donating time, money, and encouragement.

May 17—I invited Marge Onaindia and her sister Juana Malaxa to ride down to Sheep Creek. My two old friends, widows of Basque sheepherders Joe and Gus, miss country living. They and their families used to own and operate the Cherry Creek Sheep Co. These two aging but active women miss wintering down on Cherry Creek, lambing out, cooking for the shearing crew, and trailing on foot the huge flocks of sheep to their high summer pastures, where they lived in tents and baked their bread in dutch ovens.

It was a lovely canyon morning and my snowball bush was in full bloom, as were the rambling roses growing on the garden fence. Marge packed a picnic, reminiscent of former days, which we ate outside on the lawn there by the creek. Earlier we'd taken a long rambling walk beyond the Magic Garden. The clouds had parted, and rays of warm sun bathed the sweet pink phlox, and felt good on our skin. We gazed down on the creek as we followed an old wagon road. After a mile or so, we turned around and headed back.

On a hill under the rim rocks, we were startled by a loud whirring. Yep. A rattler—coiled in a clump of bunch grass, angry as anything, warning us not to intrude. We didn't, but I wished for a stout stick.

Feeling like I was coming down with Doug's cold, I cooked up a kettle of chicken soup and baked a loaf of sourdough bread. Good thing, as I spent the next two days supping soup and eating that bread. I still milked my cow, however, and cups of hot chocolate along with my fresh eggs has made me all better.

Sorry to have missed Wayne Marks' 95th Birthday Sunday at the Imnaha Church. Happy Birthday old-timer.

May 20—Last evening, as I was reading in the living room, my back to our picture window, I sensed an unusual light outside. Turning around I was struck dumb by a rainbow, one so brilliant in color, one so arched in it's wholeness, I was moved to tears. "Rowdy's rainbow," I whispered. Then ran for my camera to capture the moment.

Hough's black cattle were grazing beneath the giant bow, which bathed them in pastel rainbow-hued light. Ken's humble cow, "Clover," jerked her head up to behold the spectacle. I wondered what a cow would think of such beauty. I clicked off another shot of the giant bow, at its southern end, backgrounded by Locke's barn and our potato cellar. Dark purple clouds cloaked the eastern sky, a fine misty rain, shot with bronze light, had birthed this rainbow, which lingered, growing dim, until the sun sank behind the Wallowas.

At Rowdy's Memorial Service, son Todd had mentioned he had seen a rainbow the morning after Rowdy died. Rowdy's wife Kasey had seen the same rainbow, and there had been no rain.

We finally received some rain, not a lot, but enough to transform our valley to vivid green. Leaves on trees glisten, the song of the meadowlark fills the air, the pair of Red tail hawks take turns keeping their eggs warm, in the nest they built high in the ancient willows.

Ken has the irrigation going. Water in the ditch spills out, flooding the lower fields, and hand line sprinklers spray jets of precious water on the hill. It is hard work changing hand lines, and Ken is behind. My heart goes out to my eldest son at this time, carrying on with his life while grieving the loss of his son.

Our family gathered from miles around to attend Rowdy's two Memorial Services, one here in Enterprise and the other in Summerville. Overflow crowds filled both churches to capacity. Rowdy rests now, in his knotty pine casket in the peaceful Elgin cemetery. His soul wanders with the rainbows.

Our gnarled old apple tree is in full bloom, and today, after the rain, bees are busy pollinating. Mamma kitty birthed her spring litter of kittens in the woodshed, two baby chicks, borrowed from my friend, Stanlynn, are happily following my setting hen around the chicken yard. It's the only humane way to break a hen from setting. I tried letting her set on a clutch of her own eggs, marking them with an X, but she kept moving into other nests and letting them get cold.

Stanlynn and I joke about our a rent-a-chick deal. When the chicks

Rowdy's rainbow.

reach adulthood, I'll return them to her, meanwhile, mother hen will have resumed laying again. One old-timer ranch woman once told me how to break a broody hen from setting: "Ya put the hen in a burlap bag, swish her 'round in the crik, then hang the bag on the line, works every time," she said. Somehow I just couldn't bring myself to do that.

The day after Rowdy's memorial, there was a graveside service in Wallowa for my old friend Ruth Baremore, who passed away on May 7th. In another month Ruth would have been 98. Ruth was admired in her community, and rightfully so. An independent woman who carried on after the death of her husband in a logging accident in 1961, who raised four sons while holding the ranch together. Because of company and the emotional trauma of the day before, I didn't make it to Ruth's services. I'm sure she forgave me.

May 21—We awoke to a heavy wet layer of snow covering everything! Which is good.

This afternoon the sun's warmth is melting it all into the ground. Perhaps our stock ponds, summer ranges and dry canyons will make it yet. This morning I drove to Lostine to pick up five more chicks. Tonight I will sneak them under my other setting hen. These are fryer-types, and nothing beats homegrown fried chicken. Time for the evening milking.

May 23—The day dawned 28 degrees with a heavy frost, and patches of snow lingered from that last storm. Great-grandson Clayton graduated with honors from high school in Lodi, California. Grandma Ramona reports he was awarded several scholarships, to be applied this fall when he attends college at Cal Poly in San Luis Obispo.

May 24—After turning Fawn's calf in with her, I took off for Sheep Creek, armed with a tamale pie casserole, which was added to our monthly Writer's Group potluck. We had a good turnout and, after feasting, we got serious about our writing and read from manuscripts in progress.

Sara stopped in on her way to Horse Creek that evening and treated us to an old folk tune, played on her little "squeeze box" concertina. I was late getting home that night, but the evening was very satisfying.

May 26—I picked a bouquet of Bleeding Heart, Columbine, and a single tulip to place on grandson Bart's grave at the Prairie Creek Cemetery on my way to church.

May 27—Today Doug and I attended what has become a Triple Creek Ranch tradition, the crab leg branding, staged at the upper Prairie Creek headquarters. Several members of our family were there to help work the calves, and I added a large platter of deviled eggs to the generously-laden table. Since it threatened rain—though no one really cared, as we needed it—the food was laid out on long tables set up in the shop.

Our local cowboys and cowgirls work with extra fervor during this branding. With each toss of the loop, each wrestling of a husky calf, each scorched hair brand, they are thinking of those KING CRAB LEGS.

Brent and Connie McKinley love to entertain their neighbors. This couple and their family are most generous to us Wallowa Countians, who almost never taste fresh Alaska King Crab Legs. This seafood delight arrives from Seattle's Pike's Market, to be simmered in butter and garlic.

As if that weren't enough, we are offered thick beef steaks, grilled to juicy goodness before our eyes. Salads, fresh fruit, potatoes, beans, and an array of desserts provide more culinary treats. Brent remarked that my son Todd told him he starts thinking about those crab legs in January, while riding the frozen breaks of Big Sheep.

After the branding and feasting, we were all invited to tour the beautifully-restored octagonal barn, located to the north on Tucker Down Road, The McKinleys are to be commended for this restoration. The historic barn has graced many a magazine cover over the years, and will continue to be a local landmark and a link to our past.

May 28—I loaded a dutch oven full of rising sourdough bread, and took off for Sheep Creek.

Later, seven of us writers gathered for a salad lunch, and just as we were sitting down, here came 90-year-old Christine Anderson. Her daughter, Kris, had stolen her away from the nursing home in her wheelchair. Christine has been a member of our Write People for years.

The kitchen still smells of sourdough bread. We celebrated Maxine's birthday with a chiffon cake I'd baked earlier and frozen. We piled on frozen strawberries, peaches, and dollops of the Jersey cream.

The gals presented me with a lovely pale pink peony, which Pam planted by the front porch in memory of our grandson Rowdy.

May 29—I drove in a warm, misty rain to where my friend Ruth Wineteer lives, way up in the timber. I took Halley along and we wandered into the wet woods searching for morel mushrooms, which were everywhere! Later, after a cup of tea with my friend, we returned home where I froze most of those tasty morels.

May 30—Our Magic Garden volunteers converged at my Place on Sheep Creek, where we transplanted numerous tomato plants. I personally planted four rows of potatoes. The Imnaha school students—all four of them—along with school marm Shari Warnock, helped plant seeds this morning, too.

This afternoon I hurried back "on top" to take in the Enterprise Elementary School music program. Great-grandchildren Ashlyn, Gideon, Jada, and Lucy joined the throng of other students in performing a most entertaining and varied program.

June 1—June dawned warm and green, fresh after the rains. Doug and I hauled an old picnic table to Sheep Creek and unloaded it under a spreading Box Elder tree next to the Magic Garden. Now volunteer gardeners will have a place to spread their lunches.

At noon we drove to the Imnaha Store and Tav for fried chicken. Folks were wearing T-shirts proclaiming INDEPOOPDEHIDABEATUS DAY! Huh? Guess you'll just have to visit Imnaha to find out.

June 2—A blood orange sunrise signaled the beginning of a perfect week. After turning the calf in with the milk cow and loading my car, I headed down into the canyons again. By mid-afternoon, here came Bobbie and Barb from Portland, followed by Mary and Jessica, who pulled in from Boise via the Upper Imnaha road. We were together again—our 17th year!

Earlier, I'd baked a lemon pudding cake and, after everyone settled in, we flopped down in lawn chairs alongside the creek and caught up on our lives.

This evening I put together a shrimp and pasta dish, which we supped around Steve Arment's table. And, since we are, after all, aging friends, we turned in early.

June 3—The day was spent relaxing, reading, nibbling gourmet food, gazing up toward Middlepoint, and allowing Sheep Creek's song to wash away our cares.

June 4—This morning we pitched in to help plant more of the Magic garden. Bobbie, now in her 85th year, the oldest of our group, had planted all the cantaloupe seeds last year, and, since we'd harvested over 200 sweet melons as the result her efforts, she was delighted to plant again. I put in another row of potatoes and David Martin stretched a fence along my row of baking squash, so the tendrils will cling, climb, and produce hanging babies!

June 5—We headed to Joseph this morning, where we noticed Doug's pickup parked in front of the Cheyenne Cafe. While I hung back, the gals trooped in and each gave my hubby a hug, which naturally caused quite a reaction from the "locals table." Especially from Stormy!

Since we had time to kill before riding the tram to Mt. Howard, we took in the Nez Perce photo exhibit, then walked next door to order fruit smoothies. The drive to the lake was a treat, as the East Moraine was a-bloom with golden arrowleaf balsamroot.

Shortly after 10:00 we were floating up the slopes of Mt. Howard, riding three, and two, in two cars. It was a first-time experience for my friends. There was still a considerable amount of snow on top, but that didn't stop us from hiking the trails. Of course the views were stupendous, as the weather was warm, the sky blue, and the sun melted the snow underfoot.

We took photos of ourselves backgrounded by the High Wallowas, and stared at waterfalls leaping down from Ice Lake and B.C. Basin. We hiked up the steep Royal Purple overlook and marveled at the Seven Devils in Idaho, the cut that followed Little Sheep Creek, the far-off Divide, Marr Flat, and the V in the rim trail we knew to be Freezeout Saddle. Our sweeping view also took in the Buttes, the vast Zumwalt Prairie, and the canyons of the Imnaha and Snake. Finally, we trudged down a snowy trail in shirt sleeves.

Back at the terminal, we ate our lunch around a picnic table overlooking the Wallowas. On the return trip, we watched all of Wallowa Lake come into view, reflecting the sky, and stared downward at clumps of brilliant Indian Paint Brush beginning to bloom at the lower elevations.

At the bottom, we drove to the Methodist camp, home of Summer Fishtrap, and recalled long-ago memories of meeting there 17 years ago in Bob Pyle's workshop, writing about Syringa. Then we took ourselves to the Josephy Center for Arts and Culture, where our Write People meet on Tuesdays, and toured the Josephy Library.

On to Enterprise to visit Fishtrap House and Mary Swanson's Bookloft. Day's end found us seated at a picnic table under the aspens beside a wandering stream where children played. There we were, sipping Terminal Gravity beer brewed right there, and dining on gourmet sandwiches.

In the twilight we drove back down into the canyons while cool air wafted to us the cloying sweetness of wild Syringa.

June 6—The warm air over the creek was alive with the caddis fly hatch. Backlit by the rising sun, they flitted among a number of swallowtail and mourning cloak butterflies. There was a cacophony of birdsong, singing, singing, singing.

After breakfast eaten outside, we drove the three miles to Imnaha school, where I was scheduled to give a presentation on baking sourdough bread in a dutch oven. After letting the dough rise all night, I showed the students how it looked before I baked the bread in the school kitchen.

Busloads of children had been transported from the Joseph Elementary school as well. The little school below the rim rocks was a hive of busy bee activity. Canopy-covered booths contained learning aids that included tepee making, fish education, and a demonstration of grinding wheat and millet into flour using stone pestles and bowls.

Inside the school, Ken Hunt demonstrated creating natural colors using local clays, and a large mural was painted on an outside wall. The bread was a hit, and the smell of it baking permeated the playground. It was the last day of school!

After lunch at the Imnaha Tav, we returned to our humble abode. This evening we invited neighbors Ken and Maggie for supper. Jessica created her chicken enchiladas, and we offered a plethora of leftover desserts to be eaten outside on a mild canyon evening.

June 7—We got a Scrabble game going outside under those cottonwoods the beavers tried to take down, and the game lasted all afternoon. A table full of aging women, amidst the songs of birds, creek waters, and caddis flies. Barb won!

Ken invited Bobbie and Barb to ride his horse, Lokey, that evening. What a thrill for them. A still, golden twilight provided a perfect ending to our day.

"Syringa Sisters" L-R: Jessica White, Mary Smith, Barbara Fankhouser, Janie Tippett, Bobbie Ulrich, on Big Sheep Creek. Photo by Kathy Hunter.

June 8—We were up early to disperse on this Saturday morning, to return to our separate lives. I lingered at the cabin after the gals left, recording memories in my journal. Earlier we'd witnessed the rising sun spilling through the cleft high on Middlepoint at precisely 7:55. The rays streamed down, first on the Magic Garden and finally on us as we sipped our morning coffee. God willing, we'll meet here again next year.

At home I returned to milking my cow and weeding my garden, which is up now and growing, thanks to Doug, who irrigated in my absence.

This evening Doug and I attended the Blue Mountain Old Time Fiddlers Show at Cloverleaf Hall. It was one of the best, preceded by another one of those famous Apple Flat pork dinners.

Life is good, and a busy summer stretches ahead.

June 10—"Nothing so rare as a day in June" aptly describes my feelings this morning. Even though winter snowfields are shrinking, there is enough on the mountains to contrast with green valleys and robin's egg skies. Between irrigation and natural rainfall, gardens, crops and permanent pastures are a lush and brilliant green. Wild roses bloom along the country lanes, and a carpet of wildflowers covers our high plateaus and prairies.

Historic octagonal barn, recently restored by owner Brent McKinley. The barn is located on Triple Creek Ranch near rural Joseph.

Ken's heifers and bull mingle with my little herd, sleek and content, full of grass and chewing their cuds, drinking from cool waters and shading up under the willows. Rhubarb is due to calve. The Guernsey calf, Buttercup, is nearly as tall as her mom, the Jerz, and Rhubarb's yearling twin heifers are fat and sassy.

I'm busier than usual, catching up after spending a week down on Sheep Creek with my "Syringa Sisters." The weather couldn't have been better.

June 23—I thought of grandson James today. It was his birthday. James is still stationed in the Marines, back in North Carolina. I rang the bell in church extra long for your birthday grandson.

June 24—It was raining lightly as I lunched with my friend Pat Cason, who recently purchased a home and small acreage on Alder Slope. Pat is raising hay and bees, midst a setting that commands a view of Ruby Peak, the Seven Devils in Idaho, and the entire valley below. My contribution was a loaf of sourdough bread, still warm from the dutch oven. Which complemented Pat's morel mushroom soup. Yum!

June 25—The day dawned cloudy and coolish as I arose early to milk my cow, chore, and leave for the canyons. Due to the rains, the hillsides along the Sheep Creek highway were smothered in blooming penstemon, wild roses, and evening primroses.

It was a perfect morning for hoeing in the Magic Garden, where we managed to define and weed rows of carrots and beets, plus hills of pumpkins and cantaloupe. My winter squash plants are serious now—watch out! David Martin built a fence for them to climb, so they won't swallow the garden. Occasional bursts of sunlight filtered down on the growing vegetables, a breathtaking reward for our efforts.

Then it was back "on top," running late for my writing group but productive nonetheless. At noon we hoofed it up Main Street to Red Horse Coffee Shop for a gourmet sandwich, and then I spent the remainder of the afternoon volunteering at our Wallowa County Museum. Y'all need to visit our Tom Dorrance Family exhibit, on display now until after Labor Day. Wallowa County is proud of its Dorrance heritage.

June 26—It rained again, a bit late but good for the land.

June 27—Temps climbed into the 80s today.

While in town this morning I paid a visit to Lyman's widow, Wilma, whom I'm happy to report has purchased a home in Enterprise. Good to have you back in Wallowa County, Wilma.

June 28—Early, to beat the heat, my friend Liz Cunningham, a former Joseph resident now living in Taos, New Mexico, took off with me for Sheep Creek. We found heavy dew, left from the rains, and everything bright and fresh. We visited whilst ambling among the gardens, staring at the creek, and listening to the birds, who were extremely vocal that morning. Up the road we spied a pair of wild turkeys, their gangly babies trotting between them.

Then hot weather hit. We here in Wallowa County aren't used to temps in the 90s, so us "old folks" hunted up the shade.

Rang up grandson Buck down in Mt. Vernon.

"Been haying in 106 degrees Grandma," he said. Good thing Buck was raised on Imnaha!

June 29—I fixed egg salad sandwiches and plucked a bowl of strawberries as daughter Linda called early that morning to say she and her friend Dennis Huber were on their way up. The reason for the couple's short visit was to announce their forthcoming marriage on July 13th. Linda and Dennis live in Salem.

This evening Doug and I, along with Doug's nephew Mike, attended the Ranch Rodeo at the Harley Tucker arena in Joseph, the annual Countdown to Chief Joseph Days event. Yost Ranches swept top team honors this year. Seemed strange not having any of our family participating, but son Todd was back at the Mayo Clinic with wife, Angie, who underwent heart surgery. Buck moved out of the county and son Ken was busy haying.

June 30—Already sizzling hot at 6:30 a.m. as I milked my cow in a grassy corral.

Made it to ring the bell at church, where all the doors were thrown wide to capture any wandering breeze. Despite the heat, our evenings are most pleasant on the shaded east side of our house. Often I sit there, reading or witnessing a blood orange sunset bleed into a night sky pierced with stars.

July 1—July dawned even HOTTER. Luckily, a soft warm rain is quietly soaking into our pastures, gardens, and hills. Most welcome as we head into summer with its hot, dry days ahead. I'm hoping these late rains have helped fill stock ponds, and activated sluggish springs.

Today seems almost tropical, and my garden is leaping up! Ken's cattle, plus my little herd, can scarcely keep ahead of the grass. 'Tis the season when the cottonwoods and willows set free their drifts of "Summer Snow." It's been a busy June, and everything seems accomplished in slow motion. Granddaughter Mona Lee called from Portland and filled me in on her world.

Using gobs of chilled garden-fresh lettuce, I fixed shrimp salad for supper and we ate at the picnic table. Tall glasses of iced tea, laced with lemon, kept me hydrated.

July 2—The Big Weed again—early, before sunup. The men rototilled between rows of veggies, everything growing madly, what with our new larger irrigation pump installed. The other pump, two years old, now pumps water to my lawn and orchard, thanks to those same volunteers. I appreciate those fellas, who spent a sweltering day figuring it all out!

Later, in Joseph, you could fry an egg on the sidewalk as we writers regrouped inside the cool confines of La Laguna Restaurant, to chow down on Mexican cuisine.

July 3—A merciful coolness wafted down from the mountains. Wished a happy anniversary to grandson Buck and his wife, Chelsea, who celebrated their big day by hauling and stacking the last of their first cutting.

July 4—On this Fourth of July I sat myself down under a tree and pitted enough partially-thawed cherries to build a pie, then whipped up fixings for homemade ice cream.

This evening Doug and I joined family and friends at Kate and Heimo's lovely home on Upper Prairie Creek. Luckily, plenty of ice cream lovers took turns cranking the old freezer. It was one of those rare sunlit evenings that intensified the beauty around us as we feasted on bar-b-cued ham and potluck there at the base of Wallowa Lake's East Moraine, under Chief Joseph Mountain.

Surrounded by fertile farms and ranches, at the peak of summer's growth. Doug and I didn't take in the "Shake the Lake" fireworks display. We opted to hit the hay early.

July 5—I pushed my old hand cultivator up and do the rows of vegetables, a good morning workout, then headed over to the Liberty Grange hall, where 84-years-young Carmen and I mopped the large wooden floor upstairs in readiness for Pomona Grange next weekend.

July 8—You should see the hill beyond our house! In Doug's former hayfield, a fragrant crop of Canola, in full bloom, glows mustard-yellow against the purple snow-splotched Wallowas. My young friend, Richelle, who hiked the high trail to LeGore Lake last weekend, reports this golden field jumped out dramatically from her eagle's eye view of the farmscape below.

During the early morning hours, thunder rent the clouds asunder, and fiery flashes of lightning lit our bedroom walls. Later, a brief shower, followed by hail—yes, hail—cooled the atmosphere. In our neighbor's fields, thick, mature, alfalfa, timothy and meadow hay, fallen to the swather, lies curing in the summer sun, while other fields display rows of bales, or stacks of them, awaiting a truck to haul them away. Wallowa County is known for the quality of its hay, much of which is contracted straight from the fields.

Our recent hot spell, followed by a rainless week, has allowed for perfect haying weather. Of course there are the inevitable breakdowns, real heart-breakers when the hay is ready to swath or bale.

Numerous white-tail does graze grassy pastures during these long golden evenings, their newborn fawns hidden nearby, while the bucks, sporting velvet antlers, wander unto themselves.

My garden is a joy! We're eating strawberries on homemade ice cream, devouring lettuce, radishes and Swiss chard most every day, and waiting to taste the first tender peas, and new potatoes.

July 9—Gail Swart honored us with her presence in church, and accompanied our singing with her excellent piano playing. Gail recently played in Seattle's Benaroya Hall, which must have thrilled those present, including her five children.

Last weekend grandson Buck, wife Chelsea, and their three children, moved to Mt. Vernon. Although they are greatly missed, we are content with the move. They're doing what they love. You see, Buck accepted the job of running Widow's Creek Ranch, the ranch his cousin Rowdy used to manage. Rowdy and Kasey's children, Cutter and Nevada, are happy to have Buck's family there, particularly cousins Lucy, Katelyn and baby Cooper.

Buck reports he couldn't run the place without Cutter, who was his daddy Rowdy's constant companion and therefore learned much about the ranch.

July 13—Enterprise staged its annual Bowlby Bash, a celebration that honors the beautiful historic stone of which many of the city's buildings are constructed, including the impressive Courthouse. The stone, locally quarried, is named after a man named Bowlby who owned the quarry, which is located out the Swamp Creek Road.

Booths lined Main Street, selling wares that ranged from hand-blown glass to sausage and sauerkraut. Live music filled the air with songs played by several musicians. And, of course, the big attraction, the soap box derby, was held on South Main hill, where all manner of homemade contraptions came zooming, crawling, or stalling to the finish line.

Doug and I sat in the gazebo on the Courthouse lawn, visited old-timer Dick Hammond, and sipped cold drinks. Since the days are long and hot, Doug and I spend our evenings on the lawn, watching Hough's huge machines compress fragrant meadow hay into large "bread loaf" stacks. Occasionally a white-tail doe wanders into view, wild geese honk overhead as they seek a place to feed, and two juvenile hawks, hatched in the willows, screech for food.

July 17—To beat the heat, I arose early on the 15th to bake a loaf of sourdough bread that had been rising in the dutch oven all night. Then, while the oven was hot, I baked a mixed berry cobbler. So as not to heat the house any further, I browned a beef pot roast, added onion, garlic, and herbs, and let the meat simmer slowly all day in my crock pot.

By noon our expected guests arrived. These were folks I grew up with in the Placer County foothills, Wayne and Barbara Vineyard. We hadn't seen each other in nearly 30 years! Wayne and Barbara are members of a prominent ranching and farming family who produce rice and beef cattle. The couple pulled their motor home into our driveway and parked near the carport. I fixed sandwiches with iced tea, and we lunched out on the picnic table, catching up on our lives.

Wayne's mother Lila was a 4-H leader in our Mt. Pleasant community up until a few years before she passed away at age 98. She was a remarkable woman who touched the lives of many young people. Lila and my mother, also a 4-H leader, were contemporaries. Since Barb and Wayne's stay was short, we crammed in as much sight-seeing as possible. I drove them up to the lake, followed by a tour of upper Prairie Creek.

That evening I invited my grown children, Ramona and hubby Charley, Ken and wife Annie, and Todd and wife Angie, for supper. Todd arrived after we'd eaten, and Angie didn't make it, but we visited into the night. The pot roast, gravy, mashed potatoes, sourdough bread, salad, Ramona's watermelon and cherry cheesecake, and my fruit cobbler were a hit. I'd picked the first beets and cooked them with their tops, and plucked a salad from the garden.

Doug, not a part of my former California life, took himself off to bed, leaving us to ourselves.

The next morning we were on our way early to visit my Sheep Creek place, which was all cool and green from irrigating. While Barb and I stooped to pull weeds in the Magic Garden, Wayne disappeared. Seems he'd become acquainted with the fellows who were scratching their heads over my water pump's problem...which was not a problem for Wayne, who grew up repairing machinery in his shop.

We finally pried him away after he'd diagnosed the leak, and drove the three miles on down the creek to the Imnaha Store and Tav for a cold soda. Like all first-time visitors, Wayne and Barbara marveled at the tiny town, with its storefront wooden Indians, dollar bills stuck on the ceiling, and the rattlesnake count recorded on butcher paper taped to the side of a freezer.

Since I'd volunteered to be a docent at the Josephy Center at noon, we headed back up "on top" and bade goodbye on the Main Street of Joseph, where the couple hoped to purchase one of my books, *Four Lines a Day.*

July 18—Our old friend Allen Voortman burst through the door today. He'd been in Wallowa County doing business. Since it was nearing noon, I invited him to lunch, not knowing what to fix except salad. Then's when Allen recalled, with nostalgia, how his mom would take fresh lettuce, add hardboiled eggs and bacon then pour over a hot vinegary/sweet dressing.

"Wilted lettuce salad," I ventured, and put on a pan of eggs to boil whilst I traipsed to the garden.

"Smells awful good out there," quipped Allen, and soon we were out under the willow tree, munching our salads. Allen had many stops before heading back to Granger, Washington, so before calling his dogs, this generous man gifted us three bottles of his creamy Pride and Joy Dairy milk. Therefore, I was able to refrain from milking my Jerz for a few days. Thanks Allen!

Another old-timer passed on this week—neighbor Gardner Locke, who was in his 90s. Quite a guy, who never stopped learning a new language, nor reading to further his education. Our sympathies to wife Tappy and their family.

July 19—This evening I drove down to Wallowa Town, and on out to the Pow Wow grounds for the 23rd annual Tamkaliks celebration. Each year the event is held at the Wallowa Homeland Site on Whiskey Creek Road. I had volunteered to help in the raffle ticket booth, where, in addition to tickets (the proceeds of which go to the Homeland Project) we sold T-shirts and programs.

The booth is set up next to the pavilion where the dancers, clad in beads, buckskins, bells and feathers, form a circle and dance to the beat and chanting of various tribal drum groups. A steady breeze wafted the Wallowa river's wet coolness across the meadow, sprawled beneath Tick Hill. Tamkaliks means "from where you can see the mountains" in Nez Perce, and you can indeed, the last of winter's snow melting from their purple flanks.

Later, a waxing moon appeared through the rippling parachute canopy strung above the dancers. I am always transfixed by this peaceful scene, and touched by the observance of our Nez Perce friends' traditions, culture and spiritualism. As I drove off the grounds, the aroma of Indian frybread nearly made me turn around and buy some, but it'd been a long day, so I returned to Prairie Creek.

Now it's coming up on Chief Joseph Days week, and my applesauce is ready to can.

July 22—Usually, the aroma of simmering applesauce is associated with fall, but this morning my kitchen smells that way because Doug picked a bucket of Transparent apples down at the Sheep Creek orchard last evening. And, since I've already canned seven quarts for pie, these are being sauced. Transparents, definitely not keeping apples, make the BEST pies and sauce there is. Come winter, when the snow piles deep, this preserved fruit will be most welcome.

Later, as twilight ushered in coolness, I baked a Dutch apple pie. Yum! Our hills wear their tawny summer colors, and "Tucker's Mare," the snow-shape of a horse, has long since disappeared west of East Peak. The brilliant canola fields are fading, grains are ripening, and my garden is bearing kale, peas, lettuce, chard, and cheering my soul with blue bachelor buttons, sunflowers, and golden marigolds.

We've had day after day of cloudless blue skies, with ol' Sol nurturing all growing things, including our Magic Garden on Sheep Creek, which would gladden the coldest heart. My ancient squash vines, having enmeshed themselves in David's fence, are now exploring other areas to conquer.

Due to recent lightning, fire season arrived early, and the whirling *chop, chop, chop* of helicopters, water buckets swaying in their wake, fill our skies. As I write, a stubborn fire on the Idaho side of Snake River continues to rage east of us.

Since our church is now conducting an early summer service, I rang the bell at 8:00 a.m. yesterday morning. Later, we all met at Wallowa Lake State Park for potluck. Since it's common knowledge that Methodists are fantastic cooks, our feast featured plenty of summer salads, fruits, melons, fried chicken—and deviled eggs, my contribution.

July 8th-14th was the annual Fishtrap conference week, with its workshops and Summer Gathering, held at the Methodist Camp near Wallowa Lake. I didn't participate in this winding up of our 25th year, but managed to join overflow crowds who showed up for nightly readings offered free to the public.

It was interesting listening to authors like Judy Blunt, Bill Kittredge, and the acclaimed author of *Wild*, Cheryl Strayed. Most memorable, however, was being present when Myrlin Hepworth read a love poem, written by his father, for his mom. Then we listened to the amazing 17 young people who signed up for Myrlin's workshop. Among them were the sons and daughters of Fishtrap presenters that us oldsters had watched grow up with Fishtrap: Mateo Minato, Dawn Hunter, Guthrie Stafford, Patrick Powers, and Myrlin himself, to name a few.

I did help with the Gathering registration Friday afternoon. Although many of our old-timers are fading away, I enjoyed connecting with many longtime friends who had either been involved with the Fishtrap Imnaha Writer's Retreat, our Outpost Writing Project, or numerous writing workshops in the past. It was good to see Kim Stafford again, too.

That morning son Ken showed up with four of his grandchildren, Riley Ann, Ashlyn, plus the twins, Gideon and Jada, who helped grandpa set out hand lines for the second set of irrigation on our pastures. Since it was noon when they finished, grandma fixed their favorite tacos again.

Ashlyn commented, "Grandma, you should open a restaurant."

While we ate outside on the picnic table, they told me cousin Cutter, Rowdy's son, won the Jr. Steer Riding event at the Elgin Stampede.

"Won a huge belt buckle," they said. "At the rodeo the night before." He also won a buckle for goat tail tying. Way to go Cutter—your daddy would be proud.

July 23—I joined other volunteers down on Sheep Creek to weed, and harvest a wheelbarrow full of zucchini and crookneck squash. Robin picked cucumbers, greens and herbs. Our garden would gladden any heart! Framed by blooming zinnias, backgrounded by tiered layers of basalt, bordered by Sheep Creek, its an oasis in the dry canyon.

Not long after the sun spilled over Middlepoint, things heated up. It was HOT! Good for gardens, but we all showed signs of wilt. I made haste to drive back "on top" by 10:00 o'clock, in time for our weekly writer's group. After a quick lunch at La Laguna, I went grocery shopping.

Later that afternoon, daughter Ramona stopped by with her "Camp Runamuck" kids, grandchildren Stetson and Bailey, here to spend a week with Uncle Charley and Aunt Ramona. They'd been to the lake to cool off after moving irrigation pipe. The pair planned to stay through Chief Joseph Days week.

This evening I put together a platter of cucumber, crab meat, cream cheese finger food for the "Romance the West" event at the Josephy Center. The program included great Western music, as well as local cowboy and cowgirl poetry.

On the way home, a white-tail doe and her twin fawns appeared suddenly in my headlights—a memorable wild picture to store in my mind's eye.

July 24—I attended the Chief Joseph Days opening rodeo performance. This has become a family rite, and myriad family members and friends joined me in the stands. Doug, however, opted to stay home.

Once again the "One-Armed Bandit" was the featured entertainer. I found myself sitting next to a tourist from South Africa, who was attending his first rodeo. The fellow got very excited when two bull buffaloes loped into the arena, pawed the ground, and began rolling over in the dust. Meanwhile, the one-armed bandit—riding his mule, minus bridle—cracked a whip with his one good hand.

Later, after the first cowboy came busting out of the chute on a saddle bronc, his eyes nearly popped out of his head! An enormous full "fire moon" glowed orange over the Divide, as I made my way home, I was yet to hear the news, but our 29th great-grandchild, Beorn, finally made his appearance. Weighing in at 9 lbs, 1 oz, he joins four brothers and two sisters.

July 25—Volunteered at the Wallowa County Museum in Joseph from ten 'til one. Doug showed up at noon with hamburgers-to-go from the Cheyenne Cafe. Marine Grandson James called this morning. Said it was hot and sultry in North Carolina.

July 26—I joined other onlookers and took in the Kiddie Parade, then headed home to fix a tray of deviled eggs for Ben Tippett's surprise 70th birthday and retirement party at his home this evening at the Lake. He was surprised!

July 28—The morning of the 27th found Doug and I at the rodeo grounds, partaking of an "all you can eat" pancake breakfast cooked by the Shriners. After visiting other old-timers, we drove over to Main Street and plopped down in the lawn chairs I'd set up earlier, to take in the Grand Parade.

Lots of family there—however, little did we know it would be the last time we'd see Doug's brother Biden's wife, Betty, who suffered a heart attack and passed away a day later. Betty was 85 years old, and spent most of her life as a ranch wife down on Jim Creek, in the hills and cow camps like Cold Springs.

Son Todd and his partner were entered in the wild cow milking Saturday night. I listened to the rodeo on the radio. Although they made the first qualified time in two nights, the pair was beaten out by the next two entrants. Wild cow milking is always a crowd pleaser. This year they used long horn cows—not only hard to rope, but to milk.

This morning Doug attended the Cowboy Breakfast while I drove to the 8:00 o'clock service at church, after which I returned to the annual Chief Joseph Days Cowboy church, held in the arena. Prevailing winds filled our valley with smoke from out-of-state fires.

July 29—There was a feeling of fall in the air today; only 45 degrees in the morning. I picked ripe cherries off the little tree son Todd had given me for Mother's Day years ago. By using netting, I cheated the birds out of enough fruit for several pies.

Now we have company from Salinas, California. The Dorrances—Steve, wife Leslie, and daughter Mollie—are here to participate in a special program planned Friday evening at our Wallowa County museum. Well-known in the world of horses, Tom and his brother, Bill Dorrance, grew

Past presidents of the Wallowa County Stockgrowers riding their float in the parade at Baker City. The group was part of the 100th anniversary of the Oregon Cattlemen's Association Celebration. L-R: Back row: Scott McClaran, Phillip Ketscher, Skye Krebs, Charley Warnock, Scott Shear, Melvin Brink Perry Johnson, Biden Tippett, Bob Morse. Front row: Rod Childers, Jim Stilson, Pat Wortman, Doug Tippett, Wilfred Daggett, Jeanie Mallory, Grant Warnock, Dave Parker, Todd Nash.

up in a family of eight children born to Church and Minnie Dorrance way out on Crow Creek, here in Wallowa County. Steve is Bill's son.

It's been an extremely busy week, what with the Museum program, cooking, entertaining, Betty's funeral, the fair, and the 4-H/FFA Livestock Auction last evening, to name a few, and now it's Sunday and this column remains unfinished. So, I'll leave for now, to be continued next time.

August 1—Son Steve and children, Stetson and Bailey, drove over from Selah, Washington, following Aunt Betty's passing. The kids and I played a lot of double solitaire and Scrabble, and they helped me with chores.

Great-granddaughter Riley Ann bagged her cow elk that day too. Her mom reports she was a very thrilled young lady, helping put meat on her family's table. For the second year in a row, this little Miss has filled her cow elk tag. She was accompanied by Uncle Todd and Grandpa Ken, who took her hunting out on the Divide. They said she was a regular "Annie Oakley."

Later, after helping Riley take care of the meat, they treated her to dinner at the Imnaha Tav.

August 3—I baked a blackberry pie for the Museum benefit at the Joseph Farmer's market. Using wild blackberries picked from my Sheep Creek place, I had enough for a batch of make jam as well.

This evening I attended Caleb and Katie Howard's wedding, held at

Alder Slope hayfield.

Canola in bloom, former Doug Tippett Ranch on Prairie Creek.

Volunteers working in the magic garden on Big Sheep Creek.

neighbor Nancy's "Blue Barn" ranch up the road. 'Twas a lovely summer evening and folks converged from miles around to witness the marriage of this popular couple. The simple ceremony was performed beneath the wide Prairie skies, surrounded by grazing cattle and hay fields, and backgrounded by our beautiful Wallowas.

Randy Garnett's Apple Flat Catering provided barbecued beef accompanied by fresh salads, and a wedding cake surrounded by elaborately decorated cupcakes. Caleb and Katie are young agriculturists, fine young people to carry on after us oldies retire.

August 4—I attended the 11 o'clock church service, where all of us were happy to see former residents Don and Rosemary Green, who were visiting from Texas. Rosemary was the bell-ringer before I took over the job.

Today, while closing our upright freezer, after placing a bag of blackberries there, my left hand caught in the metal shelf of the door and scalped the thin skin from my fingers to my wrist. Not a pretty sight. I did a quick first aid and continued on with my busy life. It would be a week before I took time to see the Doc, who said all was healing fine but would leave a scar.

"At this point in life, a scar is the least of my worries," I told him.

"Just think of a good story," he quipped. "You got bit by a wolf that was attacking your dog."

The Dorrances—Steve, Leslie, and daughter Mollie—arrived this week after a two-day drive from Salinas, California. As the weather was hot, we ate outside; roast beef sandwiches with garden lettuce and Walla Walla onions, and ice cream with freshly-picked strawberries for dessert.

After everyone retired for the night, I mixed the sourdough.

August 5—This morning, Mollie and her mom were out jogging around our country block before sun-up, about three miles...which they kept up every morning for six days. They marveled at our green meadows, the quiet landscape, lush hayfields, lack of traffic, irrigation ditches rushing full of water, white-tail deer, and—always—the mountains.

Steve visited with Doug and I while I flipped sourdough pancakes and stacked waffles in the oven. The runners returned and we chowed down on a hearty breakfast to better face the day. Copious amounts of fresh strawberry jam was slathered on the hotcakes and waffles, and there were ham and eggs on the side.

Later that morning, we got ourselves to the fair in time to watch great-granddaughters Riley Ann and Ashlyn show their 4-H hogs. The Dorrances then drove north, out the Crow Creek Road, to visit the "pink barn" still standing on the site of the old Dorrance Place, where Steve's father, Bill, and uncles, Tom and Jim, spent their boyhoods.

This evening we invited son Todd and wife Angie to join all of us at the Glacier Grill at Wallowa Lake for dinner.

August 6—It's FAIR WEEK and, for the first time ever, there was no rushing in to Cloverleaf Hall in the early morning cool, to enter my veggies and flowers before they wilted in the heat. Rather, I stayed home, cleaned house, and irrigated the lawn.

Instead of driving down to Big Weed the Sheep Creek garden, or show up at our weekly Writer's Group this morning, I stayed put. There are times when one can only do so much, and this is one of them. We have company coming tomorrow, everything in the gardens is ripening at once, and there are not enough hours in the day.

So far I've kept up with the burgeoning produce; peas podded and frozen, strawberries jammed and preserved, raspberries picked, garlic dug and drying, broccoli eaten, bolted lettuce fed to the chickens, and the first potatoes unearthed and devoured.

As I write, Hough's tractor chugs around the field across the road, swathing the high meadow grasses that grew from their cattle's wintering grounds. I've turned my calf out with my milk cow for the duration of her lactation. After over four months of milking, she isn't producing enough for us and the growing calf, and although we miss the milk, my time is limited lately, and that is one less chore.

August 7—This morning I drove Mollie and Leslie to my place on Sheep Creek, a first visit for Mollie, as Steve and Leslie visited here last summer. We toured the Magic Garden and then drove down to Imnaha for a cold drink. Steve opted to stay at the ranch and work on his presentation, scheduled that evening at our Museum.

The program, featuring Steve and his family, was a success. A full house filled our new Museum annex and we had to set up more chairs. Steve, in his relaxed, laid-back way, gave those in attendance a glimpse into the early Dorrance family life, with emphasis on his famous uncle, Tom, and father, Bill, both acclaimed far and wide for their talents with horses.

Questions from the audience were answered, and Steve brought along an album containing old black and white photos of the family homestead on Crow Creek. His way of telling stories captivated the audience. Many old-timers remembered learning to dance on the 3rd floor of that massive Dorrance house, which was, sadly, torn down a number of years ago.

August 10—Nine of us gathered at the Cheyenne Cafe for breakfast. Betty Tippett's funeral was at 11:00 o'clock and the Enterprise Baptist Church was filled to overflowing, which proved to be a mini-Tippett reunion. This was a fine final tribute to a ranch woman memorialized by those her knew her best.

Betty's happiest days were those she lived at the remote cattle ranch at Jim Creek on Snake River. There, with her husband, Biden, and children, Casey and Donna, life was harder, but simpler. Many stories were told, and retold, as relatives and friends partook of a generous potluck in the church social hall. It was very hot through all of this.

This evening found Doug and I at the F.F.A. bar-b-cue, followed by the 4-H/F.F.A. fat stock auction. Luckily, swine sold first, and after we purchased Riley Ann's hog we headed home to Prairie Creek.

August 11—I mixed up biscuits and sausage gravy for our guests. Meanwhile, various out-of-town family members stopped into visit on their way home after the funeral. granddaughter Lacey, hubby Colin, and children Callen and Seely, daughter Lori and husband Larry. Mollie picked the ever-bearing strawberries and I made another batch of jam.

Thunder rumbled over the valley this evening, and a fine rain gifted us a rainbow and blessed coolness.

This year's rock jack building contest included a gal. Shown here working are Jason Cunningham and Beth McClaran, both Wallowa County ranchers.

August 12—Leslie baked a frittata in my dutch oven using supper leftovers mixed with zucchini, basil, garlic, and ten eggs, and melted cheese on top. Toasted bagels with more strawberry jam.

This morning, son Todd, who had about 20 slick-eared calves to brand at the old Dorrance place, hauled out saddled horses for the Dorrance family. There at the old corrals they had a branding. Steve said it was a great experience to be horseback out there, in the same country where his father had grown up.

August 13—The Dorrances left early this morning—that is, after they tended to a flat tire on their car. They were easy company, and fun folks to have around.

The summer continues on, with a reunion of those of us who used to work at the old hospital in Enterprise, hosted by Mary Lou Brink.

August 14—My dear friend and fellow writer, Christine Anderson, passed away today. She was 90 and living in the new Care center.

August 17—Today was the annual Wallowa County Stockgrowers day. Son Steve, wife Jennifer, and kids returned to spend the weekend for Steve's Joseph High School class reunion. Doug treated them to breakfast at Cloverleaf Hall, while I stayed home to cut a huge cabbage in my garden and grate coleslaw for the Stockgrower's dinner that night.

The annual Stockgrower's Ranch rodeo began at noon with the popular world championship rock jack building contest, which was followed by the ranch rodeo.

Grandson Stetson and great-grandson Gideon competed in the wild ewe-milking event. After a rangy black ewe drug them through the dirt, she finally settled down, whereupon the two equally tired boys labored on and on in intense concentration as they actually squeezed enough milk from those sheep teats to pour out of a pop bottle.

Son Todd and his daughter, Adele, competed with another father-daughter team in a sorting event.

Doug and I returned to Prairie Creek to rest and freshen up before the big dinner and awards night at Cloverleaf Hall. The Warnock family catered the yummy bar-b-cued beef dinner, and us old Cowbelles furnished salads. Ed and Carol Wallace, former residents who now live in Clarkston, Washington, donated two beautifully decorated cakes, which were served with ice cream.

Melvin and Mary Lou Brink were the recipients of the Honorary Stockgrowers Award, and Alder Slope rancher Jeff Parker received the Cattleman of the Year Award. The place was packed with the younger generation of ranchers, who easily outnumbered us old-timers. It was good to see children running around and having a good time.

Needless to say, we slept well that night.

August 23—Thank goodness August is a five-Friday month. I have an extra week to deal with what I call "Summer Madness." In other words, I'm more than a week behind.

A very vocal black bird chorus drifts through the open kitchen window, a sure sign of fall, as many birds of a feather are flocking together to discuss when they should head south. Earlier this morning, I noticed the birds feeding frantically on my sunflowers, raspberries, and, alas, the ripening corn.

For the first time in days, there seems to be an absence of helicopters whirling overhead. Reports are that the Sheep Creek 2 fire has been contained. However, last evening we were bombarded by a violent thunder and lighting storm. Let's hope enough rain fell to discourage future fires.

Tom Birkmaier, Crow Creek, Wallowa Co. won the rock jack contest at the Baker celebration of the 100th anniversary of the Oregon Cattlemen's Association.

At any rate, the storm provided a break from the intense heat we've experienced all summer. My kitchen smells of fermenting kraut, pickled beets, and a faint whiff of this morning's batch of strawberry jam. Definitely harvest time.

As the days shorten, our mornings are refreshingly cool, thus allowing me sufficient energy to put food by for winter.

August 24—The sauerkraut was ready to can, so went to work. All jars sealed, and I saved three gallons fresh to store in fridge. When I finished cleaning up the mess it was noon.

On a whim, I rang up friend Cathy, who lives out on the "North End."

"Wanna go to Christine's memorial with me?"

"Sure," says she.

"Be here at 3:30," I said, and hung up. And she was.

The memorial was scheduled for five o'clock at Buckhorn, nearly 50 miles from here. Cathy drove about that same distance to ride with me. 90-year-old Christine had been a member of our writing group for years. Cathy and I had talked earlier about going, but logistics seemed overwhelming.

We visited over the long dusty miles out the Zumwalt road, a first trip for Cathy. A smoky haze nearly obscured the Seven Devils mountains in Idaho, as the Big Sheep 2 fire was still smoldering. We wound down into timber at the old Steen Ranch, then passed Thomason Meadows, and soon we were climbing the rocky road to Buckhorn Lookout.

Many of my readers have been to this amazing place, where mere words fail when it comes to describing the views, which include a sweeping panorama of the Imnaha canyon that leads the eye to distant canyons beyond—all the while, you stare into depths of silence so complete, you're mesmerized. Imagine the river gleaming far below, lit by the low late August evening light, and you might get the picture.

Long tables, covered with colorful cloths, held pot luck dishes. Photos of Christine's life, clothespinned to a line secured on an old weathered building, fluttered in the breeze. Friends and family gathered to share stories about Christine.

Her four children remembered living in places like Fence Creek, Marr Flat and Mahogany Cow Camps when their cowboy daddy worked on ranches, then later for the Forest Service. They recalled living at Indian Village, not far from Buckhorn, and how they seldom went to town, "'cept when dad ran out of tobacco." Fond memories of being loved, loving the land, and learning about the land. Buckhorn was one of their mother's favorite places.

On the long drive home we talked about our friend, about how she taught in the one-room school at Imnaha, and later, after her husband passed away, how she taught schools in remote Alaskan Eskimo villages. We felt Christine's presence as a brilliant sunset flamed and died over the Zumwalt Prairie.

September 4—The days run together.

We attended another country wedding, Devin and Rebecca's, held at Devin's grandparent's home on the Butterfield ranch amidst Grandma Donna's spectacular garden, one she'd spent all summer making beautiful.

The ceremony began with non-traditional music, and here came the bridesmaids, decked out in apricot-colored dresses, skipping along in cowboy boots...followed by Rebecca's border collie, wearing a dog-collar bouquet and trotting obediently ahead of the lovely bride, radiant, in country-girl charm, holding on to her father's arm. This is so much fun to write about!

The simple service was touching, performed by a friend, to the sound of running water in the irrigation ditch and the sight of Butterfield hay fields simmering on a late August evening, the sun sinking over bare-boned mountains, Prairie Creek folks taking time off from summer labors to celebrate the union of two homegrown kids.

Add Grandma Donna's stunning garden and you have it. After Mr. and Mrs. Devin Patton returned smiling down the aisle, grandpa Tom stole the show by firing up one of his restored vintage John Deere tractors, *put-put-put*, while guests looked on in wonder.

Later, we attended the reception feast at our nearby Liberty Grange Hall. Randy Garnett's Apple Flat catering provided beef and pulled pork. All those homemade rolls, salads and pies, prepared that day by the family women. Wouldn't have missed it for the world!

Mary Lou Brink hosted yet another CowBelle reunion at the Brink ranch. There was good turnout. Wonderful to see old-time Cowbelles like Marilyn Johnson and Betty Van. Each year some are missing, and we learned that our neighbor Ardis Klages had just been discharged from the hospital.

On my way home I dropped a card off to Ardis, who lives only minutes away from us. What a trooper she is, living alone now since her husband Harold passed away last year. Glad to hear you're doing better, my friend. There are some amazing ranch women in our community.

Doug and I treated daughter Ramona and son in law Charley to dinner at Vali's Alpine Delicatessen at Wallowa Lake, the occasion being the couple's 44th wedding anniversary. Maggie was out of town that evening, but Mike Jr. and wife Dione served us hot rolls, shrimp and grits, plus a special dessert, *Happy Anniversary* scrawled in chocolate bordering the plate. After Charley yodeled for Mike, the evening was complete!

September 10—Enjoyed a brief visit with friend Phyllis, who now lives in Bend. We met on the Courthouse lawn and listened to music amidst the Farmer's Market.

Our Write Group continues to meet weekly at the Josephy House, and I still ring the bell at our Methodist Church on Sundays. All of these, and other events, were woven into my hastily-kept daily journal. Some evenings I was too tired to write.

Anyway, back to my sisters and Duane. I'd spent the day prior cleaning house, though not too seriously, and the day of their arrival, cooking. They pulled in around 3:30 on September 6th. Hugs all around. So good to see them! They live so far away.

That evening we gathered 'round the table to devour leg of lamb, roasted with garlic and rosemary, roasted potatoes with herbs, garlic, and shallots, pickled beets, sliced Imnaha tomatoes, sourdough bread, crookneck squash, broccoli, corn on the cob, and raspberry cobbler with ice cream—a feast prepared with love for my dear sisters.

We laughed a lot, washed the dishes, and went for a walk to watch a Prairie Creek sunset melt into twilight, while my cow herd looked on curiously.

The next morning sister Kathy took over my chores for the duration of their stay. She LOVES animals. After breakfast, we all left for the Wallowa County Fairgrounds, as Mule Days was in full swing.

Doug and I, as in years past, joined other former Grand Marshals in the non-motorized parade. Fred Talbott was there with his oxygen tank. "Still kick'in." he quipped.

We waved as the parade made its way down Main Street, and I spotted my sisters standing with family. After chowing down on one of those juicy Marr Flat hamburgers, we climbed in our mule-drawn wagon again and joined the grand entry.

After visiting family and watching the mule show in the arena, Caroline, Kathy and I drove down to Sheep Creek to rest up and tour the Magic Garden, which bulged with produce like ripening pumpkins and golden jubilee corn. We picked some of that corn and feasted on it that evening for supper. Yum!

We gathered at the.Cheyenne Cafe the next morning to celebrate Doug's birthday. We were joined by daughter Ramona and hubby Charley, who gave us an account of the mule and horse auction the night before. It seems Ramona had purchased a horse for her grand-daughter Brenna.

Fortified by a hearty breakfast, my sisters and I headed out north, took the Flora exit, then snaked our way down the dusty Redmond Grade to Troy, a first for my sisters. There, along the Grande Ronde River, the tiny hamlet appeared deserted except for three women sitting at tables laden with vegetables, doilies, and pies. A sign read, *Troy Farmer's Market*. Of course we had to patronize them!

We were headed for an adventure, to locate and visit grandson Buck, wife Chelsea, and great-grandkids Lucy, Katelyn and Cooper, who had only just moved into their new home on Bartlett Bench. We found our adventure as we found the steep, gravel road signed "Bartlett" and followed directions given earlier, winding around and up until we leveled out along Grouse Creek Road.

Here, I must end the story, as space and time are running out, and this column is late.

September 12—Well, it finally happened! My birthday has come and gone. I'm 80.

In our mailbox today was a belated card from cousin Marsha Wilson, from Sacramento, California. The simple greeting reads, *Hope you're feeling lucky as a dog, free as a bird, and happy as a birthday.* I am indeed, Marsha—however, this morning, I wasn't feeling any of those things.

Those of you who've had to deal with modern phone dysfunction, and the reporting thereof, like talking to a LIVE person about a real problem, can understand. STRESS describes it best. The problem is, no one can call us, 'cause the ringer doesn't ring. I don't even want to talk about it.

After I wasted an entire morning attempting to communicate, via time-saving technology, to our phone company, the frazzled woman on the other end of the line assured me that a repairman will show up next Monday. 'Nuf said.

Thunder heads build over the Wallowas. It's hot. The garden— unfrosted as of yet—continues to produce summer squash, chard, kale, beets, carrots, broccoli, corn, and cabbage. Bernice and Frank Bernatot will be here in the morning to help dig potatoes. Those noisy blackbirds and other feathered friends must've headed south. At dusk last evening, the single song of a meadowlark lingered on the hill.

Because recent rains halted harvesting and haying, Prairie Creek appears peaceful and quiet. Irrigated pastures remain green and lush. Fuzzy caterpillars criss-cross the county road; yellow jackets and grasshoppers are numerous and active. Stars, brilliant as sapphires, prick the clear night sky, while the September moon waxes over the Wallowas.

The season is changing. We are aging, Doug turned 82 the day before my birthday. Our birthdays were memorable, however, and special, 'cause sister Caroline, husband Duane, and youngest sis, Kathryn Jean, drove all the way from California to help us celebrate. Therefore, in spite of that *gxzzztt* phone, I'm filled with warm memories. For weeks I'd anticipated their visit.

The days were accomplished in typical summerly fashion, with its full calendar of events, plus all the "stuff" that just happens, like mourning the death of cousin Bob Clifford, who died peacefully at home, surrounded by family.

September 14—I chopped the head off of one of those fryers my setting hen raised, and Doug picked it. Fried chicken was his fate. It was 80 degrees today.

Cole's brother Clayton is now attending Cal Poly in California. How can my eldest great-grandchild be in college? Somewhere in the past few days, my sisters and I, plus other family members, met at the Glacier Grill to celebrate my birthday…my 19th. I wish. Sure missed them when they left, we had so much fun.

One day son Ken arrived with six of his grandchildren, my greats, to pick up irrigation pipes. I made a huge platter of tuna sandwiches, which they ate out on the picnic table. Melvilles harvested the canola and grain fields, some by moonlight, to beat the rains. Other farmers were not so lucky.

Robin and her Magic Garden crew harvested and delivered five hundred pounds of produce to schools and Community Connection. One day I canned 7 quarts of Imnaha tomatoes, and froze roasted tomato sauce, during a thunder storm.

At church we prayed for my nephew Jeff Turpin, sister Caroline's son, who is undergoing intensive chemo for cancer.

September 20—The first frost nipped the garden, but didn't kill it. Magic Garden escaped unscathed.

September 21—The season's first snow fell on the mountains. Took food to granddaughter Chelsie who was ill. Invited Ben Tippett for supper.

September 22—An astonishingly beautiful Autumnal Equinox! North-wood maple turning orange.

September 23—Visited Wilma Goucher in Enterprise.

September 24—Harvested garden at Sheep Creek.

September 25—Raining.

September 26—Cooked a roast beef, potatoes and gravy meal for the cold cowboys, sons Ken and Todd and young cowboy Clint. They'd been gathering in the forest and moving cattle to Marr Flat in a snow storm. They were most grateful for a hot meal after a long cold day in the saddle.

At noon Doug and I'd attended a birthday meal with our "old gang" at the Outlaw restaurant in Joseph, before most head south for the winter. My roast was in the oven.

Our electricity went out in one of the wind storms. Nice—no phone calls, but reporting it was another rigmarole, like the phone company.

Oh, somewhere in there Doug and I hosted friends Bernice and Frank Bernatot, and Chuck and Kris Fraser to dinner here for roast pork and sauerkraut cooked with apples, onion and bacon, mashed potatoes and pickled beets. Dutch apple pie for dessert. Good food, good friends. Bernice and Frank flew back to Germany for the winter. We'll miss them, as they helped us with so many things.

And now, at the moment, it's not raining, the sky is blue, and our Wallowas are blanketed with many inches of new snow. Blinding in their brilliance, they create a startling contrast to Prairie Creek's lush green grasses.

See you next time, as I record this slice of a very busy life.

I leave you with these farmers' words to live by: "If children live with fear, they learn to be apprehensive. If children live with tolerance, they learn patience."

October 1—This morning two bus loads of Head Start children, along with their teachers, drove 40 miles to our Magic Garden on Big Sheep Creek so they could see where the food we'd been donating for their meals came from. One little boy, digging potatoes, found his first angle worm; another, upon leaving, remarked, "I just want to stay here forever."

Amazing, in our rural area, how many children are totally removed from the land. Thank you Head Start for allowing this field trip to happen. We need more of this. Ironically, this was also the same day our government crashed, thus axing the Head Start program.

Volunteers at Magic Garden (Sheep Creek), harvest produce for schools and Food Bank in Wallowa County. L-R: Kathy, Angie, Ingrid and Caroline.

The season's first snowfall. Janie's cattle grazing in foreground. Photo taken from west window of Tippett ranch house.

Eagle Cap Excursion Train crossing the bridge at Rondowa. Note the con-fluence of the Grande Ronde and the Wallowa River—hence the name, Rond-owa.

Surprised to find out at our Extension Office that longtime Agri-Times fan, Bev Hansen, from Walterville, Oregon, received the winning bid (via the magic of internet bidding) for my two loaves of sourdough bread, my annual donation to the local 4-H Radio auction. I called Bev, who has read "Janie's Journal" for over 20 years, and she tells me she is looking forward to having those fresh loaves shipped to her via UPS.

October 5—Accompanied by Doug's cousins, Mike Tippett and Dirk Wiggins, I boarded the Eagle Cap Excursion train at the new depot in Elgin. What a fun day! Though, those two would make any day fun. We had tickets for one of several fall foliage runs. This one hosted photographers—I mean, serious photographers. Me with my simple camera had to bulldoze my way past huge cameras, tripods, telephoto lenses and such, to step out on the observation platform to photograph the amazing scenery that slowly passed by.

The view was lovely. We followed the Grande Ronde River to Palmer Junction, then on to Rondowa, where the train crossed the bridge and stopped to let us photographers out so we could photograph the train slowly going back, then slowly making its way across, just for us.

Then—all aboard! The train whistled and we made our way to Vincent, an old logging settlement, *chug, chug,* where the engine on the opposite end pulled us back to Elgin. Stunning scenery, and *surprise!* My little camera took great photos. Eric Valentine was along, offering pointers.

October 6—Mike and his dog, Oreo, spent the night with Doug and I, and Mike went to church with me this morning, and rang the bell. Since it was such a lovely fall day, Mike and I headed to Sheep Creek to pick apples…only, a bear or bears beat us to the red apple tree. You have good taste, bear.

October 10—I attended Rick Fischer's Memorial service at the Enterprise Cemetery. The sun came out from behind dark clouds, hot and intense, just as the ceremony began. It was a gift from Rick. Our condolences to the Birkmaier and Fischer families. We lost another young mother, father, and husband.

October 11—I participated in the Inaugural Fishtrap Fireside. I was the first at the podium, followed by Sara Miller, a member of our Sheep Creek writers. We represented the rural local culture which provides fodder for our writing.

Another member, Pam Royes, read at open mic, depicting a sense of place. A fire crackled in the fireplace in the living room of the old Coffin (now Fishtrap) House, and we enjoyed hot cider and donuts baked by Sophie.

This new Fishtrap event is to be held each month all winter.

October 12—I attended the last Farmer's Market in Joseph, Our Magic Garden sold pumpkins, beets, and jars of relishes and pickles made by our church ladies, using the last of the garden produce. It was a lovely day! The money earned all went back into the Magic Garden project for 2014.

Doug and I ran into the Spencers, who own the ranch across the Snake River from Doug's old ranch at Dug Bar. We walked across the street to the Red Horse coffee shop and talked about "old times."

October 13—I rang the hell at church, and following services we enjoyed a salad lunch.

October 14—22 degrees with a heavy frost. Blue sky and sunshine, so Andi Mitchell and I "seized the day" and tied to Sheep Creek. A day well spent. Our dogs had a good time too. Somewhere in there I was the guest speaker at the Josephy Center Brown Bagger. I talked about my book, *Four Lines a Day,* which, by the way, seems to be selling well.

October 17—Daughter Ramona and I drove to my Sheep Creek place to trim trees, like the black walnut that hung precariously over my cabin.

October 18—Our Sheep Creek Writers met and enjoyed leg of lamb and sourdough bread, baked in my wood cookstove, along with potluck supplied by Heidi Muller, Bob Webb, Jenny Moore and Keith Kurtz. We built a fire in the pit by the creek after supper, and watched the full "Hunter Moon" rise over Middlepoint, which didn't happen until 8:15. Middlepoint is a high steep rim that rises above Big Sheep Creek. Fitting, as Heidi and Bob have just released their latest album "Dulcimer Moon."

October 19—Another Indian summer day spent on Sheep Creek. Golden-leaved cottonwoods, sunlight on the creek. floating leaves, wild turkeys pecking grass in the meadow across the creek, and black walnuts dropping on the tin roof of my cabin. Coral-colored thornbrush thickets in the draws.

October 23—Doug's brother Biden got run over by a cow. This tough Snake River cowboy is 86. Glad to hear you are mending, brother-in-law.

October 24—I drove Jean Falbo to Dug Bar. It had been years since I'd returned to Doug's old ranch. It is a place I remember fondly, from when Doug and I were newlyweds back in '78. Jean and I had a wonderful

Gideon and his twin sister, Jada, paint pumpkins in the Magic Garden boot at the last Joseph Farmer's Market.

day with perfect weather, and I had many memories of traveling that road. We took a lot of pictures to preserve the day.

We stopped at the Imnaha Store and Tav for supper, as it was after dark by the time we returned to civilization. Then 30 more miles to leave Jean off in Joseph.

October 27—Attended the 11:00 church service and rang the bell.

This evening I joined a throng of locals at the Josephy House to listen to our Wallowa County Angel, Gail Swart, play piano selections from her newly-released CD, "Reflections." This beloved woman began and ended the concert with her soulful rendition of the Lord's Prayer, a performance that recently stunned the audience in Seattle's Benaroya Hall. We love you, Gail.

October 28—Baked an apple pie to take along with other foodstuffs to Bartlett Bench tomorrow.

October 30—Yesterday, accompanied by my writer friend Pam, who raised her two children on Imnaha along with my daughter, Jackie, out to Bartlett Bench to see Jackie and hubby Bill, who'd traveled from Challis, Idaho, to help Buck and Chelsea gather their cows and calves off the

Swamp Creek allotment. It was one of the last lingering Indian Summer days, with a crisp, frosty morning and a sunny afternoon.

On the road early, we drove out the North Highway to Flora, then zig-zagged down Redmond Grade, stopping to photograph the Arko School, built in 1910. We continued down the winding gravel road that led to the Grande Ronde River, then crossed the bridge near the tiny settlement of Troy. We switchbacked our way up Bartlett, where we were warmly greeted by family. Hugs from great-grandkids and daughter Jackie. Buck and Bill were still a horse-back, gathering miles away, and wouldn't return until well after dark.

After settling in, I took Katelyn and her little friend, Halley, for a long walk along the bench, thus creating wonderful memories with children on a perfect fall day, far above the Grande Ronde River. Upon our return to the house, the children and I, including baby Cooper, raked leaves into piles.

Later that afternoon, we drove down the bench with Chelsea to the old Richman place, where we left Chelsea milking "Bell," the family milk cow while Pam, Katelyn, Jackie and I made the 20-minute commute to pick Lucy up from school. The two-room building houses the Troy library as well as the school, where our Lucy is one of three students currently enrolled. We met Lucy's teacher, and his wife, who runs the library. This couple thinks they've landed in Heaven. Indeed they have. Troy was a-glow with fall color, a few fishermen plying the waters of the Grande Ronde. The river is famous for its steelhead fishing.

We parked near the river and walked across the old bridge, long-closed to vehicle traffic, all the while staring down at the Grande Ronde River near its confluence with the Wenaha. Golden leaves drifted silently downstream as they wafted from the cottonwoods lining the opposite bank.

Home to Chelsea's homemade clam chowder and grandma's apple pie, served up with a scoop of Bell's whipped cream. Buck and Bill pulled in long after we'd eaten. Wearily, they supped their soup, then turned in for a few hours of sleep before driving all that way back to Swamp Creek and another long day in the saddle.

Father and son left before dawn this morning. I'd gotten up early to visit my busy family. After eating Jackie's sourdough wallies, Pam and I packed up, said our goodbyes, and drove down to Troy to leave Lucy off at school. Hugs to our precious Lucy as she walked past three jack-o-lantern pumpkins, carved by each of Troy School's three students.

Returning via Redmond Grade, we stopped to visit a writer friend who lives on Lost Prairie.

October 31—On Halloween I was printing photos at Central Copy in Enterprise when a fellow burst through the door announcing.

"Did you see the moose?"

To which I replied, "what moose?"

"On Eggleson Lane" he said. "Been there since early morning. Here, look. I got a photo." That's all it took for me—I was out the door and driving to the place he'd described. I knew it was Millie Gorsline's place. A line of cars, resembling moose sightings in Yellowstone, nearly blocked traffic on Eggleson Lane. No moose.

I glassed the area with my binoculars and spied a moose ear. There she was, lying down in a stand of aspens, contentedly chewing her cud.

On a whim, I drove up to Millie's house, knocked at the door, and asked if I could photograph the moose. Then, striding boldly up to the cow moose, I asked her to get up—and she did! I got neat photos.

All that excitement made me hungry, so I ordered one of Heavenly's famous burgers cooked medium rare. Yum. Son Todd's Marr Flat grass-fed beef.

I joined my old friend Sally Akin, and we talked about years gone by, when we worked in the old hospital back in the '70s. Sally, one year older than I, was born in the Leap, the rolling hill land that lies northwest of Enterprise.

Then I paid a brief visit to brother-in-law Biden, who is still in the hospital, slowly recovering from being run over by a cow.

Just barely home from town when here came the Gray family, all dressed in spooky attire: our only trick or treaters. Pappa Doug and grandma treated them to donuts and apples.

November 1—Such a beautiful day, I fled to Sheep Creek to sit by the creek, watch the colorful leaves float downstream, and recharge my batteries.

November 2—Andi and I drove to the historic Wallowa Lake Lodge to participate in the Jo High Thespian's dinner and mystery theater, which was set in Ireland. I picked the murderer! Good acting, great food. Thanks to all those who made the evening special. Andi and I went dressed as Irish. I was the grandmother I never knew, Jenny Glennon Bachman, my paternal grandma who was raised in New Jersey.

November 3—Granddaughter Mona Lee drove in this evening from Portland. Mona is Buck's sister, who grew up on Imnaha and is now a full-fledged massage therapist.

November 7—Its 2:30 in the afternoon and a sodden wind is blowing out of the south, sweeping away our colorful Indian Summer. Frost-burned willow leaves are flying hither and thither, save for the 15 trash bags full of maple leaves given to me by the Fishtrap staff, who occupy the historic Coffin House in Enterprise. I often wonder which member of the Gwen Coffin family planted those trees. Their autumn fire has blazed its way down through the years.

When the wind dies down, I'll scatter these leaves over my garden where, over time, they will enrich the soil by their dying and, out of their dying, create more earth to produce vegetables to nourish my family and friends—just as the sight of their golden glory continues to nourish my soul.

November 9—We lost another old cowboy, Henry "Hank" Bird, who was born on May 3, 1932, on Marr Flat. Henry attended school on the Divide with the Isley boys. Hank's true loves were his fine Hereford cows, his dogs, his horses, and his family lands on Big Sheep, Coyote, and the Divide.

Hank was our neighbor and lived his life out just up the road from us, on Bird Lane. That's where Hank died, his body worn out by years of hard work. I'll always remember Hank's beautiful loose hay stacks. You were truly an artist, Hank, and I'll miss you.

Doug and I attended Hank's services on this Saturday in the Enterprise Christian Church, where he attended worship services up until his health deteriorated. I have the utmost admiration for the entire Lathrop and Bird families. They are truly fine, humble, hard-working folks, and Wallowa County natives. With the passing of each of our old-timers, a star blinks out for all of us.

Hank saddled up and rode home for the last time. His body rests in the Prairie Creek Cemetery.

This morning we arose to a brilliant sunrise. I like to think it was Hank, letting us know he's now free of life's cares, and living in peace.

December 29—It's a Sunday morning. Everything is quiet, not a person is stirring, not even a mouse—at least, not in the house. And, I suspect, not even in the barn nor the woodshed, due to the fact we didn't dispose of mamma kitty's last litter of kittens, who are all now quite large and seemed to have gotten the hang of "mousing" from their mother.

I must leave for the 11:00 o'clock service at our United Methodist Church in Joseph soon, joined by granddaughter Mona Lee, who is still here with us after Christmas. At the moment she is visiting old friends

This moose showed up just outside Enterprise on Halloween. It seemed quite at home on the ranch.

"Buck's Crew." L-R: 1-year-old Cooper, Buck's wife Chelsea, 4 year old Katelyn, and Buck's sister, Mona. Buck and Chelsea Matthews work for the Burns Brothers Ranch in Bartlett.

on upper Prairie Creek. Mona is like a ray of sunshine in our lives. She leaves today after church and, like always, I'll miss her happy presence.

Mona's mom and dad are up on Bartlett visiting Mona's brother Buck and family. They will all be here this evening to meet with more family and visit over pizza before they take off in the morning for Challis, Idaho. Son Ken and daughter Ramona are invited, too.

Last night the stars shone with a polished brightness in a clear cold sky. This morning's flamingo-colored sunrise signaled a cloudy, overcast day with a bit of snow in the forecast.

Christmas was awesome! We actually pulled it off. Family from all over converged at the Sheep Creek cabin for a most memorable time. Seventeen of us gathered around two tables and dove into prime rib, baked ham, mashed potatoes, gravy, green salad, sourdough bread, and baked beans, and still had room for pies: blackberry, mincemeat, pumpkin, and Lori's cheesecake.

The day was sunny and not really warm, but most of the snow was melted. High up on the rims up Big Sheep, the snow still clung to the highest ridges. Ice lined the creek and the beavers have taken down six more trees on the Magic Garden side.

Daughter Linda and hubby Dennis Huber, and son Brady, drove all the way from Silver Lake State Park, and daughter Jackie and hubby Bill arrived from Challis just as we were sitting the food on the table. Talk about timing.

Son Steve from Union Gap, Washington, his wife Jennifer and their two little hats, Stetson and Bailey, along with daughter Lori, arrived Christmas Eve. Steve and Bailey took right to chipping ice off our driveway, while Stetson and I took a walk with Halley around the ranch. Stetson enjoyed skating on the frozen ditches.

That evening, Christmas Eve, daughter Ramona and hubby Charley drove in with a moveable feast, which was enjoyed by son Todd and wife Angie as well as upper Prairie Creek friends. Most appreciated by yours truly, as the next day was spent cooking the dinner down on the creek. The wood cook stove really got used.

It was a memorable Christmas with family, but I'm a bit used up.

Events leading up to Christmas included a full calendar. And, since I'm not fully used to this THING yet, I hope this column doesn't get lost in cyberspace. The stress of it all was just too much. So I did the only sensible thing. I unplugged from the grid.

This is the first time in three weeks I've sat down at technology. I must say, it was like a huge load had fallen off my back. No e-mail, no aching back, no THING on the kitchen table to remind me of technology. I was so peaceful.

Now, since Allen Voortman acted as guest columnist to give me a rest, I must get back to it. But first, it's time for church. See ya later! Got to get there in time to ring the bell.

Gwenllian Nash shows off her new heifer calf from her milk cow, AnnaBelle. Looking on are her three brothers: Gavin, Kennon, and Lochlan.

Buttercup chews her hay during a February snowstorm.

2014

January 11—6:30 a.m. Sitting here at my kitchen table, I'm surrounded by items that reflect my present state: umpteen get-well cards; bottles of prescription pills placed on notes telling me when to administer them; a flashlight in the event the power goes off, as 30-mile-an-hour Chinook winds are evaporating the snow and exposing layers of melting ice, and candles to light, if that should happen; a booklet from Home Health Care; detailed transcriptions, written in pen, copied from e-mails and phone calls with insurance companies and Home Health.

No printer, yet!

Also on the table are the latest issue of Agri-Times, a bowl of fruit, and a cup of tea, cold now, since I took time to shower while Doug is still asleep. Things have been surreal around here since December 31st. That's when IT happened. Per usual, Doug left the house before six on that fateful New Year's Eve morning to join his cronies at the Cheyenne Cafe's LOCALS ONLY table.

It had rained during the night, and when he drove into Joseph the pavement was still wet. However, while breakfasting with "the boys," the temperature dropped below freezing. Therefore, by the time he left town, a frigid Prairie Creek wind was blowing across the Imnaha Highway and the road was coated in ice. Doug, apparently unaware of the change in temperature, took off for home.

Being concerned, I decided to call him on his cell phone. After much fumbling, a strange voice. "Hello." "Where are you?" I asked.

"In the barrow pit," he lisped, like he had a mouth full of applesauce.

"What happened?" I said, and he proceeded to tell me how he'd lost control of his pickup and wrecked.

"Where?" I asked, my heart pounding.

"By the old Marks' place."

"Are you ok?"

"Yeah, got a little blood in my mouth, state cop is here and they're taking my pickup to the garage."

I tried to picture this. As a freezing wind swept across Prairie Creek.

I'd just come in from choring, walking with mincing steps, placing each booted foot firmly on tufts of old grass, using my ski pole. Fortunately, I'd chored early enough, before the temperature dropped. During such icy conditions I wait for things to warm up. Since moving to Wallowa County nearly 46 years ago, I've learned the hard way to respect ice.

I immediately called son-in-law Charley, since he and Ramona live just south of the Imnaha Highway, I reasoned it wouldn't take long to reach Doug. Also realizing that if I were to drive up there, there'd be two of us in the barrow pit! This turn of events dramatically changed the course of our lives. Not a good way to start off the New Year.

Our large family rallied, and we were catapulted into the world of ambulances, emergency room visits, and finally, after a bed was made available, into our new Wallowa Memorial Hospital in Enterprise.

As an aside, Doug was assigned room 11, ironically the same room his brother Biden resided in after his "cow wreck." Biden, by the way, is running laps around Joseph, where he is still staying with daughter Donna and son-in-law Wayne. He says he's even driving again.

For me, this all meant little or no sleep, family arriving from out-of-town, cooking, holding down the fort here, making 20-mile-round-trip hospital visits, dealing with constant phone calls and e-mails, making decisions, and finally, at last, having my patient home again.

Doug's daughter Lori stayed at the hospital for a few days and nights, and spent the night here the day he was released. Lori left the next day and I've been alone with Doug since then. As always, family support is just a phone call away. We have established a routine now. Doug improves daily; however, recovery is a long, slow process when one is 82. My former nursing skills have been honed by round-the-clock caregiving duties.

At the moment, my man of the house appears content to be in his familiar surroundings, and my pureed soups and milkshakes are a hit when compared to hospital food. Doug's tongue was severely lacerated, which means no solid food. Therefore, it was a challenge when it came to fixing nutritional but tasty meals that didn't require chewing.

The day I drove hubby home, my dear friend Idella delivered a gallon of turkey soup, a loaf of sourdough bread, and freshly-baked cookies. Life continues to be a learning experience. Since Doug had other injuries, we are entering a new phase. God Bless us all.

Now, it's time to get Doug up and begin our day, our hospital day. Ken will deliver more hay this morning for my cows. Halley, my border collie, misses her milk bones. Every morning, seven days a week, Doug would walk out to his little pickup to leave for the Cheyenne Cafe, and

Halley followed at his heels, knowing he would produce a bone before leaving.

So, to reestablish this routine, I let her in of a morning and, wagging her stub of a tail, she trots over to Doug's chair to receive her treat.

Life goes on, as does winter. I've been up since 4:00 a.m., taking my shower in case the power goes out. Nearly 36 years on Prairie Creek has taught me to be prepared for such emergencies.

There are advantages to canceling everything on the calendar. Between nursing duties, I curl up in my recliner, throw a blanket over my legs, and read. At the moment I'm deep into *True Grit*, which is this year's Big Read selection. This classic novel, written by Charles Portis, was published in 1968. It is delightful. Since we live in a valley where people practice "true grit" everyday, I can identify. It isn't easy living here, especially in winter. I especially admire our cowboys and cowgirls who feed cattle during blizzards, and venture out in the middle of a frigid night to save a frozen calf, or help deliver one. Seven days a week, for weeks.

Fishtrap has supplied copies of this book to the schools, and many in our community are reading it. Book discussion groups have formed, and many events associated with the theme are being planned.

I attended another of our generational rancher's memorial services last week. Long-time Imnaha rancher, Jack McClaran, passed away recently. An overflow crowd gathered at the Baptist church in Enterprise for a very moving tribute to a fine person. Our sympathies to wife Marge, and their three children. Lots of stories died with Jack, who grew up in the canyons, a place he dearly loved.

Warm memories of Christmas on Sheep Creek surface during these challenging times. I hold such memories in my heart. How I long to be there, where it's always 10 degrees warmer than here "on top." In the meantime, I'll observe sparrows and chickadees at the bird feeder out my kitchen window, and chuckle at the fully grown kittens as they "camp out" under the feeder, in hopes they can snag a bird.

"Allen," my enormous Hereford rooster, is learning how to crow. It is a strangled attempt, which startles the hens. His sister "Alice" did lay a double yolk egg, but I'm still waiting for the triple yolker.

While I accomplish one day at a time, I dream of spring on Sheep Creek, and it WILL come, along with the daffodils, flowering quince, cherry blossoms and buttercups. And soon it will be time to plant the magic garden again. Life is good.

January 12—More icy conditions, adding to the large floes of ice that continue to cover our property. This has been the winter of ICE. Some folks, who live at the end of steep driveways, were actually ice-bound.

January 15—I came down with the flu, a light case, thank goodness, as no time for sickness. My duties as full-time caregiver never ceased. I did enlist the help of caregiver, Lucinda Olsen, so I could run errands in town and restock groceries. Doug's brother Biden and nephew Casey were of great help to us as well.

During the full "Hunger" moon, the Imnaha pack of wolves stole into our valley. Kinney Lake, Hurricane Creek, Alder Slope, Prairie Creek, Upper Prairie Creek, the East Moraine and, most recently, Findley Butte in the Zumwalt country. Halley, my border collie, hears them too, as we're awakened in the predawn hours by Hough's wildly bawling cattle, frightened and running from their bed grounds.

I opened our front door one night to see a ghost herd in starlight, hooves breaking through crusty snow, fleeing from circling dark shapes. I drove my car out onto the road and shone my lights over the pasture, silence. Hungry now, in the dead of winter, wolf sightings are numerous and we listen to their mournful howls. It is surreal. The latest kill is a sheep on upper Prairie Creek, on private property.

Daughter Linda, hubby Dennis, and sons Jordan and Brady drove over from Salem to visit Doug. I opened up my cabin on Sheep Creek for them to spend the night.

January 19—Doug treated various members of our family to breakfast at the Cheyenne Cafe, while I attended the 8:00 a.m. church service in Joseph. Directly after, I hurried home to prepare my dutch-oven pot roast and a cast-iron pan of sourdough biscuits for a Fishtrap event held that afternoon at the Josephy Center. All part of the Big Read theme based on the book, *True Grit*. Granddaughter Adele and I experienced true grit, as my girl had to leave directly after the demo to drive cattle, and alfalfa hay still clung to our boots from feeding cows that morning. In other words we were REAL.

Arriving early we transformed the Josephy Center into a cow camp. A saddle here, a cow skull there, boots, scarves, long johns hanging on hooks. We dressed Mike Midlo in old-timer Jess Earl's buckskin jacket, and Doug's worn Stetson.

Prior to the program, Adele and I were organized enough to take in the Stein Distillery tour, which proved very educational. We highly recommend it. The local distillery is just down the street from the Josephy Center. We did imbibe on a thimbleful of spirits, which made our presentation very informal and relaxed. It was fun! Especially for me, after all those days of intense nursing.

After a short question and answer period, those in attendance eagerly consumed our cow camp and trail food. Adele, our young chef, dressed in grandma's red union suit, chaps, worn hat and boots, proved a pro when it came to answering questions about cooking grass-fed beef. By the way, the beef was raised by her daddy. Yep, Marr Flat Natural Grass-Fed Beef.

Earlier I'd brewed a large enamel pot of cowboy coffee, demonstrating how I used one of Doug's discarded socks to hold the coffee grounds. Several old-timers were brave enough to drink a cup. And, one fellow asked for a refill!

Linda and her family, who had been visiting Doug, left later that afternoon to return to Salem. It was good to see those two grown grand-sons. Prayers for our old friends, Sandra and Fred Hubbard, who live faraway in Auburn, California. Fred is dealing with serious health issues, and both Doug and I wish we were closer to offer support at this difficult time in their lives. We call often, wishing to ease their burden.

January 20—I fixed Doug pancakes, which he seemed to manage without any teeth. His new dentures should arrive soon.

Our monthly Reader's group met that morning at Fishtrap House. It was a sunny 44 degrees.

January 21—Our weekly Writer's Group gathered at the Josephy Center, where I was warmly welcomed back after a long absence. At noon I fled to the canyons and hiked along Big Sheep Creek. There's something soothing about moving water.

After eating my sack lunch, I drove to the small settlement of Imnaha to visit Postmistress Bonnie Marks, who told me her father-in-law, 90+-year-old Wayne Marks, is now a resident of Alpine House, an assisted living facility in Joseph. I know Wayne misses his canyon home, but hopefully he is content to be in the company of fellow Imnaha old-timer Bill Bailey.

January 22—I drove into Cloverleaf Hall to attend the annual Stock-grower's "Dollars for Scholars." I'd spent the morning baking a mince-meat pie and raspberry cobbler, plus Jesse Tippett's sour cream raisin pie for Doug, who couldn't attend this year. The event, which included a silent auction and traditional dessert auction, raised 7,000 dollars to be used for scholarships and the heifer project.

A record 137 folks attended this year's prime rib dinner, prepared by Randy Garnett and his Apple Flat Catering. The desserts, which included elaborately decorated cakes and luscious pies, were auctioned off by Dave Yost. Bidding was lively, and rancher Doug Mallory Jr, who, along with his wife, own and operate the Troy Resort, captured the winning bid on my mincemeat pie, which sold for over $200. My cobbler went to a table full of folks who polished it off in minutes, and Peggy Brennan returned my pie plate all washed, yet!

The Stockgrowers committee deserves a hand for staging this event, which grows in popularity every year.

Neighboring rancher, Mark Butterfield, donated hay for the heifer project. Good to see my old CowBelle friend, Marilyn Johnson, there, and of course her daughter, Sara Lynn, does a stellar job of organizing the event.

Then there was the annual meeting of the Silver Lake Ditch Co, held this year at the Josephy Center, which was warmer than the old Grange Hall.

January 23—This evening found Katherine and I at the Joseph Community Center where we attended the 2014 Eagle Cap Extreme annual banquet. Wonderful fun! Great meal, featuring Marr Flat Natural beef, followed by musher's stories along the trail, plus Team Ollokot related their tales. I remembered my own adventures cooking way out there in winter wilderness on the Upper Imnaha River, at Ollokot Campground, during the 2009 Sled Dog races.

The thrill of that Saturday night, however, was being hugged by my future granddaughter-in-law, Danielle, who told me her future husband, my grandson, James, is being mustered out of the Marines and will be home soon.

Earlier, driving into Joseph from Prairie Creek, I could scarcely see the road.

Thick, frozen fog covered everything and visibility was limited. Returning home the fog lifted, and the moon led me Eastward toward Prairie Creek. Wallowa Lake is frozen over now, and hundreds of wild ducks occupy about an acre of open water.

January 24—My new friend Katherine and I drove to Ferguson Ridge ski area to watch the Eagle Cap Extreme Sled Dog Pot race. "Fergie" is also the start and finish line for the 100- and 200-mile races. It was a beautiful sunny afternoon and we enjoyed visiting other friends while waiting for the teams to finish. The sun sank behind the mountain and a bitter chill descended on the ski slopes just as Jennifer Campeau

Jennifer Campeau of Okotoks, Alberta, Canada, won the 2-stage, 31-mile pot race during the 10th annual Eagle Cap Extreme Sled Dog Race held in Wallowa Co. Shown here is Jennifer and her 2 lead dogs, "Zana" and "Paloma." Jennifer's husband, Jason, won second place in the 200-mile race.

of Okotoks, Alberta, arrived with her team. Jennifer's husband, Jason, competed in the 200 mile race.

January 29—Arising at dawn this morning, I noticed frozen rain drops plastered to the kitchen window. At first light I ventured outside to discover a thin coating of ice covering our driveway. Doug was up and dressed minutes

Later, waiting for me to drive him into the Cheyenne Cafe to join his cronies for breakfast.

"We aren't going anywhere," I announced, remembering the last time road conditions were like this.

"Ok with me," he said, heading for his recliner with a cup of coffee. I turned on K.W.V.R. just in time to hear Richard announce that all Wallowa County schools would be closed. Wise decision.

After breakfasting on oatmeal and leaving Doug to watch icy conditions elsewhere on TV, I backed our car (with studded tires) out to the feeder (to avoid my falling on ice) and forked hay to my little herd. Fragrant leafy clover hay, put up last summer by son Ken on his fertile Alder Slope ground.

They were all eagerly awaiting my arrival. My Jersey milk cow, Fawn, due to freshen with her third calf in early March; Fawn's yearling Guernsey cross heifer, Buttercup; Rhubarb and her June Bug. How I love my cows! They aren't work, they're my joy. I suspect, because they provide a link to my childhood.

Daddy taught me to milk when I was five years old, and gave me Guernsey calves to raise for my 4-H projects. He showed me, by example, that milking as well as breeding Guernsey cattle was fun. His cows were his passion, never drudgery. He was living his dream. I guess that's why I continue to enjoy my cows. They, plus my other chores, provide exercise to keep me strong as I age, as well give me the satisfaction of doing a job I've spent a lifetime perfecting.

Son Ken is feeding Rhubarb's 2012 twin heifers with his own cattle this winter.

Tending my chickens this morning proved much more of a challenge, but thanks to my ski pole, I accomplished the task safely. My hens have decided to lay again; brown and blue eggs. The largest brown ones are laid by Alice, the gargantuan red pullet sister of Allen.

Speaking of whom, Allen, as in Voortman, called the other morning to tell me his wife suspected I might have named my rooster after him because he eats me out of house and home! Allen, however, says I can't insult him, and I believe that. By the way, Allen, thanks for leaving two gallons of COW in our fridge. *Mmmmm!* Oatmeal is so much better with Pride and Joy Dairy milk.

Now, at 10:00 o'clock it's snowing. Prairie Creek appears clean and white again, as it should be in winter. Across the road I see Don and Lois Hough's cows and calves, muted through the falling snow, forming wavering black lines, munching their daily ration of meadow hay. Tomorrow, son Todd and his crew of cowboys and one cowgirl (wife Angie) will begin trailing the Marr Flat cows to the valley from Big Sheep Creek, a three-day-drive.

On Friday I will prepare the traditional hot meal for the cold crew after they make their way down Echo Canyon, which lies due east of our ranch.

As the "Wolf Moon" wanes, I look back on this departing January. It has been a very emotional month. Doug continues to improve from his accident, and enjoys returning to his "old gang" at the Cheyenne Cafe in Joseph, and eating lunch with the "old folks" at Community Connection in Enterprise. Then there are those other necessary outings like doctor and dental appointments.

Doug's new dentures have been ordered, and he is looking forward to chowing down on beef steak. He is most grateful for friends and neighbors, like Danny at the Cheyenne Cafe, for transporting him to and fro on mornings when I'm too busy. He also thanks all those who sent cards, and food, and appreciates his friends' visits.

February 2—After dropping Doug off at the Cheyenne Cafe this morning, I rushed to church in time to ring the bell. How I love early morning there, with the rising sun streaming through those beautiful stained glass windows. Fellowship afterwards, with some of the finest folks in the world.

Back to the Cheyenne to breakfast with Doug, A Sunday morning treat.

Last Friday Todd's cowboys, and his cowgirl, braved a cold snowy foggy, ice-filled trail up Hayden Creek, to arrive safely with over 300 cows, which were then trailed very slowly into the holding pasture at Stilson's ranch, just north of our place. Todd had spent the morning feeding other cattle in the valley, checking on two calving heifers, and spreading hay in the holding pasture.

After soggy slickers, gloves, boots and hats were piled deep on the porch, the crew trooped into the warmth of our kitchen, washed their hands, sat down at the table, and bowed their heads to say grace before filling their plates with the food I'd spent all morning cooking: Dutch oven pot roast, simmered with garlic, carrots, and shallots, a huge kettle of mashed potatoes, rich beef gravy, green salad, a cast-iron frypan of sourdough biscuits, with warm blackberry cobbler and cowboy coffee for dessert.

Sons Ken and Todd, wife Angie, Angie's dad Bob Thompson (an old Colorado cowboy), and Todd's younger cowboys, Cody Ross and Pat Dougherty, plus Doug and I, polished off most of the food. As in years past, I enjoyed hearing their stories, some of which were pretty scary, like when Ken's horse went down on the ice. Luckily he was leading his gelding at the time. Ken said the horse calmly sat down, then carefully gained his footing. At one point, after they topped out, it was so foggy they couldn't see their cows.

Early the next morning, those cows were trailed to their wintering grounds on the old Snyder Ranch, just east of Enterprise. Passersby will soon begin seeing the first baby calves, a sure sign of approaching spring, or of lingering winter.

Last evening at the Josephy Center, a packed house sat spellbound at a performance celebrating the release of Carolyn Lochert's new CD. Our local Blues singer is so fabulously talented, and her backup musicians were amazing. Entertainment at its finest. Really professional stuff. Congratulations, Carolyn, and thank you, thank you for treating us to your songs.

Carolyn's daughter baked the cakes, too. Oh, my, what a treat. They were delicious.

I drove back to Prairie Creek with songs in my heart. And now it's 9:30 p.m. on Super Bowl Sunday. Doug is in bed, and his Sea Hawks won. I'm tired of sitting here at the kitchen table writing down my life. Time to turn in.

February 4—Three inches of snow fell in the night, and the temperature dropped to 10 degrees. Doug is back to driving again, and early every morning he disappears into Prairie Creek's white void to make his way into the Cheyenne Cafe.

Our writer's group met this morning at the Josephy Center, where we toughed it out, as the furnace was on the blink.

February 5—It was 5 degrees. After my round of chores, I returned to the kitchen to put on a pot of beans and ham hocks. At noon I took a cast-iron fry pan of cornbread out of the oven. I invited son Ken for lunch, as he'd been hauling our garbage cans to the dump.

February 6—The thermometer on the carport registered minus twelve. I let it warm to zero before venturing outside to chore. After layering myself with clothing, I could scarcely move. A search in our coat closet yielded a down jacket my mother had purchased prior to a January visit with us many years ago. My face was covered with a baklava, and two scarves were wrapped around my neck.

We were saddened to hear that Doug's sister, Barbara Fredrick, passed away in Punalu'u, Hawaii. Barbara, an accomplished artist, was 89. She will be missed.

Our former Wallowa County friends, Carol and Ed Wallace, called from their home in Clarkston, Washington, wondering how Doug was doing.

It was 11 degrees, and snowing when I headed home that night, after watching the second film screening of *True Grit,* which was held at the Josephy Center. I enjoyed the movie; however, in my opinion, no one can replace John Wayne. I'd popped a bag of popcorn to nibble on while watching the film.

Earlier that evening Joanie Fluitt scooted in out of the cold bearing two quarts of milk "from our friend, Allen Voortman," she said. She and Mike had stopped by Granger, Washington, on their way home from Seattle. Thanks again, pard, for keeping us in fresh milk until my Jersey calves.

February 7—Snowing. 20 degrees. Since the roads were plowed and sanded over Sheep Creek Hill, I left before noon and headed to the canyon cabin. I spent the remainder of the day preparing for our monthly writer's potluck and reading. As a large duck, stuffed with bread dressing, roasted in the wood stove oven, I enjoyed being "off the grid." After the table was set, I read, took a nap and went for a hike with Halley. It's always 10 degrees warmer down there.

At five o'clock, here came my friends, bearing wild rice pilaf, pasta, fruit salad, green salad and orange chutney. As usual the meal was memorable, as were our discussions. Dishes washed and wood added to the fire, we gathered around the stove to read and critique our writing.

Luckily, I made it out "on top" just ahead of a snow storm. The first flakes pelted my windshield coming down Sheep Creek hill.

February 8—Eighteen inches of snow fell during the night, and a good foot by noon. Almost two feet before the storm moved on. Our lane was so clogged, we couldn't break through to attend Lois Blankenship's funeral.

February 9—Doug broke trail with the diesel pickup, and I followed later in the car. The snow plow, working overtime, hadn't plowed our road yet, but I did make it to church, and Doug joined "the boys," at the Cheyenne.

Received a nice card from Julie Wheeler, the owner of Divide Camp for wounded veterans. Just a quick note to let you know your story in the Agri-Times about the Divide Camp has generated more donations than the Observer, Oregonian and Chieftain stories combined. Your story and the wonderful people who read it was a big winner for us!"

So, thank all of you in Agri-Times land, who found it in your hearts to donate to this worthy cause. Julie says she can't wait to get going again in the spring.

Doug and I recently enjoyed a great visit from old friends Pat and Linde, who now reside in Butte, Montana. I drove Linde down to Sheep Creek, where we escaped the cold and snow, walked in GREEN grass, and picnicked on tuna sandwiches while remembering old times. Linde and I used to hike all over the mountains and canyons, places that stretched

Janie participates in the Big Read True Grit Dutch Oven cooking, accompanied by Mike Midlo (left) and Adele Nash (right). Photo by Debbie Lind.

from LeGore Lake to Eureka Bar, not to mention the time we took a boat ride from Dug Bar, on New Year's Day, up the Snake with our hubbies. I can still see Doug piloting his old DUG BAR boat. Wonderful memories.

Linde and I lived on the edge, always ready for adventure. So glad we did, as we couldn't manage it now.

Later, we drove on down to Imnaha, and visited Myrna Moore, another old friend, who is librarian at the little school there.

Back "on top," we bade farewell over hot mochas at Arrowhead Chocolates in Joseph. A perfect ending to a perfect day. A dutch oven pot roast, smothered in veggies, has been simmering slowly all afternoon.

Tonight is the Grand Finale for the Big Read of *True Grit*. I'm entered in the Dutch Oven Cooking contest at Hurricane Creek Grange, which begins at 5:30. Storyteller Rick Steber is the judge. I best be going.

February 10—Last time I left you with my dutch oven meal simmering slowly for the Big Read "True Grit" finale, held last evening in the Hurricane Creek Grange Hall. The event was an smashing success. Seventeen contestants entered the dutch oven cooking contest. Author and storyteller Rick Steber, assisted by the 2014 Chief Joseph Days Court, sampled all the entries, and decided "Boudin Stuffed Pork Crown Roast" deserved first prize.

Mike Baird, who calls himself "just an old river rat," prepared the winning dish. "Cuz," Stanlynn's "Boarding House Beef Stew and Biscuits" took second place. My pot roast and root veggies were a hit and not a bite was left. A counter full of piping hot ovens, featuring local meats, awaited a long line of hungry guests, who all contributed potluck side dishes. And, of course, those Grange ladies baked the pies.

We relaxed with full stomachs and listened to Rick Steber relate stories inspired by some of the more colorful old-timers he's interviewed over the years. True West stories with True Grit, all highly entertaining.

February 14—It's raining on this Valentine's Day. Raining on snow and ice, melting our white landscape. Water, water, everywhere, filling swales and gullies, pooling in pastures, clogging culverts with rotten ice, eroding country roads, swelling ditches, creeks, and rivers. All swirls in a frothy stew of winter's dirty flotsam, exposing dog bones, frozen grasses, cow pies, weeds and junk. It's all good moisture, except that the ground is still frozen, and most of the water is draining off. Hopefully it's snowing in the Wallowas and adding to our valuable snowpack.

This gray day was brightened, however, by several phone calls. The first being grandson James, en route from North Carolina to Oregon. At long last he's out of the Marines and heading home to his beloved Wallowa County. Wonderful hearing his voice, "Happy Valentine's Day, Grandma!" No text, no e-mail, my grandson's voice TALKING to me.

"Where are you, James?" I asked.

"In Kearney, Nebraska," he replied. "I've had snow all the way, and it's still snowing."

I told him how relieved I was to know he'd survived that Eastern ice storm. After visiting for awhile, James said he planned to veer north into Montana to visit a friend, wait for the weather to improve, and be home next week.

My second phone call came from the Northern Cheyenne and Crow children at St Labre Indian School in Ashland, Montana.

"Hello," a man said. "Here's a Valentine's gift from our children to you." Whereupon a chorus of clear young voices began to sing "Let Me Call You Sweetheart." I tried to visualize those precious children, miles away midst that cold Montana Prairie, snug in their warm school, a school that my meager contributions have, for many years, helped sustain.

The children's musical Valentine continued. "Let me call you sweetheart, I'm in love with you, let me hear you whisper, that you love me too, keep the love light shining, in your eyes so blue, let me call you sweetheart, I'm in love with you."

Those words and melody awakened a long-ago memory of my daddy singing that very song to HIS sweetheart, my mother, as he milked his cows. His strong Caruso-like voice floating on a summer eve, forever burned into his young daughter's memory. Valentine's Day is about LOVE. Today, that emotion was wafted over the miles between Nebraska, Montana and Oregon, to warm a grandmother's heart on a rainy winter day.

Granddaughter Chelsie and her family presented me with another special Valentine today, a red rose and a photo taken years ago at Chelsie and Justin's wedding. In the photo, grandson Rowdy has his arm around his grandma, and we're both smiling for the camera. Another example of love that endures.

Doug presented me with a box of Arrowhead chocolates, made right here in Joseph. Yum!

While out feeding my cows and calves this morning I continued to be extremely cautious. Melting patches of ice can be tricky, so best go slow and select the safest route. Perhaps this thaw is a foretaste of spring, because now we have MUD, muddy feeders, muddy chicken pen, and mud on lovely brown eggs.

I watch from my kitchen window, amused, by Allen and Alice, venturing forth in the rain, brother and sister chickens clucking along, shaking their wet feathers as they scratch in the rotting pile of lawn clippings.

On the way to Enterprise yesterday, I noticed Todd's cows have begun to calve. A sure sign of calving season are the bald eagles perched in the old cottonwoods lining Prairie Creek, awaiting their annual diet of placentas.

One evening at dusk I spied a dead yearling Angus lying in Hough's pasture. I called Lois and told her what I'd seen. At dawn the next morning, I observed a cautious coyote snatching chunks of beef, then trotting off a few feet before returning for another bite. During the coyote's brief absences, several ravens swooped in for their share of the feast. Later, after the carcass was hauled off to the dump, coyote and ravens returned to peck the bloody snow.

While driving through Joseph to attend the 8:00 a.m. church service, I was amazed at the huge piles of snow pushed up alongside life-size bronzes of cowboys, eagles, wolves, horses and Chief Joseph. Everywhere, folks were digging out driveways, clearing sidewalks, or shoveling snow from doorways. A kind volunteer had cleared the snow from our church's parking area.

February 17—Our book group met at Fishtrap House to discuss the book, *True Grit*. Following a lively discussion we all agreed Portis has authored a classic.

After the meeting, I took a drive up on Alder Slope to see the damage caused when a wall of snowmelt water came rushing off the mountain during a recent warm spell. Two of the roads turned into creek beds.

February 19—Snowed, 20 degrees. Doug and I met Marge and Juana for breakfast at the Cheyenne Cafe. It was fun visiting with our friends, who, along with their husbands, Joe and Gus, used to own the Cherry Creek Sheep Company. A familiar sight in Enterprise are these two sisters, taking their daily walkabouts.

Since February was my month to host Methodist Meals Together, I spent the remainder of the day preparing supper. By the time our guests arrived, a roaster pan of Cornish Game hens, stuffed with bread dressing, a kettle of mashed potatoes, pot of gravy, tossed salad, cranberry sauce, and molasses apple cake were ready to serve. It was a most enjoyable gathering. Inviting folks for dinner, becoming better acquainted, and taking time to really visit, is becoming increasingly rare these days.

It didn't used to be that way, especially in rural areas. When long winters provided time to get together in warm cozy homes and share a meal together. Of course, that was before TV, Facebook, and the internet. In my opinion, meals don't have to be gourmet and houses don't have to be spotless. Folks simply enjoy meeting together to exchange conversation over home-cooked food.

Grandson James is home! Welcome back, grandson.

February 21—My friend Katherine and I drove to Imnaha and turned upriver to check on the Fishtrap Writer's Retreat. Since it was a warm day, the lawn was GREEN and the birds were singing spring songs, we ate our chicken sandwiches out on the sunny deck near the river.

On our return downriver we met Barbara Warnock walking along the road with her dog, and caught up on local news. Glad to hear old-timer Wayne Marks is settled in Alpine House. A wave of nostalgia washed over me while passing Lyman's ranch, remembering the happy times we had there. Like the river, changing its course after a flood, life changes too, and like the river, life keeps right on flowing.

Lots of changes along the old Imnaha. We stopped at the Sheep Creek cabin to check on things and take a short walk up the canyon before heading out "on top."

"My young housekeeper, Amy Ramirez, took this photo of Halley and me after she cleaned and we went for a walk around the old ranch this morning," says Janie. "It was a gorgeous morning. 'A photo is worth a thousand words' says it all. Hard to describe such a morning. The mountains were drop dead beautiful.

February 23—Snowed all night. By morning Prairie Creek resembled beaten egg whites. Pristine and clean. After wading through the soft stuff to chore, I barely made the eight o'clock church service in time to ring the bell.

Later this afternoon, when the snow had melted and the sun came out, Halley and I climbed the east moraine of Wallowa Lake. It was lovely up there, looking down to the lake where a gaggle of honkers rested on the ice, at the edge of open water. The lake ice is beginning to melt, after weeks of being frozen over.

I breathed in the clean fresh air and took in the snowy ramparts of Chief Joseph Mountain, rising beyond the west moraine. Looking north, then east, I let my eyes wander over Prairie Creek far below, to where we lived.

Snow was melting on the high ridgeline and trickling down the steep slope. On my return I rested on a fallen pine. The road below was quiet, no tourists yet. The sound of silence.

February 24—I baked another loaf of sourdough bread for Bev Hansen, who purchased two loaves at the 4-H radio auction held last fall. After mailing her bread, I left another loaf off for grandson James, an excuse to hug him and meet his new puppy.

February 26—A cold fog hides our Wallowas this morning, and hangs heavy over the prairie. My cows and calves appear ghost-like, arising from their bed ground under the ancient willows. At the sound of my voice, "Good morning girls," they wander over to the feeder.

Fawn is springing. Her due date is March 10th. Soon, I'll be milking again. While I fork hay, Halley, eager to help, chases a flock of sparrows flying from garden fence to barn roof. It is a game, and one she's been playing for years, with generations of sparrows.

Late yesterday afternoon, I drove out to grandson Chad and wife Amy's place to see milk cow AnnaBelle's new calf. Traveling out the North Highway, I noticed Trout Creek was flooding. Temperatures hovered around 45 degrees, which meant those great snowy meadows up the road were melting. When I pulled in their lane, I could tell my great-grandkids were pretty excited, 'cause they'd raised and tamed AnnaBelle, their Jersey/Brown Swiss heifer, and now she was a mommy.

"She's in there," said Gavin, pointing to a stall in the barn, and there she was. Bedded in straw, the robust, tan-colored heifer calf peered at us with large brown eyes. It was pretty obvious that these children, who'd witnessed the birth, were extremely proud. Soon, daddy, grandpa Ken, and grandma Annie appeared. After photos were taken, the as-yet-unnamed baby was petted and fussed over, and Annabelle duly congratulated on being a fine mother, the older children tried their hand at squeezing milk from the first-calf heifer's ample teats.

"AnnaBelle has a fine udder," I told them. "High and wide fore and rear udder attachment, evenly-spaced teats, level udder floor." All terms for judging dairy cattle, which I learned as a child under my daddy's tutelage.

February 28—Because the sun was out, Andi Mitchell and I headed to the crik. After tending to a few chores, we hiked the steep canyon slopes of Middlepoint, checking my fence line as we went. Halley was a happy dog, joyfully sniffing around, investigating every scent. Meanwhile, we rejoiced in the sweeping views of Sheep Creek, rushing with snowmelt toward its confluence with the Imnaha. Since the sap is rising in the willows and red osier dogwood, the creek was lined with color. New bunch grass provided a green contrast to last years old growth.

Back at the cabin we ate our lunches out on the sunny deck, and soon Andi's hubby Dave Kuhlman drove in. Her cowboy was on his way out from Cow Creek on the lower Imnaha, where he works for the McClaran Ranch. He reported calving was going well, and he was taking a break to visit his "calving widow" wife, who lives "on top."

After returning home to Prairie Creek, I prepared supper for Doug before driving into Enterprise to attend "An Evening of Opera." Yep.

At Lear's Restaurant, where Eastern Oregon University's Music Department presented "Too Many Sopranos." Glad I went. 'Twas a wonderful evening that included an Italian dinner, savored slowly, while eleven joyful students of opera entertained us. Thrilling to hear those trained young voices! Each student obviously enjoyed performing. The evening was a benefit fundraiser for Alpenfest, which will be held in the county September 25-29.

March 1—March padded in like a fluffy white cat, bringing three inches of wet spring snow that melted before noon.

This evening I joined friends at Cloverleaf Hall to enjoy the Blue Mountain Old Time Fiddler's Show. Randy Garnett and his Apple Flat Catering family served up their famous bar-b-cued beef dinner, which included huge wedges of pie. An impressive crowd of locals gathered to spend the evening tapping their feet to some of the best fiddling in the Northwest.

To name a few performers: our Prairie Creek Girls, Ryya and Lexi Fluitt, who just get better every year; granddaughter-in-law Amy Nash on guitar, accompanied Rebecca Lenahan on the fiddle, and Caleb Samples providing back up. The popular local group, Homemade Jam, played their various instruments and Laura Skovlin sang folksy tunes. Young Bailey Vernam began the evening by singing the Star Spangled Banner. As usual, M.C., Denny Langford, kept everyone entertained.

My young house keeper, Amy Ramirez, took the photo of Halley and me after she cleaned and we went for a walk around the old ranch this morning. It was a gorgeous morning. The photo is worth a thousand words ', says it all. Hard to describe such as morning. the mountains were drop dead beautiful."

It didn't matter that we've heard his "Sweet Marie" joke every year! March 2, After 8:00 church service I joined Doug at the Cheyenne Cafe for ham 'n eggs. That afternoon we called our Auburn, California friends, Sandra and Fred. They are finally getting some much-needed rain. Fred says he's "hanging in there."

March 4—Cloudy, no frost, 34 degrees. Our weekly Writer's Group met at the Josephy Center, which was followed by a brown bag lunch program featuring Women in Agriculture. The panel consisted of cattle rancher, Jill McClaran, goat raiser, Wendy McCullough, and Back Yard Garden lady, Beth Gibans.

March 7—I washed clothes and hung them on the line, and they dried! First time since last fall. That afternoon I drove to Lostine to attend the World Day of Prayer, hosted by the Lostine Presbyterian Church Women. I love being in that old church, built in the late 1800s.

March 8—Clear at sunup, 29 degrees. Snow continues to melt and the creeks and rivers are running bank to bank.

Steve and Angie Rubin treated me the Friends of the Elgin Opera House production of OKLAHOMA! It was my first trip out of the county in months. Met up with several Wallowa County folks who'd also traveled out to see the musical. We had balcony seats and really enjoyed the matinee. I'm still singing "Oh What A Beautiful Morning."

March 9—After early church service, I met up with Doug, who'd been joined by other members of our family, for breakfast at the Cheyenne Cafe. Luckily, we remembered to set our clocks ahead the night before.

Doug headed to Imnaha in the afternoon, while I drove to Lostine to take in the matinee performance of "Desperate Ambrose," a play staged by the Mid-Valley Theatre Company to officially end the Big Read. The story takes place in Dead Man's Gulch, 1885.

Watching our local "wanna be" cowboys play the roles of Panhandle Jake, Stinkweed Meade, Homer the Kid, Hoot Owl Pete, Beth Malone and others, was gangs of fun. And the actors were really into it. It took TRUE GRIT to pull this production off. Thanks to Kate Loftus and her crew of volunteers who have been bringing us live theatre since 1995.

March 10—High water caused rivers like the Grande Ronde to overflow their banks and wash out roads. Traveling to the Sheep Creek cabin, I noted a washout at Lightning Creek. Sheep Creek and the Imnaha were malt-colored and running high with debris.

March 11—Catching up with my column, and now it's 11:00 p.m. and I need to wrap this up and get to bed.

Today I saw the first returning robins and red-winged blackbirds. Spring's a' coming.

March 12—This morning, my friend Amy Ramirez appeared with her cleaning supplies to wash the dusty knick-knacks that clutter my kitchen, which freed me to work on some editing. By 11:00 o'clock we finished, so I suggested we take a hike over the hill. Halley was eager to be off, and Amy had her camera ready. The views on top were stunning: snowy mountains, the east moraine of Wallowa Lake, farms and ranches scattered over the Prairie, Liberty Grange Hall, and "the hills" rolling northward. We traipsed down to the Farmer's Ditch, which was barely trickling, so the Lake would fill, we guessed.

Hiking along the bank, Amy spied a juvenile barred owl perched in an old cottonwood. The nocturnal hunter slept through many clicks of Amy's camera, so she got some great shots. A pair of wild geese honked loudly as we approached their nesting site.

Returning by way of our cow pasture, we met "Hank the Cowhorse," who belongs to son Ken, and soon approached my little "herd," lying in the sun, bellies full, enjoying the warmth.

Driving into Enterprise these days, I'm cheered not only by the sight of son Todd's calves, but by a nearby hillside splattered with buttercups.

Yesterday our Museum Board met at the County Courthouse, where a good turnout of members discussed the printing of our new Wallowa County History Book featuring family histories. We are encouraging folks to begin writing their new stories and updating older ones. Another huge undertaking, requiring hours of volunteer effort, looms ahead.

March 13—Another Bluebird Day! Two in a row. Clear sunny skies, blinding white Wallowas, meadowlarks, robins, red-winged blackbirds, hawks and honkers, all pairing up for nesting. My Jeri still hasn't calved. At first light I'm out there hunting her down.

This morning I found her bedded on the hill alongside her yearling heifer, contented as could be, chewing her cud. She barely acknowledged my presence, so I told her it'd sure be nice if she'd calve during this lovely weather, rather than wait for the next blizzard to sweep through. Upon leaving, I turned to see my two cows and their offspring rise to their feet and head for the feeder. The one thing they do understand is FOOD.

March 17—BIG NEWS. Yesterday, around 2:00 p.m. my Jersey milk cow decided to calve, and on a lovely, dry afternoon yet! I witnessed the birth through the living room window. One final push, and a strapping reddish-brown calf slithered onto the pasture. A bull. I named him Pat, in honor of St. Patrick's Day, which we celebrated today.

Arising at dawn, I baked James' favorite pie, huckleberry cream. Then, after chores, I spent the remainder of the morning preparing the traditional meal of corned beef cabbage, carrots, and potatoes. I also baked Irish Soda Bread. By noon, the meal was ready.

James' college buddy Kyle was here visiting, so it was fun to see him. James' fiancee Danielle, his dad Todd and wife Angie, also joined us. Let me tell you, that pie was reduced to an empty pie plate in less time than it takes to tell. Our Marine is home.

March 26—It's a long story, but this will be a short column. The short of it is, I'm typing with my left hand, 'cause there's a broken bone in my right one. I'll know more after my 2:30 doctor's appointment today.

After surviving hazardous icy conditions here on the ranch all winter, I should have stayed put, not gone to town. Town can be a dangerous place. Especially at night, when one is walking to the car and trips over one of those raised cement markers in a parking area. They are a stumbling block waiting for an accident, especially in the dark.

I won't dwell on the details, 'cause I'm tired of x-rays, waiting in emergency rooms, wearing this splint, and explaining what happened. In other words, it cramps my style, especially when it comes to milking the cow.

Thankfully, "Jerz," who senses my handicap, has been surprisingly cooperative, for her. She stands, patiently chewing her alfalfa hay, while I use my left hand to milk a teat into a large cottage cheese carton, which I grip with two fingers of my splintered right hand. Thus far I've managed to keep us and the cats in milk, not to mention provide relief for Fawn's swollen udder, and keep her production up until I regain the use of my right hand.

Patrick, my cow's bouncing red bull calf, is thriving, and playfully chews on my jeans while I'm milking.

My other chores are accomplished in slow motion, very carefully. The hens and two roosters are free and far-ranging, which seems to be the IN thing these days, and which does boost their egg-laying. They are happy chickens. However, as the daffodils, crocuses and other bulbs emerge, the chicken's free-roaming might come to a halt, at least during the day. I'll let them out in the evening.

Son Ken stacked my hay so's all I do is push the large flakes into the feeder with my boot. Amazing what can be accomplished due to necessity. Doug is in charge of daily dishwashing and brushing my hair, but all other chores are mine per usual. Driving isn't a problem with automatic shift.

Our old pal, Ray Combes, passed away recently, and his services were held in our Methodist Church in Joseph last Saturday. Ray was a longtime member of our church, and sympathies go out to wife Pat and his family. I will miss Ray. We were on the same wavelength when it came to milk cows. Years ago, Ray worked for Carnation Farms in Washington. Mostly though, Ray had a sense of humor and, over the years, we laughed a lot.

Grant Warnock called the other evening to tell me Marvin Sams, who lives in Milton-Freewater, Oregon, left a peach tree with him on the Upper Imnaha.

"A very special tree for you," he said, grafted with three varieties of peaches. I'll plant it near the Magic Garden on Sheep Creek. Marvin says he's read my book, *Four Lines a Day*, four times. Thank you Marvin.

The first day of spring has come and gone, and the March Moon, the "Worm or Full Sap Moon," is waning. It rained in the night. Walking to the cow barn this morning, I noticed night crawlers slithering along. The red osier dogwood limbs, cut in the canyons a few weeks ago, are now leafed-out in the living room. Makes me yearn for Sheep Creek, where I know daffodils, forsythia, apricot trees, violets and buttercups are blooming.

Friend Jo and I were down there last week. The canyons are greening up and fishermen are whipping the waters for steelhead. Although my doctor says the fracture in my hand is healing nicely, she says I'll have this splint for three more weeks.

March 28—As this is the last Friday of the month, our Sheep Creek Writers gathered at my cabin. I'd put together meatballs and sauce yesterday, using elk burger and good pork sausage, and today the meatballs roasted slowly in the oven while Halley and I spent a leisurely day enjoying the coming of spring.

The forsythia bush Andi Mitchell planted last year was glowing yellow, as were the daffodils alongside the house. The skies were rain-rinsed blue, with great white clouds scudding silently over the rims. I read, napped, and listened to Straus waltzes on my old-timey record player. This is life off the grid.

As everyone arrived around 5:30, they began cooking pasta, tossing salads, slicing bread, and frosting apple cake. After the meatballs were dumped into the sauce and heated, we all gathered around the long table and dug in. The evening was made all the more special due to the presence of grandson James, who joined our group of writers. After dishes were done, we regrouped around the stove in the living room and read our work.

It rained on the way home, a nice warm soaking that assures continued grass-growing conditions.

March 30—Today is Sunday, and I exchanged my bell-ringing job for lighting candles in church this morning. I met Doug after at the R&R Drive-in for fajitas.

Fawn's bull calf, Patrick. Just ten minutes old.

The month is nearly gone. A cold north wind blows here on Prairie Creek, and skies are mostly cloudy, with a weak sun breaking through. My little herd is roaming the hill, grazing the first green shoots of grass. What will April bring?

April 13—The sun has long since dipped behind the Wallowas and darkness is closing in. It's been a long day. Doug and I joined daughter Lori and hubby Larry for breakfast at the Cheyenne Cafe this morning, after which I attended church.

Stopped home for a brief rest before attending granddaughter-in-law-to-be Danielle's bridal shower. Daughter Ramona and granddaughter-in-law Chelsea hosted the affair, which was gangs of fun, surrounded by all those young folks. Danielle and grandson James will tie the knot in June.

Todd and his crew started trailing the cows to Big Sheep today, a three-day drive. I hope to join them on Tuesday when they leave Peekaboo along the Imnaha Highway for their final day.

Easter Sunday is coming up, and our family will gather on the creek again.

Framed by a center pivot irrigation line, a full moon sets over the Wallowas.

April 18—I'm typing this column down here along Sheep Creek. Although seated at my table inside, I can hear the sound of water outside through the open door.

On my right, the creek; on my left, blooming cherry trees and flowering quince. Why would I be anywhere else?

My used—obviously used a lot—computer died last week. I was given no choice, but had to buy a new one, which meant traveling OUT OF THE COUNTY, a 140-mile round-trip to La Grande. A friend advised me to purchase my laptop at Walmart. So, excusing myself from our Writer's Group, I headed out.

It was hot in La Grande last Tuesday. Entering the labyrinth of Walmart's cluttered aisles, I finally located the computer section and enlisted the help of an employee, who seemed well-versed in computer language. I knew nothing, but clutched a scrap of paper with scribbled notes advising me what NOT to get.

The transaction took only minutes. As I exited the store, an official-looking woman walked up to me and said, "An alarm might go off when you step outside because you have a computer. Just thought I'd warn you."

Luckily that didn't happen, but anticipating it proved unnerving. Entering Elgin on my return home, my thoughts shifted to grandson Rowdy, and how he left us nearly a year ago, in full-blown spring.

I turned up Phillips Creek Road and followed a sign to the cemetery that sits on a hill. In a large clearing, surrounded by pines, I located Rowdy's headstone. It was very peaceful and quiet there, and a meadowlark burst into song as I approached the grave site. There, in a photo image imprinted on a slab of granite, was our Rowdy a-horseback, splashing into the waters of the Grande Ronde, riding for his life, competing in the Suicide Race held each year during the Elgin Stampede.

After a stop for an iced-tea at the Little Bear Drive-In on the outskirts of Wallowa, I made it back to Enterprise by 4:30, just in time to leave the new "notebook" with a friend, who will transfer my old data to my new purchase. Since this procedure won't be accomplished until the end of the week, I am borrowing my friend Katherine's laptop to begin this column.

The two of us arrived here at Sheep Creek this morning and spent 'til noon doing chores around the cabin. The canyons are especially gorgeous today. 70 degrees now, so we've been outside the entire time, burning limbs and watering the young peach tree transplanted a few days ago by David in the young orchard across the creek. It is responding well and beginning to bloom.

I had a nice conversation the other evening with Marvin Sams, who gave me the peach tree, and assured him I would see to its frequent watering. Green leaves are appearing at creekside, and the sarvisberry bushes are bursting white over the steep canyon sides. A startling deep pink across the creek defines an aged plum tree.

The Magic Garden committee is gearing up to plant, and last week a volunteer work crew cleaned the irrigation ditch. My caretakers mowed the lawn and winter seems to have retreated into the past in the lower climes of the canyon country.

Up on top, life goes on and new life appears daily.

Last week I was totally unprepared for an-other calf, yep, Rhubarb decided to calve a big bull calf. Black and bullish, I named him Thunder. The season for thunder-rolling-in-the-mountains is nearly upon us. Rhubarb obviously bred right back after she calved last June. My herd continues to multiply as Rhubarb's two-year-old twin heifer, Caroline, now pastured with son Ken's cattle, also calved a couple of weeks ago, which means I have nine animals now.

Since the broken bone in my right hand seems to be healing on schedule, the Doc says I only have one more week of wearing this splint. Yeah!

All over the valley there is much activity in the fields. Tractors pulling harrows, discs, rollers and no-till drills churn up the spring dust. Hay stacks are shrinking and cattle anticipate the greening hills and canyons, and by May 1st most will be turned out, which means branding time is near.

The tomcats on Tenderfoot Valley road have been busy. Every one of our female cats is expecting. Something must be done, but the mothers-to-be are wild and hard to capture.

Prayers once again for the Combes family. Just a few days ago, Ray's wife, Pat, went to join him. Even though they are in a good place and together again, we'll miss seeing their happy faces in church.

Prayers, too, for my brother Jim, who lives on the ranch we grew up on, as he battles cancer. I talked with him the other day. Jim has a positive outlook, which is so important.

I'm back to taking long walks again with Halley, following the hill and making a loop around the old ranch. Big changes in the irrigation systems here on Prairie Creek. New pipelines going in, willow trees cut down, huge cement diversions being built to hold water to be pumped along miles of pipe line, and the arrival of great center-pivot sprinklers on rolling wheels, operated by computerized timers. A far cry from the hand lines moved by young people, and flood irrigating, where we chased water with a shovel.

I enjoyed my drive to the Upper Imnaha a couple of weeks ago to visit neighbors Grant and Barbara Warnock. It rained all the way, and I just had to stop at Wayne Marks' old place to photograph an entire canyon side covered with flowering plum trees. What a sight it was, seen through the softly falling rain. The canyons soaked up the warm moisture, and the grass was brilliant green.

I was invited into the Warnock's cozy home there along the river, where Barbara served me a cup of coffee along with some freshly-baked ginger cookies. Before loading my peach tree in the car, Barbara gave me a tour of her amazing garden. Grant has been building her a greenhouse and she is anxious to begin planting.

It was still raining when I dropped the little tree off at my place on Sheep Creek and headed home.

I lost my bell-ringing job in church—but have been replaced by two children, who do a great job.

April 15—I hosted our Writer's Group down at my place on Big Sheep Creek. Heading down into the canyons, a couple miles beyond the mouth of Lightning Creek, I met up with son Todd a-horseback, trailing his cows and calves. As I wove my way through the herd, I visited other riders, strung out over a mile.

Near Bear Gulch, I came upon Larry and Myrna Moore moving their pairs out to pasture.

Pulling into my place, I was blown away by the sight of full-blooming SPRING! Forsythia, flowering quince, cherry trees, and newly-mown lawn. After watering the little peach tree across the creek, Halley and I returned just ahead of the gals, who had carpooled from Joseph. They reported spitting snow over Sheep Creek Hill (on top) and since this lower elevation provided such a dramatic contrast, we strolled around outside, enjoying the warmth.

After the readings, we were in the middle of sharing our lunches when Todd's lead cows arrived. It took nearly an hour for over 300 head of cows and calves to single-file across the new bridge, just downstream from the confluence of Big Sheep Creek. Naturally, it offered another photo op for my friends, who'd encountered the cattle drive on the way down.

Halley and I lingered after everyone left, waiting for Todd's crew to return and load their horses, which didn't happen until five o'clock when the stragglers finally reached the field below Blue Meadow.

A long three days in the saddle was rewarded by Todd, who treated his cowboys and cowgirls to dinner in Joseph that evening.

April 17—Son Ken harrowed the cow pastures. I drove to the Upper Imnaha for a brief visit with old friends who were attending the April Fishtrap Writer's Retreat. Since this was the first retreat I've NOT attended since it began nearly 20 years ago, it was fun to connect with Robin, Stephen, and Cathy.

On the way back I stopped at my place and was pleasantly surprised to see Grandson James and his puppy, Claire. After James watered my peach tree, we returned to the cabin for lunch. It was a fun visit, and James related how he'd taken his sister, Becky, turkey hunting that morning up the canyon.

It rained this evening, and the Prairie Creek wind blew as I drove up our county road to attend the Liberty Grange meeting, held in neighbors Larry and Juanita Waters' cozy country home. We discussed plans for the upcoming annual Plowing Bee, to be held the weekend of May 3rd and 4th at the Waters' Ranch.

April 18—The day dawned clear and frosty cold. Ken shod his horse, Hank, in readiness for the big branding tomorrow up Big Sheep. I spent the morning building a large macaroni salad. Son Steve, his wife Jennifer, and "hats" Bailey and Stetson, arrived later that night.

April 19—A busy day! Cowboys and cowgirls, cow dogs and cow kids, all converged on Blue Meadow up Big Sheep Creek. Stock trailers, pickups, and horses took up an acre of meadow. Since Doug opted to stay home this year, I hitched a ride with Steve, Jen and the kids.

The road up the canyon is narrow and rocky, and spirals upward until it descends to cross the bridge over Big Sheep Creek and into the meadow. Todd's crew was working the last of the cows in the long, wooden chute when we arrived.

The calves had already been separated from the cows, and cowboys and cowgirls were unfurling ropes, limbering up horses, lighting the branding fire, and heating the branding irons. Soon the first calves were "headed and heeled" and drug to the fire. Youngsters and oldsters worked side by side. A couple of Rotary Exchange students, one young man from Sierra Leone and another from Portugal, were in the thick of it, taking in their first branding. Grandson James was there, having arisen at 3:00 a.m. to take a friend wild turkey hunting. He was obviously enjoying showing the visiting students how to hold down those husky calves.

The weather, although a bit breezy, was mostly clear, and the canyons provided a backdrop that rivaled scenery in those old-time Western movies. Granddaughter Adele and cousin Buck engaged in a roping competition, and James' Danielle pitched in and joined the ground crew. 11-year-old grandson, Stetson, remembering the mauling he took last year, wasn't as eager this time. His sister, Bailey, kept busy ear-tagging. Son Ken roped calves all morning, then wielded the branding iron that afternoon. Cowboys and cowgirls from neighboring ranches took turns roping and working the ground crew. A very skillful outfit, doing what they do best and loving it.

Around one o'clock everyone headed for the chow line. Three grills sizzled with Marr Flat Natural Beef burgers. The aroma of fried onions lingered in the air. I added my macaroni salad to the others; condiments were laid out on long tables, drinks in coolers, paper plates stacked, and pies cut. Pickup tailgates provided seating, and everyone ate hungrily. No matter jeans spattered with manure and the meadow littered with cow pies, food never tasted so good.

The creek rushed past, draining the high country snows, and bleached white clouds built over the rims. Crows cawed and the white sarvisberry bushes bloomed on the canyon sides. Refueled, everyone returned to the corrals until the last of 311 calves was counted out the gate to join its mamma.

Todd's wife, Angie, rounded everyone up for a group photo, and it was pretty impressive, all those on horseback, and the rest of us standing, recorded there that day. It was pretty quiet and, I suspect, everyone was thinking the same thing: this is the last Marr Flat Cattle Company branding at Blue Meadow. There are big changes up Big Sheep Creek, and at the old Snyder ranch on Prairie Creek.

As we drove away, my gaze wandered up the green canyons where the cows were grazing the lush bunch grasses. Cattle Country. What does the future hold for such lands? And what as well as for the good stewards who love them, the cattle folks, who understand grasslands and how to manage them?

I'd filled my camera's memory card with precious visual images and now write these words to record this time and place.

April 20—Easter Sunday dawned clear and warm, a rare day in an otherwise long, cold Wallowa County spring. I arose at dawn to feed my critters and dress for church. Then, leaving Doug, Steve, and the kids to eat breakfast at the Cheyenne Cafe, Jennifer and I drove in to attend the 8:00 a.m. Sunrise Service at our Joseph United Methodist church.

It was wonderful, the sun streaming through those stained glass windows onto those smiling, friendly faces. I had my bell-ringing job back, and during the service we decorated the willow cross with tulips. Afterwards Jen and I joined the congregation for a delicious brunch before heading back to Prairie Creek.

Bailey and I loaded the ham into the car and took off for Sheep Creek. The rest of the family followed

Later. Much warmer on the crik. The thermometer on the screen porch registered 70 degrees. No wind, robin's egg-blue skies, and plenty of sunshine. Leaving the ham baking in the oven, Bailey and I took a walk, then drug some lawn chairs out beside the creek and soaked up silence and sun. When Steve, Jen and the kids arrived, they hung the hammock up between trees and everyone took turns using it.

Before 2:00, our large extended family arrived, bearing food, which was laid out on a long table near the creek.

Then here came Uncle Todd carrying a pan full of mountain oysters, soaking in milk. After dipping them in crumbs and frying them crisp in a hot fry pan, he served these tasty tidbits for appetizers. Danielle and her mom weren't too sure about this, but were good sports and sampled one. The rest of us polished them off. It had been a long time since I'd eaten a good oyster. Todd admitted he'd stayed up 'til eleven the night before, cleaning them.

Our family, holding hands, formed a large circle there alongside the creek, and son Ken said the blessing before we filled our plates with ham and all the trimmings. Then Uncle Todd announced it was time for the GREAT RATTLESNAKE HUNT, which granddaughter Chelsie says is highly overrated, but the idea itself is exciting—apparently so, as young and old jumped into several pickups and took off up the canyon, leaving only three of us behind.

Over an hour later they returned, having seen two snakes retreating into their den. They admitted they had stopped to play ball in the meadow. After older cousins hid chocolate bunnies in hard-to-find places, younger cousins emerged from the pump house to search in trees, high grasses and rocks for their treats. Poppa Doug had purchased enough bunnies for the adults as well.

Arrowleaf balsamroot spattered the high rocky benches with golden color, and the wild pink ground phlox bloomed above the old orchard. All the pear trees were in full blossom. After the last carload left, Stetson and I closed everything up, and just as we pulled out of the driveway, a wild turkey hen, nesting nearby, strode out on the lawn to peck in the grass. A perfect ending to a perfect day.

April 23—The day dawned cold and gray, 30 degrees. New snow on the Wallowas.

April 24—Son Ken tore down a sagging fence in the cow pasture and set new posts.

April 25—It was snowing here on the prairie as I loaded my car and headed to Sheep Creek. I lit a fire in the stove at the cabin and baked a lemon pudding cake. No snow there in the canyons, only a fine misty rain. As I puttered around inside, I could watch our garden volunteers installing a new metal gate across the creek. Now, when we gals enter the Magic Garden, no more "lady killer" barbed wire gate.

Since I missed being Den Mom at the April Fishtrap Writer's Retreat on the Upper Imnaha, a carload of old friends, who were spending the week there, brought the retreat to me; not only themselves, but a moveable feast consisting of leftovers from their former gourmet meals. Seven of us gathered at the long table, just like old times. Thanks gals, and Tom.

After they left, I got busy browning a pot roast, peeling carrots, and setting the table for our Sheep Creek Writer's monthly potluck and meeting. Leaving the roast simmering in the Dutch oven with garlic, shallots and carrots, Halley and I took a jaunt over the bridge to inspect the new gate. Nice.

The canyons were responding to the warm rain in a positive way.

Verdant green grasses, wild Oregon grape bloomed yellow in rocky crevices, and the creek ran high, rushing to its nearby confluence with the Imnaha. The scent of new cottonwood leaves permeated the air, and a covey of quail called from a blackberry thicket.

Returning to the cabin, I actually found time to do some writing before everyone arrived. At six o'clock, here came Jenny Moore, bearing a kettle of steaming mashed potatoes. Others contributed tossed salad and sourdough bread. As a watery sun sank behind the rims, a soft green twilight appeared outside as we savored our meal inside. I made coffee and we dished up the fresh lemon pudding cake.

We tackled the dishes before seating ourselves around the stove in the living room to read our stories and discuss our writing until darkness settled in. Driving home, it continued to rain as I contemplated my day, which had been most comforting, sharing this place I love with friends.

April 26—Met Doug at the Hurricane Creek Grange at noon to sup a bowl of homemade soup. The event was a money-raiser to benefit the South Fork Grange members, who recently lost their historic hall in Lostine to a devastating fire.

A tempting variety of homemade pies were auctioned off after lunch, proceeds of which were donated to the Grange rebuilding fund. Long time South Fork Grange member, Ben Boswell, was honored for his years of service by the gift of a framed charter of the Grange. Great music was provided by Katherine Josephy and June Colony.

Later, while toting my peach pie to the car, a dark cloud zipped open and dumped nearly an inch of hail over all. By the time I drove through Joseph, however, the sun was out.

95-year-old Wayne Marks, who lived all of his life on the Upper Imnaha, died today. For the past three months he has been a resident of Alpine House, an assisted living facility in Joseph. Goodbye, old-timer, you lived a long, full life in one of the greatest places on earth.

April 27—Another frosty cold morning. A snowy blizzard erupted as I drove to church in time to ring the bell.

April 28—Doug and I met daughter Jackie and her hubby Bill at the Cheyenne Cafe for breakfast. The couple were on their way home to Challis, Idaho, having spent the week visiting their son Buck, his wife Chelsea, and grandchildren Lucy, Katelyn and Cooper, who live on Bartlett Bench up from Troy. Grandma and Grandpa filled us in on the antics of our great-grandchildren, and a branding they helped with near Anatone, Washington.

Tina Borgerding showed up today to roto-till our garden. Now I must set out the Walla Walla Sweet onion plants. Soon we'll be prepping the garden on Sheep Creek, tilling in the green manure crop. Hard to believe this will be the 4th year for our huge undertaking.

April 29—70 degrees! Write group met this morning at Josephy Center; then home to prepare a pot roast for our Methodist Meals Together.

This evening, six of us partook of another one of my homemade suppers. I'd baked a loaf of sourdough bread in the dutch oven and served the roast with veggies, simmered in the meat juices, along with mashed potatoes. I enjoy these meals, as it allows time to visit and get to know each other. This will be the last meal until we resume again next January.

April 30—Doug came down with a cold, so didn't accompany me to the 34th Annual Hells Canyon Mule Days Grand Marshal Dinner this evening.

The 2014 Grand Marshal, Dick Walker, was honored and introduced, as was the Honorary Grand Marshal, Art Galbraith. Dick Walker is a second-generation Grand Marshal, as his father, Max, along with other well-known mule skinners, founded the event in 1981. For his part, Art Galbraith was a U.S. Forest Service packer and also helped with the founding of Mule Days.

You can come to this long-eared event and see these two honored men ride in the parade September 5-7 at the Wallowa County Fairgrounds.

May 1—42 degrees, clear and sunny. Drove with my old friend Phyllis, visiting from Bend, to the "crick" to picnic outside, take a walk and visit. The lilacs are blooming now, and the snowball bushes are ready to burst into bloom. It was a lovely relaxing time, and the canyons put on a show.

Later this afternoon, I pruned the raspberries here on Prairie Creek.

May 2—After a spectacular sunny weekend, SPRING seemed to leap forward, before slipping back to its usual April self. A skim of ice on the chicken's water pan this morning proves it was below freezing. The tulips and daffodils blooming alongside the house lack luster, and our white Wallowas shiver under snow clouds. It's COLD.

Since my bales of alfalfa are few, I opened gates to our grassy corrals to let my herd graze. A pair of wild geese near the irrigation ditch flew up at my approach, honking their way overhead before returning to their nesting site.

Dick Walker, right, was named 2014 grand marshal of Hells Canyon Mule Days. Art Galbraith, left, will be honorary grand marshal. Mule Days will be held September 5-7th at the Wallowa County Fairgrounds.

My little herd loves this green grass and is ready to give up eating hay. The hens laid 11 eggs today.

May 3—Helped Carmen cook for the Plowing Bee held at the Waters Ranch just up the road. Took time off to photograph the teams of mules and horses pulling those old plows and discs. A wonderful thing. Luckily the rains held off long enough for the event to happen.

May 4—Arose early to chore before driving over on the next road to the Liberty Grange Hall to help with breakfast. The wind blew and rain splattered here and there, but we served a sourdough pancake, sausage, and eggs breakfast. Did the dishes and then I was off to the 11 o'clock church service.

May 5—I joined Leigh Dawson, Marcy Sheehy and Jan Hohmann for a history tour of the Upper Imnaha country, as my friends were curious about the places named in my book about Mary Marks.

May 6—It rained while we were touring the upper Imnaha, and has continued raining, which is great for the country. Because we gals are all involved in ranching, it didn't spoil our day; rather, we rejoiced.

May 7—To the west, purple-black curtains of cloud; eastward, thunderheads boil up over Hells Canyon. Out north I can feel the winds sweeping across the Zumwalt, spurring the galloping cloud shadows over the green hills, recalling Mays past when we held brandings out on Wet Salmon Creek. Thanks to these welcome rain showers, we live in a green world again. It's been a long winter.

Between rains, my hens and Piglet, the tiny but mighty rooster, range far out across the grassy fields. I'm sad to report the untimely death of my young rooster, Allen, who appears to have succumbed to the wrath of Piglet, who has zero tolerance for competition when it comes to courting his harem of hens.

May 10—One of my two setting hens hatched a single chick. The other hen continued to set on her clutch of eggs to no avail. Since both hens had, at some point, changed nests, allowing their eggs to get cold, I was surprised that morning to hear peeping. After waiting another day and noting no further activity, I cracked the remaining eggs, which, as I suspected, were rotten.

In due time, mother hen flew down from the nest and the chick tottered to the edge and fell out. To my amazement, so did the other setting hen. There was no confrontation, just a silent agreement between them. They'd share motherhood.

As of this date, it is still so. The chick, with its two mothers, is thriving.

The morning the chick hatched, a cold rain fell here, while on upper Prairie Creek snow created a distinct green-white line.

Tonight, a Saturday night, Doug and I drove down to the Imnaha Store and Tav, where a local band, Last Call, played great old time western songs. The music was so good folks got up and danced, even though there wasn't much room to do so.

Our friend Leita danced with Doug, and he didn't even have to leave the booth. While enjoying the music, we chowed down on Sally's hamburgers, as did others who came from up and down the river, as well as "on top." Let me tell you, Imnaha was jumping. It sure was good to see folks having such a good time.

It was also nice to get out of the rain, sleet and snow on top, and venture to canyons where the lilacs were still blooming. When we topped out on Sheep Creek Hill, just above home, we drove into a flaming Prairie Creek sunset.

May 12—I headed to Sheep Creek to transplant pansies near the cabin. Ken hauled June Bug to the vet to be Bangs vaccinated while I was gone.

This evening, while Halley and I took a jaunt up the road, we spotted 14 head of white-tail deer trailing down Hough's hill to feed in the fields, which were flooded in golden light. The deer, for some reason, have been elsewhere, until now.

May 13—Our write group met today at the Josephy Center. Warm sunlight streamed in the windows and we had a good turnout.

May 14—Grandson James picked me up early in the morning and we drove over the Blues to the Wild Horse Casino, where we, along with other grant recipients, were treated to an elegant luncheon in one of their new banquet rooms.

James and I represented the Divide Camp, as Julie Wheeler was unable to attend. The Divide Camp for wounded veterans received a generous grant to use for Julie's worthwhile project. This money is most appreciated, and will be put to good use. We were amazed to learn of all the grants awarded to adjoining counties that will, in turn, aid various community projects. For me it was fun spending time with James, himself a veteran of Afghanistan, who will be helping with the Divide Camp this summer.

It was my first trip out of the county since I purchased my new laptop in La Grande, and the luncheon was a special treat, as well as meeting new folks from all over. Naturally, we had to stop at the Little Bear Drive-In out of Wallowa for a Little Bear ice cream cone on the way home. It's a tradition!

May 15—Several of us volunteers showed up on Sheep Creek to prepare the magic garden for planting. David Martin had already tilled the ground, and the rest of us picked rocks, set out pipe, and put up fencing for tomatoes. Gary took the weed eater to the entire perimeter of the garden.

At noon, I invited everyone to eat lunch at the cabin.

May 16—Somewhere in the busy day yesterday, I found time to make a macaroni salad to take to our Methodist Women's luncheon meeting held at Jane Wiggins' lovely home. The Wiggins' house is built above the West Fork of the Wallowa River, before it empties into Wallowa Lake. Floor to ceiling windows afford views of river and alpine heights. It was a restful time for all of us.

May 17—I baked two loaves of Dutch oven sourdough bread to take to son Ken's branding, held at the Six Ranch west of Enterprise. Since Ken has no corrals, Liza, James and Adele offered their facilities, which included chutes for working the cows. All 13 of Ken and Annie's grandchildren were there that day.

My camera recorded our "herd" of great-grandchildren tugging on the end of a rope that held a struggling calf, plus kids on horseback roping, like Cutter, who is learning how to head and heel. Grown-ups, like Uncle Todd and cousin James, were there to instruct and teach. Most of the calves were big and husky, a real challenge, but the sheer numbers of kids overwhelmed them. Of course it was good to have daddy Chad and cousin James there to throw the calves down.

The branding took a long time, as all were allowed to rope from the ground, and some of those kids were pretty young. The kids loved it, and thankfully no one got hurt.

Annie spent the morning cooking ham, beans, salads and desserts, which she transported down from Alder Slope to the ranch. We added my sourdough bread and feasted on the lawn under a large shade tree. The weather was perfect, and one more branding was accomplished.

It was a long day for the adult cowboys, which included son Todd, grandsons James and Chad, and son Ken, who seemed to be everywhere at once. Wives pitched in and formed the ground crew, handing out shots and ear tags, while I rode herd on my two youngest great-grandkids, Arianwyn and Beorn.

May 18—It rained again, our old apple tree burst into pink and white blossoms, and by 11:00 o'clock I was ringing the bell in church.

May 19—Clear with a heavy frost that morning, but warmed up later when friend Katherine drove in and helped me plant three long rows of potatoes: Yukon gold, California white, and red Norlands. There's only a partial bag of spuds left in the cellar from last fall's harvest.

May 21—The thermometer registered 50 degrees, so I think it's safe to say we made it through another winter.

May 22—Ken and I worked my critters, along with some of his heifers that are pastured here for the summer. It was a hot day, and we used the long wooden chute that led to a squeeze chute with a head catch, so my job was to keep the cattle coming, and prepare the ear tags and such. Not as quick as I used to be, but the two of us got the job done.

May 23—Doug and I drove to Wallowa Lake to attend Vali's Alpine Restaurant's 40th anniversary open house. We delivered the three dozen deviled eggs I'd previously prepared for the event. Others brought salads and other goodies to add to the food.

As always, there was a huge crowd coming and going until evening. Music, good food and drink, and lots of visiting. An earlier rainy and windy spell subsided, and the evening was lovely. Maggie, along with son Michael, and wife Dione run one of the most popular eateries in all of Eastern Oregon. Reservations are required.

May 24—Another gorgeous day, the Wallowas showing off their bright whiteness in contrast with our green valley. It's Memorial Day weekend and time for the traditional Triple Creek branding, a time when local cowboys and cowgirls trailer their horses up Tucker Down Road to rope calves and generally have a good time doing it.

The first bunch was finished around noon, and another smaller bunch were trailed to the corrals. Old hands and young hands honed their skills, showed off their horses, and worked hard. Then came the meal everyone looks forward to all year. Thanks to the generous hosts and owners of Triple Creek ranch, Brent and Connie McKinley and their family, we were treated to a meal that mere words fail to describe.

Tables were set up on a green lawn with a creek splashing through it, and folks helped themselves at long tables laden with King crab legs simmered in butter, artisan bread, sizzling hot-off-the-grill steaks branded with the Triple creek brand, beans, salads, colorful bowls of fresh fruit and berries, and for dessert, Dutch oven cobblers. Let me tell you, those of us so far removed from fresh seafood really enjoyed those crab legs.

Thanks again, Triple Creek.

May 31—And now it's Saturday again, and so much more has happened, including a moving memorial service conducted this morning at the Joseph Cemetery on Prairie Creek for our friend Pat Combes. The clouds were magnificent and leaked a few drops as we remembered our friend, who passed on just a short time after her husband, Ray. We are losing so many of our old-timers lately.

Pat had chosen this spot to be buried, near a tall pine tree, with a view of the valley below, the Seven Devils range beyond, and the closeness of Chief Joseph Mountain. A very peaceful place. She had a bench installed so her friends and family would have a place to sit while visiting. Pat's family hosted everyone at her daughter Bev's and hubby Mike's lovely place on Hurricane Creek Road on the outskirts of Joseph.

May 30—Spring is here, with all of its demands. I spent the morning down on Big Sheep Creek along with other volunteers, transplanting tomatoes, peppers, and a huge variety of bedding vegetables that have been started in greenhouse conditions. Now they are at the mercy of Mother Nature.

The tomato and pepper plants I set out were grown by grandson, Chad, who is extremely conscientious, and very into heirloom varieties. He raises a huge garden for his own family in a frosty area north of Enterprise, and wanted to see how these plants would respond to the warmer climate of the canyons. Chad was very generous with his gift, and we Magic Garden folks appreciate it.

This afternoon, muscles I haven't used since last spring are protesting, but should loosen up as the season progresses.

Golden shafts of morning sun had just spilled over Middlepoint when I pulled into the garden. All was dewy-fresh with the fragrance of blooming locust saturating the air. Myriad hidden birds chirped among the canopy of cottonwoods lining the creek.

But all was not well. We seem to have a problem with either squirrels or muskrats. More specifically, their former burrows, which are transporting water from the ditch to places we'd rather not have it. After digging trenches downhill through the garden, the problem is put on hold until we can locate the underwater entrances in the ditch and deal with them.

On a happier note, I noticed the Heavenly Blue morning glories I planted earlier were all up.

Before I continue this column I want to mention that Dan Warnock's new book, *You Can't Borrow Yourself Rich,* has just been published. Dan has woven stories of his well-known ranching family with local history here in Northeastern Oregon. There will be a book signing at the Bookloft in Enterprise on June 14, at 11:00 a.m.

Dan says he is donating proceeds from the sale of the book to Julie Wheeler's Divide Camp project for wounded veterans. Many thanks, Dan; that's mighty generous of you.

June 1—The beautiful month, and there is so much to do. This evening I planted carrots, lettuce, beets and radishes in my garden here. In the morning, I'll be down on Sheep Creek again, helping the school kids plant corn in the Magic Garden.

June 2—A group of us volunteers were planting more of the garden on Sheep Creek when a busload of Joseph Charter School students pulled in. The two students at the Imnaha School, along with school marm

Shari Warnock, had arrived earlier. In a well-organized fashion, the kids planted potatoes in long rows. The children were very excited, and it was a lovely warm morning. Little girls in colorful dresses resembled flowers blooming in our garden.

Master gardener Barbara Warnock, from up river, joined me on bended knee to set out more tomato plants. Our Magic Garden hummed with activity. The squirrel hole problem has been solved for the moment, and Gary fired up his weed eater again. We certainly appreciate our volunteers, who seem to enjoy just being there in that beautiful setting.

This evening I finished planting my corn, herbs and squash here on Prairie Creek.

June 4—Granddaughter Mona Lee arrived from Portland to spend time here in the county where she was raised, before attending the wedding. Mona, who grew up on Imnaha, helped me fix fence after my Guernsey heifer decided to crawl through onto the road.

June 5—Mona left us to visit her nieces and nephew, Lucy, Katelyn and two-year-old Cooper. Mona's brother Buck and his wife, Chelsea, live way up on Bartlett above Troy, and she couldn't wait to see them.

This evening I attended the first Courthouse Concert of the season in Enterprise.

June 6—Our family gathered this evening, along with the wedding party, at the Mt Joseph Ranch for a rehearsal dinner. Son Todd grilled thick tender steaks on a portable grill he constructed himself. The remainder of the meal was catered.

We were again blessed with warm weather, and the setting couldn't have been more perfect. It was good to see Navy grandson Josh and his wife, Desiree, plus their children, Wyatt, Ryder and Vivian, who had driven all the way from San Diego. Son Steve and grandson Stetson drove from Selah, Washington, and camped with Uncle Charley and Aunt Ramona at their ranch on upper Prairie Creek.

June 8—Well, the big wedding is history. It was wonderful and all went as planned, thanks to a gigantic team effort performed by a multitude of friends and family. Grandson James and his lovely Danielle were married on June 7th at the Six Ranch, alongside the river where James spent his boyhood. It was a warm, sunny afternoon, and guests parked their cars across the road in the barn lot before wandering over to the meadow, where they were seated beside the meandering Wallowa River.

My grandson, in true James fashion, greeted each guest as they appeared along the path. His father, Todd, performed the simple ceremony wearing his jeans, cowboy boots, and hat. Great-granddaughter Riley Ann played her fiddle. James' groomsmen stood next to him, and the pretty bridesmaids, including his sister, Adele, made their way between the guests to take their place on the bride's side.

Ponderosa pines lined the opposite bank, and the cool scent of water wafted in the warm afternoon. The river swirled between green grassy banks, brilliant cotton clouds formed in a pure blue sky, and the air was filled with bird song. Danielle, lovely in her trailing white gown, joined James in front of Todd as they recited their vows. The bride, clutching a bouquet of fragrant white peonies, kissed her new husband, and since it was all so happy and right, I managed not to cry.

After the wedding, Doug and I drove down the road to the reception, which was held in the large indoor arena at the Six Ranch. There were the wildflowers granddaughter Mona and I had driven down to the canyons early that morning to pick, then help arrange. It had been a hectic morning, as others had arrived bearing buckets full of wildings gathered from all over the lower valley and hills. We'd spent until 11:00 o'clock filling fruit jars with penstemon, lupine, prairie smoke, blue bells and buttercups, which decorated the long tables. Enormous sprays of wild syringa gave off a heady mock orange scent.

The arena was transformed into a ball room with tables and chairs, complete with a dance floor constructed at one end. Two huge doors opened to green pastures beyond and provided fresh air. Suddenly the arena was full of family and friends, many of whom had traveled long distances to honor this popular couple. For me, it was a treat to rove my eyes over generations of our burgeoning family. As in weddings past, I felt truly blessed. Seeing sons, daughters, grandchildren, and a bevy of great-grandchildren all enjoying themselves filled me with gratitude.

Soon, everyone lined up to partake of a gourmet meal featuring smoked tri-tip beef and prepared by the bride's brother, a professional chef from the East Coast. The wedding cake, one that granddaughter Adele had agonized over, was cut. In spite of various set-backs, the cake was beautiful and delicious.

After the bride and groom fed themselves, the oldest married couple present, who happened to be daughter Ramona and hubby Charley, were allowed the second slice. Ramona commented she'd had to smear frosting on Charley's mustache all those years ago too.

A band appeared and the dancing began. Bride and groom first, followed by Todd and Danielle, plus James and his mom. Soon the floor was full of Western Swing dancers, who made me dizzy to watch. I was amazed at the amount of energy exerted by my grown children.

Noticing grandson Chad holding their youngest, I took baby Beorn in my arms, which allowed he and wife Amy to dance. Shortly thereafter, my youngest great-grandchild's little head nodded and plopped down on my shoulder. Consequently, mom and dad spent quite a bit of time on the dance floor.

Later, grandson-in-law Joel asked me to dance. Thankfully, it was a slow dance.

Since Doug had left earlier, I rode home with daughter Jackie. It was a lovely wedding, and now one more grandchild is married and living Wallowa County.

Long-time friend and respected member of the community, Bud Stangel, passed away recently, and we regretted missing his funeral, which was in conflict with the wedding. We also missed old-timer Wayne Marks' memorial held at the Imnaha Church a few weeks ago.

June 9—Another cloudless June morning, with no rain in the immediate forecast. It used to be we relied on "those June rains," to ensure a good grass year, especially in the hills, where natural rainfall provides the only irrigation.

Not so this June, thus far anyway.

Back when our children and grandchildren were exhibiting their 4-H and FFA beef projects at the Union Stock show, it always rained. It was a given.

While weeding the rows of potato plants in my garden last evening, I was startled by a loud snort across the fence. This turned out to be a white-tail doe, her head protruding above a lush crop of grain, nostrils flared, protecting her newborn fawn. It's the birthing season for all the little wild things. For ranchers it's the season for electric fence failure, falling-down fences, the cattle out, pump and irrigation problems, moving pipes, and, on a happier note, rhubarb pie.

June 13—So much more has happened. Like the baby shower held at the Imnaha School for Jenny, formerly Moore, who married a young man from Iceland, IN Iceland, and I can't pronounce his last name.

Jenny, from Bear Gulch near Imnaha, will be leaving us soon to go live in far-off Iceland, but promises to return often. She will be missed.

Must cut this short; am busy getting ready for our annual Syringa Sisters week down at the cabin on Sheep Creek. They'll arrive Sunday. Am so looking forward to seeing all of them.

June 20—"Get out of the way, Mary!" yelled Bobbie, and Mary scrambled over the rocks into an elderberry bush seconds before the Subaru, driven by 86-year-old Bobbie, roared past her.

Jess, Barb and I looked on in disbelief at what had just happened. But it was real. Here we were again, in our 18th year of meeting together to keep alive our friendships. Our adventures over the years have only increased in us the desire to live on the edge. With pure joy and glee written all over us, we piled back into the Subaru and proceeded up the Camp Creek road.

Upon waking up that morning, my Syringa Sisters informed me they wished to see the Zumwalt Prairie. Bobbie had this map, and the GPS showed a road that began just beyond where we were spending the week here at my place on Sheep Creek.

"Must be the road up Camp Creek," I told them. A rough road, not often traveled, we'd need a four-wheel drive. Bobbie, who is always bragging on her Subaru, said she'd drive.

Adventure, I said to myself. *Let's go.*

So we'd scurried around fixing breakfast, made lunches, and packed water, cameras, maps, binoculars and chocolate, and took off down the road to Camp Creek. It was cloudy and threatening rain, and the lower part of the graveled road was in fairly good shape. We passed the old house where my daughter Jackie and family used to live years ago, and continued on up to the turnoff to the Nature Conservancy's winter quarters.

Up and up we wound, over rough rocky patches, crossing dry Camp creek, enjoying the syringa-scented canyon. The cloying sweetness of the mock orange was wonderful after the rain, and we rolled down our windows. Other wild bushes bloomed as well, Mountain spray, pink roses, elderberry, and hillsides full of lupine and blooming yarrow. Higher and higher we climbed, until we came to a washout in the stream bed.

Bobbie stopped. We got out and looked down to the left to see a giant mound of boulders under a bank which had sloughed off in a rush of spring torrent. To the right was a path exactly the width of Bobbie's car.

We all rolled rocks to one side, sticks were tossed, and I said we needed to make a decision to turn around, because if we got stuck in the creek and couldn't climb the opposite bank, chances are we'd have to walk back and call for help. It was a mighty long walk back to the highway. And, if we walked on up, we were only half way to the top and there wouldn't be anyone there either, no phone nor electricity.

Bobbie never hesitated, just grinned and got behind the wheel. Mary said she'd guide her. Barb, Jess, and I stood way off to the side and prayed.

Little Mary, who weighs all of 110 pounds and stands 5 feet tall, stood in the middle of that steep rocky road and, using her hands, gestured to the right, to the left, then motioned straight ahead.

That's when Bobbie yelled for her to "Get out of the way!"

Dust and rocks flying, Bobbie gunned the motor and made it. A bit shaken, we all crawled back inside the Subaru, which, indeed, was a trooper, not to mention the driver, and we proceeded upward toward the vastness of the Zumwalt Prairie.

In due time we confronted three wire gates, which I dutifully opened and shut. Good thing, as the only human we would see on the entire trip was a cowboy on horseback pushing a bunch of cows near the second gate, who grinned and tipped his hat, looking a bit surprised at seeing a carload of old ladies, knowing the road they'd traveled to get there.

We traveled past the buttes, Findley and Harsin, which were clothed in cloud shadows. The scene was breathtaking, even to me, familiar with the area, as Doug used to own a large chunk of these prairie hills west of there. Acres of silence, enormous sky, the scent of mingled wildflowers, sticky pink geranium, yellow and red Indian paintbrush, the waving bunch grasses and rolling hills, limitless horizons of grass and sky. Rock jacks, fences, hawks, ponds, and the smell of rain.

We parked on a rocky hill, and looked down on Midway, the weathered remains of the old stage stop, where early settlers rested their teams, ate a hot meal, or stabled their horses and spent the night before traveling out to the valley towns. Here we took photos and ate our lunches, as it had taken all morning to reach the prairie. Top speed on that road had been about ten miles an hour.

We turned north at the intersection with the Zumwalt Road, and drove past the Tippett corrals on Doug's brother Biden's ranch, then continued on out into the heart of "the hills." Since the gals wanted to hike, we parked near a sign that read, *Horned Lark Trail. 1.09 Miles.*

We climbed a wooden stile and began walking a trail that looped around a stretch of scenic prairie. I took off in the lead, following an old road bed. Far in the distance, I could barely make out a marker with an arrow pointing in the direction I hoped we were supposed to go. I continued far ahead, leaving my trailing companions to follow. Feeling responsible for them, I wanted to make sure we didn't get off on the wrong course, which would have been easy to do.

Rain-filled clouds threatened. A wind began to blow, stirring the high lush grasses, and our feet were wet from a recent shower. However, the smells, sights, and stimulation of walking were invigorating. Eagerly,

I forged on. No trail now, only a sea of waist-high grass and wildflowers. I came to a large swampy area with a stock pond in the middle.

It got to be a game: stand at the sign, pause, and then search far off in the distance for the next arrow. I was enjoying it. At each sign I looked back to see my friends plodding along, so far away I couldn't talk to them, blindly following me. I skirted the large pond, surprising a pair of wild mallards, and headed toward a distant pole marked with its now-familiar arrow.

On and on we trudged. I supposed we'd come a mile. It was that.09 mile that would be the killer.

Emerging from the grassy meadow, I looked for the next marker, and saw that it began a steep ascent of the hill we'd hiked down. My four friends were still far behind. I stood on the last marker within view of them and waved until I knew they'd seen me, then proceeded down a swale where I nearly stepped on a mule deer doe, who appeared close to birthing her fawn. The wild animal leaped up as if on springs and sprang across the ravine, bounding up the hill to a large rock where she lay back down.

When the gals made the turn, I proceeded uphill to complete the loop. Out of breath by this time, I decided to wait for them, so I could point out the doe and her birthing spot. After a long time here they came, straggling up hill, feet soaked, but grinning at all they'd experienced. Never had they been in the midst of such beauty.

Just as they crossed the ravine, a chorus of coyote pups let loose with the most thrilling songs. Then, as suddenly as the yelping had begun, it ceased, and a meadowlark took up the music. It was perfect.

I pointed out the doe, but due to high grasses we couldn't see what was happening in the birthing department. We all congratulated our aging selves and climbed back over the stile just as the first drops of rain fell. As thunder rumbled and lightning flickered, we fled to the safety of Bobbie's good old Subaru.

That was just one of many adventures experienced during that marvelous week. We climbed the east moraine one morning, and stared down at the lake, breathing in the fresh warm air, and ate our lunches on a glacial rock. We rewarded ourselves with iced tea at the Glacier Grill and returned to our cabin to fix another gourmet meal.

During the first of the week when it rained, we played Scrabble, wrote, read, and cooked. My cabin resembled a girl's dormitory. The kitchen smelled of coffee brewing in the mornings, and the wooden table was filled with conversation as we shared our lives.

We took long walks in the evening up the road or across the creek to the garden. One rainy morning, the wild turkey hen trooped out with her eight chicks, and spent over an hour feeding on the lawn. When the sun came out, the birds sang with joy, and my three cherry trees glistened with ripening fruit.

On the last night we pooled our gourmet leftovers, invited neighbors for supper, sat at a long table by the creek, and toasted ourselves and the Summer Solstice.

Later, we kindled a fire in the pit and listened to our Story Teller, Barb, recite her version of the Frog Prince. Some of us read what we'd been inspired to write during the week. Brilliant stars appeared in a clear sky, and myriad crickets chirped their tiny tunes. Middlepoint loomed darkly above, and the water slurped along beside us. It was a perfect ending to a perfect week.

On Tuesday evening, to celebrate Doug's and my 36th anniversary, we all met at the Imnaha River Inn for dinner. I'd made the reservations a couple of weeks before. Doug drove down, and even though it rained, the canyons were lovely. Nick Vidan grilled steaks outside for us, and his wife Sandy fixed fresh salads, veggies, rolls, and cheesecake dessert topped with strawberries. She even fixed veggie lasagna for our two veggie-tarians.

We sipped wine in front of the rock fireplace and remembered this was an anniversary for us gals too. In June, 2006, after hiking the high rim trail between Snake River and the Imnaha Canyon, we had booked ourselves here to take showers, eat a fine meal, and spend the night.

Doug had stopped n his way down along the Sheep Creek road and picked me a bouquet of syringa, which was touching. It was my wedding bouquet 36 years ago.

So much more to write about, but no time. Gardens need hoeing; lots of catching up. Next time I'll report on another country wedding, and two more book signings. Enjoy the summer.

June 27—It rained, of course it did. The Brinks and other farmers had hay down. For sure, the hay was ready but the weather was not. At noon, Doug and I met at the Community Connection in Enterprise and joined other "old folks" for lunch. The entree was roast beef and Doug and I had sponsored the meat.

June 28—Up at dawn to do chores, so as to join a record-breaking crowd of run/walk enthusiasts who gathered on the grounds of our new hospital to participate in the annual Amy Hafer Memorial event.

Syringa Sisters hiking East Moraine of Wallowa Lake, June 2014.

Imnaha and Joseph school children–Magic Garden on Sheep Creek.

A sprinkling of rain cooled the air, and I wished I'd had entered the 5K, but had signed up for the one mile walk due to an issue with my heel. Consequently, the morning went very quickly, and because there weren't many other 70+ women entered, I won a blue ribbon, which is always a thrill no matter what age.

This evening was the seventh annual CM Ranch Rodeo, held at the Harley Tucker Memorial Arena in Joseph. After finding a seat in the grandstand, I was joined by grandson James, his bride Danielle, and his mom, Liza Jane. James' sister Adele won the new event for gals this year, the break away roping. Granddaughter Adele, who also competed on the Marr Flat Cattle Company team with dad, Todd, and Cody Ross, also won the Top Cowgirl Award, which included a set of custom-made spurs.

It was an entertaining little rodeo, with events like team branding, sorting, doctoring and, for the kids, goat team-roping and stick-horse races. The last event was saddle bronc riding.

As usual, it takes a lot of volunteer help to pull this event off, and the community was most generous. Scholarships are awarded using some of the proceeds, and this year's winners were Ashton Olsen, Emily Spang, and Bailey Wearin.

June 29—This morning I made the 8:00 church service in time to ring the bell. By 10:00, I was parking at the Hurricane Creek trailhead with old friend Phyllis, who was visiting from Bend. It was a lovely fresh morning after the rain, and we counted over 30 varieties of wildflowers along the trail, including Indian paintbrush, blue phlox, forget-me-nots, wild clematis, and yellow cinquefoil.

Our first adventure was to cross Falls Creek, which dashed off the mountain beneath us as we carefully placed one foot beyond the other along a large log that had conveniently fallen over the water. Lucky for hikers, another tree had wedged itself above the long trunk, and we grabbed the accommodating knots to steady ourselves. The trail was damp and therefore without dust, and to our left, the glorious presence of Hurricane Creek rushed full of high melting snows. The scene was very refreshing and in no time we had entered alpine wilderness.

The highest peak in the Wallowas loomed ahead: Sacagawea, with her gleaming flanks of snow, grew ever closer as we made our way up that lovely trail. We broke into a meadow and gazed up at the Hurricane Divide, where waterfalls cascaded down over whitened, weathered rock punctuated by reddened strata.

We stopped to eat our lunches in a meadow near Deadman Creek. There we visited other hikers who had chosen that lovely day to explore the Eagle Cap Wilderness.

On the way back, we met a group of young men wearing backpacks who had planned to hike to the Lakes Basin but had been turned back by deep snow blocking the trail. Returning to the trailhead, we enjoyed a different perspective of the creek. We noticed the turquoise pools, the frothing waters, and surprise, ripe wild strawberries, which we nibbled on. So tiny, sweet and wild.

All around us, butterflies were flitting and birds sang above the sound of the rushing waters. A time to refresh the soul. Phyllis and I gave ourselves a pat on the back, as we hadn't hiked this trail since she moved. Although we aren't the youngsters we used to be, and the trail has grown steeper somehow, we did it!

June 30—I left early for Sheep Creek to work in the garden and pick cherries. Although the birds have been feasting in my absence, there was plenty for all. At home I pitted enough cherries to bake a pie, and froze the rest for future pies.

July 1—I fetched the last of our home-grown potatoes out of the cellar to fix for supper. They were Yukon Golds and had stored well. After pulling off a few sprouts, the spuds were firm and flavorful inside. Temps climbed into the 80s that day, all of sudden, it's summer.

Our writers group met this morning at the Josephy Center, and at noon we strolled up the street to The Red Horse Coffee House where granddaughter Becky works, and ordered delicious salads to eat out on the deck. Since I had volunteered at the Wallowa County Museum that day, I spent from one 'til four surrounded by relics of Wallowa County's colorful past, and answered questions posed by visitors from several states.

July 2—Doug and I rang up our friend Fred who lives in Auburn, California, to wish him a Happy 86th Birthday. Hope you had a good one, old buddy.

July 4—Hot and sultry.

We were invited this evening up to daughter Ramona and husband Charley's ranch on Upper Prairie Creek, where we joined a small gathering of family and friends to celebrate. Charley grilled hamburgers and I contributed another cherry pie. Ramona and others provided yummy potato salad, deviled eggs, lemonade, and watermelon. We sat outside in the shaded yard, in view of the east moraine, which rises abruptly across the pasture to the west.

July 5—We were in bed before the fireworks shook the lake last night. Was a good thing I retired early, as this morning there I was again, as in years past, riding the bus up the South Fork of the Lostine River to be dropped off at the three mile mark, along with another record-breaking turnout of run/walkers. There were four bus loads this year. Two of the buses continued on up the road to transport the 10-K runners.

As usual, after the starting shot was fired, the bulk of the entrants—many years my junior—took off like a herd of antelope, leaving me to enjoy my leisurely saunter. It was a lovely morning, and the smell of ponderosa pine and the sight of the Lostine dashing along to my left were exhilarating, and renewed my energy.

The familiar course continued on, and soon I was overtaken by the 10-K runners, sweaty and panting, as they entered the final mile. My heel had healed and I felt great. The final hill appeared ahead, and the temperature was rising, but I made it, then headed into Lostine and soon made the turn to the finishing line.

Rotary volunteers, bless them, provided tables laden with melons and drinks. At the awards ceremonies, I won a second place medal to wear around my neck. I was beat out by Rochelle Danielson in the 70+ division. Way to go, Rochelle!

After the awards, I wandered up-town and into the newly refurbished Lostine Tavern, with its Bowlby Stone front. What a treat! Air-conditioned and cool, beautifully restored, this favorite gathering place for locals fills a need in the community. A great menu features locally-grown farm- and ranch-to-table fare. The Marr Flat Cattle Company, Six Ranch, and Carman Ranch grass-fed beef is all locally raised.

There is ample seating, and one can watch Lynne Curry grill those burgers in a clean, spacious kitchen. The place was packed and my sparkling lemonade and burger were delicious. A huge bar offers locally brewed drinks, and the salads were prepared using local garden produce. Just goes to show how a dream turns to reality.

Sad to report the passing of yet another old-timer. Marge McClaran has left us to join her husband, Jack, who passed away earlier in the year. Gone, but not forgotten, are these folks, who now leave the operation of the McClaran ranch to the younger generation.

Chief Joseph Days will be here at the end of the month, and although summer is nice, I hope it turns a bit cooler soon.

July 6—Our church congregation was happy to welcome Don and Rosemary Green, who were in the county visiting. The popular couple now live in Texas. We were further cheered by the presence of Malcolm and Jean Dawson, after a long absence due to aging and health issues.

Doug spent this Sunday touring a portion of the Wallowa Mountain Loop road that circles back to Imnaha. He said it was 97 at the Imnaha store.

July 7—Hay! It's HOT—as in, making hay while the sun shines, because some of these earlier first-cuttings got wet when it didn't.

This evening, as the lingering low light lay softly over Hough's hay field, I watched a white-tail doe searching for her twin fawns. Soon they came bounding out of the tall, uncut meadow hay and began to nurse. The doe, seemingly unconcerned, flicked her long white-tail as a tractor pulling a mower advanced toward her fawns' hiding place. When the twins finished nursing, they followed her out of the field.

During this hot spell I wait until the sun slips over the western Wallowas before taking hoe in hand to weed my garden here on Prairie Creek. My favorite time, the cool of evening, hoeing in the midst of my thriving potatoes, cabbages, corn, carrots, squash and onions.

Before sunup this morning, I headed down to Sheep Creek to hoe the tomatoes, peppers and squash. By the time the sun poked its head over Middlepoint, the other volunteers were just arriving.

After tending to other chores at the cabin, I returned Prairie Creek. My growing cow herd is fat and content, as they should be, what with large willow trees to seek shade, belly-high grass to graze, and fresh running water to drink. Since the cows and calves are allowed to graze the high grasses growing between the garden and yard, oftentimes I must wend my way between their large bulky bodies on the way to the chicken pen. As they sit chewing their cuds in my path, I'm reminded of the sacred cows of India.

As usual, a lot has happened since last I wrote.

Dan Warnock's book-signing of *You Can't Borrow Yourself Rich* was a success, and Doug and I have both enjoyed the book. Dan has done an excellent job of telling their family story, the ups and many downs of establishing a foot-hold in Eastern Oregon. Many ranching folks will identify with this spunky family, who never gave up in spite of hardships. Since many Warnock descendants continue to live in Wallowa County, and we are familiar with the history of the Warnock place on Crow Creek, we found it a good read. Thanks Dan, for sharing, oftentimes with humor and old-fashioned wisdom, those tales told by your father and mother, Dan and Alice.

The Saturday I returned from Sheep Creek, after spending a week with my Syringa Sisters, I caught up and rested enough to attend Colby

Patton's wedding. Colby married her Wes in the beautiful yard on the ranch where she and her twin brother Devin grew up, which is located just east of us here, up Echo Canyon.

It was a lovely evening, and the views of the Wallowas were stunning, not to mention the rolling green hills. It seemed such a short time ago when curly-headed Colby was a little girl. I'd guess her grandma Donna was entertaining similar thoughts as her lovely granddaughter danced with her daddy on the deck, then walked to the altar under the trees. Smiling Colby, grown up now and wearing a long white gown, her golden curls accentuating her country-girl charm.

After the ceremony, a long line of cars wended their way down the gravel road to rejoin everyone at a lively reception held at the old Edelweiss Inn at Wallowa Lake. Wedding guests were treated to a tasty meal consisting of barbecued pork and beef, salads and wedding cake.

A very danceable band began to play, and my neighbor, Lois Hough, and I enjoyed watching the youngsters as well as oldsters cavort about the floor. Wallowa County children love weddings. It is where many of them learn to dance, under the patient tutelage of their daddies and mommies.

July 8—At the end of another sweltering day, I drove to Wallowa Lake Camp to listen to this year's Fishtrap presenters, including friend Teresa Jordan, speaking at an event that was open to the public. A welcome relief from the valley heat, to walk into pine-scented coolness and welcome old writer friends I've made over the years.

A half moon on the way home, its reflection wavering on the waters of Wallowa Lake, hanging suspended over Chief Joseph Mountain.

July 9—A bit of a predicament today. My cow herd, plus Ken's heifers and one bull, were grazing outside the garden fence when suddenly I heard this enormous thud.

Further investigation revealed the cattle had rubbed against an old power pole, causing it to fall. The pole, so rotten its base had been reduced to sawdust, was an accident waiting to happen. What to do? The line that supplies electricity to the chicken house was draped over a row of corn in my garden.

After calling son Ken, who drove over and installed a new pole Doug had purchased in town, the problem was solved. Sadly, what's left of our ranch is showing signs of aging, like us! Sagging posts and fence wires, listing hay shed and weathered outbuildings. I see this happening all over our rural areas, as the average age of ranchers creeps up and over the 65-year mark.

Lush hay lies in field on Prairie Creek in rural Joseph, waiting to be raked. Yields are high this year timothy, alfalfa and meadow hay first cuttings are just going up.

July 11—Today was HOT. In the cool of evening, Halley and I walked up the road to Locke's, where I sat down on a stump to rest and observe the Butterfield family and friends pitch in and make hay.

Such feverish activity. Four balers thumped up and down the rows of fragrant timothy hay, cut at just the right time to preserve its green color. Two loader-stackers were picking up the small bales and transporting them to the side of the field. Two large semi-trucks and trailers drove slowly into the field and were loaded with the same precision as the haying process. All the machinery, operated by men and one woman, worked tirelessly and efficiently with not a wasted motion. Everything functioned and nothing seemed to break down. It was Agricultural Art.

The sun set but the crew continued on until the last loaded semi disappeared down the road.

As I was walking home, the full July moon appeared suddenly over the eastern horizon. By the time Halley and I turned in our lane, the setting sun's glow outlined the dark willows in fiery apricot.

A hayfield on Prairie Creek, east moraine of Wallowa Lake in background, showing a canola field in yellow bloom.

July 12—I drove into Enterprise and found John, and Mrs. Groupe seated out on the shaded sidewalk in front of the Bookloft, autographing John's latest book, *My Eastern Oregon*. Nice job, John. Reading it makes me want to head into the backcountry with a pack string.

Our Enterprise Carnegie Library was celebrating its 100th birthday that day, along with the annual Bowlby Bash. A man named Bowlby quarried stone used many years ago to build many of the city's historic buildings, including the courthouse. Each year, Enterprise celebrates its historic past by staging a street fair and other events.

Tonight I was invited back up to Fishtrap to take in what is now a tradition, referred to as Saturday Night Live, which included Word Begone, a spoof on Lake Wobegon, sponsored not with powder milk biscuits but Janie's Sourdough.

The hilarious script, written and executed by our local humor man, Jon Rombach, had us laughing ourselves silly. We were also treated to the professional Mary and Rindy Ross with their unique musical program.

Driving home, Prairie Creek was lit by the light of the full July moon, the closest to earth it would be all year.

July 14—Lightning and thunder in the night ignited fires—one up Hurricane Creek.

July 15—Met with our Write group, but left early to return to the ranch to fix hamburgers and potato salad for the pipe crew: Ken's grand-kids, Ronan, Gwenllian, Kennon, Gavin and Lochlan. All sweaty and red faced, they trooped in and I served them lunch outside under the old willow tree on the picnic table. After they set out the irrigation pipes with grandpa, they ran through the sprinklers to cool off.

July 16—A large turnout gathered at the cemetery on the hill above Enterprise, to celebrate the life of Marge McClaran, who now joins her husband Jack. The mountains provided their faithful backdrop and folks came from miles around to honor this great little lady. Sam Morgan, local veterinarian, sang comforting songs, and stories were told by family and friends. Another old-timer laid to rest.

July 17—Wild winds activated the Hurricane Creek fire, and the eastern sky was dark with smoke from the Hells canyon fire.

July 18—Cooler. Mike Tippett, Katherine Stickroth and I drove to Wallowa to attend the opening ceremony of the Tamkaliks powwow, Nez Perce for "from where you can see the mountains."

It was a lovely cool evening and a light breeze ruffled the parachute cover over the dance pavilion. The setting sun backlit the feathers, beads and bells that adorned the dancers in full regalia. It's always so colorful, Tick Hill looming over the beating of the drums and the tepees pitched in the meadow. The smell of Indian frybread was pretty irresistible so we shared a hot one, dripping with butter and honey.

July 19—Friends and members of our church family met at the picnic area of the lake to celebrate another old-timer's life, that of Jane Williams, who passed away earlier in the year. Jane loved cupcakes, so that is what we brought. Such an array.

Daughter Lori and her hubby Larry arrived then, too, as Lori had gone to school with Jane's daughter, Linda. The two of them stayed on for Chief Joseph Days.

July 20—Ramona and Charley hosted 38 of us family and friends for a feast at their ranch to meet with granddaughter Tamara and her hubby Matt, along with two of their children, Cole and Halley, who had driven up from Lodi, California, for the weekend. It was good to see everyone, and I took the makings for homemade ice cream, as there were plenty of helpers.

Great grandkids Cole, Halley, Brenna, Gideon, Ashlyn, Jada, and Riley Ann all took turns cranking, and scoops of vanilla ice cream were ladled onto cherry cobbler. Ramona provided pork and beans, and the guests contributed the traditional summer fare to feed hungry folks. Our family loves to eat.

We sat in the yard and watched the Hurricane fire boil up over Chief Joseph Mountain, and finally burn itself out above timberline.

Sadly, another old friend and local passed away this week. Bob Moore left us after a long, brave battle with cancer. Our prayers go out to the Moore family, who live up Bear Gulch. Bless you all.

July 23—Finally, relief from the heat. Skies, recently filled with smoke, have been swept clean by a cool wind, and we only hope last night's thunder storm didn't ignite new fires. Most of the first cuttings of hay have been stacked for winter feeding or hauled out of the county.

Irrigation resumes, thanks to an ample snow pack that insures a continuing source of water. Reports from the backcountry indicate there is still lots of snow in our mountains, even though it appears to be disappearing rapidly from the steep slopes of Chief Joseph Mountain and Ruby Peak.

July 27—The 27th Annual Chief Joseph Days has just ended. Son Steve, his wife Jennifer, daughter Lori and hubby Larry, and friends Debbi and Steve from California, have all left. We all gathered for a goodbye at the cowboy breakfast this morning behind the rodeo grounds. It was quite a week.

I only made one rodeo, the family night performance on Wednesday. As usual, it was thrilling, and thankfully the weather cooled off enough to make all the activity more enjoyable. We cheered on great grandson Gavin, who made an 81 score in the mutton busting event.

We also did the two parades, the Kiddie Parade on Friday and the Big Parade on Saturday, waving as grandson James drove by representing the Divide Camp for wounded vets, and his dad, Todd, rode by on a horse with the Wallowa County Stockgrowers entry. Doug and I didn't take in as much of the festivities as did the younger generation, opting to stay at home and avoid the large crowds of people who add to Joseph's population an estimated 20,000 visitors. Once again, an army of volunteers must be very glad this annual event is over!

I listened to the rodeo on KWVR radio last evening, and learned son Todd barely missed making the whistle in the Wild Cow Milking. After all that work, of being mauled around by a wild cow, that must have been a heart-breaker. This event is always the crowd pleaser, and provides some pretty humorous entertainment for the observer, albeit bumps and scrapes for the contestants.

The weather is turning hot again, and this column needs to be e-mailed. See you next time.

July 28—I dealt with my errant cow herd and tried to survive the extreme heat today.

July 29—Arose early to bake a blueberry cobbler to take to Dan DeBoie's funeral, held at the Joseph United Methodist Church. I met at the Josephy Center with our Write Group, but left early to attend the funeral at 11:00.

Talk about a life well-lived over a long period of time; that was Dan's. Born in 1918 in Joseph, Dan remembered carrying ice blocks from an ice house for the family's "modern" refrigerator, and plowing with horses. He was also present as a boy at the reburial of Old Chief Joseph's body at the foot of Wallowa Lake.

Dan married Catherine Daggett in 1946 and, the week following his death, they would have been married 68 years. An overflow crowd filled the church that hot morning, and a multitude of tributes were paid to this extraordinary man. After the service and a military burial at the Prairie Creek cemetery, we all enjoyed a pot luck lunch at the nearby Masonic Lodge.

This evening I joined other members of the Liberty Grange at a meeting in the old hall just across the road from our place. The basement was cool, and we appreciated Carmen bringing her famous "Impossible pie" for refreshments.

July 30—Our skies were filled with smoke from the Hurricane Creek fire. We did have a thunder shower, but what moisture fell quickly evaporated in the wind. I picked raspberries and tried to water the garden.

July 31—July is moving off the calendar. I made the first batch of raspberry freezer jam. Yum. Over east tonight, lightning zipped through dark clouds. Every evening, when it cools, three white-tail does and their twin fawns step cautiously down from the dry hills to feed on the green, irrigated hay fields across the road. I look forward to watching the spotted babies leaping around and chasing each other.

August 1—It was very smoky, but cooler, so Halley and I took a long walk.

On the way home, a young badger appeared out of the tall grass growing alongside the road. Whereupon it presented itself to us in such a formidable manner, we both gave it plenty of room.

This evening a cock pheasant that has been hanging around the chicken pen flew up at my approach, missing my head by inches.

August 2—I was up early baking a raspberry cobbler to take to yet another memorial, this time for Doug's sister, Barbara Fredrick, and her husband Arnold, who passed away within two months of each other. Arnold was 101 and Barb was 89. They died in Hawaii and, sadly, due to failing health, they weren't able to return to their beloved Wallowa County.

The Memorial was held in the Enterprise Baptist Church and offici-ated by Doug's nephew Bob Fauste, aka Smoke Wade, who did a great job. Attired in his cowboy garb and signature black hat, he said we were there, not to mourn, but to celebrate two lives well-lived.

Earlier, the family asked that I present the eulogy, which I gladly did. As so often happens at family funerals, the occasion proved to be a Tippett reunion with family members arriving from a-far.

In my eulogy I emphasized how, as she grew older, Barbara remem-bered her growing up years as a ranch kid on Joseph Creek with increas-ing fondness. After the memorial service, we enjoyed a feast hosted by the family in the church's social hall. It was very hot, and many folks had a long drive home.

I thought of Barbara that evening, remembering the many happy times we spent together.

Son Ken showed up that afternoon to haul several critters to another pasture, leaving my three cows and calves here. This will give these pastures a rest and time to grow again.

August 3—After our 11:00 church service, our congregation drove to the Wallowa Lake Methodist Camp to join a throng of folks from the community to say farewell to Ben and Claudia Boswell, who have impacted our county in a big way. They will be sorely missed. The popular couple are moving to Spokane due to Ben's health concerns, and to be closer to their daughter. The place was packed.

Another potluck. Wallowa County is noted for them. Ben and Claudia were roasted and honored for their years of community service, which ran the gamut from Grange to County Commissioner. We at the church will miss Claudia, as she was our long-time and most efficient choir director. Listening to the numerous organizations stand up and pay tribute to Ben was amazing.

"Oftentimes I was the only one to turn up at a meeting," quipped Ben. "I wondered, where were the other folks?"

At one time, Claudia taught school at the one-room school at Imnaha. To end the moving program, the Wallowa County choir, under the direction of Randy Morgan, sang special songs to honor the couple. A tear fell from many an eye.

Driving home in the heat of the afternoon, I noticed smoke coming from the direction of Imnaha.

August 4—Left before sunup to drive to Sheep Creek, concerned about the fire. Pulled into my place to turn off the irrigation sprinklers and saw that the water was off. A neighbor stopped by to tell me the power had gone off around 2:00 a.m., when the fire had burned a power pole.

I walked over to the Magic Garden and picked the first TOMATO. How we look forward to this yearly ripening. I also picked yellow squash, cucumbers, and peppers. The garden is thriving.

Back at the cabin, I noticed the blackberries also ripening, so spent over an hour picking several gallons to freeze at home. Soon the volunteer crew arrived to weed and till in the garden. Before I headed back up on top, I drove to Imnaha to see the fire. The air was thick with smoke and I could see the fire burning up high near the road to Hat Point.

Fires make me sad. I know all that country up there, and know how dry it is. I prayed for the safety of the ranchers and others who lived along the river. I ran over two rattlesnakes in the road on the way home.

That night we ate a homegrown meal. Hamburger steak, potatoes, yellow squash, swiss chard, Walla Walla sweet onions and cucumbers in vinegar, and tomatoes. My, how good it tasted. When it cooled off outside, I dug my garlic, as it was ready.

August 5—A murky red sunrise. The Imnaha fire, which had started upriver on Sunday afternoon between Don Marks' and the Royes' place. The Hurricane Creek fire had calmed, but later flared again. At our Write group we discussed the fires and read our work. Afterwards we met at the Outlaw Restaurant in Joseph for lunch.

When I returned home Doug was gone.

Later, he drove in with the news he'd seen 1,000 head of elk out by the Buttes.

And now it's FAIR time. Must get up early in morning and bake a pie for the Grange Day. Great grandkids will be showing their hogs. Too much going on to enter my veggies, flowers and photography this year.

August 7—I baked my raspberry pie and took it to the fair for Grange Day. It didn't last long. While there I watched great grandchildren Riley Ann, Gideon, and Jada show their hogs. They did really well: Riley Ann and Jada won reserve champion market hogs, and Gideon received a red.

Visited while eating a fair hamburger under the shade trees near the show barn. While we ate, the Hurricane Creek fire blew up, and Chief Joseph Mountain looked like an erupting volcano.

When I returned to Prairie Creek, Doug and I were pleasantly surprised by a visit from Steve and Leslie Dorrance, who live in Salinas, California. They were on their way to Canada for a vacation. They treated us to dinner at the Lostine Tav, where we had a great meal in the newly-restored restaurant, before Steve and Leslie drove up the South Fork of the Lostine River to camp for the night.

August 8—This morning is cooler, with clouds scudding above the smoke from the two fires. The Imnaha fire is far from being contained and we face another day of worry. Tomorrow night is the FFA and 4-H Fat Stock Auction at the fair. More company coming today.

August 9—The morning dawned chilly with stagnant air trapping murky smoke from the fires that ring the valley. At noon, Doug and I were invited to the Outlaw Restaurant in Joseph for a Tippett family gathering to honor Mike Tippett and his mother Janet's birthdays.

Before lunch, I strolled through the Joseph Farmer's market, listening to our local musical group Homemade Jam play their lively tunes. While there, I visited Myrna and Larry Moore, up from Bear Gulch to enjoy the festivities. After purchasing a loaf of zucchini bread at the Magic Garden booth, baked by Betty Cosgrove, and some molasses popcorn from the kettle corn lady, I walked over to the Outlaw for the birthday party.

By 3:30 I was on my way to attend the annual FFA Bar-B-Cue, held at the fairgrounds. I joined Ken's family and chowed down on smoked beef, salads and beans. Prior to the meal, a large crowd gathered in the shade outside the sale barn, where awards were presented to both FFA and 4-H members.

We were pretty proud of great-grandson Gideon, who won a trophy for reserve champion 4-H hog showmanship. The Jidge Tippett Memorial belt buckle that Doug and I sponsor, was won by Aspen Birkmaier for her outstanding beef project. Wouldn't you know, the hogs sold last in the fat stock auction order this year, so it was late when I won the winning bid on Gideon's market hog.

Driving home, the nearly full "fire moon" appeared eerily red in the eastern sky.

August 10—Smoky again, and the endless irrigating continues. We met outside after church to eat ice cold watermelon and survey the stakes marking our proposed addition to the existing building, which would include a new kitchen and space to feed 100 folks. If this happens, our church could provide adequate facilities to host wedding receptions and funeral meals on site.

This evening, after it cooled off, I baked a chocolate angel food cake using 12 egg whites fresh from the hen house. The cake was refrigerated until I frost it on Tuesday.

August 11—After a cool morning, which allowed me to pick enough raspberries for another batch of freezer jam, this afternoon's hot winds are not welcome. Especially since two fires, both visible from our place, have been fanned into renewed life. The old fire, smoldering along in wilderness up Hurricane Creek, flares up during these winds.

The more recent Imnaha fire, which began last Sunday, now blackens steep, dry canyon country and continues to grow. Our concerns are for the fire fighters, the ranchers and inhabitants who live and work in the fire's path. Irrigating seems futile due to the prolonged heat and dry winds. I noticed many lawns in Joseph were not being watered at all.

My critters are still breaking down worn-out fences and traipsing around in places they shouldn't be. Veggies are ripening in the gardens, and the raspberries just won't slow down. Mamma kitty weaned her four kittens, and they use my garden for a playground as it lies next to the woodshed where they live.

It continues to be a busy summer. I drove to Sheep Creek today to join other volunteers in harvesting our garden. This enormous plot is not only luxuriant, but beautiful to behold. Interspersed among the vegetables are colorful sunflowers, zinnias, and of course the golden squash blooms. Due to the hot days, and plenty of water, the garden appears tropical. Pumpkins and squash plants are out of control, climbing fences and sending out tendrils, creating a jungle-like effect over the garden.

Corn is as high as a cow's eye, and tomatoes and peppers are ripening. It's pure pleasure to stand in the midst it all, the rising sun streaming between the cleft of Middlepoint. As soon as it began to heat up, I walked back across the bridge and spent an hour picking another flat of blackberries in the shade near the cabin. A bumper crop this year, enough to share with friends.

Later, back on Prairie Creek, I pulled beets and canned pickled beets. A few sprinkles of rain and sultry conditions helped the gardens.

August 12—I frosted that angel food cake with a cream cheese frosting and decorated the center with a cluster of freshly-picked raspberries and their green leaves.

Our Write group met this morning at Pat Adelhart's charming cabin home above Wallowa Lake. After reading, we sat outside on her patio, surrounded by planters of blooming red geraniums, savoring a variety of potluck salads and Della Allen's warm bread. The cake was a hit, and we sang Happy Birthday to Cathy Putnam, and to Ruth Wineteer, even though she was in the hospital at the time.

I left directly to volunteer at the Wallowa County Museum until four o'clock. I fought sleep, but there were too many visitors to let that happen.

August 13—I took sister-in-law Janet Uhler and her hubby Jim to Sheep Creek, as they'd never been there before. We'd left early enough to beat the heat for a tour the Magic Garden. We also picked more blackberries. Thankfully, the 5-Mile Imnaha fire was under control, and the smoky canyons were clear again.

This afternoon I attended a museum board meeting in Enterprise.

A rather severe thunder and lightning storm materialized this evening. Although not as bad as the winds plummeting much of the Northwest, a few limbs and trees were blown about. Also spotted a Western Tanager feeding in the raspberry patch this morning—its brilliant red and yellow plumage startled me.

August 14—Halley barked at coyotes yipping in the night, and this morning several ravens, buzzards and a golden eagle led me to my missing first-calf heifer, lying in the water of an irrigation ditch as if she just dropped dead. We suspect lightning killed her. A big loss, in more ways than one.

In the habit of animals, her big steer calf, accepting its fate, didn't even bawl, and it's been eating grass and seems to be thriving.

It rained most of the day, lessening more fire hazards.

August 16—The day dawned rain-washed and clear, perfect for the annual Stockgrowers Ranch Rodeo, which began promptly at noon with the World Champion Rock Jack Building contest. I'd arisen early to grate a huge head of cabbage from my garden for coleslaw.

It always amazes me to watch the entrants in the rock jack contest perform a feat which is, to them, part of their everyday lives. Beginning with logs, these strong men and boys split fence material, and in mere minutes they are hammering nails to hold a finished rock jack in place, complete with rocks to support it. These are huge rocks. It takes muscles and endurance to build one of these fence braces. In a country where there are plenty of rocks and shallow soil not conducive to digging post holes, stays and rock jacks serve the purpose.

Cousins Ty and Clancy Warnock, Imnaha-raised boys, won the event this year. It was obvious they'd had lots of practice.

Was much entertained watching my herd of great grandkids perform. Riley Ann, Ashlyn, Jada, Gideon, Cutter and Nevada entered everything they could, which included the stick horse races and wild ewe milking. By necessity, wild ewe milking morphed into wild ewe branding. Turns out the ewes were dry! Using a stick dipped in paint, the team members pretended branding. Of course, the ewe had to be caught first, and therein was the problem. Many a kid was dragged through the dirt.

Second grader Cutter joined his grandpa Ken and uncle Todd on horseback to compete in the team sorting event. Teams were given a number, written on the critter, to begin sorting out, and then sorting continued in that order until all the critters were herded into an adjacent pen.

There were two thrilling horse races, one a half trot and the other a full-out gallop around the track. The Muley team roping event also got pretty wild. Dust boiled up in the arena as cows evaded twirling ropes of teams of four. Son Todd and daughter Adele were on the winning team.

It was good to see Ed and Carol Wallace, who drove over from Clarkston for the day. Also visited Julie Wheeler of the Divide Camp.

Grandson James sat beside me until late in the afternoon, when he left to begin grilling some SERIOUS BEEF: pounds of tri-tip for the dinner held in Cloverleaf Hall that evening. James and his dad took on the monumental task of cooking the meat. It was another one of Wallowa County's amazing volunteer efforts through the entire day, beginning with the annual breakfast meeting at Cloverleaf Hall.

After the last event, I drove home to wash off the dust, gather up my coleslaw, and join Doug and friends at Cloverleaf Hall. One could detect the luscious aroma of grilling beef all over town. The place was packed with both the younger and older generation of cattle folks. We chowed down on juicy tri-tip, a large selection of donated salads, rolls and beans, and two large decorated sheet cakes donated by Ed and Carol Wallace for dessert.

Newly-elected Stockgrowers President Alan Klages presided over the annual awards, all presented to deserving recipients. The Grossman of the year award went to the McClaran family, and the honorary Cat-

Pat Dougherty finishes the rock jack contest in the fastest time. Pat is a former World Champion Rock Jack Builder, but this time he didn't win, as the judges also select on quality and stability. The World Champion Rock Jack contest is held each year in the Wallowa County Stockgrowers Ranch Rodeo in Enterprise.

tleman award went to Tip Proctor, who was employed for years by the McClarans.

Two scholarships were awarded to local youth enrolled in agricultural studies in college, and the winning rodeo contestants received their prizes. The Rock Jack trophy was created and donated by Casey Tippett, and the winning rock jack auctioned for $1400, with the proceeds going to help the Norton family, who recently lost their welding building to a fire. Proceeds from the ranch rodeo go to raise scholarship money as well.

There were a lot of tired cowboys and cowgirls that evening. It had been a long day, but the music provided by Imnaha's "Last Call" band began to play for those with enough pep left to dance. Doug and I left, remembering the years we used to stay and kick up our heels until the early morning hours.

And now, the heads of cabbage are ready. It's time to make sauerkraut.

Amy and Chad Nash's family. From left, the kids are Kennon, Lochlan, Ronan, Gwenllian, Gavin, and Arianwyn. Baby Beorn sits in front.

August 18—As we volunteers do every Monday morning, we met at the Magic Garden on Big Sheep Creek to harvest our burgeoning crop. My heart was gladdened by the sight of my First Heavenly Blue morning glories blooming. Their color matched the canyon sky.

We are supplying produce now for the Divide Camp for wounded veterans, as well as the local school lunch program, the food bank, and those in need. The pair of wild turkeys showed up with their half-grown brood, wishing they could get into the garden. Before I drove home, I picked up more windfall pears to can.

August 19—Summer is rolling and ripening into fall. I say ripening, because that's exactly what everything is doing around here. All those hot days and mild nights, recent rains, and long hours of daylight have produced a record crop of berries, apples, vegetables and grass. The fires have simmered down, with the exception of the Snake River burn, which means our skies have cleared of smoke for the time being.

The second cuttings of fragrant alfalfa lie in windrows. Our County Fair is history, as is the annual Stockgrowers' Ranch Rodeo dinner and awards. It's been a busy past two weeks. Ken is in the middle of haying and hasn't had time to build a new fence to keep our critters from running hither and thither, so we keep the gates shut in our lane.

August 21—I took Doug into our local hospital for his second successful cataract surgery. After spending the morning there, we celebrated by treating ourselves to a Marr Flat hamburger at Heavenly's in Enterprise.

August 22—Katherine came out and we shredded, tamped and salted four huge heads of cabbage out of the garden here, and got the sauerkraut going. Then we sat down to scrambled eggs and toast with grape jelly made from the grapes on Sheep Creek.

This afternoon I baked a Dutch crumb apple pie from the transparent tree in our yard. Grandson James showed up just as I took the pie from the oven.

For supper I combined elk burger and sausage in a mixture to stuff those lovely peppers grown in the Sheep Creek garden. By bedtime, a soft warm rain was falling.

August 23—It dawned wet and cloudy. 44 degrees. Our county was full of tourists.

This evening I surprised a large barn owl that was swooping down to grab one of my hens, late going into the coop. Luckily, I saved the hen from becoming owl bait.

August 24—Doug and I headed to the upper Imnaha to our favorite "undisclosed" huckleberry patch. The purple fruit hung heavy on the bushes, and the air was saturated with the fragrance of their ripening. It was lovely in the forest, in the speckled sunshine and shade, and soon I'd gathered a gallon.

Suddenly, thunder boomed in the distance, and rain appeared to be falling all around us. We enjoyed a picnic lunch and returned home. Coming down Tenderfoot lane, we met my little cow herd, moseying along on their own outing. I jumped out of the pickup and headed them back home.

August 25—More Magic Garden harvesting. Home to can dill pickles, and start the 7-day sweet pickles. Couldn't resist picking enough blackberries to make a wild juicy cobbler. Fried corn fritters for supper.

Allen Voortman called to say he had run into another California Golden Guernsey Queen in his travels. Yours truly was queen in 1949.

August 26—Halley howled with the coyotes all night.

I cleaned out the freezer to accommodate a quarter of Marr Flat grass-fed beef while Doug drove to Wallowa to pick it up.

Our Writer's Group met this morning, and at noon we lunched outside in the sunshine at Embers Brew House before I volunteered at the museum from 1-4.

I canned pears and met with the Divide camp committee late in the afternoon, a very busy group of volunteers doing great work. Julie tells me son Todd built two rock jacks to secure a gate recently.

August 27—Canned the sauerkraut and dealt with a huge liver son Ken left with me after the mobile slaughter unit finished butchering his barren grass-fed heifer. I was able to find a home for the delicious organ meat, after saving a feed for us, which I fried and smothered in onions. Yum!

Our mornings remind us fall is coming. Clarified, rarified air, carrying a sharp cold tang. Mary Lou Brink, Lois Hough and I served for the CowBelles at the Community dining center today. After which I visited Wilma Goucher, in our local hospital recovering from a stroke.

When I got home I found a lovely box of peaches left by Myrna Moore who lives down in Bear Gulch.

August 28—This morning found me canning peaches. I love to work with this sweet, golden fruit. Windy, rainy and cold. A good day to be inside. Using some over ripe pears, I baked a crisp for supper.

August 30—My friend Pam and hubby Skip showed up to make sauerkraut. We set up on the picnic table outside and had it all done by 9:00 a.m. I traded Pam three cabbages from my garden for tomatoes from her Imnaha garden to can

Later.

This evening we joined friends and neighbors way out on Crow Creek as guests of Clint and Maureen Krebs at their annual Labor Day get-together. Lamb kabobs sizzling with peppers and onions on a huge grill, and we added potluck side dishes. Of course I brought sauerkraut.

It was a lovely evening way out there, with a full view of the distant Wallowas. I always miss the hills, since we no longer trail cattle out that way every fall and spring.

On the way home we spotted a herd of 20 elk coming down a draw at the edge of the valley.

September 1—Clear, sunny and crisp here. Down to Sheep Creek before the sun slipped warmly over Middlepoint. All the volunteers were smiling. It was so pleasant in the middle of all that bounty growing so lushly midst the blooming sunflowers and zinnias. Towering over all were the Palomino-colored canyons.

We all gathered around a trailer-load of produce for a photo. Our smiles reflected the joy we shared after weeks of toil. All volunteers are allowed to help themselves to the vegetables. I returned at noon to stir-fry eggplant, squash, onion, green beans, and tomatoes for lunch. Served with a sprinkle of Parmesan cheese: it don't get any better than that!

September 2—This morning early, before Writer's Group, I was up canning the sweet pickles.

September 3—There was a light frost, but my garden escaped.

At noon, around 20 former CowBelles met at the home of Mary Lou Brink's for their annual reunion. So many of us are gone now, and others fading away, but those of us in attendance had a great time, enjoying the potluck finger food and visiting about the good old times.

This evening Doug and I attended the surprise retirement party for our friend, Maggie Vali, who, after nearly 40 years, is retiring from the restaurant she and deceased hubby Mike started so many years ago. She will be missed, but her able son Michael, and wife Dione, will continue to serve up fine Hungarian and American cuisine, even though Maggie won't be there to kiss bald heads like Doug's.

The team of mules that pulled the Grand Marshal wagon waiting for the parade to begin

September 4—It dawned crisp and clear again, and I got the wander lust. Called Katherine, and we loaded up our dogs and drove to the Hurricane Creek trailhead. The last of the wildflowers—cinquefoil, asters, Indian paintbrush and snowberry—lined the trail, while the rushing waters of the creek supplied delight to our senses as we climbed ever upward.

The highest peak in the Wallowas, Sacajawea, appeared before us, her stark gray slopes devoid of all but a few patches of snow. We hiked and rested often, until we arrived at a spot next to the creek, sitting on a bleached log situated on a sandy beach to eat our lunches in the warm sunshine.

As we were leaving, we heard a great splashing and crashing next to us, and looked up to see a six point bull elk bounding across the creek. Kind'a took our breath away!

We savored the afternoon and paused often to gaze up at the rugged Hurricane Divide, where trickles of waterfalls drained the last of the snowmelt. We both felt blessed to be able to walk into the wilderness in less than an hour from our homes.

September 7—Due to there being five Fridays in August, a lot has happened since last I wrote. Hough's have just finished compacting the last "bread loaf" hay stack in the field across the road. Other neighbors have combined their grain and baled their straw. Blackbirds sing in concert along the fence lines, and my cow herd crunches down the apples as the wind blows them down from the old tree. Juice trickles down their jaws, and if a cow could smile, mine do. And Mule Days winds up today.

Yesterday morning found me seated alongside past Grand Marshals of Hells Canyon Mule Days, riding in a covered wagon pulled down Main Street Enterprise by two mules wearing bells on their collars. Several old-timers, including Doug, chose not to ride this year, finding it harder to negotiate those steep steps into the wagon.

At noon I joined a long line waiting for one of those grass-fed Marr Flat hamburgers prepared by daughter-in-law Angie and her daughter Becky, aided by Susan, secretary for Marr Flat Cattle Co. It was worth the wait. Juicy and grilled just right, served with caramelized onions and traditional fix'ins.

Then it was back in Julie Kooch's wagon to be pulled around the arena for the Grand Entry. A long afternoon of mule events followed, which included mule races around the track. I didn't take in the mule show, however, as was busy signing copies of my book, *Four Lines a Day*. Situated midst vendors from all over the West, I met people from out of the county and State. Thanks to friend Katherine, we did quite well.

Always a treat to visit my little family from Bartlett, who traveled from the Grande Ronde canyon to sell two mules in the auction that evening. Grandson Buck, wife Chelsea, and the cow kids, Lucy, Katelyn, and Cooper. Also visited grandson James, who just returned from a successful pack trip into the Wallowas with his dad and friends in the Marines. Sons Todd and Ken were also there.

Katherine and I stayed on for the bar-b-cued pork dinner that evening, and drove home watching a spiral of smoke boil up over East. We have since learned of another fire in the canyon country.

Our family is grieving yet another tragedy. Son-in-law Dennis Huber, husband of daughter Linda, was killed in a truck accident last week near Klamath Falls. Linda is planning on spending some time with us, and a memorial is planned down at the Sheep Creek cabin.

September 8—Doug's 83rd birthday was special, as daughter-in-law Ramona and hubby Charley treated us to a savory steak dinner at the Wallowa Lake Lodge. Great atmosphere and food.

Since my birthday was the following day, we celebrated both.

September 9—Our Write group planned another birthday for me, this one held out North, in the wilds of Flora, at Cathy's charming, restored farm house. After reading our writings, we partook of a gourmet meal featuring creative salads, an ice cream cake and two elderberry pies. Thanks, gals.

This all transpired during another one of those Super Moons, plus a wildfire that began near the Ice Lake trail in the Eagle Cap Wilderness. I continued to can pears and froze a batch of pickled/spiced crab apples picked at Cathy's.

In our mail box today arrived a box of hand-sewn red-checked kitchen curtains for the cabin. Thanks, Mary Smith, one of our Syringa Sisters. Was cool today so I whipped up a kettle of chicken soup simmered with garden veggies. There was ice coating the sprinkler water that morning. Our corn survived, but the squash is toast.

September 11—It froze hard this morning. Goodbye, garden. I got in and dug three rows of potatoes, and son Ken and Doug helped me bag and load them to store in the cellar.

The corn is still unharmed. I salvaged several squash and dug the rest of the onions and shallots. The garden on Sheep Creek, being lower in elevation, has thus far escaped. My friend Pam just gave me that flat of tomatoes. Granddaughter-in-law Danielle will help me can them this weekend.

September 12—A film crew descended on the Magic Garden to create a video of the project. The large plot never looked lovelier, and camera men and ladies were awed by the pumpkins, corn, baking squash, peppers, tomatoes, blooming zinnias, sunflowers and Heavenly Blue morning glories. A lot of footage was shot of our little Eden. I picked enough jalapenos to pickle several pints when I returned home.

September 13—Spent the morning canning more pears, then rode with granddaughter, Chelsie, and great granddaughters, Riley Ann and Ashlyn, to the Elgin Opera House to take in the musical production of "OLIVER!" Wonderful afternoon of music and entertainment in the restored historic opera house.

On the way home our car just pulled into the Little Bear Drive-in, and we slurped up Little Bear ice cream cones with gummy bears on top.

September 14—Granddaughter-in-law Danielle showed up for her lesson in canning. While I supervised, she proceeded to can all the tomatoes and another batch of pears. She was a quick learner and it was fun. I love passing along these skills to the next generation. Her new hubby, James, was out cutting wood for the winter. We had stuffed peppers for supper along with baked Yukon Gold potatoes and corn on the cob.

September 15—Today found me early down in the Sheep Creek garden, where I joined other church volunteers to host the Enterprise Head Start School. Two bus loads of children spilled out to walk in teams through the garden and harvest various vegetables. Each child was allowed to take one of each veggie home with them.

I asked all of the students where French fries came from, and not one knew the answer! They mostly said R&R Drive-In and Safeway. Not one knew they were made from potatoes. Now they know, and actually got to dig the spuds and see how they grow under the ground. Methinks this type of education is more important than book learning.

Returned home as the afternoon warmed up. Canned more peppers and dilled green beans. That evening I attended a meeting at the Liberty Grange across the road. We had a ceremony for a deceased Granger, Joyce Freudenberg, a member for 60 years.

September 16—Up early to bake a pie crust and fill it with eggplant, peppers, onions and garlic, all sautéed together, and layered with tomato slices. Then off to the west moraine with a carload of writers to the Wallowa Lake home of member Don and his wife Elane. After our usual readings, we retired to the deck and savored creative potluck and mint tea. It was a most pleasant afternoon, as a cool breeze whipped the wavelets against the shore, while gulls and kingfishers dipped over the lake.

September 17—No frost! Canned more pears. Took a long walk with Halley at sunset, circling the wheat stubble, following deer trails and watching long skeins of geese float to the fields to feed.

September 18—All in our valley awoke to the smell of thick smoke filling every available space. A warm wind had blown it in overnight from Southern Oregon and Northern California.

September 19—I canned salsa this morning and spent the afternoon volunteering at our local museum. Luckily, the smoke cleared today, after the wind shifted from the north.

Friend Allen Voortman popped into my kitchen bearing a gallon of his delicious Pride and Joy Dairy whole milk. He looked good, said he was busy, like us all, and took off. After he left, I poured myself a tall cold glass of cow juice and made it through the day much better for it. Thanks, Allen.

I drove over to Sally Brandt's to attend a Stitch and Bitch brunch. While the gals knitted, I spent the time identifying photos and recording dates in my albums.

Home to can the last of the pears. I quit! Those pear trees in my creek garden have been too prolific this year.

September 20—Doug and I, along with other birthday people Duane and Jean Wiggins, were feted to yet another birthday celebration. We all met at the Glacier Grill across from the Wallowa Lake Lodge for lunch. Our old gang is fading away, and any chance we have to connect is welcome.

Also joining us were son Steve, wife Jennifer, and our two hats, Bailey and Stetson. Daughter Linda drove in to the ranch just as we were leaving, to stay for her husband's memorial.

I'd spent the morning preparing deviled eggs, raspberry cobbler and apple pie.

September 22—a gentle warm rain soaked the thirsty land. I was down to the Magic Garden that morning harvesting apples left after a mamma bear and her cub ravished the remainder of that tree. Other varieties are still ripening higher up on the branches of two other trees.

I shook my fist at crows that flew to the English walnut trees, picked green nuts, and skittered off to a rock where they stashed them for winter meals.

A bus load of young students from the Joseph Charter School arrived to tour the garden and take home samples of the produce we are donating for their school lunches.

Later, I walked back to my cabin and picked the ripe Concord grapes growing in the arbor over the deck.

Daughter-in-law Angie loaned me her steamer/juicer, which made quick work of canning a batch of grape jelly and juice.

September 24—A gentle wind, born in the south, exhales its warm breath over Prairie Creek this morning, drying my newly-laundered sheets in minutes, ruffling chicken feathers, loosening windfall apples, and rattling withered corn stalks. My kitchen table is full of dark purple-colored Concord grape jelly and juice. All jars sealed! An Olaf vase full of zinnias from the Magic Garden, and a zillion notes to myself, occupy the remaining space.

September is leaving, which intensifies my squirrel-like rush to preserve and store for the coming winter. The autumnal equinox has come and gone, and the changing of the season shows itself in the flaming sumac and yellowing willows.

Our old friend, Frank Millar, was here this morning for a brief visit. He was on his way home after camping out on the Divide, where he reported a great time was had due to his self-contained camping equipment. Frank elaborated on the views, which were far-reaching.

The Memorial for our son-in-law, Dennis Huber, went off smoothly and memorably. Perfect weather, a great gathering of family and friends, touching eulogies, services conducted by my two sons, Ken and Todd, a tree planting ceremony in honor of Dennis, and a feast beside the creek. The highlight was when the Von Nash family, our take on the "Sound of Music" Von Trap family, gathered beside the creek and sang a fitting ballad. Chad, Amy, and their seven children, Ronan, Gwenllian, Kennon, Gavin, Lochlan, Arianwyn, and baby Beorn.

Folks lingered well into twilight visiting there in the canyons, which provided a very healing place for all. When everyone left, I stood there next to the newly-planted aspen tree and felt Dennis' presence. He so loved it there.

Across the creek lay the burgeoning garden with its long rows of giant sunflowers and sun-ripened tomatoes. Draped along the creekside, blackberry bramble, in whose vines quail called, a chorus of birds signaling the coming night. A kingfisher flew over the water and an owl hooted in the tall pine. It was hard to leave.

September 25—Another clear, cool day. Planted garlic along the perimeter of the garden, and dug horse radish roots remembering the advice given by my dear old friend, Wilmer Cook, that you dig horseradish only in the months with R.

Larry Waters, wearing his hat, drove by with the Tippetts with team of mules. He was teaching two young friends how to drive a team. The horse radish roots were milder, firmer, and not stringy. After peeling the gnarly roots, I cut them into small pieces and ground them in the blender with white vinegar. Yum. Spread on egg salad, ham and beef sandwiches satisfies my craving for its unique zesty flavor.

On a whim, since I had a gift certificate for a Gondola ride, that I had purchased during the 4-H radio auction and was about to expire, I rang up my friend Ruth Wineteer and asked if she would like to accompany me to the top of Mt. Howard.

"Sure," she said, and I headed over to pick her up.

Larry Waters, wearing his hat, drove by the Tippetts' with a team of mules. He was teaching two young friends how to drive a team.

We were soon stepping into a windowed cage and floating up a 7,500-foot vertical rise that in 15 minutes deposited us on top of a mountain in the heart of the Eagle Cap wilderness.

On the way up, a gust of wind caused the chair to swing outward, which brought forth an adrenaline rush that only subsided when the chair straightened itself out again.

The views were awesome. Reflecting the sky, Wallowa Lake glimmered far below, and across from us, waterfalls trickled down from B.C. Basin and Ice Lake. Beyond the behemoth mountains of the Eagle Cap, which include the Matterhorn and Sacajawea, not to mention the stark Hurwal Divide, the wilderness of peaks ended in sky. Since I no longer backpack into my beloved haunts, this is one way to experience it.

At the top, the wind kicked up again, and a cold front of clouds moved steadily towards us. Ruth opted to sip hot cappuccino in the covered dining area, which afforded a view, whilst I pulled my hat down firmly on my head and struck out along the trail that leads to a view point overlooking what I just described. Surprisingly, there were still tourists about, older couples, clutching each other to steady themselves against the wind that was, by then, so strong as to topple us.

After climbing wooden steps to a high vantage point, I attempted to take a photo but couldn't hold my camera steady, and if I hadn't found a bench to hold on to, would have been swept away by a gust I guessed to be around 70 miles per hour. It was exhilarating, however, and brought back memories of being on top of Aneroid Peak during one such fall storm.

Because of the cool wind, I was refreshed, and fairly ran back to the mountaintop restaurant where Ruth and I enjoyed a most delicious lunch before climbing once more into our gondola cars and descending the mountain. As luck would have it, after the clouds swam in, the wind blew itself out and our trip down was most pleasant.

After searching for, and finding, a few red Kokanee spawning in the West Fork, we returned to our lives. Homemade tomato soup for supper.

September 26—A gorgeous morning, no frost. Canned a box full of tomatoes and cooked tomato sauce. Took a long walk through the golden stubble fields alongside the irrigation ditch with Halley. Scared up a covey of Hungarian Partridge.

. At noon I joined other volunteer members of our Magic Garden crew to conduct a class on food preservation at the Joseph Charter School. My job was to demonstrate the art of making sauerkraut, while Betty Cosgrove and Robin Martin made zucchini relish and pesto. Marla Dotson, home ec teacher, made salsa. All the produce we worked with was grown in the Sheep Creek garden. Class members were allowed to participate and went home with samples of each product.

I hurried home to bake a rhubarb cheesecake pie to take to son Ken and wife Annie's ranch on Alder Slope for the occasion of a going-away party for great-grandchildren Cutter and Nevada, who will be moving soon to California.

After a traditional potluck, which included a cake baked by Ashlyn and homemade ice cream cranked by Chad's family, we fled inside away from the evening cool, and took photos and celebrated both youngster's birthdays. We will miss you two, but know you will be back to visit often.

It was a bittersweet gathering for me, as 14 great-grandchildren were in attendance. These cousins love being together.

September 27—Whiskers on the mountains, with a light dusting of snow. Katherine set up a book signing for me at the Farmer's Market in Joseph where we managed to sell a few books and visit a lot of folks, including John Groupe. Since it was Alpenfest weekend, a couple of talented women played the accordion across from us, and older couples began to polka midst the garden produce, kettle corn and goat soap lady's booths.

Pressed for time, I drove to Wallowa Lake's Edelweiss Inn and waited in line to purchase a bratwurst and sauerkraut on a bun. Lots of revelry going on, and memories came flooding back when my daddy, who so loved that Bavarian Swiss music, was there with me, a stein of beer in one hand, dancing and singing his way through the performances in that same old building.

September 28—I attended the 8:00 church service, then drove to the Enterprise fairgrounds to take in the Junior Rodeo. This event isn't advertised and has no entry fee or admittance fee. It is just a good old fashioned play day for the little ones, organized by the parents of Wallowa County's burgeoning population of wee cowboys and cowgirls. And, since I had several participating, I made an effort to be there.

I'm so glad I did. Watching two-year-old Cooper attempt to throw a rope in the dummy roping, then build sand castles in the dirt was worth it all. His two sisters, Katelyn and Lucy, were in several events, and seeing Kate, assisted by daddy Buck, complete the barrel racing, well, walking; that was special.

All the cow kids were familiar as they come to all the brandings and will, hopefully, keep the traditions alive. They came from miles around, and although the audience consisted of proud parents and relatives, the participation was amazing.

September 29—After a substantial breakfast of hotcakes, ham and eggs I drove down to the garden on Sheep Creek to greet yet one more school tour. The event was canceled because it was raining, but the volunteers, not deterred by a light rain, harvested a truck-load of produce.

By noon my friend Kathy and I were enjoying a birthday lunch at a new Thai eatery in Enterprise. Homemade spaghetti sauce on noodles for supper.

September 30—Tuesday—I arose early to bake butter sticks, a long biscuit, to take to our Write Group. We lunched on Pat Adelhart's veggie soup after 9 of us read our weekly readings at the Josephy Center.

October 1—We awoke to find our Wallowas covered with a white blanket of the season's first substantial snowfall.

Our history book committee met this afternoon at the home of Darlene Turner, where we are working steadily on the new history of Wallowa County. The deadline for submitting your local histories will be May 1, 2015, and we are encouraging all those who want to record their family histories, or update old ones that were published in the first book, to begin writing and submitting them. We know many of you now live out of the county, but would like to be included in the book, so get to work on this exciting project.

To those of you who are interested, I will be doing a book signing on Saturday, October 25, 1-3 p.m. at Looking Glass Bookstore on Adams Street in La Grande.

October 2—33 degrees; a clear, green-and-gold day.

On my weekly visit to Sheep Creek, I planted tulip bulbs and transplanted a clump of Prairie Sun perennials next to the cabin. Returned home to clean and line the chicken nests with new grass hay.

This evening I joined friends at the Josephy Center to listen to Liz Enslin introduce her new book, *While the Gods Were Sleeping*, which is about her experiences living in Nepal. Liz lives out north and is a fine writer.

October 3—We awoke to a heavy frost. I got busy this morning and canned the prune plums I'd picked earlier at Kathy's in Lostine.

As it warmed into a lovely Indian Summer afternoon, Halley and I struck off across Hough's hay meadow and climbed the dry hills, where she sniffed squirrel holes and I sank down on my jacket, staring at the intense blue sky and watching a hawk circle. The smell of sage, the quiet, the breath of the cool Wallowas lulled me to sleep. A perfect way to relax and savor these last precious days.

October 4—A sort of calmness has settled over Prairie Creek. The fields, harvested of their grain, lay in golden stubble, and the bare-boned mountains appear purple above all. Ken has hauled the irrigation pipes out of the pasture, my garden is being put to sleep, and all is quiet, save for the odd boom, which means buck deer season opened this morning.

Another warm day, in the 70s. I baked kolache plum buns.

October 5—I took a batch of those buns to church for our fellowship time. The Magic Garden committee reported on the tons of produce that had been harvested and delivered to the local schools, meal sites, food bank, Head Start and Divide Camp.

Doug headed for Imnaha and ate lunch at the Store and Tav. Reported lots of hunters—and fisherman, waiting for the steelhead run.

October 6—I drove to the canyons to clean the cabin and found a hatch of gnats, so thick in the air it was hard to keep from inhaling clouds of the tiny insects.

I picked a flat of tomatoes and peppers and delivered them to grandson Chad's family, as he had gifted us those plants in the spring to transplant in our garden.

October 7—I returned to the creek so as to be there when our Write group arrived. I spent the morning simmering a kettle of chicken noodle soup, and the gals contributed salads and dessert. The gnats were still there, so we met inside, but by noon a gentle warm breeze wafted them away and we were able to enjoy our lunch out by the creek.

The smell of ripe Concord grapes permeated the air, and yellow cottonwood leaves sailed down from the tall trees. The black walnut was shedding its leaves as well, which made for a golden afternoon, and spider webs floated through space seeking a place to snag themselves.

October 8—It was another warm day, but the nights were cold. Sisters, great-granddaughters Ashlyn and Riley both bagged their bucks today and, appropriately, the full Hunter's moon rose over the eastern hills early that evening.

October 9—At dawn this morning, that same "Hunter" moon hovered over Ruby Peak, bright and lovely against the blush of alpenglow. Piglet crowed the morning awake, and his son, as yet unnamed, answered from his perch in the maple tree.

Last week there was a confrontation between sire and son, and son was banished from the henhouse roost. Now that the nights have turned colder, son has been allowed back, but must fly out of the pen at dawn's first light, lest he lure a hen away from pop.

I took a long walk in the afternoon and Puss and Boots, our two half-grown kittens, followed along, much to Halley's disgust.

Baked a plum upside down cake to take to Fishtrap House that evening for the showing of the popular musical, "The King and I."

October 10—31 degrees, frosty and clear. We all met at the Sheep Creek garden to harvest green tomatoes, dig spuds, and glean other end-of-the-season produce. My basement is full of ripening tomatoes.

This evening I was one of the featured writers giving a presentation at Fishtrap House's first Fireside event of the season. It was cozy there, a good crowd showed up, and Mike really did have a fire going in the fireplace.

October 11—It was smoky, with periods of sun. I baked an apple meringue pie, then drove in to the last Farmer's Market in Joseph. It was very colorful with our Magic garden booth brimming with sunflowers, cornstalks, pumpkins, squash, canned jellies, pickles and pesto. Music by Homemade Jam floated out into the mild air, and I photographed before heading to upper Prairie Creek with my pie, to partake of the annual Cider press'in party at the Fraser Ranch.

Folks arrived all afternoon and into the evening bearing food, apples to press, and hearty appetites. More music, smoke unfurling from a huge barrel type cooker that was slowly roasting a hog, more smoke from under 30 broasted and basted chicken halves, folks peeling and grinding horse radish, grinding and pressing apples, straining juice and visiting and eating.

Long tables in Chuck's blacksmith shop awaited the hungry visitors, laden with salads, pickles, cobblers, pies, cakes, beans, potatoes, dips, shrimp, and breads. A large straw bale maze attracted the kids, as did a dirt pile. The creek splashed past and a warming fire blazed in a pit. It was pretty wonderful and we thank Chuck and Kris for hosting this every fall.

I left early, however, and ate sparingly at noon, as Doug and I were taking daughter Ramona and hubby Charley out for supper at the Range Rider, to celebrate our daughter's birthday. And that, too, was a great meal. Ramona and I ordered chicken fried steak, while the guys chowed down on sirloins. A good cook there, and gracious hosts. We were delighted to have great-granddaughter Brenna join us as well.

October 12—A fresh snowfall on the mountains. James' bride, Danielle, was here as planned to can plums. And then, since I had an abundance of tomatoes and peppers, we canned several pints of salsa. Danielle is quite the young homemaker, although she works in the health department during the week.

I'd canned my apple juice before Danielle arrived. In the midst of canning, son Todd texted Danielle while hunting. He'd just shot his buck. And, thanks to technology, there was the photo her father-in-law had just taken to prove it!

October 13—Clear and cold. Driving down to the garden on Sheep Creek, I noticed hunter's camps and camo-clad hunters in the canyons.

Many volunteers showed up to put the garden to sleep. We pulled vines and stacked them in the corners, gleaned pumpkins and squashes, dug carrots, and transplanted herbs in pots to winter over in the green house. There was no waste. I climbed over the stile to pick apples and check out the walnut trees. David stayed into the afternoon and tilled up the garden. I will miss seeing it there, but alas, the work is done for another year.

At noon and hungry, I drove to the Imnaha Tav, ordered lunch, and listened to hunters tell tall tales. Returned home to can seven quarts of apple slices.

October 14—The wind blew all night, wild gusts shaking the house, and the electricity was out for about an hour. Made salsa verde with the tomatillos I picked yesterday.

Attended our write group and we ate lunch at the new Silver Lake Bistro. Good soup. Joseph's streets were littered with red maple leaves, piled in great drifts by the winds.

That evening we were invited to Ramona and Charley's for another great supper of tri-tip beef, a gift from sister-in-law Nancy Tanner, visiting from California.

October 15—Prairie Creek was full of smoke from the still-smoldering fire located where Triple Creek ranches' two hay barns burned the night before. A tremendous loss and a real shame, as hay is in much demand with winter coming on.

The chicken enchiladas I made with the salsa verde were excellent.

October 16—More new snow in the higher elevations, and Ken and Charley loaded my three steers to haul to the La Grande auction this morning. I can't believe the prices they fetched: unreal! But my cows weren't happy, and went to bawling for their babies.

October 17—A flaming October sunrise. I did some house-keeping, then fed a herd of Ken's grandchildren sourdough biscuits with grilled cheese, and banana cake for dessert. They had hauled over their milk cow Annabelle's heifer calf to wean. "Tinker Bell" added her bawling to the cow chorus.

October 18—I cooked all day. Sourdough bread, raspberry cobbler, apple pie squares, and jelly from the apple peelings, all for the Divide Camp luncheon I would be catering the next day.

October 19—A beautiful day as I transported my moveable feast to the Divide Camp, located far out on the Divide that separates the two Sheeps: Big Sheep and Little Sheep Creeks. The sun came streaming through the trees from over the Seven Devils, back-lighting a flock of wild turkeys that waddled in front of me on the road.

It was such a pleasure to meet the three veterans from Afghanistan and Iraq, and very gratifying to watch our heroes enjoy the peace and solitude of that remote place. Each fellow had his own clean, private cabin, and access to the wild woods and camp surrounding them.

I served the meal inside the lodge, but folks ate outside at long tables set up in the trees. It was a hearty meal. Dutch oven pot roasts from beef raised on natural grass not far from there on Marr Flat and the Divide. All the vegetables and fruits came from the Sheep Creek garden, or mine on Prairie Creek. Pickles, jelly, sourdough bread, baked in the dutch oven, and lemonade.

So many improvements had been made since last I visited. Julie is to be commended for her vision, and the continued volunteer help and grants received have truly been a blessing to this worthwhile project.

October 25—That Saturday, Katherine and I drove over to La Grande for my scheduled book signing at Looking Glass Books. After a delicious lunch at Mamacita's, we made our way to the book store to be ready when the first guests arrived.

It was fun meeting new folks and after reading several chapters of my book, I sold and signed 20 books. Granddaughter Carrie, who lives in La Grande but was unable to attend, had called ahead to treat me to a fresh cinnamon roll and hot chocolate upstairs in the building. Thanks Carrie, it was yummy.

October 26—After breakfasting at the Cheyenne Cafe with daughter Lori and hubby Larry, plus daughter Ramona and her Charley, I went to church while Doug headed to Imnaha. Later returned to my kitchen to simmer the venison neck which I would use in making mincemeat.

October 27—I ground the good meat and refrigerated it while I attended our Write Group, after which we all attended Arnold Schaeffer and Mary Hawkins' interesting demonstration of throwing a diamond hitch, which eventually morphed into an hour of storytelling by Arnold of his many entertaining experiences over the years, while he was a packer and guide at the famous Lapover pack station up the Lostine.

Mary, daughter of Merle and Carol Hawkins of Lostine, and granddaughter of the famous Red Higgins of Red's Horse Ranch fame, is also a top hand when it comes to packing, and is now a mother of an adorable little boy.

Home to chop apples, add raisins, apple cider, and all the spices to the ground venison, and simmer until thick. Also checked on the setting hen's eggs. All rotten. Warm rain falling into the night.

Danielle Nash's six point bull elk.

October 29—I canned 12 quarts of mincemeat and baked a pie in my deep iron skillet with the leftover filling. Doug's favorite pie.

Daughter-in-law Angie e-mailed me a photo of grandson James' bride, beaming beside her first elk kill. A six point bull, downed with a single shot. Nice to know James' gal loves hunting, 'cause that's what her hubby's all about!

I joined a small crowd this evening at Fishtrap House to listen to Richard Etulain, author of *The Life and Legends of Calamity Jane,* talk about writing his book. Mr. Etulain, of Basque descent, was passionate about his subject, and his book dispels the many myths about this famous woman of the West, who was born Martha Jane Canary. After years of research and tracking down facts that other historians gave up on, he paints a truer picture than anyone has thus far of this colorful lady. Amazing that Calamity's legend lives on after all these years.

Since we were supposed to come dressed in the Wild West period, I wore the buckskin jacket given to me years ago by old-timer Jess Earl, my mule skin boots, dusty hat with the rattlesnake band, elk teeth necklace and Levis. I won the prize! I once had an Appaloosa mare named Calamity Jane.

October 30—40 degrees and sunlight sifting through our lingering Indian summer. After baking a lemon meringue pie I headed to Sheep Creek. After sweeping the large yellow leaves off the deck, I discovered my power was out. It seems a wild turkey hen, flying from her roost high in the locust tree, had fried herself on the transformer. Her lifeless body lay at the foot of the pole.

In less than half an hour, PP&L had replaced the fuse.

Since we were having potluck that evening for supper, I was able to take a long walk with Halley, sit at creekside and read, and be ready when our Sheep Creek writers arrived at five. It was a lovely day, with peace and quiet, save for the calling of numerous quail.

Later, eight of us sat down around the long wooden table and recounted our summertime adventures while savoring our delectable fare. After the dishes were done, we retired to the living room to read our work far into the night. Pam helped clean up and it was nearly eleven when I climbed in beside Doug back on Prairie Creek.

October 31—Neighboring ranchers Lois Hough and Judy Stilson joined me to serve for CowBelles at the Community Center in Enterprise. A large crowd of senior citizens showed up for chicken-fried steak and all the trimmings.

This evening we were honored by the presence of great grandkids Lucy, Katelyn and Cooper, who had traveled with parents Buck and Chelsea all the way from Bartlett, above Troy, for Halloween trick or treat. We handed out popcorn, apples, and Poppa Doug's candy corn. Good to see their smiling faces.

November 1—November arrived rainy, misty, and dark. Our power out again, due to a downed tree somewhere. When it came on I simmered beef short ribs with carrots, shallots and garlic, served with mashed potatoes, and invited Ben to supper.

November 2—We went back on standard time. Couldn't sleep in, as my internal clock didn't change.

November 3—Dug the remaining carrots in the garden, roasted more of my ripening tomatoes, baked squash for supper, and froze the rest for Thanksgiving pies. Baked a banana cream pie with my excess bananas. Son Ken hauled his critters to a different pasture and sampled the pie.

November 5—A warm rain fell in the night, soaking the leaves blown from the trees by the wild winds of fall. Good to know those leaves will rot and nourish spring's new growth. I firmly believe we should use nature's compost, rather than burn it. Our soil needs the mulch.

My kitchen table, where I write, holds yet more canned tomato sauce, a bowl of apples and pears, and a flyer on tomorrow's 4-H radio auction. I see the two loaves of sourdough bread I have donated is listed.

One of my Barred Rock hens has been setting on a clutch of eggs located under an old rusted pump near the woodshed. I see one chick hatched and promptly died, which hasn't discouraged the hen as she faithfully waits for more. The Northwood Maple is leafless, allowing me to better view East Peak and Mt. Howard from my kitchen window. My cows have quit bawling for their calves, who were weaned a couple weeks ago. The ancient willows are rusted gold, and the asters alongside the house are blooming purple.

November 6—Baked an apple cake and simmered an elk stew in the Dutch oven all day. Offered it to our history book committee after we met here at four o'clock to work on plans for the new book. The "Beaver Moon" rose full over Hough's hill early that evening. Calm after a very windy day.

I will be having another book signing at Hamley's in Pendleton on Saturday the 22nd from 10 'til 12, for those of you who are interested.

November 7—Drove down in the canyons to the creek and gloried in the 70 degree sunshine; folded up and put away the hammock that was stretched between two trees in the yard, stored the birdhouse on the porch, and walked over to the orchard to pick apples and the last of the fallen English walnuts. To bite into one of those golden apples and taste the crisp sweetness is to truly taste fall.

The garden, devoid of its lush growth, has been roto-tilled, and the green manure crop is over an inch tall. Due to the mild weather and sunshine, the canyons are greening under the dry bunch grasses. There is still plenty of color among the cottonwoods and aspen, and I was overjoyed to see my Heavenly Blue morning glories were still blooming on the fence left in the middle of the garden.

November 8—The sun streams through the living room window onto Doug, who is napping in his favorite recliner, the one he returns to each morning from the Cheyenne Cafe, where he goes to chat over coffee with the "boys." Frost carpeted the grasses when he left earlier, and the thermometer on the carport registered 25 degrees.

At sunup, when Prairie Creek awoke, the mountains gleamed whitely with fresh snow. My cattle hovered coldly beside the calving shed, Piglet and son crowed in the hen house, and Halley, sleepy from howling at coyotes all night, grinned at me when I stepped out to chore.

My kitchen smells of roasting tomatoes, drizzled with olive oil, garlic, salt and pepper and dried basil. Later, after they've cooled, I will freeze them in bags to use in sauces, stews or served tasty hot on toast. It is quiet on this Saturday morning, and since all my canning is done, I scrubbed the cooked-on goo off the stove burners.

November 8, later—I attended the popular Healthy Futures dinner and auction this evening in Cloverleaf Hall, which was decorated as elegantly as a New York nightclub. How can I say that? I've never been to such a place, much less New York itself.

Anyhoo, the old hall was transformed far above what you'd expect in Wallowa County. Linen table cloths and napkins, silverware up to gazoo, fresh flower centerpieces, and waiters and waitresses. Beth Gibans, who shares some of my Sheep Creek garden space, catered the affair. Fresh veggies and smoked salmon appetizers were followed by one of the best prime rib dinners I've ever eaten. That gal knows how to prepare beef. The event raised a substantial amount of money-to purchase modern equipment for our local hospital.

November 9—I made it to church in time to ring the bell in the old tower. Many of our members have fled to warmer climates and I can see why. A polar vortex was breathing down our necks here. Shrimp chowder for supper out on Prairie Creek.

November 10—We awoke to our familiar snowy world and the temp was 17 degrees. Clear, cold and beautiful, if you like cold. Grandsons Gideon and Ronan are working with their 4-H steers, along with Grandpa Ken, who is helping these young lads make halters. Being a former 4-H'er himself, he is instructing them during their first year.

My short-lived housekeeper, Amy, and hubby Joseph, stopped by to show off their newborn baby girl. Pretty baby, she slept through the entire visit.

November 11—Veteran's Day—Grateful, as we are every day, for the sacrifices made by our veterans. Especially proud of our own Shawn, Josh and James, who have and continue to serve our country.

Our Write People met at Katherine's home in Joseph. She made a pot of soup and we fetched potluck. I'd spent the morning baking caramelized apple bars.

Our cat population has been thinned out due to raccoons or coyotes.

I spent until late afternoon sitting at Les Schwab's, waiting to have the studded tires put on.

November 12—Five degrees when Charley and Ramona picked me up to drive to Boise. After leaving my daughter and I off at the airport, Charley headed back to Joseph and we boarded a plane to Sacramento. Soon we were up, up, and away, flying into the sunset over the Eastern Oregon desert. And in no time, swooping down to Sacramento International Airport, stepping out of the plane into a mild 70-degree dusky evening.

There was cousin Janet Feil, driving up to meet us at the curb and whisk us off down I-5, where she pulled onto an off-ramp to a Mexican eatery where we were soon enjoying a delicious meal. Then on down the freeway to Lodi, where we were happily stuck until Friday.

We spent the time resting up and visiting my oldest granddaughter, Tamara, and my oldest great-granddaughter, Halley Jane, and her brother, Cole. Daddy Matt was hunting back east, and brother Clayton was attending college at Cal Poly, where he is a sophomore. They have a charming country home situated in the midst of their wine grape vineyards.

We lunched at the Phillips wine-tasting restaurant while a gal traipsed from the kitchen with fresh pies, just out of the oven. As fast as she filled the shelves, they emptied, at $16 a pie.

Halley gave us a tour of her livestock business, mainly Boer goats, which she sells for meat and breeding purposes. She also has an emu, an alpaca, fainting goats, Suffolk sheep, a horse, a burro, a Dutch Belted heifer, chickens and dogs. She is all about animals. Cole is an active F.F.A member who has had steer projects in the past.

Tamara bar-b-cued pork loin for us on the wrap around porch. Incredibly mild weather.

On Friday morning Tamara drove us back to Sacramento where we met up with our Wilson cousins at a pastry/coffee house. We took up a long table and joined in the conversations between bites of sinful pastry. The California sunshine streamed in the window and us Oregonians shed our jackets.

Later, we went for a long walk with my sister Kathy at a nearby park that borders Dry Creek. The creek, not dry, was full of spawning salmon which we were able to view right there in the heart of Roseville. Not only did roses bloom in Roseville, but morning glories, petunias, pansies and every other kind of flower. In Kathy's yard we picked tangerines, pecans and purchased lemons from her friend across the street.

Cathy put us up in a motel, where we were most comfortable.

Later in the evening we drove to the airport again to pick up sister Caroline and her hubby Duane, who had just flown in from Wyoming, having visited their son and family. They reported 17 below in Sheridan.

We were whisked off to Roseville again, where we chowed down on Thai food.

The next morning we visited my sister, Mary Ann, who resides in assisted living in Roseville, and later picked her up to drive to the old ranch where we were all raised. My brother Jim, who still owns 80 acres of the original ranch, was there to greet us. Jim has been battling cancer for some time, and it was good to see him.

Our visit was an excuse for a family get-together, and his wife Joyce and other members of their family put on a real feed, featuring homemade enchiladas. Jim looked good. It had been several years since our last visit.

After eating, Jim took me, along with his border collie dog, for a tour around the ranch. It was like a dream, Putting around in his ATV through green grass bordered by oak trees, and seeing his fat cattle grazing in the meadow. He showed off his new bull and the fall calves.

Jim drove down across Doty's Ravine, past blackberry vines and into the old flat where my daddy used to grow alfalfa. Memories of my youth came flooding back. He took me up into the oak woods and to a knoll where he said he always wanted to build a cabin.

Back at the house, we all gathered in Joyce's lovely yard for a photo of the five Bachman kids, followed by a group photo before we left. My sister Caroline then drove me up to rural Auburn for a visit with my childhood chum, Sandra, and her husband Fred. Over tea and persimmon cookies we chit-chatted about this and that, and then bade goodbye.

That night, sisters Caroline and Kathy joined Ramona and me in our motel room for a girls party. My sisters ended up spending the night after we played a game of Scrabble. Caroline won!

In the morning, we all went to Kathy's little house and looked at family photos until it was time to catch the plane home.

On our way to the airport, we stopped in Sacramento to visit our 97-year-old aunty Carol Nunn. Had a nice visit and once again connected with a few of the Wilson cousins. Aunty Carol is my heroine, she still lives in the same house she did when we were young.

Upon our arrival at the airport, we were informed the plane had been delayed due to an Eastern storm and we would have to fly to L.A., and possibly Pasco or Lewiston. Finally, after a considerable wait, we boarded a plane to Salt Lake City, where we would have to deplane and run to catch the flight to Boise. We did, run, that is, only to be informed that our plane had left! Other folks scheduled for that flight arrived, so they brought the plane back.

We ran aboard and finally arrived safely in Boise. Stepping out of the terminal was like opening a door to Siberia until we climbed into Charley's warm pickup for the ride home.

Home was a shock for a day or two. Creeks and ponds frozen over, icicles hanging from all the buildings, and sub-zero temps for days. All had survived, including Doug, and the fond memories of being with family still linger.

November 17—10 degrees. Saddened to hear of the death of Theo Grote. "Ted" was an extraordinary man, and led an adventure-filled life. I remember once, when I had hiked from Moss springs into the Minam Lodge, joining Ted at breakfast. He was in his later years, and he had been flown in by a friend. Let me tell you, that man had many tales of flying into Red's Horse Ranch, and he had a terrific memory. Rest well, my friend.

In my absence, one of our out-of-state friends had left two boxes of lovely apples on our carport. Of course they froze solid. What to do? I discovered it worked just fine to run hot water over them, then peel, slice them into a kettle, and simmer 'til tender. I made applesauce and pies, and froze the other slices. I managed to salvage most of them. The frost sweetened the apples and they needed no sugar.

November 18—After Writer's Group, we enjoyed soup at the new Silver Lake Bistro in Joseph, and then I drove to the creek to check on things. All was well.

November 19—An owl hooted in the old Willow to signal snow. It was right! More long walks with Halley. Much warmer.

November 21—Helped set up our annual Bazaar in the Methodist church. I baked an apple and two mincemeat pies for us, and a crust for a lemon pie for the bazaar.

November 22—Up early to chore and finish the lemon pie, made from California lemons, and headed to church. My lemon pie sold within the hour for 15 dollars. Helped all day with the bazaar, which was very successful.

The ice cracked and boomed and swept away in the large irrigation ditches and creeks. I cracked walnuts to put in the freezer. Doug watched football and took long drives to the hills to look for elk. The latest count for Thanksgiving is 24 family members here, best get busy!

November 24—First, I would like to apologize for canceling my trip to Pendleton for the book signing. Must admit, when it comes to icy roads, I'm pretty much a chicken. And although the roads were good early on, we would have returned over mountain passes in a snow storm. I promise to be there in the spring.

On this Monday morning it is clear, sunny and 25 degrees. My kind of weather! Had fun crunching through snow to feed the chickens, the cats in the woodshed, and my three pregnant ladies, Fawn, Buttercup and Rhubarb! I especially love forking fragrant clover hay to my cows. Although a long winter stretches ahead, that simple chore stimulates my blood and starts my day better than a cup of coffee.

The sparrows at the feeder outside my kitchen window are a brown flutter against a white world.

November 28—Slept in until 7:00, and then hurried through my chores to drive to Joseph to help our Methodist church committee serve soup and grilled cheese sandwiches at the big bazaar held at the Community Center. There it was, only the day after Thanksgiving, and we were plunged into Christmas. The center bulged with fresh wreaths, handmade pottery, hand-knitted caps and mittens, homemade fudge and myriad creative crafts. It was very festive.

November 29—Snowed this morning and the snow plow roared past early on. Took a long hike over the hills and fields with Halley, to walk off some of that turkey dinner. They buried Ted Grote in the Prairie Creek cemetery that afternoon, in the midst of a blizzard. A few brave souls trudged up there, but I opted to join all
Later, at the LDS church for the meal and memories that followed.

November 30—Dipped to 5 degrees this morning. Clear, cold and sunny. I filled the feeder for the wild birds, and simmered a kettle of turkey soup. And November rolled off the calendar.

December 1—15 degrees when I drove into Central Copy to have my friend, Richelle, print our Christmas cards. While our car was being serviced, Doug and I ate with "the old folks" at the Community dining center.

December 2—It was 12 degrees and clear. Worked on Christmas cards and wrote letters. The Wallowas were astounding in their cold white beauty. Cut Doug's hair, not much of a challenge, but like he says, "Anyone can have hair, but God only made a few perfect heads."
Much warmer, so headed for Sheep Creek to check on the place. All was well, so Halley and I struck off across the creek and wandered up an old road that follows the creek toward its confluence with the Imnaha. It was lovely and the canyons enfolded us in their silence. No rattlesnakes to worry about, lots of fresh air, and the creek itself swirled in December coldness below. Halley nosed every inch of ground, sniffing her way along deer and elk trails.
Long after lunch when we returned to the cabin, so I drove to the Imnaha Store and Tav and ordered a hamburger. Lots of fishermen and hunters coming and going, the bell over the door pinging each time. While in the canyons I found the perfect Christmas tree, and since it was growing on my own property, took my trusty little saw and cut it down.

December 4—The roads were very icy in the morning, but quickly melted. Daughter Ramona delivered a lovely fresh evergreen wreath, great granddaughter Ashlyn's class project, which now graces our back door.

December 5—Attended Fishtrap's Christmas open house at the Coffin House. Fire crackling in the fireplace, readings, good cheer, and a tree decorated with little book ornaments. The staff served a punch that really packed a punch, with cranberries floating on top. I baked crackers for the occasion.

December 6—It rained, was warm, and then turned into a bright sunny day. At 10:00 I was seated in Mary Swanson's independent little book store, the Bookloft in Enterprise, signing my books. For me it was a treat to visit friends and hug granddaughter Becky and granddaughter-in-law Danielle. What a pair! Mary treated me to an Irish Creme latte.

After, I drove to the annual bazaar held at Cloverleaf Hall. There I purchased one of Hope McLaughlin's pot holders she sews from scraps left over from her quilts. Also bought a creatively covered journal crafted by the gal who cooked me a hamburger at the Imnaha Store and Tav.

On the way out I ran into great grandchildren Lucy, Katelyn, and Cooper with their mommy. More hugs!

This evening I drove to the Wallowa Lake Lodge, which was warm and festively decorated for Gail Swart's annual caroling dinner party. Lights glittered everywhere in the great room, where a tree had been trimmed and wreaths hung from the dark wooden pillars, bowls of Christmas candy graced side tables, and wood heat radiated from the fireplace insert.

We all gathered there to sing carols, accompanied by Gail herself at the piano, and the bell chorus played their magical chime-like songs. We made our way into the dining room to find another tree trimmed and glittering, and long tables set with silver, tablecloths, and cloth napkins. After a very filling meal, huge trays of homemade cookies baked by Gail were passed along, and the entertainment began.

Local talent, singing and playing instruments, capped off with Duff Pace singing his heartfelt spiritual songs. Gail, at the piano, turned and said "Merry Christmas," and her warm heart was reflected in her smile. That said it all. We were all in the Christmas spirit.

Driving along the shores of Wallowa Lake on the way home, I was struck again with the beauty presented by the full December moon's glow as Chief Joseph Mountain's white slopes were reflected in the water. Our little home town of Joseph winked with lights as I made my way slowly through it and then turned east on the moonlit road to Prairie Creek.

December 8—It's hard to believe we're into December, weather-wise and otherwise. Especially this morning, with the temperature hovering around 40. Our ground is bare of snow, there is mud in the chicken pen, and a mild breeze rattles the mountain ash leaves that still cling to the tree. Halley says it's time for a walk: there are trails to sniff, dead muskrats to roll in, and deer bones to chew on, so I suppose I'll have to keep my promise and strike off across the stubble field hill when I get back from my dental appointment.

Thanksgiving made us all feel truly thankful, for our family, this special place we call home, and for an abundance of food. Our plates and our hearts overflowed with gratitude. Around 20 of us gathered here on our Prairie Creek ranch to devour a 20-pound turkey and all the traditional foods that go with.

After baking one mincemeat and two squash pies, simmering cranberries, and mixing up the dressing the day before, I was well into preparation of the feast by Thanksgiving morning. Even threw my cows extra hay, before closing the oven door on that stuffed turkey. By 2:00 p.m. our house bulged with bodies as family after family drove in. Per usual, son Todd mashed the spuds. He uses warm milk and lots of butter, and they ARE good.

The family carried in their own specialties, and soon we formed a long wavering line to bow our heads for the blessing. Then filled our plates at the stove and sat at tables decorated with dried maple leaves and ceramic pilgrims. We didn't go to the crik this year. Some said it was too far to travel.

What a treat to have our Marine grandson, James, home this year for good, and his bride Danielle around the table. After everyone was stuffed with pie and whipped cream, we somehow managed a group photo, quite a feat in itself. Some of the great-grandkids caught one of the wild woodshed kittens, which now has a new home.

The weather was so warm I opened the kitchen window. Daughter Ramona and daughter-in-law Annie washed all the dishes and cleaned up the kitchen, which was most appreciated.

Our dear Auburn, California friends sent a box of mandarin oranges up to us, which are nearly all eaten, savored to their last juicy bite. Thanks much.

December 10—The white December moon and the hollow roar of the wind conspired to keep me awake most of the night.

Later in the morning, after a refreshing nap, I called some of our family and friends to invite them to dinner. My plan was to use some of this overabundance of stored food in our freezer and cellar. It worked.

I baked frozen strawberries and raspberries in a cobbler, roasted a small pork and lamb roast, cooked mashed potatoes, opened a jar of sauerkraut, and Ramona contributed a salad. Nine of us enjoyed a hearty meal, as well as stories around the kitchen table.

In our mailbox that afternoon: a box of freshly-picked sweet tangerines from sister, Kathryn, who lives in Roseville, California. Thanks, sis!

December 11—Wind carried on all night. Storms on the coast and California made the news. Discovered a mystery wreath left on our carport, thanks to whomever left it. UPS delivered a box of cookies from niece Pat. I love Christmas!

December 12—40 degrees and a sprinkling of rain. Fed my cows and headed to the crik with that lovely fresh wreath to decorate the cabin for our annual Sheep Creek Writer's party.

Dealt with a few dead mice, scrubbed and cleaned, then took a long walk with Halley to collect pine boughs and cones. Noticed one of the Warnock boys is building a good fence down the creek to keep his cattle in. The green feed is coming and the old bunch grass looks good.

On the way home it poured down rain, and later turned to snow. Great for the country!

December 13—Snowed in the middle of the night; four inches by morning. Cows wait for their hay, their heads aimed at the back porch door. Sloshed through deep snow to shake it off the hay.

Baked a chocolate applesauce cake to take to Mike and Kristy's party that evening high up on Alder Slope. The view from their house is astounding. Kristy says she sees some awesome sunrises over the Seven Devils not to mention moon rises. The village of Enterprise sprawls below, and at night the winking lights remind me of a poem. *I see the lights of the village, gleam through the rain and the mist.*

I think the title is *When Day is Done.* I was especially pleased to chat with my old friend Hope McLaughlin, who lives next door.

December 14—Clear, brilliant snowfields blanket the Wallowas and Prairie Creek. I sipped tea and stared out the window, fed my cattle, then took a long walk around the old ranch. Our tree is decorated and the inside of our house reflects the season.

I baked spice cookies, using my frozen squash, for the gook group tomorrow morning. Potato, corn and bacon chowder for supper.

December 15—Our book group met this morning at Fishtrap House, where we discussed the book *Out Stealing Horses*, and munched holiday goodies at the long table.

December 16—Our weekly writers group met here at our house. We all contributed sandwiches, chips and dips, no sweets. Taking a break. Huge gobs of snow plop off the roofs as the snow melts. After our readings, we watched the video *Heartland*, which is based on the true story of Elinor Pruitt Stewart.

Ken hauled some of his critters here to feed, until he can fix a place for them on the Slope.

December 17—The day began with a flamingo-colored sunrise over the frozen prairie. Fog in the night coated the landscape with hoarfrost, delicate and beautiful.

I baked Christmas Stollens and took a hike while the dough was rising in the bowl. Delivered one to our dear old friend Scotty, whom I visited on the way to the OK Theatre to watch two of my great granddaughters sing in the combined choir from the county's three schools. Randy Morgan, director extraordinaire, will be retiring next year, and a pity it is. He knows how to exact the best from his pupils.

The place was packed, and music from the choir and the band was perfection, exhibiting hours of practice. Riley Ann and Ashlyn made their great grandma proud.

December 18—Ken hauled me a load of hay. Our Methodist women hosted a salad luncheon that noon at our church. Tasty salads, followed by a brief program reflecting this holy holiday.

December 19—I arose early to bake a blackberry cream pie, do chores, load the car with kettles and food ingredients, and head for the crik for our traditional Sheep Creek Writer's annual Christmas party. I spent a relaxing day preparing for the evening.

The weather showed off with sun one minute and fine misty rain the next. Dark skies and snowy rims contrasted with green grass and, just before dusk, a golden light flooded the canyons. I watched it all whilst preparing for our meal. In the midst of that special light, twenty mule deer does and one buck grazed across the creek near the garden. All visible from my kitchen window.

When it rained I let Halley in the screened porch. I placed an old '60s record on my phonograph player, set out bowls and silverware, then concocted the rich broth for our seafood Cioppino dish. For a base I used a package of roasted tomatoes I'd frozen, clam juice, wine, bay leaf and other herbs which simmered all afternoon. When the guests arrived, they added their shrimp, scallops and crab. Some brought steelhead and salmon, which I cooked separately. Jim's wife baked a large round loaf of artisan rustic bread, and Pam tossed a Caesar salad.

I fixed a kettle of Wassail, which simmered on the wood cook stove next to the stew. The cabin still smelled spicy, as I'd baked tiny whole apples, rolled in honey, cinnamon, and sugar, which I then floated on the top of the apple cider-based punch. Of course I dumped in a bottle of Three Blind Moose, a fruity white wine, and created a hot, hearty drink. After all, this is the season.

Nine of us dished up our tasty repast and at at the long wooden table to sup supper. After which I served coffee and blackberry cream pie. It was nice to have Sara Miller and Mike Hale there, as it turned out they were on their way with a load of hay to Horse Creek, many miles down the Imnaha River on the steep, rim-hugging road to Dug Bar.

After dishes were washed, we retired to group around the wood stove, read poems and tell stories. I especially liked Mike's version of one of Robert Service's poems. There's nothing like hearing tales of the Alaskan north country while sitting around a wood stove during the canyon winter.

When the cabin was in order and the last car left, Halley and I headed home. The pavement glittered with frost, which turned to snow near the top of Sheep Creek hill, and it was nearly midnight when I crawled wearily in bed next to Doug.

December 20—I drove to Enterprise to watch four of my great grand-kids, Ronan, Gwenllian, Kennon, and Gavin, perform in their school's annual Christmas program. They all took turns singing and Gwenl-lian played her violin. Of course this great grandma was just as proud as all the other grandmas in that packed room. I sat next to Lochlan and Arianwyn and grandson Chad, who held baby Beorn on his lap. I thought about great-granddaughters Lucy and Katelyn, who had played the piano way down in the one room school at Troy, and wished I could have attended that too. Troy, along the Grande Ronde River, boasts four pupils.

This afternoon, daughter Ramona and great-granddaughter Brenna showed up with homemade peppermint fudge for Doug and a wrapped present for me. They will be traveling to Lodi, California, to be with their children for Christmas.

Because beef short ribs roasted in the oven, I rang up Ben and invited him for supper. Which was nice, as we enjoyed visiting, and since his wife Jackie passed away several years ago, he spends a good deal of time alone.

December 21—The 21st was the longest day in Earth's history, said our radio. It was mild, with a drizzly rain when I drove to the Josephy Center and joined half the county for the program described at the beginning of this column.

December 22—A spattering of snow is all that's left of last night's storm and subsequent mini-blizzards that sporadically sweep over the prairie. In between squalls the sun shines, making it seem more like March than December. However, daylight will last a bit longer than yesterday, as we have passed the Solstice.

The Solstice bells were ringing last evening at the Josephy Center as a goodly portion of our community gathered to celebrate the Christmas season. Bob Webb announced the passing of the Solstice around 6:00 p.m. What a wonderful program that was!

It began with an Alpenhorn solo, followed by a trumpet duo, Gail Swart at the piano, families singing carols, bassoons, oboes, guitars, violins, dulcimers, autoharps and little ones singing right into the microphone. Many thanks to Janis Carper and her Wallowa Valley Music Alliance for staging this annual event. We all went home with warm hearts.

My cows munch their hay, the chickens venture out into their pen between showers, the two kittens in the woodshed curl up together, waiting for mamma to bring them a field mouse, and Halley says it's time for a walk.

December 23—Tomorrow is Christmas Eve and last count for dinner was 23. We pray for those on the road, coming and going to be with family.

December 24—I was in the kitchen, having just finished chores and flipping a sourdough hot cake, when to my wondering eyes who should appear but jolly Santa Claus himself, his eyes all a twinkle, his white beard framing his cheeks and a red tasseled cap covering his head. In each hand he held a jug of Pride and Joy milk.

You guessed it: Allen Voortman, our Dutch friend, who popped in to wish us Merry Christmas. His Dutchman friend, our neighbor Mike Fluitt, was waiting in the pickup so he couldn't stay. I fixed a large hotcake to go, slathered with grape jelly, rolled and cut it in half, so he and Mike could share it.

This evening I used that rich creamy milk to make scalloped oysters for our Christmas Eve supper. Thanks, Santa!

A busy day for me. I baked two huckleberry-cream pies and one mincemeat. Also a loaf of sourdough bread. Plus, I readied beds for family who arrived that evening for supper. Son Steve, wife Jen, and hats Bailey and Stetson, drove in from Yakima late and hungrily slicked up the scalloped oysters.

I didn't make the Christmas Eve service at our church, but just as well, as it was snowing heavily and the wind was blowing.

December 25—Christmas Day found Prairie Creek drifted in, large snowbanks having formed around the house, the chicken pen and our driveway. I fed all of us sourdough waffles, bacon and eggs for breakfast and then began preparing for Christmas dinner planned for 3:00 that afternoon.

Jen and the kids helped set up extra tables. I made a huge green salad, mixed up horseradish, peeled potatoes, and took a walk, as the sun was out, weak though it was. Prairie Creek squeaked with cold and glistened with light.

Son Todd arrived to plunk a huge prime rib into the oven, with instructions of what to do after he left. He kept calling to make sure we did as bid.

Three o'clock came and went. Everyone was here, except daughter Jackie and hubby Bill, who had left early that morning to drive from Challis, Idaho.

Last we'd heard they were leaving Stanley and it was 13 below 0. We decided to wait for them. As they drew nearer, Todd cut the prime rib and mashed the potatoes, granddaughter-in-law Chelsea's bread was sliced, and suddenly, there they were!

After hugs all around, we held hands while son Ken said grace, and then we sat down to our long-awaited meal. I always get a bit teary-eyed at this point, feasting my eyes on our family and being eternally grateful for their safe arrival.

After everyone left, except for those who filled our beds, we were visited by another grandson, Ethan, his mother Shannon, and brother Gideon. They'd invited sister and brother Bailey and Stetson to spend the night on Alder Slope, where they were staying with their grandma.

December 26—We were all asleep in our beds when the phone rang. It was Steve.

"We're at the emergency room with Bailey. She had an accident in the snow, damaged her knee, and we're on our way to Lewiston where there is an orthopedic surgeon on duty." We hadn't even heard the cell phone ring downstairs, nor had we heard Steve and Jen leave.

Long story short, Bailey was operated on and returned the next day, a bit sore but now healing nicely. It was a wonderful Christmas, and after Bill and Jackie and Mona departed for Bartlett Bench to visit Buck's family, and Steve and Jen returned home, we settled down to something resembling normal.

During this time I did a lot of cooking and visiting. Among our visitors were Myrna and Larry Moore from Bear Gulch, and their daughter Jenny and hubby who are visiting from Iceland, and their new baby girl. A real doll baby, and after watching Jenny grow up, we are pleased to see her happily married and enjoying motherhood.

Granddaughter Mona Lee stayed for a short visit before returning to Portland. She now owns a half-grown puppy, Boomer, who is a half-brother to my Halley, as they share the same mother. Boomer's father, however, is a black lab, so you can imagine how rambunctious he is. He had never seen a cow before and wasn't sure what to think, but decided to leave them alone.

Son Ken popped in often with his grandson Cutter, who was visiting from California for the holidays. After feeding cattle they were always starved, so I cooked up elk steak sandwiches and served apple pie and ice cream.

December 28—A new snowfall added to the old. 10 degrees on the 29th, and again on the 30th. Clear, with a veil of fog over the mountains. Long John weather.

December 29—After enduring zero temps, snow storms and all the inconveniences associated with severe cold, we are now basking in relatively mild conditions. Our snow has been reduced to a white mosaic spread across the fields, and an occasional wind-drifted pile in the yard. While forking hay to my critters this morning, the high-pitched wavering wails of coyotes echoed off Hough's hill. Over the Wallowas hung the waning wolf moon, the hunger moon, and those wails meant empty stomachs.

On the way into Enterprise this morning, to pick up Doug at the Davis Body Shop where he left his pickup to be repaired, I spotted three cock pheasants feeding in a grain field. Up our own road yesterday, hundreds of wild mallards and Canada geese landed on our neighbor's stubble field. Numerous white-tail deer trip their dainty way across the road every morning and evening, but now there is at least one less, and all that remains is a tattered hide on our lawn.

I raised the blinds in the living room early one morning into the New Year to witness a startling sight. Three coyotes had recently made a kill only a few yards away, and were busily tearing the deer apart. I stepped outside to call Halley, and when she didn't appear I was alarmed, and found my border collie in her dog house. She was way in back, cowering and shivering, and not with cold. Whew! I was relieved. Apparently she has learned that coyotes can gang up on a dog and kill it just as well as a deer.

As dawn gave way to daylight, each coyote trotted off carrying a huge chunk of venison to enjoy elsewhere. While flocks of ravens and magpies converged to slick up the remains, Halley drug the hide home.

Yesterday was one of those rare December days when you have the urge to go camping. I mean, it was 40 degrees and not a cloud to be seen, the sky so cold-cleansed it was a joy to breathe, and the sun held real warmth. After duties here, Halley and I fled to the canyons, where it was so mild I took off my jacket. Chores done in the cabin, I ate a sandwich and then the two of us crossed the bridge and went through the gate to the field beside the Magic Garden.

We stepped over the wooden stile and rambled along the old road down the creek. At first the path leads upward, then down almost to creek level before climbing again. Every step reveals lofty views of canyon, creek and high, frosty rims. Water caught in clefts is still frozen and the creek is lined with milk glass-colored ice chunks. The water flows fast with melting, and kingfishers seek quarry in the frigid waters. I was glad to see cattle grazing the steep slopes while bedded down in sunny swales chewing their cuds.

Seeking a flat rock, I sat down and soaked up sun and view and counted myself among the luckiest in the world.

December 31—Woke to ice on the inside of our bedroom windows.

Daughter Linda appeared this evening, having driven from Salem. While she celebrated New Year's Eve with old school chums in Joseph, Doug went to bed at 7:00 and I made it to nine.

Kathryn Cole and Caroline Rueb, Janie's two sisters visiting from California loved being down on Sheep Creek

2015

January 1—Well below zero and I was glad not be plunging into Wallowa Lake with the brave (or crazy) souls who do this every New Year's morning.

January 3—Doug and I attended Betty Van Blaricom's funeral at our Methodist church in Joseph. It was 15 degrees and the sun streamed through the stained glass windows to brighten the woodwork and many large bouquets of flowers surrounding her casket. Betty met her husband Van when she was only 16, and they had been married for over 70 years. I will always remember Betty as someone who had a sense of fun.

We were once involved in a skit to promote beef for the CowBelles, and Betty and I were dressed as a cow. We came on stage, she the tail, me the head. Somehow, Betty tripped and down went the huge udder, teats splayed this way and that, and I got one of my fits of uncontrollable laughter and, finally, Betty got up and straightened out the udder, then went down again, as she couldn't see. The audience went wild seeing this giggling cow. At least we got their attention, and created a memory I shall not forget.

While munching cookies in the church kitchen I hugged Van, who said he felt like only half a person, now that Betty was gone.

"May her sweet soul rest in peace," he said.

Another friend, Mike Brennan, turned 93 this week. His friend Shirley Doud had purchased the two loaves of sourdough bread I donated to the 4-H Radio Auction last fall, so I got up early Tuesday morning to bake the bread, and delivered it warm to Mike on my way to town.

Mike, whose famous father is Walter Brennan and lives just up the road, declared one loaf would go to him and one to Shirley, who was due to visit that day. Mike showed me some wonderful photos of his dad, taken while making films with movie stars our younger generation never heard of. Happy Birthday, Mike.

January 6—Attended my friend Ellen Morris Bishop's book signing this evening in Joseph's Wallowology log building. Ellen's latest book on geology, entitled *Living with Thunder* is beautifully written and easy to understand, and her photographs, shot all over the northwest, are stunning.

January 7—I took my Halley dog to the Red Barn Vet to update her rabies shots, then headed for the creek to work and play.

January 8—30 degrees, and I baked cookies for the Big Read's kickoff this evening at the Joseph Community Center. Leo Arenas, from El Bajio restaurant, fed us tacos and other Mexican dishes, in keeping with the theme of the book *Into the Beautiful North*. A large crowd turned out for the popular event, including children, who delighted in striking down a loaded piñata.

January 10—Drove down into the canyons to meet up with Todd's Marr Flat cattle drive. At Lightning Creek I ran into Todd's wife, Angie, who was driving a pickup loaded with hay. She said Todd had a meeting that day so she was taking his place. At the entrance to Walter Brennan's old ranch, Halley and I waited until nearly 400 cows ambled past. Then, joining son Ken and Sheep Creek neighbor Ken, plus Todd's cowboy, Cody Ross, we brought up the drag.

The sun shone briefly, highlighting the muted colors of willows and dogwood lining the creek. Since son Ken took Rowdy's two dogs after his untimely death, they were busy doing what cow dogs do best. However, one of the dogs, Jim, runs on three legs and therefore tires easily, so Ken lifted him up on his saddle, and there he rode while Ken led his horse.

The day made for very pleasant walking, staring up at the rims and listening to the creek splashing merrily alongside. It was well after noon, and since the crew had lunch waiting at Brushy, Doug appeared and we drove on down to the Imnaha Tav and ordered something to eat. Warmed by the barrel stove and entertained by old re-runs of "Gunsmoke," we munched our lunch. Visitors and locals trickled in and out, and all agreed: What would we do without the Imnaha Store and Tavern? So glad it hasn't changed in all these years.

January 11—I didn't make church, but stayed here in the kitchen where I roasted three pot roasts that son Todd had contributed for the occasion. I also baked a fry pan full of sourdough biscuits, peeled potatoes, baked two huckleberry cream pies, and put together a salad. Todd's cattle were trailed up on top from Brushy this year, which proved a shortcut from years past, so the cowboys and one cowgirl were here by 12:30.

Grandson James, home this year from the Marines, was among them. He had called on the cell phone to say they were only 45 minutes out, which put me in gear to mash potatoes and make gravy. Let me tell you, that food was devoured pronto. How I love cooking for hungry cowboys. Nine of us around the table today.

January 12—It was snowing lightly as the cows made their final way along the Crow Creek Rd to the old Snyder ranch out of Enterprise.

January 18—On the 13th, son Ken and his crew began tearing down the old hay shed here on the ranch. For several years now the building has been listing earthward with each new wind storm. I fed the cold hungry crew a hot noon meal all this week, which was most appreciated.

On the last day, I treated them to roasted Cornish game hens with dressing, apple cabbage salad, and buttermilk biscuits.

Today I joined our Stitch and Bitch group at the Lostine Tavern for a birthday brunch for Lynne. Mucho delicious, and since it was after 11:00, I ordered steak and eggs, which I highly recommend. This historic building has been lovingly remodeled, and Lynne and her crew do a great job of preparing wholesome local food.

January 19—Our book group met to discuss *Into the Beautiful North*, by Luis Urrea, a story woven around Mexican immigration. This evening our Liberty Grange met at Larry and Juanita Waters' ranch up the road.

January 25—A wedge of weak January sunlight falls on the kitchen table where I write. At 3:00 in the afternoon it's the first sun I've seen all day. Up 'til now fog has smothered Prairie Creek in a damp misty chill.

After church let out around noon, on a whim, and because I had worn my hiking boots, I decided to take a hike. I drove to the terminal moraine of Wallowa Lake and parked my car near an interpretive trail that makes a loop through what used to be the old Marr Ranch. As I wound my way up the zig-zag path to a ridge, the fog lifted enough to expose occasional peeks of snowy peaks. Signs placed along the trail illustrate where the Silver Lake and Farmer's irrigation ditches run, where the Marr Ranch house used to stand, as well as Nez Perce history, which precedes early white settlement.

I treaded carefully along the snow and ice-covered meadow trail until I climbed to the frozen pond. Pausing to rest on the wooden bridge that spans the creek, I let the silence sink in. My only encounter was a magpie, who screeched at me from a large ponderosa pine. I made my way up the final hill and thence back to my car.

At home I warmed up beef stew, and shortly thereafter Doug returned from Imnaha, where he'd spent the morning in sunshine! Quite a contrast to yesterday, when I hiked the high trail that follows Sheep Creek: jacket

The Eagle Cap Extreme Sled Dog Races. The Junior events began at Ferguson Ridge Ski area.

off, sleeves rolled up, basking in 55 degree sunlight, where robins chirped in the willows, quail and wild turkeys, who have escaped the jaws of coyotes, were numerous. Halley and I had a glorious day.

Last night I drove into the Joseph Community Center to attend the Musher's banquet, staged by the Eagle Cap Extreme Sled Dog Race folks. The hall was filled to capacity with volunteers, mushers, their families and helpers, and lots of locals. A home cooked meal, served up by the Chuck Wagon Sisters, was devoured before the awards were presented to the mushers.

All of the winners raved about how well they were treated here, how they loved the scenery and the well-marked trails, but most of all, the people, who made them feel like family. The winner of the 200-mile race generously donated his winnings back to the race committee for next year. Several mushers and their teams were headed for Alaska's famed Iditarod. Listening to their tales of the trails brought back memories of when I cooked at the Ollokot checkpoint several years ago.

Katherine and I had driven up on Friday to Fergie, our local ski area, to watch the juniors and pot racers take off with their teams. We were below the ski slopes and above the fog, and the backdrop of the snowy Wallowas was breathtaking. Although the mushers would have preferred colder conditions for their dogs, it was great for spectators. We were pretty proud of our own local junior racer, Morgan.

After photographing, Katherine and I sat on the sunny deck near the warming hut and gobbled down sourdough biscuits filled with ham and cheese.

As the daylight hours lengthen, my hens have begun to lay again. My milk cow, Fawn, and her two-year-old daughter, Buttercup, who will be calving in March, munch heartily on the hay son Ken raised on Alder Slope. The big black cow, Rhubarb, is also growing big in the belly.

January 27—Our Write Group met at the Josephy Center that morning and there was a heavy frost under a cloudy sky. We had a great session. I returned home for lunch, then struck off up the hill and down along the irrigation ditch, where Halley found a deer leg to chew on and drag home.

January 28—I noticed the first robins returning to Prairie Creek, which is early. It was a mild 45 degrees. Doug attended our local ditch company annual meeting.

January 29—I headed to Big Sheep Creek and my cabin, where I spent a relaxing day cleaning and cooking. Leaving Swiss steak simmering in the Dutch oven, Halley and I walked along the creek on the cabin side, bushwhacking our way through willows and rotten, beaver-felled trees, over rock jacks and up and over stiles to wind around at creek level, just exploring.

Back in the cabin, I brewed a cup of tea, put on a record of relaxing music, and read.

At five o'clock the Sheep Creek Writers began to appear, bearing potluck salads, sourdough bread, and pie. We were eight around the table, and per usual the food and conversations were superb. Full, and warmed by the wood stove, we retreated to the living area to read and discuss our work until quite late.

Joanna stayed to help with the dishes, and Halley and I drove back to Prairie Creek. As I walked to the car I gazed up at the nearly-full January Moon, encircled in a huge watery halo, a wide, rainbow-colored ring which disappeared when I arrived back up "on top."

On a sad note, Doug had called just as we were about to eat our meal, to tell me my childhood chum, Sandra, had just informed him of her husband Fred's death. Although expected, it is always sad to realize someone dear has left.

I spent the night remembering my long association with Fred and Sandra—from the age of 17, being Sandra's matron of honor at their wedding, raising our children together, crying and laughing together. Sandra and Fred had celebrated their 63rd wedding anniversary last year. We'll always remember all the good times: elk and deer hunting, celebrating their and our anniversaries, spending time with the couple in their rural Auburn home, and how Fred loved my pickled beets and raspberry cobblers. I will treasure the gifts he left, like the deer antler-handled knife he made for me. So long, old pardner.

Prayers for my brother, Jim, who lives in rural Lincoln, California, as he continues his brave fight against cancer; also for sister, Mary Ann, who has been dealing with health issues. Growing older isn't easy, and we must enjoy each day as it comes.

January 30—Son Ken hauled the two steers, recently purchased from our neighbor, Alan Klages, here so grandsons Gideon and Ronan can begin breaking them to lead for their 4-H projects. Neighbors, Lois Hough, and Judy Stilson, helped me serve a meat loaf meal for the CowBelles at the Community Connection at noon that day.

January 31—The morning dawned clear and 20 degrees, and that afternoon it warmed into the 40s, so Halley and I walked across the fields to Hough's hill where I sat on a high rock and surveyed the Prairie below. I was surprised to see the green leaves of buttercups poking through the snowless soil.

Veggie beef soup for supper with cheese biscuit bread.

February 2—Snowed lightly yesterday, on Super Bowl Sunday. Got an e-mail from my soon-to-be 98-year-old auntie Carol Nunn on this Groundhog day.

Walked to Klages' corner and back before attending my Writer's Group this morning. We dined at the Old Town Cafe in Joseph, while large soft flakes of snow turned the town white.

February 7—I drove to the canyons to see if there was any wind damage there. Found none that I could see; it appeared the wind wasn't as wild there. The creek was full of muddy snowmelt from slides in the mountains, due to the higher level of rains. I noticed my tulips are coming up, and the canyons are greening.

Halley and I enjoyed our hike across the creek. The wind had scrubbed the sky so clear, it defined the color blue. White clouds slid silently over the rims and swam into a wild dark mass, so we retreated to the cabin. And, now, it is time to e-mail this column.

February 11—After the winds ceased, I resumed my daily walks to Klages corner and back with Halley. The grass that had begun to green during our warm spell is now dulled by morning frosts. Earlier, I noticed several frozen night crawlers on the road. This afternoon I drove into our new elderly care facility to visit friend Wilma Goucher (Lyman's widow) who has been a resident there for some time.

Our visit on the 11th would be the last time I'd see her, as Wilma passed away a few days

Later. She was 84 and had been in failing health. Now both she and Lyman are gone, but fond memories linger of fun times at Lyman's log home on the upper Imnaha. Especially those crab feeds, when we spread newspapers on the table and had at it.

February 12—The morning dawned clear and warm, so after chores I stuck two oatmeal cookies in my pocket, filled my water bottle, loaded up Halley, and drove to Sheep Creek Hill. After parking my car at the entrance to daughter Ramona and hubby Charley's grass ranch, I climbed the wooden fence and this aging lady and her dog struck off across the open hills.

The entire Wallowa chain can be seen from up there and, due to a recent snowfall, the mountains glared white against the dark timbered slopes at tree line. We wandered beneath a wide space of blue sky with not a single sign of human habitation around. Nothing moved, save for several meadowlarks, a hawk or two, and a raven. Not a breath of wind to stir the air, and the sun so warm, I shed my jacket.

A herd of mule deer appeared over the next hill. Walking up toward the highest point on the property, my eyes were drawn to a patch of creamy yellow. Buttercups! The first ones of the season, most unusual to be blooming this early. It was noon by the time we reached the spot where granddaughter Carrie was married to her Joel, so I plopped down on a flat rock and munched my cookies.

Off to the north rose the Buttes, beyond which sprawled the undulating Zumwalt prairie, melting into the timbered Chesnimnus Country. At my feet began the breaks of the Imnaha canyons, and to the southeast lay the Divide that separates Big and Little Sheep Creeks. The Seven Devils of Idaho framed the eastern horizon.

I am always humbled during these times, and thankful that I chose NOT to clean house, but to take myself to these special places, only minutes from home. Thankful too, that at my age, I'm able to navigate and get myself there.

Back home I got in and pitted a package of half-frozen cherries I'd taken from the freezer to thaw. Something about presidents and cutting down a cherry tree drives me to bake a cherry pie in February. All the while singing, "Can she bake a cherry pie, Billy Boy, Billy Boy," which made the pitting go faster.

February 13—Ken stopped in with grandsons Gideon and Ronan, who had been working with their 4-H projects, which had included forking manure into the spreader, as well as leading and grooming their steers, "Lucky," and "Sirloin." Of course, Great Grandma gave her boys a bag of homemade cookies to munch on.

This evening I joined a literary crowd at Fishtrap House for the monthly Fireside event and enjoyed listening to the readings of Lynne Curry, Ralph Swinehart, and Mary Emerick. While flames licked logs in the fireplace, we settled back for an evening filled with stories written by our local authors.

February 16—Valentine's Day was celebrated all weekend long. Son Steve and children Bailey and Stetson, plus daughter Lori and hubby Larry, paid us a visit, and some were house guests until today, it being Presidents Day. We all gathered at the Outlaw Restaurant Saturday night for dinner, which was most delicious.

The town of Joseph was hopping, since Valentine's Day fell on a Saturday. If you didn't have a reservation, you either had to wait or go on to the next eatery. Rare in our area during winter. We ran into other members of our family treating their spouses to dinner.

On Sunday morning we gathered at the Cheyenne Cafe for breakfast, and that evening I cooked,a huge kettle of meatballs and spaghetti, and invited daughter Ramona, hubby Charley, granddaughter Brenna, and her friend Jenna to join Steve's family and us for supper. I'd baked two long loaves of sourdough bread and put together a salad. Ramona furnished a decadent ice cream brownie dessert.

This morning found me on a road trip to Clarkston, Washington, where I arrived safely for my three o'clock dental appointment. It was a lovely day, and the only snow I encountered was coming up Rattlesnake Grade to Field springs Park.

After a dizzying drive down Buford, I'd pulled into the Oasis to see the sign: *Steelhead running 8:00 to 6:00!* I wondered what they did the rest of the time! Walk?

Lots of fishing activity and the conversations were all about fish. How big? Lures used? Photos taken? Clarkston boasted green grass and bulbs poking through the flower beds, and best of all, good news for me.

I DIDN'T need a root canal.

A tired dog rides horseback during a Marr Cattle Company drive.

February 18—We invited granddaughter Adele and her friend Trent for supper. Adele recently celebrated her 27th birthday. Can this be? I remember writing about Adele and brother James in this column, when they were toddlers.

I spent the day cooking: blackberry cream pie, bread, green salad, and a roaster pan full of bar-b-cued spare ribs. We had a great time visiting, as we find young people invigorating and this pair were obviously interested in us! Doug enjoyed talking about his youth, and his experiences running a cattle outfit in the canyons. He'd been in the hills this afternoon and reported seeing a large herd of elk.

February 19—Attended our U.C.M.W. (United Methodist Church Women) meeting.

February 20—It snowed two inches and the temperature dropped to 33 degrees when our Magic Garden committee met to plan the 2015 year. This will be the fifth year for our garden project. Since we met there in the church until 2:30, lunch was served by Robin and David. We supped soup concocted with dried and frozen veggies from our fall garden on Sheep Creek, which was yummy and nutritious. Snow continued to fall, which was good.

Baby calves are appearing in the Wallowa Valley. Shown here is a herd of mother cows pastured south of Enterprise.

February 21—Raindrops cling to the east-and south-facing windows of our house, swept there by a weird warm wind, which is now heading into its second week. It is not unusual to experience a brief so-named "Pineapple Express" in February, but this is ridiculous. There is no snow or ice left here on Prairie Creek.

The obvious effects of a terrific windstorm that hurled through the county are everywhere. Trees are down, tatters of plastic caught on fence wire wavers in the wind, center pivot and wheel line irrigation systems lay twisted in the fields, and what used to be the roof of the Joseph High School is scattered along the Imnaha Highway below. Luckily, our damage was minimal compared to most. During the height of the storm, our house shook and shuddered as the wind vented its fury across the prairie. Windows rattled and limbs flailed in the ancient willows.

Early the next morning, I heard a knock at the door: our neighbor, Nathan Locke.

"I was fixing my coffee when I looked out the window to see sparks coming from your calving shed." he said, coffee cup in hand, and together we walked out in the front yard to watch tin peeling off the shed roof. Closer inspection revealed the tin had cut the electric line, which was now dangling in the pasture where my cows were.

Nathan said he was without power, while ours, out earlier, had returned. He is on a different line, so it was obvious this wasn't causing his outage. Nathan reported our problems, as our phone was out, but repairmen were so busy with the storm that no one was available. Son Ken arrived, and we drove the cattle to another field and shut the gate. Nothing could be done until the wind calmed down and Joseph Electric could deal with the hot wire. So, we waited.

Late that evening, our local electrician sealed off the dangling wire and I was able to turn the cows back into their enclosure. Thankfully, the winds abated and damage could be assessed.

Now it is windy again, so repairing the shed will have to wait. Our phone remained out all weekend, but we did have power.

Last evening, as I made my way through Joseph, I noticed trees and old buildings down, but most of the scattered roofing from the Joseph School had been cleaned up. I drove to the Hurricane Creek Grange to attend the Grand Finale of the Big Read. The old hall was filled with folks who carted salads and side dishes up the steps into the kitchen to add to long tables displaying potluck.

On the kitchen counter reposed steaming pans of chicken and pork tamales, prepared that day by the owners of La Laguna Restaurant in Enterprise. You see, the theme this year is Mexican, as the Big Read Book was *Into the Beautiful North,* by Luis A. Urrea. And, for the first-time-ever Big Read finale, we had the author with us last night. Authors in the past have included folks like Mark Twain and John Steinbeck.

So, Luis' first remark was: "I am the only author so far that's alive." Alive he was, and such a storyteller. Luis had the audience captivated as he told how most of the characters in his book were based on people he knew or was related to. The hall was decorated with colorful Mexican art objects created by the county school children, Mexican music added a fiesta-like gaiety, two long tables held slices of pies baked by the Grange Ladies, coconut cream, blackberry, apple. Tough decisions.

After an entertaining question and answer period, Luis stepped down off the stage amid a clamorous applause, and we all left to drive home on another windy night.

In church yesterday, I climbed the stairs to the bell tower and was startled when I opened the door to find a starling imprisoned in the belfry. The black bird circled the old tower a couple of times, then flew out past my nose to flutter in frightened flights above the cookies on the fellowship table.

In due time, someone kindly opened the door and the hapless bird flew to freedom.

February 24—At 3:00 in the afternoon, thin clouds threaten to blot out the sun, ice that formed on the irrigation ditches is still frozen along the edges, father and son rooster crow back and forth across the chicken wire fence, one free to roam and the other protecting his harem, mamma kitty drags yet another field mouse up to her half-grown kittens in the woodshed, my three milk cows chew their cuds under the old willows, Doug has taken a break from working on the income tax, and I sit down to write my column.

This morning it was 12 degrees when I bundled up to chore. Yep, back to our normal weather again. After breakfast I put together a salad for our Writer's lunch, held at Katherine's house in Joseph.

While I'm thinking about it, I'd like to correct an error in my last column, which concerns the roof of the Joseph High School. Doug had come home with the news that it had blown off, when in fact, it wasn't the roof, but the bleachers. In any case, it was a mess and littered the highway below.

I noticed a lot of activity in Joseph today, such as tree trimming and the clearing away of fallen limbs.

February 26—I fed my critters with heavy frost covering my pitch fork handle. By 10:00 am, I was headed down into the canyons to Sheep Creek, where quince, forsythia and daffodils were beginning to flower...much too soon. The old apricot tree, in full bloom, was obviously damaged by frost. Lavender violets sprinkled the lawn, which was green and needed mowing. I spent a relaxing day preparing for our monthly Sheep Creek Writers potluck meeting that evening.

Halley and I took a long walk down the creek and, after mixing up the ingredients for tamale pie, I listened to old records, read and napped. By 5:30 folks began to assemble, set the table, and sit down to another feast. Then followed our readings which, in time, morphed into major story-telling that continued into the night. It was so warm we let the wood stove die down and opened the windows to the mild air.

By the time Maggie and I washed the dishes and cleaned up the cabin, the February moon had heaved itself over the canyon rims. That full "Snow Moon" resembled more the waning March "Sap Moon," as the sap rises in the Osier Dogwood limbs. Earlier, I had picked a bouquet of flowering quince, forsythia, and dogwood twigs.

By the time I climbed into bed beside Doug, it was nearing midnight.

February 27—We lost another old-time cowboy yesterday. Dick Hammond passed away at our local hospital here in Enterprise. Dick, born on Grouse Flats, possessed a remarkable ability to recall events that happened in the past. He worked for numerous outfits and ranches all over Wallowa County, was a former Grand Marshal of Mule Days, and will be missed. It will be like closing the pages of a history book now that Dick has left us.

Another past Mule Days Grand Marshal passed away on the 25th. Carmen Kohlhepp, who was a faithful member of the Liberty Grange and another repository for history. Carmen and her husband ranched on Snake River, and used to own the popular Kohlhepp's Kitchen in Joseph, a forerunner of the Cheyenne Cafe.

May Wilma, Dick and Carmen rest in peace.

February 28—Son Ken, his son-in-law Justin, and grandsons Gideon and Ronan, showed up to repair the wind-damaged roof on the calving shed. While the men were up on the roof, the boys worked with their 4-H steers, who have gentled to the point where they are riding them! Typical boys.

At noon I fed them homemade chicken noodle soup and sourdough bread. March frolicked in like a gentle lamb, clear and sunny, with no wind. I did a wash before church and hung flannel sheets on the line. That afternoon Halley and I wandered over the old ranch, where she found a dead something or other, and rolled in it!

March 2—17 degrees, and later went to spitting snow.

March 3—Snowed today, and Doug and I had an appointment with the tax accountant. In the waiting room we noticed a copy of Agri-Times N.W. on the coffee table.

March 4—It dropped to 12 degrees, and had cleared in the night. I peered out the bedroom window at first light to see a black calf nursing Rhubarb! A nice big bull, which I promptly named "March." Before feeding hay to the cows, I splashed iodine on the sleeping calf's navel.

Since we were expecting company for the coming weekend, I spent the day cleaning house, ugh! By day's end the rugs were washed, the bathrooms cleaned, the house swept and dusted, and I must say it needed it!

March 5—Today dawned clear with thin clouds as I did chores and admired my new calf. In the kitchen I baked two loaves of sourdough

A morning scene during the Lee Scott Memorial Plowing Bee held at the Waters' ranch on May 2nd and 3rd near Joseph. Wallowa Mountains provided a stunning background for the event.

bread and a blackberry-raspberry pie, and later in the afternoon I cooked up a kettle of beef soup loaded with veggies.

Jack and Karen Hooker from Ovando, Montana, arrived just at supper time. They had driven over to attend Dick Hammond's Memorial. Dick and Jack used to work together a long time ago here in Wallowa County, when Jack owned a pack outfit at the head of the lake. Retired now, Jack and Karen used to own and operate a large guide service known as white-tail Outfitters out of Ovando, Montana.

March 6—I fixed sourdough waffles, sausage and eggs for our guests before I did my chores. 'Twas a beautiful day for Dick's Memorial, which was held at Cloverleaf Hall at 11:00 a.m. The hall was packed with Dick's many friends. Wayne, Casey, and Tim Tippett were pallbearers, and Biden, Jack, and Doug were among the honorary pallbearers. Dick's casket reposed near the stage, and his worn saddle, bridle, and blanket graced the top. His rope, boots and hat were also nearby.

The simple service was very moving, with everyone agreeing Dick was a living history book, who could recite stories, dates, and names with amazing clarity and accuracy. It was said if you wanted to visit Dick, just sit down and listen! And because Tim and Wayne brought their wives, Marlene and Diane, as well as their mom, Blanche, over from Clarkston, we had a mini-Tippett reunion. Karen and I put together a salad for the potluck that followed the service, and the ladies of the Community Church had prepared ham and a long table full of cookies.

That evening Karen helped me deliver pizzas to the Josephy Center for the opening of the Women's Art exhibits. Since our Write Group meets there, we, in turn for the use of the space, provide refreshments for various functions.

March 7—Doug treated us to breakfast at the Cheyenne Cafe, after which we drove to Sheep Creek for a look around there, and Imnaha.

On the way back we visited Larry and Jake Moore at Bear Gulch. Jack had also packed with Larry many years ago.

Back home from the canyons, I put out snacks of cheese and crackers, and we rested until it was time to drive to the cemetery on Prairie Creek to attend Carmen Kohlhepp's Memorial service. We stopped at Mike Brennan's ranch to join a procession behind a mule drawn wagon, owned by Larry Waters, that was transporting Carmen's casket to the cemetery. It was a lovely warm afternoon as the team clomped its way up the cemetery hill.

The brief service was conducted by Brinda Stanley, a friend of the family, who stood there beside the casket under a pine tree, and with tears in her eyes remembered Carmen. George Kohlhepp, Carmen's son, read his very touching and well-written eulogy. His mother, he said, "was born in a tepee on November 4, 1930, and didn't want to take her first breath, so the woman stepped outside, rubbed her in snow, then put her in warm water and, after several attempts, she took a deep breath and started her life journey.

"She married Morris Kohlhepp in 1970 and moved to Kirkwood on the Snake River where Morris worked for Bud Wilson tending sheep camps." George, born in November, 1970 was taken to the Snake River when he was 12 days old. George told how his mother taught him kindergarten in a one room log cabin that for years had been vacant.

"The pack rats had three feet of grass and twigs in the cabin. Mom cleaned it out and made a home, and lined the walls with alphabet letters. At recess we played kick-the-can, and during lunch we'd walk up the creek to check our raccoon traps.

"After we moved to the valley," recalled George, "and I was working on the 3V ranch, Mom went along to help on the Divide. We were gathering bulls and my horse was totally worn out. The bulls split at the catch trap, and I grabbed mom's horse to get around them.

"As I turned the bulls, I heard her yell and looked over my shoulder to see her and Hollywood in the middle of a bucking horse ballet. Mom was in the middle, but my stirrups were ten inches too long and she only had one rein. That horse had bucked with me and he was no slouch.

On this day he was really cranking. She rode him till he quit. She was 72 years old."

After the service George asked, "Are you ready boys?" And six tall lanky cowboys, wearing their worn working hats, jeans, boots and spurs, gently lifted Carmen's casket from the wagon and carried her to her final resting place. The breeze rustled the pine needles, and the warm sun shone on the fertile Prairie Creek fields below.

With the lake moraine to our backs, and the cool breath of Chief Joseph Mountain wafting down upon us, young Bailey Vernam played a fiddle tune. Some of us scribbled a final goodbye on Carmen's casket before it was lowered by the "boys" into the ground.

Carmen and her husband, Morris, ran what was known as Kohlhepp's Kitchen, even after Morris' death. Today, it is known as The Cheyenne Cafe.

Doug and I rested up, and then the four of us drove to Cloverleaf Hall to partake of another one of those Apple Flat Catering bar-b-cued pork dinners, before enjoying a full evening of no less than 25 fiddle players who performed at the Blue Mountain Old time Fiddlers show.

What a wonderful toe-tapping time we had! Jack, who had been feeling a little poorly, said the music made him all better. Emcee Denny Langford kept the show going with his quips and giveaways. The fiddle players included a gal who took her shoes off to sing Milk Cow Blues with her little granddaughter; our local "Homemade Jam" musical group; the Samples boys, Caleb and Tyson; among others, like Ryya Fluitt and sister Lexi, plus Bailey Vernam, who is growing up playing the fiddle, and many more.

March 8—We turned our clocks ahead, our company left, and I hurried to church to ring the bell.

This afternoon the county Chorale staged a rousing concert at the Lostine Presbyterian church, which I wouldn't have missed for the world. And now it's March 12th and as dawn gave way to day, my Jersey milk cow, Fawn, gave birth to a nice cinnamon-colored heifer calf, named Patly, after St. Patrick's Day, which is coming up. Better get my milking hands in shape.

March 13—Friday the 13th. Caught up Fawn and milked out her hind teats, as her heifer calf prefers the longer ones in front, leaving the short ones for me. Since Fawn's milk still contained colostrum, I treated the cats and chickens to a warm breakfast.

Later, on my morning walk down the road with Halley, I stopped to visit the 4-H'ers working with their steers.

That afternoon I spread dry manure on the emerging rhubarb, and cleaned out more dead corn stalks in the vegetable garden. Windy, cloudy, no rain.

March 14—Dark clouds opened up enough to spit rain and it was 56 degrees. Discovered one of my Barred Rock hens is laying her eggs in the raspberry patch.

March 15—55 degrees, warm and weird.

After church I drove to the Lostine Tavern and met grandson Buck, wife Chelsea, and great-grandkids Lucy, Katelyn, and Cooper for lunch. After my family treated me to a bowl of clam chowder, I joined them at the nearby Lostine Academy to take in the performance of "Anne of Green Gables."

This play was staged by the Mid-Valley Theatre Company. The story is based on the book of the same name, about Anne, an orphan girl, sent by mistake to live with a family who had a farm on Prince Edward Island in 1905. The cast, full of familiar faces, including many children, proved a delight to my great-grandkids. It was an entertaining and pleasant way to spend Sunday afternoon.

Returned to the ranch to find Doug just home from Imnaha.

March 16—50 degrees, a very mild morning when, still wearing my nightie, I ventured forth from my bed to check first calf heifer, Buttercup. She hadn't calved yet, so returned to the house to enjoy a cup of hot tea.

Later this afternoon I enjoyed a visit from grandson James, who brought over a book he'd made of photos taken on his hunting trip to Africa. Pretty amazing stuff. I remembered when James was a little boy and, to keep him amused, I would make up hunting stories about elk and deer and bear. And now, here he was, all grown up, out of the Marines, off to Africa to hunt big game. It gave me chills to see him posed beside an enormous hippo, and listen to the stories he told grandma, which were for real.

I'd just taken a loaf of pizza bread from the oven, but James declined any, saying he had to get home to his wife's cooking.

Later, I served the bread to our history book committee when they arrived for a meeting at 4:00.

March 17—On St. Patrick's Day morning, I again strode out to the pasture in my nightie and rubber boots to check my heifer. And this time I found her bawling frantically at something, which turned out to be her newly-born calf, who had slid under the panel fence, downhill. So, naturally, I got all gooey pulling baby up to mamma. You can imagine how this white-haired grandma must have looked. Thankfully, no one drove by!

Since Buttercup's calf was a heifer born on St. Patrick's Day, she became Patty 2.

After chores were completed and the calf's navel swabbed with iodine, I indulged in a hot shower before continuing on with my day, which included preparing the traditional corned beef 'n cabbage meal for company this evening. I also baked a raspberry pie and a loaf of Irish soda bread.

March 18—It rained a bit in the night, and I saved Fawn's milk for the house.

Later this morning, I fixed a sandwich and headed to Sheep Creek, where my faithful border collie and I took a walk across the creek. The old plum tree was in full bloom and it was another warm shirt-sleeve afternoon. If this early warmth continues, methinks snakes will venture out of their rocky dens.

Back home I discovered the starling that had been trapped in the stovepipe of our wood cook stove had escaped via the open firebox door and was flying around the house. I finally captured the bird and set it free.

Wolves are still in the news locally, and our heart goes out to the Birkmaier family who underwent a horrific experience recently when a pack of them got into their pregnant cows on Crow Creek, and chased them for miles. Now, according to Mack, the cows are aborting calves, and many are backwards or turned around, which is proving to be a rancher's worst nightmare. The ramifications of this needless harassing will be felt for years.

It is hoped those who praise the return of the Canadian Gray Wolf to Eastern Oregon will someday realize the reality of living with them.

March 20—The first day of spring &wised 27 dogma, clear with a light frost. My new calves were running around the pasture, delighting in the day.

March 21—I baked a key lime pie after chores, using 16 fresh limes. Late that afternoon, daughter Lori and husband Larry arrived to spend the night. They gifted us a new TV, one of those long skinny ones, and then proceeded to install it. Now, we are really uptown with the latest technology and, thanks to them, know how to operate it.

I served our family a pot roast with parsnips, carrots, mashed potatoes and gravy.

March 22—This morning Doug treated us to breakfast at the Cheyenne Cafe, after which we took a tour of Imnaha, driving as far as Fence Creek, where the pavement ends. We paid a visit to Sandy Vidan, who, with her husband Nick, own the Imnaha River Inn.

This huge log structure is situated 5 miles downriver, and if you ever want a getaway from the modern world, this is the place for you. Built on a bluff above the Imnaha River and surrounded by beautiful canyon views, you can spend the night and be served a country breakfast in one of the best-kept secrets in Oregon. For the benefit of Lori and Larry, Sandy gave us a tour. Mere words can't describe the workmanship in this beautiful Inn.

March 26—Time to get this column e-mailed. Since Fawn is broke to lead, I am now able to lead her into the barn and lock her in the stanchion. Yesterday morning, she munched her hay and stood still. This morning she wanted out and fought it the entire time I was milking. Typical female; can't figure her out. Oh well, the fresh milk is worth the effort.

Yesterday, the Magic Garden Committee met in our church to make plans for the fifth year of our garden. We all can't wait to get dirt under our fingernails again, and, mainly, to taste the veggies of our labors.

March 27—Arose early to milk my Jersey, who unwillingly put her head in the stanchion, with the aid of a halter. Feed the chickens and loaded the car with ingredients for Dutch oven Shepherd's Pie. Arriving down at Sheep Creek, I was pleased to see the tulips I planted last fall in full bloom alongside the cabin. My three blossoming cherry trees appeared to be wearing garlands of popcorn, and the temperature rose to 80 degrees by afternoon. I wasted no time opening the window and doors to air out the place, and to let the bird song and creek sounds inside.

With Halley for company, I ate my lunch seated in a chair near the creek, and listened to the quail call in the blackberry bushes.

Later that afternoon, I began preparing my Shepherd's Pie—browned chunks of blade roast, sautéed onions, garlic, shallots, carrots and celery, all simmered until tender, with frozen peas added

Later. After covering this mixture with a kettle full of hot mashed potatoes, the casserole baked for 30 minutes. The potatoes form a crust over a meaty, veggie gravy that seeps through.

This savory concoction was ready when folks arrived bearing potluck. Pam contributed one of her home-grown squashes, baked whole in the shell, and a bowl of marinated asparagus. Others brought salads, and Joanna carried in a towel-wrapped, warm-from-the oven cherry-rhubarb pudding cake.

Per usual we feasted on this delicious fare, spiced with wordsmiths' words. Pam and I washed the dishes and we all retired to the other room, where no fire was needed in the wood stove and the windows remained open to the warm, summer-like evening. After all eight of us read our writings, everyone left after yet another memorable meeting.

On the way home I listened to the loud, then fading, croaking of frogs, as I passed marshy areas alongside the road, Halfway up Sheep Creek heavy dark clouds rolled in, and by the time I pulled into our lane here on Prairie Creek the waxing moon was completely obscured.

March 28—It rained in the night, and new snow brightened our Wallowas. The temperature dropped to 33 degrees. Son Steve and Steve's daughter Bailey, having arrived late the night before, were occupying two of our spare beds. They had left grandson Stetson off at Uncle Todd's earlier, so he'd gotten in on branding 150 calves. Sister and brother would spend their spring Break week here in the county. Bailey would be staying with Aunt Ramona and Uncle Charley.

After Steve left for home, I baked a batch of oatmeal flax meal cookies. It was windy and cold, a radical change from yesterday.

Doug treated me to supper at the Range Rider in Enterprise that evening, where I ordered the special, chicken fried steak. I highly recommend it.

March 29—Attended the 11:00 service of our church, then came home to take a long walk with Halley. I hung a wash on the line and Doug drove to the hills to check on the elk.

March 30—I took Halley to the Red Barn Vet on Alder Slope for her Parvo/distemper shot, and then treated her to a walk in the nearby Pioneer Alder Slope cemetery. It was a beautiful afternoon and, while Halley sniffed for squirrels, I visited the graves of my old neighbors, Wilmer and Mary Cook.

March 31—Windy and raining, as opposed to its lamb-like entrance, March went out like a not-so-gentle lion. Spitting sleet pinged against my windshield as I drove to meet with our weekly writer's group at the Josephy Center, and when we came out it was snowing. We warmed ourselves at the Silver Lake Bistro in Joseph over bowls of hearty potato soup.

At home, seated in a warm tractor cab, son Ken, was busy harrowing the pastures. I cooked up a chocolate pudding using some of my excess creamy Jersey milk.

April 1—No April Fools on this April first. 29 degrees, with a heavy frost on the pastures and an icy skim on the irrigation ditches. A raw wind, with spats of sleet, announced an unsettled beginning to April.

April 2—It was 10 degrees in Enterprise; 15 here. Baked a yummy Easter bread filled with raisins and a hint of lemon zest.

Late tonight, son Steve, and wife Jennifer drove over from Selah, Washington, and crawled into bed. They will stay until Easter and then take their children home.

April 3—While milking my Jersey cow this morning a raw wind tunneled its way under my woolen cap to my neck. *Burrrr.* What did I say about the weather being mild? Well, it has since returned to its usual March sell, including, mini-blizzards.

By leaving a rope halter and trailing a long lead rope on my cow, all I have to do in the morning is catch and tie her up to the feeder, fork her a flake of alfalfa hay, and milk her in peace while the other cows are eating at the feeder. That is, if one of the calves doesn't decide to nibble on my pony tail.

Up until this morning, it has been very pleasant outside, but now I am considering putting her in the milking barn. However, just the mention of the word stanchion and Fawn goes ballistic. The only thing good about this unpleasant weather is that we are receiving much-needed moisture, mainly in the form of mountain snow.

A sure indication that spring is near is that mamma kitty is pregnant.

Later, friend Katherine and I drove to Pam's place, and she gave us a ride to Sheep Creek, dropping us off at my cabin while she continued on to her place upriver. K. wrote while I tended to some chores.

After lunch, Pam picked us up. It was a relaxing get-a-way, and allowed me to ready the cabin for Easter.

Later, at home, Steve and Jennifer told us they'd had a picnic in the hills.

April 4—It snowed today, but didn't stick long. I spent the day cooking our Easter Dinner.

April 5—Our family was blessed yesterday, when 17 of us gathered down on Sheep Creek for our traditional Easter Sunday. Although it was a bit brisk outside, we partook of a feast inside, comforted by the warmth of the wood stove and the homey aroma of baking ham. I had spent the day prior preparing potato salad, deviled eggs and wild blackberry cobbler. Therefore, most of the cooking was done when I loaded our car Sunday morning. Grandson Stetson, who'd ridden down with granddad, began a challenging game of scrabble with me while we waited for the rest of the family to arrive.

I'd started a fire in the wood stove before putting the ham in the oven, and picked a bouquet of flowering quince and cherry blossoms for the dining room table. Daughter Ramona arrived with hubby Charley, bearing a roasted turkey, plus a generous supply of chocolate eggs, which were added to the marshmallow chicks Doug had stashed away for the Easter Bunny. Angie walked into the kitchen with a crockpot full of her famous beans. She and son Todd had ridden down with grandson James and bride Danielle.

Once again, our family seated themselves at the long wooden table, plus a card table, and counted our blessings. After we all ate too much, the sun steamed through breaks in the clouds and the greening canyons beckoned little ones outside in anticipation of the promised Easter egg hunt.

We were delighted to have great-grandkids, Seely and Callen, this year, along with their parents, Lacey and Colin, who drove over the Blues from Pendleton to join us. Little ones are very necessary for Easter egg hunts, and those two youngsters really whooped it up. The not-so-young grandchildren hid the eggs among the blooming cherry trees, grasses, and in crevices under fences and rocks. Due to cooler weather, the Great Rattlesnake Hunt was canceled. Uncle Todd opted to indulge in a well-earned nap instead of leading the troops up Big Sheep Creek. Since it is still calving time, ranchers never miss an opportunity to catch up on their sleep.

After everyone left, I tidied up the cabin and relaxed. Pushed by a chilly wind, dark wet clouds swept over the rims and, on the drive up Little Sheep Creek, rain began, a lovely soaking rain to make the grasses grow, the arrowleaf balsamroot to flower, and the canyons come alive with spring time.

Our house on Prairie Creek, which had been full of out-of-town family, was strangely quiet when I returned, and during the night, quieter still, as the rain turned to snow.

April 6—By ten thirty this morning, Prairie Creek's white landscape returned to green again as last night's snow vanished in mere minutes. This is how April should be, bringing moisture to our hills, valleys and canyons, while adding to our stored snow in the Wallowas.

Son Ken was here this morning with great-grandson, Cutter, to help feed cattle. It was good to see Cutter while he is visiting grandma and grandpa, along with sister Nevada, during spring Break. Cutter and Nevada now reside in northern California.

April 7—Although not very warm outside, there are spurts of sunlight. Our weekly writers group met at the Josephy Center this morning from ten 'til noon, and once again enjoyed a gourmet lunch at the Silver Lake Bistro. Time to take Halley for a promised walk on the hill.

April 9—35 degrees, no frost. Out to do chores and milk the Jerz. This afternoon I baked a rustic peach pie in my cast-iron skillet, loaded it in the car, and left the Easter ham bone simmering in a pot of beans for Doug as I took off for the upper Imnaha. At Lightning Creek it began to rain, but ceased by the time I reached the store and turned up the gravel river road. Golden Arrowleaf Balsamroot bloomed profusely in the burn area, and there appeared to be a good crop of thistles as well.

While the new grass on the east side of the river was a brilliant green, where the large 2014 bum had scorched the landscape, the west side slopes wore the dull color of winter-killed grasses. I passed Lyman's old place, and continued on up past Mary Marks', then down the hill to Dr. Driver's log lodge where the Fishtrap Writers Retreat was in its first week.

I was surprised to see the old boards in the swinging bridge replaced with new ones. The lawn was freshly mowed, and apple and cherry trees were in full bloom. The beaver-killed trees had been removed, the river rushed past full of snowmelt, and it made me happy to see another generation of dippers had made a nest on the rock wall alongside the river. I paused to watch the pair of water ouzels fly back and forth, feeding their young.

Inside the kitchen I was greeted by Tom and Woesha Hampson, old friends, who had invited me down to supper. They were preparing a feast, to which I added my peach pie. Lorna and Cathy soon joined us, and we lingered over the meal, recalling retreats past, like hikes up Freezeout, and enjoying writing together.

After I did the dishes, we all grouped around the fireplace and I settled back to listen to their stories. Therefore, it was very late when I made my way back across the bridge, carrying my empty fry pan to the car, and paused to savor the stars. There is nothing as bright as a deep canyon night to observe the constellations. It was later still after I drove the 45 miles home to Prairie Creek.

April 10—Windy today, so I hung sheets on the line.

Later, in Enterprise, I drove to the Grain Growers and purchased wheat for my chickens, plus two bags of seed potatoes to plant next month in my garden.

April 11—40 degrees with a light rain. The Jersey seemed nursed out by her calf, so didn't milk her, as had a good supply in the frig. From my kitchen window I glimpsed the snow line on upper Prairie Creek. The wind was freezing and we had a brief hail storm in the afternoon. I called my brother, Jim, in California and it was good to hear his voice. We talked about our cows.

April 12—A new layer of snow lay on the Wallowas this morning. A good thing. In church we welcomed back another one of our "snow birds," Jane Wiggins, who, with her hubby spent the winter in Arizona. Like I do every Sunday, I climbed the stairs up to the bell tower and rang the bell.

April 13—The day dawned cloudy with an icy wind. The Jerz lost her halter again, and I still haven't found it! Son Todd and crew started his cows and calves to Big Sheep this morning, a three day drive. My heart goes out to the cold cowboys and cowgirls on horseback. They will trail them to the top of OK gulch today, down South Lightning tomorrow to Peekaboo, then on up big Sheep on the 15th.

April 14—29 degrees, snowing and windy. My daffodils are shivering! Snow squalls all day. Went to our Writer's Group this morning, there were 10 of us.

April 15—20 degrees, with more freezing wind. After chores I began to clean house in anticipation of my sisters' visit. Good thing we have company now and then, as it seems to be the only time my poor house gets a serious cleaning.

Took a long walk in the afternoon around the old ranch with my dog Halley.

April 17—Clear and sunny, really nice, but things are drying out and we need rain. I made a large macaroni salad for the branding tomorrow, and at five o'clock Doug and I joined members of our church and others at the Lostine Tavern for an appreciation dinner for the Magic Garden volunteers, hosted by Robin and David Martin. Lynne Curry, well-known food author and chef, and part-owner of the restaurant, outdid herself on the five-course meal.

Lynne, the author of the well-known cookbook, *Pure Beef*, started us off with a presentation of cheeses and salami served on a board, followed by crackers, bean and veggie dip, and golden pickled beets, then a spring salad made with local greenhouse greens. The main course was melt-in-the-mouth salmon, caught in the Columbia River, served on a zucchini, garlic, onion fritter with a wheat berry and kale dish on the side. For dessert, a tasty cake served with sarvisberries, foraged locally and frozen, in a sauce. Everything was farm-, field-, forest-, and river-to-table. We fairly waddled out of the place. It was delicious, and fun! Thanks, Lynne.

Lauren passed around a flyer containing information about our local Head Start program that our Magic Garden donates produce to. Local teacher Kris Fraser offered several statistics on the project. In addition to field trips to the Sheep Creek garden, where the kids pick and take home produce, the Magic garden staff delivers vegetables throughout September and October. Surplus produce that the students can't eat fresh is frozen for winter meals.

The kids connect their food to a beautiful place they love, and Kris says 100 percent of the children now eat and enjoy vegetables. The Magic Garden is a volunteer-led community garden in a dramatic setting. Golden canyon slopes surround the garden, a creek gurgles by, sunflowers tower, and an old orchard grows just beyond the fence. The kids see a watermelon growing for the first time as they visit each fall, and they eat the produce all year long. A preschooler once grabbed a volunteer's hand and said, "I never want to leave this place." That says it all, and makes our hearts glad.

We all enjoy working with teachers like Kris, who says, "Everything we do is an encouragement for the whole family to eat differently, to try a different recipe, and to see a local food source."

April 19—The last squash, picked in October down at the Sheep Creek garden, bakes in the oven. It is over 60 degrees in yet another warm, dry day. I've just finished pruning the raspberries and began irrigating them. Mamma kitty has hidden her spring litter of kittens.

After I returned from church this morning, Doug announced he was driving over to Pendleton to attend great-grandson Callen's fourth birthday party. And, because my two sisters, Caroline and Kathy, are on their way up from California for a visit, I opted to stay home, work on this column, and clean house.

Yesterday, down in the corrals at Blue Meadow, there was a great deal of activity as Todd and his crew of cowboys and cowgirls branded MANY calves. It was a warm, lovely day, but those of us in the cattle business agreed we sure need rain. The canyons are extremely dry, which means the grass growth is not what it was last year.

After a brief stop at my place on the creek to irrigate a few plants, I bumped my way up the rough rocky road that winds steeply above Big Sheep Creek. I spent most of the morning fence-sitting and photographing the action, of which there was plenty. When you have a corral full of cowboys and cowgirls racing around on horseback, twirling ropes, it gets pretty wild.

These seasoned hands make it look easy, but once in a while there's a wreck, like when a ketch rope gets snagged under a horse's tail and the cowboy lands in a rock pile. Not good. Granddaughter-in-law Danielle was a real trooper when it came to ear tagging, sticking with it all day as part of the ground crew. And Todd's wife, Angie, not only rode behind the cows and calves the three days it took to get them to Blue Meadow, she helped give shots, then grilled hamburgers for a LOT of hungry folks.

It was nearly 2:30 when the crew took a break and trooped over to eat. I brought out the macaroni salad I'd made the day before. The food was spread out on pickup tailgates, and cowboys hunkered down around stock trailers or sat on the ground. As in years past, the canyon setting provided a stunning backdrop for our photos. Some left after lunch, while a few hardy souls returned to work the final thirty calves. Since son Ken had stayed on top to help his grandchildren take delivery of their 4-H hogs, he wasn't able to rope this year. I left soon after lunch, as had a long way to drive home, and much to do.

April 21—In the midst of writing my column and the phone just rang: "Hi, this is Caroline, we are just driving into Wallowa!"

Must go check the sourdough bread, rising in the dutch oven.

Sisters Caroline, and Kathryn arrived shortly before lunch. It was so good to see them! I had just taken the round loaf of sourdough bread out of the dutch oven, so we pooled our leftovers and made sandwiches. I brought out the mustard pickles, preserved last summer, and since one of our favorite pastimes is eating, we fell to it.

Kathryn, who couldn't wait to see my critters, was out visiting the calves when she looked up in the ancient willows and spotted three baby great horned owls. Out came the cameras, and during the following six days, those fluffy little guys received constant attention.

April 22—I lured Fawn into the barn, haltered her again, led her into the stanchion, and milked her.

After Kathy fed the chickens, we returned to the kitchen to fix scrambled eggs with sausage, and sourdough toast with strawberry freezer jam. Kathy packed a lunch and we took off for Sheep Creek. Just past Bear Gulch, we ran into son Todd, and his cowboy, Cody Ross, on horseback, moving a small bunch of cows and calves. We pulled off the road so Todd could visit his white-haired aunties.

Arriving at my place, we were delighted to see the old apple tree, growing in the small orchard back of my cabin, was in full bloom. The gnarled old tree was spectacular, at the peak of its blooming beauty. More photos. The tall locust trees rang with the singing of hundreds of small birds as they fed on locust pods.

We enjoyed a restful day, playing Scrabble on a card table carried out beside the creek, eating our picnic lunch, taking a walk through the old and new orchards across the creek, admiring the Magic Garden, lush now, with its green manure crop soon to be mowed and tilled under.

While crossing the bridge, Caroline stopped suddenly and said: "Look," and she pointed downstream to where three large steelhead were spawning.

That night, back up on Prairie Creek, I fixed baked potatoes to go with some of those Marr Flat grass-fed sirloin steaks. During supper my sisters admitted, while on their way up, among other things they anticipated was savoring REAL BEEF and my pickled beets.

April 23—After chores, we took a walk up on the hill with my dog Halley, and noon found us at daughter Ramona and hubby Charley's, enjoying a delicious salad lunch. Leaving their ranch, which lies below the east moraine of Wallowa Lake, we spotted a pair of ospreys whom, we learned, had been displaced from their nest by a pair of eagles.

On into Joseph for a visit to Arrowhead Chocolates, where we feasted our eyes on chocolates being created as we watched, and sampled several tasty morsels. I purchased three coconut chocolate macaroons for a future picnic, and we returned home to play more Scrabble. During their entire stay, I was never able to win a game with my sisters!

April 24—There was a heavy frost, and after chores we met Doug at the Cheyenne Cafe for breakfast, where my sisters got a kick out of all the "banter and bull" at the local's table. Home to put together lunch and head to Sheep Creek again, where we played another game of Scrabble, then took a long walk up Big Sheep Canyon as pink phlox bloomed alongside the dirt road and lilacs, gone wild, filled the air with their lavender fragrance.

It began to rain on our return, then hail, so we hurried to the cabin and listened to the rain falling on the tin roof as we brewed tea and ate our lunch. Earlier, on a tour up Camp Creek, we were watching several wild turkeys when a mule deer wandered into their midst.

That evening, back at the ranch, at my sisters' request, I cooked up a kettle of chicken and dumplings. Doug was happy about that one.

April 25—We walked around the old ranch, then rested up for the big evening ahead, the Divide Camp benefit staged by Julie Wheeler's hardworking volunteers.

Daughter Ramona, Katherine Stickroth, and Johnna Marcum had spent many hours organizing this first annual dinner and auction, which was a sell-out. It was like a family reunion for us. Former Marine grandson, Shawn, had flown up from San Diego for the event, and he, and another former Marine grandson, James, gave short talks.

Also there were Grandson Buck, his wife Chelsea, and their three children, Lucy, Katelyn, and Cooper, drove down from Bartlett, above Troy; grandson Chad, son Todd and wife Angie, daughter Becky, and granddaughter Carrie, hubby Joel, and daughter Brenna. Great visiting for the aunties, who don't see much of our Oregon tribe. The meal, organized by noted local chef Tom Swanson, was wild! Wild-caught salmon, grilled to perfection, by Joe McCormack, who supplied the fish, and elk stew prepared by Tom. An impressive table full of pies drew everyone for dessert.

When the Western musical group "Last Call," began to play, James's wife, Danielle, and I headed for the dance floor, which, as we intended, brought out others, including great-granddaughter Brenna, who danced with her papa Charley. It was great to see Agri-Times N.W. editor Sterling Allen and his pretty wife, Cheryl, as well as others from Pendleton, supporting Divide Camp. Over $13,000 was raised, a commendable community effort, which will enable veterans to participate in activities like hunting and fishing, as well as their stay at the camp. Kudos to those volunteers who pulled off this first annual event, which included both a silent auction as well as a live one.

April 26—Some of our family met this morning at the Cheyenne Cafe to visit with grandson Shawn, before he flew back to San Diego and his family. Before he left, I gave him some raspberry freezer jam and he brought us morel mushrooms, picked the day before by grandson-in-law Joel, who lives in La Grande. Yum!

My sisters and I returned home to pack a picnic lunch, jump into Doug's pickup, and head for the hills! It was a lovely morning, with clouds floating in an azure sky. Heading out the Zumwalt road, our first sighting was of a mountain bluebird perched on a rock jack. We were quite alone out there, with the high prairie all to ourselves, and views in all directions of acres and acres of open country beginning to green up. The hawks soared above, their keen eyes hunting ground squirrels below.

We passed the Buttes—Findley, Harsin, and Brumback—and caught glimpses of the canyon country off to the east, backgrounded by the snow-clad Seven Devils range. Up and down those roller coaster hills, and then we pulled off to park beside the Horned Lark Trail head. Where we all piled out and climbed up and over the wooden stile and hiked the nearly two-mile, untrodden trail, marked only by arrows painted on rock jacks, that made a loop down around a pond before returning up a draw to our rig.

Every wildflower was cause for celebration, and photographed: grass widows, owl's clover, the purple pasque flower, yellow bells, blue bells, carpets of yellow cous. Out of breath, we gained the final rock jack, and headed for the pickup, where we broke out the picnic and enjoyed the miles of bunch grass prairie under those glorious clouds!

We drove on to the edge of the timber before we turned around, and soon Kathryn spotted a small herd of elk grazing to the east of us. More photo ops. I took them home via the North Pine road that led past Doug's old ranch on Wet Salmon creek, then down Dorrance grade to the pink barn and the junction with the Crow Creek Road.

All the way, I remembered this route, all those springs and falls on horseback, trailing our cows to the hills and back again.

While the girls drove into Joseph for a rustic pizza we ordered for supper, I sautéed those morels in butter and garlic to spread on top.

A note of sadness this evening, word that our brother, Jim, was in ICU due to complications connected to his battle with cancer. Our prayers are with you, brother.

April 27—I treated my sisters to sourdough waffles before we took a final walk and they left for home. I miss them still.

The day turned unseasonably hot, and while I attended a history book committee meeting at Darlene Turner's, I missed a visit from Ed and Carol Wallace, who'd driven over from Clarkston. Thanks Carol, for the plum jam, and Ed for that "board fish."

April 29—Today is Auntie Carol Nunn's 98th birthday.

April 30—I headed to Sheep Creek and spent an enjoyable day cleaning, pruning, and falling asleep in my chair alongside the creek. The rambling yellow rose and the snowball bushes are now in bloom.

Later, I placed a pot roast in the oven, along with shallots, garlic, onion and carrots and let it cook slowly until supper at six. Another golden evening, great potluck, and companionable writer friends to share our work with. Lingered after everyone left, enjoying the waxing moon. This was our final meeting until October.

May 4—Last evening the full, May "Flower" moon slipped silently up and over Locke's hill. Due to the dryness and dust particles in the air, it appeared orange and thirsty. Since our pastures do have some grass, I turned my little cow and calf herd out to graze. No more feeding hay. Son Ken was here this morning to move his heifers and bull over to a neighboring pasture, so mine now have the run of the place.

This past weekend was the annual Lee Scott Memorial Plowing Bee, held just up the road at neighbors Larry and Juanita Waters' ranch. There weren't as many teams of horses and mules as in years past, but those who showed up had a good time. And, even though we wished for rain, it made for a pleasant plowing bee, and since meals for the teamsters were served in an open garage near the field, it was comfortable weather-wise.

I joined them for lunch on Saturday, which was a very busy day for everyone I met. Doug and I had attended the memorial service for Wilma Goucher that morning at the Enterprise Christian Church, which was conducted by Wilma's brother, Rev. Raymond Bates. He entertained us at length with stories of growing up in the midst of 18 children. He said his sister, Wilma, was the sibling responsible for him, and therefore figured prominently among his earliest memories.

Saturday evening was the Speakeasy event, held at the Josephy Center to raise money for the maintenance of the Coffin House in Enterprise, which serves as the headquarters for Fishtrap. Many folks dressed in clothing of that era, which was fun! Lots of feather boas, head bands, black mesh stockings, high heels, and short skirts. Men wore suits and loud ties. Food and libations were available, and entertainment was tops.

Jon Rombach, with Mike Midlo providing sound effects, staged an old time radio show featuring Guy Noir, which brought down the house, as Wallowa County was substituted for "the city that never sleeps." Among the raffle items was "a dinner for two" at my Sheep Creek kitchen, which was won by Iva Lindsay and her husband.

Pianist Gail Swart and blues singer Carolyn Lochert provided period music.

May 6—This evening we attended the annual Hells Canyon Mule Days Grand Marshal dinner, held this year at the VFW Hall in Enterprise. It was a fun event, as usual, gathering together with other former Grand Marshals, including those who traveled from out of the county, like Fred Talbott and Dick Walker. Dennis and Peggy Brennan, husband and wife from Enterprise, were selected as the 2015 Grand Marshals.

This year's Mule Days will be held the weekend after Labor Day, September 11-13, at the Enterprise Fairgrounds. This deserving couple have worked with and supported Mule Days over the years. Dennis, a Wallowa County native, remembers his boyhood working on grandfather Walter Brennan's 12,000 acre ranch on Lightning Creek. Peggy rides for several different ranchers, and Dennis is generally busy shoeing horses.

After a ham dinner, prepared by the VFW ladies, we all posed for a group photo—and when we stepped outside to go home, it was raining, and hasn't stopped since.

May 8—Doug and I hauled our lawn mower to Sheep Creek, then drove on down for lunch at the Imnaha Store and Tavern.

May 9—Grandson-in-law Justin and great-grandson Gideon repaired the wind-damaged calving shed.

May 10—Mother's Day dawned clear today, with no frost. I appreciated the cards, phone calls, and gifts from our combined seven children, and felt truly blessed and loved.

This evening, Doug and I drove to Wallowa Lake and partook of a delicious meal at the Glacier Grill, which is located across from the historic lodge. The carpet of golden arrowleaf balsamroot was just beginning to bloom on the east moraine, and the eaglets could be seen in their nest in the old cottonwood growing at the head of the lake.

May 12—Raining when I drove into attend our weekly writer's group at the Josephy Center. We lunched that day at the Old Town Cafe in Joseph. That afternoon, wild winds blew limbs off the willows and the rain poured incessantly for over an hour. My cows and calves huddled together, water streaming off their backs, to wait it out. The dry ditch out front, suddenly filled to overflowing as a wall of water came foaming through the pasture, did a great job of flood irrigating.

A brief clearing revealed a rainbow arching over Locke's barn as a watery sun wavered between dark clouds. Our thirsty land drank it up to saturation, and the water pooled in low spots seeded to grain, and washed down the gullies. My newly transplanted cabbages quivered under the deluge. Culverts clogged, and barrow pits ran with muddy water. Unfortunately the warm rain melted a great amount of mountain snow too early, which filled our creeks and rivers with frothy water.

May 13—Early morning snow freshened the highest peaks. I met friend Kathy for a promised birthday lunch at the newly-restored Lostine Tavern, where we enjoyed tasty Reuben sandwiches and slices of decadent beet-chocolate cake.

Stepping outside, we marveled at those enormous brilliant white clouds swirling above a bright green countryside. Heading home, I glanced up the South Fork of the Lostine River to see the canyon enveloped in wet clouds.

Home to bake a batch of blueberry muffins filled with flax seed, wheat germ and almond flour, to freeze for future breakfasts.

This evening I joined son Ken, wife Annie, and granddaughter Chelsie for the dinner and academic awards night at the Enterprise High School. We proudly watched great-granddaughter Riley Ann receive her awards, along with her classmates, all of whom impressed us. Over 30 student body members belong to the National Honor Society, and those same students excel in sports and other activities, like F.F.A. It was a great tribute to the school's dedicated teachers, who gave credit to the parents and grandparents who supported their children in their endeavors. For whatever reason, I went forth with renewed faith in our young people.

Prayers continue for my brother, Jim, who underwent surgery today.

May 15—Another drizzly day. Worked in the garden, pulling weeds in the mud.

May 16—Still raining; son Ken's branding canceled. Fixed bar-b-cued short ribs in the Dutch oven, and invited our neighbor, Ben, to supper.

May 17—I arose early to bake a huckleberry cream pie and take a long walk with Halley before church.

This evening I drove into Enterprise, climbed the stairs to the Odd Fellows Hall, and stepped into a Hootenanny and Shoo-Fly-Pie Social, an event staged by the Wallowa Valley Music Alliance to raise money for their musical programs throughout the year.

Janis Carper and her crew had done an excellent job of lining up local talent, talent that just continues to come out of the hills, canyons, valleys, and small towns of our county. The old hall was filled to capacity.

I added my pie to 28 others that were being cut into small slices, so folks could pay a dollar to sample before casting their vote for the three top pies. You voted by using a number stuck in each slice of pie.

Before long, the music began. M.C. was Dan Maur of Washington State University Public Radio, who, with his seeing eye dog at his feet, entertained us with his vast knowledge of the history of country music. Dan also introduced the performers, whom he had memorized. The songs, sung and played by folks we knew, were all familiar, of the '50s and '60s, sung in words we understood and knew by heart. Our generation had listened to them on the radio and played those old records. Remember?

It was like hearing the original Sons of the Pioneers when Ted Hayes and John McColgan belted out "Tumbling Tumble Weeds." It blew us away and took us away to that long-ago time. Groups like our popular "Homemade Jam," and others too numerous to mention, treated us to an evening of music we could have listened to all night.

During intermission we dove into those pies, and my huckleberry cream won 3rd place. I received an old flour sifter and an antique dish towel for a prize.

May 19—Following our writer's group meeting at the Josephy Center, Katherine and I joined the brown bag lunch gang in the front room, which featured neighbor and fellow CowBelle member Mary Lou Brink, who told us stories about her coming from the Philippines, marrying Melvin, her husband of all these years, and moving out to Zumwalt—quite a change for a doctor's daughter, used to servants and housemaids.

Way out on Zumwalt, Mary Lou had no running water and no electricity; miles from town, she raised a family in comparative isolation. Today, Mary Lou, a retired R.N., and her husband Melvin, live in a lovely house in rural Enterprise, and their family is engaged in a large farming operation.

May 20—After chores I drove into our Wallowa County Museum in Joseph, and joined other members of our board cleaning, in preparation for opening on Memorial Day Weekend. I volunteered to weed the flower beds, situated on the sidewalk. I finished just before it began to rain.

May 23—Today, Saturday the 23rd, was the Big Day. The traditional "crab leg branding." No, they don't brand crab legs, but eat them after the work is done. Cowboys and cowgirls arrive with their horses from miles around and the fun begins. Due to the rains, the corral was a bit muddy, but those big husky calves were all worked by 1:00. As usual I had my camera to capture the activity, of which there was plenty.

The branding is also a time to visit family, like grandson James and wife Danielle, sons Todd and Ken, daughter-in-law Angie, great grandchildren Ashlyn, Jada, and Gideon, all of whom were helping in one way or another. The showy Wallowas were gorgeous, and the acres of green pastures and the red barn provided an awesome setting for photos. And, best of all, it didn't rain, in spite of threatening to.

This all happens every year on the Triple Creek Ranch, located on upper Prairie Creek. Ranch owners Brent and Connie McKinley generously provide a much-anticipated lunch that includes King crab legs fresh from Alaskan waters, steaks, bowls of fresh fruit, and Dutch oven-baked peach and berry cobblers. Some of us contributed salads and beans, and in my case, a rhubarb pie.

It is amazing, seeing those plates loaded down with such fare. Watching those hungry gals and guys dig in. Brent, Connie and their family outdid themselves on this special branding day. Which is most appreciated by those of us who rarely, if ever, savor such a treat.

Memorial Day brought in a wave of tourists, the streets of Joseph were full! So much more to write about, but must put a period here.

May 26—Since May was a month of five Fridays, it's been a long time since I've written a column. Precious rain has fallen upon our parched land in the meantime. We live in a giant greenhouse: Prairie Creek is now brilliant green; every blade of grass, every pesky weed, every leaf pulses with green life. Stock ponds are filling, dry creeks are running, birds are full of worms, wildflowers are prolific, and mushrooms are still numerous at higher elevations.

And it's still raining, a warm, jungle-like, tropical rain, causing every living thing to bolt. I can't keep up with the rhubarb, its tart succulent stalks have been baked into juicy pies and crisps. Wild roses and prickly pear cactus are riotous in the canyons, loving this moisture-laden warmth. Lawns are out of control, and my contented cows and calves are basking in their grassy bovine paradise.

Son Ken was so busy with other chores, he didn't get around to starting the irrigation, but not to worry: Mother Nature intervened.

I planted potatoes between storms, set out cabbage plants and onion sets, and transplanted strawberries. After nearly drowning, the cabbages are finally showing signs of new growth. Yukon Gold and red potatoes are pushing through the moist earth, and of course you can't discourage radishes, no matter what. The other evening I planted carrots, lettuce, beets and set out the Walla Walla Sweet onion plants I'd tilled in earlier.

On Memorial Day I visited the Wallowa County Nursery and, using the gift certificate given to me by daughter Ramona for Mother's Day, picked out petunias and marigolds for my planters, and a Sun Rose perennial to plant near the cabin.

James Nash fends off a mamma cow while holding her calf during branding.

Three of Janie's great grandchildren, Lochlan, Beorn, and Arianwyn Nash.

I'd gone to the Alder Slope Nursery the week before to pick up the hanging flower basket given to me by daughter Jackie. Thanks, girls!

The juvenile owls are nearly as large as their parents, and have apparently decided to take up permanent residence in the giant willows that grow alongside the irrigation ditch in the cow pasture. Every evening, the trio fly off to hunt and return at daylight to sleep the day away. I observed them during our violent thunder storms, hanging on to the swaying limbs with their claws, waiting patiently for the rain and wind to subside.

May 29—We CowBelles, Lois Hough, Judy Stilson, Mary Lou Brink and I, served the Friday meal at the Community Connection in Enterprise.

I turned my milk cows and their calves, plus son Ken's heifers and bull into the machinery yard to eat down the tall grasses. Thunderheads built up and a light rain fell.

May 30—I drove into the Farmer's Market, where I visited our Magic Garden booth, purchased a few plants from other peddlers, and enjoyed listening to "Homemade Jam" play their toe-tapping music. It was beautiful weather and very festive there.

I then headed to the crik, where I transplanted petunias and herbs next to the cabin.

David Martin was busy roto-tilling the big garden across the creek. A huge job.

This evening, Doug and I drove into the Range Ryder in Enterprise and treated ourselves to a tasty meal. Good food, friendly service, and nice folks run the place. Muggy and warm, light rain.

May 31—On the last day of May the skies were cloudy when I went to church to ring the bell. What a surprise for all of us! Ben Boswell was the choir, and wife Claudia played the piano. Boy, how we've missed them. They were just visiting however, as they now reside in Spokane.

This afternoon I attended a celebration of what would have been Alvin Josephy's 100th birthday, held at the Josephy Center for Arts and Culture. So glad I did. Got to visit Alvin's daughter, Diane, and hubby Mr. Peavy, who drove over from Idaho for the celebration, plus Alvin and his wife Melissa, who live near Seattle. There were Indian drums, emotional tributes, and refreshments, a wonderful affair for a very deserving historian, who was also a friend. The lovely display of Indian bead work, clothing and time line of Alvin's life was well done.

June 1—The wind was out of the east, clouds formed and it rained. I took my friend, Nancy Locke to the cabin for a little relaxation and peace. Across the creek David and his crew were hard at work preparing the garden for planting. Glorious clouds floated in a blue sky and the weather was warm and beautiful, and the three cherry trees in the front yard were ripening.

June 2—Rain sluiced down in sheets as our Write Group made its way up the street from the Josephy Center to "The Red Horse" for lunch. Home to bake a rhubarb crisp. Yum.

June 3—Today would have been grandson Rowdy's birthday. Happy birthday, Rowdy. May you rest in peace, our precious young man, who died too young.

Great grandson Cole, who graduated from high school in Lodi, California, was awarded some pretty impressive college scholarships. Very proud of you, Cole.

Grandson Buck, wife Chelsea, and Lucy, Katelyn, and Cooper honored us with a surprise visit. It had been the last day of school for Troy, and when school resumes in the fall there will only be two students, Lucy and Katelyn. The 4th was "the wolf incident" at Sheep Creek.

Later, I also enjoyed a brief visit with neighbors, Myrna and Larry Moore, who live up Bear Gulch. A tiny pair of birds were carrying worms to their young in my birdhouse built on a shovel.

June 5—Clear and sunny. Planted beans in the Prairie Creek garden.

June 6—Today is the Wallowa Valley Festival of the Arts in Joseph and the Farmer's Market, and son Ken branded his calves on Alder Slope, aided by 18 members of his family, three generations, and four, counting me, who photographed it all. A very hot day!

This evening Doug and I enjoyed a visit from Dinah and Mr. Hemphill from Pendleton this evening,, sorry, his name escapes me, who are the parents of our granddaughter, Lacey's, husband, Colin, and grandparents of Seely Jo and Callen.

June 7—The 7th was my oldest son Ken's 62nd birthday. And grandson James and wife Danielle's first wedding anniversary. Congrats, you two!

At church this morning, we had a party for departing Pastor Kaye Garver. I rang the bell for the 11;00 service, then left for Sheep Creek to host "Stitch and Bitch." It was hot. We enjoyed salads on the lawn in the shade by the creek, and visited the afternoon away. Some knitted, while others, me included, were sorely tempted to jump in the crik.

But that didn't happen until I hosted our write group on Tuesday. You'll have to wait 'til next time to hear about THAT. Time to quit.

June 8—The roses alongside the bunkhouse burst into full bloom.

June 15—June is not only "busting out all over," as the song sings, it's completely out of control! I mean the grasses are as high as a giraffe's eye, ranchers are haying before the 4th of July, my cows are so fat they can hardly walk, their calves so full of milk and motherly love they want for nothing, the old fashioned yellow rose blooming alongside the bunkhouse is nearly spent, and on June 17th Doug and I will have been married 37 years. So, you see, I've spent that many years here on Prairie Creek, watching the seasons come and go with great regularity and, as I age, with increasing speed.

Those roses always bloom on our anniversary, however, and by June 17th the petals will have fallen. Spring this year was, well, different. We actually had one, and now it's suddenly summer. And all those five inches of rain worked their magic, but then the sun came out and got really hot, and it's drying out again, so it's back to irrigating. Ditches, full to the brim with water from Wallowa Lake, which is also full to the brim, are diverted at a dam, where the waters carried by those ditches ultimately sprinkle out of center pivots and wheel lines.

The lake is full, really full, as recent warm rains have caused premature snow melt. Those of us who planted our gardens early are very happy folks. Rain, warm nights, and hot days have contributed greatly to rapid growth. I've just come inside from hilling up my potatoes, and pushing the hand tiller up and down the rows of cabbage, lettuce, onions, strawberries, beets, carrots and squash. The beans I planted last week are all up, and we will eat the first radishes for supper this evening.

The Magic Garden on Sheep Creek is coming along nicely due to our wonderful volunteers, who put in long hours down there. And now it's June 15th and I'm actually down here on the crik, writing. I talked to Sterling Allen this morning, who called wondering where my column was. I told him this past week has been, to put it mildly, a bit hectic. I mean, even more than usual.

For starters, we had a little excitement here last Thursday, when Robin, David, Rob and I were transplanting 100 heirloom tomato plants in the garden. We were also transplanting zinnias, to feed the soul, and I was dipping water out of the irrigation ditch to fill a watering can to sprinkle on a row of sweet peas, when my neighbor's horse, who had come down to drink at the same ditch that flows inside the garden, suddenly bolted. Aren't you glad you are through reading this epic sentence?

At first I thought the horse was spooked at seeing my colorful hat, but then, suspense—the horse stumbled into the water, twisted its leg, and ran trembling uphill to join two other horses, who we could see were also trembling, their ears turned in the direction of some tall grasses growing just yards away from the four of us. Suddenly, here it came, a large tan-colored wolf, with an obviously newly-born fawn in its massive jaws.

The jaws of the four of us hung open as we watched the drama unfold, not unlike the horses, who stood transfixed just uphill. The wolf, not in any real hurry, turned away and trotted up the canyon, slipping under my line fence and entering the National Forest land that joins my property. We watched until the wolf disappeared under a sarvisberry bush that grew at the foot of a rocky draw.

Our attention was drawn to another wolf, perhaps a mate, who ambled up under the fence and looked back at us as if to say, "Wanna join us for breakfast?" Then it, too, vanished behind the sarvis bush.

Meanwhile, the terrified doe ran around our young orchard, confused and sad, searching for her fawn. Which made us feel distressed and sad too.

More movement caught my eye near the sarvis bush, and out trotted a wolf, to loll on the slope and watch us. A bit unnerving. This all happened around 11:00 a.m. in broad daylight, and even more disturbing, we had been there since 8 o'clock, working in the garden only yards away, whilst this pair of the Imnaha pack of wolves had been patiently waiting for the doe to birth her fawn, then snatch it before it could take its first breath.

Knowing there is safety in numbers, plus we were standing INSIDE the garden's seven-foot fence, we felt reasonably safe. When the wolf that had been lying on the hill side, returned to its mate, we never saw the pair again, and so continued working in the garden. However, none of us would ever be the same again. My camera had been in the car, parked at my cabin. Darn, as I would've had ample time to record this surreal scene.

Even though other adventures pale in comparison to the above tale, my life has nevertheless reached the limit of living, especially for an 81-year-old woman, who should be slowing down. Right? WRONG.

June 28—At 7:00 o'clock on this Sunday evening, the thermometer on our carport registers 90 degrees. I've just returned from a meeting of our church. Thunderheads formed earlier, and occasional lightning zig-zagged across the sky. Now it's hot and sultry, like living in a giant hot house, and my garden is fast-forwarding to early maturity. Luckily, I have kept up with the weeds, as my garden here on Prairie Creek is small.

My garden is a source of solace, not work, when I arise early to take hoe in hand and stand in the midst of lush potato plants and cabbages, cabbages I am growing for our church's Magic Garden sauerkraut project. There are 30 plants. Lately, I need all the solace I can get. Everyone I run into feels the same. It is a busy time in Wallowa County. Make hay while the sun shines, so to speak, and the "boys," as Doug calls them, are hard at it.

Because of the abnormally hot temps, the hay matured earlier and cured instantly, and therefore balers can be heard *chunk-a-thump*ing all night long, as record crops of hay are baled, stacked, and hauled out of the fields, and the irrigation began again. And it's not even July yet.

Normally, my column would have been e-mailed by now, but due to many intervening events in my life, I am just now sitting down to write. Because of time restrictions I won't elaborate on all of these happenings, but I would like to tell you about one of the most fabulous things that ever happened to me.

For years I have wanted to go on a float trip down a wild river, in a raft. When Doug and I were married in 1978, he took me in his Dug Bar Ranch jet boat up and down the Snake, which was wonderful and fun, but every time a raft full of folks drifted by, I longed for that experience, mainly for the quiet and serenity, not to mention the speed. But I was in love, and much younger then, and the jet boat with Doug was a thrill.

So I put a raft trip on my bucket list, where it stayed until I was nearly 82. Now. This all came about after my grandson, James, called to ask if I wanted to go on a raft trip he was guiding for Divide Camp, taking four veterans on a three-day trip down the river. It seems there had been a cancellation. My writer friend, Katherine Stickroth, who had been scheduled to go along and write an article, became ill at the last minute.

I was totally unprepared. Guests were to be arriving here at our place at 10:00, I had this column to write, I was scheduled to volunteer at our Museum from 1:00 to 4:00, and at 4:30 I had a meeting about Fishtrap Outpost. Plus, I was hesitant to leave Doug here on such short notice. However…James said he thought I should go, and his dad, my son Todd, agreed. That's all I needed. James was very happy with my decision, as was his dad.

"Be at the Winding Waters boat house at 9:00", said James.

"Or earlier," added Todd, who was, at this time, waiting with James at Old Town Cafe in Joseph, where they were to meet, over breakfast, with the four veterans who were staying at Divide Camp. Prior to making the decision to go, I had driven in to wish James "Happy Birthday" and now here I was going on a raft trip.

"What should I pack?" I asked James.

"Nothing" he said. "It's all provided."

"What about a toothbrush?" I offered.

"Bring that," he said, and I drove home, walked into the living room, told Doug I was leaving for a three-day raft trip, to which he replied, "Good, have fun."

I made several phone calls, not canceling my life but putting it on hold, and grabbed my toothbrush, camera, a change of clothes, pen and writing tablet. I arrived at the boat house before the appointed time.

After the four vets arrived, a great flurry of activity followed, all fascinating to observe. Rafts were loaded on a trailer, food prepared in the kitchen was loaded into coolers, and then decisions had to be made. We were told to put our stuff in two bags, one we would carry on, and the other we wouldn't see until that night in camp. This required quick thinking, which I somehow managed to do, and label "Grandma Janie," a name I acquired for the entire trip.

Actually, I was everyone's gram, including Robin, the beautiful cook, and her 16 year old assistant, Izzie. I have nothing but admiration for Robin, who is a most amazing young woman, who not only cooked, but paddled the larger raft down the river, loaded with gear and food. A real challenge, as the water level of the river was dropping fast due to warm weather.

My heart overflowed with joy and gratitude at this rare opportunity. I was as excited as a child and showed it. My exuberance was contagious, and we were all in a jovial mood as we stuffed our bags, became acquainted, and boarded the expedition shuttle.

Then I remembered I'd had no time for breakfast, whereupon James brought me a bowl of granola and yogurt, which I ate en route. Then we were pulling into the "put in" spot at Minam. How many times I'd driven past that spot, and glanced down to see happy folks paddling off down that wild river, and yearned to go. And now, here I was, going. It was a dream, surely not real, but a dream it wasn't, and all our gear and four rafts were launched, and there I was with Mark Keffer at the oars, paddling down the Wallowa River.

The air was saturated with the wild scent of syringa. A perfect June morning, warm and lovely, as we slipped into the current and swirled our way through gentle rapids. All my cares and obligations melted away. I savored every moment of those floating miles as we became acquainted. Our river guide, Mark, turned out to be the newly-hired schoolteacher who taught my twin great-grandchildren, Gideon and Jada, in his class!

Further conversation revealed that Mark had spent time with grandson Chad in Alaska, working in the salmon harvest. A grueling job. I'd remembered Chad talking about it. James, the expedition leader, paddled his raft before us, giving two of the vets pointers on fly fishing as they floated along. They, like me, were mesmerized by the scenery, the river, the solitude, and the wildness, far from the madding crowd.

Then there was the expedition photographer, Shelly Tippett. Another co-inky-dink. Shelly is one of Doug's relatives, and a fine photographer. Also, Shelly will be hired on as my future housekeeper. *Yeah!* for both of us!

Soon we floated under the bridge at Rondowa, where the Grande Ronde flows into the Wallowa and becomes the Grand Ronde River— hence the place name, Rondowa. Since I had ridden the local excursion train to Rondowa, the river beyond was all new territory for me. After living in Wallowa County for nearly 50 years, I was seeing new country. Exciting stuff.

Now we were floating a wild river, accessible only by boat. Words fail when it comes to describing the country. It was invigorating: the wild life, including bald and golden eagles, mergansers flying low over the water, wild geese with their young staring as we floated past, mallards bobbing up and down in the wavelets, their duckling between them. Then we were pulling into Clear Creek Camp. It had turned hot, so I'd slipped into the water to cool off.

An evening coolness came upon the river, along with a breeze.

"Camp wherever you want," Robin said, as I stepped ashore. Bushes beckoned. I located my long term bag and did as bid. Then I overheard our guide remark that the last campers here, at noon, killed a rattlesnake. A timber rattler. I must say, it wasn't a pretty sight to see an 81-year-old grandma attempt to remove her wet clothes in brush, while wary of snakes, well you get the picture. Thank goodness I was in good shape due to hoeing the garden, which helped a lot.

I found my campsite near Shelly, marked by a sleeping bag and mattress. That was it, no tent. Not much to setting up camp. I mastered the Groover, an ammunition can containing toilet paper, handi-wipes, antiseptic soap, etc. which you then carried further down a trail that supposedly led to a port-a-potty. It was like a scavenger hunt. I eventually got the hang of it.

Wearing dry clothes, I sought out the kitchen, where I fixed myself a cup of hot tea. Robin and Izzie were preparing the first of several gourmet meals and we were hungry. Delicious smells wafted through the forest, and the vets, who had been fly-fishing all the way down the river, were too. James said there had been a golden stonefly hatch that day, a good thing, in fly-fishing jargon. While James grilled lemon salmon, Izzie and Robin prepared smashed potatoes (baked earlier) and grilled with butter. Dessert was berry cobbler with whipped cream.

There was a special bowl for James, with candles, and "Happy Birthday" had been sung at the noon lunch stop. Since it was dark by this time, I crawled into my sleeping bag under the stars, and sort'a slept, only to awake at four to a sleeping camp. First light revealed the river below, dimples of rising trout. I gave into temptation and headed up the trail toward the kitchen, passing snoring vets along the way, when something white in the dawn's early light caught my eye.

On the other side of the river, white birds. Could it be? Yep. Pelicans. 15 of 'em. Oh my gosh! I ran back for my camera, but they flew off upriver.

I made my way quietly to the raft, where I grabbed the fly rod James had given me earlier. I walked along the shore where I'd seen the trout dimpling the water. It's been many many years since I'd held a fly rod in my hands, and longer still since I cast a fly into the waters. Just me, in the cool dawn on the river, me and God.

I confidently let out line and cast, like my wrists used to know how to do. It wasn't bad, but not good, and the fish I'd seen earlier weren't impressed. Then, after an especially brilliant cast, I reeled in to discover I'd snagged James' hand-tied golden stonefly on a rock. I'd been told if this happened to let it be. James would wade in and retrieve it. The fly was that valuable. So, I did. And returned to camp. No one up yet, so I jotted notes in my notebook until the cooks and guides came to life.

Announced by a cow's horn blown, well, sort'a, by Robin., breakfast was awesome, made with fresh eggs laid by hens kept by the Winding Waters folks, along with sausage from their hog, both of whom were fed leftovers from previous trips. The food was nutritious, home-grown and delicious. Even the coffee rivaled Red Horse Coffee House in Joseph.

James retrieved my fly, the crew pitched in with dishes, and we packed up and pushed off into more wild water, leaving all sense of time behind. There was absolutely no need for it. Mile after mile of rapids, glassy stillness, and rocks, upon which we often became stranded, as the level of the river was dropping dramatically due to hot weather.

Actually, I found it gangs of fun being stuck on a rock, as it involved our paddler, Mark Keffer, slipping into the river and pushing us off. This made for much hilarity. We yelled *Ya-hoo!* as we washed over rapids, loving the spray in our faces, living the dream.

In my last years, I was becoming a river rat. I was hooked.

We camped that night near Sickfoot, a place name given to a crippled homesteader by the Nez Perce. Another gourmet meal, more camaraderie, and I nearly maxed out my camera's memory card. So did Shelly.

That night, Mark gave me his tent, and I slept like a hay hand. The stars were magnificent. The four vets relaxed, told stories, laughed, ate, fished, and the next day, when we put out at Mud Creek at the end of 39 river miles, we were forever changed by this experience of a life time.

It was hot at Mud Creek, near Troy, where our shuttle met us, and after the rafts and gear were loaded in a sweltering heat, we drove through Troy and past the little school where my two great-grandchildren are the only two students. Divide Camp vets Robert from Maine and Steven from Florida were experiencing the Wild West.

Wide-eyed they all were, when not far from the small settlement of Troy, the vets and James (also a vet) became little boys again. You see, a young bear that had just swam the river, appeared alongside the road. All bailed out of the van, but the bear disappeared in the bushes.

We returned via the Oasis, for milk shakes. It was 100 degrees! The air-conditioned van was refreshing. After another stop at the Joseph Creek viewpoint, we headed back to the boat house in Joseph, where I again plunged into my former life. A life so full, I am behind on everything. Therefore I will have to report on we four Syringa Sisters being at my cabin for two nights at a later date. Not to mention the Ranch Rodeo and other events. I am just too sleepy. Like the hay balers, I, too, work in the cool of night.

Thoreau said, *My life is a poem I would have writ, if I had time to live and utter it.* My mother printed this quote out for me once, as she understood what it meant. Well folks, that's all. I know I haven't done justice to our wondrous trip, and left out so much, but there are only so many hours in a day.

Fishing on the Grande Ronde with veterans on a Divide Camp float trip.

Index

Doug Tippett appears too frequently to be included in the index.

Photos of Doug appear on pages 51, 55, 62, 151, 159, 208, 263, and 347.
Photos of Janie appear on pages 73, 74, 99, 145, 159, 263, 266, 321, 336, and 384.

CPSIA information can be obtained
at www.ICGtesting.com
Printed in the USA
LVHW020045121021
700156LV00002B/13